NT Enterprise Network Design

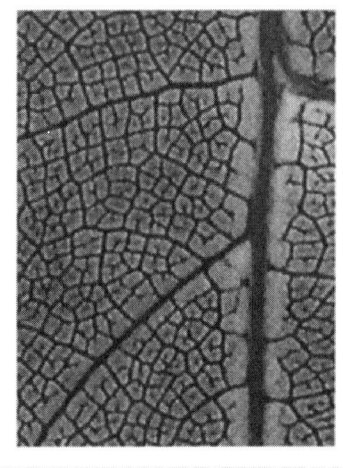

Morgan: For my dad
Gary: To my wife Michele, who provided unconditional love and support while simultaneously keeping the dogs at bay...literally
Vahan: For Olga

Acknowledgments

We would like to thank everyone who contributed to this work in one form or another. To our wives and significant others, thanks for your patience and understanding while we spent the better part of the summer with our faces in our computer screens. Remind us to never start a book at this time of year again.

Our gratitude to our families and friends who, supplying selfless support, will end up buying a copy of this book even though most won't know what it's about—and aren't sure exactly what it is we do for a living.

Thanks also to everyone who gave helpful suggestions and ideas for how we could make this a better publication. Your enthusiasm and input helped guide our vision to a reality.

Thanks especially to everyone at Sybex who helped make this book possible: Neil Edde, our acquisitions & developmental editor; Kim Wimpsett, project editor; Vivian Perry, editor; Jennifer Foley, editorial assistant; Charles Mathews, production coordinator; Tony Jonick, desktop publisher; and Nancy Guenther, indexer. Thanks also to our technical editor, Fred Collett, who kept us honest and in line by making a number of insightful suggestions.

Finally, to "you know who" at "you know where," thanks for nothing. (Just kidding, but you still don't get mentioned in this book.)

Contents at a Glance

Introduction   *xvii*

Part I	**The Design and Evolution of Microsoft Windows NT**	**1**
Chapter 1	Windows NT: Developed with a Clear Goal in Mind	3
Chapter 2	The NT Architecture	25
Part II	**The Foundation for a High Performance NT Enterprise Network**	**55**
Chapter 3	The Principles of Network Design	57
Chapter 4	Dynamic Domain Design	91
Chapter 5	Forming the NT Network Infrastructure	137
Chapter 6	Incorporating Windows NT into the Enterprise Network	171
Part III	**NT as a Net Platform**	**223**
Chapter 7	Introduction to Net Concepts and Services	225
Chapter 8	Internet Information Server in the Enterprise Network	259
Chapter 9	DNS, Mail, and News	291
Chapter 10	Firewalls and Proxy Servers	317
Chapter 11	Virtual Private Networking: Private Conversations in a Public Network	357
Part IV	**NT as a Remote Access Program**	**377**
Chapter 12	Remote Access Concepts and LAN to WAN Design Issues	379
Chapter 13	Designing a Remote Node Implementation	413
Chapter 14	Designing a Remote Control Implementation	439
Part V	**Managing the NT Enterprise Network**	**491**
Chapter 15	Performance Tuning and Optimization	493
Appendices		**509**
Appendix A	The Future of NT	511
Appendix B	The OSI Model	531
Appendix C	Glossary	541
Appendix D	Acronyms	557

Index   *566*

Table of Contents

Introduction — xvii

Part I **The Design and Evolution of Microsoft Windows NT** — 1

Chapter 1 **Windows NT: Developed with a Clear Goal in Mind** — 3

The Curse of Operating System Development — 5
Not So Humble Beginnings — 6
Windows NT Design Goals — 7
    Extensibility — 9
    Portability — 10
    Reliability — 12
    Compatibility — 14
    Performance — 18
The Windows NT Evolutionary Ladder — 20
The Future Direction for Microsoft Windows NT — 21

Chapter 2 **The NT Architecture** — 25

Establishing the Model — 26
    Client/Server and Layered Internals — 28
    A Modular Approach Throughout — 29
    Symmetric Multiprocessing — 32
Internals of NT — 41
    The Windows NT Executive Layer — 42
    The Hardware Abstraction Layer — 47
    The Environment Subsystems — 48

Part II	**The Foundation for a High Performance NT Enterprise Network**	**55**
Chapter 3	**The Principles of Network Design**	**57**
	Design: A Definition	59
	Basic Design Principles	59
	Meet a Business Requirement or Need	59
	Avoid the Use of Technology for Its Own Sake	61
	Consider Organizational Objectives	63
	Respect the Budget	63
	Leverage Existing Infrastructure When Feasible	65
	Utilize Components from Reliable Vendors	67
	The Five Elements of a Successful Design	70
	Installable, Manageable, and Supportable	70
	Works in the Real World	74
	Simple and Straightforward	76
	Reliability through Fault Tolerance and Redundancy	77
	Best of Breed Technologies Whenever Possible	79
	Considering the Alternatives	80
	The Pilot Project—Making Sure Everything Works Before It's Too Late	82
	Why Implement a Pilot Project?	82
	Planning a Successful Pilot Project	84
	The Phases of a Pilot Project	86
Chapter 4	**Dynamic Domain Design**	**91**
	Exposing the Myths of Domain Design	92
	Debunking the Domain Model Design Myth	93
	Demystifying the Number of Users for a Single Domain	96
	When to Implement the Multi-Master Domain Model	99
	Naming Standards and X.500	102
	Why Establish Naming Standards?	103
	The X.500 Directory Service	114
	Understanding Trust Relationships	119
	How Many Trusts?	122

	Unveiling the Mystery of Browsing	125
	Domain Master and Master Browsers	126
	Backup Browsers	129
	The Timing of It All	130
	The Election Process	131
	The Preferred Master Browser	134
Chapter 5	**Forming the NT Network Infrastructure**	**137**
	Capacity Planning	138
	Understanding the Limitations of a PDC	140
	Not All PDCs Need to Be Created Equal	141
	BDCs Support of PDC	142
	Platform Design	149
	Crafting the Domain Controllers	150
	Crafting the Member Servers	154
	Network Protocol Support	157
	TCP/IP: The Enterprise Protocol	158
	Planning Your TCP/IP Network	161
	Dynamic Address Allocation with DHCP	165
	Finding Servers with WINS	167
Chapter 6	**Incorporating Windows NT into the Enterprise Network**	**171**
	The Native Transport Protocols	173
	NetBEUI	174
	NetBIOS over TCP/IP	178
	IPX/SPX	182
	TCP/IP in a NetWare Environment	183
	Protocol Interoperability	188
	Integration and Interoperability	190
	Microsoft's View on Integration and Interoperability	190
	Novell's View on Integration and Interoperability	193
	Closing Comments on the Native Transport Protocols	194
	Novell's Support for Microsoft Windows NT	195
	Novell IntranetWare Client for Windows NT	196
	Novell Workstation Manager	199
	The Novell Administrator for Windows NT	206

	Microsoft's Support for Novell NetWare	214
	Gateway Services for NetWare	214
	File and Print Services for NetWare	216
	Directory Services Manager for NetWare	220

Part III — NT as a Net Platform — 223

Chapter 7 — Introduction to Net Concepts and Services — 225

Crucial Net Definitions	227
Internet: The Network to the World	227
Intranets: Leveraging the Technology of the Web	228
Extranets: Sharing Intranets with the Outside World	229
Core Net Services	230
The Client/Server Model	232
Web Protocols: HTTP and HTML	233
DNS: The Domain Name Service	235
SMTP, POP3, and IMAP: Net Mail	242
FTP: The File Transfer Protocol	244
Gopher: A File Navigation Service	246
NNTP: The News Protocol	247
Secure Networking in an Insecure World	250
Proxy Servers: The Network Middleman	251
Firewalls: Gatekeepers of the Corporation	252
Virtual Private Networks	254
Net Design Issues	255
Select the Right Tools for the Job	255
Understand the Network Infrastructure	255
Put Your Eggs in the Right Baskets	256
Design a Maintenance Plan	256

Chapter 8 — Internet Information Server in the Enterprise Network — 259

IIS: The Internet Information Server	261
Core IIS Services	261
Active Server Pages	268
Index Server	269

	NetShow	270
	Optimizing IIS	271
	Streamlining Your Services	271
	Typical Bottleneck Areas	272
	Microsoft Analysis Tools	273
	Managing IIS	276
	IIS Security	276
	IIS and SNMP	282
	Reporting Utilities for IIS	283
	IIS Design Considerations	285
	Utilizing Virtual Directories	286
	Creating Virtual Servers	287
	Load Balancing with DNS	288
Chapter 9	**DNS, Mail, and News**	**291**
	The Microsoft DNS Server	293
	Doing It Right	294
	DNS/WINS/DHCP Integration	300
	Dynamic DNS/DHCP Considerations	302
	Configuring Workstations for Dynamic DNS	303
	Third-Party DNS Servers	304
	BIND for NT	304
	MetaIP	306
	Design Considerations	308
	Looking at Your Topology	308
	Considering Your Internet Strategy	309
	Mail and News Protocols: SMTP, POP3, IMAP, LDAP, and NNTP	310
	Choosing from Mail and News Server Options	312
	The Big Debate: Proprietary vs. Open Messaging Systems	312
	Exchange 5: A Step in the Right Direction	313
	Choosing a Third-Party Server	314
	Design Considerations	316
Chapter 10	**Firewalls and Proxy Servers**	**317**
	Network Security Threats	319

External Threats	319
Internal Threats	322
Developing Your Security Strategy	324
Determining Your Security Objectives	325
Developing a Security Policy	328
Implementing Security Strategies	333
Guidelines for a Secure Network	337
Passwords Are a Must	337
Educating Users	338
Regular Backups Are Mandatory	338
Test, Test, Test!	339
Enforcing Your Security Policy	339
How Does a Firewall Work?	340
How Does a Proxy Server Work?	345
Proxy Servers vs. Firewall Servers	348
NT-Based Firewalls	349
Checkpoint Firewall-1: An NT Firewall	349
The Microsoft Proxy Server	353
The Web Proxy	354
The Winsock and SOCKS Proxies	354
Reverse Proxy Support	355

Chapter 11   **Virtual Private Networking: Private Conversations in a Public Network**   **357**

Who Needs Encryption?	359
Leveraging the Internet as a Dial-Up Infrastructure	359
The Internet as WAN	361
Building Extranets	362
How It Works: Elements of a VPN	363
The Public Network	364
The Data Source	365
The VPN Server	366
The VPN Client	367
Putting It All Together	367
Creating a VPN with PPTP	368
PPTP Server Configuration	369

PPTP Client Configuration (Windows 95) 371
PPTP Design Considerations 373
Third-Party Products 373
AltaVista Tunnel 374
VPNs and Firewalls 375

Part IV NT as a Remote Access Program 377

Chapter 12 Remote Access Concepts and LAN to WAN Design Issues 379

Remote Access Network Technologies 381
Plain Old Telephone System (POTS) 381
Leased Line Systems (Analog) 384
The T-Carrier System 384
Fractional T1 System 388
PSDNs: Packet-Switched Public Data Networks (X.25 Protocol) 388
Integrated Services Digital Network (ISDN) 389
Frame Relay 392
Remote Access Concepts 392
Communication Servers 394
Remote Node 395
Remote Control 396
Remote Node vs. Remote Control 400
Remote Access: Emphasis on LAN to WAN Internetwork Design 402
Designing the LAN/WAN Connection 403
Leased Line Network Configurations 404

Chapter 13 Designing a Remote Node Implementation 413

Windows NT Remote Access Service 414
What Is RAS? 414
Remote Node vs. Remote Control Revisited 415
Connecting through RAS 417
RAS-Supported Access Technologies 419
Designing a Remote Access Solution with RAS 422

	Server Preinstallation Considerations	422
	Designing the Proper Hardware Configuration	426
	Pros and Cons of Protocols and Their Impact on Performance	426
	Installing RAS on the Server	427
	When to Use RAS	436
Chapter 14	**Designing a Remote Control Implementation**	**439**
	Citrix WinFrame and Remote Access	441
	What Is ICA?	442
	Designing a Remote Access Solution with WinFrame	443
	When to Use WinFrame	443
	Server Preinstallation Considerations	450
	A Sample WinFrame Project	451
	Widget's WinFrame Capability Requirements	452
	Predicted Number of Concurrent Users	454
	Understanding the Applications	457
	Configuring the Hardware: RAM, Hard Drive, and the Rest	465
	Connectivity Options (ISDN, Frame Relay, Dial-In)	471
	WinFrame Management Options	473
	WinFrame Server Administration	473
	WinFrame User Setup	475
	WinFrame Licensing	476
	WinStation Configuration	477
	WinStation Administration	479
	The WinFrame Client Tool	480
	Other Client Support	481
	WinFrame Questions and Troubleshooting Tips	481
	New Features in WinFrame 1.7	488
Part V	**Managing the NT Enterprise Network**	**491**
Chapter 15	**Performance Tuning and Optimization**	**493**
	The Fundamentals of Performance Tuning	494

		What Performance Tuning Is	495
		What Performance Tuning Is Not	495
		Where to Begin	496
		Inspecting Application Performance	496
		Performance Tuning	498
		Optimization	505

Appendices 509

Appendix A The Future of NT 511

The Future: NT 5 — 512
Active Directory — 513
    Site Structure — 514
    Directory Structure — 515
    Administration — 518
Hydra — 519
The Zero Administration Initiative — 520
    The Zero Adminstration Kit — 520
    IntelliMirror Technology — 521
    Microsoft Management Console — 522
Routing and Remote Access Service — 523
    Routing Protocol Support — 524
    Demand-Dial Routing — 525
    RAS Enhancements — 525
Wolfpack Clustering Technology — 527
    The Wolfpack Concepts and Architecture — 527
    Management of Wolfpack Clusters — 528

Appendix B The OSI Model 531

The Need for a Common Language — 532
Encapsulation and Peer Communication — 534
The Seven Layers of the OSI Model — 536

Appendix C Glossary 541

Appendix D Acronyms 557

Index — 566

Introduction

If you've ever felt ripped off after spending too much money on a Windows NT book only to find that it is essentially a reprint of Microsoft's NT documentation and help files, then this book is for you. We guarantee that you will find a wealth of valuable information and techniques throughout the chapters that follow—information and techniques that you won't find in any of the Microsoft literature, because most of it comes from our own experience. We are pleased to share this experience with you.

From the beginning of this project, we wanted to create a book for people who know that to install Windows NT within the enterprise requires more than just pulling off the shrink wrap and inserting a CD. Our goal is to help the people whose job is (or will be) to design all aspects of their enterprise NT network. In other words: Our goal is to help you!

We recognize that you don't need information on where to configure your server's TCP/IP address, but that you do need to know how to create a "real world" NT domain design, develop capacity planning strategies for your NT servers, secure your network, and design an effective remote access implementation.

We want to equip you with the tools, techniques, and concepts that you'll need to understand when it comes time to design your NT enterprise network.

If you've read this far, you've already seen the title of the book: *NT Enterprise Network Design*. We're sure that we don't need to explain the first part of the title. Windows NT has taken the network world by storm, and while not every company has begun to deploy NT, experience has shown us that at least every company is thinking or talking about it. Some early implementers are on their second attempt at deploying NT throughout their networks. Now that they've learned some valuable lessons, they're trying to do things the right way. We've worked with a number of these companies, and we've incorporated many of those lessons throughout the book so you can do things right the first time.

The second part of the title, the *Enterprise Network*, is a term that is used very frequently these days in the press and in the offices of CIOs, but what exactly is an enterprise network? We like to think of an enterprise network as including all the elements of networking technologies that are required to run your business. The network operating system, a means for Internet access, and a remote access solution immediately come to mind.

The final part of the title of the book focuses on network design. As network designers ourselves, we understand the importance of a well-thought-out network game plan, and our goal in this book is to share with you our philosophy of network design. We'll talk about how we approach a network design, the issues to consider, and how to test your design to ensure ultimate success. The layout of this book reflects our approach to design, so it's a good idea to read carefully through the first parts so that you'll cover the important background information first.

This book was not written for NT network administrators—the people responsible for maintaining user accounts and deleting print jobs, although many will find this a helpful resource. We have written this book for the people whose responsibility it is to create a corporate Windows NT infrastructure. We know you are out there, and that you're looking for help. Otherwise, we'd be unemployed because a big part of our job is to work with people like you in companies like yours to develop successful enterprise NT implementations. This book is about learning through shared experiences. We are pleased to be presenting it to you.

What This Book Covers

This book is divided into five parts. In Part I, *The Design and Evolution of Microsft Windows NT*, we discuss the evolution and architecture of Windows NT. In Part II, *The Foundation for a High Performance NT Enterprise Network*, we focus on designing your core Windows NT infrastructure. Part III, *NT as a Net Platform*, discusses how to use Windows NT as the foundation for Internet, intranet, and extranet services. In Part IV, *NT as a Remote Access Program*, we cover the concepts and issues related to creating optimal remote access implementations with NT. In Part V, *Managing the NT Enterprise Network*, we describe some tools you can use to optimize your NT servers. Here's a more detailed list of what you'll find in the book:

In Chapter 1, we discuss the origins of Windows NT. We describe its growth from a twinkle in Bill Gates' eye to its emergence as the hottest networking platform on the market. We'll also talk, in detail, about the driving design goals of Windows NT and why they're important.

In Chapter 2, we discuss the Windows NT architecture, including the concepts and systems that turned Microsoft's design goals into reality. If you've been an NT user for a while but still don't fully understand what's going on beneath the hood of the operating system, we encourage you to read this chapter.

We discuss our philosophies of network design in Chapter 3. You'll learn many of our proven techniques for developing successful network designs, as well as the questions to ask before you approach any type of network design. You'll also learn how to develop a pilot project to ensure a successful production deployment.

In Chapter 4, we tell you all of the things you didn't learn in MCSE school about designing the right kind of NT domain model for your organization. You'll learn about developing effective naming standards, the real story on trust relationships, and we'll unlock the mysteries behind browsing.

We discuss how to design and plan your NT network infrastructure in Chapter 5. After discussing domain controller capacity planning, we continue with a collection of the best practices for building optimized domain controllers. Then we discuss how to deploy TCP/IP as your enterprise network protocol.

In Chapter 6, we discuss how to integrate NT into your existing enterprise network by focusing on Windows NT/Novell NetWare coexistence issues. We discuss all of the latest tools and techniques to get your network operating systems to work together instead of against each other.

In Chapter 7, we introduce the concepts associated with the Internet, corporate intranets, and multi-corporate extranets. We also introduce the major services, such as WWW, FTP, DNS, and Mail.

Chapter 8 covers Microsoft's Internet Information Server, from its early days to its emergence as a multipurpose mega-Web server. We discuss the core IIS features and functions, as well as offering some tips for optimizing and managing your IIS server once it's up and running.

In Chapter 9, we discuss the services that provide support for other open-standards-based protocols, such as the Domain Name Service (DNS), Internet Mail, and News discussion groups. We also discuss how to implement dynamic DNS that integrates the Windows Internet Naming Service (WINS) and DNS.

Chapter 10 contains our conceptual approach to network security. We discuss the importance of a corporate security policy, as well as how to implement that policy with proxy servers and firewalls from Microsoft and other third-party developers.

In Chapter 11, we discuss the emergence of virtual private networks (VPNs). We discuss the concepts behind VPNs, as well as how to implement a VPN using Microsoft's Point-to-Point Tunneling Protocol (PPTP).

Chapter 12 contains an introduction to remote access concepts. We discuss the difference between remote control and remote node implementations, as well as providing some guidelines for choosing the right type of remote access solution to meet the needs of your organization.

In Chapter 13, we concentrate on designing remote node implementations utilizing products such as the Remote Access Service (RAS) that is included with NT Server 4.

In Chapter 14, we discuss how to develop high-performance remote control implementations using software from Citrix. This chapter contains a number of helpful techniques and practices that you can use to optimize Winframe to its fullest potential.

In Chapter 15, we teach you the essence of server performance tuning and optimization using tools such as the Performance Monitor and the Task Manager. You'll learn what performance tuning is and, just as importantly, what it is not.

In the appendices, we get to talk about all of the stuff we wanted to put into the book that wouldn't fit. We talk about the future of NT in Appendix A, including the release of components such as Wolfpack, Steelhead, and the Active Directory.

PART I

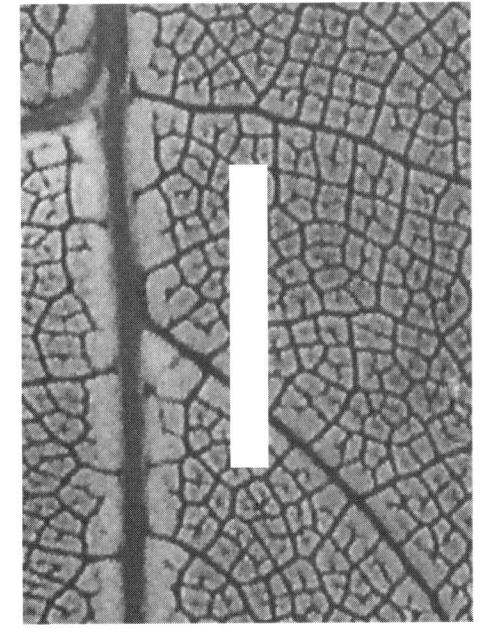

THE DESIGN AND EVOLUTION OF MICROSOFT WINDOWS NT

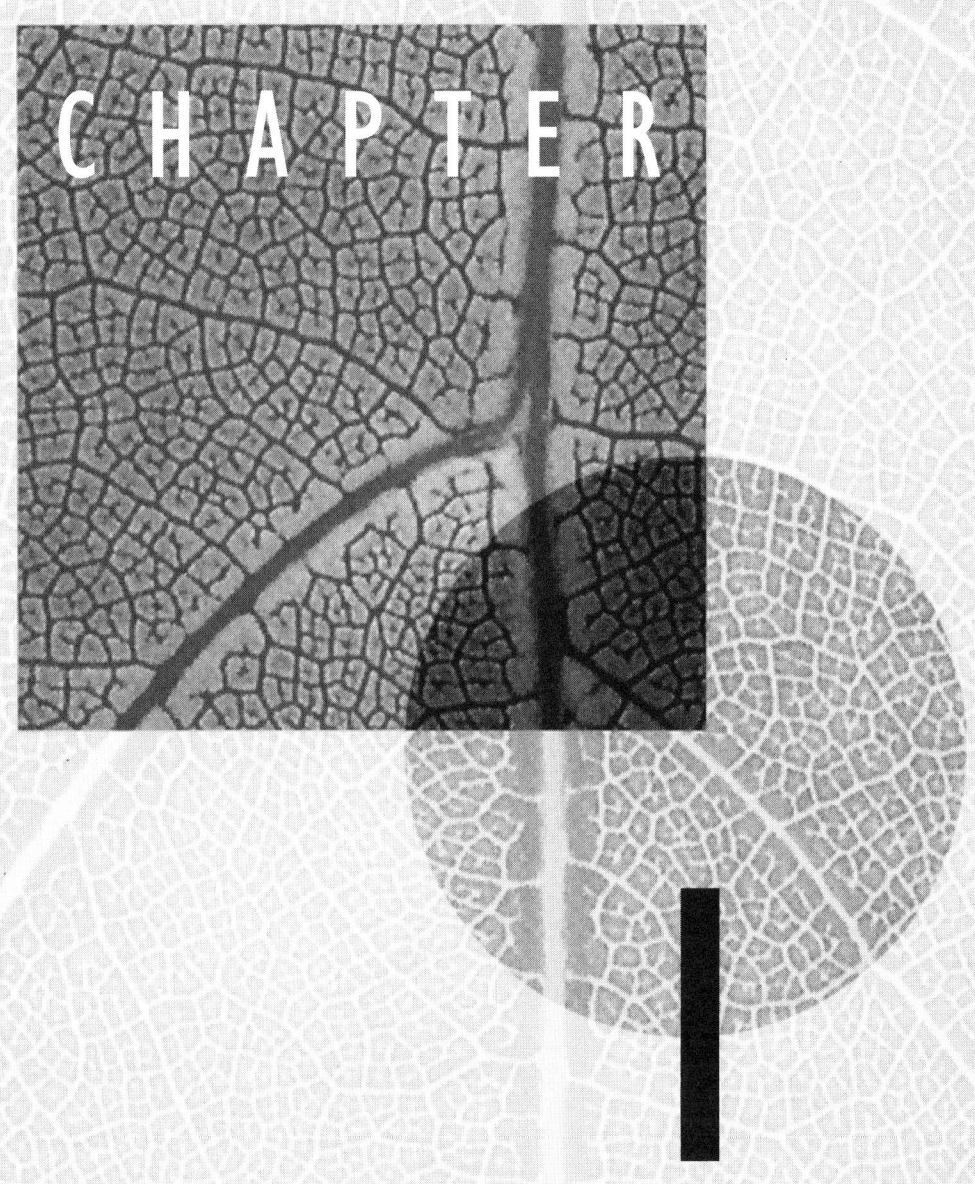

CHAPTER 1

Windows NT: Developed with a Clear Goal in Mind

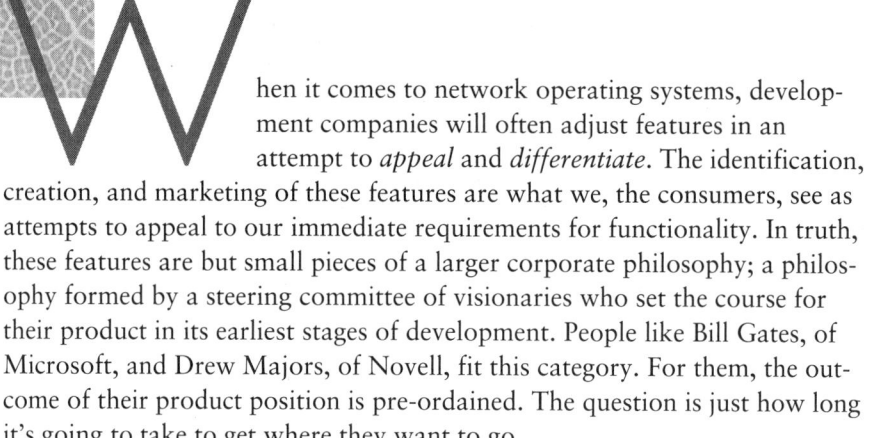When it comes to network operating systems, development companies will often adjust features in an attempt to *appeal* and *differentiate*. The identification, creation, and marketing of these features are what we, the consumers, see as attempts to appeal to our immediate requirements for functionality. In truth, these features are but small pieces of a larger corporate philosophy; a philosophy formed by a steering committee of visionaries who set the course for their product in its earliest stages of development. People like Bill Gates, of Microsoft, and Drew Majors, of Novell, fit this category. For them, the outcome of their product position is pre-ordained. The question is just how long it's going to take to get where they want to go.

By understanding the assumptions, goals, and philosophies of a manufacturer, you can select the product that was designed to meet your requirements. The purpose of this chapter is to provide you with insight into Microsoft's design philosophy for creating Windows NT. In the process we will uncover:

- The curse of network operating system development

- The early objectives for Microsoft Windows NT

- The design goals for this enterprise network operating system

- The philosophical direction this product intends to take in the future

Insight into the minds of the developers becomes extremely important, particularly when competition is heated, as with the recent battles between Microsoft, Novell, and Sun Microsystems for control of the corporate network. By understanding the philosophy underlying an organization's product development, you can make a sound decision about whether your business objectives align with that philosophy.

It is also extremely important that, as a network designer, you have a clear understanding of the concepts and capabilities of Windows NT, so that you can understand how to best apply NT technology throughout your enterprise.

The first part of this book is designed to provide you with a conceptual framework, and the remaining parts are designed to provide you with the technical information you'll need in order to make informed decisions.

The Curse of Operating System Development

"Users run applications."
—*An operating system developer's curse*

Imagine it is the year 1981. Joe Poweruser is stretched out in his office chair, flipping through a department store catalog, while Space Invaders downloads at 300bps to his Atari 800XL. He has just completed a report using Bank Street Writer and needs a break. Focusing on the catalog, he notices a brand new computer model, the powerful IBM Personal Computer. Featuring a whopping 512KB of memory along with DOS, a user-friendly operating system, the IBM PC makes the 64KB 800XL look like a toy. Joe's interest is piqued, so he begins to feverishly flip through the catalog looking for all the great software that would run under control of the mighty DOS. He continues to flip through the pages to no avail. Much time would pass and many catalogs would be printed before Joe would finally find something that would make the purchase of the IBM worthwhile. That something was Lotus 1-2-3. Lotus 1-2-3 was the original "killer application." Users didn't buy a computer because it ran DOS, they bought it because it could run Lotus 1-2-3 and other programs like it.

It was through Lotus 1-2-3 that Joe, and many other users like him, discovered what it meant to have an under-powered operating system. Frequent lockups and mandatory backups became a way of life, as users like Joe began to discover the need for an operating system that was robust enough to provide a stable computing environment. Alas, this is the curse of the operating system developer; for it is only through the availability of applications that the need for a robust operating system becomes obvious, but since the operating system doesn't yet exist, neither do the applications.

Developers that focus on providing a robust operating system before the applications exist put themselves at tremendous risk. What happens if they build the "Super OS" but nobody comes?

Not So Humble Beginnings

Flash forward to 1988 when Bill Gates and Dave Cutler meet to take on the curse. Their goal is to develop a rich operating system capable of running the *anticipated* base of applications that are being downsized from the mainframes and mini-computers of the 1980s, while simultaneously supporting the existing desktop suite of products—and winning favor with an expanding computer-literate society.

Dave Cutler joined Microsoft in October 1988 as director for the Microsoft Windows NT development team. By joining Microsoft, Cutler ended a 17-year career at Digital Equipment Corporation, where he was recognized as the chief architect for two of Digital's most popular operating systems: RSX-11M for the PDP-11, and VMS for the VAX.

At first glance, Cutler's PDP-11 and VAX background might have seemed an odd match for Microsoft's personal-computer-driven business. However, his most recent project before joining Microsoft was the development of a MicroVAX workstation (the MicroVAX1). The MicroVAX1 was designed to host high-performance CAD/CAM applications for the individual user.

Cutler began his assignment at Microsoft by forming a team that would be capable of capturing the vision of Bill Gates. It was a vision in which the business community could rid itself of the anxiety typically associated with running mission-critical applications on a personal computer—a vision where Microsoft could create the operating system that would turn that anxiety into confidence. This vision began to take shape through a clear set of objectives established for the operating system in the earliest phases of planning.

The objectives for the operating system were to provide:

- Support for 16-bit applications

- A 32-bit application-development platform

- Portability

- Security

- Internal scalability

- Extensibility

- POSIX compliance

- Ability to internationalize

At the time these objectives were considered, it was generally accepted that the first two items were mutually exclusive. Operating system developers chose either to provide compatibility within the restrictive requirements of 16-bit DOS, or to write the most robust 32-bit system they were capable of, hoping that applications would be developed for it once other developers recognized the power of their OS. To place both items on the list of goals shortened the roster of candidates for the development team.

As if this weren't enough, Gordon Moore's Law, which predicted the exponential growth of transistor density for microchips, proved to be alive and well, taking us from the 8086 to the 80386 in eight years. The development team needed to consider how they were going to develop for the rapidly evolving microprocessor architecture. Through contact with Intel's Andrew Grove, the Microsoft Windows NT development team ensured itself that they would be able to deploy a network operating system capable of leveraging the most current microprocessor technology available. This relationship, developed in the early phases of this project, has proven to be very beneficial to Microsoft and Intel.

Windows NT Design Goals

In the early 1980s Microsoft and IBM were continuing their business relationship through the development of OS/2. This operating system held great promise for the future of personal computing and was highly touted by both companies—right up until the moment they announced a parting of the ways. As you might suspect, both sides had valid reasons for the separation, most political, some politically technical, and just a handful that were actually technical. We'll avoid the political differences and their derivatives and focus on one of the more interesting technical issues.

OS/2 was written in assembly language to the Intel 80286 instruction set. This unavoidable fact locked OS/2 to a single platform, which was in direct violation of Microsoft's vision for a portable operating system. Whether or not this was the main factor for the breakup is now beside the point. What it shows is how early in the process Microsoft was committed to a portable next-generation operating system.

It is this type of insight that allows us to realize why Microsoft eventually ported NT to the PowerPC platform. Portability has been—and will continue

> **Foolishness or Philosophy?**
>
> It was around the time of the late 1980s that I was at a trade show in New York City. I was coming out of a conference session when a rather odd-looking fellow handed me a leaflet. This leaflet came with an invitation to meet with a group of individuals dedicated to exposing the supposed "unholy" agreement between Andy Grove of Intel and Bill Gates of Microsoft (an agreement designed to make them billionaires). It went on to describe in detail how Andy and Bill had agreed to establish complimentary releases of technology whereby the operating system would within one year be inefficient compared to the microprocessor technology.
>
> As the theory went, Bill would release a new, more robust and more demanding operating system. The masses (or lambs, if I remember correctly), would purchase the new operating system, not realizing that it would overdrive their existing hardware platform and subsequent microprocessor technology. This would result in another one-year cycle where the microprocessor architecture was incapable of keeping up with the operating system requirements. Andy would then release a new microprocessor for the lambs, and the cycle would continue. I threw the leaflet in the trash can and laughed, back then. . . .

to be—a critical part of the NT philosophy. In the end, understanding the philosophy of a company with respect to its operating system design enables us to fully comprehend the current product and anticipate the direction of future releases. This will become powerful information as you begin the task of *architecting* (meaning hands-on designing) enterprise networks.

With this point in mind, let's examine some of the early design goals for Microsoft Windows NT in more detail, beginning with the higher priority goals. Throughout the NT development period, Microsoft strived to fulfill the higher priority goals, even if that happened at the expense of a lower priority goal.

The choice of priority for these design goals is documented by Helen Custer, one of the original members of the NT development team, in her book *Inside Windows NT* (published by Microsoft Press).

Extensibility

Windows NT was designed from the onset to be flexible and open to change and growth in order to keep pace with emerging technologies. If this had not been the first priority, NT would have been left to suffer the same fate that DOS faces today. Designed as a 16-bit operating system for the 8086, DOS's features remained all but unchanged until version 5.0. By then Microsoft Windows had begun to increase in popularity and the promise of moving away from the DOS command line and into a full graphical operating environment became a reality. DOS remained stagnant while Windows continued to evolve.

In order to become extensible, NT needed to ensure that it could be flexible in its architecture so that it could adapt to the point where support for future microprocessor technology and hardware peripherals could be easily incorporated into the operating system.

At the time, one operating system that was considered to be very extensible was UNIX. In fact, UNIX was so extensible that it ultimately led to many variants, such as BSD (Berkeley Systems Development), Hewlett-Packard UX, Digital ULTRIX, and SUN OS, that exist to this very day. The extensibility that existed in UNIX occasionally led to instances of instability and weak security, because by design, the core, or kernel, of the operating system could be directly manipulated. The thought of developing a variant of UNIX was certainly not very appealing to Microsoft.

What Microsoft wanted was an architecture that sat somewhere between the tightly coupled ideals of DOS and the loosely coupled architecture of UNIX. At the time, Dr. Richard Rashid of Carnegie Mellon University had developed the Mach operating system with similar intentions. Onto a compact, core set of functions (or *primitives*, to borrow from the world of TCP/IP), Dr. Rashid had snapped service-based modules, or servers, to extend the capabilities of the operating system. New servers could be added or expanded through a set of APIs. All this flexibility occurred a layer above the operating system primitives, adding a great degree of stability to the system.

The early architects of Windows NT chose a similar approach by establishing a kernel mode and a user mode of operation. The integrity of the operating system would be guaranteed by isolating the NT kernel below a series of executive services. All application and non-privileged processes would run in user mode, out of the way of the operating environment. Figure 1.1 provides a general view of this architecture. The internal architecture of Microsoft Windows NT will be covered in more detail in Chapter 2.

FIGURE 1.1
Microsoft Windows NT internal architecture

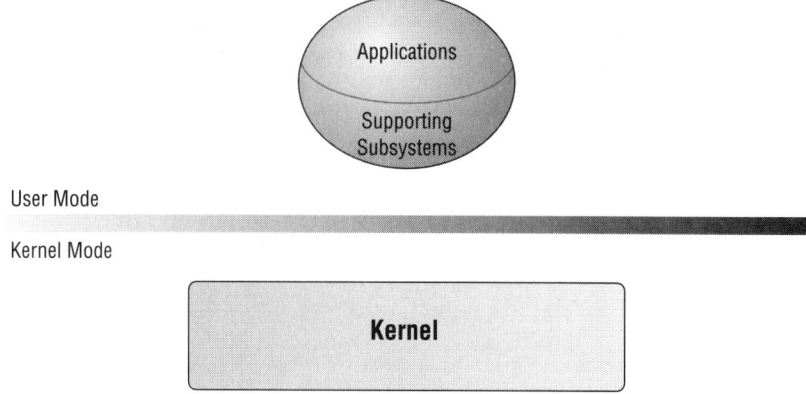

Portability

Lack of portability for OS/2 was arguably one of the main reasons why Microsoft broke from its IBM partnership to launch the NT project. OS/2 was written in assembler (assembly language), and as such it was closely tied to the hardware platform, making it a weak candidate for migration. This is not to say that it would have been impossible to port OS/2 to other platforms (including the emerging RISC architecture), but it would have required a lot of effort. The moral of the story is that the more tightly the language that creates the operating system is coupled to the hardware platform, the less likely it is to be portable.

Enter Dennis Ritchie, forefather of the C programming language. As a high-level language, C was designed from the start to be modular and *portable*, a nice fit for the NT programmers, ultimately providing them with the right tool for the right job. C would become the language used in the majority of NT code. Assembler would only be invoked where speed of execution and direct access to the hardware were priority requirements.

The use of assembler ultimately brought up questions of manageability. Understanding that using the language was required, the architects of NT began to consider how its shortcomings might be effectively dealt with. The first decision was to keep the assembler code in self-contained modules. This would allow for easy replacement of these modules as NT was ported across various platforms. The second point of consideration dealt specifically with the hardware architecture of various PC manufacturers, including those whose design was based on the same microprocessor. This is where the real question of portability comes into play. To solve this problem the NT team turned to HAL.

Portability Is Not a Game

Last Christmas, my brother leaned toward me to ask a question as my nephew opened his third Nintendo 64 cartridge. "Why is it that I have to buy a DOOM II cartridge for Nintendo 64 and a separate DOOM II cartridge for the Sega Saturn?" he asked. "These aren't the only games where I've got duplicates, either—you know these things are about 50 bucks apiece. What's the story?" He rambled on.

I responded by explaining to him that the operating system that runs on Nintendo is not portable, nor is the one that runs on the Sega Saturn. If either were, it would go a long way toward alleviating this problem. "I don't understand what you just said, but in the end it still sucks," he stated, simultaneously ending the conversation and highlighting the importance of portability.

The Hardware Abstraction Layer (HAL) isolates the executive services of NT from the computer hardware. Figure 1.2 provides a view of this service. HAL's objective is to provide a single point of reference to the computer hardware. In this role it preserves the investment made in the kernel and executive services, enabling them to maintain their integrity by not having to change for each platform that chooses to run NT. In summary, HAL provides machine-independence to Microsoft Windows NT.

FIGURE 1.2 The Hardware Abstraction Layer

User Mode

Kernel Mode

Executive Services
Kernel

Hardware Abstraction Layer

Hardware

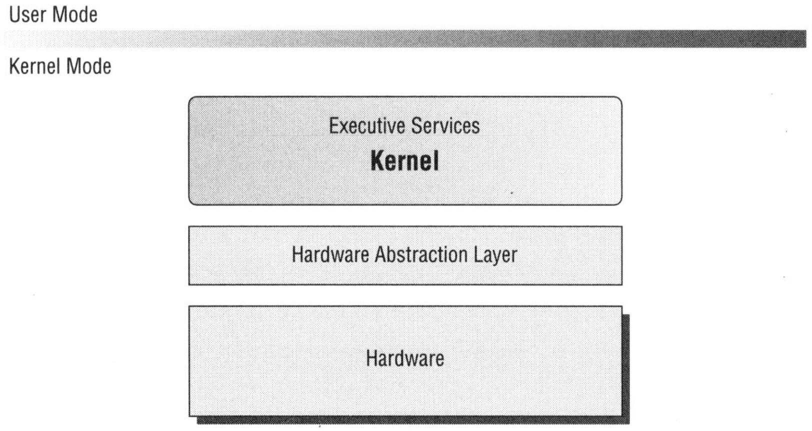

Reliability

Interestingly enough, it is not until we reach this third design point that we get to a design goal that translates directly to user acceptance of the NT operating system. Extensibility and portability are extremely important, but it was the reliability of the operating system that won over the CEOs, giving them the confidence to select NT as a viable platform upon which to run their mission-critical applications. At the time, Microsoft's flagship product was Windows 3.1, and the network-enhanced Windows for Workgroups was slowly emerging from the labs of Redmond, Washington. Neither of these products was taken as a serious platform suitable for downsizing legacy applications. Echoes of a product code-named *Chicago* might have held promise, but as more details were released, it became apparent its direction was toward the mid-range desktop and consumer market—more of a migration path from Microsoft Windows than a robust workstation platform.

> ### Designing by Deadlines
>
> The product code-named *Chicago*, which later became Windows 95, was under development in a separate branch of the Microsoft organization from Windows NT. Initially little interaction occurred between the Windows NT and Chicago development teams. When the release schedule was stepped up for Chicago, many developers from the NT organization found themselves transferred to the project, leaving NT development to a skeleton crew for a period of time. The good news is that Chicago was released as promised (as Windows 95), in August of 1995, thanks to the Herculean effort of the Microsoft programmers. The backlash from this shift of staff focus can be seen in the lack of features and peripheral support in the first release of Windows NT as compared to the first release of Windows 95. Many of us probably have stories of how we obtained the necessary video, printer, and peripheral drivers from the Windows 95 CD, when they couldn't be found on the Windows NT media. Other features that exist in Windows 95 such as PC Card drivers, Plug-and-Play support, and Power Management, are still lacking in the most recent releases of the NT product.

Our design points become more significant when we consider that the reliability of an operating system is based on perception as much as fact. In the networking technologies business *perception is truth*. Therefore it was important for Dave Cutler and his team to develop an operating system that would obtain market share through *mind-share*. To do so, he would have to enhance the exception handling process of Windows NT, such that it exceeded the expectations of his audience, an audience whose only experience with Microsoft exception handling came from Microsoft Windows.

For those not familiar with Microsoft Windows 3.*x* exception processing, it was managed through an interface known as Dr. Watson. The information provided by Dr. Watson was usually cryptic and rarely helpful. In the end, with or without Dr. Watson the treatment was the same—REBOOT. As if Dr. Watson itself did not provide enough of a challenge, Dave Cutler and his team found themselves having to enhance the image of Windows NT security beyond the screen-saver/password protection that Microsoft Windows 3.*x* provided.

The internal architecture of Microsoft Windows NT was crafted in a way that provided a solid foundation for handling exceptions in a predictable and structured manner. It was decided that at no time should an unexpected error condition result in the instability of another application program or, worse yet, of the operating system itself. This foundation was established early on in the project when it was determined that NT would be built as a *preemptive* multitasking environment.

Preemptive and Non-preemptive Operating Systems

Generally speaking, a *preemptive* multitasking environment places the operating system in control of resources (memory, CPU cycles, etc.), where it can determine which services obtain resources and for what duration they can retain them. This concept can be contrasted to a *non-preemptive* multitasking environment where all services work in a cooperative fashion to request, share, and release resources. Non-preemptive multitasking works outside the direct control of the operating system, placing a greater dependence on the services and on the developers of them, to ensure that they do not compromise the integrity of the system. At the time of NT's development, Novell NetWare 3.*x* was the most popular non-preemptive multitasking system.

Other key elements of reliability include the following:

- Executive Services
- Virtual Memory Manager
- Structured handling of abnormal endings (ABENDS)

The executive services of NT work in a coordinated effort through the operating system to ensure that interaction with the kernel happens in a very predictable manner. This carefully choreographed model allows for the structured handling of exceptions, resulting in a more stable and predictable operating system.

The integrity of the operating system has additional support through the Microsoft Virtual Memory Manager (VMM). The VMM provides each user-mode service with a dedicated block of virtual addresses. The VMM then takes the responsibility of placing each user-mode service into actual memory, ensuring that one program does not overwrite the memory area of another.

More esoteric, but none-the-less important, features such as event logging, auto-restart, and memory core dump trapping provide an audit trail from which to troubleshoot if system integrity should become compromised and an abnormal ending should result. In the event that this situation should occur, the NT File System (NTFS) comes complete with transaction logging, lessening the chance of data corruption. Additional information on NTFS can be found in *Mastering Windows NT Server 4* by Mark Minasi (published by Sybex, 1996).

Further information on C2 security can be obtained through the NCSC publication Department of Defense Trusted Computer System Evaluation Criteria, DOD 5200.28-STD, December, 1995. This book is commonly referred to as the Orange Book. Further information is available at www.fedworld.gov/ntis/ntishome.html from the National Technical Information Service.

Compatibility

It's interesting to note that it isn't until the fourth design goal that we reach the subject of compatibility. Somewhere between the early design objectives and final design goals, the subject of compatibility began to take on less importance.

C2 Security

All of the features described thus far, while important, are not obvious to the individual considering Windows NT as a reliable platform. Therefore, Microsoft took the bold step of applying for a U.S. government security designation. As such, Microsoft Windows NT 3.5 went through the process of being designated C2 certified. This designation indicated that the NT operating system *has the ability* to provide discrete protection through the auditing of objects, thereby allowing for the accountability of the subjects and their actions. This certification was meant to provide Windows NT with instant credibility, enabling it to break away from the weak security precedent established by the earlier versions of Microsoft Windows. The C2 designation is certainly quite impressive; but with all due respect, consideration needs to be given to some important details:

- Microsoft Windows NT is not C2 secure by default. Upon completing the default installation, the C2CONFIG.EXE program (available on the Microsoft Windows NT Resource Kit Utilities CD) must be run against the installation. This utility will make note of where C2 compliance is lacking. The administrator is responsible for making the appropriate changes, aligning the platform with the C2 security specification.

- A C2 security designation is only one level above the bottom of the scale, where D signifies a product under review, not necessarily a security designation. In essence, this makes a C2 security designation the first and lowest level of classification, while B and A designations, including their sublevels, impose more stringent requirements.

- The C2 security designation applies to the version of software tested, in accordance with the platform upon which it is tested. In essence, just because Windows NT 3.5 was C2 certified does not mean that 3.51, 3.51 service pack 1, or 4 and its associated service packs are automatically certified. Each version or service pack release would need to go through the same certification process as the original.

> - There are several features available within Windows NT that, if invoked, automatically disqualify it for C2 certification. NT must be the only NOS installed on the system, OS/2 and POSIX support must be removed, and networking services must be removed. Of all those mentioned, that last is certainly the most glaring. To remove networking services from Windows NT is to strip it of some of the very features that it was designed to provide.
>
> The point of this section is to provide the reader with the information necessary to make a valued decision, where C2 compliance is a determining factor in deciding whether to deploy Microsoft Windows NT. For this reason, it is important that we understand that Microsoft Windows NT is not C2 secure by default. In fact, to tailor Windows NT after installation so that it becomes C2 secure is to rid it of some of its most important features. Many network consultants, including the authors, consider C2 security within Windows NT to be more of a marketing feature than anything else.

Before we continue with our discussion, we need to define exactly what we are considering when we use the term *compatibility* as applied to an operating system like Windows NT. Let's think about some of the different levels of compatibility. For instance:

- Compatibility can occur at the source-code level or binary level when we consider executable programs.

- Compatibility can occur at the file system level, when we take into account the way that data is stored and secured.

- Compatibility can also occur at the interface level, when we think about the way in which we will interact with this new operating system.

The area of compatibility is where the market-research branch of an organization really earns its money. Ultimately, compatibility means that the operating system you are asking users to switch to supports whatever they are currently working with, whether it is an older version or a competing product. The closer that Windows NT can get to supporting the majority of features and functions of the widely accepted operating systems, the better chance it has of converting users to its platform. The job of finding out what the majority of users are running falls on the shoulders of the market research analyst.

Source-Code and Binary-Code Compatibility

Source-code and binary-code compatibility are handled by the Windows NT subsystems operating in the user-mode layer of the architecture. Binary-code compatibility provides a means for the application to run natively on Windows NT without any modification. On the other hand, source-code compatibility requires that the application be recompiled in order to operate properly on the Windows NT platform. At the time of its release, Windows NT provided binary-code compatibility for the more popular operating environments. These included DOS, 16-bit Windows, 32-bit Windows, and OS/2. Source-code compatibility was provided for the POSIX application suite. The support for these operating environments was handled primarily by the Win32 subsystem. Figure 1.3 provides an overview of this architecture. (More details will follow in Chapter 2.)

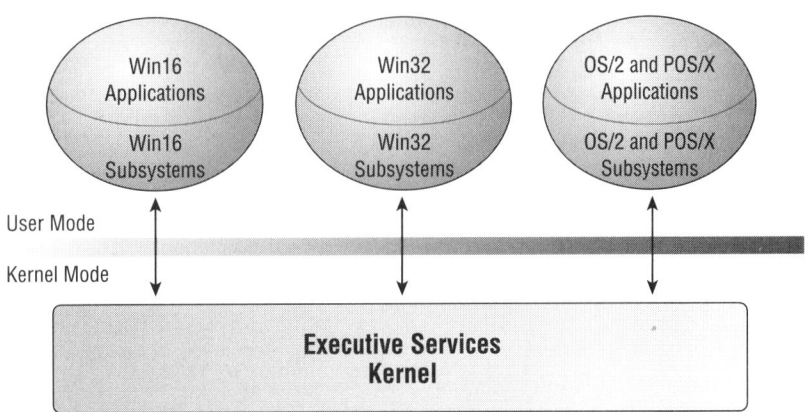

FIGURE 1.3
The original Windows NT subsystems

File System Compatibility

It makes sense that if you are going to support DOS/Windows applications, then you'd better support the File Allocation Table (FAT) file system. You'll win great favor with OS/2 fans should you choose to support the High Performance File System (HPFS) in addition to OS/2 character-mode applications. Microsoft certainly had a desire to win over OS/2 consumers from its former partner, IBM. Therefore it chose to support HPFS within the Windows NT file systems suite.

HPFS support appeared as promised in the first and second releases of Microsoft Windows NT (3.5 and 3.51). In truth, only partial support was delivered, as hot fixing and security could not be applied to an HPFS volume. With the release of Windows NT 4 HPFS support was discontinued.

Those without any ties to former file systems could choose to deploy NT's New Technology File System (NTFS). Lastly, CD-ROM support would be handled through the CD-ROM File System (CDFS).

> Conversion of a file system to NTFS is a one-way process. Once the conversion takes place there is no means of recovery to take you back to the former file system. This is a prime example of where corporate philosophy becomes an operating system feature—or fault, depending on your perspective.

User Interface

At the time of Windows NT's development, Microsoft Windows 3.*x* was the leading desktop operating environment. It made perfect sense that the user interface should mirror the popular program manager interface pioneered by Microsoft Windows 3.*x*. When Windows 95 was released, the interface style changed from Program Manager to the Explorer. It wouldn't be until Windows NT 4 was released that we would find ourselves working with a common interface once again.

Performance

High performance was the final design goal of the Windows NT team: 3-D modeling, CAD/CAM, and simulation packages would place a great demand on NT as a high-performance workstation, while network services would need to run efficiently on NT Server if it had any hope of breaking into the corporate enterprise network.

With this in mind, focus was placed on optimizing various elements in the NT kernel mode layer, including:

- **The NT Kernel:** Architected by Dave Cutler, the NT kernel provides a set of strong primitives (the lowest level of calls within the operating system) that could be built upon nonintrusively. This enabled the kernel to be coded in an efficient and optimal manner without a need to allow for services that would enable direct manipulation.

- **Executive Services:** As they would be constantly communicating with one another in kernel mode, the NT team established a messaging scheme known as a Local Procedure Call (LPC), to handle the efficient communication between these services.

> **Back to Chicago**
>
> Early on we made a point of mentioning that it became increasingly apparent that Chicago was going to be the upgrade path for Microsoft Windows 3.*x*. By default, we can assume that compatibility went to the top of the list of design goals for Chicago. The legacy suite of 16-bit applications running on Windows 3.*x* desktops would have to be fully supported if there was any hope of making Chicago a success.
>
> This proved to be a blessing for the developers of Windows NT, as it released them from the burden of having to apply such stringent requirements on its operating system for compatibility with 16-bit applications. Windows NT was being designed to support an emerging set of 32-bit applications. For those looking to support their legacy 16-bit services on a new operating system, Chicago was an option.
>
> This philosophy exists to this day as Windows 95 (formerly Chicago) remains the preferred platform for 16-bit applications. Microsoft is not as committed (philosophically speaking) to providing 16-bit application support on Microsoft Windows NT.

- **Networking Components:** These were built into NT from its inception. Placed in the kernel-mode layer, they were designed to be run optimally.

Testing began to take on increased importance as a release date for Windows NT approached. The "critical path," comprised of system calls, virtual memory management, and environmental subsystems, was tested in part and as a whole to ensure that each individual element, as well as cooperative elements, would run optimally.

Despite the fact that NT performs well, we still need to consider that performance was last in the series of five design goals. As you may recall, when two or more design options conflict, the option that adheres to the higher priority design goal wins. This infers that in some instances performance may have lost out where extensibility, portability, reliability, or compatibility had higher precedence. To help you get the most performance from your NT Servers, we'll discuss performance tuning and optimization in Chapter 15.

The Windows NT Evolutionary Ladder

Windows NT did not enjoy immediate widespread success. With each version released, corporate acceptance of NT has grown. In this section, we'll outline the evolution of NT since its inception. Figure 1.4 illustrates the evolution of this product as described in the remainder of this section.

FIGURE 1.4

The evolution of Microsoft Windows NT

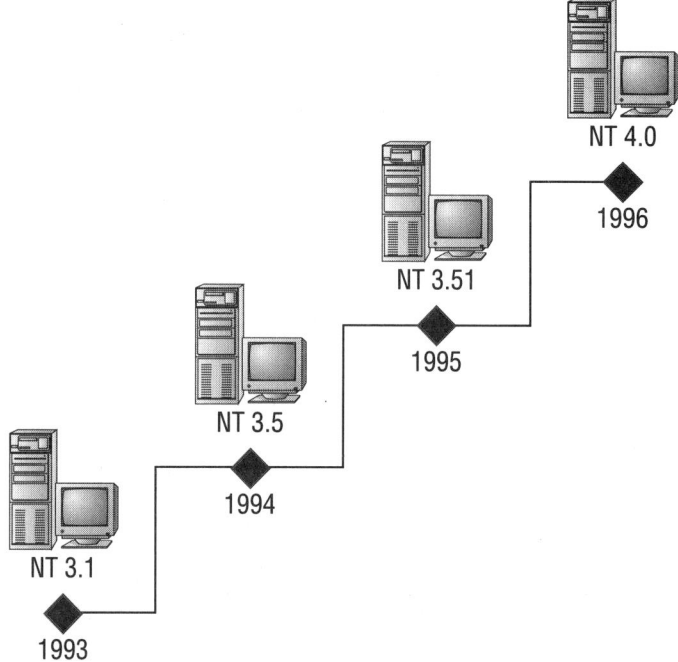

Windows NT Advanced Server 3.1

Windows NT Advanced Server 3.1 was released in 1993, five years after Bill Gates and Dave Cutler first met. This first release contained 7 million lines of code that delivered on the basic design principles established by the NT development team. NT Server 3.1 offered the following services:

- File and print services
- Application services
- Single network logon

- Symmetric multiprocessing support (up to 4)
- Intel, Alpha, MIPS platform support

Windows NT 3.5

One year later, under a new version number and with a slight name change, Microsoft introduced Windows NT Server 3.5. This 1994 model was followed shortly with a 3.51 release in 1995. By then TCP/IP support had been enhanced and was being touted as the best protocol for an enterprise deployment. Internal routing surfaced in a later service pack and the system as a whole began to stabilize.

Most interesting of all was that with this release, Novell began to fight back. The question of the year was on the mind of every CIO: "Which direction should I go, NetWare or NT?"

Windows NT 4

With the release of 4 in 1996, Windows NT source code had increased to 16 million lines. It was during this time that Bill Gates redirected his entire organization toward a new focus—the Internet.

Windows NT 4 was rolled into this frenzy, and came bundled with the Internet Information Server and Internet Explorer Web browser. In response to popular demand, the user interface was redesigned to match the Explorer style released with Windows 95.

At the time of this writing, NT 4 continues to be enhanced with strong Internet support. Microsoft Commerce Server, Microsoft Site Server, and third-party firewall vendors have all chosen NT 4 as their platform. Part III of this book, *NT as a Net Platform*, will explore this topic in much more detail.

The Future Direction for Microsoft Windows NT

The intent of this chapter has been to show how the philosophy of a company drives the direction in which a network operating system develops. Additionally we've tried to introduce the development of the product as it has evolved to its current state. To understand the future of NT we need to reconsider the philosophy of Microsoft with respect to its premier network operating system.

As you'll recall, in 1988 Bill Gates met with Dave Cutler to discuss an opportunity for him to join the development team at Microsoft. Cutler would take charge of developing a *portable* operating system—one that addressed any concerns that the business community had with running *mission-critical* applications on personal computers.

What we can infer from this meeting is that Microsoft has *always* intended for NT to be the operating system upon which companies will be willing to run their core business applications. NT was never intended to provide *just* file and print services. Therein lies the future direction for Microsoft Windows NT.

Consider the following:

- In 1991 Jim Allchin and six others joined the Dave Cutler NT team with the goal of bringing NT to the next level—*distributed computing*. Within two years, NT began to erode the market share held by Novell (for file and print services) and, to a lesser extent, by UNIX (for application and Web services).

- In 1993 David Vaskevitch and more than eight others joined the core team with the intent of enhancing Windows NT through a *distributed applications infrastructure*. During this time, the Microsoft BackOffice Suite was developed to embellish the network operating system. BackOffice has continued to evolve, providing us with Microsoft SNA Server, Microsoft SQL Server, Microsoft Systems Management Server, Microsoft Internet Information Server, and Microsoft Exchange Server, to name a few.

On May 20, 1997 Microsoft hosted Scalability Day in New York City. In the course of this program, attendees were provided with live demonstrations of:

- **Terabyte-size databases:** Windows NT 4 was the platform of choice for Microsoft's next generation SQL server, code-named *Sphinx*. Onto this platform, Jim Gray of Microsoft established a 140-million-row, 1.4TB database of information. This demonstration was aimed at showing the extent to which NT Server and Microsoft SQL Server are capable of scaling. At the time of this demonstration most of the larger databases were in the range of 3GB (Human Genome Project) to 300GB (Dayton-Hudson Sales Records).

It is worth noting that Jim Gray was one of the original team members who joined Microsoft in 1993 under the leadership of David Vaskevitch.

- **A billion transactions per day**: The equivalent of over 1 billion banking transactions in a 24-hour period were processed, using a multinode configuration of 20 Compaq ProLiant 5000 servers accessing 2.5TB of total disk storage. Microsoft provided NT server 4, SQL Server 6.5, and Transaction Server 1.0 for the operating system along with BackOffice software. This volume exceeded that processed by the five largest U.S. banks in the same 24-hour time period.

- **Large-scale Internet Web Servers**: 100 million hits per day were taken by a Hewlett-Packard NetServer LX equipped with dual 200MHz Pentium Pro processors. Microsoft Internet Information Server 3.0, running on NT Server 4, demonstrated that it could withstand this load.

- **Large-scale messaging systems**: Microsoft Exchange Server 5 was configured to run on a digital AlphaServer 4100 which housed four 466MHz Alpha Processors and 1GB of RAM. This "single-box" configuration serviced 50,000 active users, sending/receiving 1.8 million messages in a single day.

In summary, we need to ask ourselves: "Is Microsoft still committed to the same philosophy for Microsoft Windows NT that it has stated from the very start, when Bill Gates first sat down with Dave Cutler?"

At Microsoft Scalability Day, we listened in earnest as Bill Gates delivered the keynote address. Focusing on his presentation, we could not help but notice phrases that surfaced, like "...any business of any size can now run its enterprise applications on Microsoft software and industry-related hardware" and "combining enterprise-class scalability with PC-industry volume economics will radically reshape the enterprise market."

We left this presentation contemplating how similar words were probably used in Gates' meetings with David Cutler. Lost in conversation we hardly paid attention to the conference assistant who handed us a package on Microsoft's soon-to-be-released *Windows NT - Enterprise Edition*. It was only later in reviewing this package that we read of its promise to run "...mission-critical business applications such as airline reservation systems, online banking" and to "...optimize return on corporate computing investments by easily integrating with and adding value to existing mission-critical systems and applications, while offering a low cost of ownership." These are words that continue to echo a philosophy established nine years ago.

CHAPTER 2

The NT Architecture

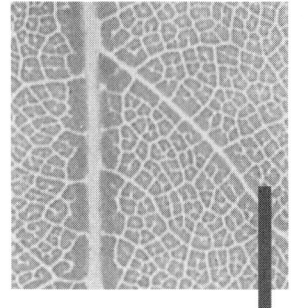

I n the first chapter we discussed motivations that shaped the design goals for Microsoft Windows NT. Now we'll continue by taking a look at the architecture that resulted from implementing those goals.

As we discuss the NT architecture, you'll notice ho2w the priority goals for the NT design team—extensibility, portability, reliability, compatibility, and performance—are reflected within the Windows NT operating system.

Throughout this chapter we'll examine the client/server, object-oriented model that Windows NT was designed to embrace. We'll fully discuss key elements, such as symmetric multiprocessing, preemptive multitasking, and built-in networking, so you can gain an appreciation for the elements of NT with which you may never directly interact.

We'll discuss:

- The methodology and model that was the foundation for Windows NT
- The internal architecture of Windows NT, including:
    - Windows NT Executive Layer
    - Hardware Abstraction Layer
    - Environment Subsystems

Establishing the Model

Windows NT was designed to support three models of operating system design:

- Client/server
- Modular components
- Symmetric multiprocessing

These three models would have to be coordinated in a way that would enable Windows NT to break from the monolithic models of operating system design that were common during the years of NT's development. For example, early operating systems, such as DOS, and dedicated operating systems, such as those that control the Nintendo video game units, were often developed as monolithic systems. Because monolithic systems are comprised of a series of nested procedure calls, one can never tell where one process leaves off and the other begins.

While this approach may have been suitable for small, dedicated operating systems, its lack of flexibility and scalability made it impractical for enterprise operating systems like Windows NT. Instead, NT developers broke from the monolithic model and chose to take a layered approach to operating system design. Figure 2.1 depicts the system structure of a layered operating system. For our purposes, it is compared to a monolithic model. Note that the layering enables us to separate common functions that can be built on top of each other. Through this approach we are able to more easily enhance or replace an element of the operating system with minimal impact to the other elements. Dave Cutler brought this approach to Microsoft through his experience in developing Digital's VMS operating system.

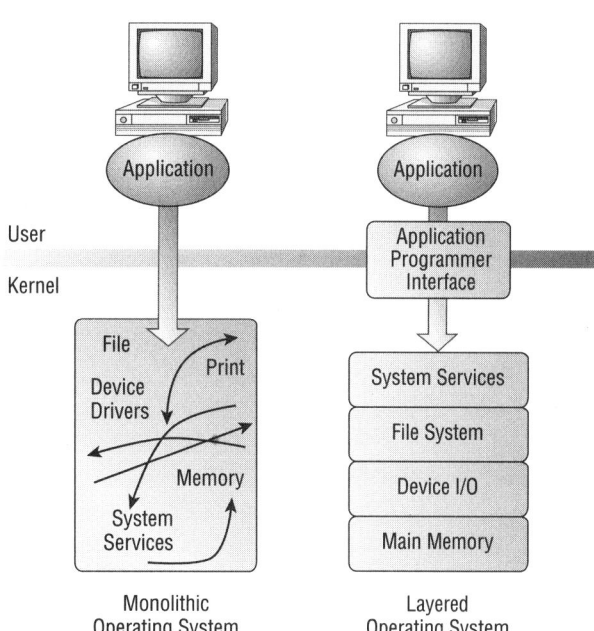

FIGURE 2.1

Monolithic vs. layered operating system models

Client/Server and Layered Internals

Client/server operating system design is a natural extension to the layered model. Through this approach, elements of the operating system are divided into services such as file, print, and communications. Each service has a dual relationship with the rest of the operating system. In its first role, the service interacts with the user interface, accepting requests for processing. Once the request is received, the service switches roles by interacting with the system kernel. Through this interaction, the service will deliver the request for processing. Once the request is complete, the service will return the result to the user interface, as shown in Figure 2.2. Notice that the service calls convert from user mode to kernel mode, as the service interaction changes from the user interface to the operating system kernel.

FIGURE 2.2

Client/server processing

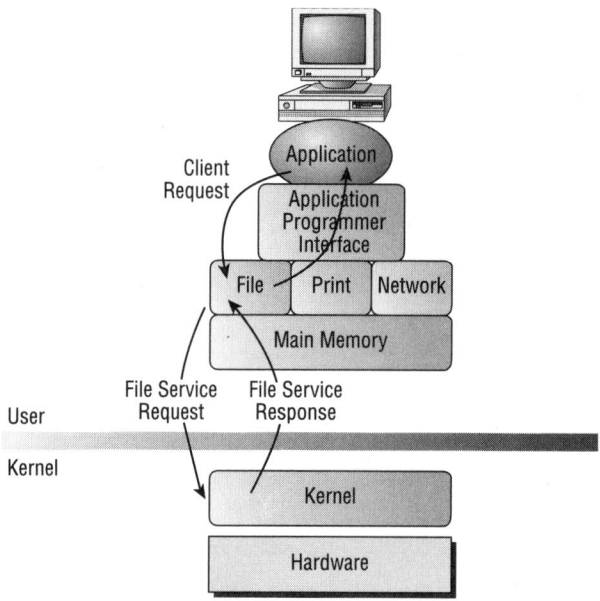

After some consideration, it may become confusing to distinguish between what constitutes a user mode service (client) and what constitutes a kernel mode service (server) in our client/server model. Ultimately, it is up to the operating system designer, who must weigh what impact to the operating system services in user mode will have, should they become unstable. The penalty for this comes with the speed at which they will execute.

> ### A Mini-Glossary for States of the Microprocessor
>
> As you read through this book and others, you may notice the terms *kernel mode* and *privileged processor mode* used interchangeably. For this reason and others that follow, we present a mini-glossary:
>
> - **Protected Subsystem = Non-Privileged Processor Mode = User Mode:** Describes a state of the microprocessor where the instruction set is limited, access to memory is not allowed, and direct access to the hardware is not permitted. Faulty programs running in this state provide little threat to the integrity of the system as a whole. If they become unstable, they can usually be dealt with in a structured manner, with little impact to the operating system kernel.
>
> - **Non-Protected Subsystem = Privileged Processor Mode = Kernel Mode:** Describes a state of the microprocessor where all instructions are allowed, full access to memory is available, and direct access to the hardware is permitted. Programs executing at this level need to be reliable and efficient. Should they become unstable, they may jeopardize the integrity of the entire operating system.

All things being equal, a service running in user mode will execute more slowly than the same service running in kernel mode.

After careful deliberation, Dave Cutler and his team began to develop a model for Microsoft Windows NT that leveraged the best features of the client/server and layered methodologies. Figure 2.3 shows a graphical representation of the early model for Windows NT.

A Modular Approach Throughout

A modular approach with Windows NT results in an operating system that is built of components that work cooperatively in providing services. These components are an extension of NT's system resources which are represented by objects. For instance, print services are an object; file services are an object; communications services are an object. This object representation occurs wherever there is an opportunity that the resource may be shared by more

FIGURE 2.3

The Windows NT high-level model

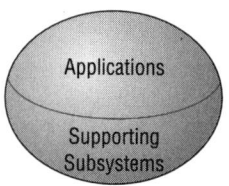
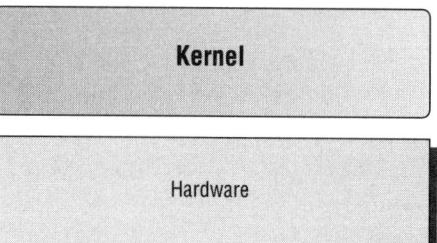

than one process. Shared resources such as memory, file systems, and peripherals all fit this criteria and as such are implemented as objects.

This technique of implementing shared resources as objects was borrowed in part from UNIX. It provides great flexibility to the operating system, enabling the OS to adapt to changing peripherals, emerging technologies, system fixes, and system enhancements.

Windows NT leverages this modular approach by first separating those shared elements from the kernel, moving them to the layer just above it. This layer, known as the Executive Layer, is then divided into objects with similar functions. Each object has the ability to stand on its own as a runtime service; these services are referred to as Executive Services. As for the kernel, it has been streamlined to the point where it contains nothing but primitive system calls, leading it to be referred to as a *microkernel* at times. This process of separation and division of the kernel is depicted in Figure 2.4.

In summary, this architecture provides the following benefits:

- The NT Microkernel exists as a compact and efficient set of primitives, which are accessible only through the Executive Layer. While running in kernel mode, the Executive Layer will issue calls in a structured and secure manner, using its Executive Services.

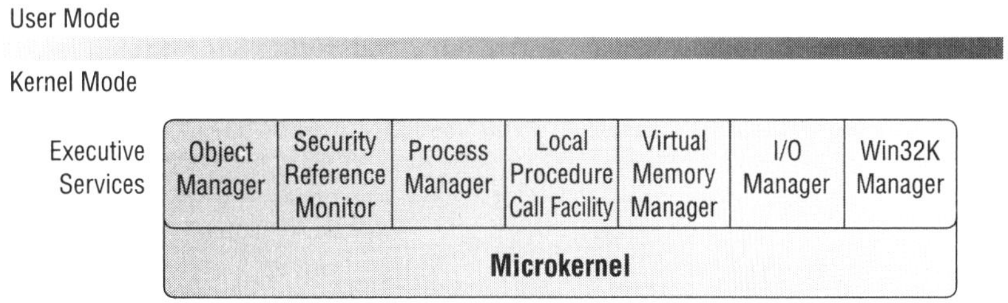

FIGURE 2.4

The emergence of Executive Services and formation of the microkernel

	Object Manager	Security Reference Monitor	Process Manager	Local Procedure Call Facility	Virtual Memory Manager	I/O Manager	Win32K Manager
Executive Services							

User Mode / Kernel Mode / Microkernel

- The NT Microkernel, I/O Manager, and Win32K Manager are the only portions of the operating system with privilege to access the hardware, which provides a greater level of stability than previous DOS/Windows environments. It is also the reason why 16-bit programs that attempt direct hardware access are not permitted to run on Windows NT.

The Executive Layer is actually a set of objects working cooperatively as an interface between the system services and NT kernel. As requirements change, the object providing the service is the only one that needs to be updated. Objects requesting services can remain intact.

One of the more interesting aspects of this object-oriented approach to the Executive Layer comes when we consider the manner in which it can be extended by third-party developers. Consider this—by separating the shared services from the kernel and implementing them as manageable objects, Microsoft has opened up an opportunity to provide access to NT's kernel mode for select third-party developers. These developers are then able to create a richer set of applications that combine the stability of user mode services with the speed of execution of kernel mode. As you will see in Chapter 14, Citrix was quick to partner with Microsoft, where they could leverage this support to their advantage.

The NT development team continued in their modular approach by providing application support through protected mode subsystems. In doing so, they were able to provide the User Mode layer with all of the benefits that object-oriented design afforded them at the kernel mode. An operating system subsystem could be added, modified, or removed without affecting the other subsystems. Communication between subsystems would happen through the Executive Layer, ensuring that the messages would pass in a reliable and

> ### Riding with the Devil
>
> A line from an old blues song goes, "If you choose to ride with the devil, eventually he's going to want to drive...." Developers choosing to accept the invitation to write to the kernel mode of NT need to clearly understand that this layer belongs to Microsoft. As such, they have the ultimate authority in permitting or denying access at any point in the evolution of NT.
>
> Citrix was faced with this dilemma in early 1997, when there was a question as to whether Microsoft would license them for NT 4 in the same manner as they had for NT 3.5. The word coming out of Redmond was that Microsoft had decided to develop its own multiuser version of NT similar to what Citrix had pioneered. Not wanting to support its partner-turned-competitor, Microsoft pulled back on licensing the 4 Executive Services code. Citrix stock dropped, while everyone held their breath for a couple of nerve-wracking months. Eventually, Microsoft reconsidered and agreed to recommit to its partnership. A deal was inked for the 4 code and the Citrix stock jumped more than 30 points. Citrix was back in business, no longer having to sing the blues.

secure manner. Access to the Executive Layer happens either natively or through the CSR Subsystem:

- **Natively:** A native service is detected by the hardware that returns control to the Executive Services. All elements of the Executive Layer work in a cooperative manner to provide authentication (Security Reference Monitor), memory resources (Virtual Memory Manager), and processor support (Process Manager) as needed.

- **CSR Subsystem:** The CSR Subsystem is responsible for the console which provides text window support, hard error handling, and shutdown.

Figure 2.5 illustrates this interaction and architecture.

Symmetric Multiprocessing

As we discussed in Chapter 1, NT was designed as a multiprocessing operating system from the very beginning. Although it required much more effort, the choice was made to establish NT as a symmetrical multiprocessing (SMP) operating system, as opposed to an asymmetrical one. Let's take a moment to examine both models.

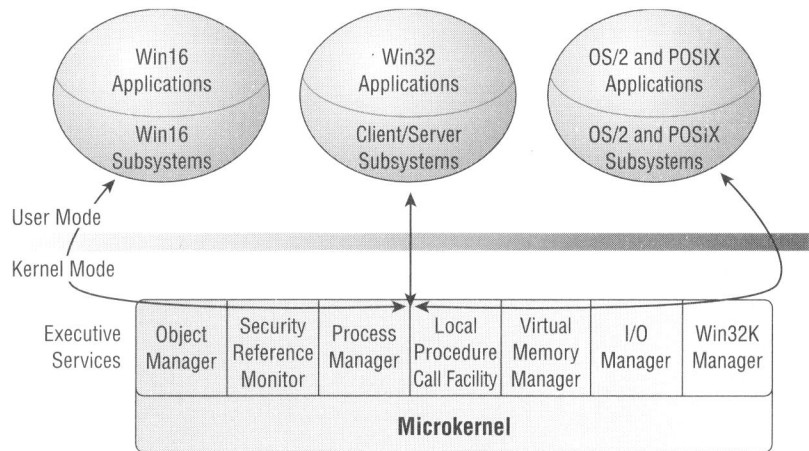

FIGURE 2.5
The User Mode subsystems

The Asymmetrical Model

In an asymmetrical multiprocessing (AMP) model, one or more processors are dedicated to supporting the operating system. All other processors are dedicated to supporting peripheral functions such as network, application, or storage services. Otherwise, they would share the load of application services between them. The advantage to an AMP model is its rapid development time for companies looking to provide a higher level of service for their operating system. The disadvantage is that the whole system could be rendered inoperable following the failure of the processor dedicated to supporting the operating system.

Industry examples of asymmetrical multiprocessing systems include the Power Mac 9500/180MP and the DayStar Digital Genesis MP600. Both of these systems are exclusive to the MAC operating system. Developers are required to implement Apple's multiprocessing extensions to their applications in order for them to take full advantage of the multiprocessing capabilities of these systems; otherwise the applications will run as if they were on a single processor machine. Figure 2.6 illustrates the asymmetrical multiprocessing model.

Asymmetrical processing systems are traditionally tightly coupled to the hardware on which they are running. This essentially requires that the operating system be redesigned for each platform it intends to support. Though easier to create through its tightly coupled nature, the asymmetrical model conflicted with NT's portability design goal and was dismissed as an alternative.

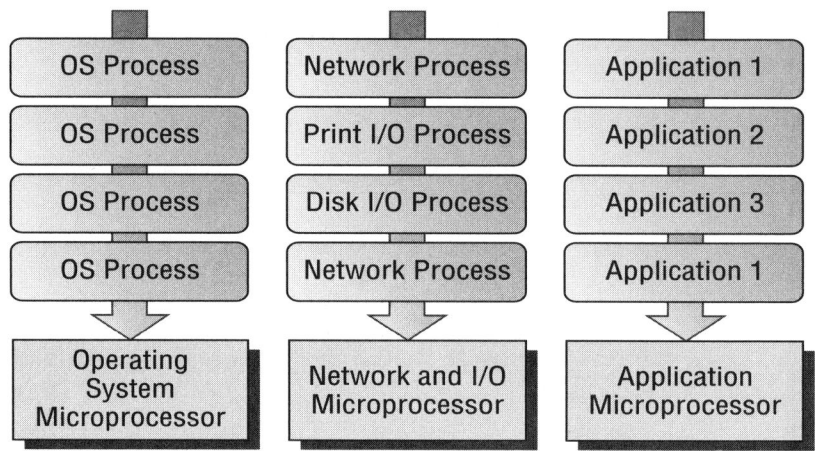

FIGURE 2.6

Asymmetrical multiprocessing model

The Symmetrical Model

In a symmetrical multiprocessing model, the operating system and application services are spread evenly across any available free processor. This even distribution means the operating system will not be bottlenecked by a single microprocessor, as could happen in the asymmetrical multiprocessing model. The symmetrical multiprocessing model allows the operating system to derive the full benefit of all available microprocessors.

In symmetrical multiprocessing, the operating system describes its needs to the kernel's dispatcher. This service will then take the responsibility for scheduling threads to run across the available processors. Refer to Figure 2.7 as the components of symmetrical multiprocessing are described in more detail.

Multitasking Supports Multiprocessing Multitasking describes the ability of a microprocessor to handle more than one task at the same time. This ability is a cooperative effort between the microprocessor and operating system. For example, we can run DOS on a four-way SMP system and try as we may, only one task at a time will be carried out. The truth of the matter is that DOS will not even realize that the other processors exist. By the same token, we can attempt to start Windows NT on an 8088 microprocessor, only to discover that the lack of multitasking support would be just one of the reasons why we are unable to get it running. In the end we realize that a multitasking operating system running on a multitasking-capable microprocessor is the only way to achieve true multitasking.

FIGURE 2.7

Symmetrical multiprocessing model

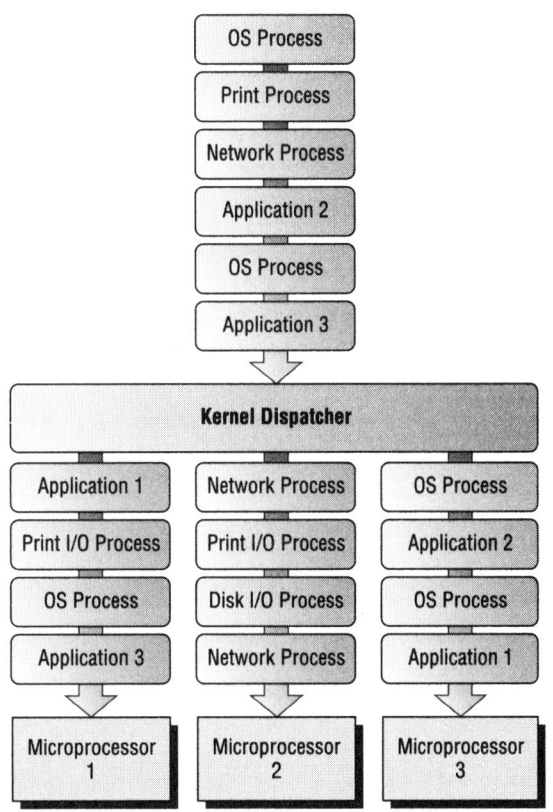

 Multitasking is not multiprocessing, yet multitasking helps to support multiprocessing. Read on as we attempt to clarify this often-misunderstood concept.

Let's take this concept and imagine that we are operating on a single-processor system. Within this system, the microprocessor will take the responsibility of splitting its time between all of the tasks requesting services. The speed at which the microprocessor can switch between these tasks is what gives the illusion that it is accomplishing more than one task at a time—in essence multitasking.

36 Chapter 2 • The NT Architecture

It could be argued that the only true task is the one that is being executed. Essentially, all others are being held in a dormant state. As such, *current context* is the unique name applied to the active task. The idea of switching between the current context and the dormant ones is referred to as *context switching*.

If we extend this concept of multitasking and scale it to machines that contain more than one processor, it may then become clear how multiple tasks can truly be accomplished at the same time (multiprocessing). True multiprocessing is the result of incorporating multiple processors, each with multitasking capability.

Figure 2.8 illustrates a dual microprocessor system. Processor 1 is multitasking tasks 1, 2, and 3, where 1 is its current context. Processor 2 is multitasking tasks A, B, and C, where A is its current context. The system as a whole is multiprocessing tasks 1 and A at this time.

FIGURE 2.8

A multiprocessing system

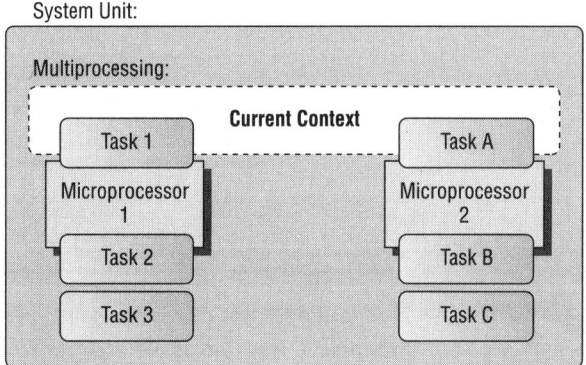

All of this talk about multitasking and multiprocessing might leave you wondering who is responsible for coordinating the effort between all of the microprocessors. The answer can be found at the Executive Layer of our model, in the form of the Process Manager.

You might be asking yourself, "Why is this object called a Process Manager, when its job is to control all of the current contexts, or tasks. Why not call it a Context Manager or Task Manager?" Fair question. If we go back to the previous section we discover that we can replace the word *task* with *process*, since they are terms that can be used interchangeably when describing the current context.

Processes and Threads Even though processes run on their own unique microprocessor, they still share the same physical memory of a machine. As such, it becomes the responsibility of the operating system to ensure the processes do not overwrite one another. The operating system accomplishes this by providing each process with its own area in memory from which it can execute, effectively turning the process into a kind of container.

To access this area of shared memory, the process needs to be authenticated to the operating system. Once this occurs, the process is equipped with a security token from which it can gain access to file, print, application, and other system or network resources. Each resource that the process desires is identified by a unique handle. Figure 2.9 shows a caricature of an authenticated process with handles to all desired resources.

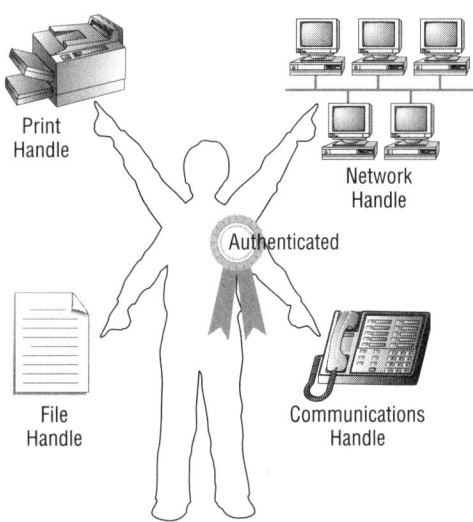

FIGURE 2.9

The authenticated process

At this time, work is still not being accomplished, as the process alone is incapable of servicing the application. The real work in servicing the application is handled by the thread of the process, implying that each process must have at least one thread of execution. We say "at least" because more than one thread may be executing within a process at the same time. All new threads generated in this way will become children of the first, or *parent,* thread.

Wherever possible, a programmer will choose to launch a new thread within an existing process instead of generating a new process. The reason for this, as you probably suspect, is that the overhead in creating a new process is much greater than in creating a new thread. Additionally, interprocess communication is much slower than between threads within a process. These combined reasons are what makes multithreaded processing beneficial to the programmer and end user. Figure 2.10 expands upon the process shown in Figure 2.9 to show the threads executing within this process.

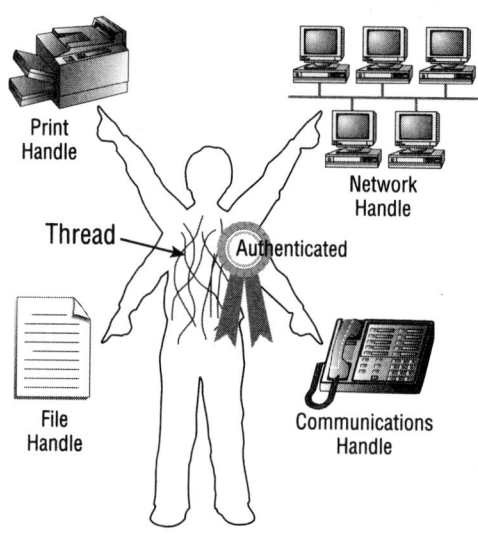

FIGURE 2.10
A multithreaded process

The following list shows the composition of processes and threads:

Process   Private address space in memory where the process's code and data are stored

A Security Access Token provided by Windows NT

Handles to system and network resources such as file, print, and application services

At least one thread to execute the code

Thread	A processor state including the current instruction pointer
	A stack for use when running in user mode
	A stack for use when running in kernel mode

Prioritizing Processes and Threads   One of the responsibilities an application developer has is to assign a priority class to a process within that application. These priority classes are taken into consideration when the Process Manager schedules a process for execution. Once scheduled, the Process Manager passes control to the kernel dispatcher who prioritizes and manages the threads. The kernel dispatcher will utilize a 32-bit prioritization scheme for this purpose. Figure 2.11 provides a view of this classification scheme.

Let's take a moment to consider the life of a thread:

1. A program requests services of the operating system in the form of a process. This service request is handed to the Process Manager, whose job is to find space in memory for the process to execute. The priority of the process has much to do with the speed at which this request for memory address space will be fulfilled.

2. Once the address space is allocated, the parent thread enters a *ready* state and is placed in the priority queue of the kernel dispatcher. When prompted to reschedule, the dispatcher will examine all threads relative to their priority in contrast to all other threads in the queue, threads currently executing, the process's default base scheduling priority and a default set of microprocessors on which the thread may have been scheduled to run.

3. Threads with higher priorities will preempt those with lower ones. This action is what characterizes Windows NT as a preemptive operating system. The threads with the highest priority enter a *standby* state, meaning they will run next on a particular microprocessor. The number of threads in standby can never be greater than the number of available microprocessors.

4. At the appropriate time, the kernel dispatcher will perform a context switch to the high-priority threads. The thread will then enter a *running* state from which it can execute and spawn child threads.

FIGURE 2.11

Thread prioritization classifications

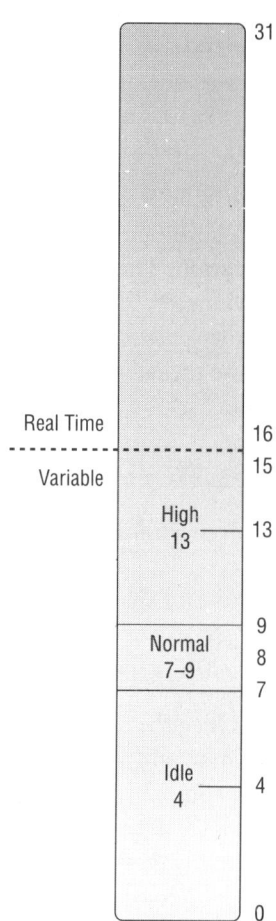

5. When a thread finishes executing, it is *terminated*. It is the determination of the Object Manager as to whether the thread will be deleted or be reinitialized at another time.

Windows NT will handle the policy associated with ensuring that a thread does not grab too much CPU time or, on the other hand, that a thread does not become preempted so many times that it is ignored by the CPU. It accomplishes this by adjusting the base priority of a thread. The base priority is adjusted after a period of evaluation that results in a subsequent action. These are identified as follows:

- Threads waiting for input and threads in the foreground will get a priority boost. This will ensure that the system remains responsive to the console operator.

- Threads that take a voluntary wait will get a priority boost.

- CPU-intensive threads will get their priorities lowered. This prevents them from obtaining an exclusive lock of microprocessor time and/or system resources.

- All threads will periodically get a priority boost to prevent lower priority threads from locking shared resources that may be needed by higher priority threads.

This concept of priority boosting can also be controlled, to some degree, by the thread itself. Each thread within a process has the ability to adjust its priority plus or minus 2. Anything greater or less than this becomes the responsibility of Windows NT, under the aforementioned guidelines.

We conclude this section by highlighting two main points:

- Microsoft Windows NT follows the symmetrical multiprocessing model, allowing the operating system to derive the full benefit of all available microprocessors.

- Microsoft Windows NT handles the policy associated with ensuring that a thread does not grab too much CPU time by preempting its execution in favor of a higher priority thread.

By understanding these points it becomes clear why Microsoft Windows NT is often referred to as a preemptive-symmetrical multiprocessing system.

Internals of NT

In the previous section we provided insight on how the architectural model of NT evolved. Now we'll continue our discussion by examining this architecture in more detail, beginning with the Executive Layer. Later in this chapter, we'll look below to the Hardware Abstraction Layer and then above to the Environment Subsystems. Figure 2.12 illustrates the relationship between the layers.

FIGURE 2.12

The internal architecture of Microsoft Windows NT

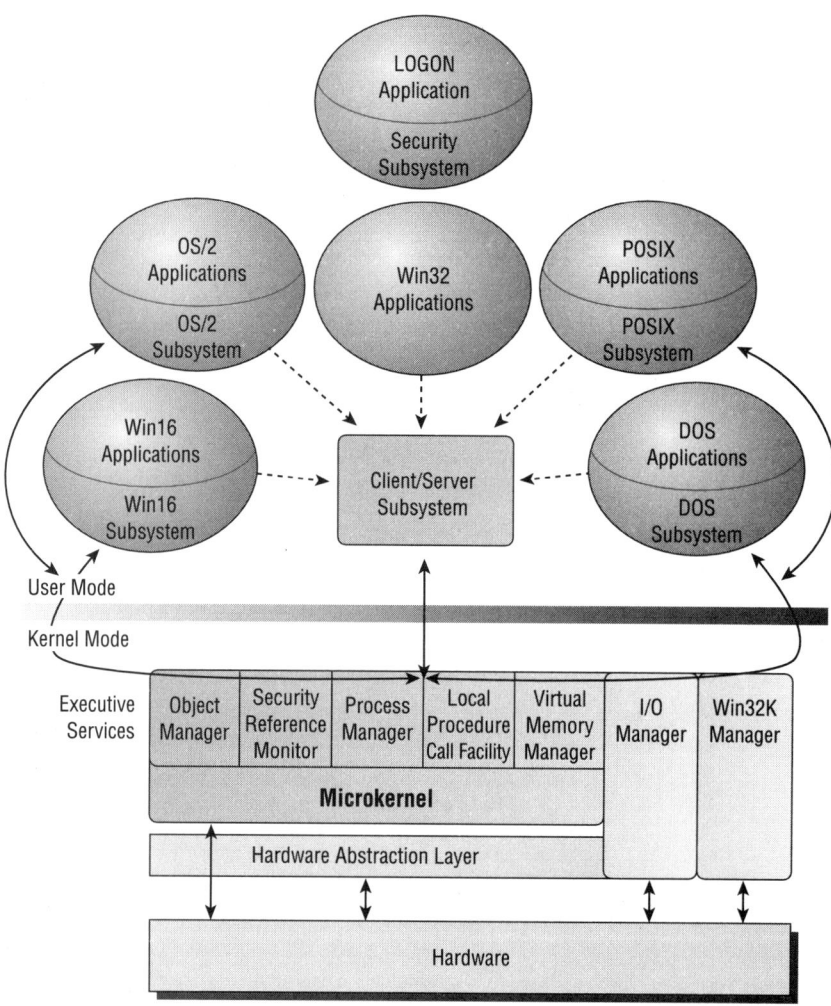

The Windows NT Executive Layer

The Windows NT Executive Layer exists at the kernel mode layer of the architecture. Because of this, independent objects of the Executive Layer are in the best position to service the Environment Subsystems. Executive Layer modules service the subsystems by working cooperatively among themselves, communicating with the microkernel as appropriate. This modular design of the Executive Layer provides great flexibility and extensibility to the operating system. The following sections describe the components of the Executive Layer in more detail.

Object Manager

The Object Manager is responsible for creating, securing, and auditing objects, which are logical representations of resources. In our earlier discussion on processes and threads, we discussed how the Object Manager is responsible for creating the process in which the thread will run.

Security Reference Monitor (SRM)

The SRM is responsible for setting and managing the security policy of the NT operating system. It determines whether a request to create or access an object is valid before authorizing the activity. Since almost everything within the NT operating system exists as an object, the SRM has tremendous power and responsibility.

Process Manager

The Process Manager is responsible for creating and deleting process objects. The process itself is a virtual address space with handles to shared resources, in which the threads will execute.

Local Procedure Call Facility

In the client/server model of the NT operating system, client processes and server processes communicate through message passing. These messages appear as procedure calls of two types: Remote Procedure Calls (RPC), where the client and server communicate across a network, and Local Procedure Calls (LPC), for client/server communication within a system. The NT operating system supports both types, with LPCs being the means of communication between objects within the system.

Virtual Memory Manager

A virtual memory architecture enables the operating system to allocate memory to processes beyond what physically exists in the machine. In Windows NT, each process is allocated address space of 4GB. The application is given 2GB, while the remaining 2GB is reserved as a "scratch pad" area for system files. The Virtual Memory Manager will map this address space to actual physical memory, using a page size of 4KB. As the upper limits of physical memory are reached, the Virtual Memory Manager will "swap" (or "page") the Least Recently Used (LRU) memory pages to physical disk.

I/O Manager

Structured access for peripheral devices is handled by the I/O Manager, an Executive Layer object that helps to achieve the long-sought-after objective of all operating system designers—the ability to uncouple a monolithic device-specific driver from the operating system. Windows NT accomplishes this task by including as much generic I/O code as possible in the I/O Manager. This code is then separated and stacked in a layered design that fosters code sharing and efficient communications.

Within the I/O Manger we discover the following elements:

File Systems   These handle file-oriented access to and from a particular device. Built into NT is support for the FAT, NTFS, and CDFS file systems (HPFS is no longer supported as of version 4). NFS support is also an option through third-party developers.

Cache Manager   This enhances the performance of the file system by storing the most recent requests in system memory. It will also work cooperatively with the Virtual Memory Manager, coordinating the writing of cached data during idle system time.

Device Drivers   These communicate directly with the hardware for read/write access to the network or a physical unit. Uniform Device Drivers exist at this layer where NT has created objects with as much general code as possible relative to activities such as printing, modem communications, and media drive access. This leaves the device manufacturer with the reduced task of writing a SMP "mini-driver." The mini-driver only needs to contain code relative to the unique functions of the device. This mini-driver is designed to hook onto a published set of Application Programmer Interfaces (APIs) that tie to the more general code of the Uniform Device Driver and I/O Manager.

Network Drivers   These are a form of file system drivers that handle I/O requests through the network.

The I/O Manager is one of the only Executive Layer objects with the ability to communicate directly with the hardware without going through the kernel (the Win32K Manager is the other). This design prevents the kernel from having to include primitives relative to specific hardware peripherals, while at the same time adding portability and stability to the operating system.

The I/O Manager is one of the Executive Layer objects that has the ability to not only communicate directly with the hardware, but also with a virtual representation of what it believes to be the hardware—an interface known as the Hardware Abstraction Layer.

Win32K Manager

With the release of NT 4, Microsoft made a change to the positioning of the Win32 graphical components. In earlier releases, these were deployed as a User Mode Subsystem. Figure 2.13 depicts this early architecture.

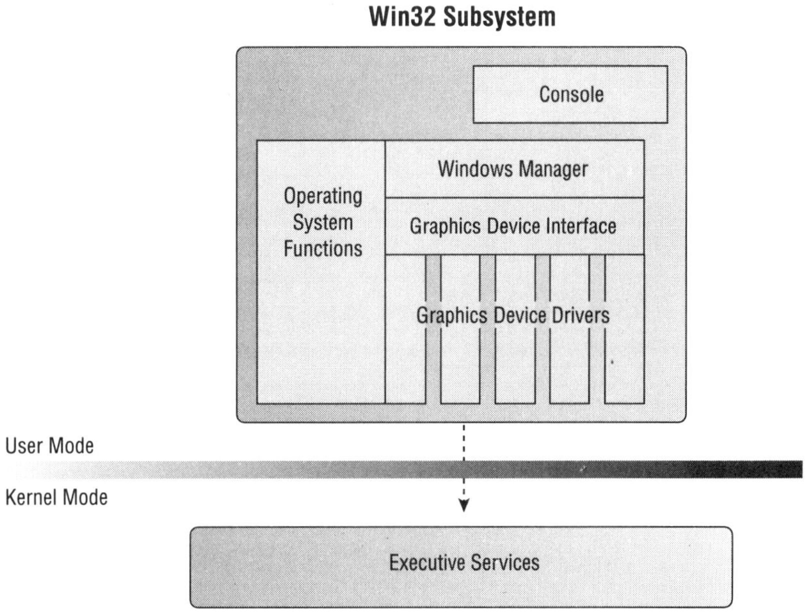

FIGURE 2.13

Pre-Windows NT 4 Win32 Subsystem

With version 3.51 and earlier, Microsoft had noticed that all other subsystems were continuously interacting with Win32 for their graphics and windowing API calls. This seemed appropriate, since NT is built upon the concept of *windows*—but nevertheless, there was concern that this constant activity might be causing a bottleneck.

This issue took on more importance because Windows NT 4 was going to be released with its new (windows-graphic intensive) interface in the style of the Windows 95 Explorer.

Recognizing that something needed to be done, Microsoft took the step of relocating many of the elements of the Win32 subsystem to the faster performing Kernel mode. This was accomplished through the creation of a Win32 Manager object that would become part of the Executive Services. Figure 2.14 illustrates this.

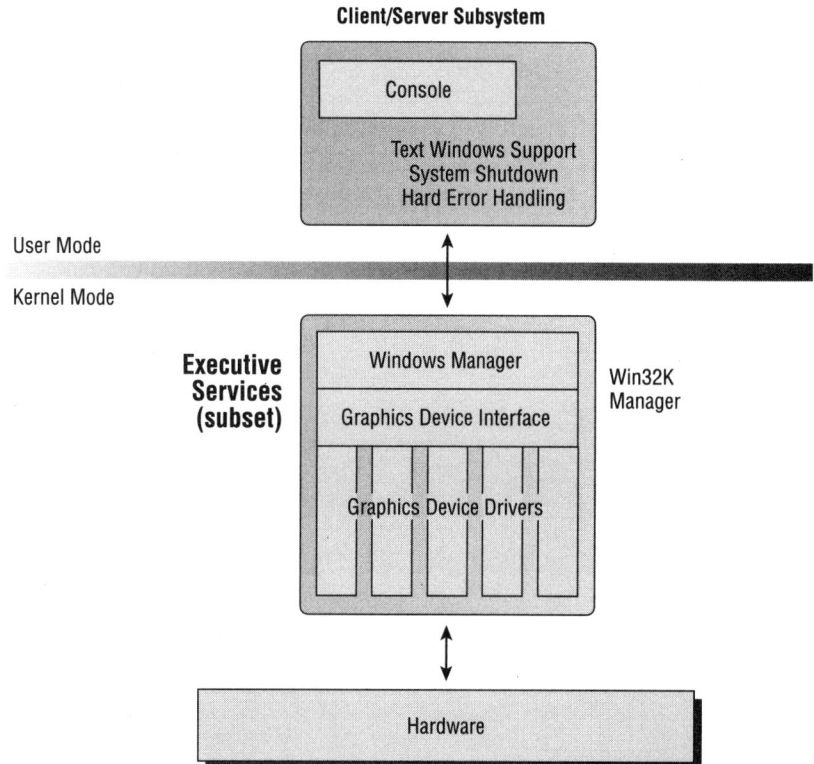

FIGURE 2.14

The Windows NT 4 Win32K Manager

The only element of the Win32 subsystem that remains in User mode is the console. It has appropriately been renamed to the Client/Server Subsystem (CSS), signifying its function of coordinating activity between the other subsystems using local procedure calls (LPCs). The CSS also handles responsibility for text windows support, system shutdown, and hard error handling.

The elements of the Win32 subsystem that moved to the Kernel mode have been packaged together in the Win32K Manager. These elements include:

- **Window Manager:** Manages the windowing elements and handles input
- **Graphics Device Interface (GDI):** A drawing library used by graphics output devices
- **Graphics Device Drivers (GDD):** Graphics drivers which are hardware dependent

The *Operating System Function* element was no longer needed in this new architecture, since the communications services it provided were not required now that the Window Manager, GDI, and GDD components were moved directly into the Executive Services layer.

The benefit of this new architecture is that the graphical drivers have the ability to write directly to the hardware, speeding execution time. The detriment is that these same drivers now have the ability to take down the operating system, should they write to an address space occupied by other Executive Services. Microsoft feels that its comprehensive testing policies will prevent this from becoming an issue. Only time will tell if this is the case.

The Hardware Abstraction Layer

As mentioned previously, one of the major design goals of Windows NT was portability. The Hardware Abstraction Layer (HAL) helps NT achieve this goal by providing a machine-independent layer between the kernel and the computer hardware. HAL provides machine independence by establishing a set of virtual processors that can communicate directly to the kernel.

Virtual processors are necessary because, while HAL is machine-independent, it is not necessarily microprocessor-independent. Code tied to a particular microprocessor architecture does exist, though in a limited quantity, and where necessary it will communicate directly with the hardware.

The microkernel is the only layer that communicates with the system hardware through the HAL. It does this only when direct access to the hardware is not required. Figure 2.15 provides an illustration of the relationship between the HAL and the Executive Services Layer.

48 Chapter 2 • The NT Architecture

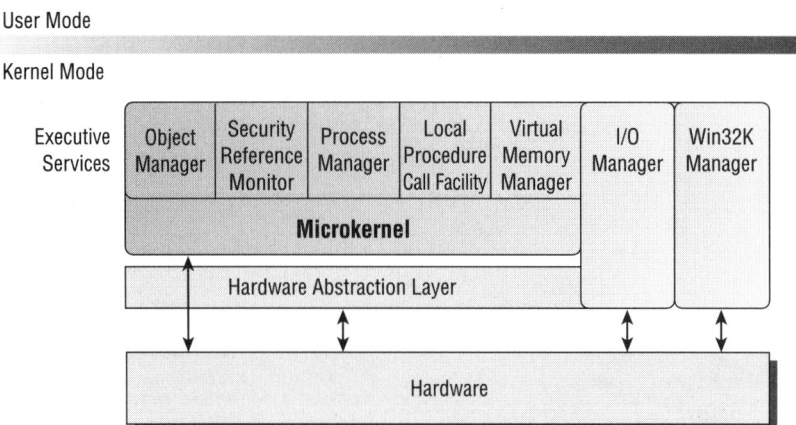

FIGURE 2.15

The Hardware Abstraction Layer

The Environment Subsystems

The Environment Subsystems exist above the Executive Services in the User Mode layer of the model. These subsystems provide a link from the APIs of a particular operating environment to the Executive Services of NT. Where common operating system functions exist, they only need to be implemented once in the Executive Layer rather than for each Environment Subsystem. This means that existing subsystems can be modified and new ones added with little impact to the others.

Environment Subsystems exist for most of the popular operating systems, each of which we will review in more detail. You may find it useful to refer to Figure 2.16 during the review of these systems.

Security Subsystem

The Security Subsystem is where all activity begins for the user. Any user's first interaction with an NT system is the logon screen that interfaces directly to the logon process. From this point, the user will enter the appropriate ID and password, which will be parsed to the Security Subsystem. The Security Subsystem takes this request and checks it against the Security Accounts Management Database (SAM) of the NT operating system. Assuming that the logon is valid, the Security Subsystem will generate an access token, which will be used to authenticate the user to all other system resources that the user may request.

FIGURE 2.16

The Environment Subsystems

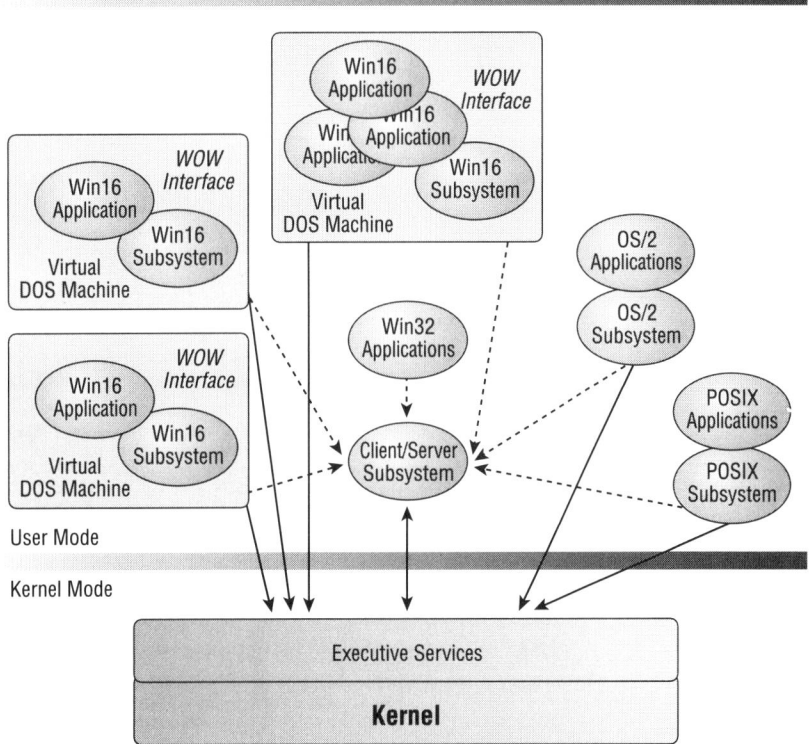

The executive service known as the *security reference monitor* is the object that will actually use this access token when the request for services occurs. Figure 2.17 illustrates this process.

Each object in NT has a security descriptor known as the Access Control List (ACL) associated with it. The ACL contains Access Control Entries (ACE), which are a list of permissions granted or denied to a user or group for the object. The SRM is responsible for overlaying the access token onto the ACL, where it will subsequently check for a match between the Security ID (SID) of the access token and an ACE for the object. All permissions will be aggregated,

50 Chapter 2 • The NT Architecture

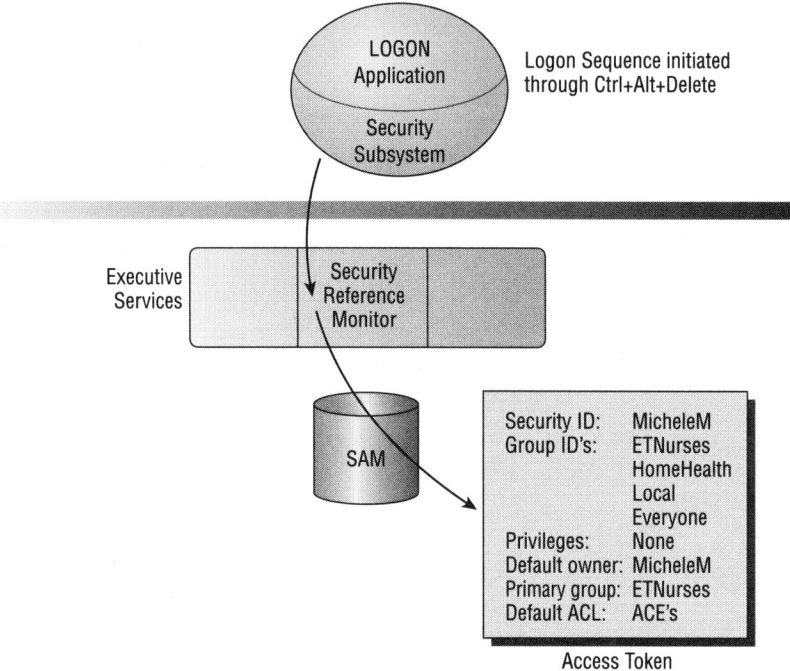

FIGURE 2.17

Object authentication through use of the access token

and the end result will be a definition of the explicit permissions that the user has to the object. At this point the user is granted a handle to the object.

The access token is valid for the duration of the logon. New permissions that the user may receive will not become active until a new access token is generated (at the next logon). Also, any changes made to the ACE for the object while a handle exists will not become noticeable until the existing user ends the current process and starts a new one. This new process will result in the generation of another handle based on the new or modified ACE.

Client/Server Subsystem

The Client/Server Subsystem (CSS) of Windows NT 4 is a shell of what was formerly the Win32 subsystem in Windows NT 3.51 and earlier. The only element that remains is the *console*. This component retains responsibility for text windows support, system shutdown, and hard error handling.

The CSS also coordinates messaging between the various User Mode subsystems and the Kernel Mode Executive Services. This interaction occurs through Local Procedure Calls under the guidelines of client/server communications. It is from this client/server role that the subsystem gets its name.

MS-DOS Subsystem

MS-DOS-based applications are supported through a subset of the Win32 subsystem known as a Virtual DOS Machine (VDM). The VDM functions as the equivalent of a self-contained MS-DOS environment. In this role it provides structure as the NTVDM.EXE user mode program. As such it interfaces with the NT equivalents of the IO.SYS and MSDOS.SYS, known as NTIO.SYS and NTDOS.SYS.

The VDM is designed to support DOS 5.0, including the system files CONFIG.SYS and AUTOEXEC.BAT. Within Windows NT, these files exist as CONFIG.NT and AUTOEXEC.NT, and are stored in the \SYSTEM32 directory.

Access to hardware for the VDM is provided through a set of Virtual Device Drivers (VDDs), which pass their requests through the Executive Services I/O Manager. MS-DOS programs are not permitted direct access to the hardware as this would violate system integrity.

Each MS-DOS program is launched in its own VDM. Should the integrity of the VDM become compromised, it will be terminated without impact to the other VDMs or subsystems.

Win16 Subsystem

The Win16 subsystem is designed to support applications built to run in the DOS/Windows 3.*x* environment. Logically, it follows that these applications will run within a VDM since this will provide support for the DOS portion of this emulated environment.

As you may recall, Windows 3.*x* was designed as a 16-bit, non-preemptive, multitasking environment for single-processor systems. Application programmers designed 16-bit Windows 3.*x* applications to run within this environment where they would share system resources in a cooperative manner (most of the time). Due to the popularity of Windows 3.*x*, the developers of Windows NT chose to support this architecture through the Windows on Win32 (WOW) component of the Win16 subsystem. WOW is responsible for translating those 16-bit calls to the equivalent 32-bit calls and back again. This process, known as *thunking*, has an associated overhead that goes along with this translation process. Some believe that this overhead can be offset by the speed gain obtained through running elements of the program as 32-bit instructions.

Windows 16-bit applications can utilize the VDM/WOW interface in one of two ways:

- By default all 16-bit Windows applications run in one VDM, utilizing the services of a single WOW interface. These applications utilize a shared memory area and features like Object Linking and Embedding (OLE) and Dynamic Data Exchange (DDE) are fully supported. There is an associated risk with running in this manner, as there was in the native Windows 3.*x* environment. Essentially, should the integrity of a 16-bit Windows application become compromised, there is every chance that it will hang the WOW or VDM, thereby adversely affecting all other applications sharing that same WOW/VDM interface. All other subsystems will remain unaffected should this occur.

- Optionally, each 16-bit Windows application can run utilizing its own WOW/VDM interface. Operating in this manner, there is no risk that a faulty 16-bit Windows application will adversely affect any other WOW/VDM interfaces or Windows NT subsystems. Additionally, the Win32 subsystem will be able to more efficiently manage the multitasking of the application within an SMP-based system. The penalty for operating in this manner comes in the form of the additional memory required (approximately 1MB of RAM and 2MB of PAGEFILE space per WOW/VDM interface).

The default WOW/VDM interface always exists, regardless of whether a 16-bit Windows application is running within it. The same cannot be said for WOW/VDM interfaces launched for applications choosing to run in their own separate memory space. As soon as the application terminates, the WOW/VDM interface closes.

OS/2 Subsystem

By default, OS/2 character-mode applications are the only ones supported within the OS/2 subsystem. Presentation Manager applications will not run within this subsystem and are only supported through a snap-in available from Microsoft. Applications that start in character-mode, yet make calls to the Presentation Manager, must run within a VDM. The FORCEDOS.EXE command can be used to launch an application within a VDM.

It is worth noting that the OS/2 subsystem will not load by default. Only upon executing an OS/2 application will this subsystem load. This policy reserves system memory for more commonly used Environmental Subsystems.

Portable Operating System for Computing Environments (POSIX) Subsystem

The POSIX subsystem is designed to meet the IEEE 1003.1 standards for multithreaded character-mode applications. This subsystem conforms to the U.S. Federal Information Processing standard 1521. Designed as a means of establishing a government standard for portable computing environments, POSIX failed to include API support for networking and security. As such, operating system developers must often resort to non-POSIX-compliant APIs in order to add this support.

Interestingly enough, Windows NT is one of those operating systems. What is even more interesting is that according to the U.S. Federal Information Processing standard 1521/IEEE 1003.1, POSIX support must be removed in order for Windows NT to conform to U.S. Department of Defense C2 security requirements. (Go figure...)

Similar to OS/2, the POSIX subsystem will not load by default. Only upon executing a POSIX application will this subsystem load. This policy reserves system memory for more commonly used Environmental Subsystems (further reinforcing the concept that next to C2 security, POSIX becomes our second *marketing* feature.)

In this chapter we've explored the internal architecture of Microsoft Windows NT by following the evolution of this operating system from the original model to its current design. Throughout this book we have purposely avoided using the term "final design," as Windows NT is an operating system that is far from being complete.

In the process of exploring the internal architecture, we introduced concepts that will become critical throughout the process of designing, extending, and optimizing an enterprise network. In the next chapter, we'll discuss some of the principles of network design so you can begin to understand not only how NT operates on a conceptual level, but also how to best apply NT technology within your enterprise.

PART II

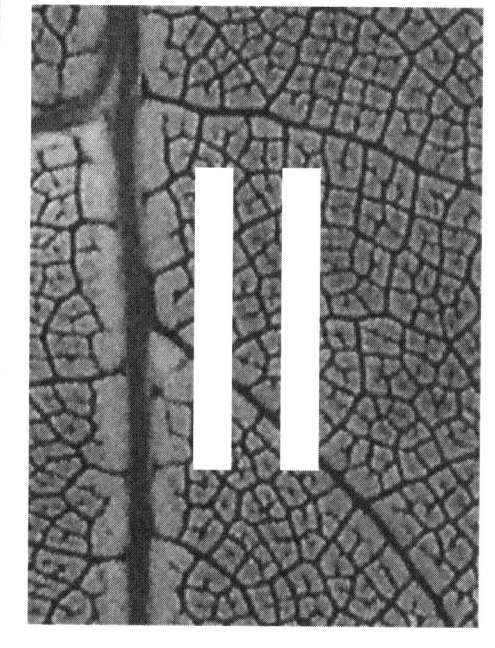

THE FOUNDATION FOR A HIGH PERFORMANCE NT ENTERPRISE NETWORK

CHAPTER 3

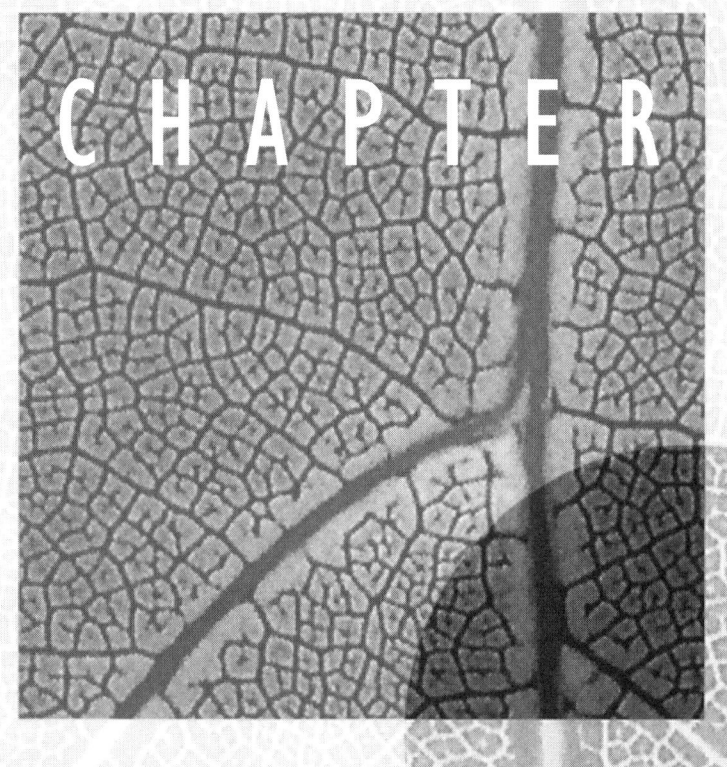

The Principles of Network Design

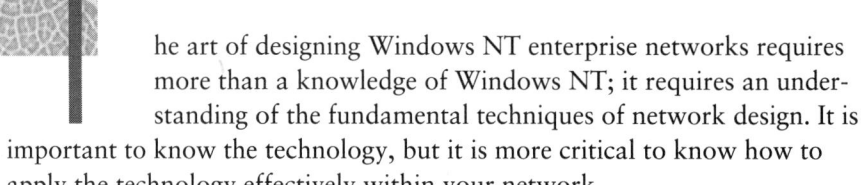

he art of designing Windows NT enterprise networks requires more than a knowledge of Windows NT; it requires an understanding of the fundamental techniques of network design. It is important to know the technology, but it is more critical to know how to apply the technology effectively within your network.

The most important phase in any technological implementation project is the first phase: the design. Without a sound design, few projects make it past the testing stage, and those that do rarely meet the expectations of users and management.

Your ability to successfully deploy Windows NT throughout your organization depends upon a number of factors: your knowledge of NT fundamentals and supporting technologies, a firm understanding of your company's existing infrastructure and business objectives, and your grasp of the fundamental concepts of design. Now that you've read the first two chapters and understand the fundamentals of the NT architecture, we're going to begin to discuss how to develop designs that take advantage of NT's flexibility, performance, and power.

Before we begin our discussion of NT design issues, however, we'll look at the design process itself. This chapter presents many of the techniques utilized by the most successful design consultants in the business.

In this chapter, you will learn:

- What the term *design* really means

- The questions to ask before you approach a design

- Proven techniques for developing a successful design

- The five elements of a good design

- How to plan a pilot project to ensure a successful implementation of your design

Design: A Definition

In general terms, a *design* is a plan. It may be a plan for building a tree house or a plan for building a nuclear reactor. Because you're reading this book, we assume you are interested in learning how to develop plans to implement NT technology within your enterprise. Maybe we'll talk about nuclear reactors some other time.

A good design is the result of paying close attention to assumptions, considerations, and constraints with respect to a technology implementation. If you ask the right questions, have the right background information, understand the technology, and plan efficiently, you're well on your way to creating effective network designs.

Basic Design Principles

Almost everyone who develops network designs for a living has a slightly different approach to the design process, but the most effective designers follow the same basic principles. The following sections discuss some basic design principles that you should keep in mind throughout the design process. As you read the principles, you'll begin to understand that a good design provides more than a technological implementation; it provides the answer to business needs.

Meet a Business Requirement or Need

Any design an organization undertakes that has been created without considering how the organization operates is a waste of time and money. Today's competitive business arena has made it increasingly important to review all processes within an organization with respect to their contribution to the bottom line. If a process does not ultimately contribute to saving money or better servicing the customer, it probably needs to be eliminated, or at least reengineered.

Implementing network technology is no exception. Chief Information Officers have become fond of terms like *return on investment* (ROI) so that they can attempt to show the financial impact of information technology deployment. Projects that offer a low return on investment or an ROI that is difficult to quantify may never be deployed, while those that promise an easily quantifiable ROI are sure to become priorities.

For example, if a CIO can easily demonstrate how a $10,000 project will save the organization $1,000,000, that project is more likely to be initiated than a project that costs $500,000 but will only save the organization $50,000.

If your primary responsibility is day-to-day network administration and operations, you're probably more concerned with making your network run more efficiently than with business concepts like ROI. However, when you first approach a network design, you should always consider why you are being asked to do the project.

The First Questions to Ask

When you begin a design, before you even begin to think about a particular technology or implementation, ask yourself and your management one simple question: "What is the compelling business requirement or need driving this project?" What processes does your organization need to make it operate more efficiently?

The answers to these questions are the most important considerations for your design. You should never begin work on a network design that does not provide a solution to a real business need. If your organization will not realize a tangible benefit from the project, it is not worth doing.

Keep in mind that there are many types of valid business needs. For example, a business unit may have a need to share resources or data with another business unit. By sharing this data, both business units may be able to reduce by half the time it takes to generate sales proposals. Your design might involve utilizing a traditional file-sharing implementation, or it might involve building a corporate intranet. Your final design will be based on a number of factors, which we'll discuss in more detail later in this chapter, but your ultimate consideration will be whether your solution helps your customers (the business units) share data in the most efficient way.

Other categories of network designs may not be as easy to trace directly to a business need. For example, as the network administrator you might be responsible for providing 100 percent network availability. One component of your toolset that you'll need in order to guarantee maximum uptime is a network management platform. Every aspect of the design of your network management system should be developed with this purpose in mind. If a component of your design does not contribute to maximizing network availability, it probably should be left out.

As your design process progresses, you'll find yourself becoming less involved in the "big picture" and more involved in the details. Don't let the details distract you from the driving force behind the project. It's always a good idea to take a step back from your work once in a while to consider who will be impacted by your design and how it will enable them to do a better job.

Always think in terms of the customer. Your customer may be the accounting department, the international sales business unit, or it may be the companies who pay your organization for products or services. In the network management system scenario, the customer is you. The ultimate criteria for your design is how well it serves the customer.

Determine the Definition for Success

Once you have identified the business requirement that will drive your design, you may want to work with your customer to identify the criteria that will be used to determine whether the design can be considered successful. The success criteria may be as simple as a single statement, such as, "The project will be considered a success if the users of the sales department can access their electronic mail from the road." For other projects, the success criteria may be more complicated. In fact, it may be difficult for your customer to verbalize all of the factors that need to be present for the design to be a success. Be patient and try to assist them in filling in the blanks.

Once you have identified all of the success factors, spend some time prioritizing each element.

It is extremely important that you develop concrete issues that must be satisfied in order for the project to be considered a success. By developing a set of issues upon which you and your customer can focus, you can ensure everyone involved in the project is operating under the same set of assumptions about the goals of the project.

Avoid the Use of Technology for Its Own Sake

Any time you are asked to design a network, it's always a temptation to include some exciting new product that just became available or is still in beta testing. After all, one of the reasons you went into this line of work was to work with the latest technologies, right?

While you might be itching to try out something new, now is not the time to get your feet wet with a new product or technology. Avoid the temptation to use something just because it sounds cool. If you have to look for excuses to use a product, or have to stretch the product's features to accommodate your project, you need to stop and rethink your solution. The success of a design is not measured by how many brand-new products it involves, it is measured by how well it works, and how well it meets a need.

A successful network designer has the ability to weigh the temptation to use bleeding-edge technology against the desire for a solution that is mature, time-proven, and stable. When you use technology for its own sake (or for your own curiosity's sake), you are putting the cart before the horse. Let the business requirement drive the design, not the technology.

Keep in mind that you may have no alternative but to use unproven technology, particularly if it is the only product that will meet the business requirement. If you find yourself in that situation, be sure the management and the customer are aware that the benefits of using the technology may be outweighed by the risk associated with using an unproven product. Incorporate a pilot project (which we'll discuss later this chapter) into your design so that everyone will have sufficient opportunity to discover any bugs and to determine if the design provides a real answer to the need.

Fools Rush In

A number of years ago, when computer fax boards first became available, I was working for an organization run by a CEO who felt compelled to implement the "latest and greatest" technology at every opportunity. He mandated that the entire corporation be converted over to network-based inbound and outbound faxing. While outbound faxing worked fine, the odds of someone getting a fax that was addressed to them was approximately one in four. Within two weeks, everyone reverted back to real fax machines for all inbound faxes. Had the CEO stopped to see the limitations on inbound network faxing at the time, he could have saved the organization a considerable amount of time and money.

Consider Organizational Objectives

Once you have identified the business requirements that your design must meet, you should stop and identify the factors that created those business requirements. Try to recognize the forces behind the need. By digging into the problem and identifying the root causes of the requirements, you can obtain an understanding of the drive for design.

Whenever you are creating a design, you'll need to consider how your design will fit within the "big picture." The business requirement that drives your design may be only one of a group of requirements that have been driven by a large project or shift in corporate direction.

For example, if your organization has decided to move in a new direction and is beginning to sell widgets internationally, a number of requirements will arise in order to make global widget sales a reality. Your involvement in the overall project may be at a high level, in which case you would already be concerning yourself with the big picture; or your involvement may be at a much lower level, in which case you might be focusing on a relatively small task such as designing a network fax system for a workgroup.

Regardless of at which level you will be working, understanding the ultimate goal of your organization is significant, which in this example is to become the leading supplier of widgets to the world. By having a broad perspective, you will be able to understand how your project will coexist within the infrastructure, and what impact your project will have on other projects.

To achieve a broad perspective, think about not only your goals, but your department's goals, and more importantly, your organization's goals. If you are a manager, try to help those who report to you to develop a better understanding of the corporate direction. If you are not a manager, identify people within your organization that can help you understand what is driving the business requirement.

Avoid operating in a vacuum. Be aware of the corporate direction, and your designs will be more successful.

Respect the Budget

The greatest technical design in the world is useless if it will cost too much money to implement. If the money for a project is not in the budget, no amount of creativity will make the design work. Before you become involved in a project, find out about the budget. Know the monetary parameters for the design and work within them. If you think the budget for the project is unrealistic, say so up front. You may be able to modify the budget, or the project, to be more appropriate.

If you find yourself having to create a design that is subject to budgetary constraints, be creative. Remember that necessity (and a limited budget) is the mother of invention. You may find that you can offer nearly the same amount of functionality within a design by substituting less-expensive components for more costly ones. However, whatever you do, do not use substandard products. You'll only end up spending the money you saved initially on increased repairs and support costs.

If you have scaled back your design to the point that you can no longer offer the same level of functionality that was initially envisioned and the project will still go over budget, you'll need to inform management that you'll need to sacrifice low-priority features. It's better to provide a stable set of core functionality and cut out less important features than to skimp on the entire project.

As your design progresses, remember that for most projects, the costs for the hardware and software are not the only costs. The costs for tangible items, like equipment or applications, are easily calculated. The costs that are tougher to identify are the less tangible ones, such as the costs associated with training, installation, configuration, and ongoing administration of the products specified in the design.

When you create a design, make an effort to identify both the fixed costs (the hardware and software) and the hidden costs (the training and administration). In management-speak, the total cost for a device, network, or design is referred to as the *total cost of ownership*. If your design includes components that are difficult to administer, be sure to indicate the costs associated with training someone for the administrative tasks or the cost to hire someone to do the job. Management will appreciate your attempt to approximate the total cost of ownership, because they will be able to understand the long-term impact of the design.

If you are forced to make a decision between a product with a low sticker price that is difficult to administer and a product that has a higher sticker price but is easier to administer, remember that you will only pay for the product once, but your organization will pay for administration of the product for as long as they own it. When you consider the two products in that light, the one that is more expensive initially may actually cost your company less in the long run.

This factor is extremely important, particularly if you or your department will be responsible for the day-to-day maintenance of the implementation.

When you consider that you not only have to deploy your design, but that you also have to live with it every day, that decision to go with the less-expensive design that requires daily administrative attention seems like less of a bargain.

Leverage Existing Infrastructure When Feasible

Unless you are asked to install a new network from the ground up, your design will have to be integrated into a living, operational production network. Keep this in mind when you approach your design. If you fail to, you may encounter critical compatibility issues between your new design and the existing network.

Successful consultants and network designers recognize the need for their design to mesh with the existing production network. Before you put pen to paper (or fingers to keyboard) on your design, be sure you have a solid understanding of the existing network infrastructure, including all hardware, software, and internetworking devices.

Every production network has existing issues that should be addressed. These issues may be in the form of performance bottlenecks, improperly configured devices, or intermittent failures. Since your design will impact the network in one way or another, you'll need to identify those issues and address them before the implementation of your design if possible. Even though an issue may not be "your fault," once your design is implemented, most end users (and managers) point the finger at the newest software or hardware on the network when their applications do not work properly. Your design may be the proverbial straw that breaks the overloaded router's back.

The advantage of working with a pre-existing network is that you can utilize the parts that work well to your advantage. For example, why design a high-speed backbone to allow your servers to communicate if one already exists? By effectively leveraging an existing network's infrastructure, you may significantly reduce the cost of implementation while preserving the initial investments already made into the network.

If It Ain't Broke, Don't Fix It

Although it is always a temptation to expand the scope of your design, avoid the tendency to redesign existing network components that already work the way they are supposed to. For example, your design may include a Microsoft Internet Information Server-based Web server that communicates with an existing SQL database. If the SQL server has sufficient capacity to fulfill its current requirements and the future requirements of the Web server, leave it alone.

If something already works, leave it alone. Your good intentions may have serious repercussions. Every component that you modify on your network may in turn affect other components. Before you attempt to redesign those components, be sure to have a comprehensive understanding of how those components function within your internetwork. In very large network environments, gaining a comprehensive understanding may be a considerable undertaking. Take the time to discover what's happening with all of the devices that will become involved (in one way or another) with your design. That workstation-based mail gateway may be doing more than you think. Before you remove if from the network, be sure of what the impact will be.

Recognizing Potential Bottlenecks

If the existing network has been properly designed to support its current applications, be careful to anticipate what new requirements your design will place on the network. For example, if a gateway or other device is already operating at near 100-percent utilization, you may need to include an upgrade to those devices within your design. For server-based applications, you may need to plan for a RAM upgrade, or you may need to add a second or third CPU.

Don't make the mistake of underestimating the impact your design will have on the network. If you need to perform a comprehensive analysis to determine the current operational environment of the production network, do the analysis before you begin your design.

Before the analysis begins, you should have already identified the areas within the network that your design will have the most impact on. For example, if you plan to add a new server-based application to an existing server, you'll know that the application will place requirements on the CPU, on memory, and on the disk channel on the server. Network traffic associated with application usage will also increase. Focus on these areas during your initial analysis to determine what stresses the devices involved are experiencing.

One way to predict how your design will impact the network is to closely analyze how your design operates once it is implemented in the pilot project (we'll discuss how to plan a pilot project later in this chapter). Utilize tools like Performance Monitor and network protocol analyzers to get a clear view of your design's performance requirements.

Even if you don't have the budget to upgrade the components that will be operating beyond operational efficiency, identify those impacted areas in your design. Some parts of your network may fall outside your department's responsibility. Communicate with management and other departments so that they understand what the impact will be. Be prepared that your project may be put on hold, or that it may be delayed until the necessary upgrades have been put in place. In some situations, management may tell you to go ahead with the design anyway. If that is the case, put your concerns in writing so you and your management team have sufficient evidence to make an educated decision.

What If It Won't Work?

There will be times, however, when you will be unable to leverage the existing infrastructure due to the unique requirements of your design. For example, if your new design will require a high-speed backbone and the network currently only utilizes 10Mb technology, no amount of network readjustment will make your design work unless you install that fast backbone.

If you anticipate that your design will require significant (and expensive) upgrades to the network infrastructure, be sure to communicate the cost of the upgrades to management. It is extremely important to identify the total cost of the implementation, including the costs associated with infrastructure upgrades, so that management can make the decision to move forward with the project. In some cases the additional costs for the upgrades may exceed the budget for the project. In those situations, try to break the project up into smaller projects. For example, by separating the upgrade tasks into a stand-alone project, you may be able to identify additional business requirements for the upgrade, or you may be able to receive budget dollars from additional departments.

If your design will require upgrades to network devices, such as routers, speak with the people who are responsible for those devices to determine if they have already planned for the upgrade. Chances are, they already have a plan to replace the hardware. If so, work with them to determine a timetable for the upgrade, and plan your design around that calendar.

Utilize Components from Reliable Vendors

If you are faced with a restrictive budget, avoid the temptation to substitute generic components for proven, reliable, (and more expensive) brand-name components. That clone computer may look like a budget saver when you compare it to a high-end, brand-name server, but you should always remember that there are reasons why those no-name systems cost one-quarter to one-third of the price of a high-end server. You may save dollars on a clone system, but you will almost certainly pay a price in three key areas: performance, reliability, and support.

If you haven't already defined standards for your networking equipment and software, now would be a good time to do so. It is unlikely that you will be able to select a single vendor to provide all of the components that will comprise your network, but you should try to keep the number of different vendors to a minimum, and you should try to select vendors who have common corporate goals and visions, as well as strong business partnerships.

Performance

Clone systems are typically built from commodity components that have been selected more because of their low cost than their performance. When you opt for the cheapest system, you will never be sure what you paid for.

Brand-name server manufacturers such as Compaq and Hewlett-Packard engineer their servers from scratch to provide the fastest possible performance for server applications. They may feature high-speed backplanes, improved bus architectures, or specially optimized logic boards. The cost associated with the engineering of this performance is reflected in the price. Brand-name systems built to be servers cost more than systems built to be workstations.

Reliability

Because they are built from commodity components, the reliability of clone systems may be very good, or it may be very poor. You can never be sure if the hard drive in your clone system was selected because of its reliable track record, of if it was the cheapest hard drive the day your clone builder bought it.

Brand-name server vendors have not only engineered their servers for fast performance, but they have designed their systems to take advantage of devices that offer improved fault tolerance such as redundant power supplies and drive arrays. Most servers built by brand-name manufacturers undergo a more thorough "burn in" period to ensure that none of the components contain manufacturing defects.

Support

High-end servers are manufactured by well-known companies that have been in the computer industry for years. Most come with extensive on-site warranties and offer enhanced programs for quick replacement of failed components. They maintain warehouses to store replacement parts for older systems, so when your server dies three years from now they will be able to send you the right part. Clone systems are typically built from a parts pool that varies from day to day, depending on which brand of components was the cheapest that day. If your hard drive dies two week after you buy your clone system, the dealer may not be able to replace it with the same model. This factor might not be a big deal if you had only one drive in your system, but if it was part of a drive array, installing a different brand of hard drive may not be possible.

Few clone systems carry more than a one-year warranty, and even fewer clone dealerships stay in business for more than five years. When a brand-name server dies, you know who to call, because the server manufacturer will service all of the parts within the system, regardless of whether they manufactured a component or not. When a clone system dies, you may have to contact a different company for support of each of the components. You might call the hard drive manufacturer for a hard drive replacement, the video card manufacturer for video card problems, or the motherboard manufacturer for a motherboard issue. You might even have trouble identifying the manufacturer of a particular component.

A Bad Time for Experimentation

Even if you plan to utilize brand-name components within your design, it is never a good idea to include vendors or products you have not worked with before. Trying out new products or brands because they looked interesting in the network trade journals is a bad move. Your success as a network designer depends on your ability to specify products that work the way they are supposed to work. You don't want to learn about a problem with a vendor's product line after the systems have already been deployed.

Your network design is not an experiment. You should have the ability to feel confident about anything you include in your design. If you use products with which you are not familiar, you are adding uncertainty to the design. Stay away from products that you have not personally used and feel comfortable with.

If you are unhappy with your current vendors, resolve those issues before you include someone else's components in your design. You should never specify a device within your design until it has been tested within your network environment.

If you have no choice but to use a new vendor, brand, or product type, clearly identify a time period in which you will thoroughly test the product for compatibility, performance, and effectiveness within your environment. Include component testing within your pilot project so that you can feel confident the devices will operate the way you intend them to.

Before you select a product, spend time researching the vendor in general, and that product in particular. Talk to other people in the industry to see what they think of the vendor's support track record and of the product's reliability. If you have Internet access, search through Usenet newsgroups to see if anyone is mentioning any good or bad experiences they have had with the vendor or the product. Once you locate the appropriate newsgroup, feel free to ask questions; most Internet users are happy to offer anecdotes and advice.

The Five Elements of a Successful Design

Now that you understand some of the considerations involved in developing a network design, let's discuss some of the elements common to successful network designs. After speaking with a number of the top network designers in the world, we have identified five of the most important elements of a successful network design.

A good network design possesses the following qualities:

- It's installable, configurable, manageable, and supportable.
- It works in the real world.
- It's *clean*, by which we mean it accomplishes its objectives in a simple, straightforward manner.
- It ensures reliability through fault tolerance and redundancy.
- It favors *best of breed* technologies whenever possible.

We'll look at each of these qualities in more detail in the following sections.

Installable, Manageable, and Supportable

The first quality that all successful designs have in common is that they were suitable for the environment into which they were deployed. A successful design not only fulfills a business requirement, it reflects a consideration of the organization and the support personnel who are responsible for the installation, configuration, management, and support of the implementation.

Simplifying Installation

As you create your design, ask yourself the following question: "Given the skill sets and availability of the people in my department, will a successful installation of my design be possible?"

Before you begin the implementation phase, you'll need to estimate the number of hours required for the installation in addition to identifying the skill sets required to complete the installation process. To do this, try to break up the design implementation into smaller, more quantifiable tasks. Make a list of the tasks, one task to a line. Next to each task, estimate the amount of time required and identify the skill level required to complete the task. For example, if you wanted to install a new NT server on your network, the first task might be to configure the server hardware. A reasonable estimate for server hardware configuration might be six hours, and the person configuring the hardware would have to be familiar with server hardware standards.

As you develop this list, and the other lists mentioned in this section, avoid using actual names of employees within your organization. Identify roles for the tasks, such as "installer" or "administrator," and define the skills and job functions associated with those roles. Later on, during the implementation of your NT enterprise, you can create NT groups related to these roles and add the appropriate employee user IDs to the groups.

Once you have completed the list, tally up the number of hours for completion. This number will be a rough estimate of the number of hours you'll need to schedule for the installation. If the number of hours for the installation or the skill sets required to complete the tasks exceed the resources you have available to you, you will have to make a decision—either you must scale back the scope of the project so that it can be completed with your available resources, free up the previously busy resources, or bring in outside help to complete the project.

If, after reviewing the task list, you determine that a successful deployment is too expensive with respect to time or skills, you may want to get a second opinion. Review the tasks and time frames you have identified with a coworker or supervisor, and ask for input from a specialist. For example, if you plan to install Ethernet switches, try to review your project with someone who has installed them before. They may be able to help you confirm or modify your assumptions and estimates. You might also try contacting the manufacturer of the equipment directly to speak with field engineers who have installed the devices. Often, pre-sales organizations make things sound easier than they actually are, so be sure to confirm their claims.

If the second opinion confirms that the project is unfeasible, it's time to consider scrapping the design and starting over. Reconsider all of the areas of the network and the organization that your design will impact. Can you reduce the scope of the project so that it can be installed more easily, but still meet the business requirements? You may need to split the project into smaller, more manageable sub-projects so that you can simplify the installation process.

Add the task list, along with the time and skill requirements, to your design documentation. You can use the task list during the implementation phase for project management purposes.

Assessing Management Needs

After you have resolved the scheduling and availability issues related to the installation process, you'll need to consider the resources needed to maintain the design implementation on a day-to-day basis.

At this point, you must ask yourself the following: "What are the day-to-day management requirements of the design? Who will be responsible for managing the system? Do they have sufficient available time to perform the management functions?"

Think through all of the elements of your design in an attempt to anticipate how someone will manage the implementation. For example, if you plan to install an NT Server as a file server, identify the skills necessary to maintain the user accounts, manage the file systems, modify access controls, and maintain the server hardware.

Develop a document that identifies the daily, weekly, monthly, and annual maintenance procedures for your design and add it to the design documentation. Next to each procedure, note the amount of time required to complete the procedure as well as the skill level required to do the job. For example, if you think that an administrator should review file system access controls on a monthly basis, add "file system access control review" to the administrator monthly checklist. Note that the review will take approximately two hours and that the administrator must be a level-two administrator or higher.

TIP

You may find that more than one person will become involved in the scheduled maintenance of the system. If that is the case, make multiple maintenance lists, one for each role. For example, you may have a server administrator maintenance list for NT server administrators and a network administrator maintenance list for the overall network administrator.

Once you have completed the maintenance procedures, you'll need to determine if it will be possible for your organization to provide people with sufficient skill levels and availability to provide the day-to-day management of the implementation. If it will not be possible to manage the implementation under your current system, you'll need to determine the feasibility of restructuring your support infrastructure to meet the new management requirements. In some cases, restructuring your support infrastructure will not be possible, so you may have to reduce the scope of the design so that it can be properly managed.

> **Taking Stock of Skills**
>
> Developing an accurate estimate of the skill levels required to manage an implementation can be a tricky process. Early in my career, I assisted in the design of an online shopping system that utilized a number of components, operating systems, and products from multiple vendors. Since I had worked with all of the products before, I assumed that the system could be managed by a single person. I failed to recognize that the only single person that could manage the job was me, because no one else had had the opportunity to develop the same combination of skill sets that I gained while the system was in development. A year after I left the job, there was a staff of five people managing the system—a UNIX administrator, an NT administrator, a NetWare administrator, a database programmer, and a Web developer.

Providing Adequate Support

As you develop your design consider not only the day-to-day schedule maintenance procedures, but the unscheduled, emergency support scenarios as well. During your evaluation of products and technologies, be sure to ask each vendor about their support policies.

You'll need to answer the following question: "How will the organization receive support for the components within the design if something goes wrong with one or more components?"

Quality support is more than a warranty. You'll need to work with each vendor to determine what level of support you can expect to receive. Ask about technical support hours of availability and whether support calls are free. If support calls cost extra, ask about alternative support channels such as e-mail or a corporate Web site. Ask about a vendor's return policy. For mission-critical hardware devices, you'll want to ask if the vendor includes a service to cross-ship replacement hardware in the event of a device failure. Also work with the vendor to locate local authorized service/repair facilities, and contact the local representatives to establish a service account. Ask the facility for references, and call the references to determine if the company provides adequate support for the products you'll be using in your design.

It is in your organization's best interest to utilize those vendors that provide the best products with the best support infrastructure. Even the most reliable devices can fail; you need to be sure you can repair the device or replace it in as short a time as possible. Choose products and vendors that will help you minimize downtime, and your design will be more successful.

Once you have identified the vendors and products you plan to use in your design, document the warranties, service agreements, and support policies within your design documentation. Include contact names, phone numbers, addresses, and URLs in your documentation as well as a support checklist for each vendor's products.

While you consider these three areas: installation, management, and support, remember that any design may look good on paper, but if an organization doesn't have the resources or skills to complete and manage the implementation, that design is worthless. As you begin to design your NT enterprise network, remember that the most successful designs have been developed after a thorough consideration of installation, management, and support issues. Ensure success by creating a design that will work both today and in the future.

Works in the Real World

The second element common to all successful designs may sound like common sense, but it is an element that escapes many rookie network designers. A successful design is not only conceptually sound, it works the way it is supposed to once it has been implemented.

Successful designers understand that products do not always live up to their manufacturer's claims. Specification sheets and advertisements may seem to indicate that a particular product may be ideal for a particular design, but they never mention the bug that will be fixed in the next release or the README file that informs you that the software won't work with your hardware.

Many times, these bugs do not show up until late in the implementation phase of the project. If the bug is minor and does not affect the solution to the business requirement, the bug is trivial. However, most bugs are not so trivial. Some can prevent the implementation of your design from meeting its objectives. If the bug appears late in the implementation, it is usually too late in the project to start over from scratch. Your options will be limited to finding a product that will fill the gap until the bug is fixed. In some cases, there will be no alternative product and the project may have to be scrapped.

Jumping to Conclusions

One of my customers chose a different vendor for their Internet Web site development. That vendor assumed that the Web server (located on the insecure side of a firewall) would be able to FTP files to an internal database server. They spent six months developing an interactive site based upon this assumption. What they didn't realize is that the firewall software that another person from their organization had selected did not support inbound FTP sessions. When the customer complained that the system didn't work, they fired the vendor. If the vendor had tested their assumptions in some type of pilot project, they might still have that client. (And no, this isn't one of those "I have a friend who has this problem" kind of story—it really did happen to another vendor, although I've made my share of mistakes in the past.)

To avoid unforeseen bugs and incompatibilities, try to use components with which you are already familiar. If you already know that you'll need to download a special driver to make the 100BaseT network interface card work with your server, you'll save yourself a significant amount of time during the implementation. Stick to what you know, and you'll encounter fewer problems.

If you are in a situation where you must incorporate a new product into your design, document and test the configuration and operation of the product during the pilot project. The pilot project is your last chance to be sure that the product operates as advertised, so go above and beyond your normal testing procedures to make certain that you won't get burned.

Simple and Straightforward

In most design scenarios, multiple possible solutions exist for a single business requirement. The most successful and effective designs are those that meet the requirement simply and efficiently. A *clean* design is a design that accomplishes its objectives in the most simple, straightforward manner.

When you develop network designs, strive for simplicity. Avoid the temptation to throw in extra features or functionality. Stick with the minimal feature set that will meet the business requirement while also meeting the larger objectives of the organization and the standards set forth for the network and networking devices.

The most successful network designers always attempt to minimize the number of components in the design. By minimizing the number of components, you effectively reduce the number of points of failure within the system.

One way to simplify your network designs is to minimize the use of translation devices such as gateways or transceivers whenever possible. Every design that utilizes a gateway introduces a potential bottleneck or point of failure.

There will be situations when you have no alternative but to install a gateway product. For example, if the business requirement is to connect the electronic mail systems for four offices that utilize different mail systems, you'll have to install some sort of gateway. How you approach the requirement, however, will have a significant impact on the simplicity of the design.

Using this example, let's look at two possible design solutions. Imagine that Office A uses cc:Mail, Office B uses GroupWise, Office C uses Lotus Notes, and Office D uses Exchange. One possible solution would be to install three mail gateway products on each of the four mail systems. For example, Office A would install a GroupWise gateway, a Notes gateway, and an Exchange gateway. Assuming each mail system supported gateways for each of the other three, the design would involve installing and maintaining 12 gateway products. A cleaner solution would be to utilize a single mail protocol, such as SMTP, as a backbone protocol to connect all of the offices. In this scenario, each office would install a single gateway product, the SMTP gateway. Now, instead of installing and maintaining 12 different gateway products, the design would only call for four separate gateways. Figure 3.1 illustrates the more complex design, and Figure 3.2 illustrates the clean design.

FIGURE 3.1

The complex approach

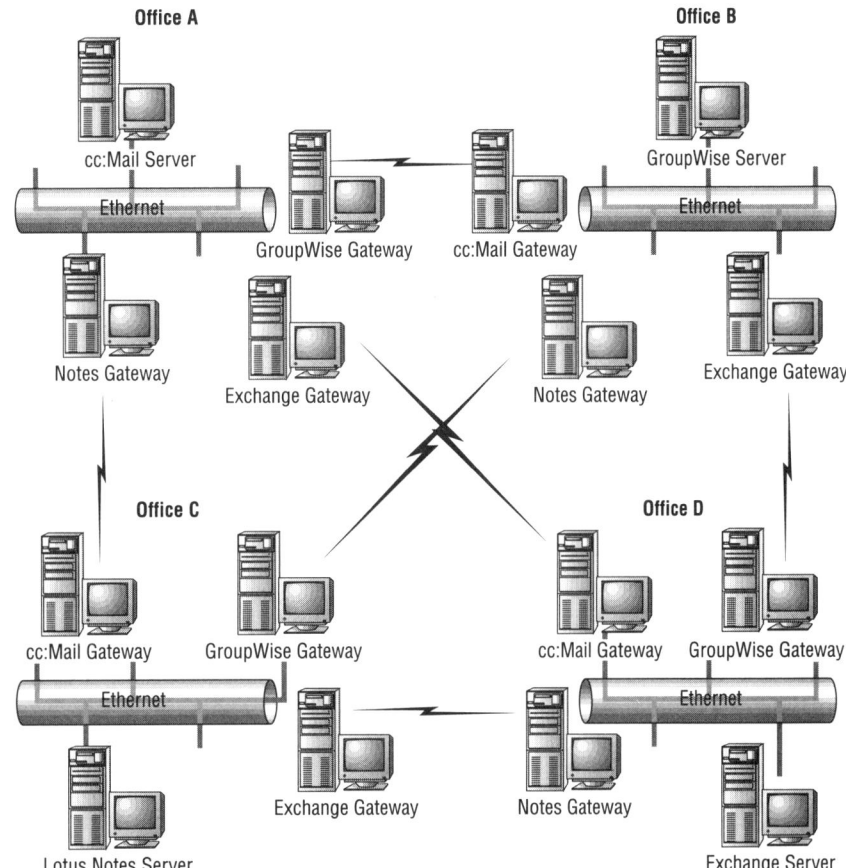

Reliability through Fault Tolerance and Redundancy

System failures are inevitable aspects of any network. A successful designer recognizes that components will occasionally fail and creates designs that incorporate redundancy to avoid downtime whenever possible.

At the physical layer of a network, designing for fault tolerance may involve planning for extra cable runs between network devices, such as routers and hubs, to prevent a connectivity outage that might arise as the result of a cable break. Within servers, designing for fault tolerance may involve the implementation of a RAID disk array or a clustered server approach. Designing for redundancy may even be as simple as planning to buy one extra set of every component to have a spare handy in the event of a failure.

78 Chapter 3 • The Principles of Network Design

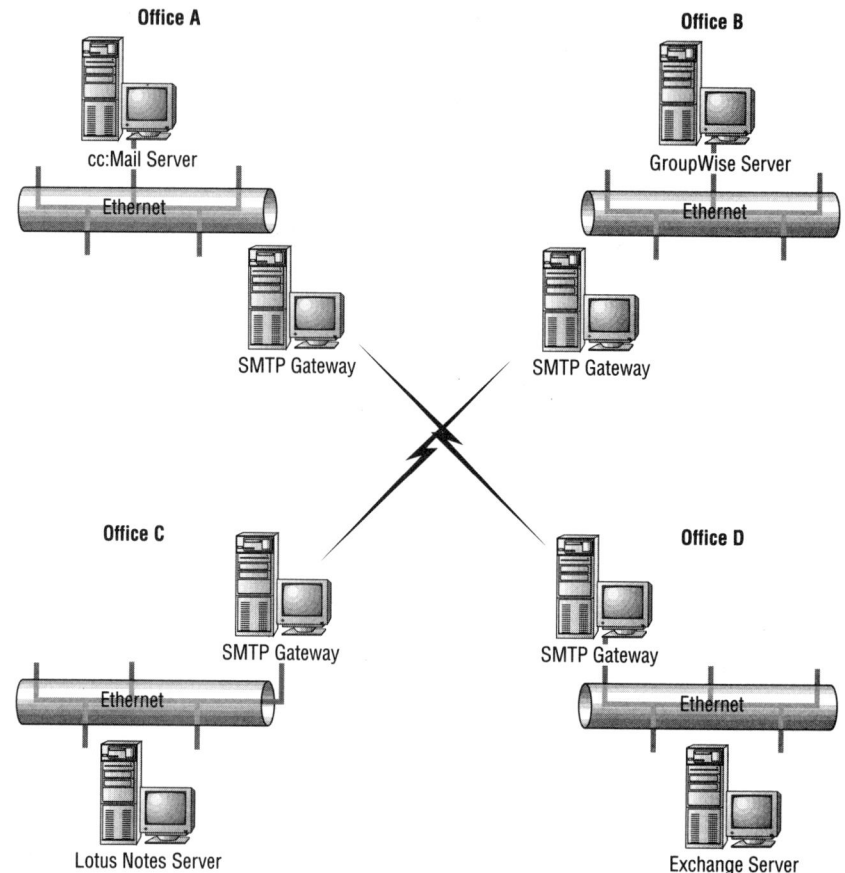

FIGURE 3.2

The clean approach

At first glance, the concept of ensuring reliability through fault tolerance and redundancy seems like a contradiction to creating clean, simple designs. After all, if you add redundancy to a design you'll require additional components, right? While it is true that creating a redundant system will require additional components, the extra components do not add significantly to the complexity of the design because they merely duplicate existing functionality. For example, if you design a server to contain a second, redundant power supply, you are not adding to the complexity of the design by including the second power supply. The server will provide the same functionality with or without the second supply, but by adding the supply you will be providing a backup should the primary power supply fail.

Another technique for improving fault tolerance within a design is to identify and eliminate any single points of failure. *Single point of failure* refers to any single element within a design that could cause the failure of the entire system if it were to cease to operate. For example, the single point of failure for most corporate Internet electronic mail systems is the Internet connection itself. Most organizations have only one connection to the Internet. If that connection were to lose service, the entire organizational Internet electronic mail system would become unavailable. If the organization depended on Internet mail to conduct business, it would begin to lose business as soon as the connection failed. One way to eliminate an Internet connection as a single point of failure is to design a second, backup Internet connection. Say, for example, that the primary corporate Internet connection was a 128Kbps frame-relay link. A redundant design might include a dial-up POTS or ISDN connection as a backup should the primary link become unavailable.

> **The Costs of Nearsightedness**
>
> An organization that I worked with spent about a hundred thousand dollars to design a mirrored server implementation so they would have the highest level of fault tolerance available. Every night, the mirrored servers would be updated by a process that ran on a single computer. One night, something went wrong with that computer and the data was corrupted on both of the mirrored servers, causing the company to lose approximately one million dollars worth of transactions. The mistake the organization made was that they focused only on the servers themselves, not the entire system. Had they designed in a failover for the computer that ran the process, they probably wouldn't have lost all of those transactions.

Best of Breed Technologies Whenever Possible

While this point may also seem like common sense, it is worth discussing. Successful designers recognize the importance of utilizing products and technologies that are considered to be the best in their class.

Typically, products that are at the top of their class are there for a reason. Compaq did not become the top PC server vendor by accident; their servers became the most popular because they offered the best combination of performance, reliability, and fault tolerance. Most other products that enjoy the same type of popularity provide users with a compelling reason, or reasons, to choose them over the competition. They may have become the most popular because of their feature set, performance, overall quality, or low price.

Because they are installed on a large number of networks, products that are at the top of their class are usually the most well-known by support personnel. Put a seasoned technician in front of a Hewlett-Packard LaserJet printer, and you can bet that they will be able to repair any component in a few minutes. Put the much less popular Brand X printer in front of the same technician, and they may not even be able to fix a paper jam.

Products that enjoy a broad user base also receive the most attention from third-party developers. If a developer has to make a decision between developing a reporting program for the number one Web server on the market and the number three Web server, most will opt to develop for number one to appeal to the largest user base. The same principle applies to applications, utilities, and development tools.

However, don't fall into the trap of selecting a vendor or product simply because it is the most popular. If you buy a type of printer simply because it is made by the number one vendor in the market, but fail to determine whether the printer can print the type of forms that the tax department requires, you are neglecting the golden rule of design—meeting the business requirement. Ultimately, you need to create a design that meets the need. If you locate two printers that will do the job and one of them is the top-rated laser printer, your customer will be better off with the more popular printer.

Considering the Alternatives

Before you begin to formalize any design, think twice about your alternatives. Your solution may not be the only one, and it may not be the best when you consider all of the factors. For example, the cost to implement your design may be so high that a business unit will choose not to do anything and will instead stay with the old way of doing the job. When you weigh all of the factors, a non-technical alternative may be more appropriate for certain scenarios.

In some situations, the best design may not be the simplest one. If one of the business units within your organization utilizes non-networked IBM XT computers and has a business requirement to share data with other members of the organization, you will have an opportunity to approach the problem in a number of ways. One solution might be to install 5.25-inch floppy disk drives in all of the computers within the organization. Another solution might be to install network cards in the XT systems so that they can connect to the corporate network. A third solution might be to attach external modems to the XTs to allow them to upload files to the corporate BBS. A fourth, but more expensive, solution might be to upgrade all of the computers to Pentium-class, networked computers. As you can see, there are many alternatives. The best choice depends on a number of issues. Once you fully understand the business requirements and the organizational objectives of the business unit, you can weigh the advantages and disadvantages of each alternative.

Once you have arrived at a conclusion, discuss your design with some of your colleagues. They may be able to provide you with valuable suggestions, valid criticisms, or helpful feedback. They may even suggest an entirely new approach to the design. Keep an open mind, and understand that your design is but one approach to a complex issue.

Whenever possible, avoid jumping to conclusions early in the design process. Try not to choose a product first and build the design around the product. Let the requirements drive the design. Once you have selected a product that meets the requirements, take some time to research similar but competing technologies. Complete the research and identify the strengths and weaknesses of each of the products. Then determine which product you'll use by selecting the one that best matches the requirements. Document your findings and include them in your design documentation.

You may find that your final decision includes products or technologies that you have not originally thought of. That's okay, as long as you feel confident that you can work with the product and that the end users can support it.

This approach will not only help you to create the most appropriate design, it will also help your end users to understand that your design is the best possible approach to the business requirement. You should develop enough evidence so that you can defend your design against anyone.

The Pilot Project—Making Sure Everything Works *Before* It's Too Late

By this point, you should have a good idea of the issues you'll need to consider before approaching a network design. As we've been mentioning throughout this chapter, the best network designs result from applying the most appropriate network technology to solve business problems. Before you can be certain that your design will utilize the most appropriate technology, you (and the end users of your design) need to be sure your solution will work within the environment it will be deployed in, and that it will work the way it should.

Even if it does work well, almost every design can benefit from some measure of refinement. Frequently, the areas that will most benefit from improvements and refinements are not apparent until the design has been installed. Once the project moves from concept to reality, it becomes easier to identify the elements that don't work quite the way they should, or the elements that could operate more efficiently.

The wrong time to discover the limitations of your design is during the implementation phase of the project. If the flaws of your design don't show up until you have installed the components onto the production network, your organization may be in trouble. If your company has made an investment in technology that doesn't work based on an incomplete design, the cost to remove that technology and successfully deploy an appropriate solution can be considerable.

The best time to determine if a design needs to be refined or if it needs to be scrapped altogether is before it is deployed on the production network. By implementing your design in a test environment as part of a pilot project, you'll have the opportunity to confirm that your design elements work the same way in the real world that they do in theory.

Why Implement a Pilot Project?

The purpose of a pilot project is to provide everyone involved in the project the opportunity to determine that a design will meet its objectives. The scope of a pilot depends on the scope of the design itself. For example, a pilot project for a new application might involve installing the application on a test server on the existing network, or a pilot for a new router might involve the creation of an entirely separate test network.

In smaller network environments, the advantages of a pilot project are not always obvious. Pilot projects take time to conduct, and they require resources that are in constant demand throughout your organization. Planning an effective pilot can be difficult. Regardless of the size of your network, two significant advantages of including a pilot project as part of your design are as follows:

- It will enable you to learn lessons early in the course of the project.

- It will protect your network from unanticipated mishaps or misconfigurations.

Learn Lessons Early

Specification sheets, trade journal reviews, and product literature are no substitute for experience. No matter how much time you may spend researching a particular product or technology, you will always learn more about a product when you install it and try to make it to work on your network. You'll never know exactly how a component will react with existing components on your network until you connect them.

By working through the installation and configuration process during a pilot project, you can learn the tough lessons early, before you and your staff have to work under a tight implementation deadline. From the experience you gain during the pilot, you will be able to more accurately project the amount of time it will take to deploy the design on your production network.

Pilot projects also allow your end users to see the results of your design for the first time. It gives them the opportunity to learn whether the technology will allow them to do what they want to do. In some situations, the pilot project will enable them to realize that their original vision for the project may not have been the best approach to the problem. They may ask you to revisit the design, placing an emphasis on a different aspect of the problem.

Protect the Production Network

The second most significant advantage of conducting a pilot project is that it will provide a buffer zone between your design and the production network. It is always a good idea to avoid performing any type of testing on equipment that is designated to serve the needs of the active production network. Any changes associated with testing could have unpredictable results, and the last place that you want to introduce unpredictability is your production network.

Establishing a separate test network will enable you to test all of the elements of your project without concern for service disruption. The pilot project is your opportunity to test every aspect of your design regardless of the consequences, so be sure to test every element thoroughly.

Your test environment should be as similar to your production network as possible. If your departmental budget will allow, try to purchase equipment that is identical to the components that are deployed on your network. Unfortunately, many budgets do not allow for such flexibility, so you may have to be more creative. Minimally, you should order the equipment specified within your design early and use it during the pilot for testing. By testing your design on the same equipment that will be used later on in the production environment, you will be able to avoid compatibility problems.

Planning a Successful Pilot Project

The success of a pilot project depends on more than whether the design works properly. Designing a pilot is similar to creating a network design. Every pilot project you conduct should have a clear objective and a clear definition of the factors that must be met in order for the pilot to be considered a success.

A pilot project that lacks objectives will not be as effective as a project that has been carefully planned to test all critical design elements.

Identify the Objectives

Begin your pilot project plan with a clear definition of the objectives you want to meet. First, review all of the elements, functions, and components specified within your design. Next, develop a list of each of the elements, being sure to define each objective in concrete and measurable terms. Your goal should be to define each objective so that it can become the basis for a test you'll conduct during the pilot.

For example, if you have developed a design for a mail system to link two remote offices, you may have a list of objectives like the one shown here:

- Install and configure e-mail server software on two mail servers

- Test e-mail system for compatibility with existing network operating system

- Install and configure e-mail client software on two workstations

- Configure mail servers to communicate with one another
- Send 300 messages between mail servers in a 10-minute interval and determine if server utilization exceeds 50 percent.

Your objectives should be specific enough to cover all of the areas of functionality you'll need to test during the pilot. Before you begin the pilot, you may find it helpful to further refine the list of objectives by creating smaller sub-objectives.

Document the Process

Once you have identified the objectives for the pilot, spend some time developing and documenting your test plan. Using the list of objectives as your outline, clearly define the processes you will employ to test key functionality for each of the objectives. By creating a detailed set of testing documentation and following the documents throughout the pilot project, you will be able to easily reproduce your results.

While the pilot project is in process, you should take detailed notes throughout the configuration and testing phases. Document the entire installation process, and carefully note any steps of the installation that may be unclear or confusing in the documentation provided by the product manufacturer. Your documentation will be useful once the pilot is concluded and you wish to implement your design on the production network.

Determine What Constitutes *Success*

Finally, develop a clear definition of the criteria that will be used to evaluate whether the pilot is successful, and whether the design provides sufficient functionality to proceed with implementation.

You can use the objective list you created earlier in this section as the basis for your success criteria. For example, if you wanted to determine whether the inter-office e-mail system pilot was successful, you might list one of the success criteria as "Each mail server can transfer 300 messages in a 10-minute interval while remaining below 50 percent utilization."

Keep in mind that your definition of a successful pilot project will influence whether the design is deployed on the corporate network, so you'll want to create a definition that is an accurate model of the performance expected in the real world.

For some designs, performance issues will not be considered in the definition of a successful project. In those cases, your only interest may be that a product works the way it is supposed to and provides an adequate level of stability. For other products, such as redundant drive arrays, issues such as fault tolerance are more critical than performance. During a pilot project for a drive array, you may focus on objectives such as the drive array's ability to function when one or more of the devices experiences a hardware or software failure.

The Phases of a Pilot Project

Most pilot projects have at least three phases: the *proof of concept* phase, the testing phase, and the sign-off/approval phase. Depending on the scope of the design and the scale of the implementation, the entire pilot project may last a week, or it may last a number of months.

The Proof of Concept Phase

The purpose of the proof of concept phase is to demonstrate that the design is conceptually sound, and that all of the components specified within the design will work together.

Your objective in this phase is to prove that your design will satisfy the basic functionality required to fulfill the business requirement, so focus only on the core functionality of the design during the proof of concept phase. Don't concern yourself with thorough documentation, simply install and configure the components to confirm that they will operate the way you envisioned them to in your design.

By the end of the proof of concept phase, you will know if your design will be able to achieve its objectives. You may find that nothing worked the way you thought it would, or that a previously unknown bug or incompatibility caused your design to fail. If you find yourself in that situation, you'll need to either modify your design so that it will work or start over at the beginning.

On the other hand, you may discover that your design worked exactly the way you had planned it to work. If so, congratulations! However, even if your design had all the right pieces in all of the right places, chances are that you learned a few lessons while you were connecting everything together.

Once you and your customer are satisfied that your design is fundamentally sound, you can begin the next phase of the pilot project, the testing phase.

The Testing Phase

Once the design has been validated by the proof of concept phase, the next step is to thoroughly test all of the elements of the design. During testing, you'll want to discover the optimal way to install and configure the components of your design, and you'll want to analyze how the implementation of your design will perform. You'll also want to determine how your design will impact the existing production network.

Tuning the Installation   The first portion of the testing phase involves the steps and procedures related to the installation of the software and hardware specified in your design. During installation tuning, your goal will be to thoroughly understand and document the installation process.

As you begin to install each of the components, it's likely that you'll discover that the documentation provided by the manufacturers of the components is either incomplete or inadequate. One of your objectives is to fill in the blanks in the documentation, not only for common installation steps but also for customizable portions of the installation process, such as for dialog boxes where you are prompted to enter network and addressing information.

Your second objective during the installation tuning phase is to streamline the installation to make the process as simple as possible. For software applications, you may want to work with installation tools such as SYSDIFF, or you can use scripting tools to automate installations.

By the end of the installation-tuning portion of the testing phase, you should have documentation that is complete enough so that anyone in your department could perform a full installation of all of the components specified in your design.

Mastering the Configuration   After you have completed installation tuning, the next step of the testing phase is to focus on configuring the components you have just installed. For some components, such as network cards, there will be few, if any, additional configuration steps following installation. For other devices, such as Windows NT Server, the configuration process will be an ongoing challenge.

Your objective during this portion of testing is to determine the best way to configure individual components for optimal operation with respect to fault tolerance, performance, and manageability. In most situations, arriving at the optimal configuration will only come after considerable research and testing. Use information resources such as Microsoft TechNet, the Microsoft Web site, and Usenet news groups to learn more about ways you can optimize device configuration.

When you have completed the configuration process, capture all of the configuration information and add it to the installation documentation you created earlier.

Optimizing Performance   The performance optimization step of the testing phase is closely related to the configuration phase. During the configuration phase, you should focus more on tuning each of the components individually and optimizing each device on its own. However, during the performance optimization phase, you should focus on optimizing the performance of all of the interrelated components of the design.

To fully optimize the implementation of your design, you'll need to create a set of performance monitoring and measurement tools so that you can understand how each of the components interacts with the others. Use the tools and performance measurements to model how well your design will scale once it has been installed on your production network.

Pay close attention to major subsystems such as the disk, CPU, memory, paging files, and network channels. Your findings may lead you to additional reconfiguration of individual components, or you may discover that you underestimated the capacity requirements of your design. At this point, you may need to make adjustments to your original design to satisfy the additional requirements. For example, you may discover that an imaging application uses high amounts of network bandwidth, so if you plan to deploy this application to hundreds of users, you'll need to specify a 100Mb Ethernet network adapter instead of a 10Mb network adapter in your design.

Determining the Impact   Once you have completed installing, configuring, and optimizing your design implementation, the final step is to determine how your implementation will impact the existing network.

Determining impact is a complicated process, and it requires a thorough understanding of the normal operating utilization levels of the current production network. Using server-based tools such as Performance Monitor or network-based tools such as Systems Management Server or a network protocol analyzer, carefully measure all relevant performance statistics on your existing network. Once you have determined baseline performance information for your network, install the monitoring tools on your test network and measure the performance statistics associated with the components installed in the course of your testing.

The more closely you can approximate the operating conditions of your production network on your test network, the more accurate your overall results will be.

Review the impact analysis results carefully, because they may indicate that your design will overload the existing network infrastructure.

The whole point of conducting the pilot project is to avoid surprises when you begin implementation of your design on the production network, so take the time to be thorough during your pilot project.

Customer Review and Sign-Off

The final step in the pilot project is to review the results of the proof of concept and testing phases with the customer. The review portion of the project might involve a written report that highlights the findings from the project, or it might include a demonstration of the functional components of the design. Carefully review all of the steps of the pilot project with your customer so that they understand what you have tested and how you have tested it.

At the completion of the review, you should work with the customer to determine if the project will proceed, and if so, you should begin to plan the implementation.

In this chapter, we've discussed how to approach a network design, including the importance of creating designs that focus on meeting business requirements. In the next chapter, we'll begin to discuss the technical information you'll need to know to begin designing NT enterprise networks.

CHAPTER 4

Dynamic Domain Design

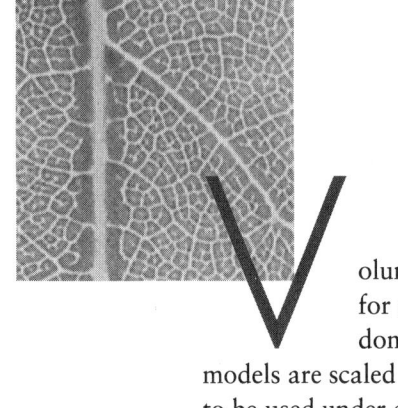Volumes of literature exist about Microsoft's recommendations for domain model implementations. The single domain, master domain, multi-master domain, and complete-trust domain models are scaled based on user population and spoken of as if they are tools to be used under clearly defined circumstances. Not so!

In this chapter, we'll explore the factors that will influence your choice of domain model, and we'll see how you can combine the best elements of multiple domain models to develop a design that best meets your network management strategy. Most importantly, we'll describe how to develop a design that will work as well in the future as it will today.

This discussion will naturally lead us to explore other areas of subsequent interest to domain modeling. These include:

- Naming standards and an overview of X.500

- Understanding trust relationships

- Our attempt to unveil the mystery of browsing (once and for all!)

Exposing the Myths of Domain Design

Allow us to begin this section by asking a fundamental question that often goes unanswered or—worse yet—is answered incorrectly.

Question: "Why do we need domains in the first place?"

Answer: "Domains provide a single network login that enables universal access to resources."

Alas, the promise of the single-network login is probably truly appreciated only by those whose networking experience is with server-based authentication. Novell NetWare 3.*x*, with the classic "Login, attach...attach...attach... attach..." model, is the best example of what we are trying to get away from.

Ideally, Windows NT will give us an authentication scheme where we log into the network, not the server. Once access to the network has been granted, we should be able to reach out to any resource for which we have permission.

Interestingly enough, we architect our domain model for reasons that are mostly different from what determines our need for it. This leads us to consider the top three myths associated with domain design:

- Myth: Domain models are designed around users and their need to access particular resources.

- Myth: The single domain model is best for organizations of up to 40,000 users.

- Myth: The multi-master domain model is best for organizations with more than 40,000 users.

Around the time of the release of Windows NT 4, Microsoft began referring to its domain model architecture as "Windows NT Server Directory Services." Changing the name was a feeble attempt to defer some of the criticisms by Novell and its supporters, who were pointing out the shortcomings of Microsoft domain modeling, as compared to the Novell Directory Services architecture. Let there be no doubt, nothing has changed in Windows NT from 3.x to 4 that would make it a true directory service. Domain modeling by any other name is still domain modeling.

Debunking the Domain Model Design Myth

This myth is the reason domain design can become so complex for a network architect. The designer may proceed with the best intentions, trying to draw logical circles around groups of users and their resources, only to discover most users belong to more than one group. The second stumbling block occurs when the designer realizes that members of the same business unit are spread across multiple geographic sites. When seen in this light, categorizing network resources becomes an equally challenging task because users of a single device, such as a network printer, may belong to any number of groups. Trying to accommodate all of the users, groups, and locations, the designer must apply trust relationships to ensure that everyone can get to what they require. The end result is a domain model like the one shown in Figure 4.1.

Chapter 4 • Dynamic Domain Design

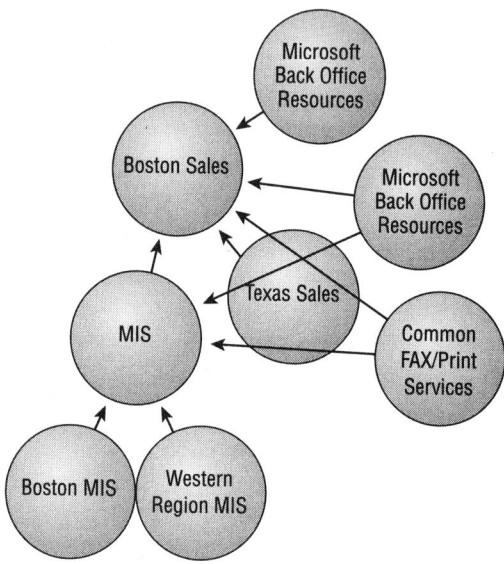

FIGURE 4.1

The messy-multi-master-complete-anarchy domain model

Actually, the best domain models result when you consider the following:

- The means by which you'll administer the Microsoft network as a whole

- Your intent in integrating Microsoft BackOffice and/or third-party application services

- The underlying network infrastructure and subsequent process that Windows NT will follow in replicating the Security Accounts Management Database (SAM)

In the sections that follow we'll explore a series of case studies to show you how to most effectively apply these principles. For now, let's consider their fundamental aspects.

If the goal is to provide centralized administration of user accounts, we should strive to keep the SAM database within a confined area. The single domain and master domain models fit this criteria, while the multi-master domain and complete-trust domain models do not.

Microsoft BackOffice products, along with certain third-party applications, bring their own requirements to domain design. We could certainly have a philosophical argument about this, since some might consider it sacrilege to have an application service dictate the architecture of the underlying network operating system. Others might consider it to be just annoying.

Whatever your perspective, consider a product such as Microsoft Systems Management Server 1.2 (SMS). It is a requirement of SMS that it be installed on a domain controller. The network architect considering a single domain is in a situation where the SMS server will also be providing account authentication and browsing services to the user population—in addition to SMS services. This begs the question as to whether it would be best to move SMS into its own domain. Doing so will ease the account authentication burden on the SMS platform, by separating it from the domain where the user accounts reside. Poof, our single domain has just been transformed into a master domain, courtesy of SMS.

Imagine a small insurance company with almost 800 users. In learning more about the business model of this company we discover that alternatives to Microsoft BackOffice products will be deployed and that the administration of the user community occurs centrally from their home office. On first thought, it seems like a perfect fit for the single domain model, that is, until you consider the underlying network infrastructure.

Figure 4.2 depicts the hub and spoke arrangement of this company, where four regional offices link back to the home office via 9.6Kbps data communications circuits.

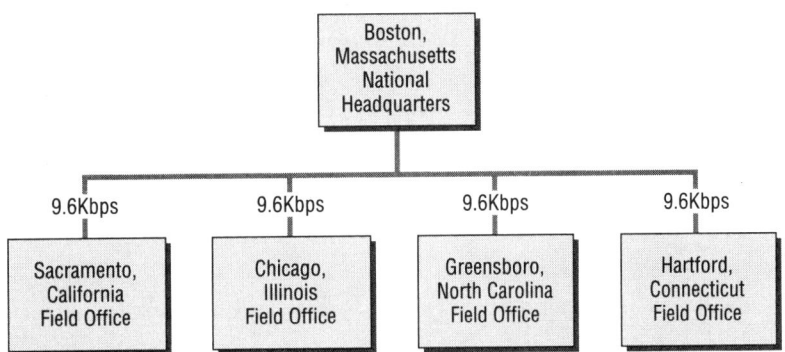

FIGURE 4.2
Network infrastructure of our theoretical insurance company

Deployment of a single domain model will result in a lack of logical grouping of users or resources, delays in authentication, and sluggish browsing. (We'll cover the reasons for this poor performance in the sections that follow.) Our alternative would be the master domain model, with the home office functioning as the master site and each of the field offices taking on the role of a resource domain. This model logically groups users and resources, and it will improve browsing performance. We can also reduce delays in authentication by deploying a BDC for the master domain in each of the resource domains. While overall performance will improve, the cost to deploy a master domain model solution will be more expensive than deploying a single domain model because of the cost of the backup domain controllers. Figure 4.3 illustrates the master domain model for our insurance company.

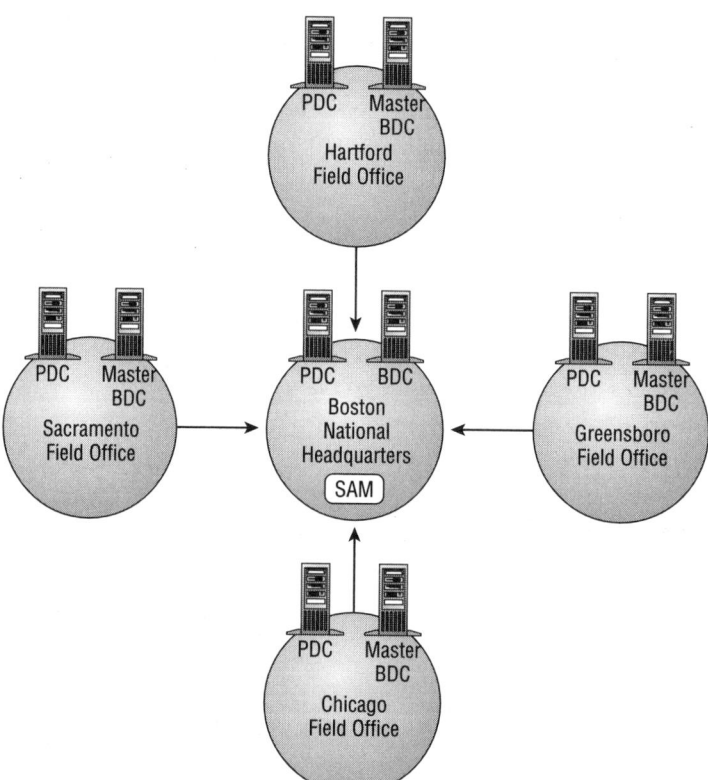

FIGURE 4.3

Master domain model for the insurance company

Demystifying the Number of Users for a Single Domain

Forty thousand users for a single domain might seem an odd number to those who've worked with Windows NT since its inception. Over the years, Microsoft has recommended a number of values, such as 5,000; 26,000; 40,000; and unlimited.

The question comes up, "So how many users can you actually fit in a single domain?"

Instead of picking a number at random, let's answer this question from a mathematical and design standpoint. First, let's do the math.

Within a domain, the PDC will replicate the contents of its SAM (directory) database to all BDCs. Issues with database corruption existed in the earlier versions of Windows NT, when the database size approached 20MB, or approximately 10,000 users and their supporting groups, domain controllers, and member servers. Therefore, with the release of Windows NT 3.1 through 3.51, the recommended number of users for a single domain was cut in half to 5,000 users. Over time this issue with corruption has been resolved to the point where a database of 40MB in size can be replicated successfully. What we can learn from this is that the population of a domain has more to do with the size of the database and less to do with the number of users.

At the present time, Microsoft has successfully replicated directory databases of a size greater than 90MB. The published recommendation for a directory database is curbed to a size of 40MB or less, however, to limit the number of incidents that might occur with 90MB databases.

Every object that exists within the directory database, including user accounts, group accounts, and computer accounts, contributes a certain amount to the size of the database. Table 4.1 provides an overview of the sizing.

TABLE 4.1 Size Occupied by Account Objects

Account	Size
User Account	1KB
Group Account	4KB
Computer Account	500B

Note: Group size assumes an average of 300 members.

You can probably tell by now that the database size can vary greatly, depending on the mixture of users, groups, workstations, domain controllers, and member servers. Let's examine the following scenarios and the resultant sizes of the databases by looking at Table 4.2.

TABLE 4.2 Sample Directory Database Configurations	User Accounts	Group Accounts	Computer Accounts	Database Size
	1,000	250	1,006	2.5MB
	5,000	300	9,000	10.7MB
	26,000	250	26,000	40MB
	40,000	0	0	40MB

Imagine that you are a member of the Microsoft marketing group. Now examine Table 4.2 and ask yourself what you would publish as the maximum number of user accounts supported by a domain. Being an enthusiastic marketer, you'd probably say that a domain can theoretically support 40,000 users. (Of course you wouldn't point out the fact that the 40,000-user domain doesn't contain any group or computer accounts.)

Unfortunately, what has occurred as a result is that the 40MB database size has been thought of synonymously with 40,000 users. The thought that this database can exist on a single PDC is what generated the myth that a single domain can support 40,000 users. The word *theoretically* continues to be conveniently dropped from this myth, whenever it is stated.

Whether you would ever want to have 40,000 users in a single domain is another issue to consider. What type of a hardware platform will be required to support replication and authentication of a 40MB database supporting 40,000 users? Is it really cost effective to architect a super-server whose sole purpose is to provide authentication and browsing services?

Question: How many Microsoft engineers does it take to screw in a light bulb? Answer: None, it's a hardware problem.

Microsoft recommends only 2,000 to 5,000 users ever be contained within a single domain due to the limitations of hardware and network infrastructure. In practice we have seen this number hover somewhere between 1,500 and 3,000, depending on the additional application servers and network services contained within the domain.

What does it take to administer a 40,000-user single domain? Consider the time involved in browsing through a list of this size looking for user accounts or client workstations. Any natural groupings of users that would have been handled by resource domains will now need to be handled through the creation of groups. These additional groups result in a larger database and are thereby self-defeating. All of these elements need to be considered before you take the time to architect an excessively large single domain.

When to Implement the Multi-Master Domain Model

Having taken the time to debunk the 40,000-user statistic, let's consider the reasons why you might craft or avoid a multi-master domain. These reasons include:

- Administration of the network
- Geographical diversity of the business
- Size of the directory database

Above all, you should consider that a user account and computer account can exist only once in the entire Microsoft network, to avoid any conflict that might occur through the assignment of more than one SID to the same user or computer. This rule applies not only to the multi-master domain, but to all domain models. We mention it here only because it is most likely to occur when architecting a Microsoft network with multiple-user account databases.

A number of factors may influence your decision to create a multi-master domain model, but administration of the network will most likely be the main factor because the multi-master model provides a more natural division of user accounts. Once you've decided on the multi-master model, the difficult part is determining where to create the division of accounts.

Early recommendations for the Windows NT multi-master domain model resulted in many businesses dividing their directory databases alphabetically based on account names. This is certainly *not* our recommendation. Instead we suggest you consider the organizational structure of your business. Ask yourself questions such as: "Are there business units that will need to maintain some degree of organizational autonomy within the Microsoft network?" If so, you can craft a design like the one shown in Figure 4.4.

FIGURE 4.4

The organizationally autonomous multi-master model

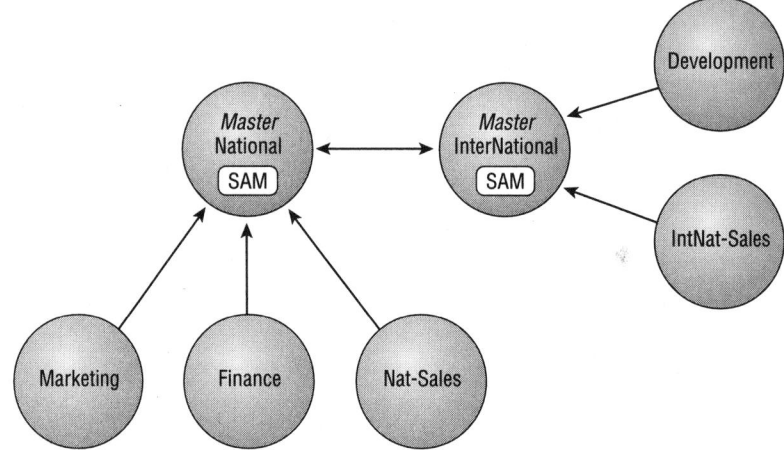

"Am I crafting a domain model to fit a national network, built upon many small field offices, connected through various high- and low-speed telecommunications circuits?" If this is the case, then you might want to deploy a multi-master model tied more closely to geography than organization. Figure 4.5 depicts how this might present itself.

FIGURE 4.5

The geographical multi-master model

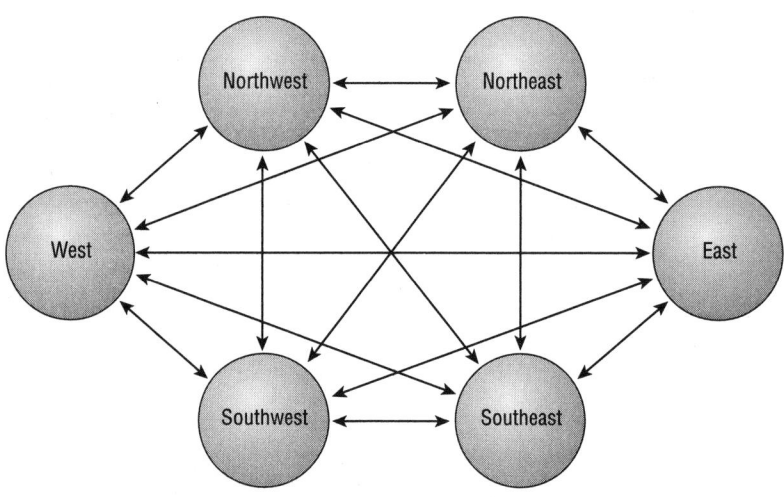

You should also consider that some organizations lack a centralized information technologies staff and are subsequently built around political boundaries. It is our experience that more multi-master domains have been created for this type of organization than any other. If you begin to work within this kind of environment, you'll discover that political posturing will prevent you from drawing clear lines between business units so it becomes difficult to develop a domain model built upon organization.

For this reason, we have found it best to build upon a geographical multi-master model, diffusing some of the more politically charged, animated discussions that would ensue over organizational control. In some situations, some of the political tussling can be settled by talking about individual, instead of organizational, control. Your end result may become a geographical multi-master model controlled by a committee of administrators, selected from each of the political parties.

Now consider an international organization, in which sites located within different countries communicate infrequently with one another. A geographically dispersed business will lend itself rather cleanly to a multi-master domain model, particularly when each location has its own information technology staff, as is most likely in a global organization. Figure 4.6 shows how a business of this type might architect its Microsoft network.

FIGURE 4.6

The multiple-masters domain model

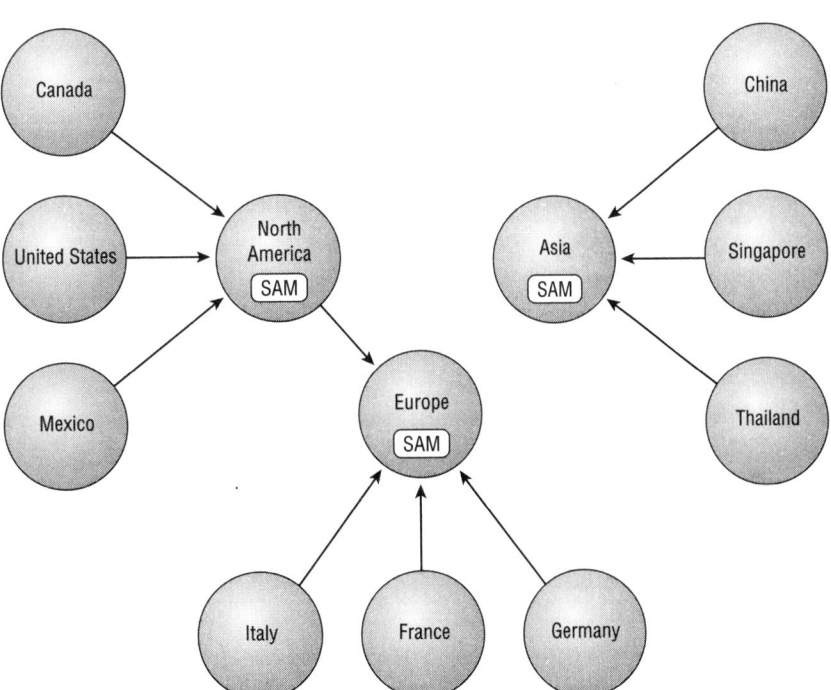

In Figure 4.6 you'll notice that not every domain has a two-way trust to the other. For that reason, this type of model is sometimes referred to as a *multiple-masters domain model,* instead of a multi-master domain model. The naming is to show that this structure sits somewhere between the single-master model and multi-master model.

In discussing the second myth, we learned that the directory database does have a physical limitation of 40MB. Theoretically, we would need to consider this as a factor in deciding whether to split the database in half when moving toward a multi-master model. In practice we most often find ourselves dividing the database into a multi-master model for political reasons long before we reach the physical limitations of the database.

The intent of this section has been to expose some of the myths associated with Windows NT domain design. These myths have been responsible for leading many a designer down a dead-end path, only to discover their error during the implementation phase.

Experience shows that it is much easier to change a design during the "whiteboard" sessions than it is during the deployment phase. With this in mind, let's begin the process of whiteboarding a solid and scalable Windows NT domain model—a model that can be crafted with a clear thought process free of myth, magic, and the demons associated with sinister domain design. (OK, so maybe the last sentence is a bit too dramatic.)

Naming Standards and X.500

As we do our work as network designers, naming standards have become our personal soapbox. The benefits associated with solid naming standards are countless, and we strongly encourage you to establish standards that are flexible without being loose, scalable without being complex, and descriptive without being verbose. Now before you call us mad, we're going to provide you with examples of how to make all of this possible.

In the process, we'll explore the X.500 naming standards. The X.500 standards will become increasingly important because of Microsoft's stated direction for Windows NT 5, which will feature the Active Directory, a combination of X.500 and Domain Name Services (DNS). We'll discuss DNS in more detail in Chapters 7 and 9.

Why Establish Naming Standards?

The importance of artful naming standards is never so obvious as when it comes time to troubleshoot a problem within a network. Once you spend some time cruising through Windows NT Explorer, you'll discover that all of the icons appear the same, regardless of the function of the computers they represent. PDCs, BDCs, member servers, and workstations all appear exactly alike. Without a descriptive naming standard it would be challenging at best to tell a PDC from a workstation.

Failure to develop and publicize logical naming standards results in domains, servers, and workstations being named after individuals' dogs and leisure activities. Over the years we've clicked on Explorer within our clients' networks only to discover names we're sure the owner never thought anyone else would ever see!

As you'll recall from Chapter 1, Microsoft Windows NT relies heavily on identifying devices through the NetBIOS name. For this reason, a solid naming standard is imperative to the success of any project. Additionally, Microsoft's stated direction for its future Active Directory is to deploy it within an architecture that embraces the X.500 and DNS standards. You'll notice that our sample naming standards have been designed so they prepare you to scale toward the emerging technology of Active Directory. We've placed special attention on limiting character usage to A–Z, a–z, 0–9, and hyphen (-), as these are the only legal characters for DNS naming.

We begin this section on naming standards by considering those elements of Windows NT that need to be named. Objects such as domains, servers, workstations, printers, users, and groups all need to be covered in the conventions that we establish. Limitations in character lengths and types are also factors and are highlighted in Table 4.3.

TABLE 4.3 Object Maximum Character Lengths

Object	Maximum Character Length
Domain	15 characters
Server	15 characters
Workstation	15 characters

TABLE 4.3 (cont.)

Object Maximum Character Lengths

Object	Maximum Character Length
Printer	31 characters total (includes the server name)
User	20 characters
Group	20 characters

Note: Illegal characters include: ? \ / * " <> | [ ] ; : , + =

In addition to the limitations imposed by Windows NT, you may also discover that integration with other network operating systems and certain applications will restrict the length of a device name. You should explore these limitations prior to finalizing your naming conventions. When in doubt, the best rule to follow is to be short and descriptive.

Domains

You've probably already begun to think about the domain model you are going to deploy—at least at a high level—by the time you begin considering a naming standard. With this in mind, you'll want to consider a logical hierarchy to your domain name similar in nature to the X.500 standards that we explore later in this section. Generally speaking, X.500 begins with a Country Name followed by an Organization Name, Organizational Unit Name, and Common Name for the remaining objects in the Directory Information Tree (DIT). Likewise, you may establish domain names that appear as in Table 4.4, where the country of origin is included or excluded depending on your business requirements.

TABLE 4.4

Sample Domain Naming Standards

Syntax	Name	Notes
CCOOOUUU	USCDMPVD	8 characters, X.500-like
CC_OOO_UUU	US_CDM_RI	10 characters, *not* DNS compliant
CC-OOO-UUUU	US-CDM-PROV	11 characters, X.500-like, hyphen delimiter

TABLE 4.4 (cont.)

Sample Domain Naming Standards

Syntax	Name	Notes
USOOO-UUUUUU	USCDM-PROVRI	12 characters, X.500-like, hyphen delimiter
CC-OOO-UUUUU-##	US-CDM-PRVRI-01	15 characters fixed, X.500-like, hyphen delimiter
CC-OOO-UUUXX	US-CDM-PRVRI	12 characters, variable last field

These naming standards have been put in place for a fictitious company, the Capo di Monti Winery, which has locations in Providence, Rhode Island, USA, and Naples, Italy. Because the winery is an international corporation, the country code takes on special importance when we may have more than one domain, geographically dispersed. You'll also notice that a hyphen makes it easier to separate the individual components of the name, enhancing readability. We also prefer a hyphen because it is DNS compliant, positioning us well for Microsoft's future Active Directory. Of all the options in the sample standards, we like the sixth one (US-CDM-PRVRI). The last five-character field provides an element of flexibility for defining the components of the domain. City, State, Region, Winery Location, and Manufacturing Plant ID are all possibilities for this field. In truth, we could use any of the samples, but we wanted to allow for future growth while keeping in mind the future direction for Microsoft Active Directory.

Servers

You'll recall that the icon that displays in Windows NT utilities is the same for all servers and workstations. Because of this, we'll need to place special importance on the naming standard for our servers. A second issue to consider is that the server name will be appended to the name of each printer. Therefore we'll want to keep this name as concise as possible to avoid exceeding the recommended 31 character total length.

OOOT-FFF##

OOO   =   Organization

T	=	Server type	
		P = Primary domain controller, B = Backup domain controller, M = General member server	
FFF	=	Functional descriptor	
		A = Archival, C = Citrix, D = DHCP, E = Exchange, F = Fax, I = Internet, N = DNS, P = Print, Q = SQL, S = SMS	
##	=	Fixed-length sequence number	

Some examples that follow this standard appear in Table 4.5.

TABLE 4.5 Sample Server Naming Standards

Name	Notes
CDMP-DNW01	PDC running DHCP, DNS, and WINS
CDMB-01	BDC (supporting the domain in the USA)
CDMM-E01	Member server running Exchange
CDMB-02	BDC (supporting the domain in Italy)
CDMB-QS01	BDC running SQL server and SMS
CDMM-P01	Dedicated print server

You'll notice that the server field length may vary, but the maximum number of characters that can be used is 10. CDM is a constant organizational field that will be helpful in distinguishing our servers from our workstations when they are listed together. The role of the server will be easily identifiable by glancing at the character to the left of the hyphen, while the codes to the right of the hyphen list the services being deployed on the device. A fixed-length numeric field assists in uniquely identifying those common servers with common services.

As a side note, you should also consider what we have intentionally excluded from the server naming standard. We have excluded the domain name because it will appear either as part of the fully distinguished name by Microsoft Windows NT, or it will be obvious because the user will have navigated into the domain hierarchy to gain access to the server. Other obvious descriptors like "NT" and "Server" are also excluded from the naming standard.

Workstations

Workstation naming standards exemplify why "personal computer" is an oxymoron. Primarily we find ourselves defining who has ownership of the workstation and from there determine the appropriate naming standard. Once past this hurdle, we'll need to decide whether peer-to-peer networking is part of our plan. The reason is while a serial number might be a great way to ensure uniqueness of the workstation name, it makes a lousy identifier when trying to browse through a list of workstations looking for a shared directory. Let's examine some workstation naming standards in Table 4.6. Comments will follow.

TABLE 4.6 Sample Workstation Naming Standards

Syntax	Name	Notes
UUUUUUUU-##	MONTIA-01	Derivative of Anthony Monti's user name
S##########-CC	S120034578-US	Serial number guarantees uniqueness
LLLLLLLL-BBB	PROVEAST-097	Building and data port location
CDM-######	CDM-874531	Corporate asset tag number

Examining the standards in Table 4.6, we favor the first and third (MONTIA-01 and PROVEAST-097). A variant of the user's name will enable us to easily identify workstations through their natural alphabetical listing. For the purist who believes the workstation belongs to the company and not the user, we ask you to consider two issues: Users share files with other users, and users call for help when they have trouble with the workstation. It is much easier for users to think about sharing information between individuals than between serial numbers.

We like the third standard in instances where the workstation may be a public resource. These types of public work areas and kiosks are becoming more common as society gets comfortable with using computer technology.

> ### From Caffeine to Chop Sticks
>
> About two summers ago I had the opportunity to travel to California on business. It was during this time that the Internet and trendy coffee bars were starting to reach their peak in popularity. It seems only fitting then, that as I was passing through Venice Beach, I came across the Cyber Café. Eight public Internet workstations were spread throughout the café, enabling one to navigate the information highway while sipping an espresso or café latte.
>
> We often hear that it takes time for Californian trends to reach us on the East Coast. That experience two summers ago certainly confirms this, but what is most interesting is the transformation that occurs as the trend passes from the Pacific to Atlantic Ocean. The next time you are in New York, take a moment to look up the Surf 'n' Sushi, where you can check out the NYSE Web site while getting your sashimi and California rolls to go.

Printers

Our experiences have shown that the most successful naming standard for a printer is one that encompasses its location. Nothing is more frustrating to a user than having to search through the building for their print job.

Another item to consider when developing a printer naming standard has to do with the recommendation that the total server name and printer name be kept to 31 characters. Spaces and backslashes (\) associated with the Universal Naming Convention (UNC) should be included as part of this 31-character limitation. Since the printer will become a shared network device, keep in mind that you may wish to limit the share name to eight characters in length for your MS-DOS and Windows 95 users.

When we talk about naming a Windows NT printer, we are actually naming the logical printer, or "print queue" as it is more commonly referred to. Microsoft chooses to refer to the unit that actually performs the printing as a printing device.

Consider the standards for print services outlined in Table 4.7, bearing in mind our earlier points relative to emphasis on location. Examples using these standards follow.

TABLE 4.7 Standard Print Services Naming Conventions	Standard Syntax		Full Name (Including Server)
	LLFFDDD##-MC		**\\CDMP-DNW01\PV08MIS01-HA**
	LL	=	Location
	FF	=	Floor
	DDD	=	Department
	##	=	Fixed-length sequence number
	M	=	Code for manufacturer of printer
			H = Hewlett-Packard, O = Okidata, X = Xerox
	C	=	Code for model of printer (A-Z)
			A= Hewlett-Packard 4SI, B = Okidata OL-810, C = Okidata OL-600e, D = Xerox 4230, E = Xerox MajestiK with Cyclone RIP

Examples that follow this standard appear in Table 4.8.

TABLE 4.8 Sample Printer Naming Standards	Printer Name	Share Name	Notes
	PV08MIS01-HA	PV08MIS1	Providence, RI building, eighth floor MIS
	NP01MAN01-OC	NP01MAN1	Naples, Italy, Okidata printer
	ML02FIN03-XD	ML02FIN3	Milan, Italy, Finance Printer #3

Notice that these standards place heavy emphasis on the physical location of the printer, which is different from most standards we've seen, which tend to emphasize make and model. The manufacturer code does not appear until the end of the standard and is encoded at that. Granted, these names appear a bit cryptic at first glance; however, over time users begin to refer to them by department code and sequence number rather than the full name. "I am printing to MAN1 and FIN3," will most likely be heard by those individuals who are in the general vicinity of these printers. The full name will usually only come into play during instances of troubleshooting and driver installation.

The Capo di Monti Winery intends to send print jobs across the wide area network (WAN). This is why the location code is included in the syntax. Were this not a business requirement, then there would be an opportunity to eliminate this from the standard.

Lastly, you'll notice that the total length of the server name, delimiters, and printer name has been kept to less than 31 characters. At 25 characters total, we are within the recommended Microsoft guidelines. You will also note that the printer share name was truncated to eight characters to keep it compatible with older MS-DOS applications, as well as MS-DOS and Windows 95 shares.

User Accounts

We highly recommend that user accounts be kept as short and descriptive as possible. If you are going to make the workstation name a derivative of the user name, then you may wish to use the last name first in the naming convention. This will provide a natural alphabetical listing of the user workstations, as discussed in the previous section on workstation naming conventions.

Let's take a few moments to examine the following standard:

Standard Syntax	Notes
LLLLLLLF	First seven characters of the last name, single character first initial

If duplicate names exist, the following rules will apply to each successive user after the first (no changes will be made to the initial user account):

- If the duplicate user's last name is less than seven characters, the middle initial will be used.

Standard Syntax	Notes
LLLLLLFM	Substitute X, Y, or Z for duplicate users who do not have a middle initial.

Example:

First instance of Laura Monti = MontiL

Second instance of Laura Monti = MontiLJ

- If the duplicate user's last name is greater than or equal to seven characters, then the first six characters of the last name will be used. The first initial and middle initial will be appended to this subset of the last name.

Standard Syntax	Notes
LLLLLLFM	Substitute X, Y, or Z for duplicate users who do not have a middle initial.

Example:

First instance of Michele Mildner = MildnerM

Second instance of Michele Mildner = MildneMM

Table 4.9 provides additional examples of this user account naming standard.

TABLE 4.9 Sample User Account Naming Standards

User Name	Account Name	Notes
Joseph Luigi Capodimonti	CapodimJ	Truncated last name, first initial
Joseph Mario Capodimonti	CapodiJM	Truncated last name, first and middle initial
David Steven Monti	MontiD	First instance of this name
David Chianti Monti	MontiDC	Second instance, use middle initial

TABLE 4.9 (cont.)
Sample User Account Naming Standards

User Name	Account Name	Notes
David Monti	MontiDX	Third instance, no middle name, use X
Rosanne Scungio	ScungioR	First instance of this name
Rosanne Bianca Scungio	ScungiRB	Truncated last name, first and middle initial

In each of the examples you can see where our naming standards and rules were applied for user accounts. While the character length was capped at eight, we use a combination of truncation and middle initials to ensure that each name is unique throughout the Microsoft network.

Group Accounts

Within the Windows NT security model, rights to the system and access to resources are provided through groups. Keeping this in mind, you'll see that a descriptive naming standard takes on special importance because it enables us to easily identify who has permissions within the Microsoft network. Think about group naming standards by first considering those categories of groups that need to be named. For example:

- **Functional groups,** such as Backup-Only Operators and Take Ownership of Files
- **Application groups,** such as Excel, Visio, and Word for Windows
- **Departmental groups,** such as MIS, Accounting, Finance, and Human Resources
- **Shared Groups,** such as Executive Secretary's, Auditors, and Lawyers
- **Policy Groups,** such as General User, Super User, and Laptop Computer

By properly assigning users membership to these groups, followed by a logical nesting of global groups into local groups, we can attain a degree of understanding over who has permissions within our Microsoft network.

In the past, we have seen a loose structure assigned to group naming. The emphasis is more on ensuring that the name is descriptive and easily recognizable.

Where restrictions do exist they are usually in the form of a maximum length. The syntax and subsequent examples in Tables 4.10 and 4.11 might provide some insight as to what we meant by *loose*.

TABLE 4.10 Sample Group Account Naming Standards

Standard Syntax	Notes
GGGGGGGGGGGGGGG	15 characters used for Functional, Application, and Departmental groups
S-GGGGGGGGGGGGG	15 characters beginning with S- to identify a shared group
POL-GGGGGGGGGGG	15 characters beginning with POL- to identify a policy group

TABLE 4.11 Sample Group Account Names

Group	Group Account Name	Notes
Backup Only	Backup-Only Ops	Members allowed to backup, not restore
Microsoft Excel	ExcelApp	Members allowed to run Excel
Year End application	YearEndApp	End-of-year financials application, local group
Finance Department	Finance	Finance Department group
Executive Secretary's	S-ExecSecretary	Cross-departmental secretary's shared global group
Tax Attorney's	S-YearlyFinance	End-of-year financials shared global group
Interns	POL-Interns	Special policy group for interns
Shared Notebooks	POL-ShareNotebk	Special policy for shared notebook computers

Imagine that it is the end of the year. The tax attorneys and executives are eager to receive a synopsis of the financial results for the fourth quarter. Assuming that the Year End application will provide this information, we might nest the shared global groups *S-YearlyFinance* and *S-ExecSecretary* into the application server local group known as *YearEndApp*. Appropriate permissions will be assigned to ensure that each group could gather just the information that it requires.

In closing this section we hope we've provided you with some general methodologies for implementing naming standards in your own network. The syntax and examples we have chosen are certainly not the only right answers. They are merely intended to provide a foundation upon which you can build to suit your own particular situation.

The X.500 Directory Service

Two weeks prior to Microsoft's annual developers conference, TechEd 1997, an announcement was made that the next version of Microsoft Windows NT would include the long-anticipated directory service. The directory service would resolve some of the complexity associated with designing under a domain architecture. Additionally, Microsoft announced it would deploy this directory service utilizing open standards. X.500 would provide the structure, while DNS would provide the naming syntax.

In anticipation of this new architecture we'd like to take some time to introduce these technologies. We'll begin with a discussion of X.500. In Chapters 7 and 9, we'll discuss DNS.

The Role of Directory Services

A *directory service* is a hierarchical distributed database that provides universal access to resources, without regard to their physical location. Directory services provide this functionality by:

- Providing a single, unified naming space for all network entities

- Providing translation of network names to addresses

- Identifying network resources in a universally unique manner

The naming space provides a set of rules defining how each network entity will be named and identified. The location in the directory database is recognized through a name-to-network address cross-reference. This model provides flexibility to the administrator, in that they can relocate network entities within the directory database without the concern of having to record their locations. Each user of the directory database can continue to call the network entity by its name, knowing that the translation to the proper address will take place.

For this to happen, each entity must be identified uniquely. It is the responsibility of the administrator to ensure that a unique friendly name is supplied, while the directory service will take responsibility for providing a unique network-entity identifier.

Current implementations of directory services include Novell Directory Services (NDS) and Microsoft Exchange server. Microsoft Windows NT 4 does not provide directory services. This can be proven by glancing back at the previous bulleted list, discovering that NT 4 fails the first test in that it does not provide a *single* unified name space for all network entities. Under the Windows NT 4 domain model, each domain is a separate name space unto itself. We attempt to collaborate between these name spaces through the use of trust relationships. Nevertheless, the trust relationships do not integrate these domain name spaces to the point where we can refer to them as a unified directory service.

The Emergence of X.500

X.500 was developed by the International Telecommunications Union (ITU, formerly CCITT) in their 1988 and 1992 specifications describing the interconnection of differing information systems. From its initial conception, X.500 was designed to become the foundation for a unified global directory for all objects of interest to humankind. (The ITU was never the type of group that could be accused of thinking small....)

To understand how the ITU proposed to accomplish this, we need to understand the fundamental components of X.500 and how they are interconnected to provide us directory services.

The Directory Information dataBase (DIB) resides at the core of the X.500 specification. Its duty is to manage the objects of the network. Users, groups, resources, and other network entities are all contained within the DIB. As you might imagine, the DIB can grow to be quite large, especially under the specifications of X.500, where all objects of interest to humankind would be contained within it. For this reason, X.500 allows for the partitioning and replication of the DIB, such that it might be shared amongst various agents. Please see the related sidebar for a bit more information on partitioning and replication.

> ### A Story of Partitioning and Replication
>
> Imagine, if you will, the size of a DIB that contains information on all of the network objects at the Massachusetts Institute of Technology. Now consider that it would be the responsibility of each DSA to house a complete copy of this DIB in order to service its local DUAs. Wouldn't it be easier if each DSA could contain just a portion of the DIB, yet have it arranged in such a way that it appears as if it has access to the database as a whole?
>
> If you have ever been to a multimedia slide presentation, then you have already experienced what X.500 is proposing. Imagine three slide projectors each pointing to the exact same spot on the projection screen. In this first scenario projector 1, projector 2, and projector 3 all contain slides of a bicycle racer on a track passing a cheering crowd. Each projector contains a copy of the entire scene as would be the case if each DSA contained an entire copy of the DIB. As long as each projector stays focused, we the users (DUA) see a single picture where a cyclist is racing toward the finish line to the encouragement of a cheering crowd.
>
> Now imagine a second scenario where the scene is partitioned such that projector 1 contains slides of a bicycle racer, projector 2 contains slides of a race track, and projector 3 contains slides of a cheering crowd. As long as each projector stays focused, we the users (DUA) see a single picture where a cyclist is racing toward the finish line to the encouragement of a cheering crowd. The difference is that the projectors (DSA) are not required to store the entire scene, just a portion of it. This all seems fine until we consider what happens if the bulb burns out on projector 1. The result is that we have a cheering crowd alongside a road without anyone racing on it!
>
> The way we solve this problem is through replication. In other words, each primary projector has a secondary one stacked on top of it. The secondary points to the same spot on the screen and contains a copy of the same slide as its primary. In this way we are guaranteed that if a bulb should burn out on the primary, the secondary could step in and the whole picture would still be visible to our user community.

The Directory System Agents (DSA) are the devices that provide structure to the DIB. They are the network servers that share the responsibility of maintaining a valid copy of the DIB partition. The DSAs need to provide for the seamless flow of information between their peers, such that uninterrupted access to the DIB is always provided. They accomplish this through a series of protocols identified in the X.500 specification.

Directory User Agents (DUA), in the form of applications or end users, utilize the Directory Access Protocol (DAP) to make requests of the DSAs that house information contained within the DIB. The DSAs will then use the Directory System Protocol (DSP) to communicate among themselves to gather the information, as it might be distributed among multiple DSAs (partitioning). This information is gathered as a single response to the query and is returned as such to the DUA. Figure 4.7 illustrates the communications process between the fundamental components of X.500.

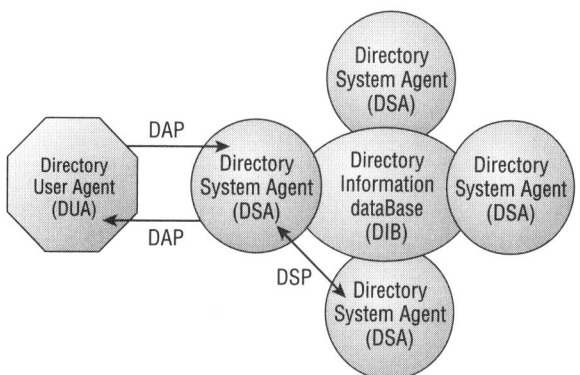

FIGURE 4.7

Communication among the fundamental components of X.500

Whereas the DIB represents the physical structure of X.500, the Directory Information Tree (DIT) represents the logical structure of X.500. Each element in the DIB can be identified as a point on the DIT. Let's examine a DIT that might be created for the Capo di Monti Winery (see Figure 4.8).

The name spaces specified by the X.500 standard are obvious:

- C = Country Name
- O = Organization Name
- OU = Organizational Unit Name
- CN = Common Name

The International Organization for Standardization (ISO) and the ITU crafted the name space with the intent of providing global directory services. Hence, the reasoning for the Country Name. The Organization, Organizational Unit, and

FIGURE 4.8

The X.500 DIT for the Capo di Monti Winery

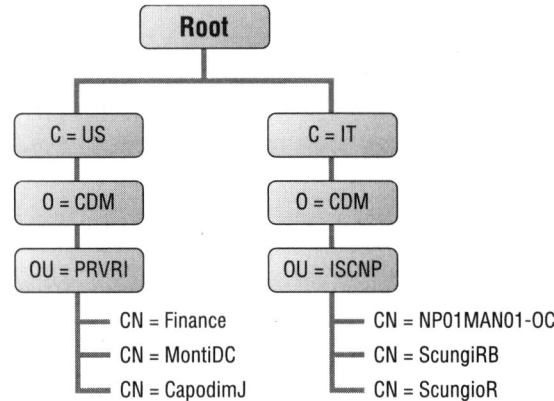

Common Name extend the concept of establishing a universally unique name space, one that was built to support a future global messaging infrastructure based on X.400.

 Locality (L) is also part of the X.500 specification. This container object is designed to reside under the Country Name but above the Organizational Unit. In truth, the Locality is seldom used since an Organizational Unit assumes the role of a Locality in most commercial implementations of the DIT.

Each object in the DIT is named according to the order in which it resides in the tree. The name of each object at the point which it exists is referred to as its Relative Distinguished Name (RDN). In Figure 4.8, the first RDN = C = US. The second RDN = C = IT.

The Distinguished Name (DN) is derived by concatenating all of the RDNs from the root to the object being identified. Table 4.12 provides examples of RDNs and DNs.

TABLE 4.12

Examples of Relative Distinguished Names and Distinguished Names

Relative Distinguished Name	Distinguished Name
OU = PRVRI	{C = US, O = CDM, OU = PRVRI}
CN = ScungiRB	{C = IT, O = CDM, OU = ISCNP, CN = ScungiRB}
CN = MontiDC	{C = US, O = CDM, OU = PRVRI, CN = MontiDC}

Some interesting points relative to the X.500 specification:

- There are no limitations surrounding the length of names.

- The syntax representation used to depict a Distinguished Name is not specified. (However, the syntax shown in the examples in Table 4.12 is the style most commonly used.)

- The structure of the DIT layout is left to the designer of the X.500 directory.

The lack of structure surrounding the naming of X.500 objects is what Microsoft wants to strengthen by integrating DNS in the formation of its X.500-like Active Directory. For further information on the X.500 Directory Service specification I suggest you pick up a copy of *X.500 Directory Services*, by Sara Radicati, International Thomson Computer Press.

In the next two sections we'll explore what many administrators find to be the two most confusing concepts in Windows NT: trust relationships and browsing. If these subjects have been a cloudy for you, then hang on—the clouds are about to part.

Understanding Trust Relationships

Trust relationships provide a level of congruity to a domain-based architecture like Windows NT. The establishment of trusts enables name spaces to be shared within an environment that lacks a directory service. (Please see the previous section on the X.500 directory service for any questions on the differences between directory services and domain modeling.)

Domains trust each other for the purpose of centralizing the user accounts database, while distributing the resources. This model provides for a single login to the network, with the ability to access all resources. For this reason it seems fitting that the domain that contains the user account is referred to as the *trusted* domain, while the domain that is requesting validation of the account is referred to as the *trusting* domain. Figure 4.9 illustrates this concept invoking Microsoft's standard, where the arrow points to the trusted domain.

A cooperative decision is made between the administrators of both domains when deciding to establish a trust relationship. It does not happen naturally, as might occur in a unified directory service. For this reason, careful planning

120 Chapter 4 • Dynamic Domain Design

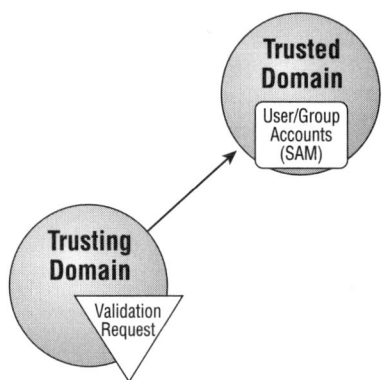

FIGURE 4.9

Communication between a trusted and trusting domain

ensures that all accounts are established in the trusted domain. With this administrative policy in place, we can explore what occurs when the trust relationship is established. We will use Figure 4.9 as an example in the explanation.

The process begins when the administrator of the Capo Di Monti trusted domain (CDM) goes to the User Manager for Domains utility. From within here he or she selects Policies → Trust Relationships → Add Trusting Domain. The administrator is prompted to enter the name of the trusting domain (CDM-RESOURCE) along with an initial password and confirmation of the same. After clicking on OK, CDM-RESOURCE is added to the trusting domains list. Then the following will happen:

- Windows NT will contact the Local Security Authority (LSA), asking it to go through the process of generating a secret object in the SAM database of the PDC for the trusting domain CDM-RESOURCE.

    - This secret object is named G$$CDM (where CDM is the name of the trusted domain) and contains the password specified by the administrator.

    - This secret object is replicated to all of the BDCs in CDM-RESOURCE.

- Windows NT continues by generating a hidden user account in the SAM of the PDC for the trusted domain CDM.

    - This account is named after the trusting domain (CDM-RESOURCE$) and it is unique in that it has the USER_INTERDOMAIN_TRUST_ACCOUNT bit in the control field set. This account also contains the password specified by the administrator.

- This account is replicated to all BDCs in the trusted domain (CDM). As an account it is hidden from the User Manager for Domains utility.

The process continues when the administrator of the Trusting Domain (CDM-RESOURCE) goes to the User Manager for Domains utility. From within here he or she selects Policies → Trust Relationships → Add Trusted Domain. The administrator is prompted to enter the name of the trusted domain (CDM) along with the initial password entered earlier by the administrator of the trusted domain.

- Windows NT will contact the Local Security Authority (LSA), asking it to go through the process of generating a secret object in the SAM database of the PDC for the trusting domain CDM-RESOURCE.

  - This secret object is named G$$CDM (where CDM is the name of the trusted domain) and contains the password specified by the administrator.

  - This secret object is replicated to all of the BDCs in CDM-RESOURCE.

- The PDC in CDM-RESOURCE will attempt to establish a session to \\CDM\IPC$ using CDM-RESOURCE$ as the user account. This will result in an error, 0xc0000198, Status_Nologon_Interdomain_Trust_Account

- This error indicates that the supplied credentials were valid, but that this account does not allow a network style login. This information is important because it indicates that the trust account at CDM does in fact exist; it just does not allow an interactive login.

- The PDC in CDM-RESOURCE will then continue by establishing a null session with the PDC in CDM. It will use remote API calls to establish the trusted domain relationship over a secure channel.

- After the trust is established, the PDC in CDM-RESOURCE will change the password of the trusted domain object (G$$CDM) password. This updated trusted domain object will then be replicated to the BDCs in both the trusted and trusting domains.

- Maintenance of the trusted domain object accounts occurs every seven days. The process is always instituted by the trusting domain (CDM-RESOURCE) PDC, who changes the password of the trusted domain (CDM) PDC. This updated trusted domain object will then be replicated to the BDCs in both the trusted and trusting domains.

There you have it, the complete process for establishing a trust relationship between domains in a Windows NT 4 network. With the trust in place we can now explore the areas of the registry where the trust information is stored.

HKEY_LOCAL_MACHINE\Security\Policy\Secrets is responsible for storing the trusted domain (a.k.a. LSA secret object). This object contains the password for the trust from the perspective of the trusting domain. The key is replicated between all of the BDCs within the trusting domain. (In our example the LSA secret object was identified as G$$CDM.)

HKEY_LOCAL_MACHINE\SAM\SAM\Domains\Account\Users\Names is responsible for storing the INTERDOMAIN_TRUST_ACCOUNT that contains the common password for the trust from the perspective of the trusted domain. The key is replicated between all of the BDCs within the trusted domain. (In our example the INTERDOMAIN_TRUST_ACCOUNT was identified as CDM-RESOURCE$.)

How Many Trusts?

As network consultants, we receive many questions on whether there actually is a limit to the number of trusts that can be established within a Microsoft network. This topic is particularly relevant for anyone contemplating the master, multi-master, or complete-trust domain models. Now, we'll respond to the question.

Response #1

In the previous section we learned that HKEY_LOCAL_MACHINE\Security\Policy\Secrets is the key that contains the LSA secret object responsible for the establishment of the trust relationship.

Prior to Windows NT 4, the maximum number of LSA objects that could be stored in this key was fixed at 256. As we learned in the previous section, the trusting domain is responsible for storing the LSA object, and therefore it is with the trusting domain controllers that we need to be concerned with reaching the 256 maximum value. Consideration also needs to be given that LSA objects are created for other reasons besides trust relationships, most notably for storing service account passwords. This means we may be incapable of allocating 256 LSA objects for trust relationships. Due to this level of unpredictability, Microsoft has published a recommendation of no more than 128 trust relationships per trusting domain.

Beginning with Windows NT 4, the maximum number of LSA objects that can be stored in the key has been increased dramatically. A comment from Microsoft has this value fixed at 4096, although no documents have has been published that confirm that number.

Response #2

Upon initialization, trusting domain controllers will attempt to contact each of their trusted domain controllers. The response from the trusted domain will be stored in the nonpaged-pool of memory on the trusting domain controller that initiated the contact. This response will remain in the nonpaged-pool of memory until the NetLogon service can attend to it.

Memory classified as being from the nonpaged-pool cannot be paged to disk, and therefore in this example, it will have to refuse responses from trusted domains, should its maximum capacity be reached. The result is that the trusting domain controller may not be able to successfully establish trust relationships with all of its trusted domains.

In Windows NT 3.1 the default amount of nonpaged-pool memory was fixed at one of three values, depending on whether your machine was considered:

- Small: less than 16MB of memory

- Medium: between 16MB and 20MB of memory

- Large: greater than 20MB of memory

the actual default values for each classification of machine were never made public.

Beginning with Windows NT 3.5 through Windows NT 4, a complex set of algorithms were developed to calculate the values for nonpaged-pool and paged-pool memory (Microsoft PSSID:Q126402 explains the formulas used in calculating these values). The result is that we can achieve a reasonable number of trust relationships for domain controllers whose memory size is greater than 32MB. With a DefaultMaximumNonPagedPool equal to 1MB, we can build Table 4.13.

TABLE 4.13 Nonpaged-Pool Memory Calculations

Physical Memory (MB)	Nonpaged-Pool Size (MB)	Theoretical Number of Trusts Supported
32	1.2	140
64	2.125	250
128	4.125	500
256	8.32	1050

As was the case with Response #1, the actual number of trusts supported may be much less than the theoretical value calculated. This is due to the level of unpredictability that exists when we consider other objects that may also be utilizing nonpaged-pool memory. A conservative estimate would be to assume half the number of trusts for each physical memory calculation. This would mean that a minimum of 64MB of memory would need to exist for each trusting domain controller in order to establish 125 trusts with reasonable certainty.

Response #3

Consider that you may have detected a bug that was corrected in a previous service pack. Many times problems that surface with trust relationships have been corrected in the more recent versions of Windows NT and their associated service packs.

PSSID: Q135692, "List Name From" List Box Shows Only 20 Trusted Domains, is a problem that was finally corrected in Windows NT 3.51 SP5. Upgrading to Windows NT 4 also resolves this issue, where only the first 20 domains would be visible from within File Manager or User Manager for Domains.

From a designer's standpoint, it never hurts to review the trouble calls associated with an element of a design, trust relationships included. Knowing the issues that others have had with an implementation may enable you to design around a particular shortcoming in the product. This comment is not meant to be directed solely to Microsoft Windows NT, but to all products with which you may work.

Unveiling the Mystery of Browsing

The evolution of browsing began with the idea to establish a means of enumerating servers and workstations within a workgroup. The process begins with the LAN Manager client issuing a NetServerEnum API call, forcing the issuance of a series of Server Message Block (SMB) broadcasts onto the network. These broadcasts are issued as connectionless \Mailslot\Lanman datagrams. All devices running the Server Service respond at once upon receiving this packet. This usually results in LAN Manager servers flooding the network with broadcast (\Mailslot\Lanman, class = connectionless) datagrams. Ouch! Let's think about what we are trying to accomplish.

Enumeration is the process of building a list of domains, workgroups, and servers in a LAN Manager or Windows NT environment. It is important to understand that any device (server, workstation, printer) capable of sharing its resources on the network is considered to be a server and is added to the list. This list is then distributed throughout the network where it is made available for viewing by clients wishing to obtain access to the services registered.

How can we establish a means of identifying services within a Windows NT network without carrying forward the legacy of the LAN Manager enumeration technique? Don't get us wrong, it probably worked fine in a workgroup (10 node, 1 server) environment; but across a WAN? No thank you.

Consider the Internet for a moment. Imagine what it would be like if once we launched our Web browser, it began broadcasting datagrams requesting that all servers report in so it could enumerate them and build a list of available services. We probably agree that it wouldn't be the best idea for us, or the rest of the Internet community. In lieu of this, the concept of *search sites* has evolved. These search sites retain indexes of popular services on the Internet, serving as a point of reference for us when we have a desire to explore a topic of interest but don't want to search every server on the Internet looking for it. Keeping a list of two to three of our favorite search sites, we point our browsers at them interactively and request the list of services that we desire. Once presented with this list, we have the opportunity to attach to the site hosting the service that we had in mind.

The search sites themselves run a process whereby they conduct an automated scan of the Internet, during off-peak hours, looking for new service sites. Web administrators may also follow a process in which they can register their service sites with the search engine, instead of waiting for the automated search to find them. Yahoo!, Lycos, and Excite are all popular search sites structured in the manner previously described. The benefits they provide are that they point us to the services of the Internet without requiring the individual Net surfer to maintain responsibility for obtaining their own enumerated list. If this concept appeals to you, then you'll be pleased to know that Windows NT functions in a similar manner.

Domain Master and Master Browsers

Within a Windows NT network, every NT server is a potential browser. This can be verified by confirming that the BROWSER.DLL and SERVICES.EXE files exist within the \WINNT\system32 directory and that the Computer Browser services is started. This being the case, it should come as no surprise that Microsoft has developed a hierarchy for these browsers to avoid a situation where each server would attempt to provide browsing services, flooding the network with broadcast traffic as was the case with the older LAN Manager technology.

We begin to develop this hierarchy by considering that a separate browse list needs to be built for each protocol that exists in the domain or workgroup. As such, a server may appear in one browse list, but not the other depending on:

- Which protocols are running on the server

- Which protocols are running on the client used to view the browse list

Figure 4.10 provides some perspective to the view a client will receive based on the dispersion of protocols within the domain. You will note that only the servers running TCP/IP appear visible to the client. The server that is running NetBEUI will not appear, as it is registered in a separate browse list, a list that is not visible to our exclusive TCP/IP client.

With this in mind, we can examine the domain and workgroup architecture to gain insight as to how devices establish the pecking order for maintenance and distribution of the browse list.

Windows NT leverages its domain modeling architecture in this process by electing the highest order server in the domain to function as the *Domain Master Browser*. It seems fitting that this role will be assumed by the PDC.

FIGURE 4.10

Scenario showing separate browse lists per protocol

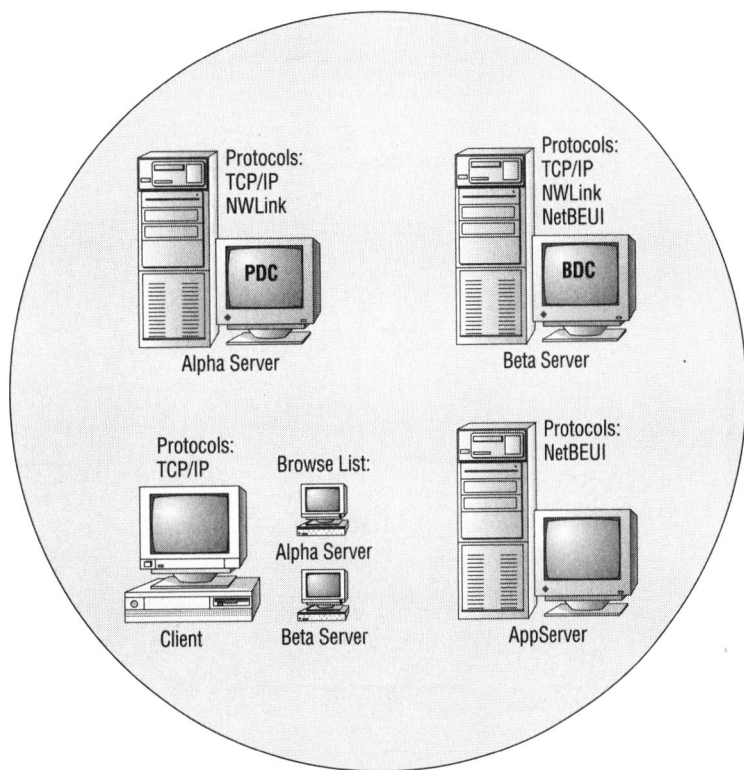

Keeping our *one list per protocol* concept in mind, we need to examine whether the PDC in the domain is able to maintain a list for each of the protocols running within its domain. Assuming it is not, then the highest order device that is running the excluded protocol will establish itself as the *Master Browser*. You'll notice that the word "Domain" is dropped from the title, signifying that the PDC is not fulfilling this role. Please glance back at Figure 4.10 and note the titles associated with each of the servers in the diagram:

- The PDC is the Domain Master Browser, maintaining the list for the TCP/IP and NWLink protocols.

- The APPSERVER is the Master Browser, maintaining the list for the NetBEUI protocol.

Master Browsers can also be elected for reasons other than protocol support. Let's assume that our domain crosses a WAN. That being the case, we will discover that browser announcements will not traverse through routers. The result is that a Master Browser will need to be elected for each subnet outside of the one where the PDC exists. Once again this must occur for each of the supported protocols. Each of these Master Browsers will be responsible for sending browser announcement requests to the Domain Master Browser. The Domain Master Browser will respond with a remote NetServerEnum API, after which it will collect the list from the master, merging it with its own. Refer to Figure 4.11 for an illustration.

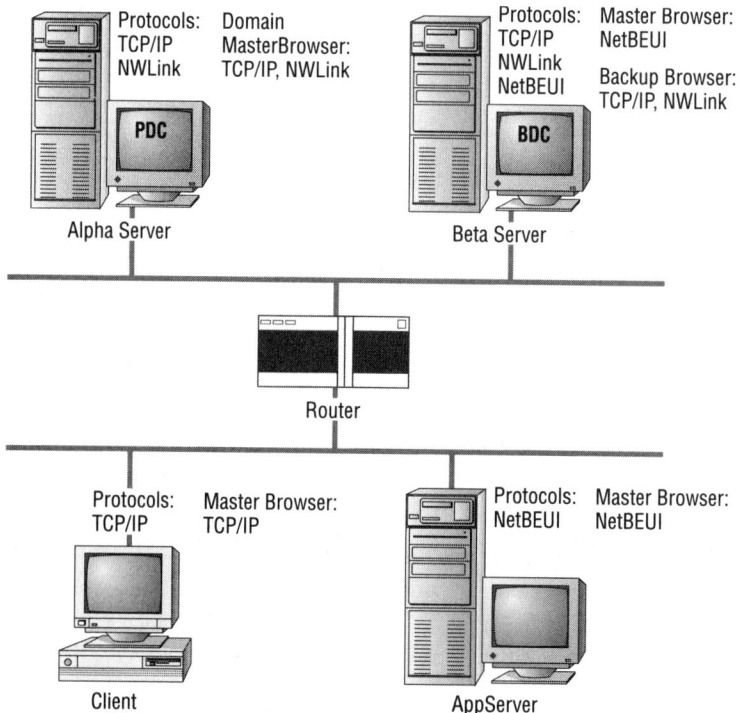

FIGURE 4.11

Browser elections across a wide area network

We should clarify an earlier point regarding browser announcements traversing the network. It is not that these announcements are unable to pass through the routed network, it's just that in most cases they have been purposely filtered out. (NetBEUI is excluded from this discussion as it is a nonroutable protocol, leaving us to focus on TCP/IP.) Exploring this further we discover that the browser broadcasts are sent as NetBIOS over TCP/IP (NetBT) frames, utilizing UDP port 137 as the transport. Most routers will filter out this port as a means of reducing broadcasts across the WAN. Those that feel this is not an issue will find that they can avoid electing a Master Browser for their individual subnet. Instead, each client will broadcast its NetServerEnum API onto the WAN, waiting for the appropriate Domain Master or Master Browser to respond.

We do not recommend this architecture. It is described in detail for educational purposes only. The detriments of this configuration far outweigh the benefits, as we will discover in Chapter 15, "Performance Tuning and Optimization."

When it comes to Workgroups, we discover a similar browsing architecture. Conforming to the rule of a unique browse list per protocol, we discover that each workgroup will elect a Master Browser to support each of the protocols functioning within the workgroup. Assuming that NetBEUI, TCP/IP, and NWLink are running in the workgroup, we discover that up to three Master Browsers may be elected. This would occur, for instance, if only one protocol was installed per workgroup node.

Backup Browsers

It's pretty obvious by now that the browsing function with Windows NT is critical to its ability to advertise service for the clients of the network. This being the case, we'll now introduce the concept of fault tolerance, in the form of *Backup Browsers,* into our browsing infrastructure.

The rules of protocol support apply to Backup Browsers in the same manner as they have to the Domain Master and Master Browsers. Backup browsers will be elected for each of the supported protocols within workgroups and domains. They are elected based on the following criteria:

Domains

Each Windows NT Server within the domain has the potential to become a backup browser.

A maximum of three backup browsers will be elected per domain.

 This explains why browsing will be sluggish in a large, 40,000 theoretical node, single domain. There just aren't enough browsers to support the number of requests that would be generated in a single domain of this size.

Workgroups

Two workstations in a workgroup will result in the election of a Backup Browser.

An additional Backup Browser will be elected once the workgroup reaches a population of 32 workstations.

From this point on, every 32 workstations added to the network will result in the election of another Backup Browser.

The Timing of It All

All of the building blocks are in place. Domain Master, Master, and Backup browsers all have a home in our NT network. Their purpose is clear, and now is the time to discover how they share information among themselves. Refer to Figure 4.12 for a view of this process.

Here is how our browsers will share information:

- Upon startup, servers (devices capable of sharing resources on the network) will announce themselves at one minute after full initialization, two minutes after full initialization, four minutes after full initialization, eight minutes after full initialization, 12 minutes after full initialization and every 12 minutes thereafter. This is referred to as the 12-minute heartbeat and occurs as a <domain>[1E] NetBIOS broadcast.

- Every 15 minutes the Domain Master Browser and Master Browsers will broadcast and receive domain announcements on the local subnet. It is through these announcements that they learn of other domains and the Master Browsers for those domains. From this information the Microsoft Windows NT network is fully enumerated for each essential protocol. These MasterBrowserAnnouncement packets appear as <01><02>_MSBROWSE_<02><01> broadcasts.

- Every 15 minutes the Backup Browser will contact the Domain Master or Master Browser for a copy of the browse list. The Backup Browsers are primarily responsible for servicing the client requests for the browse list.

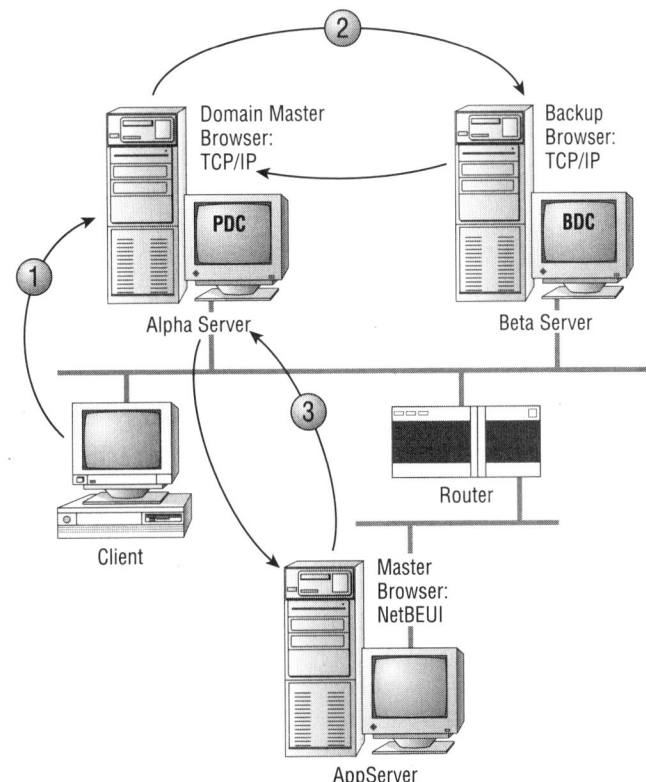

FIGURE 4.12

Timed communication among the browsing infrastructure

1) Keep Alive Announcements: 12-min. cycle
2) Domain Master/Backup Synchronization: 15-min. cycle
3) Domain Master/Master Synchronization: 15-min. cycle

The client issues a GetBackupListRequest message, sent as <domain>[1D] unicast packets to the Master Browser, who returns a list of browser servers to the client. The client will cache up to three of these named servers. This update timing between the Master and Backup browsers ensures that a reasonably recent copy of the list will be available to fulfill the client's request.

The Election Process

All of this time we have been talking about the election process. Elections for Domain Master, Master, and Backup browsers are on a per-protocol basis. With a clear understanding of the browsing infrastructure and timing, we introduce you to the election process.

Elections are used to establish the browsing/pecking order within Windows NT. An election will occur under the following conditions:

- A Windows NT Server comes into the network.

- A Backup Browser attempts to synchronize its browse list with the Master Browser but is unable to locate it.

- A client is unable to locate the Master Browser.

- A Preferred Master Browser comes into the network.

Once one of these conditions is triggered, an election will be forced. This occurs in the form of an election packet that is broadcast as a <domain>[1E] onto the subnet by the node requesting the election.

The election packet is 6 bytes in length. It consists of a 2-byte election version and 4-byte election criteria. A graphical view of this packet including a description of its elements is shown in Figure 4.13.

Using Figure 4.13 as a reference, we would like to review the process involved in determining the winner of the election. Please keep in mind that this applies to the selection of Domain Master, Master Browser, and Backup Browser, per unique protocol:

1. The originator broadcasts the election packet onto the subnet after stuffing it with its election version and criteria: <domain>[1E] NetBIOS broadcast.

2. Any active browsers on the subnet will examine the election version portion of the packet. This value is a constant and equates to the current version of the browser-election protocol. The version is not bound to the operating-system version of Windows NT.

3. If the receiving browser's election version is greater than the originator's election version, then the receiver will declare itself the winner and enter a *running election* state. Otherwise it will continue by checking the election criteria.

4. If the receiving browser's election criteria is lesser than that of the originator, then the receiving browser will enter a *listening* state where it will attempt to learn the outcome of the election, registering the new Master Browser appropriately.

FIGURE 4.13

The browser election packet

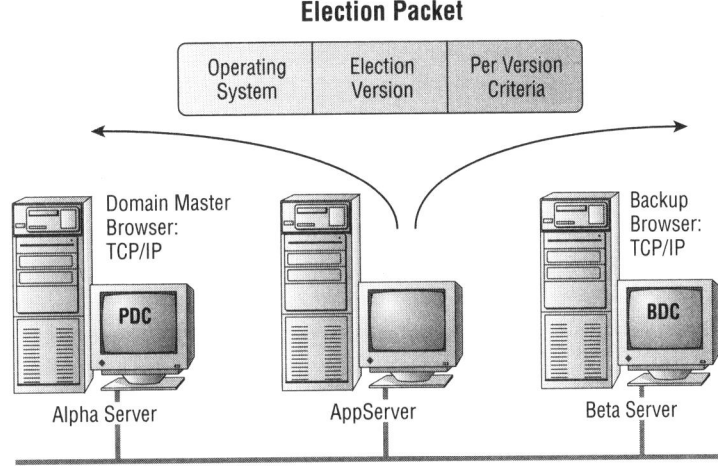

5. If the receiving browser's election criteria is greater than that of the originator, then the receiving browser will issue its own election packet with the intent that it might win the election.

6. Assuming that a tie occurs, at this point we would move to the next level of criteria, where the winner would be the node who has been powered up for the longest period of time.

7. If a tie still exists, then the final criteria would be invoked, where the winner would be chosen through evaluation of a lexical sort of the

node's NetBIOS names. The node with the lowest lexical name (A is lower than B) would be declared the winner. It is not possible that a tie would exist at this point, since it is a requirement of Windows NT that each node be named uniquely.

Once a browser wins an election it will enter a running-election state. When in this state, it will attempt to broadcast four election datagrams at 200 ms, 400 ms, or 800 ms intervals depending on whether you are vying for a seat as a Master, Backup, or Other browser.

Should the node in the running-election state be challenged by another device before its four packets have been released, then the node will be demoted and it will force an election by issuing an election packet.

The Preferred Master Browser

This special node exists so that it will be favored in an election when compared with its peers. This means that a Windows NT Workstation running as a preferred Master Browser will win when its election criteria is compared to other Windows NT Workstations. It does not mean that this device will win over a higher order node, as would be the case if its criteria were compared to a Windows NT PDC.

The preferred Master Browser setting is configured manually within the Windows NT registry:

HKEY_LOCAL_MACHINE\SYSTEM\CurrentControlSet\Services\Browser\Parameters

Value:	IsDomainMaster
Type:	REG_SZ
Value Entry:	True (To establish the node as a Preferred Master Browser)
	False (Default, node is not set as a Preferred Master Browser)

The preferred Master Browser setting can come in handy when you want to pre-establish the Master Browser in a subnet or workgroup. Establishing a designated Master Browser in accordance with a hardware platform that is up to the task can help reduce the amount of network traffic devoted to the browser-election process. However, we recommend that the device set as the preferred Master Browser be properly documented. This will avoid troubleshooting what appears to be an unpredictable election process should the device need to be taken offline for upgrades or repairs:

In this chapter we had the opportunity to dispel some old myths, bring clarity to misunderstood technologies, and establish new design ideals. Not bad for an afternoon's read.

In the following chapter we will build on this foundation, forming a tangible infrastructure of domain controllers and communications protocols. Concepts in theory will now be put into practice.

CHAPTER 5

Forming the NT
Network Infrastructure

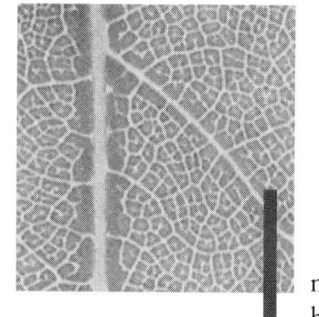

In the previous chapters, we've explored design principles that we hope will bring you success in the deployment of Microsoft Windows NT within your own environment. In this chapter, we'll focus on the elements of the NT infrastructure that will bring substance to your domain. In particular, we'll discuss:

- Capacity planning for the Microsoft Windows NT Domain Controllers

- Platform design of the Microsoft Windows NT Domain Controllers and member servers

- Protocol support, concentrating on Microsoft's preferred wide area network protocol, TCP/IP

By the time we conclude this section, we'll have provided a foundation upon which you can choose and deploy your own architectural elements in building your domain. Remember that your choices should always be based on the requirements of need and anticipated growth. By designing your network based on business needs, with an eye to the future, you will be able to have confidence that your design will perform as expected.

Capacity Planning

While it's easy to think conceptually about proper domain design, sooner or later you'll need to think about how to build the devices within your infrastructure to support the design. These devices, known as *Domain Controllers* (DC), should be deployed to ensure the highest possible performance and fault tolerance for authentication and browsing of the Microsoft network.

The Primary Domain Controller (PDC), as its name implies, is the primary controller of the domain—it contains the master copy of the user accounts database. Without a Primary Domain Controller, you can't have a domain. Figure 5.1 illustrates the structure of a master domain model.

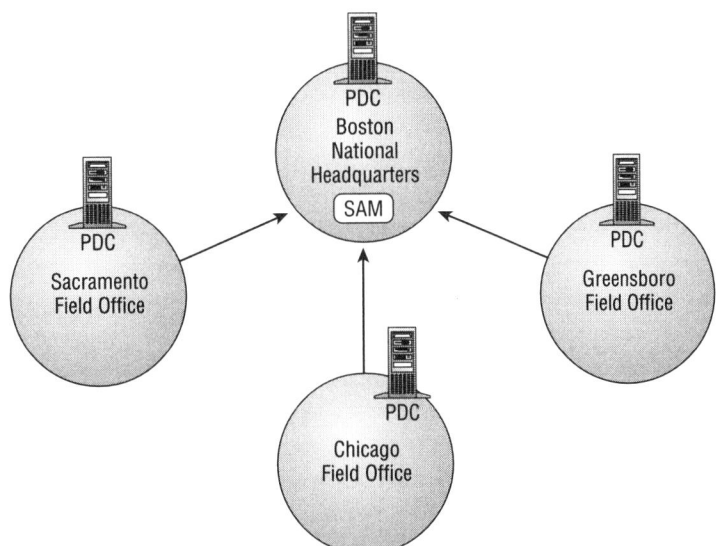

FIGURE 5.1

Minimum NT requirements for the master domain model

By examining Figure 5.1, you can visualize the hierarchy that would be established based on this master domain model. The Microsoft Network sits at the top of the tree, with the first tier given to the five domains within the network. Below each domain is a PDC and, optionally, any NT workstations or servers that have membership within that domain.

Figure 5.2 illustrates the structure of a single domain model. The domain itself is constructed around the minimum requirement of a PDC. Accompanying this domain is a workgroup known as CHAOS.

By examining the screen shot of the Windows NT Explorer in Figure 5.2 you'll notice that the workgroups and domains appear at the same level to each other. Drilling deeper into the US_ALPINE_CT domain, you'll notice a PDC named DESKPRO_SRV. If there were any other member servers or workstations in this domain, they would appear at the same level as this device. Our workgroup CHAOS has but one member, a Windows 95 workstation named Dell.

FIGURE 5.2

The structure of a single domain model and workgroup

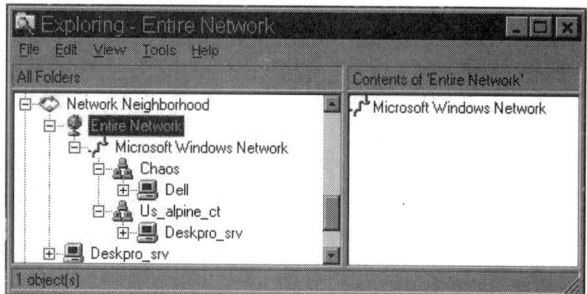

Figure 5.2 demonstrates the importance of naming standards. From the screen shot you can see that the symbols Microsoft uses for domains and workgroups are the same, as are the icons used for workstations and servers. While our choice of a naming standard for the domain is respectable, the other choices are not. The general naming standards chosen for the workgroup and computer systems do not accomplish the prime objective of identifying the role and purpose of the object.

In truth, the minimum requirements that we have examined are just that, *minimum requirements*. Undoubtedly, consideration needs to be given to performance and fault tolerance in order to determine where we need to extend these minimums. We begin this exercise by focusing on the core component of the domain, the PDC.

The fundamental role of the PDC is to provide access to the User Accounts Database (a.k.a. SAM) for authentication purposes. In this capacity, it must be capable of handling requests in a timely manner. This ability to perform in a timely manner is based on the performance of many objects, including the software, hardware, and physical infrastructure of the network. The thought of considering so many objects leaves many NT designers baffled when it comes time to establish a starting point. For this reason, in true engineering fashion, we have broken down this problem into a series of criteria which you'll need to evaluate to determine the optimum high performance/fault tolerant design.

Understanding the Limitations of a PDC

The PDC's prime responsibility is the authentication of user accounts. It accomplishes this through interacting with the SAM database. It seems logical that a PDC built upon a high performance platform will be capable of completing a transaction with the SAM much more quickly than a PDC built upon a less robust platform.

So, the question becomes, "How do we know what type of computer has sufficient horsepower to handle the SAM?" The answer depends, in a large part, on the size of the SAM. Table 5.1 contains some guidelines based upon our own experience combined with some of Microsoft's recommendations.

TABLE 5.1 Authentication PDC Platform Recommendations

SAM Size	Recommended Minimum CPU/Level 2 Cache	Recommended Minimum Memory
5MB	Pentium 90MHz	64MB
10MB	Pentium 133MHz/256K	64MB
15MB	Pentium Pro 166MHz/256K	96MB
20MB	Pentium Pro 200MHz/256K	128MB
30MB	Pentium Pro 200MHz/512K	256MB
40MB	Dual Pentium Pro 200MHz/512K	512MB

Note: Determining the size of the SAM is a function of calculating the number of users, groups, and computers that will be stored within it. The process is covered in Chapter 4.

Not All PDCs Need to Be Created Equal

In a master domain model the most heavily utilized PDC is the one that exists in the master domain. This device houses the SAM database for the users of our network and should be sized according to the guidelines we have just mentioned. But what about the PDCs in the resource (trusting) domains? These devices provide user authentication services, since that is handled by the Master PDC. Figure 5.3 depicts two scenarios where this will occur.

The first scenario is the classic master domain model, as might be developed for a national organization. The second scenario would occur when a product such as SMS, which recommends its own private domain, is brought into the network.

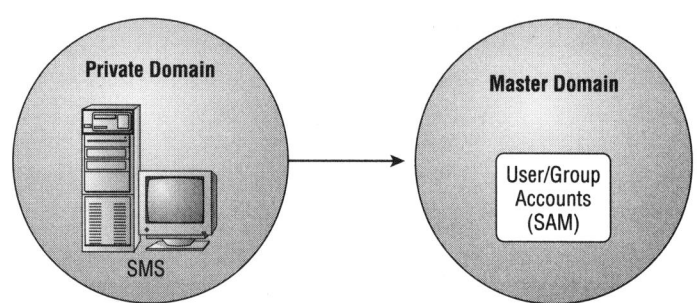

FIGURE 5.3

Master domain model through creation of a private domain

From our perspective, we determine the sizing of our resource PDCs in the same manner as we did for our master PDC. The difference is that the size of the database will be determined more by the number of computer accounts—and less by the number of user and group accounts. Our experience has shown that the size of a SAM in a resource domain rarely approaches anything greater than 3MB.

Please refer to Chapter 4, which discusses the myth that the single domain model is suitable for organizations of up to 40,000 users, for information on how to determine the size of the SAM based on the number of user, group, and computer accounts contained within it.

Using the 3MB guideline, we have successfully outfitted many resource domain PDCs under the specifications shown in Table 5.2.

TABLE 5.2

Resource PDC Platform Recommendations

SAM Size	Recommended Minimum CPU/Level 2 Cache	Recommended Minimum Memory
< or = 3MB	486 DX/66MHZ	32MB

BDCs Support of PDC

Ask two different individuals the reason for a Backup Domain Controller (BDC) and you will get two different answers:

- "BDCs provide authentication to the network in the event that the PDC should fail."

- "BDCs speed up the login process for large enterprise networks."

The first answer places the emphasis on fault tolerance as the reason to implement a BDC, while the second answer focuses on performance as the reason for the BDC. Though the reasons may be different, the message is the same:

- "The platform design of a BDC should be equal to the PDC it is supporting."

By following this guideline, you'll have the ability to ensure that in the event of a failure, you could promote a BDC to the role of a PDC without experiencing any domain controller performance loss.

To the second point, relative to speed of authentication, we know that each BDC will have an equal opportunity to service the authentication request of the client (the speed of the network, notwithstanding).

Now that we've answered the question of size, we need to consider "How many?"

Let's answer this question in two ways, from a mathematical perspective and from that of a designer. First the math.

Determining the Number of BDCs Mathematically

Assuming that our entire Windows NT user community existed in a single domain, on a single-segment local area network, we would calculate the number of BDCs required based on the criteria shown in Table 5.3. These values ensure that the authentication process will be evenly distributed among the PDC and its supporting BDCs.

TABLE 5.3 Recommended Number of BDCs Based on Number of User Accounts

Number of User Accounts	Recommended Number of BDCs
≤ 2,000	1
2,001–3,500	2
3,501–5,000	3
5,001–7,000	4
7,001–9,000	5
9,001–11,000	6
For each additional 2,000 users	+1

Determining the Number of BDCs by Design

Determining the number of BDCs required from a mathematical perspective can be useful, though the true number required usually depends upon the requirements of the domain design and the underlying network infrastructure.

Deployment of BDCs in the Single Domain Model   Figure 5.4 provides an illustration of a single domain model. The answer to the question of how many BDCs are required depends upon whether this domain encompasses a single segment local area network or a multisegment wide area network. In the case of the former, we can use Table 5.3 to calculate the number of BDCs that are required. However, in the latter case we need to more closely examine the network infrastructure that this single domain encompasses.

FIGURE 5.4

The single domain prior to implementation of supporting BDCs

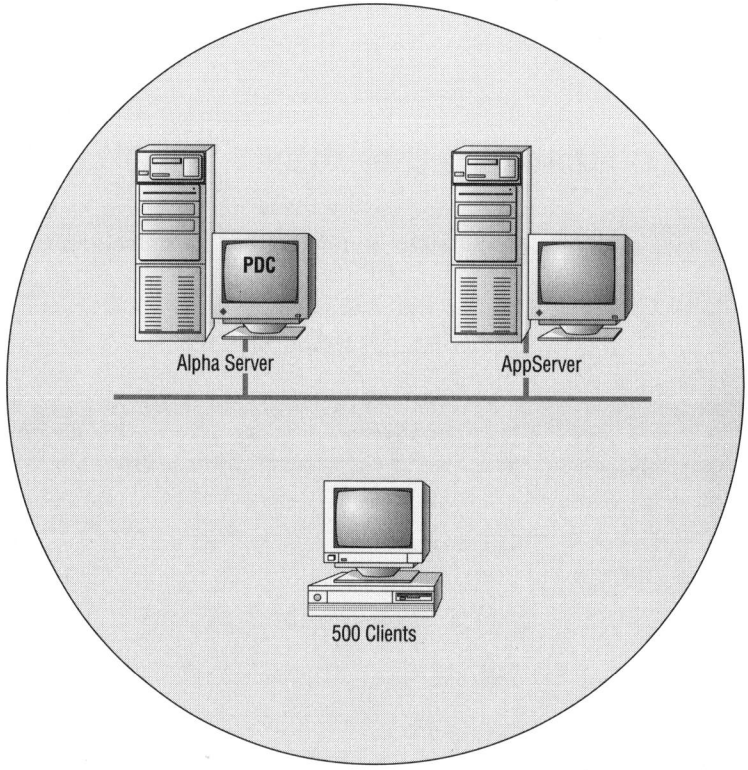

Figure 5.5 reveals that this single domain encompasses three individual segments interconnected by a pair of routers. One of the segments connects at the speed of 19.2Kbps and, for this reason, it is in our best interest to place a BDC on that segment. Doing so will ensure timely authentication for the 500 users in that location. The second segment is attached via a T-1 circuit. Due to the high-speed characteristics of the link and an assumed low user population, we opted not to install a BDC in this location. Lastly we chose to deploy a BDC on the same segment as the PDC so as to provide a local backup to this critical device. In summary, two BDCs were deployed: one for performance considerations and the second for fault tolerance.

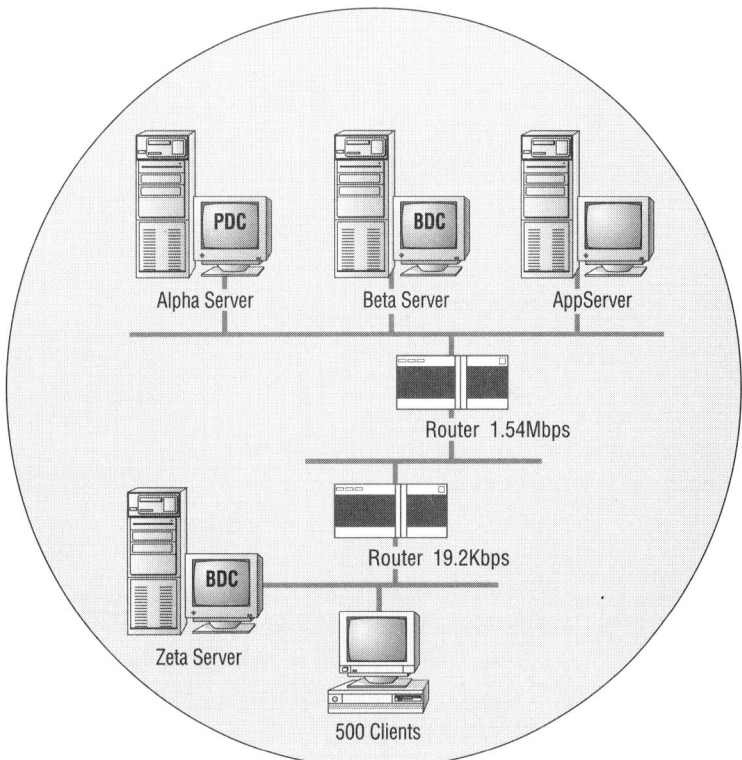

FIGURE 5.5

The single domain following implementation of supporting BDCs

Deployment of BDCs in the Master Domain Model We'll continue this design exercise by analyzing Figure 5.6. Please refer to this figure as we continue our discussion. In this illustration, a master domain model envelopes a wide area enterprise network. For performance and fault tolerance reasons, we have chosen to place a Master-BDC in each of the resource domains. Note that this BDC exists in service of the PDC located in the master domain, not the PDC in the resource domain! This design ensures that the user population in each of the resource domains will be guaranteed a timely login by having an authentication device local to their own segment. The design also provides a measure of fault tolerance. The local Master-BDC will continue to provide authentication services to the user community in the resource domain, in case the telecommunications circuit that links the resource domain to the master domain should fail.

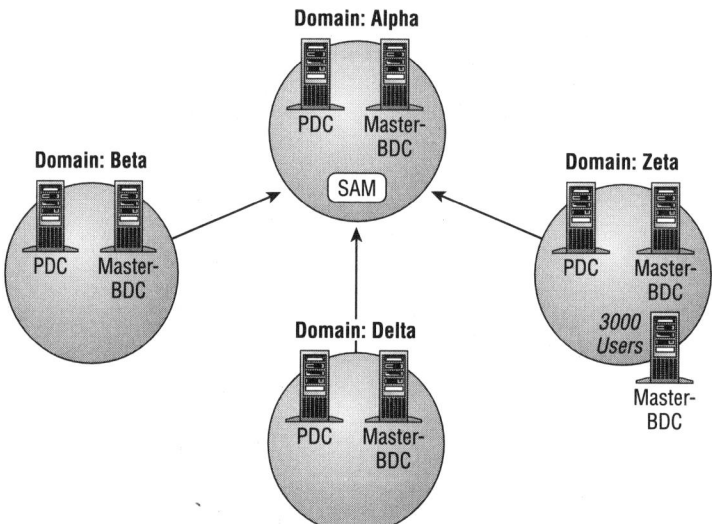

FIGURE 5.6

Deployment of BDCs in the master domain model

We have added an additional twist to this example by assuming that the resource domain known as *Zeta* encompasses a segment that contains 3,000 users. For this reason we have referred back to Table 5.3 and added a second Master-BDC in order to ensure timely authentication for the users of this domain.

In summary, we deployed a total of 5 BDCs based on a combination of our design and mathematical criteria. These devices were deployed to satisfy performance and fault tolerance requirements.

Considering the Number of BDCs for the Resource Domain During a process known as *pass-through authentication,* a workstation with membership in a resource domain will contact the domain controller for that resource domain. Once contact is made, the workstation will establish a secure connection. Through the trust relationship, the resource domain controller will pass the user authentication request to the most responsive master domain controller. Figure 5.7 provides an illustration of this process using the domain Zeta as an example.

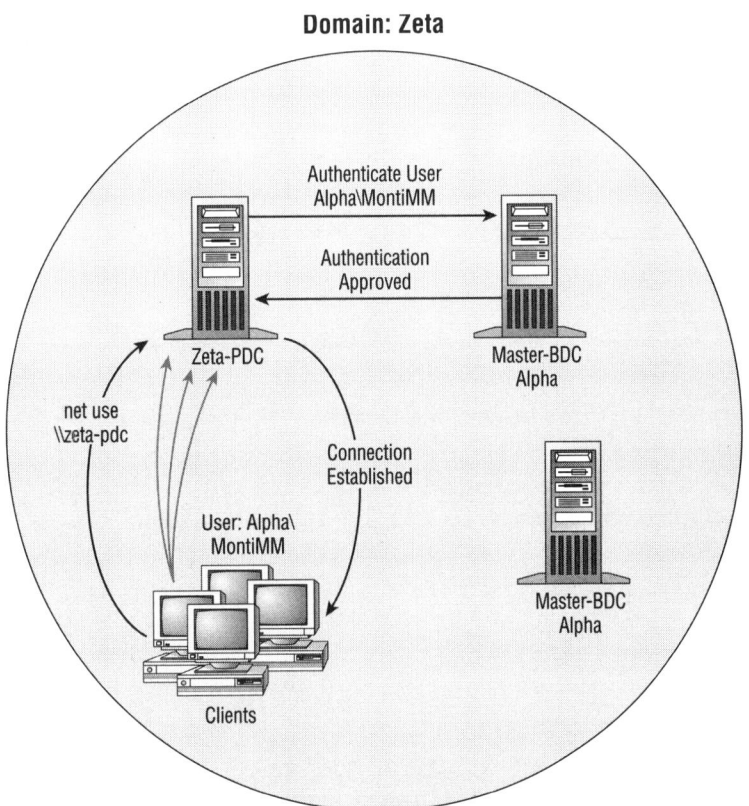

FIGURE 5.7

Pass-through authentication

You will notice that pass-through authentication occurs even though the Master-BDC is located on the same segment as the Zeta Resource PDC. This is due to the fact that the workstation is a member of the resource domain Zeta, while the user account is contained in the Master Domain Alpha.

Based on this new information, you can see that requests for authentication may be bottlenecked by an overabundance of secure connections to the resource PDC. Slow response times for login requests may result, even though we have added additional Master-BDCs to the Zeta segment.

The solution is to implement a resource BDC to share the burden of establishing secure connections for the workstations that are members of Zeta. Figure 5.8 depicts the modified architecture.

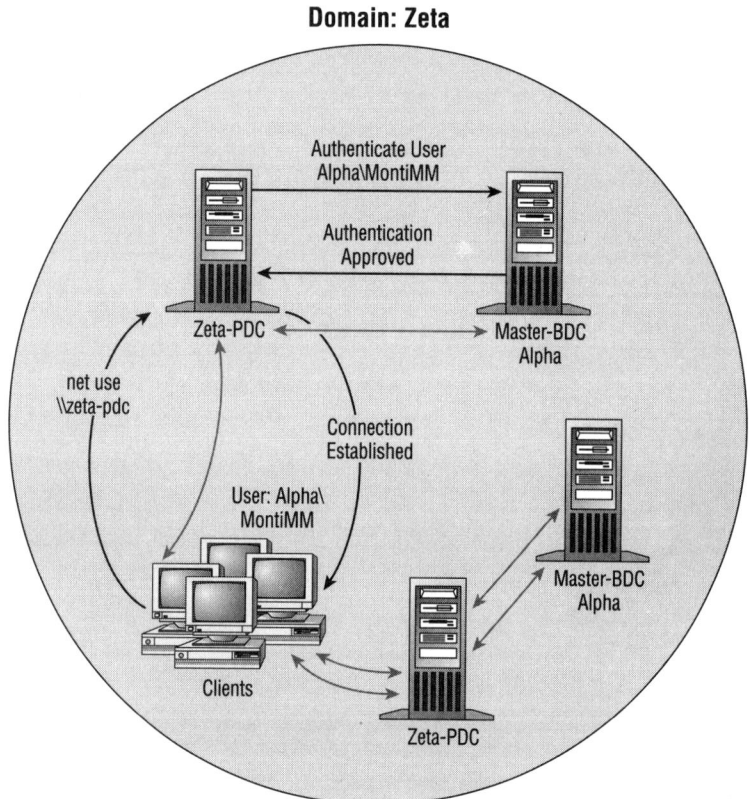

FIGURE 5.8

Load balanced pass-through authentication

In most instances, the resource PDC is more than capable of handling the load for establishing secure connections between itself and member workstations for pass-through authentication to a Master-BDC. Only in cases where multiple Master-BDCs are deployed do we find it beneficial to establish resource BDCs. Otherwise we have found it difficult to justify the cost of yet another dedicated server.

Platform Design

The goal of the platform design is to provide a scalable hardware architecture in support of the Windows NT operating system and its supporting infrastructure elements. To support this objective, it is imperative that any hardware platform candidate be included on the *Microsoft Hardware Compatibility List* (HCL). Too often we have run into instances where a particular hard drive or SIMM was not registered on the HCL and therefore was deemed incompatible and non-supported. While this is merely an annoyance when it happens with one machine, it can quickly become a catastrophe if the same nonapproved part is used in all NT servers in the enterprise.

Remember that it doesn't matter what the hardware vendor promises you. If the parts are not on the HCL, they're not recognized or supported by Microsoft. *Caveat Emptor!*

With that disclaimer given, we can now focus on elements of the design. Essentially, we are trying to craft a platform that supports the domain controllers we so carefully selected for type and quantity in the previous section. Ample attention has already been given to the proper amount of memory and type of processor; we won't rehash that discussion. Instead we will focus more on the crafting of a disk subsystem designed to compliment the other components of the Windows NT Server.

Let's use the following case study to provide some reality to the discussion, so that you'll be able to draw some parallels between our selection of hardware for the Capo di Monti Winery and your own network.

The Capo di Monti Winery

Single domain environment encompassing a three-segment wide area network

Single domain supports approximately 1,000 users, 1,800 computers, 200 groups

One PDC and two BDCs provide substance to the single domain

A resource domain has been established in support of SMS

Resource domain supports approximately five users, two computers, eight groups

One PDC provides substance to the resource domain

Figure 5.9 provides an illustration of our case study.

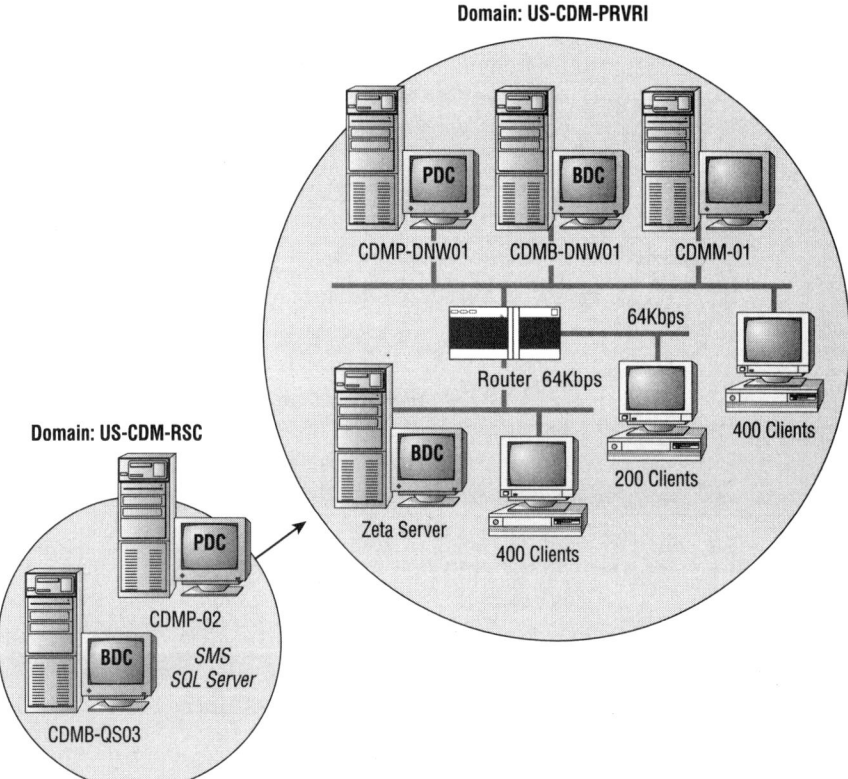

FIGURE 5.9

The Capo di Monti Microsoft Network

Crafting the Domain Controllers

We'll begin this exercise by determining the size of the SAM database for the single domain and resource domain. Table 5.4 shows the results of our calculations.

TABLE 5.4 Capo di Monti Database Configurations

Single Domain

User Accounts	Group Accounts	Computer Accounts	Database Size
(1,000 × 1KB) +	(200 × 4KB) +	(1,800 × 500 bytes) =	2.7MB

Resource Domain

User Accounts	Group Accounts	Computer Accounts	Database Size
(5 × 1KB) +	(8 × 4KB) +	(2 × 500 bytes) =	38KB

Using these statistics we refer to Tables 5.1 and 5.2, which lead us to selecting device configurations for each of the domain controllers in the US-CDM-PRVRI domain. Our selections are shown in Table 5.5.

TABLE 5.5 US-CDM-PRVRI Domain Controller Configurations

US-CDM-PRVRI PDC/BDC Hardware

Processor	Memory	Storage	Comments
Pentium 90MHz	64MB	(2) 1GB SCSI Hard Disk SCSI CD-ROM	RAID Controller

US-CDM-PRVRI PDC/BDC Disk Partition Information

Device	Type	Channel #	Size	Description
Disk 0	SCSI	0	1GB	RAID 1 for Disk 0 – 1
Disk 1	SCSI	0	1GB	RAID 1
CD-ROM	SCSI	1		8X CD-ROM

TABLE 5.5 (cont.) US-CDM-PRVRI Domain Controller Configurations

US-CDM-PRVRI PDC/BDC Disk Configuration Information

Drive letter	Disk #	Partition #	Disk Size	File system	Description
C:	0, 1	1	200MB	FAT	NT Boot Loader
D:	0, 1	2	800MB	NTFS	OS, Pagefile
E:	CD			CDFS	8X CD-ROM

Notice in Table 5.5 that a pair of 2GB drives have been selected, supported by a RAID controller. We selected this sizing by considering the size of the SAM (2.7MB); plus the requirements for the Windows NT operating system (110MB minimum); plus additional storage for Service Packs and a memory core dump (200MB); plus storage for the paging file, equivalent to twice the amount of memory (128MB); for a total minimum storage requirement of 440.7MB. Knowing this value we determined that we could use 1GB drives that would provide us with more than enough room for growth.

These drives are set up in a RAID 1 (mirrored) configuration to provide fault tolerance for the SAM database. While we are aware that Windows NT provides software-level RAID as part of the operating system, we still prefer to implement it at the hardware layer whenever possible. Our philosophy is that the hardware faults occur at the physical layer and as such should be corrected at that point. To push the burden of monitoring and correcting a fault onto the operating system is not a wise use of system resources. Placing these comments aside for the moment, we've chosen to implement the software-level RAID bundled with Windows NT, where the size of the network (less than 100 users) and economics of implementing a hardware-based solution could not be justified.

We continue by partitioning our mirrored pair into two logical partitions C: and D:. Partition C: is implemented as a 200MB FAT partition. 200MB allows us enough space to house the NT Bootloader files as well as an alternative operating system such as DOS. It also provides us with enough room to store a memory core dump. We always recommend that a small FAT partition be established as the first partition on the NT Server. Doing so provides a number of benefits:

- There is the opportunity to boot under an alternate operating system such as DOS. This can be beneficial when attempting to troubleshoot a system that is unable to boot under NT.

- Keeping the NT Bootloader files on a FAT file system enables us to easily uninstall and re-install NT, without having to back up and restore the entire system. The exact procedures to accomplish this can be found in the Microsoft Windows NT Workstation 4.0 Resource Kit.

- Establishing a FAT partition enables us to redirect the memory core dump to this area rather than to the default NTFS system partition, so that we can boot under DOS and be able to gain access to the core dump file (MEMORY.DMP). This might not be possible if the MEMORY.DMP file were stored on the default NTFS partition and we were unable to boot under NT.

The remaining 800MB is established as an NTFS partition to support the SAM database, operating system, service packs, and the paging file. We prefer to keep the paging file as close as possible to the OS because, as we learned in Chapter 2, the OS is the primary requester of virtual memory services and therefore PAGEFILE.SYS.

Proprietary system designs, such as Compaq's Tri-Flex architecture, will usually enable better performance when compared to similarly configured, standard ISA/PCI servers. You can count on the hardware vendors to provide the most up-to-date performance statistics for their servers. Your challenge will be to keep them within the guidelines shown in these tables.

Keeping the previous comments in mind, we move on to introduce the platform architecture for the US-CDM-RSC resource domain controller, as shown in Table 5.6.

TABLE 5.6 US-CDM-RSC Domain Controller Configuration

US-CDM-RSC PDC Hardware

Processor	Memory	Storage	Comments
486DX/66MHz	32MB	(2) 1GB SCSI Hard Disk SCSI CD-ROM	RAID Controller

TABLE 5.6 (cont.) US-CDM-RSC Domain Controller Configuration

US-CDM-RSC PDC Disk Configuration Information

Device	Type	Channel #	Size	Description
Disk 0	SCSI	0	1GB	RAID 1 for Disk 0 - 1
Disk 1	SCSI	0	1GB	RAID 1
CD-ROM	SCSI	1		8X CD-ROM

US-CDM-RSC PDC Disk Partition Information

Drive letter	Disk #	Partition #	Disk Size	File system	Description
C:	0, 1	1	200MB	FAT	NT Boot Loader
D:	0, 1	2	800MB	NTFS	OS, Pagefile
E:	CD			CDFS	8x CD-ROM

You may find it interesting that we chose the same storage configuration for our less robust resource domain PDC as we had for our US-CDM-PRVRI authentication domain. Our justification for this comes from comparing conformity to cost. Wherever possible we recommend that the domain controllers be kept as uniform as possible. This will ease the burden for the administrator who has to manage these devices during both normal operation and times of crisis.

Nothing is more frustrating then having to deal with a unique storage and file system configuration for each device on the network. This frustration is amplified when attempting to troubleshoot a stalled BDC or offline PDC. Storage is often the least expensive part of a server. For this reason we recommend that the configuration be kept constant across all domain controllers.

Crafting the Member Servers

Each member server in a Microsoft network is going to have its own unique system requirements. Processor, memory, and storage requirements will all depend on the function of the device and recommendations of the developer.

Nevertheless, we highly recommend that these servers adhere to a similar standard as the domain controllers wherever possible.

In the Capo di Monti winery we need to consider just one member server. The CDMB-QS01 server which, because of the requirements of SMS, was installed as a BDC for the resource domain. Because of the lack of account authentication occurring in the resource domain, the demand on this server is extremely light, enabling it to almost fully devote its system resources to the functions of SMS/SQL. For this reason, we are considering CDMB-QS01 as a member server, although it was installed as a domain controller in compliance with SMS 1.2.

With the previous points in mind we present the platform design for our SMS/SQL server in Table 5.7.

TABLE 5.7 CDMB-QS01 SMS Server Configuration

CDMB-QS01 SMS Server

Processor	Memory	Storage	Comments
(2) 200MHz Pentium Pro	256MB	(6) 2GB SCSI Hard Disk SCSI CD-ROM	RAID Controller

CDMB-QS01 SMS Server Disk Configuration Information

Device	Type	Channel #	Size	Description
Disk 0	SCSI	0	2GB	RAID 1 for Disk 0 – 1
Disk 1	SCSI	0	2GB	RAID 1
Disk 2	SCSI	1	2GB	RAID 5 for Disk 2 – 4
Disk 3	SCSI	1	2GB	RAID 5
Disk 4	SCSI	1	2GB	RAID 5
Disk 5	SCSI	1	2GB	Hot Spare for Channel 1
CD-ROM	SCSI			8× CD-ROM

TABLE 5.7 (cont.) CDMB-QS01 SMS Server Configuration

CDMB-QS01 SMS Disk Partition Information

Drive Letter	Disk #	Partition #	Disk Size	File System	Description
C:	0, 1	1	500MB	FAT	NT Boot Loader
D:	0, 1	2	1.5GB	NTFS	OS, Pagefile
E:	2, 3, 4	3	4GB	NTFS	SMS, SQL
F:	CD			CDFS	8× CD-ROM

NOTE: The actual process for determining the processor, memory, and storage requirements for SMS can be found in the *Microsoft BackOffice Resource Kit* in "Part 1, Systems Management Server."

Notice that we've attempted to stay as close to our domain controller configuration as possible. As mentioned earlier, this is a philosophy we follow for all of our member server installations.

We also chose to separate the OS from the SMS/SQL services very early on, by establishing them on separate channels of the RAID controller under different RAID guidelines. RAID 1 was kept as the standard for the FAT and OS partitions, while RAID 5 was selected for the SMS/SQL partition.

We could have chosen to create the storage subsystem as one large five-drive RAID 5 configuration. In doing so we would have striped the OS and page file across all five drives, drives that are also being used to support the disk I/O intensive operations of SQL server. Past experiences have proven to us that this is a poor configuration. Based on the fact that RAID 5 stripes data across all drives, it is obvious that whether it is the OS or SQL server, all five drives are constantly spinning in a struggle to service the myriad of requests coming into them. The end result is a disk I/O bottleneck for the entire system.

Understanding the downside of this configuration, we chose to separate the OS from SMS/SQL by placing a pair of 2GB drives onto a channel that was separate from the channel chosen for the three 2GB drives that comprise the SMS/SQL RAID 5 configuration. This architecture keeps the access of the drives isolated between the OS pagefile requests and SQL remote procedure call requests. By isolating these requests we have created a high performance/modular system—one where we can easily monitor, identify bottlenecks, and surgically correct problem areas.

· Lastly, you will notice that we have specified a Hot Spare for Channel 1. A *Hot Spare* is an online drive that is designed to *stand-in* for a failed hard disk. The use of a Hot Spare helps to eliminate one of the shortcomings of a RAID 5 configuration—how to deal with a two-drive failure.

As soon as one drive fails, the Hot Spare assumes the role of the failed drive. It begins to rebuild itself as a mirror of the failed unit by using the information available through the RAID 5 configuration. Should a second drive fail, the system will still remain online as a classic RAID 5 configuration. It is only after the third drive fails that we would have a catastrophic incident, one that the RAID 5/Hot Spare configuration would be unable to automatically recover from. Wherever it is economically feasible, we highly recommend the use of a Hot Spare drive for mission-critical NT Servers.

This concludes our review of the Capo di Monti infrastructure components and our coverage of platform design. With the NT infrastructure in place, we move on to examine the preferred protocol for enterprise communications: TCP/IP.

Network Protocol Support

As you develop your domain model and plan out the location and size of your domain controllers, you'll need to spend some time considering how these domain controllers will communicate with one another, and how they'll communicate with end users.

As Microsoft has worked to position Windows NT as an enterprise operating system, one issue has become increasingly clear—NetBEUI simply is not a viable enterprise network protocol due to its inefficiency and inability to operate over a routed network. While it may be easy to implement on a small, single-segment network, NetBEUI is impractical for large networks, because there is no facility to route NetBEUI across multiple network segments.

To overcome this and other limitations of NetBEUI, Microsoft shifted it's networking strategy. Taking a cue from the growing popularity of the Internet, Microsoft began instead to promote the TCP/IP protocol suite as the Windows NT network protocol of choice.

TCP/IP: The Enterprise Protocol

Microsoft's decision to embrace TCP/IP as the enterprise-worthy protocol for Windows NT was based upon a number of factors. In order for Windows NT to compete in the enterprise network OS arena, it had to utilize a protocol that was efficient, resilient, and could operate on large, routed networks. Instead of starting from scratch and developing its own enterprise protocol, Microsoft decided to utilize a protocol that offered all of those features; one that had seen global implementation and had been tested on thousands of computers all over the world—the TCP/IP protocol suite. TCP/IP is the protocol suite of the Internet. Every day, people from every corner of the earth communicate with one another on computers that use TCP/IP. The TCP/IP suite had already proven itself as a worthy enterprise-level network protocol, so it was an easy choice for Microsoft to make.

TCP/IP Basics

Generally, when technologists refer to TCP/IP, they are referring to a group, or suite, of protocols that utilize the Internet Protocol (IP) for delivery. Each of the protocols fulfills a different purpose, and each relies on other protocols in the suite to fulfill its purpose. If your network already utilizes the TCP/IP protocol suite, or if you have a connection to the Internet at home, you are probably familiar with some of the higher visibility TCP/IP protocols, such as the File Transfer Protocol (FTP) or the Hypertext Transport Protocol (HTTP), which is commonly used to transmit documents from Web servers to Web browsers.

In this section, we'll review some key TCP/IP concepts. For a more detailed discussion of the TCP/IP protocols see *Building Intranets on NT, NetWare, and Solaris: An Administrator's Guide* by Morgan Stern and Tom Rasmussen (Sybex, 1996).

The IP Protocol The Internet Protocol (IP) is considered the most important in the TCP/IP suite because it is the protocol upon which all other protocols depend for their delivery across a TCP/IP network. If IP is not configured properly, data sent by other protocols will never reach its destination. The IP protocol contains specifications for how IP packets, called datagrams, are formatted, addressed, and transmitted between IP networks. Each IP datagram contains source and destination address information, which IP routers utilize to direct traffic through an IP network.

Each IP address uniquely identifies a network and a host computer on an IP network. An IP address is usually expressed as a twelve-digit number, represented in four groups of three digits, separated by periods (*xxx.xxx.xxx.xxx*). Each of the three-digit numbers represents a byte (an 8-bit binary value).

It will be important to remember that an IP address actually represents a binary number, if you are forced to utilize variable-length subnet masks on your network. We'll discuss subnet masks shortly.

The numbers zero and 255 have special meanings in the IP world. A zero (0) is used to specify a network address number (if it is at the end of the address) or to specify a node address (if one or more zeroes are at the beginning of the address). For example, 192.168.32.0 would designate the network number 192.168.32, while 0.0.0.232 would designate the computer assigned with the IP address 232 on the network.

While the IP address identifies networks and computers on an IP internetwork, it is the function of routers to direct traffic between the networks and nodes. IP routers utilize routing protocols, such as the Routing Information Protocol (RIP) or the Open Shortest Path First (OSPF) protocol to calculate the most efficient paths to direct IP traffic.

The Transmission Control Protocol (TCP) and the User Datagram Protocol (UDP) While the Internet protocol contains specifications for the addressing and delivery of datagrams, it does not contain any provisions to determine that the information contained within the datagram has not been corrupted during its journey.

Two protocols provide delivery services for IP: the Transmission Control Protocol (TCP) and the User Datagram Protocol (UDP). Each protocol fulfills a specific role, and each is suited toward a specific type of transmission.

Transmission Control Protocol (TCP) is a protocol designed to provide guaranteed delivery. When a computer attempts to communicate with another computer, the TCP software module within the originating system will establish a virtual connection to the destination computer. Each piece of information is transmitted within a TCP packet, called a *segment,* that contains a unique sequence number. The destination computer will examine each segment's sequence number to determine the correct order in which to reassemble the transmitted information.

While the advantages of guaranteed delivery are significant, the communications overhead associated with establishing, maintaining, and destroying virtual connections can also be significant. Some types of transmissions, particularly ones that are extremely brief, do not benefit from the guarantees of TCP because the amount of overhead is greater than the amount of information that must be transmitted. The User Datagram Protocol (UDP) was designed for these types of transmissions. UDP has very little communications overhead. However, it does not provide any of the guarantees that TCP does.

UDP is considered to be a *connectionless* protocol, unlike TCP, which is a *connection-oriented* protocol. UDP is best suited for applications that transmit relatively small amounts of data in a short period of time, or for applications that send quick bursts of back-and-forth traffic. DHCP (a protocol that automatically assigns IP addresses to workstations) is a good example of a protocol that utilizes UDP. A workstation configured for DHCP sends quick requests to a DHCP server to receive an IP address. The server receives the request, matches the workstation's network interface card hardware address to one in its IP address table, and replies with the correct IP address. The entire transaction takes place very quickly.

Ports: An Address Extension Both TCP and UDP provide delivery services for all of the higher level protocols in the TCP/IP suite. Both protocols utilize a mechanism called a *port number* to identify to which application or protocol they will deliver incoming information. Port numbers typically correspond to well-known protocols. For example, most Web servers listen for connections on TCP port number 80, and most SMTP mail servers listen for inbound mail connections on TCP port 25.

A port number is an extension of an address, almost like an apartment number is an extension of a street address. The combination of IP address and port number is frequently called a *socket*.

Higher-Layer Protocols Once TCP or UDP have processed incoming data, they transmit information to higher-layer protocols according to the destination port specified within each packet. These higher-layer protocols provide services such as terminal emulation (Telnet), file transfer (FTP), electronic mail (SMTP, POP3), and network management (SNMP). We will discuss a number of these higher layer protocols in Chapter 7.

Planning Your TCP/IP Network

If you have not already configured your network and Windows NT servers for TCP/IP, this next section will outline the steps you'll need to follow to do so. Proper deployment of TCP/IP on your network will depend on a number of factors. Most importantly, you'll want to have a comprehensive plan for network addressing, protocol routing, and workstation address allocation. We'll begin with a discussion of how to assign network addresses

First, if you do not already have one, you'll need to prepare a comprehensive network diagram. This diagram should include each server, router, switch, dial-in device, and network segment. If you have any NT or NetWare servers that are providing routing services, be sure to note how many network interface cards are in each server.

Identify the Number of Segments

For the earliest phase of TCP/IP planning, your first task is to identify the number of segments on your network. For the purpose of this discussion, we use the term segment to represent a single, non-routed, physical network. For example, an single Token Ring or single Ethernet is a segment.

If your network does not contain any routers or routing devices (such as an NT server routing between two cable segments), the number of segments on your network will be one. For example, if your network contains an Ethernet switch, but not a router, the number of segments is one. Depending on how your wide area links have been designed, you may have to count the connection between sites as a segment.

The number of segments on your network is important because it will dictate how many IP network addresses you'll need to accommodate on your network. For example, if your network contains five segments, you'll need to utilize five IP network addresses. Remember not to pick addresses at random. Either work with your Internet service provider to implement registered Internet IP network addresses or use special reserved IP addresses, such as the 192.168.0.0 block of addresses, as specified in RFC 1918.

RFC 1918, titled *Address Allocation for Private Internets* defines groups of IP network addresses for used on private (non-Internet connected) networks. Any organization that wants to create a TCP/IP network but doesn't plan to connect to the Internet can use these addresses instead of (potentially) using someone else's registered network address. That way, if the organization eventually does connect to the Internet, their network addressing will not cause routing problems.

If you plan to use registered IP addresses on your network, you'll have two options for implementation. First, you can use variable-length subnet masks to divide your registered network address into enough smaller network addresses to accommodate your network segments. Your other option, one that is becoming more popular, is to implement some sort of Network Address Translation (NAT) device on an Internet-connected segment of your network.

As its name implies, a Network Address Translation (NAT) device operates by translating network addresses contained within all traffic that passes through it. For example, you could utilize a registered IP address on the Internet-connected side of the NAT device, while utilizing RFC1918-compliant addresses on your internal network. The NAT device would examine all traffic leaving your internal network and rewrite the packets to make them appear to come from the registered address network. There are a number of advantages to utilizing NAT, one of the most significant is that you can avoid having to re-address your entire network should you connect to the Internet or change Internet service providers.

Utilizing Subnet Masks

Effective variable-length subnet mask implementations can be tricky. Subnet masking is a technique that enables network devices (and humans) to determine which portion of an IP address pertains to the network address and which to the node address. You will configure a subnet mask on every device that you install on an IP network. In a typical network, the subnet mask is the same for all devices (such as 255.255.255.0).

A subnet mask is actually a 32-bit combination of 1s and 0s. A 1 in a subnet mask represents the network portion of the address, while the 0 represents the node address. For example, the binary representation of the 255.255.255.0 mask would be:

11111111.11111111.11111111.00000000

Where subnet masking becomes tricky is when you need to create multiple network addresses out of a single one. For example, if your network contains five segments but only 150 nodes, it's likely that an Internet service provider will only allocate to you one class C network address (for this example, let's say they give you the address 192.168.122.0). If you wish to configure each of the five segments so that users on any of them can communicate with the

Internet, you'll need to extend the network portion of the subnet mask to create additional network addresses. If you need to create at least five network addresses from a single Class C address, you'll need to utilize a subnet mask of 255.255.255.224.

Here's why: Consider the binary numbering scheme. If you had an 8-bit binary number (a byte), the maximum possible number that you could express would be 255. The placeholders in binary are powers of 2 (1, 2, 4, 8, 16, 32, 64, 128), where the leftmost bit represents 128 and the rightmost bit represents 1. When you begin to use variable-length subnet masks, you traditionally use numbers beginning with the leftmost bit (the one in the 128 placeholder). Your goal is to take as few bits as possible to create enough combinations of 1s and 0s to assign a unique one to each segment. For example, the 224 subnet mask is the result of taking the 128 bit, the 64 bit, and the 32 bit (11100000); so there would be a total of eight possible combinations of those three bits (000, 001, 010, 011, 100, 101, 110, 111). You want to take the fewest number of possible bits, because you'll need the remaining bits for your workstation IP addresses.

There is one catch, and that is that any of combination that is all zeros or all ones cannot be utilized, so you effectively gain six possible combinations (001, 010, 011, 100, 101, 110). These would translate to the following network numbers:

00100000	192.168.122.32
01000000	192.168.122.64
01100000	192.168.122.96
10000000	192.168.122.128
10100000	192.168.122.160
11000000	192.168.122.192

Each network would contain 30 usable node addresses. For example, on the 192.168.122.32 subnet, you could utilize node addresses from 33 to 62.

Subnet masking can be tricky, and our goal in this book is only to introduce you to some of the concepts.

Assigning Network Numbers

Your next step is to assign network numbers to each of the segments on your network. If you plan to use subnet masks, your network number may look like the example on the left in Figure 5.10; if you plan to use reserved addresses, it might look like the example on the right in Figure 5.10. The important point to recognize is that each segment must have a unique network address.

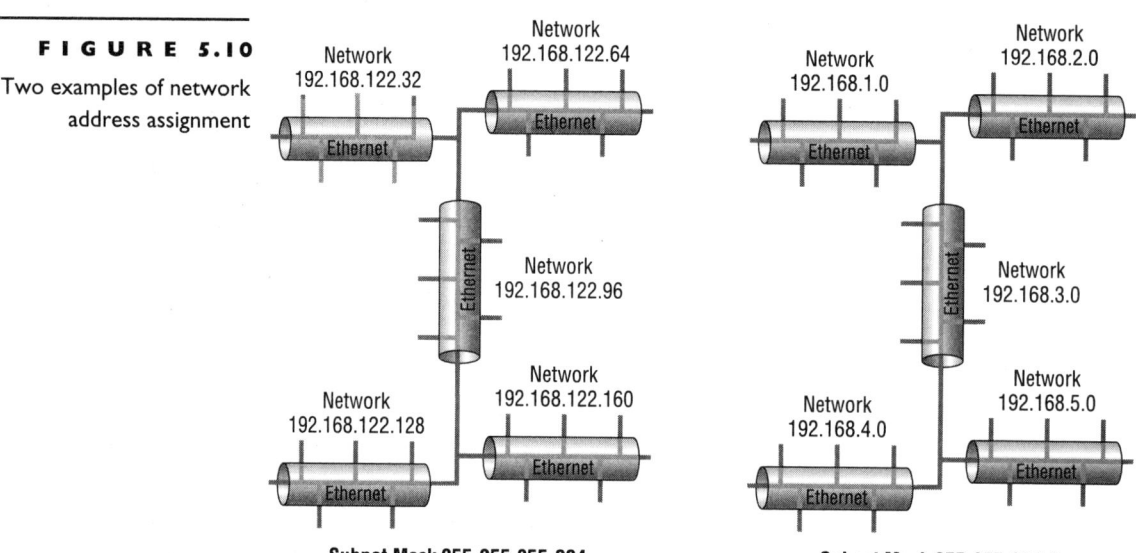

FIGURE 5.10

Two examples of network address assignment

Selecting a Routing Protocol

Once you have developed your network addressing, you'll need to determine which routing protocols to implement on your network. Your choices may be limited by the types of routing devices you plan to implement. For example, some routers only support Routing Information Protocol (RIP) version 1. If so, you'll have to utilize RIP as your network routing protocol. If your routers support multiple IP routing protocols, it may be helpful to work with your router vendor or Internet service provider to determine which protocol(s) will work best.

In some situations, you may need to implement static routing in addition to utilizing a routing protocol. A static route defines a path that all traffic should follow to reach a particular destination. For example, you might configure your

Internet-connected router with a default static route that will send all outbound traffic to the Internet. If you plan to utilize one of your Windows NT servers as a router, you can configure static routes with the ROUTE command.

Assigning IP Addresses to Nodes

The final step is to determine how you will allocate addresses to network nodes, including servers and workstations. Your node addressing scheme will need to be consistent with your network addressing plan (each workstation address must correspond to the network segment on which it exists).

Every device that will communicate via TCP/IP will require an IP address. Unlike the NetBEUI or IPX/SPX protocols, where workstations automatically receive a node address, each node on an IP network must receive an IP address in one way or another.

One way to configure a workstation's IP address is to perform the configuration manually. This process involves configuring the address, subnet mask, and other information through the Network applet within the Control Panel. While this procedure may be effective on servers and a small number of workstations, it quickly becomes difficult to manage on a large network.

If done manually, IP workstation assignment and configuration can be a time-consuming task, and managing the addresses once they've been assigned can be even more of a challenge. However, you can implement mechanisms such as the Dynamic Host Configuration Protocol (DHCP) to automate address assignment for workstations.

Dynamic Address Allocation with DHCP

The Dynamic Host Configuration Protocol (DHCP) is an address-assignment protocol based upon an earlier protocol, the Bootstrap (bootp) protocol. The purpose of DHCP is to provide a mechanism to transfer IP configuration information, such as IP address, default gateway, and DNS server information to workstations.

DHCP is a client/server protocol. A DHCP server maintains a table of available and used IP addresses, and responds to requests from DHCP clients who need to obtain or renew a reservation (called a *lease*) for an IP address. The DHCP server transmits the address and the related information to the DHCP client, who then uses the address for the duration of the period specified in the lease. At the halfway point of the lease duration, the DHCP client will contact the server to renew the lease.

The advantage of implementing DHCP is that it frees network administrators from the burden of manually assigning and managing the IP addresses, DNS server information, WINS server location, and default gateway information on all of the workstations throughout their network. Once the DHCP server is installed, an administrator simply defines a scope, configures a few options such as the router, DNS servers, domain name, and WINS/NBNS servers. Configuration on the client end is extremely simple. For example, an administrator simply selects the Obtain an IP Address Automatically checkbox within the TCP/IP Properties dialog box of the Network applet within the Control Panel.

After the server and clients have been configured, the entire DHCP system operates transparently. Users can receive new IP addresses automatically, with no administrative intervention.

Another benefit of DHCP is that it allows administrators to change other IP-related configuration information, such as the IP address for the closest DNS server, without having to make a visit to every workstation on a segment. If you've ever administered an IP network where workstation IP configurations were managed manually, you'll immediately appreciate the benefits of DHCP.

Limitations of DHCP

While the benefits of DHCP are significant, the protocol has one limitation that should be considered before you begin to plan a DHCP implementation. DHCP client requests are transmitted as network broadcasts, so they are not automatically forwarded by network routers. If you plan to implement a DHCP server on a network that has multiple network segments connected by a router, this will pose a problem because the server will only respond to those workstations that are on its segment.

Fortunately, many routers, including the software routing feature of Windows NT, have the ability to forward DHCP requests. To configure a Windows NT Server to forward DHCP requests, you must first enable packet forwarding, then enable the BOOTP relay agent for DHCP.

DHCP Planning Considerations

Although an NT Server provides DHCP server services, DHCP operates independently of the Windows NT domain structure. The advantage of this is that you can deploy DHCP servers on any NT server and it can service users from any of the domains within your network.

According to information published by Microsoft, a DHCP server should be able to serve 10,000 clients. While this number may be possible, our experience has shown that in most environments, the number of clients served by a DHCP server will be far fewer than 10,000.

Use the domain independence of DHCP to your advantage in your deployment of DHCP servers. While the traffic generated by DHCP requests and replies can be tuned for maximum efficiency, try to avoid situations where DHCP traffic might travel over a wide area network link. Each site that contains more than a few users should have its own DHCP server.

In larger sites, you will have more flexibility in your deployment of DHCP servers. It is always a good practice to have at least one spare DHCP server to provide fault tolerance should your primary DHCP server become unavailable.

When you define DHCP scopes, it's easy to think in terms of Class C-type network addresses (Class C networks can support 250 IP addresses). In older, routed networks, it was rare for a single segment to contain more than 250 users. With the growing popularity of switched Ethernet and Token Ring technology, the number of users on a particular segment may be much, much higher than 250. You may find that you'll need to define multiple scopes for a single segment, or you may need to utilize unusual variable-length subnet masks to support these types of segments.

Finding Servers with WINS

While DHCP is good for assigning IP addresses for workstations, it does not provide any type of directory to help workstations locate other network resources, such as servers that existed on non-local segments. Standard browsing processes, due to their broadcast nature, are only effective on a single network segment. Microsoft had to develop a service that would provide a dynamic map of a workstation's (or server's) IP address to its NetBIOS name, regardless of the segment on which the device was located. Without this service, no one (including servers) would be able to locate Microsoft network resources unless they were local. The service that Microsoft created to solve this problem is called the Windows Internet Naming Service, or WINS.

How WINS Works

To use WINS, you'll need to configure a WINS server on an NT server. Each WINS client workstation contains the IP address of its WINS server (or it receives the WINS server information through DHCP). When it connects to the network, it contacts the WINS server and submits a name registration request. If the workstation's name is unique, the WINS server will add the name to its database. When the workstation shuts down, it will send a request to the WINS server to release its name. For the duration of the session that the workstation is online, the WINS server will provide name-to-IP-address translations for any other nodes that request information about that workstation.

Like DHCP, when a workstation registers its name with a WINS server, the registration has an associated lifetime. The client must renew the name registration with the WINS server before the lifetime expires.

Because the communications between the WINS client and server are unicast (point-to-point, not broadcast like regular browsing), the WINS client can be on a totally different segment than the WINS server. In addition, the WINS database can be replicated to other WINS servers, similar to the way an NT domain is replicated between a PDC and BDCs. However, WINS is independent of the NT domain accounts database, so a single WINS server can serve devices from multiple domains.

WINS Planning Considerations

Determining the number of WINS primary and backup servers to implement on a network is similar to planning for PDCs and BDCs. A typical WINS server can provide lookup services for up to 10,000 workstations, but this does not take into consideration other factors, such as slow wide area network links, excessive lookup traffic, or overhead associated with other server applications.

Plan to deploy at least two WINS servers, a primary and a secondary for fault tolerance purposes.

When a WINS client submits a registration request, it submits a separate request for each of the services running on that computer. For example, as a minimum a client will submit a registration request for the computer name, the user name, and the workgroup or domain name when it connects to the network in the morning. On large networks, this early morning traffic can become substantial, particularly if the requests will travel over slow links. If you have a number of large sites that are connected by slow wide area links, you should consider placing a WINS server in each location. By implementing a server at each site, the traffic associated with registrations and releases will remain within the site, at LAN speeds. The only traffic that will traverse the slow links is the traffic associated with replication between the WINS servers.

WINS Alternatives

Because it provides name to address mappings, WINS is frequently compared to the Domain Name Service (DNS). One of the major differences between WINS and DNS, however, is that WINS is a dynamic protocol. Workstations can register names and release those registrations automatically. With DNS, on the other hand, a DNS administrator must manually add, modify, and remove entries from the DNS server. Recently, however, a number of third-party products have been introduced that will provide dynamic DNS/DHCP interaction with NetBIOS name registration functionality.

WINS and DNS One of the most significant problems with WINS is that it only works with Microsoft networking clients. UNIX systems and Macintosh users will be unable to use WINS to resolve host names. Typically, these types of systems rely on DNS to resolve host names.

In NT Server 4, Microsoft provided a solution that attempted to address the relative strengths and weaknesses of WINS and DNS. The Windows NT DNS Server that was included with NT 4 had the ability to forward DNS name lookup requests to the WINS server. For example, if a workstation registered the name MONTIA-01 with a WINS server, and a UNIX host attempted to resolve the DNS name MONTIA-01.COMPANY.COM, the Microsoft DNS server could utilize WINS to resolve MONTIA-01 and then provide the IP address of the workstation within the response to the DNS request. We'll discuss DNS in more detail in Chapters 7 and 9.

Using an LMHOSTS File In some situations, implementing a client/server WINS configuration may not be the most cost-effective solution for providing IP-address to NetBIOS name translations. For example, if you wanted to access a number of different NetBIOS computers on a number of computers located throughout the Internet, it would be more efficient to create a table of only those computers you wished to access. An LMHOSTS file is almost identical in function to an /ETC/HOSTS file in the UNIX world—it contains computer hosts' names and the IP addresses associated with those hosts.

Keep in mind that an LMHOSTS file should typically be your last resort, because it cannot be updated dynamically.

In this chapter, we discussed two important areas that you'll need to focus on to design your Windows NT network infrastructure: how to effectively plan the capacity of your NT Servers and how to plan your network protocol implementation to support those servers and the workstations that will access them. In the next chapter, we'll discuss the techniques and software that you can utilize to integrate Windows NT with the rest of your enterprise network.

CHAPTER 6

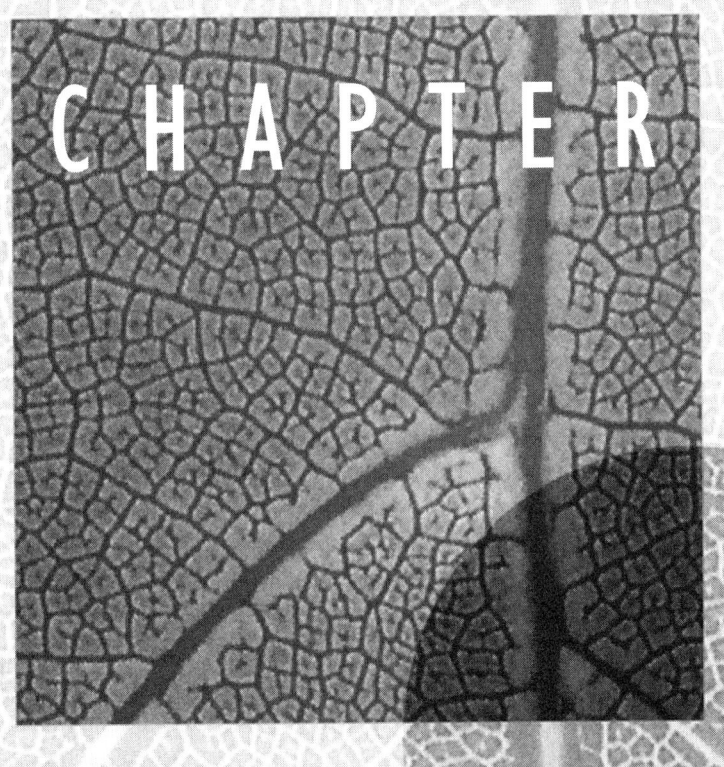

Incorporating Windows NT
into the Enterprise Network

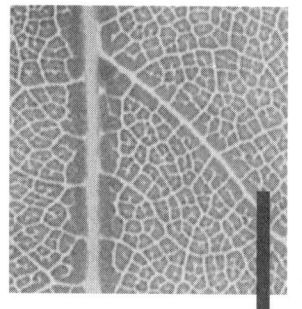

It's not often that we find an enterprise network that contains only a single operating system. By their very definition, networks are designed to enable people with different business requirements to share information. Each business requirement often brings with it a unique platform upon which to conduct that business.

Current networking technologies enable us to link heterogeneous platforms together, provided that the platforms can communicate using a common language or protocol. While this concept might sound simple, we quickly discover that the challenge comes in determining which one of the platforms should take the lead in setting the standard for the common language that both will use. For example, when we consider the leading network operating systems, Novell IntranetWare shares top honors with Microsoft Windows NT. Both vendors recognize this and each offers its own unique blend of products and integration services, such as Novell's NT Administrator and Microsoft's Gateway Services for NetWare.

Beginning with version 4.11, Novell began to refer to its network operating system as *IntranetWare* rather than *NetWare*. The purpose was to draw attention to the additional services that were bundled with the soon-to-be-released NetWare 4.11 operating system. DHCP Server, NetWare Internet Access Server, multiprotocol router and NetWare/IP, along with NetWare 4.11, are part of the product suite now known as *IntranetWare*.

Our objective in this chapter is to introduce you to these services so that you can make your own decision about which best meets your integration and interoperability needs. In this chapter, we will discuss:

- Support for the native NT transport protocols: NetBEUI, NetBIOS over TCP/IP, and IPX/SPX

- The differences between integration and interoperability

- Windows NT's support for IntranetWare
- IntranetWare's support for Windows NT

The Native Transport Protocols

In our introduction we mentioned that networking technologies have evolved to the point where we are able to join dissimilar platforms onto a common network. So often we take this for granted, and then we realize that it was not very long ago that the thought of connecting something like IBM and Digital hardware onto a common network was virtually impossible. Each platform had its own unique physical interfaces—interfaces that weren't designed to interconnect with one another.

Over time, standardization of physical interfaces and their associated physical protocols began to occur. For example, it's now possible to interconnect IBM and Digital hardware onto a common 10BASE-T network. However, if you take a look at the larger picture, this interconnection is merely the first step required in enabling these devices to communicate.

Imagine that you and a friend have built a network made of two tin cans linked by some wet string. Grasping these cans, you realize that you both exist on a common network. With this first objective met, you now need to select a common means of communication, bound by certain rules. You might choose the English language, framed by CB-Radio commands like, "What's your twenty?" or "Over and out!" Or perhaps you might choose to speak in Italian, framed by a Sicilian dialect like, "Come sta lei?" or *...actually I had better stop there*. Whatever you choose, it has to be a *common* language, one that you both agree to and are capable of understanding.

These same considerations need to be given to Novell IntranetWare and Microsoft Windows NT. If both operating systems are to communicate on a common network then they need to choose a common language. This common language is known as the *transport protocol,* and each vendor chose its own unique variant when they gave birth to their network operating systems. In the next two sections we introduce NetBEUI and IPX/SPX, the native transport protocols for Microsoft Windows NT and Novell IntranetWare.

NOTE No discussion on networking protocols ever occurs without some reference to the layers of the OSI model. While the following section is no different, we have kept our references to a minimum. If you would like additional detail on the OSI model, then please refer to Appendix B.

NetBEUI

Before we begin, we ask that you bear the following in mind:

- NetBEUI is not NetBIOS.
- The term NetBIOS should not be used interchangeably with NetBEUI.
- NetBIOS is not a transport protocol.

Please forgive us for taking a moment to get those items off our chest. It's just that we have found some of the greatest confusion in understanding Microsoft's NetBEUI protocol occurs when NetBEUI and NetBIOS are spoken of as if they are one and the same. For this reason, we would like to begin this section by discussing the NetBIOS *interface* and NetBEUI *transport protocol.*

NetBIOS as an Interface

Network Basic Input/Output System (NetBIOS), was developed as a software interface and naming standard to support IBM's PC Network LAN. Designed by Sytek Inc. for IBM in 1983, its purpose was to provide developers with a variety of hooks for interapplication communications and data transfer. Subsequently it provided those same programs with a link to a network operating system. Figure 6.1 presents a layered view of NetBIOS.

NetBIOS exists at the session layer as an Application Programmer Interface (API) for developers to utilize in submitting network I/O control directives. These directives take the form of Network Control Blocks (NCBs). NetBIOS optionally makes available the NetBIOS Frames Protocol (NBFP) in order to perform the network I/O to accommodate the interface.

It's also worth noting that NetBIOS ends where the network operating system and its transportation mechanisms begin. In essence, NetBIOS's major emphasis is on interfacing, with very little concern for transporting. As such, it becomes the responsibility of the network operating system developer to frame a transport protocol around the NetBIOS interface.

FIGURE 6.1

The NetBIOS Interface

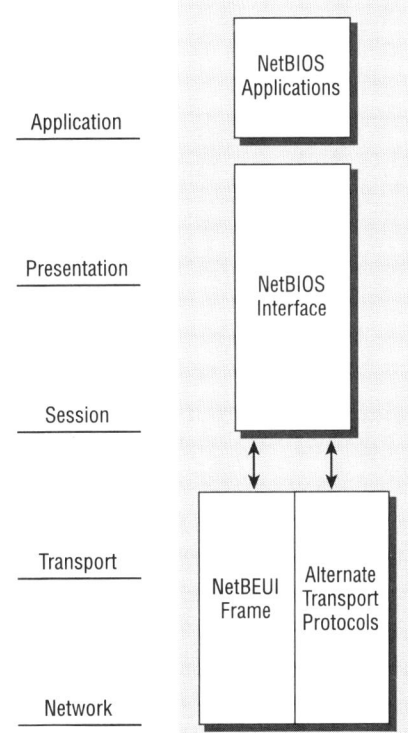

In doing so, the developer will need to decide whether or not to use NBFP. As we'll see, a protocol such as NetBEUI opts to support NBFP, while transport protocols like TCP/IP and IPX do not. The consequence of this is that transport protocols like TCP/IP and IPX must develop their own process for mapping each of the NetBIOS control directives to their own transport protocol's frame type.

Over time many vendors developed their own framing techniques for accomplishing this. The result was that NetBIOS evolved into a variety of proprietary versions as each network operating system vendor *tweaked* it to work with their own hardware or transport protocol.

NetBIOS as a Naming Standard

NetBIOS also defines a naming standard. This standard requires that each device within the network have a unique name. Groups of devices can also have names assigned to them, where all group names must be different from other group and individual device names. The NetBIOS standard limits names to 16 characters. Microsoft's implementation of this standard allows the administrator to assign the first 15 characters, while it reserves the 16th to identify a resource type. Table 6.1 lists these 16th-character definitions for your reference.

TABLE 6.1
NetBIOS 16th-Character Naming for Microsoft Networking

Name Type 16th	Character (1 byte)	Definition
Unique	<00>	NetBIOS Computer Name
Unique	<03>	Messenger Service for sending/receiving messages
Unique	<1B>	Domain Master Browser
Unique	<06>	RAS server service
Unique	<1F>	NetDDE service
Unique	<20>	Server service for identifying shares
Unique	<21>	RAS Client
Unique	<BE>	Network Monitor Agent
Unique	<BF>	Network Monitor Utility
Group	<1C>	Domain Group Name
Group	<1D>	Master Browser
Group	<1E>	Normal Group Name, local subnetwork
Group	<20>	Internet Group Name, logical group across WAN
Group	_MSBROWSE_	Appended to Domain Group Name <1C>, announcement of domain to other master browsers.

Every NetBIOS device registers itself upon startup. It accomplishes this by either registering with a centralized NetBIOS Name Service or broadcasting its existence onto the local network. This broadcast nature of NetBIOS can be a major cause of network traffic, and it is usually limited to the local network. The registration process enables NetBIOS devices to locate one another for resources.

 Microsoft supports NetBIOS name services through its Windows Internet Naming Service (WINS), which we discussed in Chapter 5.

As we conclude this section, please bear in mind the following:

- NetBIOS is an application interface for interapplication communications and data transfer.

- NetBIOS is a naming standard.

- NetBIOS must be wrapped in a transport protocol frame prior to transmission through the network.

NetBEUI

NetBEUI stands for NetBIOS Extended User Interface and is pronounced "net-booey." NetBEUI formalizes the transport protocol frame that was never standardized in NetBIOS, accomplishing this while supporting NBFP. For this reason, it is also referred to as NetBEUI Frame (NBF). It was released by IBM in 1985 as a compact, efficient protocol designed to run on local departmental networks. From this philosophy, we can understand why NetBEUI was built to be nonroutable. The presumption was that connectivity to external hosts would be provided by protocol gateways. After all, distributed local area networking was still in its infancy, with segment populations under 100 nodes. Everyone still had a need to communicate with mainframe and minicomputers for their mission-critical applications. NetBEUI and protocol gateways appeared to be a fine solution for providing this connectivity from the emerging LAN environment to the legacy mainframe environment. Figure 6.2 provides a layered view of NetBEUI.

NetBEUI does not specify the physical and data link layers, enabling it to use a Data Link Control (DLC) protocol that is compatible with IEEE 802.2's Logical Link Control (LLC) protocol. Ethernet, Token-Ring, IEEE 802.3, and IEEE 802.5 are all examples of DLC protocols that can be used with NetBEUI.

NetBEUI has been widely accepted for use with network operating systems such as Microsoft LAN Manager, IBM LAN Server, and Microsoft Windows NT. Up until version 3.5, it was the default protocol for Windows NT. After that version, Microsoft began focusing on the corporate enterprise for Windows NT and subsequently promoted a routable transport protocol capable of supporting the WAN. TCP/IP was selected, supplanting NetBEUI as the default beginning with version 3.51.

FIGURE 6.2

The NetBEUI Protocol

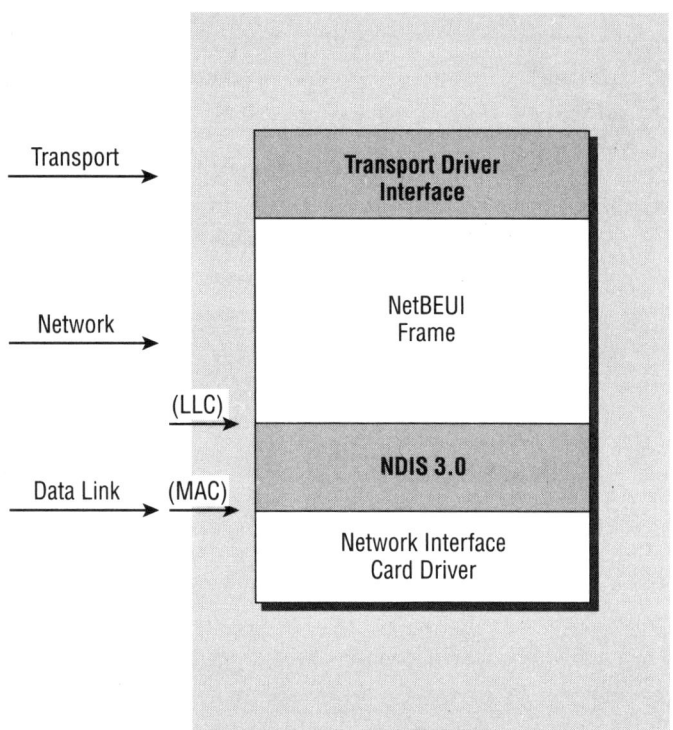

NetBIOS over TCP/IP

More often than not, we're seeing TCP/IP implemented as the sole protocol in a Microsoft Windows NT network. Attribute it to corporate America's fascination with the Internet, or NetBEUI's inability to route. Either way we look at it, TCP/IP comes out as the protocol of choice.

Based on this you may find yourself hearing the following comment, as we so often have: "My network runs only TCP/IP. I removed NetBIOS, so I don't have to deal with that chatty protocol."

After you've read the previous section, we're certain you'll educate the misguided individual by informing him or her that TCP/IP is not a replacement for NetBIOS. In fact, the two shouldn't really be compared since one is a transport protocol while the other is a software interface and naming standard. This is proven by examining Figures 6.3 and 6.4, which show how Net-BEUI is listed under Protocols while NetBIOS is listed under Services.

FIGURE 6.3

The Windows NT 4 display of network protocols

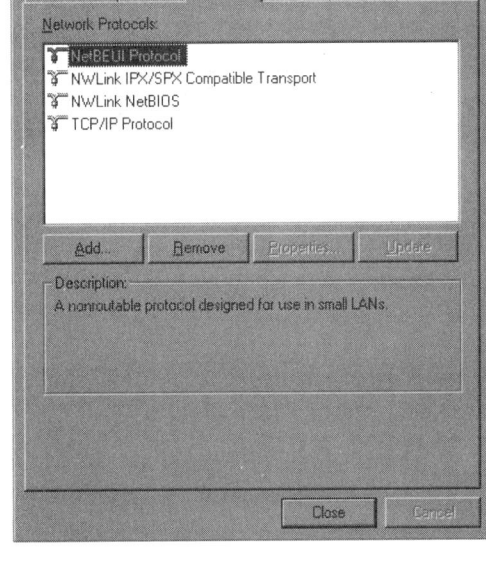

FIGURE 6.4

The Windows NT 4 display of network services

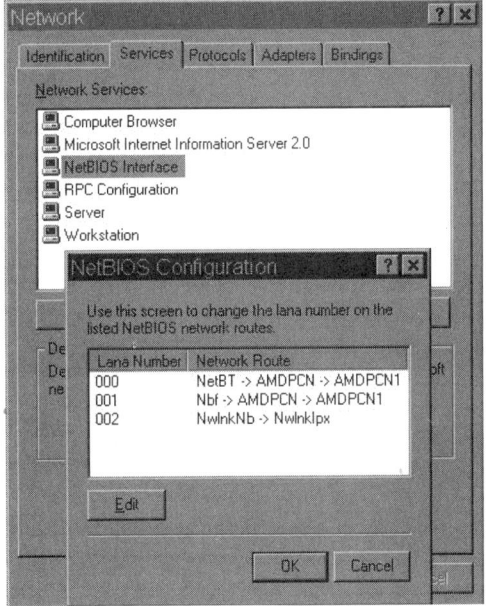

That being said, the earlier comment will likely change to, "Okay, fine, what I really did was remove NetBEUI as a protocol. Now all I have to do is get rid of NetBIOS as a service and I will be running only TCP/IP, right?" Ever the diplomat, you would answer, "In theory, yes—in practice, that's not such a good idea."

Before we remove any service, especially NetBIOS, we have to consider who or what depends on the service. You'll recall that NetBIOS is an application interface, and applications such as `net use` and `nbtstat` make extensive use of NetBIOS, as do supplemental NT services such as WINS. Other TCP/IP applications, like ping and route, weren't designed to interact with NetBIOS and would be unaffected by its removal. To understand this difference we refer to Figure 6.5, which provides a layered view of the TCP/IP protocol in an NT environment. An in-depth discussion of this concept follows.

FIGURE 6.5

Windows NT implementation of TCP/IP

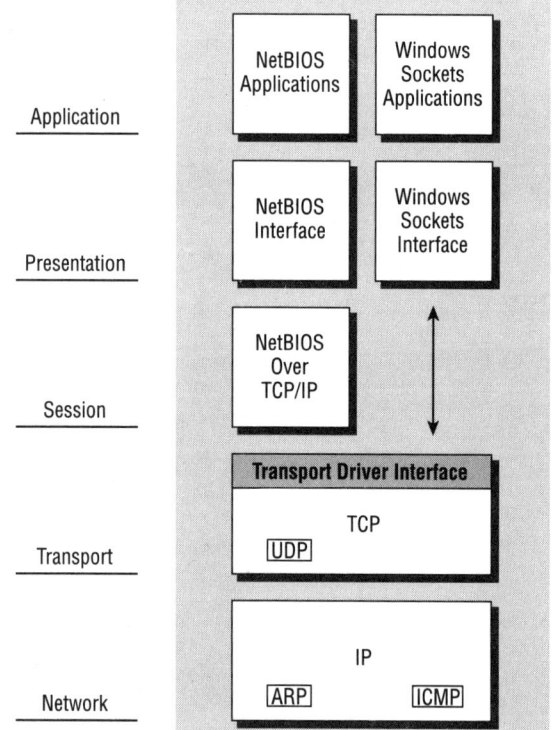

As we examine Figure 6.5, we recall our earlier discussion of NetBIOS where we referenced the NBFP and how it provides network communication services for the NetBIOS interface.

As we expand upon this concept, we discover that software programs wishing to take advantage of NBFP are required to write a transport driver that will open them into the NetBIOS interface. The effort required to develop and implement this transport driver often offsets any advantage gained through NBFP.

Instead, most developers will take advantage of the extensible Transport Device Interface (TDI) that Windows NT provides. The TDI comes complete with a NetBIOS emulator to support applications written for use with NBFP. The NetBIOS emulator will provide services to cross-reference NetBIOS commands to TDI commands. This occurs as follows:

1. An application issues NetBIOS commands as network I/O control directives. These commands take the form of Network Control Blocks (NCBs).

2. The NCBs are passed to a NetBIOS emulator that is responsible for mapping the NBFP request to a TDI request. (NETBIOS.SYS is the system program responsible for this task.)

3. The TDI request is then passed to the NBF transport driver. (NBF.SYS assumes this task, optimizing the TDI call for the 32-bit Windows NT kernel.)

This entire process is generally referred to as NetBIOS over *Transport Protocol*. Where *Transport Protocol* refers to any of the following:

- NetBEUI operating as NetBEUI frame (Nbf)

- TCP/IP operating as NetBIOS over TCP/IP (NetBT)

- IPX/SPX referred to by Windows NT as NWlink, operating as NetBIOS over NWlink (NwlnkNb)

Please refer back to Figure 6.5 for a view of these NetBIOS emulator services.

Continuing with our analysis of Figure 6.5 we discover that there is another way for us to communicate with our TCP/IP protocol stack, outside the realm of NetBIOS: through the use of Windows Sockets (WinSock).

Windows Sockets is part of the Windows Open Systems Architecture (WOSA). Originally developed for TCP/IP, it has been extended to provide transport-independent interprocess communication services for a variety of common transport protocols. These include IPX/SPX, DECnet, and XNS.

WinSock is an API that exists at the session layer. In this position it provides application developers with an alternative to NetBIOS. The majority of applications written to the WinSock standard come from the TCP/IP protocol suite. WinSock-compatible TCP/IP applications included with Windows NT are listed here:

arp	finger	FTP	hostname
ipconfig	lpq	lpr	nbtstat
netstat	nslookup	ping	Rcp
rexec	route	rsh	telnet
tftp	tracert		

Execution of any programs listed here occurs through the WinSock interface, exclusive of NetBIOS. As such, the programs would continue to operate without incident if the NetBIOS service were removed.

While removal of NetBIOS is possible, it certainly isn't practical, because the NetBIOS interface provides support for crucial NT services—services that do not yet exist in a WinSock-compliant form. It is not yet possible to run *only* TCP/IP in our Windows NT network, because the Windows NT system services which require NetBIOS restrict us from doing so.

Microsoft has committed to move toward more flexible and open standards, like WinSock, beginning with Windows NT 5. The promise of the future is that the next generation of Windows NT will be written to these standards, enabling us to rid ourselves of NetBIOS emulator services, like NetBT. If this happens then we will be able to fully agree when someone comes up to us and says, "My network runs *only* TCP/IP."

IPX/SPX

As a network operating system, Novell NetWare has an architecture that is quite similar to Xerox Network Services (XNS). Released in the early 1980s, NetWare provides file, print, messaging, and database services to its clients through a server-centric networking model. In this model, clients of the network make requests of devices dedicated to the role of server. The clients find these servers through their periodic announcements on the network. Once found, a client makes contact with a server of interest using Novell's IPX/SPX protocol.

XNS was developed by Xerox in their Palo Alto, California research center and was introduced in 1981. It forms the foundation for many present-day networking technologies, such as the Ethernet protocol and the Banyan Vines network operating system.

The Internetwork Packet eXchange/Sequenced Packet eXchange (IPX/SPX) protocols evolved from their XNS parents, IDP/SPP. IPX is a Network-layer protocol, derived from Xerox's Internetwork Datagram Protocol (IDP). SPX is a Transport-layer protocol, derived from Xerox's Sequenced Packet Protocol (SPP).

An IPX packet traveling through the network contains all of the addressing information it needs to reach its destination. Chances are, it received this information from a partner protocol called the Routing Information Protocol (RIP). RIP works cooperatively with IPX enabling it to move quickly to its destination without having to check directions along the way.

IPX is categorized as a *connectionless protocol*. By their very nature, connectionless protocols transmit without first checking to see if the destination is available to receive. If the destination does not respond within a certain interval, IPX will retransmit the packet a set number of times before considering the destination unreachable.

SPX provides connection-oriented services, enhancing the dependability of the IPX protocol by providing reliable delivery. It accomplishes this through the establishment of virtual circuits known as *connection identifiers*. Information sent over these connections will be acknowledged as received or non-acknowledged with a request for retransmission.

TCP/IP in a NetWare Environment

Similar to their Windows NT adversaries, champions of NetWare have been awaiting the day when TCP/IP will supplant IPX/SPX as the native protocol. The roadblocks to this are similar to those that exist for NT. Essentially, many of the legacy NetWare Core Protocol (NCP) API calls are tied very closely to the IPX/SPX protocol. These "hard-wired hooks" make it a difficult task to uncouple IPX from the NetWare operating system.

> **Protocols and the Postal Service**
>
> Connectionless protocols provide nonguaranteed delivery of information. They function similarly to the way that first class mail is delivered. After putting a letter in an envelope, we apply all of the destination and return addressing information before dropping it in the mailbox. This letter is then sent without regard to whether the recipient is able to receive it, or whether it may get lost along its way. We hope that our recipient will respond, but should this not occur, we will assume that the letter did not arrive as planned. At this point we either write another letter, or decide the information is no longer worth resending.
>
> Connection-oriented protocols provide guaranteed delivery of information, for those instances where it is critical that a package arrive safely. Using our earlier first-class mailing analogy, we would say connection-oriented protocols function as if we called up our recipient prior to mailing the letter. "Hello Maria, this is Michele. Stay on the phone; I am going to send you a letter." After a couple of days on the telephone, Maria notices a postal carrier arrive at her door. "Michele, the letter just got here, thanks!" Maria and Michele then both hang up, breaking the connection that was established to confirm receipt of the message.

That's not to say that TCP/IP is unable to function in a NetWare environment. This is far from the case, and with the release of IntranetWare 4.11 our choices have been expanded.

TCP/IP Server Support

NetWare support for TCP/IP begins at the server, through the loading of the TCPIP.NLM. This protocol must then be bound to at least one network interface adapter to support communication on the network. Configuration of a proper IP address and subnet mask is a requirement during the binding phase to ensure proper implementation of the TCP/IP protocol. Additional information on the implementation of TCP/IP can be found in *The Complete Guide to NetWare 4.11/IntranetWare* by James Gaskin (Sybex, 1997).

Once the TCPIP.NLM has been configured, the NetWare server has the ability to identify and route any IP traffic received by any IP-configured interfaces. In addition, the server can utilize IP utilities such as PING. Keep in mind that loading TCPIP.NLM does not allow NetWare clients to access services such as file- and print-sharing on the NetWare server.

NetWare/IP

In response to overwhelming customer feedback, Novell developed NetWare/IP to allow clients to communicate with NetWare servers via TCP/IP instead of their native IPX/SPX. One might wonder why a product like NetWare/IP is even required. If the server is running TCP/IP and the client is running TCP/IP, then why aren't they able to communicate?

The answer can be found in the way services are advertised in a NetWare environment. Early on, we mentioned that NetWare servers make their services known by announcing themselves to the clients of the network. This announcement takes place through the Service Advertising Protocol (SAP), using IPX as the transport for *getting the word out*. The Routing Information Protocol (RIP) lends a hand by making sure that the advertisements can make their way through an IPX-routed network.

TCP/IP was not designed to hold information about NetWare services and the routes to those services; TCP/IP has no way of dealing natively with the SAP/RIP information. This is where NetWare/IP steps in. Introducing a name service known as *Domain SAP/RIP Service* (DSS), NetWare/IP establishes a distributed fault-tolerant database for holding SAP/RIP information.

Rather than broadcast their services throughout the network via SAP/RIP, NetWare/IP-enabled servers will direct this information to a DSS server. This DSS information is then shared with all other NetWare/IP servers, thereby building a comprehensive view of the NetWare/IP environment. Figure 6.6 illustrates this process.

The DSS servers can be arranged in a *NetWare/IP domain of services*. This domain is built upon a hierarchy consisting of primary and multiple secondary DSS servers, enabling the designer to establish an efficient means of replication and fault tolerance for the NetWare/IP servers' service offerings.

The NetWare/IP configuration begins on the server through the installation of the NetWare/IP software. It's a prerequisite that TCP/IP (TCPIP.NLM) is loaded on this server prior to the installation of NetWare/IP (NWIP.NLM).

Once installed, NetWare/IP appears to the server's internal router as an IPX protocol stack. It accomplishes this through establishment of a unique, virtual IPX address (assigned during configuration of the primary DSS). The virtual IPX address sits at the uppermost layer of the NWIP.NLM, where it

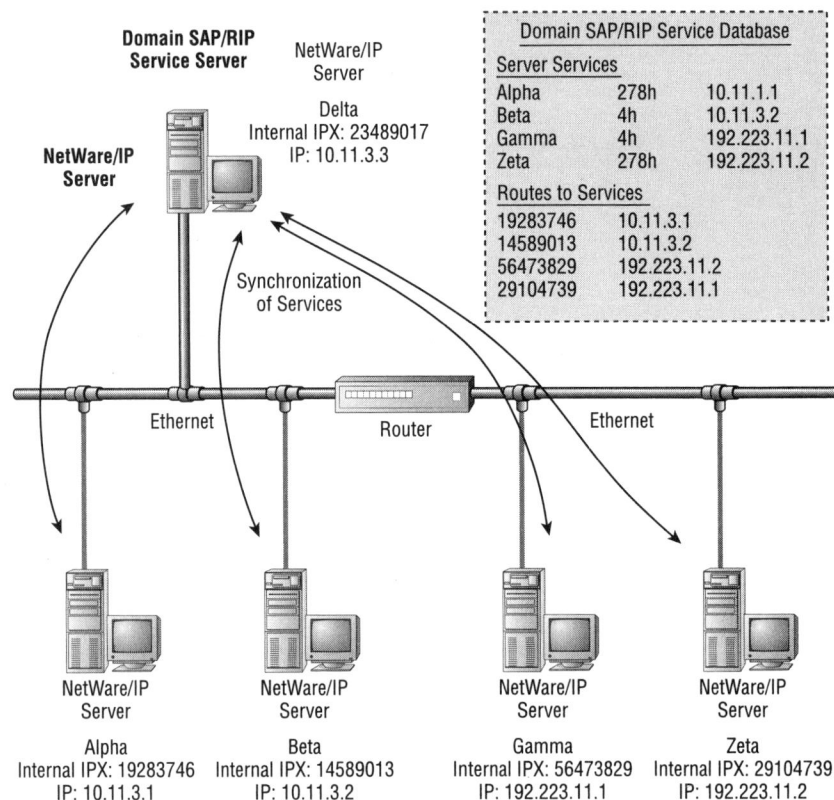

FIGURE 6.6 The NetWare/IP Domain SAP/RIP Service

can provide support for API calls written exclusively to IPX. Figure 6.7 depicts the layered view of this server architecture.

The NetWare/IP client configuration is designed to support the server concepts of NetWare/IP domains and DSS. It accomplishes this through a layered-protocol architecture similar to that on the server. Please refer to Figure 6.8, which is described in more detail below.

In Figure 6.8 we have a view of the protocol stack as it would appear for a DOS/Windows client attempting to establish TCP/IP as its sole protocol. Above the Open Data-Link Interface layer (ODI) we encounter the TCP/IP protocol stack: the actual name and type of stack. This stack replaces the IPX protocol stack as the network transport. Well...actually, it replaces most of it, exclusive of a piece known as the *IPX Far Call Interface*. The IPX Far Call Interface provides binary compatibility for all API calls written to IPX at the client.

FIGURE 6.7
NetWare/IP server architecture

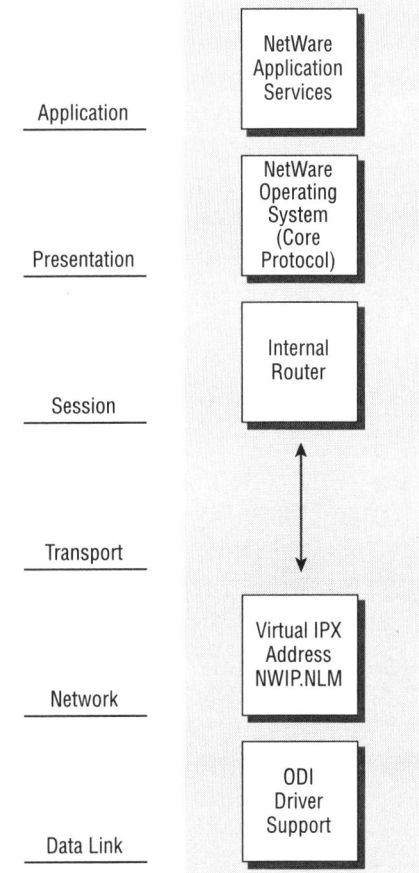

The NetWare/IP client software (NWIP.EXE), takes advantage of this compatibility interface by shimming itself between the IPX Far Call Interface and the TCP/IP protocol stack. The result is that we have a TCP/IP client that appears to the upper layer NetWare protocols as if it were an IPX client.

 The NetWare/IP client architecture, sometimes referred to as *IPX over TCP/IP*, is similar in concept to *NetBIOS over TCP/IP*, covered earlier in this chapter.

All of this slick protocol manipulation courtesy of NetWare/IP is what provides the TCP/IP client/server support in Novell NetWare. Novell envisions a

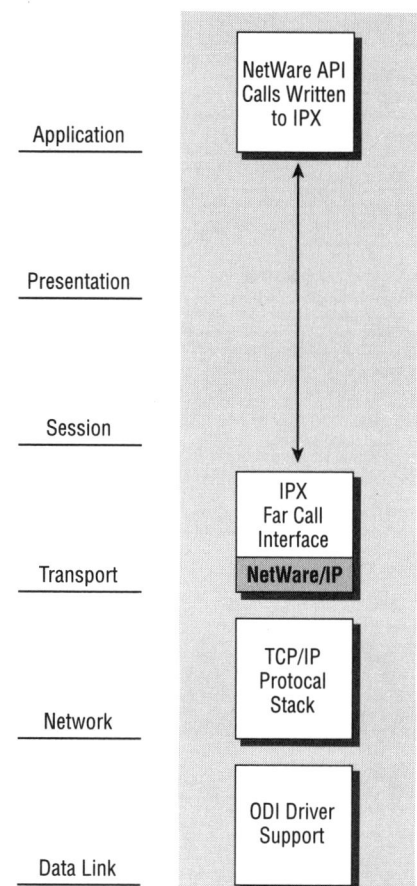

FIGURE 6.8
NetWare/IP client architecture

day when NetWare/IP will no longer be required. In this scenario, NetWare services will be advertised in a manner that does not require the SAP/RIP protocols and native IPX applications like MAP and NDIR to be written to TCP/IP open standards.

Protocol Interoperability

Thus far we have learned that for local area networking, Microsoft favors NetBEUI, a protocol born of the desire to establish a framing standard for the NetBIOS interface. When it comes to enterprise networking, Microsoft changes its tune and recommends that we deploy TCP/IP for WAN communication.

Novell, on the other hand, took the lead from Xerox and embellished upon XNS in creating the IPX/SPX protocols. Designed to support local and wide area networking, their visible drawback is that they are proprietary. For an open solution we turn to TCP/IP and discover that Novell supports this protocol through NetWare/IP.

Windows NT and NetWare interoperability begins with the selection of a common transport protocol. If we are unable to link at this layer then it matters little that we are able to integrate onto a common network backbone. We know which transport each NOS favors, let's see if we can pick a common one from this list:

- **Microsoft NetBEUI** gets the briefest of considerations due to its non-routable characteristic. Novell appears to agree since this protocol is essentially not supported. (Critics please note: We are referring to NetBEUI, not NetBIOS). An individual could spend their entire career administering a NetWare network and never hear of NetBEUI.

- **Novell IPX/SPX** appears attractive, especially when we consider that it has been widely tested in the industry for over a decade. While not the best choice for wide area networking, it does provide a routable alternative to Microsoft NetBEUI.

- **TCP/IP** is synonymous with interoperability. This open standard protocol has been used to link more heterogeneous network operating systems together than any other. Supported by Microsoft and Novell, it is only compromised by the distinctive manner in which each vendor chooses to implement this standard—creativity can at times lead to incompatibility. When compared to IPX/SPX, TCP/IP can appear as a less attractive option due to the administrative overhead associated with managing the IP addresses. DHCP serves as an attractive complement for those bothered by this.

Choosing a mutual transport is the first step in the quest for interoperability. From this platform we build a common suite of file, print, messaging, and database services all wrapped up in a universal management interface. Universal interoperability and management—this is our Holy Grail; the next section describes the progress Microsoft and Novell are making in this divine quest.

Integration and Interoperability

For the past year and a half we have been aware of and participated in the competitive sport of network operating systems. What we are referring to is the proliferation of documentation and seminars with titles like *NetWare vs. NT*, *From NetWare to NT—Without a Hitch* and *Migrating to IntraNetware from NT Server*. This non-contact (sometimes) sport gave birth to legions of fans, each taking sides with their favorite network operating system. In great anticipation they entered the arena, hoping that their champion would win the fight, claiming ownership of the title World's Greatest Network Operating System.

What a disappointment when the result of the contest turned out to be a draw.

Reflecting back we realize that the outcome was inevitable. Consider if you will that at no time has the science of one product been able to *fully* supplant another in a common technology. Phonograph records still occupy shelf space with compact disks, gas stoves are found under microwave ovens, and paper datebooks continue to be published—no matter how many types of electronic organizers are produced. As such, the outcome of the NetWare/NT skirmish was preordained. Destiny would see to it that they would be subjected to a lifetime of integration and interoperability. Lucky for us.

Microsoft's View on Integration and Interoperability

Microsoft chose to provide integration and interoperability support for Novell NetWare with the very first release of Windows NT. This was never a question, because in 1993 NetWare was the leading network operating system.

If Microsoft had any hope of winning market share from Novell, it would have to come from a strategy that feigned support before attempting to supplant this popular network operating system. See the sidebar on "The Ethics of Bicycle Racing" for insight into this strategy. We will continue by taking a historic look at Microsoft's strategic support for Novell NetWare.

Windows NT 3.1

Released in 1993, NT 3.1 included support for NetWare in the form of the NWlink protocol. This Microsoft version of Novell's native IPX/SPX protocols would provide NT the means of communicating with NetWare through a common language.

> **The Ethics of Bicycle Racing**
>
> One of the most exciting spectator sporting events is the Tour de France. This multi-day event attracts the world's best cyclists to a series of grueling races for the coveted "yellow jersey." Each day, this jersey is awarded to the racer with the lowest aggregate time for all of the races to date. Those that have worn this jersey are considered to be the greatest cyclists in the world. It only seems fitting then that the competition is fierce. Even so, the ethics associated with the sport result in races that are rather companionable.
>
> Often a team will break off from the front of the pack with the objective of outdistancing the main pack of cyclists. This dash to victory does not usually go unchallenged. A cyclist or two from an *opposing* team will jump out of the main pack and *integrate* themselves with the breakaway group. Once within this group they will *interoperate* with the opposing riders for the common benefit of all. This temporary allegiance is necessary if they hope to stay away from the main pack. Working cooperatively, all riders in the breakaway group will take turns at the front, bearing the brunt of the headwind so that the others can rest. Once they are at the front for a reasonable period of time, they'll communicate with the other riders and move to the back to rest. Someone else from the same team or another will now take a turn at the front.
>
> Riders that choose not to *integrate* and *interoperate* in this manner will find themselves exhausted and caught somewhere between the main pack and the breakaway group. In this position they are left to battle the headwind alone.
>
> As the race nears its conclusion, the rider who feels superior will often split from the breakaway group. With victory in sight, this rider's mindset is such that he no longer feels a need to integrate or interoperate with the others. Instead he will set the pace for the others to follow in the final dash toward the finish line.

Windows NT 3.5

Focus turned to Windows NT Workstation with this release and its ability to communicate directly to NetWare servers through a combination of NWlink and Client Services for NetWare (CSNW). NWlink provided the transport, while CSNW provided access to the file and print services of NetWare.

Those clients unable to meet the resource requirements for running NT Workstation could take advantage of Gateway Services for NetWare (GSNW). Running on an NT Server, GSNW acted as a proxy for clients of the Windows NT network who wished to access the NetWare network for file and print services.

> ### GSNW in the Courtroom
>
> It was around the time of the release of Windows NT 3.5 that Novell's lawyers first became involved. Early claims by Microsoft that you could operate hundreds of clients through a *single GSNW connection* did not go unnoticed by Novell at their home in Orem, Utah. A single GSNW connection equated to a single NetWare license. Corporations would be able to reduce their NetWare licensing costs 100 fold by passing their clients through GSNW rather than establishing a direct licensed connection to the NetWare servers.
>
> The resolution came as a technology restraint rather than a legal one. GSNW had a nasty habit of doubling the response time for each user of the service after the first. With performance through the gateway deemed less than robust, GSNW has been delegated to the ranks of infrequent users of NetWare services or for use as a migration tool from NetWare to NT.

Windows NT 3.51

Release 3.51 brought with it TCP/IP as the default transport protocol.

On the interoperability front, Microsoft announced two new products, File and Print Services for NetWare (FPNW) and Directory Services Manager for NetWare (DSNW). These were spoken of as a toolset to help compliment the NetWare Convert (NWConv) utility bundled with Windows NT since version 3.5. More than anything else, these products reflected a shift in Microsoft's view of Novell NetWare from an operating system that they wished to interoperate with to one that they wished to help users migrate from.

FPNW allows a Windows NT server to appear as a NetWare server, while DSNW provides for the synchronization of passwords between a Windows NT domain and NetWare server bindery (NetWare 3.*x*). (Enter Novell lawyers, for the second time).

It's worth noting that DSNW did not support synchronization between a Windows NT domain and NDS. We might speculate that Microsoft released DSNW to assist users in migrating from NetWare 3.x to Windows NT. If you were running NDS, then that meant you had already made your choice to migrate to NetWare 4.1, instead of Windows NT. Microsoft had already lost you, so what benefit was there in providing synchronization between itself and a competitor? Migration was in, interoperability was out!

The idea behind Microsoft's strategy was that these tools would allow an administrator to bring NT (disguised as a NetWare server) into their NetWare network. Sort of the way a shepherd might innocently bring a wolf (dressed in sheep's clothing) into his flock.

Windows NT 4

What a difference a version makes. Having established a foothold in the networks of corporate America, Microsoft did little to embellish upon their ability to interoperate with Novell NetWare. The only change occurred in the bundling of FPNW and DSNW into a single product known as Windows NT Services for NetWare.

The emphasis instead was placed on establishing Windows NT as the preeminent network operating system for running mission critical applications. Enhancements in the form of Internet services, transaction services, and commerce services might lead one to believe that Microsoft had shifted their focus away from Novell NetWare and toward UNIX.

Novell's View on Integration and Interoperability

Novell has laid out a very clear strategy for integrating and interoperating with Microsoft Windows NT. This strategy is broken into three phases.

Phase 1: Initial NT Integration from Novell

After a slow start, Novell released the Novell Workstation Manager as a compliment to its IntranetWare Client for Windows NT. The combination of the two supports Novell Directory Services (NDS) authentication for clients operating Windows NT Workstations. NDS authentication eliminates the need for domain authentication (SAM) and, essentially, for domain modeling.

Novell Dynamic Host Configuration Protocol (DHCP) server was released in this phase to provide dynamic IP addressing. The Novell DHCP server supports IntranetWare as well as NT clients. The Novell server also integrates with Microsoft WINS by providing a storage area for the data necessary for this service.

Novell's server management product, ManageWise, was also enhanced to interoperate with Windows NT. Beginning with 2.1, ManageWise agents for Windows NT Server and Workstation could be obtained from Novell.

Phase 2: Increased NT Server Integration

Novell Administrator for Windows NT was released to provide centralized administration for users and groups in a mixed IntranetWare and Windows NT environment. It accomplishes this through the synchronization of NDS and Microsoft domain account information.

The Novell Application Launcher (NAL), first appeared with the release of Client32 for Windows 95. It was designed to provide centralized management for application services in a NetWare environment. Beginning with this phase, NAL was enhanced to include further support for NT Workstation. Users can now invoke the services of NAL through the Explorer, Desktop, or Taskbar. Additionally, NAL now includes an administrative tool known as snAppShot. This tool handles the automatic update and synchronization of NT Workstation registry settings, .DLL files, and program files. (Further information on NAL can be found in a Novell research document by Dave Eckert titled *Using the Novell Application Launcher with Windows NT*).

Phase 3: Full Integration with NT

NDS for Windows NT: In this third phase, Novell envisions a world where NDS is accepted as the global directory service for distributed networking. Leading network operating systems like Windows NT and UNIX will embrace NDS for the value it provides in enabling them to manage network resources across the Internet and intranets.

At least for now, Novell has managed to make IBM a believer. NDS for IBM AIX was announced at the beginning of 1997. It remains to be seen whether other converts will follow.

Closing Comments on the Native Transport Protocols

Microsoft and Novell have considered numerous factors in their quest for a common transport. They too have recognized that TCP/IP holds the greatest promise for the future, while IPX/SPX is the best choice for immediate interoperability needs.

That said, our discussion on interoperability isn't about to end. While a common transport protocol is important to communication, it doesn't inherently provide access to the resources of an integrated Windows NT and NetWare network. Neither does it allow for the seamless administration of the same.

In the next two sections of this chapter, we'll examine the products that have been developed by Microsoft and Novell to support clients and administrators of a heterogeneous NT/NetWare environment.

For our clients, these products need to build upon the common transport in delivering a seamless interface between both NOSs. The clients should not be aware that they have switched from one NOS to the other, whether printing a document, downloading a file, or accessing an application.

For our administrators, we need to provide a toolset that integrates the management of accounts and resources between NT and NetWare. The last thing an administrator wants is to support two different networks where every task has to be completed twice: once for the NT users and again for the NetWare users. The fact that the clients may view this as one network is small consolation.

With the requirements in place, we invite you to continue with us as we explore the products designed to enrich NT and NetWare with the promise of seamless management and access to resources.

Novell's Support for Microsoft Windows NT

Novell has often been criticized for moving too slowly in defending against NT's attack on the enterprise network that NetWare 3.*x* had defined and NetWare 4.*x* had extended. From 3.1 to 3.51, Novell did little more than dismiss Windows NT out of hand as an operating system that was less than capable of supporting enterprise networking. The attitude seemed to be, "After all, Microsoft owns the desktop, do they sincerely believe that they can own the network as well?"

Eroding market share, compliments of Windows NT 3.51, helped to answer this rhetorical question. On November 1, 1996, Novell released the Novell NetWare Client for Windows NT.

In the months that followed, we would be bombarded by a bevy of products designed to simultaneously provide NT clients access to NetWare networks while blocking access to NT Server networks. The logic was that

Novell would recognize Windows NT as a viable desktop operating system, one that would compliment their NetWare networks. Making a business case for supporting NT Workstation in a NetWare network, Novell had no intention of releasing software that would support NT Workstation in a NT Server network.

This concept can best be understood by continuing with our discussion on the products that comprise Novell's support for Microsoft Windows NT.

Novell IntranetWare Client for Windows NT

Novell came to realize that some of its market share was being lost to businesses that were deploying NT Server domains for the sole purpose of supporting NT Workstation. Within the domain model, businesses were able to centrally manage NT Workstation accounts. This was a much more attractive approach than the distributed management model that would result by deploying NT Workstation as standalone units or in a workgroup.

Novell responded to this situation by releasing the Novell IntranetWare Client for Windows NT. This client supports NT Workstation authentication to an IntranetWare network. It is designed to replace Client Services for NetWare (CSNW), which comes packaged with NT Workstation. (CSNW only supports authentication to bindery-based NetWare servers, i.e. NetWare 3.*x*.)

Businesses choosing to deploy Windows NT Workstation with the Novell IntranetWare Client for Windows NT would now have the option of authenticating to NDS, eliminating the need for NT domains and essentially for NT Server. NDS authentication meant that the user would have full access to all IntranetWare services, including Novell login script execution, multiprotocol support, security, file, print, and messaging services.

The Novell IntranetWare Client for Windows NT also supports *some* benefits of NT domain authentication. This includes the ability to store user profiles on the network, rather than on the local NT Workstation.

User profiles specify a desktop configuration associated with the user authenticating at the NT Workstation. For instance, a profile may define the type of wallpaper, screen saver, and color scheme that a user will see.

The Novell IntranetWare Client for Windows NT is certainly attractive if our only purpose in moving to NT Server was to support NT Workstation. However, not all of us are in this situation. Many still want to run a mixed environment of NetWare and NT servers. Recognizing this, Novell designed the Novell IntranetWare Client for Windows NT to support simultaneous authentication to a Windows NT domain or local workstation, as well as to NDS.

The purpose for this was to provide the users of NT Workstation, in an integrated NetWare/NT environment, with an integrated security model that allows them to employ all of the tools associated with NT Workstation, such as Explorer, My Computer, and Network Neighborhood. Figure 6.9 shows the integrated login screen for the Novell IntranetWare Client for Windows NT.

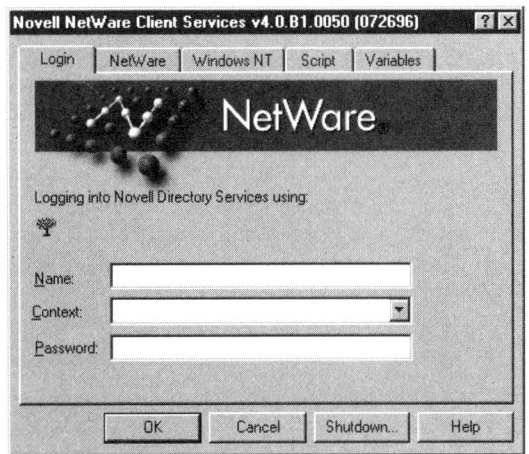

FIGURE 6.9

Integrated NDS and NT authentication through the Novell IntranetWare Client for Windows NT

Let's summarize the authentication options available through the Novell IntranetWare Client for Windows NT:

- NDS authentication with support for NT Workstation profiles
- Windows NT Domain authentication
- Windows NT Workstation local authentication
- NDS and Windows NT Domain integrated authentication
- NDS and Windows NT Workstation integrated authentication

This type of flexibility probably leaves us feeling more confused than relieved. With so many options available, how do we know which is best? For this answer we refer you back to Chapter 1, where we discussed the importance of considering the philosophy of a company before implementing networking technologies. That said, we need to ask ourselves, "Although the IntranetWare Client for Windows NT supports NT Domain authentication, is it truly in line with their philosophy of promoting IntranetWare as the premier network operating environment?"

Anticipating a resounding "No," we can eliminate any of the options that have the word *Domain* associated with them. This reveals Novell's true plan for the IntranetWare Client for Windows NT, namely to support NDS authentication of clients using NT Workstations.

Match the Client Software to the Authenticating NOS

Whether the client software is NT Workstation or Windows 95, we always recommend that it be associated with the backbone network operating system.

In other words, if IntranetWare has been selected as the backbone NOS, then IntranetWare clients should be used for all of the workstations (IntranetWare Client for Windows NT and Client32 for Windows 95 respectively).

If Microsoft Windows NT Server has been selected as the backbone NOS, then Microsoft clients should be used for all workstations (Client for Microsoft Networks). Following this tip will save a lot of trouble as the network is expanded with additional services. Consider these examples of centralized, desktop-administration services as testimony:

- Microsoft Systems Management Server will only recognize workstations running the Client for Microsoft Networks client software. Workstations configured for Novell's IntranetWare Client for Windows NT or Client32 for Windows 95 are not supported.

- The Novell Application Launcher leverages NDS in the creation of application objects built to service the users of the network. Workstations configured for Novell's IntranetWare Client for Windows NT or Client32 for Windows 95 are fully supported. There is no provision for the Client for Microsoft Networks as a replacement.

Our entire conversation so far has focused on supporting our user community with seamless authentication to a heterogeneous network, comprised of Windows NT Workstations on an IntranetWare network. While this is great news for users of the network, we need to consider the administrative implications of this design:

- A user must have an established account on an NT Workstation in order to log into that workstation. This account information is stored in the local SAM database. This means that the user must log into the NT Workstation as well as the IntranetWare network.

- Recognizing that a local account needs to exist on each NT Workstation is only half the battle. Getting that account there is the real problem. This essentially requires that a trip be made to each NT Workstation, so the administrator can add the accounts of all individuals that might use that workstation to the local SAM database.

- What about roaming users? These individuals would require an account on any NT Workstation they might access.

- Eliminating domains also eliminates the ability to establish system policies for NT Workstation. Policies provide a measure of security and standardization to the NT Workstation. Removal of the RUN command and hiding Network Neighborhood are examples of policies that are beneficial to an administrator responsible for NT Workstations.

After considering all of these administrative issues, the idea of establishing NT Workstations and Novell IntranetWare doesn't seem like such a great idea. This reinforces our earlier point that the use and administration of the network needs to be thought over before any decisions on integration are made.

Novell realized it needed to provide the same services to NT Workstation users authenticating to NDS, as the users have when authenticating to NT domains—in particular, policy support. They also recognized that a means of integrating user account creation with NDS and the local SAM database would be a requirement before anyone would embrace the idea of NT Workstations running on an IntranetWare network.

Novell Workstation Manager

The Novell Workstation Manager provides for the centralized management of all user account information for both Windows NT and NDS. It was developed to extend the benefit of the IntranetWare Client for Windows NT (by supporting Windows NT policies) and of integrated account creation for NT Workstation and NDS.

The Novell Workstation Graphical Identification and Authentication (NWGINA) module is the heart of this product. Built as part of the IntranetWare Client for Windows NT, NWGINA runs in the context of administrator at the local NT Workstation. In this mode it can dynamically create and delete NT user accounts, using the information entered at the login screen. (Please refer back to Figure 6.9 for a view of this interface.)

It is NWGINA that eliminates the need for the administrator to manually enter user accounts into the local SAM database for every NT Workstation on the network. To accomplish this it needs to work cooperatively with NDS to obtain the proper user name, NT group memberships, and profile and policy information. Let's examine this process in more detail.

The Novell Workstation Manager is actually composed of two parts; the first, NWGINA, has already been mentioned. The second, a snap-in Dynamic Link Library (DLL), attaches into the 32-bit version of the NetWare administrator (NWAdmin). For additional information on installing these components we suggest that you obtain a copy of the Novell Application Note *Installing the NWAdmin Plug-Ins for Windows NT Workstations and Servers* (April 1997), available from Novell Press.

Once the installation is complete, the administrator will have the ability to create NT Configuration (NTC) objects within NDS. NTCs hold the information that NWGINA looks for during authentication. The fundamental concept is as follows:

- The network administrator will create an NTC object with the appropriate profile, policy, login script parameters, and group membership information. The total number of NTC objects that the administrator will need to create depends on the number of unique NT Workstation configurations that are desired. In our experience, we create a minimum of two NTC objects: one for the administrator, and the other for all general NT Workstation users.

- NDS accounts are then associated with the NTC object. Users, Groups, or Containers are all valid NDS objects that may be associated with the NTC object.

- When a user authenticates to NDS through the IntranetWare Client for Windows NT, NWGINA checks the account to determine whether an association exists with an NTC object as an individual, through group membership, or as part of a container.

- Once NWGINA locates the associated NTC object, it will retrieve the configuration information for use in creating an NT user account in the local NT Workstation's SAM database.

The result is that the administrator only needs to create the user account once, in NDS. NWGINA and the Novell Workstation Manager take care of the local account creation and the application of the appropriate profile and policy information.

The NT Configuration Object

In the remainder of this section we will explore the interior of an NT Configuration object. Each of the tabs will be examined in detail in terms of their purpose and support for NT functions that might otherwise only be available through domain authentication.

The Identification Tab This tab allows you to uniquely name and describe the NTC you are creating. From this tab you also have the ability to disable the authentication of the NT Workstation should the network become unavailable.

The Associations Tab It is through this tab that you achieve centralized management of NT Workstation users. Users will gain an association with the NTC either as an individual, a group member, or affiliation with a container. It is worth noting that NWGINA will check for this association in the order just described. Figure 6.10 shows the Associations tab.

The Dynamic Local User Tab The use of this tab is dependent on whether the user has a pre-existing NT account on the NT Workstation they are authenticating from. If so, then the Enable Dynamic Local User box can be left unchecked. Doing so will allow NWGINA to query the local SAM database for the user account information, using those credentials for authentication.

If this box is checked (as is the case in Figure 6.11), then NWGINA would begin the authentication process by checking the local SAM database for the user account information. Not finding it, NWGINA would create the user account. The credentials associated with this NT account would be the same as those that exist for the NDS account (accomplished by checking the Use IntranetWare Credentials box). Otherwise the administrator will uncheck the box and enter the NT Username, Full Name, and Description manually.

202 Chapter 6 · Incorporating Windows NT into the Enterprise Network

FIGURE 6.10

The Associations tab

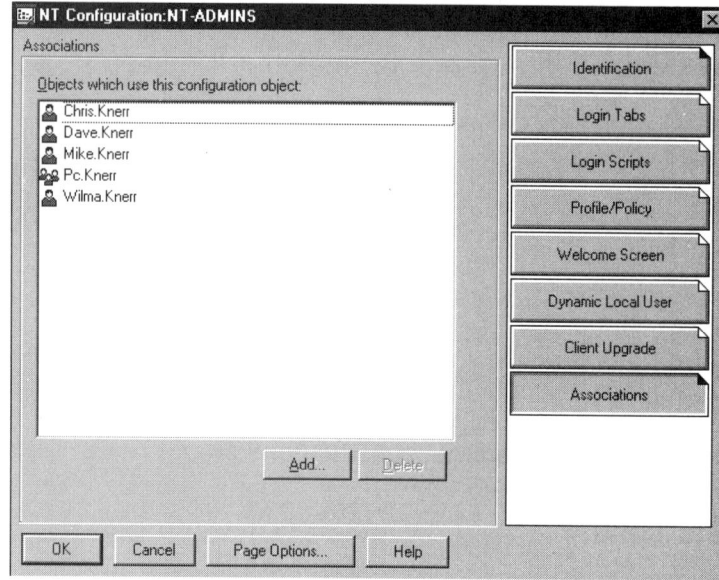

FIGURE 6.11

The Dynamic Local User tab

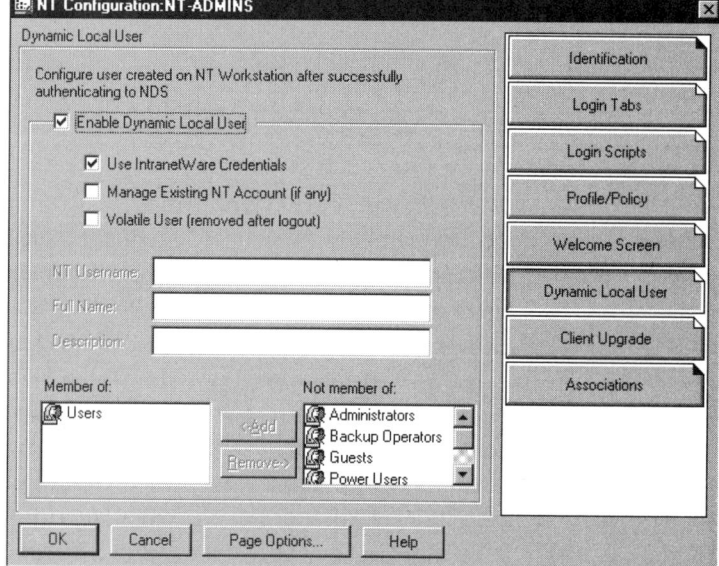

Enabling Manage Existing NT Account (if any) will allow NWGINA to overwrite existing NT Account information contained in the local SAM database, with the information contained in the NTC object.

User accounts created by NWGINA can be either volatile or nonvolatile, depending on whether the Volatile User (removed after logout) is checked. Volatile user accounts will be deleted by NWGINA as a preventive measure to avoid cluttering the local SAM database with *one-time* only users, and as an additional security provision. On the other hand, accounts that are created utilizing IntranetWare credentials have the option of becoming nonvolatile. A user with a nonvolatile account can access the NT Workstation regardless of whether the network is available.

When NWGINA creates the NT Workstation account, it can also add the user to any of the default NT user groups. The account will be added to Users by default, but membership is possible in other groups, such as Administrators, Backup Operators, and Power Users.

The Profile/Policy Tab Figure 6.12 shows a view of the Profile/Policy tab. This tab provides support for features that were previously available only through domain authentication. It is a major coup for Novell to support these in an NDS environment.

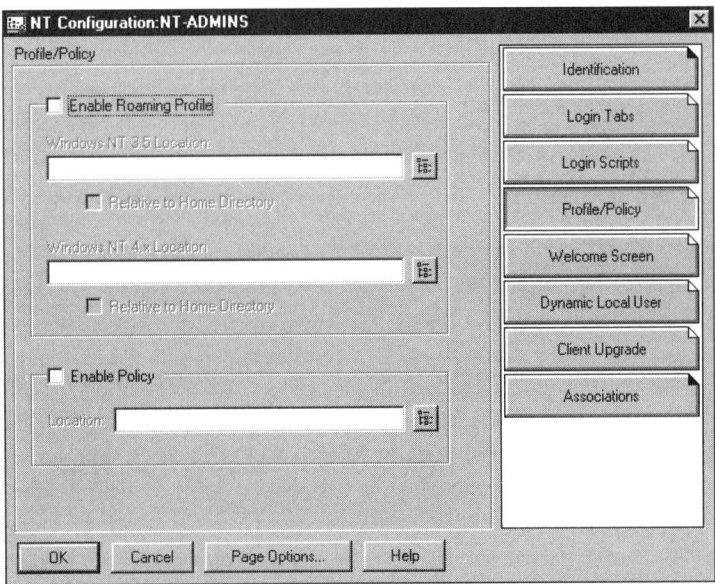

FIGURE 6.12

The Profile/Policy tab

Enable Roaming Profile allows the personalized profile of the user to be stored on the network. This profile contains user preferences for wallpaper, cursors, color schemes, and shortcuts. Different preferences are available, depending on whether the user is attaching through an NT Workstation 3.51 or NT Workstation 4. This is the reason why two separate network locations are provided.

The check box titled Relative to Home Directory allows us to keep the NTC object generic and the profile personalized by establishing a pointer to the user account home directory for retrieval of the profile information. Otherwise, we can establish the equivalent of a mandatory profile by unchecking this option and hard coding the name of a common profile into the location field.

NT system policies are also supported through this tab. NWGINA will search for the \\<preferred server>\SYS\PUBLIC\WINNT\NTCONFIG.POL file, using it as the default during the authentication process. Administrators who wish to modify this policy or create their own will need to have access to the Microsoft System Policy Editor that comes bundled with Windows NT. Once a satisfactory policy is created, the administrator can then reference it through the Policy Location field of the Profile/Policy tab.

The Login Tabs Tab NWGINA will display different tabs to support various login and configuration options during the authentication process. Most administrators find that it is not necessary to display all login tab options to their users. Prior to Novell Workstation Manager, this required that the administrator make a trip to each Windows NT Workstation for individual customization of the NWGINA login tabs.

The Login Tabs tab now centralizes this process, allowing administrators to predefine which login tabs will be displayed. Their choice is made by enabling or disabling check boxes that appear in the Login Tabs tab.

The Login Scripts Tab The Login Scripts tab controls the login script processing at the NT Workstation. Unless the Enable Login Scripts box is checked, no login script processing occurs. However, once checked, all other fields become important.

Alt. Login Script and Alt. Profile Script allow for the execution of alternatives to the scripts associated with the NDS user object. Please note that the term *profile* refers to a common set of login script commands affiliated with the NDS Profile Object. It has no relationship to Windows NT user profiles.

Login Script Variables offer the ability to customize login scripts for particular users or groups. Up to four unique variables can be centrally administered through NDS, and they will be parsed to the NWGINA variables tab. Their values can be set in the Login Script Variables page.

The Welcome Screen Tab   The initial screen displayed by NWGINA is known as the Welcome Screen. The Welcome Screen tab allows the administrator the option of changing the bitmap image displayed. An alternative title message can also be entered, replacing the default `Begin Login`.

The Client Upgrade Tab   This tab provides support for the automatic upgrade of the IntranetWare Client for Windows NT Workstation. The process begins with the administrator creating an alternate login script, one that includes the setup commands for the new software. The simplest login script might contain just one line, `SETUPNW /U[\\<preferred server>\path\filename]`, where the `filename` is the unattended file that will assist in the installation.

This login script is then saved to a location that is identified in the Alternate Login Script Location field. All that is left is for the administrator to check the box labeled Enable Automatic Client Upgrade. Please refer to Figure 6.13 as we continue our explanation of the Client Upgrade tab.

FIGURE 6.13

The Client Upgrade tab

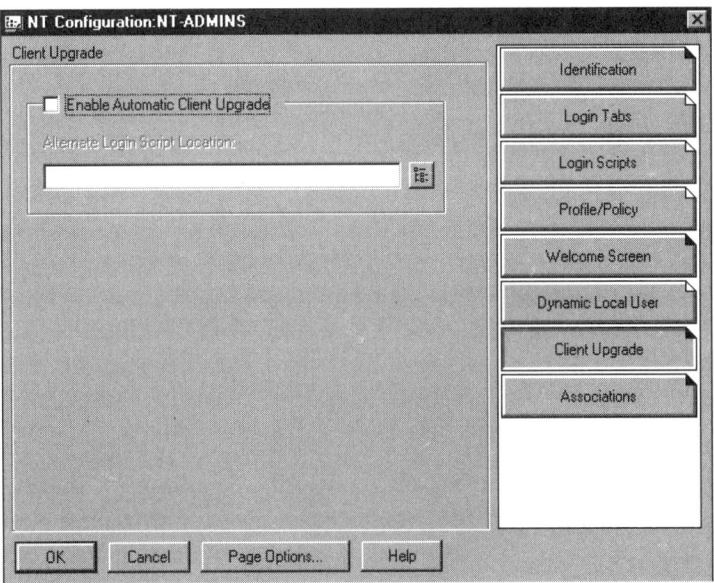

As part of the authentication process, NWGINA checks the time/date stamp of the NTC object to see if it is different from the last time it was used. If so, then NWGINA will continue further by checking the Client Upgrade tab to see if a software upgrade is in order. NWGINA will then refer to the location specified in the Login Script Location field and begin execution of this client upgrade login script.

Checking the Enable Automatic Client Upgrade box is usually enough to cause the time/date stamp to be updated, triggering NWGINA into upgrade mode. Nevertheless, if it appears that the upgrade is not occurring and you have already checked and rechecked your login script, you may want to alter some other field in the NTC object. Even if you change it back to its original state, you will have most certainly caused the NTC object to update its time/date stamp. Doing so will allow the client upgrade process to occur as expected.

The Novell IntranetWare Client for NT Workstation complimented by Novell Workstation Manager provides a solid foundation for those businesses that wish to deploy NT Workstations within an IntranetWare environment, yet don't want to deal with NT domains. Not wanting to deal with domains doesn't necessarily mean we don't want to deal with NT Servers. If at all possible, we would like to allow NT Servers into our IntranetWare network—but manage them from within NDS. Only recently, Novell has made this possible through the Novell Administrator for Windows NT.

The Novell Administrator for Windows NT

Keeping with Novell's NT integration strategy, Novell Administrator for Windows NT (NAdminNT) was released in the middle of 1997 as a tool to help reduce the redundancy associated with administering an NDS/NT domain environment.

NAdminNT uses replication as the technique for synchronizing the SAM database of NT with NDS. Links or associations, through which management of common properties can occur, are created between NT users and NDS users. Essentially NAdminNT allows for integrated administration in the following ways:

- **Management of "hybrid" users:** Individuals that have accounts in NDS and the NT domain. Synchronization of common properties will occur between these user accounts.

> **Visine Helps Clear Tabasco Sauce Out of Your Eye**
>
> On the surface Novell and Microsoft were publicly making attempts to integrate with one another. This didn't prevent the developers from having a bit of fun in the back office. File and Print Services for NetWare (FPNW) was part of a Microsoft project code-named *Visine*, as in "get the red out." Not to be out done, *Tabasco*, as in "red hot," was the code name given by Novell development to the Novell Administrator for Windows NT.

- **Management of NT users and groups:** NAdminNT can be used as a tool to replace some of the functions available in the NT User Manager for Domains administrative tool. The creation, deletion, and modification of NT users, global groups, and local groups are all possible once an NT domain has been integrated to NDS.

In the paragraphs that follow we will examine NAdminNT in more detail. Please focus on the concepts and criteria associated with *ongoing* replication between NDS and the NT domain, as you consider the feasibility of this tool in your own network. As with any replication technique, there are limitations on what information can be replicated and extenuating circumstances dictating when it can be replicated. System accessibility, sufficient bandwidth, and database integrity all weigh into the successfulness of this technique. Sufficient time should be allowed for evaluating this product in an Alpha lab environment to be certain that it meets your needs and expectations, before moving it to the production network.

The Building Blocks of NAdminNT

NAdminNT is actually a series of modules that work cooperatively in allowing integrated management of NDS and the NT domain. Figure 6.14 provides a view of how these elements communicate, and a more detailed description follows.

Schema Extension occurs to allow for the additional NT domain objects that will need to exist within NDS. Objects for NT Domains, NT Workgroups, NT Users, NT Local Groups, NT Global Groups, and Hybrid users are all accommodated for during the installation of NAdminNT. It seems fitting that the NWAdmin utility is also modified to provide support to these objects as part of the installation process.

208 Chapter 6 • Incorporating Windows NT into the Enterprise Network

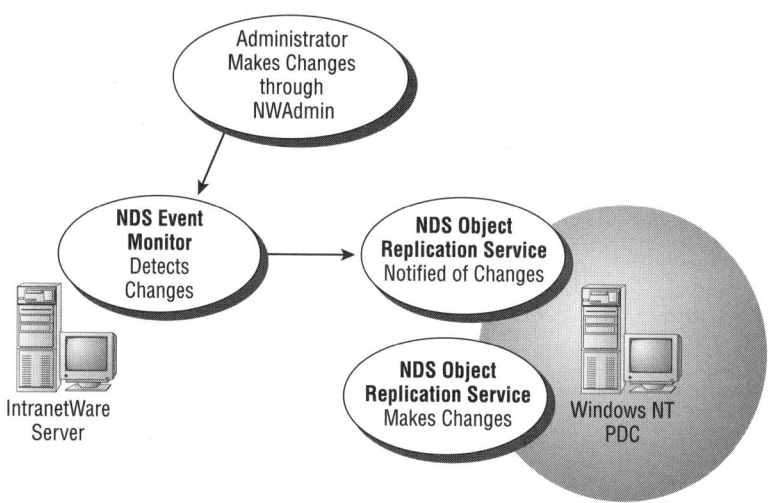

FIGURE 6.14

Novell Administrator for Windows NT components

Schema is a term used to define the objects that can be created, and whose properties can be manipulated within Novell Directory Services.

NDS Event Monitor is an NLM which resides on the IntranetWare server. Its purpose is to track and monitor changes to NDS that need to be replicated to NT. It communicates these changes directly to the NDS Object Replication Service that dwells as a service within NT. The NDS Event Monitor is designed to work with the master copy of the NDS partition that contains the NT objects being monitored. This means that a requirement exists to install the NDS Event Monitor NLM on the same server as that master copy. It is recommended, in addition, that the NLM be installed on any other NetWare servers that contain read/write copies of the master.

NWAdmin allows for the configuration of the synchronization between NDS and NT. The NDS Event Monitor will hold a copy of the changes until the time when the synchronization is scheduled to occur. NDS Event Monitor will also hold pending changes in instances where they are unable to complete due to unavailability of either the network or the NT domain. These changes will be posted once the systems become accessible.

NDS Object Replication Service works cooperatively with the NDS Event Monitor in posting changes to the SAM database. This service needs to exist on the PDC and each BDC for every domain integrated into NDS. On the

PDC, the service should be set to *start automatically*, while on the BDCs it should be *stopped* and left in *manual* mode. The service only really needs to be started on a BDC after it has been promoted to a PDC.

This configuration makes clear what we feel to be one of the shortcomings of this product. *All* changes take place *through the PDC*—the BDCs are *not* part of the process. This means the positioning of the NDS Event Monitor as it communicates with the PDC is an important aspect of designing for NAdminNT. The data communications path between these two devices needs to be investigated to ensure that sufficient bandwidth is available to replicate the changes between NDS and the NT domain.

The replication of NT workgroup-user accounts to Novell Directory Services is even more... how shall we say...*interesting*. We recall that in a workgroup environment, the user accounts database is kept local to each workstation. The end result? If we wish to replicate a workgroup to NDS through NAdminNT, we need to run the NDS Object Replication Service on every machine in the workgroup where user accounts reside!

One final point on workgroups. By default we can determine that Windows 95 workstations are not supported—for two reasons. The first is because *services* do not run on Windows 95 workstations. The second reason can be found in the requirement for the IntranetWare Client for Windows NT. Windows 95 Client32 is not supported.

Steps to Integration

NAdminNT includes the Integration Utility to assist the administrator in integrating existing NT domain users into NDS and vice versa. It is also possible to manually initiate the synchronization process between NDS and the NT domain from this utility. See Figure 6.15 for a look at this utility.

Preparation for Integrating Object Information The process begins with the creation of an NT domain or workgroup container within NDS. In most instances this container was created during the installation of NAdminNT. As part of the installation process, there is an opportunity to install the NDS object replication service on existing NT domains and workgroups. Doing so will result in the creation of an NT object for each within NDS. When placing NT objects within the NDS tree, we recommend that consideration be given to the following:

- A basic tenet of NDS design is to keep the resource objects closest to the users utilizing them. An NT domain or workgroup object is a shared

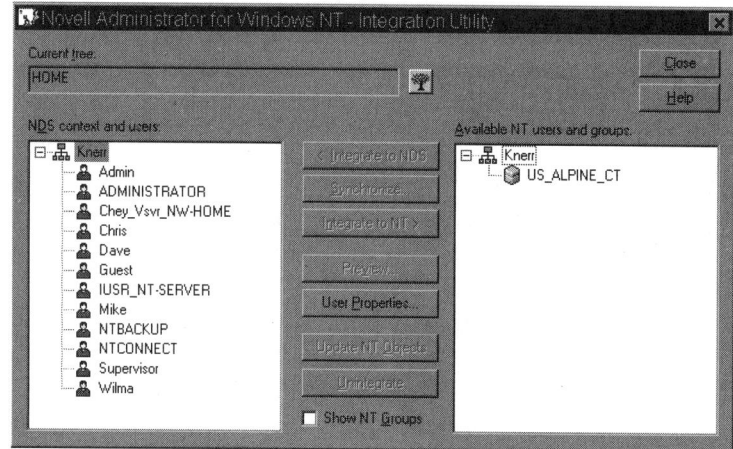

FIGURE 6.15

The Novell Administrator for Windows NT Integration Utility

resource for users of NDS. As such it should be placed in the tree near the greatest population of NDS users that you anticipate will become hybrid users.

- Be aware of the existing number of user and group accounts in the domain—especially due to the fact that each will become an additional object within NDS. Novell recommends that a single partition contain no more than 2,500 NT objects. Separate partitions should be created to service domains that exceed this value. This rule exists in addition to the exclusive NDS rule that states no single partition should contain more than 5,000 objects, after which a separate partition should be created. For example, if by adding a domain of 1,000 NT user accounts to a pre-existing NDS partition, you exceed 5,000 total NDS objects, it is time to create a new partition.

- NAdminNT was designed to support 5,000 total user and group objects per domain. This value should be considered for large NT domain installations when deciding whether to integrate to NDS.

With the NT domain object in place, we continue by uploading information into NDS. This upload process can be viewed as placing the NT objects into a staging area from which they are accessible to NDS, but are not truly part of NDS.

The process for uploading is accomplished by selecting the domain or workgroup from within the integration utility, after which the Update NT Objects button is selected. Figure 6.16 illustrates this process.

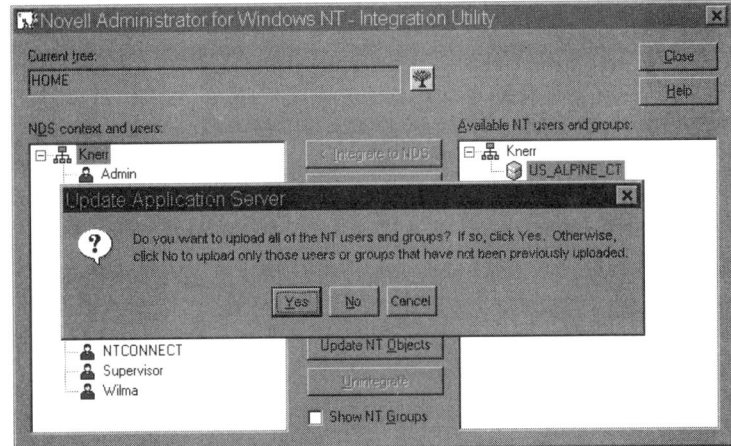

FIGURE 6.16

Updating NT objects from within the Integration Utility

Integrating NT User Accounts to NDS Now that we have a view of our NT domain or workgroup objects, we can continue by extracting the user account information from the SAM database of the domain PDC to NDS. This can be accomplished by:

- Selecting existing NT users from within the Integration Utility
- Choosing a container for the NT user accounts
- Selecting the Integrate to NDS action button

See Figure 6.17 for an integration example.

Integrating NDS User Accounts to NT Alternatively, we can export NDS user objects to the NT domain by:

- Selecting existing NDS users from within the Integration Utility
- Selecting the NT domain or workgroup where the user account information will be copied.
- Selecting the Integrate to NT button

See Figure 6.18 for an example of this procedure.

FIGURE 6.17

Integrating NT user accounts to NDS

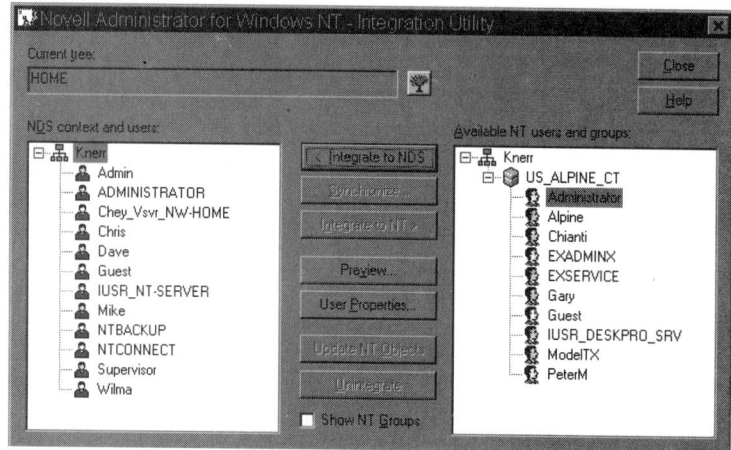

FIGURE 6.18

Integrating NDS user accounts to NT

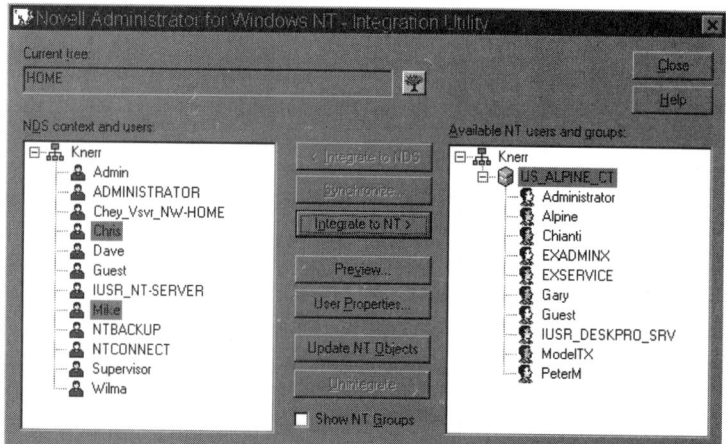

In either the NT to NDS user account integration or the NDS to NT user account integration, we have the option of using a template for the creation of the users. The template provides a form for common properties, default password, etc. These users, which exist within both NT and NDS, are now referred to as hybrid users.

Managing the Integrated Environments Once the Update NT Objects action has taken place, the administrator has the ability to manage the NT objects from within NDS. This is advantageous in that the NWAdmin tool can be used for this purpose, eliminating the need to jump between it and Microsoft's User Manager for Domains. The creation, deletion, and modification of properties for users, global groups, and local groups are all possible from within NWAdmin.

Manual synchronization between an NDS and NT user account can occur at any time, one pair at a time. This is accomplished by selecting the accounts from within NDS and the domain, and selecting the Synchronize action button located inside the Integration Utility. Figure 6.19 illustrates how this might appear.

NDS user account information will overwrite the NT user account information during this synchronization process. For example, if the NT user account conforms to a naming standard that is different from NDS, then *it will be renamed to the NDS standard.* This is something you may wish to notify your users about.

FIGURE 6.19

Manual synchronization of an NDS and an NT user account

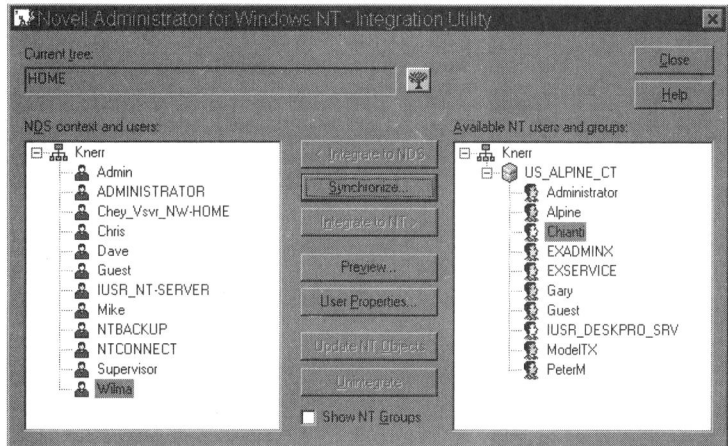

The NAdminNT utility is a first of its genre. The ability to replicate information between the SAM database of NT and NDS is an impressive feat of engineering. Nevertheless, the practicality of deploying this utility is questionable, due in part to its lack of scalability, but even more so when we consider whether it provides enough benefits to make it worth implementing rather than waiting for NDS for NT. We understand that there is always going to be a technology to *wait for*; we just question whether NAdminNT is the technology we were waiting for.

In recognition of your attentiveness to this section on Novell / NT integration products, we offer this brief, opinionated summary: "Use NT Workstation Manager whenever it's possible to, use NAdminNT whenever it's impossible not to."

Microsoft's Support for Novell NetWare

Those with an eye for detail may have noticed that the title of this section references NetWare and not IntranetWare. The reason is that while *IntranetWare* is used exclusively when referencing the current directory services version of Novell's network operating system, *NetWare* is historically associated with bindery-based versions like 3.*x*. We would like to highlight that Microsoft's support for Novell begins and ends at the bindery. Limited support exists for IntranetWare 4.11 and, subsequently, Novell directory services.

If we were to read too deeply into the reasoning for this we might hypothesize that Microsoft wants to win the NOS battle by grabbing Novell customers before they make the switch to IntranetWare 4.11. The time and commitment necessary to craft an NDS tree within IntranetWare is too great to casually throw it away in favor of another operating environment. The goal, therefore, is to turn Novell customers on to Windows NT while they are still in the bindery world of NetWare 3.*x*. It's here that Microsoft's greatest chance for conversion lies. Its integration tools provide the avenue for making that conversion.

Gateway Services for NetWare

Released with Windows NT 3.5, Gateway Services for NetWare (GSNW) provides a means for clients of the Windows NT network to access Novell NetWare servers for file and print services. GSNW accomplishes this by establishing a share to a NetWare file server directory or NetWare print queue. To access the NetWare server, clients of the Windows NT network then attach to the share point of the Windows NT GSNW server. NetWare 2.*x*, 3.*x*, and 4.*x* (in bindery emulation) servers are supported. Figure 6.20 provides a view of GSNW and the share points it has established.

Microsoft's Support for Novell NetWare 215

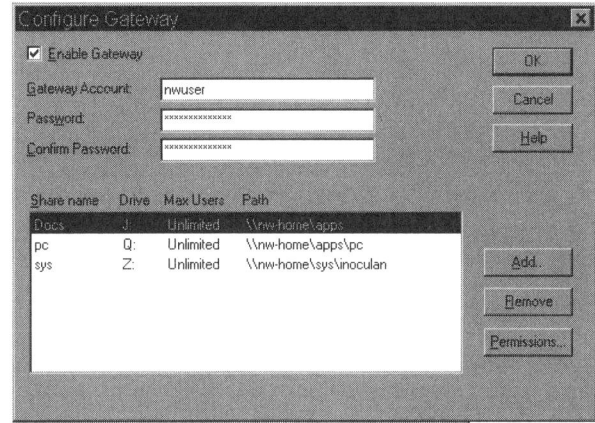

FIGURE 6.20

Microsoft Gateway Services for NetWare

GSNW functions by translating the Server Message Block (SMB) calls of Windows NT to NetWare Core Protocol (NCPs) calls recognized by NetWare servers. Figure 6.21 illustrates this process.

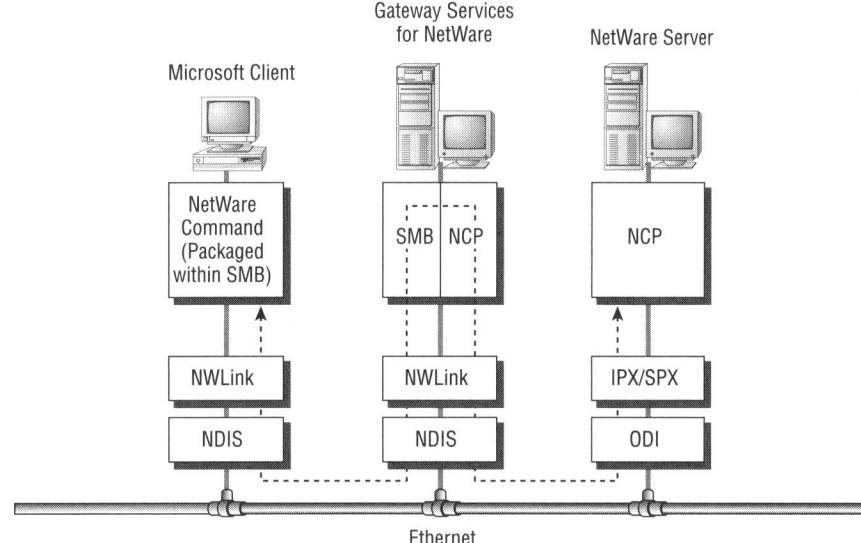

FIGURE 6.21

An internal protocol view of Gateway Services for NetWare

The following description of the protocol translation and gateway processes sheds some light on Figure 6.21:

- In essence, the NT client will issue a request for NetWare services by connecting to the GSNW server using its redirector (workstation service). What it is actually connecting to is a share on the GSNW server that maps to a NetWare directory or print queue. This request will be packaged in an SMB frame for interpretation by the GSNW server.

- Recognizing that the request is for a NetWare server, the GSNW service will repackage the client request into an NCP frame and deliver it to the NetWare server. This is accomplished by utilizing the NWLink transport protocol to establish a channel to the NetWare server. Permission to establish this channel is granted by the NetWare administrator, who creates a GSNW user account with the proper permissions to select NetWare directories and print queues. A NetWare group called NTGATEWAY, of which the GSNW user account is a required member, must also be created. Additional access permissions may be applied to the NTGATEWAY group.

- The NetWare server will fulfill the request, utilizing the established GSNW channel to issue the response. The response will be packaged within an NCP frame that reaches the GSNW server, where it is converted to an SMB frame before it is passed onto the Windows NT network.

- The Windows NT client will take in the SMB frame on it's Server (server service), completing the transaction.

Most of the standard NetWare utilities, such as MAP, SYSCON, NDIR, and RCONSOLE can be executed through GSNW in addition to standard file and print access. Consideration should be given to the fact that these NetWare services are being provided through a gateway, and as such, performance will not be comparable to what it would be if they were being provided directly.

File and Print Services for NetWare

File and Print Services for NetWare (FPNW) was released shortly after Windows NT 3.51. By enabling the FPNW server to interpret SMB as well as NCP requests, it takes Microsoft one step closer to supporting Novell's NCP. In essence, the FPNW server appears as both a Microsoft Windows NT and Novell NetWare 3.*x* file server. (Figure 6.22 provides a view of the FPNW internal architecture.) While FPNW on NT is not a true NetWare file server (using it, we cannot load NLMs), it does offer some benefits to us, as we shall see.

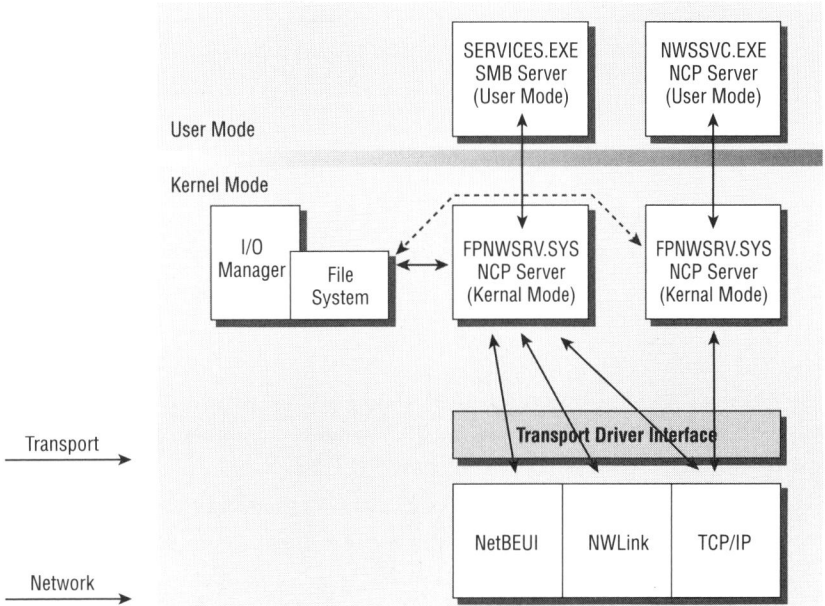

FIGURE 6.22

The internal architecture of File and Print Services for NetWare

Since the release of FPNW, Novell has always said that it closely emulates a NetWare 2.x file server—not 3.x, as Microsoft claims. They qualify this based on the less-than-optimal performance that FPNW provides to NetWare clients when compared to a native NetWare 3.x file server.

FPNW requires the installation of GSNW and NWLink. GSNW provides the Service Advertising Protocol (SAP), which Novell uses to advertise availability of its file servers. Therefore it seems appropriate that FPNW utilizes SAP to advertise itself as a NetWare server. NWLink is installed to provide the IPX/SPX transport that FPNW will use in communicating with the NetWare clients. Both GSNW and NWLink set the stage for the FPNW installation.

As part of the installation process we are required to choose a location for the emulated NetWare SYS: volume. We will also need to select a name for our emulated NetWare server. This is where we defer back to our naming standards. Often we will take the current Windows NT server name and overwrite our functional descriptor area with an -FPNW extension. For example, CDMP-DNW01 will become CDMP-FPNW01.

You'll notice that we used the example of a domain controller (by virtue of the P for PDC), for installation of FPNW. This is a requirement, since it is the location of the SAM database, and thereby the central point of authentication for the domain. Pondering this a bit more, we realize that BDCs also provide authentication services, and for this reason, installation of FPNW on these domain controllers would be required as well. It doesn't matter whether the client is native to NetWare or Windows. All authentication in a domain occurs through the domain controllers and, therefore, it is a requirement that FPNW be installed on them.

Thus far, we have installed FPNW on our PDC, and on each of the BDCs that provide authentication services. We're not done yet, because unless our domain controllers also provide file and print services, we'll need to locate all Windows NT member servers in our Microsoft network that we would want to access with a NetWare client. On these servers we will need to install—you guessed it—FPNW.

Once FPNW is fully integrated within the Windows NT domain, we can go about configuring our user accounts to access these servers as if they were natively NetWare.

In our experience, we've found FPNW to be quite useful when migrating an enterprise from Novell NetWare to Microsoft Windows NT. The two following scenarios generally describe our process, which is taken from the methodology discussed in Chapter 3.

FPNW Used to Duplicate the Novell NetWare Environment on Windows NT

The conversion of the client workstations is often the most challenging aspect of a migration. With FPNW, we have the ability to slowly migrate the user population over to NT, leaving the conversion of the client workstations to later. Essentially, we attempt to duplicate the existing Novell NetWare environment utilizing FPNW on Windows NT. The clients remain as they are while the back office conversion takes place. Once it is completed, all clients will be authenticating to the FPNW NT environment as if it were a native Novell NetWare environment. File, print, and application services are provided with the Microsoft network as they were within the Novell network. For this reason, the Novell network is no longer necessary.

At this point we can strategically go to each client under a plan designed to provide them with a new desktop (hardware and software as appropriate) and native Windows NT authentication. Once all clients are converted, we disable FPNW.

It's important to realize that we move quickly once all clients are authenticating to FPNW upon Windows NT. Let there be no doubt, there is an associated overhead that comes with FPNW. For this reason, we tend to oversize the hardware platforms that are going to support this service. We also strive to migrate the clients quickly so that they are authenticating natively to Windows NT as soon as possible. For reasons of having to oversize the hardware platform and the associated overhead that comes through FPNW authentication, we take this approach to migration only in instances where the customer has not yet determined a new workstation configuration, yet has determined an immediate need to upgrade the network operating system.

FPNW Used to Support Common Applications and Shared Data for NetWare and NT Clients

More often we use FPNW in NetWare to NT migrations to support those applications that are common to all users, as well as data shared by all users. These are the types of applications and shared data stores that cannot be migrated to the new Microsoft Windows NT network until all users have migrated to that environment. These are the applications and data that need to be accessible throughout the migration phase by both the NT and NetWare clients. These are the applications and data that can drive you out of your mind during a migration.

We deal with this situation by taking the common applications and shared data and placing them on an FPNW NT server during the first weekend of the migration. In this location they will be available to the existing NetWare clients as well as the smaller population of migrating clients authenticating to NT. As the migration continues, more and more clients will authenticate natively to Windows NT. Once all clients have been migrated, FPNW is no longer required.

This approach assumes that a new workstation configuration has been selected and that it is being deployed at the same time that the client is changing their network services from Novell NetWare to Microsoft Windows NT. This approach also requires that the user accounts exist in two locations: on the Microsoft network as well as on the Novell network. This is required because clients that are authenticating natively to NetWare will need to also authenticate to Windows NT for access to the common applications and shared data on the FPNW server. Usually this is not too much of an issue, since the accounts would have been created within NT anyway, once the user had migrated. In this scenario the account is created earlier, before they fully migrate to NT, so that they can gain access to the common applications and shared data on the FPNW server. This approach puts the least dependency on FPNW, utilizing it as we feel is appropriate—selectively and for migration purposes only.

Directory Services Manager for NetWare

In the previous scenario (*FPNW Used to Support Common Applications and Shared Data for NetWare and NT Clients*), we mentioned that duplicate accounts would have to exist within the Microsoft and Novell network during the migration process. Directory Services Manager for NetWare (DSMN) was released by Microsoft at the same time as FPNW to assist with the management of these duplicate accounts.

DSMN accomplishes this by synchronizing the Windows NT user and group account information with the NetWare server user and group account information. Essentially, the SAM database of Windows NT is synchronized with the bindery account database of one or more NetWare servers. Figure 6.23 depicts this synchronization.

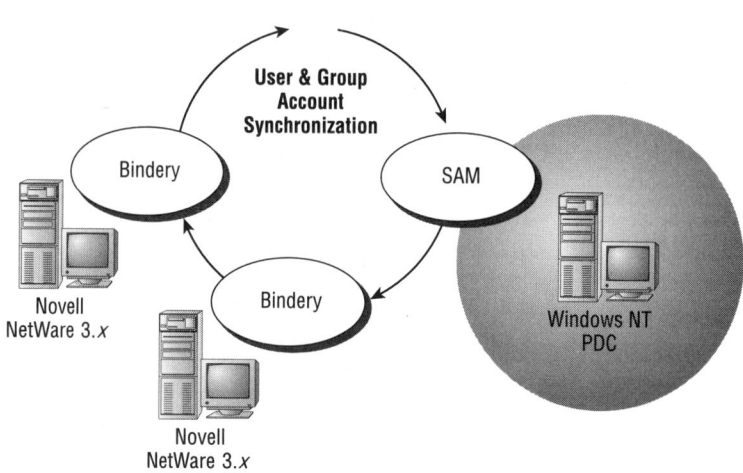

FIGURE 6.23

Directory Services Manager for NetWare synchronization

While DSMN does not require FPNW, it is most often used with that product. What DSMN does require is GSNW and, subsequently, NWLink. NWLink provides the transport that GSNW uses to create a channel to the NetWare server. DSMN will then use this channel to establish a connection to the NetWare server. Its connection is authenticated by the NetWare server using the Winnt_Sync_Agent account whose password is synchronized with the Sync Agent Account in the Windows NT domain. Through these accounts and over the GSNW channel, DSMN will synchronize user and group account information between Novell NetWare and Microsoft Windows NT.

Microsoft's Gateway Services for NetWare, File and Print Services for NetWare, and Directory Services Manager for NetWare are tools designed to allow interoperation and the staging of a migration from Novell NetWare to Microsoft Windows NT. Effective in their own right, they were designed for the bindery world of NetWare 3.*x*. This is a contrast to the Novell toolset, which includes Novell's IntranetWare Client for Windows NT, Novell Workstation Manager, and Novell Administrator for Windows NT, all of which were designed to integrate NT with the directory services world of IntranetWare. If you find yourself not too surprised by any of this then we invite you to continue on. Otherwise, if you are asking, "Why the contrast?" then we suggest you return to Chapter 1 for a refresher on corporate philosophy and its effects on network operating system development.

Integrating and interoperating with Novell NetWare was critical to the success of Microsoft Windows NT. This leading network operating system brought with it a large audience of which all were exposed and many were converted to the Windows NT sect. Yet while Novell NetWare was the leading network operating system, it certainly wasn't the only one. In the next four chapters, we'll discuss the products and technologies that will enable you to integrate your Windows NT systems with a wide variety of other operating systems.

PART III

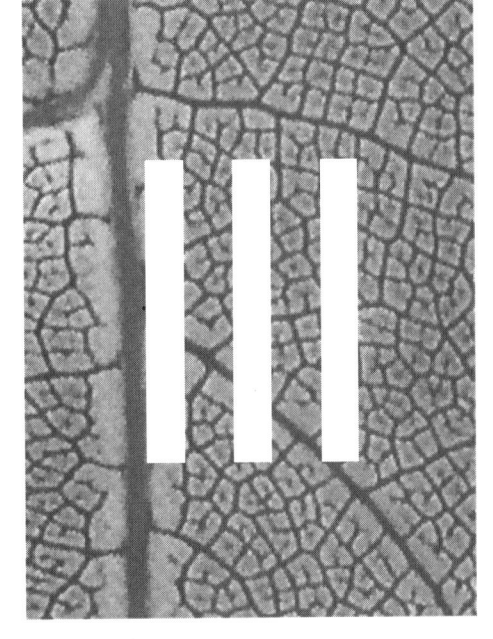

NT AS A NET PLATFORM

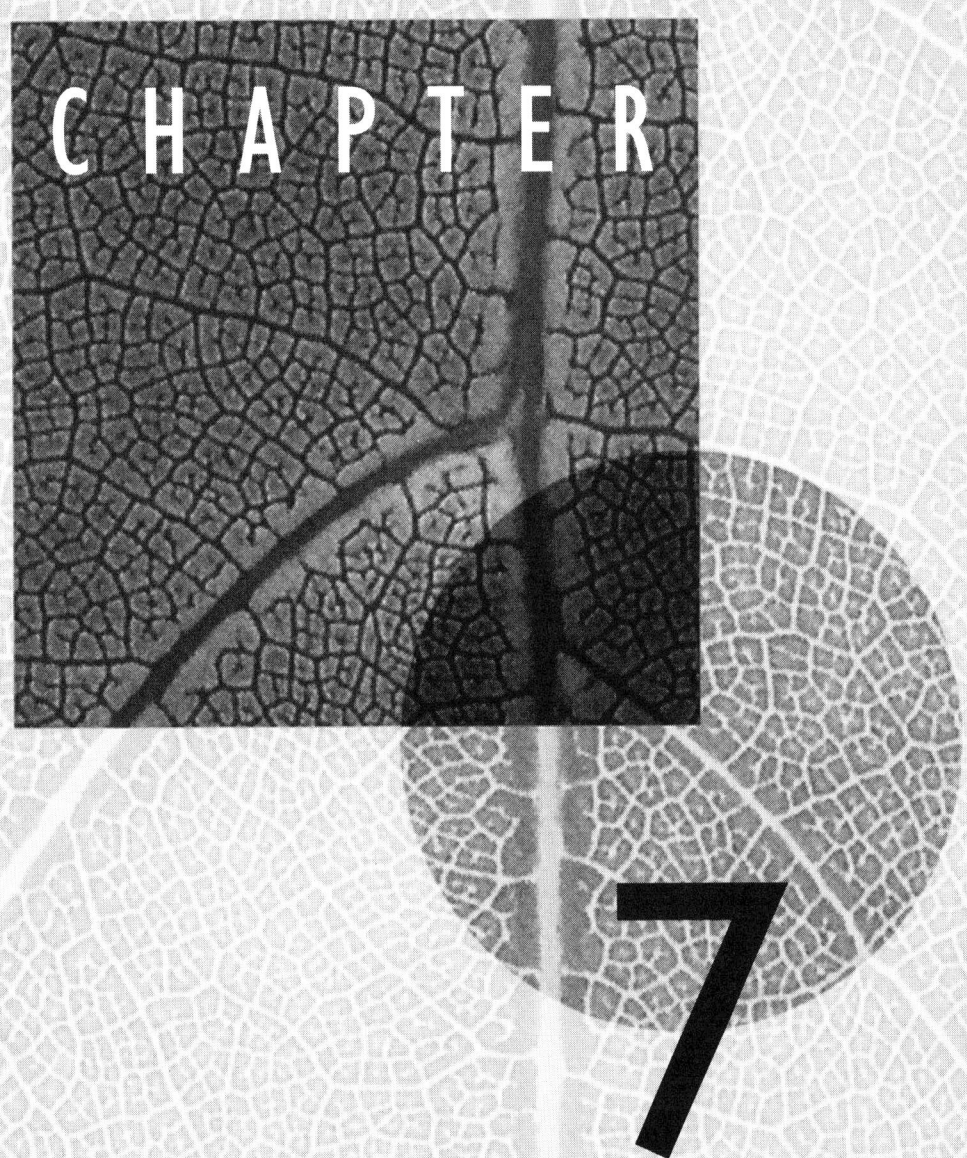

CHAPTER 7

Introduction to Net Concepts and Services

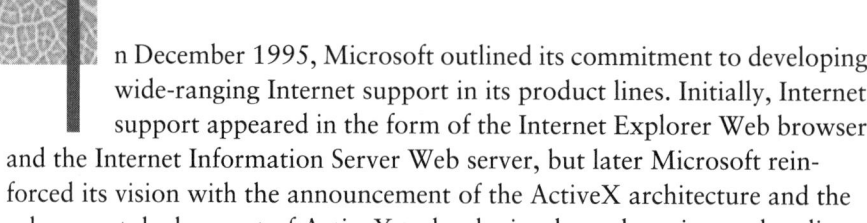In December 1995, Microsoft outlined its commitment to developing wide-ranging Internet support in its product lines. Initially, Internet support appeared in the form of the Internet Explorer Web browser and the Internet Information Server Web server, but later Microsoft reinforced its vision with the announcement of the ActiveX architecture and the subsequent deployment of ActiveX technologies throughout its product line.

Windows NT Server, with its robust kernel and inviting graphical interface, emerged as the foundation of Microsoft's Internet server product line. With the introduction of the Internet Information Server, Webmasters and Web developers had a viable alternative to UNIX-based, configuration-file-driven Web servers. Soon after, Microsoft and many other software developers began to release additional Internet server products for NT. As the technologies matured and feature sets expanded, Microsoft NT became the platform of choice for IT professionals who were new to Web-based technologies.

This chapter provides an introduction to concepts related to the Internet, intranets, and extranets (we'll use the term Net for short, because the fundamental technologies of the Internet, intranets, and extranets are identical). In this chapter, we'll discuss the following topics:

- Similarities and differences between the Internet, intranets, and extranets
- Core Net services such as HTTP, DNS, FTP, and SMTP
- Net security concepts and issues
- Proxy servers, firewalls, and virtual private networks
- Net server design issues

Crucial Net Definitions

Before we turn our spotlight on individual NT Net server applications, such as the Microsoft Internet Information Server, let's begin with a detailed description of the core concepts and issues upon which those applications are based.

Net services, like HTTP or FTP, represent a radical departure from vendor-specific services, such as Novell NetWare file sharing, because they are based upon protocols whose specifications have been made publicly available.

Because the details of these services are in the public domain, anyone can develop software that operates according to the specifications, and one vendor's implementation of a protocol can communicate with another vendor's implementation. The term *open standards* is frequently used to describe protocols based on these publicly available specifications.

Open-standards-based application servers, like Web servers, owe a large part of their popularity to their ability to allow users of any type of computer system to access information on any server computer, regardless of the operating system the server happened to be running. For example, a Macintosh user could access a Web page from a UNIX server because both computers were using an agreed-upon common protocol based on an open standard.

Now we'll trace the evolution of open standards-based applications from their beginnings on the global Internet, through their introduction into corporate intranets and multicorporate extranets.

Internet: The Network to the World

Open standards first became popular on the global Internet, the origins of which can be traced back to the late 1960s. The earliest form of what would later be called the Internet was developed by the U.S. Department of Defense (DOD) as an experimental network that would expedite communication between government agencies, the military, universities, and other research institutions.

The goal of the organization chartered to build the Internet, the Defense Advanced Research Projects Agency (DARPA), was to create a network that would be sufficiently fault-tolerant to withstand a major catastrophe, such as a natural disaster or an act of war. Key components of the network, or ARPAnet as it was known at the time, were designed with the ability to route network traffic around heavily congested or out-of-service links.

In order to facilitate communication between the dissimilar types of computers that were located within the various government offices, the founders of the Internet developed a vendor-neutral family of protocols, which would come to be known as the *TCP/IP protocol suite*. The protocols which comprised the TCP/IP suite were the first truly open protocols, and were based on published standards documents called Requests for Comments (RFCs).

ARPAnet later graduated from experimental status and was given the name Internet to reflect its role as the network that connected networks throughout the world. Implementations of the TCP/IP protocols quickly became available for virtually all computer platforms, and the popularity of the Internet began to grow. However, since a number of the protocols were originally developed for UNIX systems, many users found it cumbersome to use command-line utilities in order to locate information stored on the thousands of connected computers.

In the early 1990s, thanks to an easing of restrictions on commercial traffic and the development of the protocols that would make up the World Wide Web (WWW), use of the Internet skyrocketed. Web protocols, such as Hypertext Transfer Protocol (HTTP) and Hypertext Markup Language (HTML) made it simple for anyone to navigate through the volumes of information available on the Internet using a graphical browser-based interface. Suddenly anyone who could use a mouse had the ability to jump from information resource to information resource to locate the information they wished to retrieve.

Intranets: Leveraging the Technology of the Web

As users and developers began to recognize the tremendous data publishing and communication benefits made possible by the Web, many began to apply Web technology to improve communication not only to the general public over the Internet, but also to improve communication within their organizations to their coworkers. These private, internal, corporate Webs, called *intranets*, contained corporate information not meant to be viewed by anyone outside of the corporation.

Intranets became wildly popular for a number of reasons. Not only did they provide an ideal medium to replace expensive and wasteful information distribution practices such as the quarterly printing of the corporate telephone directory, intranets could be easily set up by the average computer user. Only later did many organizations realize that intranet Web servers had the ability to grow like weeds. Building an intranet was easy; managing one was not.

The intranet movement came at a time when the tools for building Web sites and managing servers were just beginning to mature. Web pages, which initially could only contain static, unchanging information, could now be generated dynamically by server-based scripts or applications. The data contained within these dynamic pages could come from corporate databases or other legacy data sources, and each user suddenly had the ability to access and manipulate corporate data from multiple sources, all through a single Web browser.

Thanks to their reliance on open standards, intranets eliminated the compatibility issues that had previously forced developers to create a different version of their application for each type of operating system. Intranet users were given standard Web browsers, and developers focused on building application functionality on the Web server end. Since the browsers spoke a common language, regardless of which type of computer they were installed on, a single Web server application could run on any type of computer that had a browser.

Since the application itself resided on the intranet server, the difficulty of distributing new versions of the application was greatly reduced, because all of the revisions and changes happened on the server itself. Database system vendors and other software developers created interfaces to mediate between intranet Web servers and existing databases or legacy applications. Intranet servers became the all-purpose method of access to entire corporate data warehouses.

Extranets: Sharing Intranets with the Outside World

As the popularity of intranets increased, many organizations soon recognized that they could benefit by sharing the information available on their intranet with their business partners or with their customers. By linking their intranets with the intranets of their business partners, organizations began to create what has been called an *extranet*.

Although extranets share a number of similarities with intranets, they also possess some notable differences. Intranets, by definition, are designed to share information; they are meant to be as open as possible so that all members within an organization can quickly and easily communicate and publish information. Extranets are also designed to share information, but they are not meant to be as freely accessible as intranet services.

Because they contain only the information an organization wishes to make available to its business partners, extranets take a more controlled approach to sharing. Typically, an extranet server will require some sort of user authentication or other method to restrict access to potentially sensitive information.

Extranets rely on security mechanisms to protect the host organization as well as to protect the host organization's business partners. For example if an organization creates an extranet order entry server for its customers, it must secure the information on the server so that only authorized users can access sensitive data such as credit card numbers or other billing information. Extranet developers use a number of mechanisms to control access to extranet resources, such as firewalls, login authentication, and virtual private networks.

Typically, organizations connect to their extranet partners in one of two ways; either through a private data network or through a public data network such as the Internet. A private data network may be comprised of a number of point-to-point dedicated circuit links, or it may be a combination of virtual circuits within a frame-relay network. Regardless of which technology is being used, a private data network ensures that extranet servers can be accessed only by other users on the private network.

When an extranet host allows users to connect to extranet servers through a public data network, some method must be used to ensure that only authorized users can access the server. One of the most popular methods for connecting securely over a potentially unsecure, public link is the use of an encrypted communication channel, called a virtual private network (VPN). We'll discuss VPNs in more detail in Chapter 11.

The use of public data networks, such as the Internet, illustrates the interconnected nature of the Internet, intranets, and extranets. In the end, many organizations use some combination of the three, depending on their business communication requirements.

Figure 7.1 illustrates the relationship between the Internet, a corporate intranet, and an extranet.

Core Net Services

The Internet, intranets, and extranets (we'll use the generic term *nets* to refer to all three) all rely upon the same basic set of protocols from the TCP/IP suite. When most people think about nets, they immediately associate them with the World Wide Web. However, many organizations have expanded upon their basic Web servers to offer open-standards-based services such as the Domain Name Service (DNS), SMTP mail, the File Transfer Protocol (FTP), and news discussion groups.

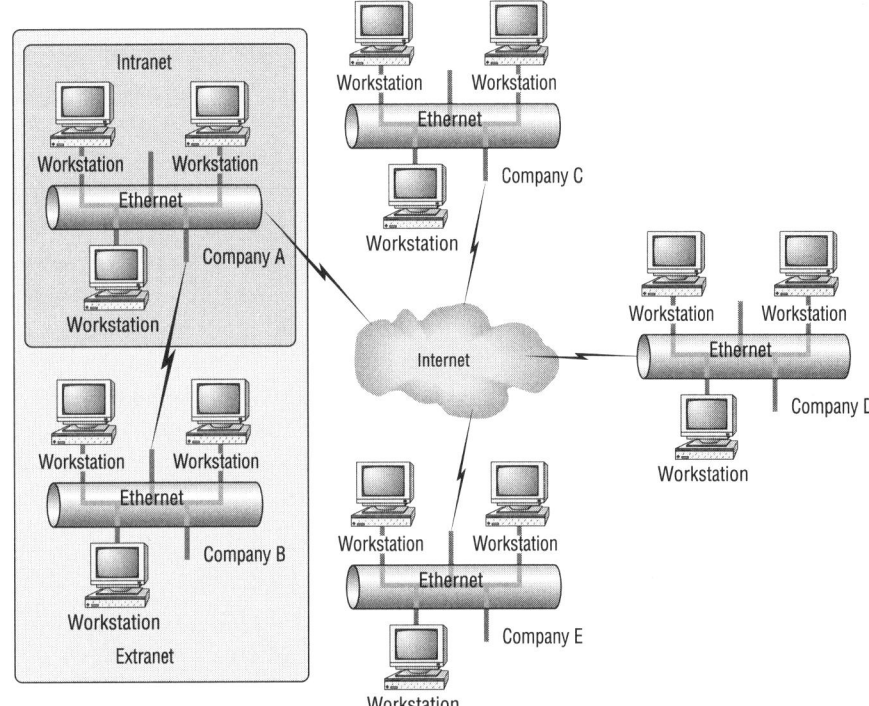

FIGURE 7.1

Many organizations combine aspects of the Internet, their corporate intranet, and multi-corporate extranets.

As a NT enterprise network designer, it is important for you to have a clear understanding of how these protocols and services operate and interrelate so you can know when it might be appropriate to deploy a net server to solve a particular problem. This chapter, and the four that follow, were written to provide you with enough information so that you can select the proper tools in the right situations.

As part of Microsoft's commitment to the Internet, the NT Advanced Server 4.0 distribution included a number of open-standards-based services, including a Web server, FTP server, Gopher server, and DNS server. A number of third-party developers have offered enhanced versions of these services and have developed additional net services for NT 4.

The Client/Server Model

Net services and protocols follow the client/server computing model. In the client/server model, the term *client* refers to a process or a program that submits a request to a server, and the term *server* refers to a process or program that receives the request from the client, processes it, and returns the results to the client. In a true client/server environment, some processing occurs at both ends of a transaction (the client and the server). Figure 7.2 shows a graphical representation of the interaction between a client and a server.

True client server applications operate independently of connections established at the Network Operating System level. A direct connection, network share, or drive mapping is not required for the application to operate. Applications which do require this type of connectivity are simply shared applications residing on a network resource available to multiple users. Instead, communication occurs at the application layer of the OSI model. The end user is most often not even aware of where the server is located or even what its name is.

FIGURE 7.2

A client submits a request to the server; the server processes the request and returns the results.

Many of the newer database environments use the client/server model. For example, in a Microsoft SQL server implementation, the SQL server receives requests from and submits responses to a client, which may be written in Visual Basic.

Client/server computing has advantages over host-based or server-based applications for two reasons. First, since the server processes the query and only returns the results, the amount of information that has to be sent over the network is minimized. Since most WAN connections operate over leased lines or lower speed connections, client/server computing provides an enormous performance benefit for applications that run over wide area networks.

Second, since the client and server must each conform to specific protocols, the operating system or hardware platform of either becomes irrelevant. The protocol itself becomes the common ground through which the client and server communicate. Any FTP client software, running on any platform, can communicate with any FTP server running on the same or on a totally different hardware platform.

Once a given protocol is established, development of client and server modules for a particular application can be done independently of one another. Some developers can concentrate on developing only the client software, some can concentrate on only the server software, and some can develop both the client and the server. As a network designer, you are free to pick and choose the clients and servers that best meet your needs. If a particular developer offers the best Web server, you can implement their server while utilizing a different vendor's browser for the client.

Web Protocols: HTTP and HTML

Because of its ease of use and integration of multimedia file types, the World Wide Web (WWW) protocol is clearly the most popular net service.

With WWW, a Web browser (the client) submits requests to a Web server (the server) using the HTTP protocol. The Web server examines the request from the browser, processes the request, and then submits a response back to the browser, again using HTTP. The response may contain text formatted according to HTML standards as well as graphics, sounds, or other binary files. It may also contain *hyperlinks* (links to other documents that may be on the same Web server or on a different Web server).

The HTTP Protocol

Web browsers and servers communicate via HTTP, an application-level protocol designed to run over TCP. The standard port number for HTTP is 80, but you can configure your Web server to listen on any other available port.

HTTP is based on the concept of a transaction. Each transaction consists of four parts:

1. The client establishes a TCP connection with the server.

2. The client submits a request to the server.

3. The server processes the request and returns the requested information or a response that it cannot answer the request.

4. The server or the client closes the TCP connection.

In Figure 7.3, you can see these four parts of a typical HTTP transaction.

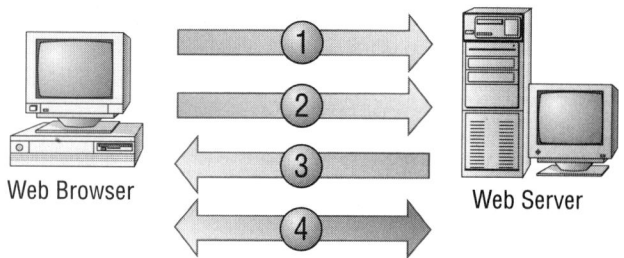

FIGURE 7.3

The four elements of an HTTP transaction

HTTP is considered to be a *stateless* protocol, which means that each transaction is considered to be a distinct and separate session. A Web server makes no attempt to maintain information about a client other than what it needs to know during a transaction to deliver the response. Neither the browser nor the server store any information about a session during the time between transactions, because neither one knows *if* there will be a next transaction. For example, if you visit a Web site and download the home page, the connection is open only long enough for the contents of the home page to be delivered to you. Once you click a link on the home page, the client considers the request as the beginning of a new transaction, so it initiates a new request.

This type of approach was necessary because a typical Web browsing session is substantially different from other session-oriented services. Once you download a Web page, you might request another page from the server, but you also might request a page from a different Web server.

By creating HTTP to be a stateless protocol, the developers could be assured that Web servers could work more efficiently. The Web server doesn't have to worry about maintaining a connection for a given period of time; it can simply receive and respond to requests. This allows the server to serve more requests in a shorter amount of time.

While this approach works well in situations where a Web user might jump from Web site to Web site, it doesn't work well in situations where information about a user must be tracked between Web pages on a single site, such as a Web-based shopping service. A number of techniques have been employed to track information about users once they leave a particular page, the most popular of which is the use of *cookies*. Cookies are bits of information that a Web server attempts to store on a Web browser's local workstation. The cookie may contain user preferences, order information, or information about the number of times a particular user has visited a site.

The HTML Protocol

Hypertext Markup Language (HTML) is the second of the two protocols associated with the Web. HTML, an application of the Standard Generalized Markup Language (SGML), is a language used to define documents using generic commands, called *tags*, to indicate document elements, such as headings, paragraphs, and highlights. By using these generic tags, interpretation of how the document should appear (such as which font to use) is left up to the Web browser. This allows HTML documents to be platform-independent—Web authors only need to create one document that can be viewed and interpreted by Macintosh systems, IBM-compatible PCs, and UNIX systems. The Web browser on each of the machines receives the HTML document, and processes the tags to determine the best way to represent the information when it displays it on the screen.

The tags within HTML documents may specify a heading, a paragraph, a list, a group of highlighted characters, or a link to another document. Each tag begins with a start tag that is delimited with angle brackets (<) and (>). Some types of tags must contain an end tag that is delimited with a </ and a >. For example, an HTML title within a document would look like this:

    <TITLE>This is a document title.</TITLE>

The <TITLE> tag indicates that the following text should be interpreted as the title of the document. The text *This is a document title* is the actual title for the document. The end tag </TITLE> indicates the end of the title. Anything that follows the title requires another tag to indicate its function within the HTML document.

You can view the HTML source code for any Web document with a Web browser by selecting View from the menu bar and then selecting the Source option.

DNS: The Domain Name Service

In the early days of the Internet, users found it easier to identify computers with names instead of IP addresses. For example, it's much easier to locate a computer called www.company.com than it would be to always have to remember the computer's IP address; so users began to assign hostnames to their computers. Each host had a hostname and a corresponding IP address. Initially, these host-to-address mappings were maintained by the Stanford Research Institute Network Information Center (SRI-NIC). The SRI-NIC compiled all host information for all of the computers on the Internet into a single HOSTS file that they placed on their FTP server to be downloaded by the Internet community. As the number of Internet hosts grew, so did the file. Eventually new hosts were being added faster than the HOSTS file could change, and the file became too large to be managed easily. The Internet community recognized the need for a more dynamic, distributed method to disseminate Internet hostname and address information.

The solution was the Domain Name Service, a hierarchical, distributed name database. DNS is made up of three components:

- The domain name space
- Name servers
- Resolvers

Let's examine each of the three components in more detail.

The Domain Name Space

The domain name space is the name for the entire DNS hierarchy. The domain name space looks just like an upside-down tree. Each branch point, called a *node*, is considered to be a domain; and each domain has a *name*, or label. The top domain, called *root*, has a zero-length (null) label and is represented as a single dot (.). Branching off the root domain are the top-level domains. The top-level domains are comprised of general categories of the subdomains that fall within them, such as .com for commercial sites or .edu for educational ones.

You can see a graphic representation of the domain name space in Figure 7.4.

The term *domain* refers to a subtree of the domain name space and the contents of the subtree. The domain name is the name of the root node of the subtree. A domain is a logical, not physical, grouping of network resources. For example, workstations within a single domain do not have to be on the same network, in the same building, or in the same country.

Domains at the same level (sometimes called *brother* domains) must have unique names, in much the same way that file system directories at the same level must have unique names. For example, on a DOS system you can only have one directory called TEMP at the root of your C: drive. However, you

FIGURE 7.4

The structure of the domain name space resembles an upside-down tree.

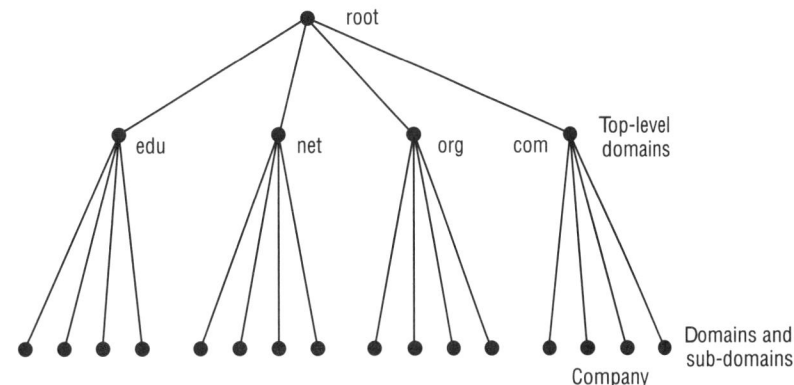

create subdirectories at different levels with the same name, so you could have a C:\WINDOWS\TEMP directory at the same time you had a C:\TEMP directory and a C:\SAMPLE\TEMP directory.

Name Servers

The second element of the Domain Name Service is the name servers. Name servers contain information about a domain's tree structure and host information.

The entire domain database is divided into *zones*. A zone may contain a single domain or multiple domains. For example, the zone for Company, Inc. might contain only information for the domain company.com, but it may also contain information for other related domains such as east.company.com and west.company.com. Also, the zone that contains information on the company.com domain and its subdomains may be divided into multiple zones to simplify administration. For example, if the east.company.com domain began to grow, the administrator of the company.com domain could create a subzone for east.company.com that could be administered separately by the administrator for the east.company.com domain.

The primary reason for the existence of zones is to create a way to divide sections of the domain name space into more manageable chunks. For example, when an organization is given its own domain, that domain is given a zone so that the organization can manage its own portion of the domain name space. If that portion becomes large enough that it is difficult to manage, the administrator of the zone can divide it up further into multiple zones, so that each one can be managed by a different person or group. Zones are usually identified by the name of the highest node (or domain) that is contained within the zone.

Unless you are designing a DNS strategy for a very large network with thousands of nodes, it is unlikely that you will need to worry about creating a subzone.

A name server's job is to answer queries about the objects contained in its zone. In addition, a single name server may be responsible for answering queries for multiple zones. Each zone, however, must have at least two name servers: a primary name server and a secondary name server.

Root Name Servers When a query comes in to a name server, it examines its tables to determine if it contains sufficient information to answer the query. If it does, it sends a reply. If it does not, it defers its answer to a more informed name server (this more informed name server is usually one that is one step higher in the DNS hierarchy). For example, the name server for east.company.com might defer to the name server for company.com. Eventually, requests may be submitted to a top-level name server known as a *root name server*. A root name server contains domain information for one of the top-level domains such as gov, org, or com. (Each top-level domain has a root name server.) They also contain the addresses for the name servers of the subdomains that fall under the top-level domains.

The root name servers are geographically spread out, mostly throughout the United States.

As you can imagine, the root name servers receive a great number of requests on an almost continual basis. Most name servers perform some level of caching of DNS information to minimize the number of requests they must pass on to the root name servers.

Zone Transfers In order to provide fault tolerance and redundancy, every zone should have at least two name servers. In this type of configuration, one name server is set up as the primary server, and the other servers are configured to be secondary servers. Secondary servers update their DNS information directly from the primary server using a mechanism called a *zone transfer*. Secondary servers periodically check with the primary server to determine if any changes have been made to its DNS tables. (Each time a change is made on the primary, it updates a field called the *SERIAL* field—the secondary checks the number of the SERIAL field on the primary server and if it is newer, it requests a zone transfer.)

Resource Records   Hostname and IP address information reside in master files, which the name servers use to answer DNS requests, maintained by administrators of individual domains. For example, the network administrator for Company, Inc. would maintain the master files that contain the hostname and IP address information for the systems within the Company domain. The Company name server would then use the files to resolve DNS name requests. These files contain entries, called *resource records*, that identify network resources within a domain. Resource records are arranged by their function, or *record type*. For example, if a resource record belongs to the NS record type, the computer named in the resource record is the name server for a particular domain.

The in-addr.arpa Domain   In addition to containing name-to-address maps, name servers contain information that maps addresses to names. The part of the domain name space that contains address-to-name mappings is called the in-addr.arpa domain. When a process needs to determine a hostname from an IP address, it performs a lookup using the in-addr.arpa domain. For example, some FTP servers insist that users access their site from a host that has a valid DNS name so they can track from where the FTP user is accessing their server. Since the FTP server only sees the IP address of the user, its resolver performs a reverse name lookup.

Entries in the files that contain the in-addr.arpa information look like a normal IP address with in-addr.arpa appended to them. For example, the entry for the host www.company.com that had 192.168.202.10 as its IP address would look like the following line:

```
202.168.192.in-addr.arpa www.company.com.
```

Notice that the IP network address is listed backward—instead of being 192.168.202, it is listed as 202.168.192. That is because of the way lookups are performed. DNS hostnames are listed beginning with the most specific element (such as a hostname like www) to the least specific (such as the top-level domain, like root). IP addresses are listed in the opposite way; from least specific (the network address) to the most specific (the host address). In order for reverse name resolutions to work, they need to reverse the IP address to begin with the most specific number instead of the least specific.

Resolvers: Name-to-Address Resolution

The third element of the Domain Name System, the *resolver*, is the mechanism that extracts the information from the name servers to perform the hostname-to-IP address translation. When a hostname is entered into a client application such as FTP or Telnet, the client application passes the hostname to the resolver. Depending on the workstation configuration, the resolver then examines the HOSTS file for a hostname or contacts a DNS name server with a request.

> The process of converting a hostname to an IP address is called *resolving* the address, or *name resolution*.

As we mentioned, name resolution begins at the workstation. If the workstation is configured to use DNS for name resolution, the resolver, which is part of the TCP/IP stack, examines a file that contains the name of the local domain and the IP addresses of a few name servers. Most systems contain a file called RESOLV.CONF or RESOLV.CFG that indicates the IP address of the name servers.

Once the resolver determines the IP address of the name server, it submits a name resolution request to the server. If the server contains IP address information for the hostname sent in the request, it sends the information in a reply to the resolver. If it does not contain information on the hostname requested by the resolver, it first contacts the root name server to determine the address of the name server that is responsible for the domain. If the request sent by the resolver contains multiple domain names (for example, www.north.company.com) the original name server will first have to contact the root name server for the com domain, then the name server for company, and finally the name server for north to resolve the IP address for www.north.company.com. Figure 7.5 shows a graphic representation of how the hostname is resolved.

Name servers also provide the ability to cache information once they have conducted a search. If another user requested an IP address for ftp.boston.north.company.com, the name server could consult its cache for the IP address of the boston.north.company.com name server instead of beginning the search from scratch.

The length of time this information remains in a name server's cache depends on something called a *time to live* (TTL) value. Each DNS zone administrator configures the TTL for his or her own zone. A long TTL value will mean that other name servers will cache information about hosts in that

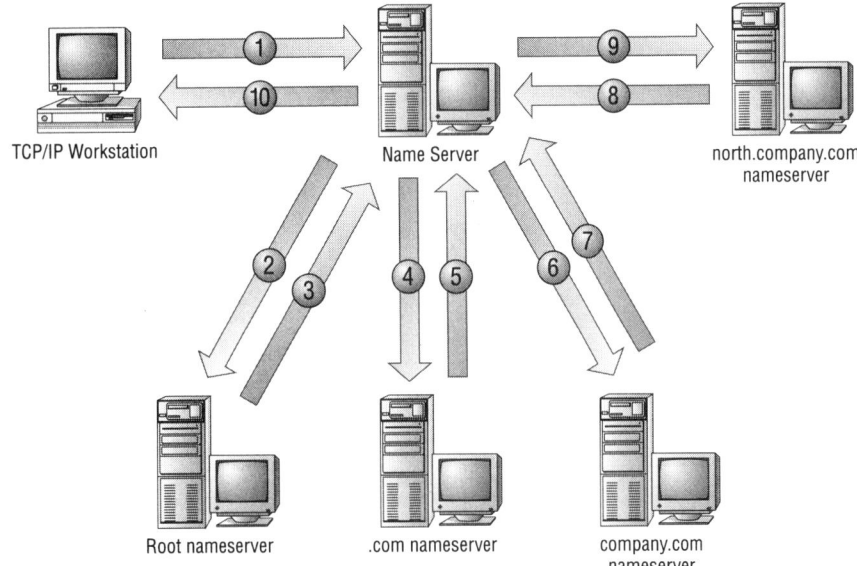

FIGURE 7.5
An example of hostname resolution

domain for a longer period of time. The advantage of a long TTL is that DNS information for that domain will remain in the cache longer, so frequent lookups won't be necessary. This can reduce the load on a name server because it doesn't have to keep checking back with requests for the same information. The disadvantage to a long TTL is that changes will not be updated as quickly, because the other name servers will continue to rely on cached information.

DNS Design Considerations

If your network is already connected to the Internet, chances are you have some type of DNS service in place: either provided by a server within your corporation, or by your Internet service provider. However, you'll most likely want to design a separate DNS service for the organizational intranet or an extranet. Why? Primarily because the intranet or extranet should support only a small group of users—there is no point in advertising the net servers to the rest of the world. In this type of scenario, you'll need to maintain two DNS configurations, one for Internet-accessible hosts, and one for intranet/extranet-accessible hosts.

If your network is not connected to the Internet, you may or may not have any type of DNS service in place. Either way, your job will be less complicated because you'll only have to maintain a single DNS server.

If you choose to design a DNS implementation, don't worry about assigning a DNS name to every computer on the network. Only the ones that offer services, such as FTP, Web, Gopher, and News servers require a DNS name.

SMTP, POP3, and IMAP: Net Mail

Along with the Web, electronic mail is one of the most widely implemented net services, but if you asked most network designers, they probably wouldn't consider e-mail to be a true net service. One reason may be that they have chosen to use one or more of the many popular proprietary e-mail systems such as cc:Mail, Microsoft Mail, Exchange, or GroupWise. Each of these packages works well if it is the only mail system in use by an organization. However, in some cases, large corporations may have implemented more than one of these mail systems and have had to configure an array of gateway products to connect each system.

This is one area where the open standards of net services can help bridge the gap between mail systems. By implementing open e-mail protocols such as the Simple Mail Transfer Protocol (SMTP), the Post Office Protocol version 3 (POP3), and the Internet Mail Access Protocol (IMAP) as backbone protocols between mail systems, administrators can minimize the number of mail gateways required to connect each mail system. In this type of scenario, each mail administrator would configure an SMTP gateway for their mail system. SMTP would act as the common backbone protocol for all corporate e-mail.

If your organization does not already have an electronic mail system in place, you may want to consider designing an open-standards-based e-mail system that supports SMTP and POP3 or IMAP. By selecting products that natively support open standards and protocols, you avoid being "locked-in" to a proprietary mail system. You'll have the freedom to evaluate and select the right components that will work best in your organization.

End-users access e-mail though any one of a number of e-mail client applications. The client software may be part of an internal corporate e-mail system, it may be an e-mail package running on a host system, or it may be a standalone POP3 or IMAP-compliant mail package. The mail client transmits the completed mail message to a mail server that examines the destination address in the mail header to determine where to send the e-mail next. The mail server then performs a DNS lookup to find out the IP address of the mail server responsible for the domain of the e-mail recipient. Next, the sending mail server establishes a connection to the receiving mail server and transmits the mail message. Once the transmission is completed, the receiving mail server determines how the mail message will be delivered. If the recipient is a local user to the mail server, the server passes the mail message to the appropriate mail program for local delivery. If the recipient is not local, the mail server passes the mail message on to another mail server for local delivery.

Electronic mail delivery is similar to the way regular mail gets delivered. First, you write the letter and put an address on the envelope (your workstation). Next, you deliver the letter to the post office (mail server #1). Then, the letter handlers examine the ZIP code on the letter to determine to which post office it should be routed and send the letter to the next post office (mail server #2). From there the letter is routed on to another post office or delivered to the recipient (workstation).

SMTP, as specified in RFC 821, is the protocol that defines the rules for communication between mail servers. Its sole objective is the reliable and efficient transfer of electronic mail. SMTP does not define the actual format of e-mail messages, only how to transfer them. RFC 822 defines the standard format for electronic mail messages.

RFC 821 describes how two mail servers should communicate to transfer e-mail. When a mail server processes a message to be sent to another mail server, it contacts the destination server via TCP port 25 and creates a connection that lasts long enough for the mail messages to be sent. The originating server greets the destination server, and then transmits information including the sender of the message, the recipient or recipients of the message, and the text of the message. After each piece of information is sent, the destination server replies with an OK to let the sender know to proceed. The sending server waits at each step for an acknowledgment before sending the next piece of information.

Let's take a closer look at the three protocols you will encounter when designing a net standards-based e-mail system: SMTP, POP3, and IMAP.

SMTP

As we mentioned earlier, the SMTP protocol defines the communication between mail servers. It is also the protocol that most mail client software uses to send outbound mail messages to other users. To receive mail, most clients use either the Post Office Protocol version 3 (POP3) or the Internet Mail Access Protocol (IMAP).

POP3

POP3 mail servers listen for incoming mail client connections on TCP port 110. When a POP3 mail user contacts the POP3 server, a conversation similar to an SMTP communication session is established. The command structure is different, however, and the commands should not be confused with SMTP commands. Most POP3 servers are configured to communicate via SMTP on port 25 and POP3 on port 110, to accommodate both types of mail transmission.

IMAP

The IMAP protocol includes a number of improvements over the POP3 protocol, the most significant being that it allows users to create and manipulate mail folders directly on the IMAP server. Once an IMAP mail client authenticates to the server with the username and password, it downloads only basic information about each mail message stored on the server, such as who sent the message and the subject of the message. Once users view the mail messages in their mailboxes, they can determine which (if any) messages they wish to receive. When users connect to a POP3 server, they have no choice whether to download individual messages; all incoming mail is downloaded completely.

Figure 7.6 illustrates the communications between mail servers, other mail servers, and mail clients.

FTP: The File Transfer Protocol

According to RFC 959, these are the objectives for FTP:

1. To promote sharing of files

2. To encourage indirect or implicit use of remote computers

3. To shield a user from variations in file storage systems among hosts

4. To transfer data reliably and efficiently

FIGURE 7.6

The interaction between mail servers, other mail servers, and mail clients

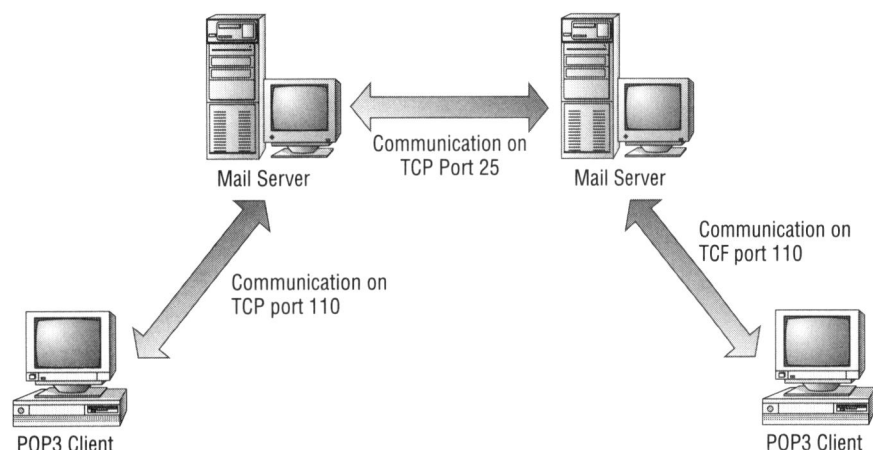

Make note of the third objective—what it means to you is that FTP provides a common language to simplify file transfer between file systems on dissimilar systems. You can use FTP to transfer files between mainframes and PCs, Macintosh computers and PCs, UNIX and Macintosh, or any combination of systems as long as they all run FTP. If your network environment contains only one operating platform, this may not seem like a big deal to you, but if you've ever had to try to transfer files between different platforms using something other than FTP, you already know what a benefit FTP can be.

An FTP server listens for incoming FTP requests on TCP port 21. When an incoming request arrives, the server prompts the FTP user for a username and password combination. If users enter valid usernames and passwords, they can then access the FTP server to upload or download files according to the access rights associated with those usernames. Most FTP servers provide a special type of access for the username *anonymous*. The anonymous ID is similar to the NT GUEST user ID, in that it allows nonregistered system users access to public files.

Figure 7.7 shows the interaction between an FTP server and client.

Just as different user IDs have different file access rights on NT, different user IDs on an FTP server can be configured to access different files and directories. Administrators use the anonymous ID to make it easier for users to download commonly accessed files. Without the anonymous account, administrators would have to add an account for every person who wanted to download files from their FTP servers.

FIGURE 7.7

The FTP client initiates connection to the FTP server on TCP port 21, and then the FTP server transmits the requested information on a higher numbered TCP connection.

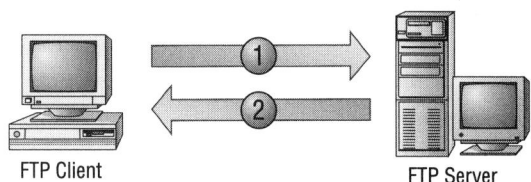

FTP Design Considerations

Many organizations have integrated FTP services with WWW services to allow Web browsers to download programs and files from Web servers throughout the organization with point-and-click ease. All it takes is a link within an HTML document that points to the FTP server, the file path, and the file name.

Other organizations have implemented FTP services as a quick-and-dirty means to transmit software and document files through the use of automated scripts and batch files.

Whether or not you plan to include FTP in a design is up to you. Keep in mind that it is the best method for your users to transmit files to one another, or to offer downloaded files to groups or individuals.

Gopher: A File Navigation Service

Gopher is a text-based file navigation service, the popularity of which has been eclipsed in large part by the World Wide Web—primarily because, unlike the Web, Gopher was designed to display text only, not graphics.

Gopher was developed to provide a service that could present files, directories, and information in a hierarchical tree structure, similar to a file system with its nested directories, subdirectories, and files. This approach allowed users to easily navigate through Gopher menus by selecting links to locate files they wished to view or download for use on their local systems.

Gopher links may point to directories, files, or other services such as Telnet sessions on the host computer or other computers. Files may be text (including HTML files) or binary files. When a Gopher client receives a file, it examines the file to determine what type it is (text or binary), and then processes the file according to its type. For example, if a Gopher client accesses a text file, it will display it on the user's screen. However, if the file is a binary, it will retrieve the file in its binary form and prompt the user for a location in which to save the file.

Most Web browser software (Netscape, Microsoft, Mosaic) includes native support for Gopher, so you can use any of these to access Gopher servers. The Microsoft Internet Information Server includes a built-in Gopher server as well.

Gopher Design Considerations

You're probably wondering why you should even consider designing a Gopher service, especially when you consider all of the advantages of the Web. However, there are situations when it might make sense to use Gopher, in addition to other services like WWW or FTP, such as:

- Your customers have a large number of text documents that they would like to make available to their users immediately. By putting these documents on a Gopher server, you give users instant access to the files.

- You would like to provide an easier method than FTP for your users to download files. With Gopher, your users can more easily navigate through directories and subdirectories to find the files they're looking for.

- Your customer has existing Gopher servers that they would like to migrate to Windows NT.

NNTP: The News Protocol

News is the generic term for the articles, bulletins, conferences, and conversations that are carried through large news systems like Usenet on the Internet.

Usenet is a loosely organized network of news servers and news providers that contains thousands of news groups organized in a hierarchical manner, each with its own unique topic.

The primary protocol responsible for the transmission of news is the Network News Transport Protocol (NNTP). NNTP, which operates on TCP port 119, defines the parameters for the distribution and retrieval of news articles between news servers and news clients.

Figure 7.8 illustrates the operations that take place during an NNTP connection.

FIGURE 7.8

A sample NNTP connection

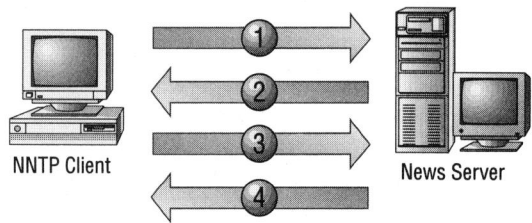

1) Client initiates connection request on TCP Port 119
2) Server – "Server: 200 newserv news server ready – posting ok"
3) Client requests a list of newsgroups – "LIST"
4) Server responds with list "215 list of newsgroups follows..."

Users can use a news system to create a hierarchical, topically-based database to share information and conduct virtual conversations on any topic they choose. Users access news with a news client (called a *news reader*). The news reader software first requests a list of newsgroups, arranged by topic. Then, the user can select a topic that interests them and view a list of messages contained within the newsgroup. At this point, they may respond to current messages or create messages of their own. In their responses, they can include text from the original message, imparting a conversational feel to the message.

In a news system, messages are categorized and saved in news groups according to their subject matter. For example, you might have a group of C++ programmers who discuss programming notes in a newsgroup they have created called `mis.programming.C++`.

Advantages of News Systems

News systems, such as Usenet, have a number of advantages over e-mail for distributing information to large groups.

- Mail-based information services such as mailing lists begin to require significant computing, network, and storage resources as the number of list subscribers grows because a separate mail message must be sent to every subscriber. With a news system, messages are stored on a centralized server, so a separate message does not have to be sent to each reader. When access to a news message is desired, a user simply starts up his news client software and accesses the newsgroup containing the message.

- Mail messages sent via mailing lists reside in the recipient's mailbox until the message is manually deleted by the recipient, providing an opportunity for cluttered mailboxes and wasted storage space. With news, message authors can assign expiration dates to time-sensitive messages. Once a message expires, it is purged from the mail system.

- While e-mail is a good medium for conversational communication between two users, it is not a good medium for multiple users to use to communicate. News messages can be grouped by topic, and any authorized user is free to respond to the message. Other users can respond to the original message, or to a response, thereby creating a message *thread*. This conversational aspect of news makes it an ideal service for your users when discussing issues or technical problems, or brainstorming on important projects.

History of News

Prior to the development of NNTP, a protocol known as the UNIX to UNIX Copy Protocol (UUCP) was the protocol used by news servers to distribute news. With UUCP, news servers used a technique called *flooding* (sending all new messages to all other hosts that the server fed) to transmit news messages. While flooding was a good technique to ensure that news servers got all of the new messages, it was inefficient because many servers were configured to receive multiple feeds (which meant that many messages were received more than once).

The NNTP protocol overcomes this inefficiency by creating an interactive mechanism for receiving file updates. When a news server (Server 1) wants to receive or send new news, it contacts a predefined news server (Server 2) using NNTP. Server 1 will initiate the transaction by first checking to see if any new groups have been created. If new groups exist, Server 1 may add those groups to its existing list. Then Server 1 will query Server 2 to determine if any new messages have been added to groups it already receives. If new messages exist, Server 1 then requests a transmission for those messages. Then, if Server 1 has any new messages, it transmits the messages to Server 2 and closes the connection.

News Design Considerations

Because most browsers provide support for accessing news, designing a news service implementation is a relatively straightforward task. All that is required is for you to establish a news server and inform the users where to point their news client software for the connections.

As we discussed before, news provides a high level of group interactivity that is missing from most of the other services. For example, publishing information on a Web server is a one-way conversation by design, while e-mail is more suited for one-to-one correspondence. News gives your users the ability to collaborate with one another.

If your company has a connection to the Internet, you may already have news on your network. If so, you can create internal newsgroups (for distribution within your organization) so that users can use news to communicate not only on your intranet, but on the Internet as well. You may decide to maintain all of the newsgroups on a single server, or you might dedicate one server for Internet news and one server for intranet news.

Secure Networking in an Insecure World

Net services make it easy for users to access data resources located anywhere on the Internet, on your corporate intranet, or on an extranet. The downside is that they also make it easy for non-authorized users to access your data. For example, a system cracker can use the same type of Web browser that your authorized users use to access sensitive corporate data on intranet and extranet servers.

Applications written with proprietary protocols had a certain, inherent basic level of security. After all, a user had to use the correct type of software to access the data, and not everyone had access to every type of application. Because net services utilize common, publicly available protocols, this type of security is no longer an option.

When you begin to design networks based on net services, you will be forced to implement alternative security methods. Typically, these security mechanisms work by creating some type of barrier between authorized users and unauthorized users.

The three categories of security products that we'll discuss in this book are proxy servers, firewalls, and virtual private networks. Each of these is discussed briefly in the sections that follow. We'll discuss firewalls and proxy servers in greater detail in Chapter 10, and we'll discuss virtual private networks in more detail in Chapter 11.

Proxy Servers: The Network Middleman

A proxy server is a system that has been configured to act as an intermediary between two or more networks. Any traffic destined for a network on the far end of a proxy server will be received by the proxy and retransmitted on the appropriate subnet. All outbound traffic will have the proxy servers' address identified as the source and all inbound traffic will be directed to the proxy server. In effect, hiding the identification of the "true" source and destination from each other.

Specific types of requests, such as requests for a Web page from a browser, will be intercepted by the proxy server, which will then generate its own request for the page. The remote Web server will send the reply to the proxy server, which will in turn send a reply to the originating browser. While an end user may only perceive a single request, two requests are actually generated; the first from the user to the proxy server, and the second from the proxy server to the destination Web server. The proxy server effectively stands in for the user. Figure 7.9 illustrates how a proxy server works.

FIGURE 7.9

Interaction between a user, a proxy server, and a Web server

1) Browser sends request to proxy server
2) Proxy submits request to Web server
3) Web server responds to proxy
4) Proxy caches reply and sends response to browser

Because no traffic actually travels between the internal network and the unsecure Internet, system crackers cannot gain direct access to internal resources or servers. Proxy servers can be configured to work in both directions; they can be configured to allow internal users to access external servers, and they can be configured to allow external users to access selected internal servers. The ability of a proxy server to provide access to an internal server is called a *reverse proxy*.

 Many proxy servers also provide the ability to selectively permit or deny certain types of access or to limit access to specific Web sites, so that organizations can have control over how employees access the Internet.

In addition to providing security between networks, proxy servers can be configured to cache the contents of the information they are asked to retrieve. For example, if a user accesses Microsoft's home page through a proxy server, the proxy server will retain the contents of the home page in a cache. When a subsequent user requests access to the home page, the proxy server will fulfill the request by transmitting the cached version of the home page back to the user.

Many corporations take advantage of the caching features of proxy servers to reduce the amount of traffic that must travel over wide-area links or slow connections to the Internet. The larger the amount of cached files on the proxy server, the higher the chance that a Web page requested by a user will be served locally by the proxy server. Every time a file is served locally, it means that the request doesn't need to be sent over the Internet, so less bandwidth is consumed. One additional benefit of caching is that the pages served by the proxy server are transmitted at LAN speeds, typically anywhere from 4 to 100Mpbs, while pages that must be retrieved over the Internet will be transmitted at slower speeds.

Firewalls: Gatekeepers of the Corporation

A firewall is any device or group of devices that provides a single point of control to permit or deny the flow of traffic between networks. Note that a firewall may not only be a single device, but a group of devices configured to provide the firewall functionality. For example, some corporations use filtering rules configured on multiple routers for their firewalls. Technically, it is the configuration of the hardware, not the hardware itself, that is the firewall.

For a firewall to be effective, all traffic that flows between the two networks must pass through it. The firewall examines the traffic and compares it to the set of rules for which it has been configured. If the traffic matches the rules for traffic that can be transmitted between the networks, the firewall forwards the traffic. If the traffic matches the rules for traffic that should be blocked, the firewall blocks the traffic.

 Technically, a proxy server can be considered a firewall because it serves as a single point of control for the flow of traffic between networks. The firewall products that we'll discuss in Chapter 11 may use a combination of techniques to enforce network security, some of which may be considered to be proxies.

Most commercial firewalls provide access logging so you can monitor the traffic that passes between the networks, allowing you to make adjustments in the firewall configuration as needed. The level of logging varies from firewall to firewall; some provide the ability to control which types of protocols will be logged and the amount of detail the logs provide, others only track the IP address and port number of the traffic.

Some firewalls also offer the ability to monitor access to TCP and UDP port numbers on a given network interface. Once the number of attempted accesses exceeds the value you have preconfigured, the firewall will send a notification of a possible attempted break-in on your network. These attempts are detected by a mechanism known as *port scanning*.

Port scanning works to thwart system crackers who attempt to gather more information about your network and the services available on it by using programs that are configured to quickly scan the entire range of TCP and UDP ports. The scanner logs any responses, which the system cracker can then use to attempt to compromise the network through one of the services. For example, SMTP mail servers operate on TCP port 25. A system cracker could configure a scanner to check port 25 on every host within a network address. If an SMTP server were configured and operational on any one of the hosts, it would respond to the port scanner. The cracker could then attempt to compromise each system that was running SMTP by utilizing a known security hole in older SMTP implementations.

The two most prevalent types of firewall implementations are *dual-homed hosts* and standard IP routers configured with packet filtering rules. A dual-homed host is a computer configured with firewall software and two network interface cards, one connected to network A and one connected to network B. The firewall software on the host may provide packet filtering, application proxies, or a combination of the two.

The biggest limitation of installing a firewall and a dual-homed host is the cost. Commercial firewall software prices range from a few thousand dollars to tens of thousands of dollars, depending on the features they offer and, for some, the number of internal network users they will support.

The other type of firewall implementation is through the configuration of access lists and filtering rules on the pre-existing routers. Packet filtering is a popular approach with administrators of smaller networks because it doesn't cost anything to implement other than the cost of the time required to configure the rules.

Virtual Private Networks

As the use of public data networks to access internal, corporate networks has increased, many corporations have begun to consider removing their internal dial-up servers and selected WAN links and replacing them with Internet connections. For example, an employee would connect to the corporate network by first connecting to their Internet service provider and then connecting to the corporate network through the Internet.

While these organizations can realize significant cost savings by eliminating the costs associated with purchasing, installing, and maintaining an internal dial-up infrastructure, many are concerned about permitting sensitive corporate data to travel over the Internet. Corporations are justifiably insecure about transmitting data within view of anyone with a packet analyzer.

A number of software and hardware developers have taken different approaches to provide data privacy. Web server vendors have enabled the use of the Secure Sockets Layer (SSL) to encrypt data being sent between Web servers and Web browsers. Other vendors, including Microsoft, have focused on encrypting entire network transmissions, instead of protecting application-layer communications, by implementing entirely encrypted connections.

The term *virtual private network* (VPN) is used to describe the use of encrypted, private communications over a public network. In a VPN scenario, each remote user uses encryption software to connect to a specially-configured router or other network device over a public network like the Internet. The router decrypts the transmissions sent by the remote user and routes the user's traffic to the internal network. Figure 7.10 illustrates how a virtual private network works.

While the intention has been to provide encryption by IPSec (a protocol specified in IPv6), many organizations have decided not to wait for widespread IPSec availability and have instead chosen to implement one of a variety of the available VPN solutions. We'll discuss VPN concepts and implementations in more detail in Chapter 11.

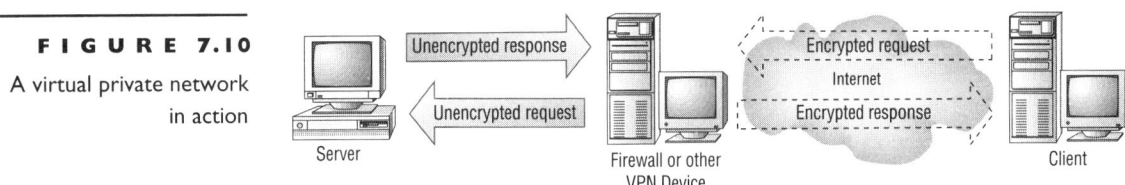

FIGURE 7.10 A virtual private network in action

Net Design Issues

Many of the issues you must consider when creating designs that use net services and servers are identical to the issues you face when undertaking any type of network design. However, there are some elements that you should consider more carefully when you begin to introduce open-standards-based services into a network. This section will identify those elements.

Select the Right Tools for the Job

Before you rush to deploy Web servers throughout your organization, take a few minutes to remember the issues we discussed in Chapter 3. Successful network designers avoid using technology for its own sake, and instead focus on providing designs that solve business requirements. Net technology is exciting, and it fits well in a number of situations. However, Web technology is not well suited for one-to-one communication or group discussion. For example, it may be more appropriate to implement an e-mail-based mail distribution list on an existing mail system than to attempt to deploy a group of new NNTP-based news servers.

Strive to select the most appropriate type of service for the requirement. Once you've selected the type of net service to use, evaluate the products that will provide the service. Weigh the pros and cons of each product, and select the one that offers the best combination of features, performance, manageability, and price.

Understand the Network Infrastructure

Where you ultimately locate your servers within your network can have as much impact on server performance as what type of Web server you use. For example, you may be able to provide a much higher level of performance if you use a caching proxy server at a remote WAN-connected site, because the majority of Web requests will be served from files stored in the proxy server cache.

Before you begin to deploy servers, review your entire network structure. Map the topology of the network to a map of the users which will access your net servers, and try to understand how data will flow throughout the network. Because of its emphasis on multimedia file types, net traffic typically consumes more bandwidth than traffic associated with typical file- and print-sharing services. Anticipating the increased network utilization will help you plan for the most effective deployment of server resources.

Put Your Eggs in the Right Baskets

Avoid the temptation to load up your net servers with too many services. While NT Server was designed to perform well while running multiple services, most net applications place substantial load on the server at peak usage times. If you try to run too many services on a single server, none of them will perform adequately.

Use tools such as the performance monitor to measure how a particular net service will impact your server. Try to simulate varying levels of usage to determine how your server will operate under light, medium, and heavy loads.

Distributing services to multiple servers will add to project costs, but you'll significantly improve overall service performance. Not only will each server be able to dedicate resources to a particular service, but you'll also gain the ability to customize each of the server's operational parameters to match the tasks they'll provide.

Design a Maintenance Plan

Web servers and other net servers tend to grow quickly. Once users begin to learn how easily they can add and manipulate Web pages, the amount of Web content will skyrocket. One thing that most users fail to learn is how to manage that content.

Developing a comprehensive server maintenance plan is as important as designing the server itself. Identify who will be responsible for managing server content, and work with the Web server manager to define a corporate policy for employee-content submissions.

Managing an enterprise-wide Web can be a formidable task. As the number of Web servers within a network increases, the likelihood that a user can find the exact document they are looking for decreases. Develop a strategy to organize server content so that users can quickly and easily locate resources throughout the enterprise.

In this chapter, we've discussed the issues and concepts associated with the Internet, intranets, and extranets, including services such as WWW, FTP, DNS, and News. Throughout the next four chapters, we'll discuss design considerations and technical overviews of products that will enable you to deploy net services on your Windows NT enterprise network.

CHAPTER 8

Internet Information Server in the Enterprise Network

Ask most network administrators about the Internet, intranets, and extranets, and they'll immediately begin to talk about the World Wide Web, Web servers, and Web browsers. During the early days of the Web, most of the major sites ran on UNIX-based systems, and UNIX was the dominant operating system on the Internet. As the user population of the Internet began to include more commercial than academic institutions, many of the new Internet users searched for better and faster servers, and more importantly, they began to search for servers that were easier to use.

In 1994, the European Microsoft Windows NT Academic Consortium (EMWAC) released the first HTTP server for Windows NT. This server provided basic Web functionality, and was available as part of the Windows NT Server Resource Kit or as a free download on the Internet. A short time later, a number of commercial Web server implementations for Windows NT were released, and Web designers and administrators began to discover that they didn't need to maintain a UNIX server to provide Net services. As of this writing, more than 40 different Web servers have become available on the NT platform.

In 1995, Microsoft announced their intention to take an active role in the Internet. Windows NT 4 was the first release that provided Net services as a standard component. The core of these services was the Microsoft Internet Information Server, or IIS.

In this chapter, you will learn:

- Which fundamental services are provided by IIS

- Tips to optimize IIS performance

- Tools you can use to manage IIS

- IIS design considerations

- How to extend the functionality of IIS with Site Server and Enterprise Site Server

IIS: The Internet Information Server

In early 1996, Microsoft made a commitment to promoting the Internet Information Server as the Windows NT engine for Net services. Initially, IIS only supported three core services: HTTP, FTP, and Gopher. Later revisions of IIS began to boast additional services, including Active Server Pages, the Microsoft Index Server, and support for SMTP mail and NNTP newsgroups. In this section, we'll examine how Microsoft has implemented each of these services within the IIS framework.

Core IIS Services

In retrospect, the first version of the IIS was rudimental: it offered basic Web, FTP, and Gopher services. In later revisions the functionality of IIS had been enhanced, but up until version 4, the management interface had remained essentially the same.

IIS versions 1–3 utilize the Internet Service Manager (as shown in Figure 8.1), which reflects a minimalist approach to server management. While some features were added to IIS in versions 2 and 3, most were minimal. Some, like Active Server Pages, were more significant, but all of the changes essentially snapped onto the existing framework.

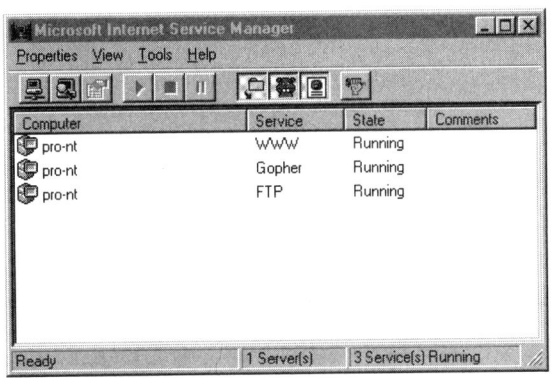

FIGURE 8.1

Managing IIS through the Internet Service Manager

From the main Internet Service Manager screen, you can start and stop services, as well as view service status and manage services running on multiple servers. To manage a particular service, you can simply double-click the service icon.

Microsoft made major changes to IIS with the release of version 4. Overall, the new version provided significant improvements in the areas of manageability, performance, and application development/support. In version 4, Microsoft introduced a new management interface, the Microsoft Management Console (MMC), shown in Figure 8.2.

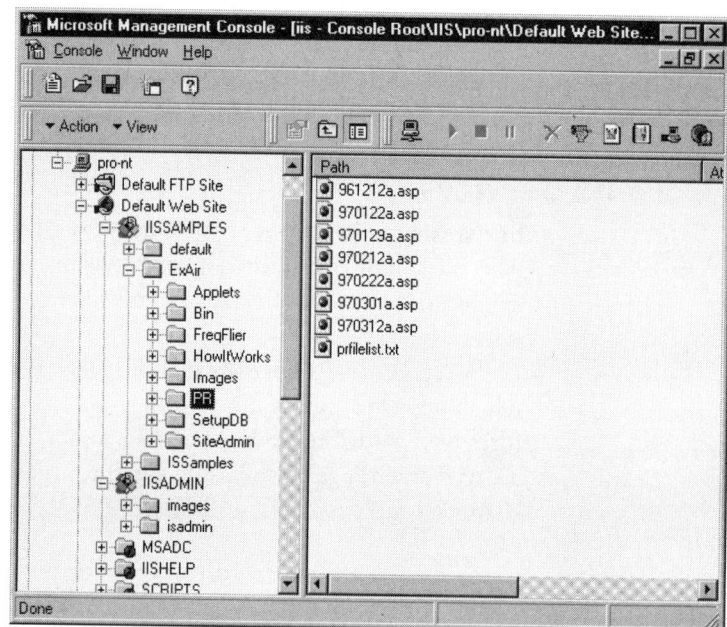

FIGURE 8.2

IIS 4 is the first revision to use the Microsoft Management Console

As a network designer, it's important for you to understand the core capabilities of IIS, as well as the features that have been added or enhanced since earlier versions. We'll discuss IIS design considerations later in this chapter. For now, we'll describe some of the more notable IIS basic configuration elements.

HTTP

The service that is most frequently used in most environments is the IIS HTTP service. Based on the HTTP 1.0 standard, the IIS HTTP service is tightly integrated with the NT operating system in a number of ways, most notably in user authentication and Web server directory configuration.

User Authentication   All of the IIS services, including HTTP, utilize the Windows NT Server user database to provide the ability to restrict access to IIS Web sites only to authorized members of the Windows NT Domain. For IIS versions 1–3, there are two ways a user can authenticate to an IIS server, either through basic (and unencrypted) HTTP authentication, or through Window NT Challenge/Response (NTLM) authentication. IIS version 4 includes a third authentication option, SSL (Secure Sockets Layer) Client Authentication. To configure authentication options, select the Service tab page from the HTTP service dialog box within the Internet Service Manager, as shown in Figure 8.3.

FIGURE 8.3

Authentication configuration options for HTTP

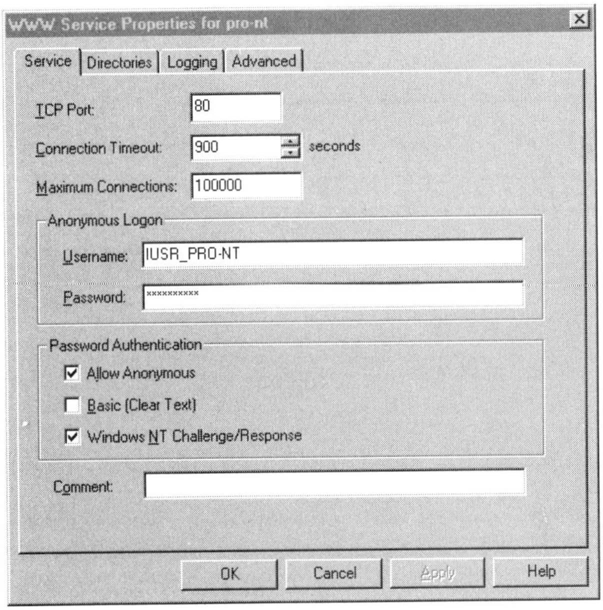

If the HTTP service is configured to use basic authentication, users will receive a username/password dialog box if they attempt to gain access to a restricted directory. When the user enters their name and password, IIS will use the input to attempt to access the requested resource. If the username and password are valid in either the IIS server local user's database or the domain database, and that user has access control permissions to access the resource, IIS will return the requested document.

In basic authentication, passwords are *not* encrypted over the network.

The Challenge/Response (NTLM) authentication method is only supported by the Microsoft Internet Explorer browser, but it allows background, uninterrupted authentication in certain situations. For example, if a user is authenticated to the same domain that the IIS server exists within and the user attempts to access a restricted resource on the IIS server, the Internet Explorer browser will authenticate automatically to the IIS server in the background. If the user's account exists within a different domain than the IIS server, that user may have to type in a valid username and password for the IIS server's domain.

In NTLM, the password is never sent over the network; a cryptographic exchange is conducted to authenticate the password.

SSL Client Authentication is only supported in IIS version 4, but it too allows background, uninterrupted authentication if both the server and the client have the appropriate digital certificates.

In IIS 4 the Client Certificate Required checkbox on the Authentication Methods dialog box is used to indicate the use of digital certificates. If the client cannot present an X.509 certificate, the client connection is rejected.

A *digital certificate* is in essence an electronic document, signed by a trusted third party, that confirms that a person is who they say they are. A digital certificate may contain information about a person such as their name, their e-mail address, and where they work or live. It also contains the public encryption key for the person, as well as a unique signature for the trusted third party, called a *certificate authority*.

Directory Configuration IIS is also tightly integrated with the Windows NT file system. For example, if IIS Web documents are stored on an NTFS file system, IIS will utilize NTFS access controls to restrict or permit access to IIS Web documents or entire directories. Once a user authenticates to IIS, either through basic HTTP authentication or through NTLM authentication, IIS will only permit users to access those directories to which the user has NT permissions to access.

Having the ability to utilize the NT user account database and the NTFS file access controls allows network designers and IIS administrators to leverage existing NT server objects instead of having to establish a completely separate user authentication structure for IIS.

Virtual Directories   IIS utilizes a concept known as *virtual directories* to simplify the way in which directories and documents are presented to browsers. A virtual directory is a logical mapping of a directory path name to a virtual directory name, called an *alias*.

To understand the value of virtual directories, it is important to first understand some fundamentals of how IIS treats directories. When you install IIS, you'll be prompted to enter three directory path names that will become the root directories for each of the three primary services. Typically, these root directories will be \InetPub\wwwroot, \InetPub\ftproot, and \InetPub\gophroot. When a user submits a request to the IIS WWW service but does not explicitly specify a directory or document name, the IIS server returns the default document from the root directory (in this example \InetPub\wwwroot). Users can request documents from the server root directory, but they can also submit requests from subdirectories of the server root. For example, if you created a directory called \InetPub\wwwroot\tests, and copied a file called summary.htm to the directory, users could submit the following URL to access the file: http://www.server.net/tests/summary.htm. Notice that the user does not have to type in the entire path to the file, only the name of the subdirectory of the WWW server root directory and the name of the file. Figure 8.4 shows examples of some already configured server directories from within the Internet Service Manager utility. In IIS version 4, virtual directory management is integrated into the Microsoft Management console, which presents services and directories in a Windows Explorer-like style. Figure 8.5 shows an example of a directory configuration dialog box within MMC.

In the example above, we described how to create an actual subdirectory off the server root. One of the more useful features of IIS is that you can use an alias to create a virtual directory off the server root, when in reality the alias may point to a totally different subdirectory on the NT server, or it may point to a directory on another server altogether. For example, if you wanted to set up a single IIS server that would serve existing documents from a number of servers on your network, you could use virtual directories to create a single logical Web server directory tree that actually pointed to directories all over your network. We'll discuss how to use virtual directories more effectively later on in this chapter.

FIGURE 8.4

The Directories tab page of the Internet Service Manager

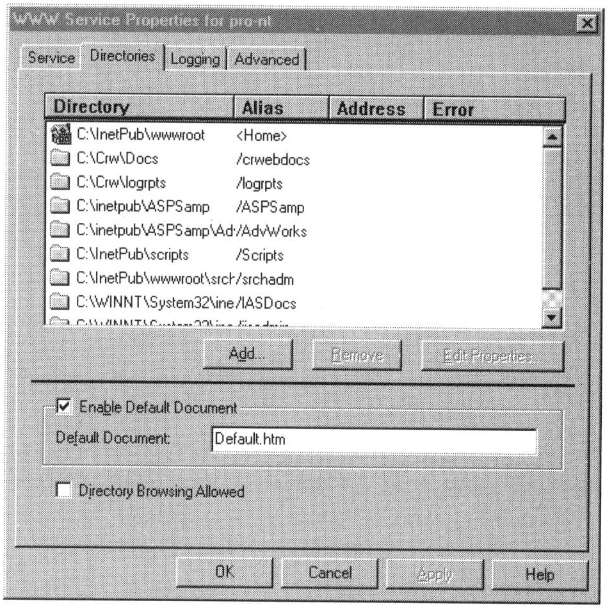

FIGURE 8.5

Configuring directories with the Microsoft Management Console

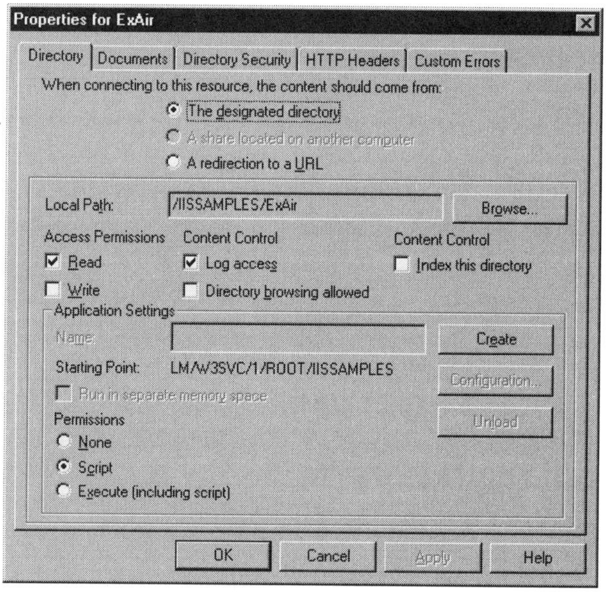

Server-side Processing Server-side processing functionality is available on IIS through a number of mechanisms. IIS supports the Common Gateway Interface (CGI) standard and works with WinCGI programs, as well as with languages like Perl (Practical Extraction and Report Language). In addition, IIS supports the Internet Server Application Programmer Interface (ISAPI) for extensions that require more resource efficiency and performance. ISAPI extensions are typically written as Dynamic Link Libraries (DLLs). The most recent addition to the IIS server-side scripting options is Active Server Pages, which we'll discuss shortly.

FTP

Like the HTTP service, the File Transfer Protocol (FTP) service within IIS has the ability to use the Windows NT Server user database to control access to restricted FTP directories. For basic file transfer operations, the FTP server excels over the other IIS service.

One of the more useful aspects of running an FTP service is that you can provide a low maintenance service to your end users for their basic file transfer needs without having to go to the trouble of creating custom Web pages and pointers to documents and files. Simply enable the FTP service and configure the appropriate directories. For example, if your network contains multiple domains and you want to limit the number of trusts between domains, you can still provide some level of file sharing by creating a `\shared` directory on one server in each domain. Then configure a virtual directory for the `\shared` directory on one IIS server in each domain, and allow anonymous access to the directory. Users within their own domain can copy files to the `\shared` directory using standard tools such as the Windows Explorer, and if they want to share these files with users from other domains, all they need to do is provide those users with the FTP server address or URL.

Gopher

The Gopher service is probably the least used of the IIS services, and many IIS users wonder why a Gopher server was included in the first place. When IIS was originally created, many Internet sites still relied heavily on the Gopher service to provide access to documents and file system directory structures. The makers of IIS wanted to provide a migration path to these existing Gopher site administrators, so they added the Gopher service to IIS.

Typically, Gopher provides many of the same functions as the WWW service, only in a much less graphical, and less visually stimulating, manner; so many Site designers skip Gopher altogether. However, Gopher does a good job of performing the functions it was designed to perform, namely in allowing users to navigate through directory structures of file systems and text files. If you find yourself in a situation where you need to publish a large number of existing text files and you don't have time to convert them to HTML format, you can instead publish them quickly and easily using the Gopher service. Simply create a virtual directory within the Directories tab page on the Gopher Service Properties of the Internet Service Manager, and point your users to the appropriate URL. All Web browsers include support for the Gopher protocol, so you won't have to do anything special on the client end to provide access to the files.

Active Server Pages

Version 3 of the Internet Information Server boasted a number of new enhancements to existing features as well as some entirely new features, such as Active Server Pages (ASP).

Active Server Pages is an ActiveX-based application environment that allows Web developers to utilize scripting languages such as VBScript or JScript to create dynamically generated Web documents. Active Server documents can reference objects such as databases or applications running on the local IIS server, or on other servers throughout the network.

When a user requests a document that contains Active Server scripts from an IIS server, the server will first process the script and then send the results of that processing to the user. For example, a developer might write a script to determine what type and version of Web browser a user has and then format the page appropriately for that particular browser. The end user may only see a Web page that is optimized for their browser, not the code that made the optimization possible.

Active Server Pages provide a number of advantages over other server-side scripting mechanisms such as the Common Gateway Interface (CGI), because the Active Server code itself exists within the HTML documents. In a typical CGI scenario, a user passes input to an external program, which processes the input and submits the output to an HTML document. With Active Server Pages, the functionality provided by the external program is embedded within the HTML document, so in many situations, no external program must be run.

Active Server Pages closely interact with ActiveX components, so if your organization has made a commitment to the ActiveX architecture, you can quickly and easily Web-enable many of your database and other applications with ASP. A complete ASP development environment is available in Microsoft Visual InterDev, part of the Visual Studio product line.

IIS version 4 includes a number of ASP-related enhancements and additions for developers. Microsoft has begun to bundle the Microsoft Transaction Server as part of IIS, so that ASP developers can create transaction-based scripts. If the script encounters an error during processing, the Transaction Server aborts the entire transaction. Another new development feature in 4 is the Microsoft Script Debugger. The Script Debugger provides a mechanism for developers to test and fix errors in ASP scripts.

Index Server

Another server that was bundled with IIS beginning with IIS version 3.0 was the Microsoft Index Server. The Index Server was created to work the same way that the large Internet search services work. On the Internet, users can go to large Web indexes such as Digital's AltaVista site (www.altavista.digital.com) or Excite's site (www.excite.com) to search Web sites that contain information in which the user has an interest. Typically, a user will conduct a search by entering relevant words, called keywords, into a search form on the site. For example, if a user wanted to find Web sites on the Internet that contained information about IIS, they could enter IIS as a keyword. Once the user has entered the keyword, the search site will query its extensive database of Web sites to determine if any sites contained the word *IIS*. If the database contains sites that have documents with the word *IIS* in them, the search engine will return a list of those documents and sites.

Microsoft Index Server provides the same two functions as the large Internet search engines. First, the Index Server will search through all of the documents contained on the IIS server and it will create an index of those documents. Second, the Index Server will respond to queries from IIS users who want to search for documents by keyword. Figure 8.6 shows the Index Server Search page.

One of the most useful features that the Microsoft Index Server provides is its ability to index all types of documents, not just those documents that are saved in HTML format. For example, you could configure the Index server to index a shared directory that contains all of the Microsoft Word and Excel documents related to customer proposals. Users could search by keywords such as the customer's name, the author's name, or the date the document was last revised. Since the Index Server is part of IIS, it offers the same integration with the NT user account database and file access controls, so you can limit

FIGURE 8.6

The Microsoft Index Server Search page

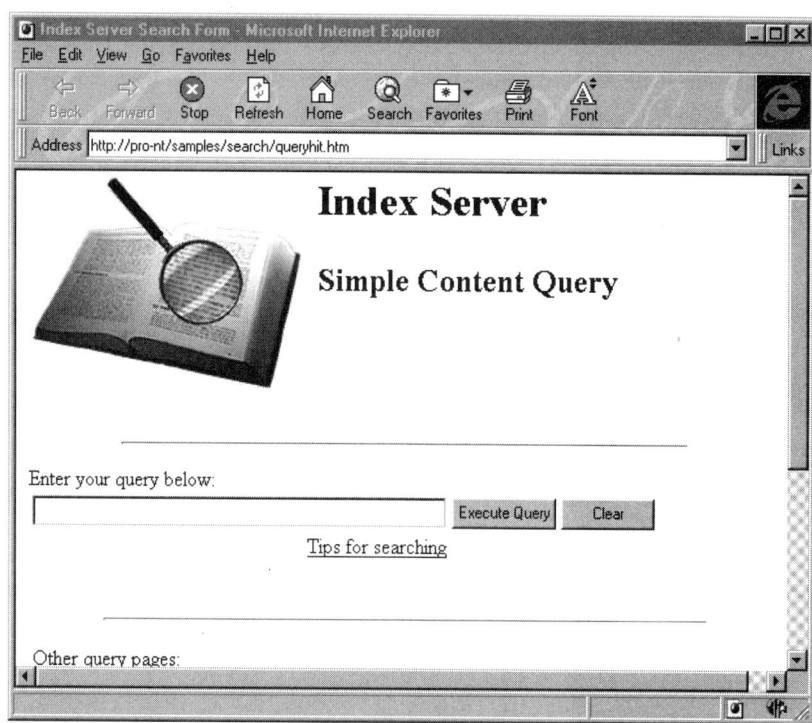

the types of documents that users can access by setting access controls on directories or individual files.

Index Server performs all of its indexing functions in the background. As documents are added, deleted, or modified, the server will update its indexes dynamically. A single Index Server can provide indexing services for multiple IIS servers.

NetShow

Microsoft NetShow is a collection of components that are designed to provide streaming multimedia content through IIS. Video, audio, and other types of multimedia content can be transmitted by a NetShow server either through a live data stream or on an on-demand basis to NetShow clients.

To use NetShow, users simply click on links within standard Web documents. (NetShow documents are stored as Active Streaming Format, or ASF, files). Once the document transfer begins, the NetShow client, an ActiveX control, will initiate automatically and begin to show the contents of the file immediately. Since NetShow is designed to stream files, users can begin to view their requested files while the download is in progress.

To conserve network bandwidth, NetShow can utilize a technique known as *multicasting*. During a multicast transmission, a single data stream is transmitted from one source to multiple, selected sources. Since only a single data stream is sent, the total amount of network traffic generated is much less than if the server had to send a separate transmission to each receiving client. In addition, NetShow has the ability to utilize a number of audio and video compression standards.

NetShow is an ideal tool to use if you plan to provide multimedia files to users of your Internet, intranet, or extranet sites. For example, if your network has the available bandwidth, you can use NetShow to distribute real-time video presentations and conferences.

Like the standard IIS services, NetShow can be administered through the Internet Service Manager application. NetShow supports virtual directories, so NetShow documents can be stored either locally on the server or on a remote host.

Optimizing IIS

If you plan to implement IIS as your primary Internet or intranet Web server, chances are you'll end up spending significant amounts of time tuning the performance of your IIS NT server. While heavy Web activity can push the limits of your server's ability, you can improve overall IIS server performance if you concentrate on a few key areas. We will discuss performance optimization in much greater detail in Chapter 15. The purpose of this section is to provide a basic introduction to IIS-specific issues.

Streamlining Your Services

Before you begin to use tools like Performance Monitor to locate and resolve bottlenecks, do your server a favor and remove any unnecessary services or protocols that may be running on it. For example, if your NT IIS server will be serving Web clients only, remove the NWLink protocols. With some experimentation, you may find that you can remove a number of other services, such as the Network Monitor Agent, the UPS service, the WINS client, and the DHCP client. Remember, however, to be absolutely certain about the functions your server is supposed to provide. Keep thorough records of which services you disable so that you can easily restart them if necessary.

Typical Bottleneck Areas

While IIS provides a number of unique services, how it impacts your NT server is similar to many other server-based applications. The three areas that are most likely to cause a performance bottleneck are the CPU, the memory, and the network bandwidth. Let's examine each of these three areas, and then we'll discuss some tools you can use to identify how well (or poorly) your IIS server is operating.

CPU

While the CPU usage associated with IIS itself is relatively low, the overall load that IIS places on your server's CPU may be significant, especially if the server handles a high number of connections, or if you utilize client authentication or Active Server Pages. If you plan to utilize standard Common Gateway Interface scripts, keep in mind that the CPU utilization impact can be as much as five times more than if you use ISAPI or Active Server Pages to process user input.

If you determine that your CPU is the bottleneck for server performance, you have a number of options. If your server will support multiple processors, you can install an additional processor. If your hardware will not support an additional processor, you can either upgrade to a faster CPU or add additional level 2 cache memory. If a hardware upgrade is not possible, try to distribute CPU-intensive operations to other IIS servers, or look for other alternatives for those operations. For example, if your server contains an old Perl CGI script, install the Perl ISAPI DLL or convert the script into an Active Server Page script.

Memory

While IIS is operating, it tries to store static pages in the memory cache. If your server will store a relatively small number of static documents, the server impact on available memory may be relatively minimal. However, if your server contains a large number of documents, or if you plan to provide dynamic documents through ISAPI, Active Server Pages, or CGI, the amount of required memory may be significantly higher.

If you determine that memory is the bottleneck for server performance, you can add more physical memory to your server. At minimum, your server should have at least 32MB of physical memory, but if you plan to do any server-side processing of dynamic documents, you should add an extra 32MB.

Once you have added extra physical memory to your server, you can further improve performance by selecting the Maximize Throughput for Network Applications option within the Server service.

Bandwidth

Estimating how much bandwidth will be required by an IIS server is sometimes a complicated task. For most organizations that plan to create an Internet Web server, the speed of the network interface in the NT IIS server is usually the highest bandwidth portion of the connection to most of the Web browsers, particularly if users are connected to the Internet through their telephone lines. The challenge for these organizations is to try to accurately predict what speed of Internet connection their application will require. These predictions are difficult to make, particularly if no historical information is available. Predict too high, and the organization will end up paying too much for their Internet connection. Predict too low, and users will become frustrated due to the slow connection to the IIS server.

One way to limit how much bandwidth IIS will use is to configure the Limit Network Use by all Internet Services on This Computer option from the Advanced tab page on the WWW Service Properties dialog box. This option will allow you to specify the maximum amount of bandwidth (in Kbps) that all IIS-related services will be allowed to use. This option can become extremely useful if you wish to reserve a specific amount of bandwidth on your Internet connection for other services, such as SMTP mail or outbound Web traffic from your network users.

If you plan to use IIS on an intranet, you may not have to contend with slower leased lines, but you will need to keep an eye on your server's network connection. If your IIS server will be extremely active in an intranet setting, you may want to consider installing a 100Mbps network interface card.

Microsoft Analysis Tools

Now that you know which areas may be the cause of a performance bottleneck, you'll need to know which tools you can use to find out exactly how your server is operating, and how to determine where the bottlenecks are. For a more thorough discussion of how you can use these tools to configure your NT IIS server for optimal performance, see the *Windows NT Server Resource Kit, Version 4.0 Supplement One* from Microsoft Press.

Performance Monitor and Task Manager

When you install IIS, it will add a number of objects to the Performance Monitor that will allow you to analyze the performance of IIS and it's impact on your NT server, such as the Internet Information Services Global object, the Active Server Pages object, and the FTP, HTTP, and Gopher Services objects.

In general, you'll want to tune your IIS NT server the same way you would tune any other NT server. First, pay close attention to the three typical bottleneck areas: CPU, memory, and bandwidth.

You can use the Task Manager to view CPU time, usage percentage, and memory usage for the main IIS process, Inetinfo.exe. All of the services (FTP, HTTP, and Gopher) run within the Inetinfo process.

For more information on the ins and outs of Performance Monitor and the Task Manager, see Chapter 15.

Process Monitor and Process Viewer

The Windows NT Server 4.0 Resource kit includes a number of additional performance analysis tools, including the Process Monitor and the Process Viewer. Both utilities will provide more detailed information about processes running on your NT server. Process Viewer is a graphical, interactive utility, as shown in Figure 8.7, Process Monitor (pmon.exe) is a character-based utility.

The main screen of Process Viewer contains a list of processes running on the NT server, as well as Processor Time values and percentages of user and privileged processor time for each process. If you select a particular process, you can view privileged and user processor time for each thread of the process. To view additional memory details for a particular process, you can either double-click on the process itself or select the Memory Detail button.

Benchmark and Capacity Analysis Tools

Another extremely useful tool for analyzing IIS performance is the Microsoft Web Capacity Analysis Tool (WCAT) included with the Windows NT Server 4.0 Resource Kit. WCAT is a client-simulation tool that allows you to test how your IIS server will respond under a variety of circumstances. With WCAT, you can determine the exact impact of adding elements such as Active Server Pages, SSL encryption, or authentication to your Web site.

FIGURE 8.7

The Process Viewer

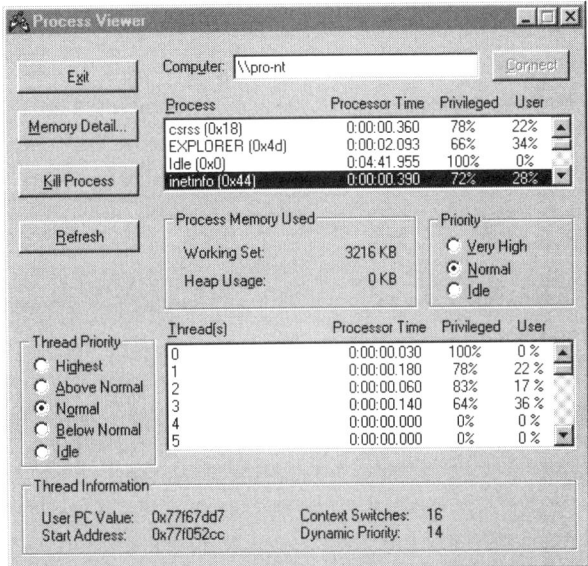

WCAT includes a number of predefined workload simulations to test some of the more frequently utilized features of IIS, or you can define your own performance tests. Once you run the tests, you can identify bottlenecks with Performance Monitor, then you can experiment with your server's hardware and configuration to achieve an optimal configuration.

To install WCAT, you need to prepare three computers; a client workstation, a controller, and a server. The client workstation will transmit the predefined requests to the IIS server and will simulate up to 200 Web clients. If you wish to test for more than 200 clients, you can add extra client stations. The controller station communicates between the server and the client. By removing controller functionality from the other two stations, the amount of test administration overhead on those stations is minimal. The server portion of the WCAT test is your IIS server. During the WCAT installation procedure, you will copy a number of sample content files to your /wwwroot and /scripts directory.

Since WCAT is IIS specific, it's designed to give you the tools you'll need to test many of IIS-specific functions. However, WCAT isn't meant to be used with other Web server platforms, so you may want to incorporate some non-server-specific benchmarking tools to see how IIS fares against its competition.

 There are a number of Web server benchmark tools currently available, ranging in price from free to thousands of dollars. Two of the free tools are WebStone, from Silicon Graphics, Inc. (www.sgi.com/Products/WebFORCE/Resources), and WebBench, from Ziff Davis (www.zdnet.com/zdbop/webbench/webbench.html).

Managing IIS

No two Web servers are alike. Each has its own security and management requirements. Some sites, including the majority of Internet sites, are designed for general public access. Users from all over the world are free to surf through these sites, and few restrictions are placed on what the users can see. Other sites, such as online shopping services, require a higher level of security. Users may be forced to log in to these sites, and sensitive information such as credit card numbers is transmitted securely through the use of encryption.

At the other end of the server management spectrum, IIS administrators require an increasing level of information about how their sites are used. By gaining an understanding of the types of users that access the site, as well as the ways in which they access the site, an IIS administrator can streamline how the site is organized.

Managing IIS servers is a complex task, and a full discussion of IIS management is better left to other books. However, we'll discuss some of the IIS management issues you may encounter during a network design.

IIS Security

Depending on the type of content you wish to offer on your IIS Web server, you may need to plan to implement one or more security measures to keep that content secure and accessible only to authorized users. IIS versions 1–3 provided three types of security mechanisms; authentication, access control, and encryption, and version 4 added SSL Client Authentication. Which mechanism(s) you choose to implement within your design depends in large part on the audience for the server and the nature of the information that will be provided by the server. We will discuss other types of security, such as firewalls, proxy servers, and virtual private networks, in later chapters.

Authentication

As we discussed earlier in this chapter, IIS has the ability to restrict access to controlled documents and directories only to valid, authorized users. Users can authenticate to an IIS server in one of three ways: through basic HTTP authentication, through Windows NT Challenge/Response (NTLM) authentication, or through SSL Client Authentication (IIS version 4 only). Each method has advantages and disadvantages, and your choice should be based upon the requirements of the users of the IIS server.

When users authenticate to IIS either via basic HTTP or via NTLM authentication, IIS will assume that the username and password information is valid for the domain in which the IIS server exists or within the local user database. All accounts required for authentication must be given the Log On Locally user right to the IIS server.

Basic Authentication The first type of authentication, basic HTTP authentication, is based on the standard method for HTTP authentication. When a user requests a restricted resource, their browser will open a dialog box to prompt the user to enter their username and password. Once the user logs on, inputs information, and clicks the OK button, the information is transferred to the IIS server in UUEncoded format. This information is not encrypted, so any information transferred via basic HTTP authentication is susceptible to network eavesdropping.

UUEncode is a process that was originally developed to allow network users to send binary file attachments through SMTP-style electronic mail. Since SMTP mail messages are limited to text characters only, a user must first convert any binary file attachment to a text file by processing the original file through a UUEncode program. The result of a UUEncode process is a text file that looks like a bunch of random text characters. When the recipient receives the UUEncoded attachment, they can run the UUDecode process on the file to return it to its original state.

Once the IIS server receives the login information from the browser, it will attempt to access the restricted resource using the username and password submitted by the browser. If the login name and password are correct, and the corresponding NT user has sufficient access rights to the resource, the server will return the requested information. If the login information is somehow incorrect, or the user is valid but does not have sufficient rights, the request will be denied.

The advantage of basic authentication is that it is supported by nearly all Web browsers currently on the market. Any user of any Web browser can request access to restricted resources and authenticate to your IIS server through basic authentication.

The disadvantage of basic authentication is that it is a far less secure authentication method than NT Challenge/Response authentication. Any login information sent as the result of a basic authentication attempt will be transmitted over the network unencrypted. A rogue user could potentially intercept a login attempt and use the legitimate user's login name and password to gain access to the IIS server or to any other server that the legitimate user can access.

Challenge/Response (NTLM) Authentication The second type of authentication, Challenge/Response Authentication (NTLM), is supported only by Microsoft Internet Explorer version 2.0 or later browsers. When a user submits a request to a restricted resource on an IIS server that is configured for NTLM authentication, and the user's workstation has already been authenticated to a domain that is supported by the IIS server, authentication will occur automatically in the background.

One of the most significant advantages of NTLM authentication is that it does not involve the transmission of a user's name and password over the network for authentication. Instead, the browser and server will transfer user-related information based upon challenge-response algorithms.

The biggest disadvantage of NTLM is that all users must access the restricted resource using Internet Explorer version 2.0 or newer. However, IIS does support a dual-authentication configuration (i.e., both basic and NTLM methods). If a server has been configured to support both basic and NTLM authentication methods, it will first attempt to authenticate a user through NTLM, and then, if the attempt fails, it will authenticate the user through basic authentication.

SSL Client Authentication The third type of authentication, available only in IIS version 4, is SSL Client Authentication. When a user submits a request to restricted resources on an IIS server that is configured for SSL Client Authentication, the IIS server will only permit that user to access the resource if their Web browser contains a valid Secure Sockets Layer (SSL) digital client certificate.

The advantage of SSL Client Authentication is that the user will never receive a prompt to enter their username and password, provided they have an appropriate SSL client certificate. Instead, the browser will transfer the appropriate authentication information directly to the server with no human intervention required.

The disadvantage of SSL Client Authentication is that the server and all users must have been assigned digital certificates. In a large network environment, the overhead and cost associated with assigning a certificate to every potential user may be significant. However, IIS 4 also includes the necessary certificate management software so that an organization can create and manage their own certificates without having to work with an outside certificate authority.

Access Control

The second type of security mechanism built into IIS is support for access control according to the IP address of the user. IP address access control is available through the Advanced tab page of the Service Properties dialog box for each of the IIS services within the Internet Service Manager application in IIS versions 2 and 3. There are two components to IP address access control configuration. First, you must specify the default access rule, then you must indicate if any exceptions to the default will exist. Figure 8.8 shows an example of the IP address access control options within the Advanced tab page.

Upon installation, IIS is set to allow default access to all users. If you wish to deny users from specific IP addresses or users from entire IP network ranges, you can add those addresses to the except list. If you wish only to permit access to specific addresses or to specific IP networks, you must first set the default access to denied access, then input those addresses in the exception list.

Like authentication, IP address-based access controls have a number of advantages and disadvantages. One advantage is that you can restrict access to your IIS server without having to force users to log in to the site by adding only the authorized users' addresses to the exception list. However, this type of configuration assumes that your users' workstations all have predictable IP addresses. If the workstations utilize DHCP to receive their addresses, you may have to permit access to the entire IP subnet, because you won't have the ability to know exactly which address a particular user will receive.

The biggest disadvantage to IP address-based access control is that access is permitted or restricted only by the IP address of the user's workstation, not by the identity of the user who is using the workstation. If you plan to implement IP address-based security, you will have no mechanism to determine the exact identity of the user.

FIGURE 8.8

Configuring IP address access controls within the Internet Service Manager

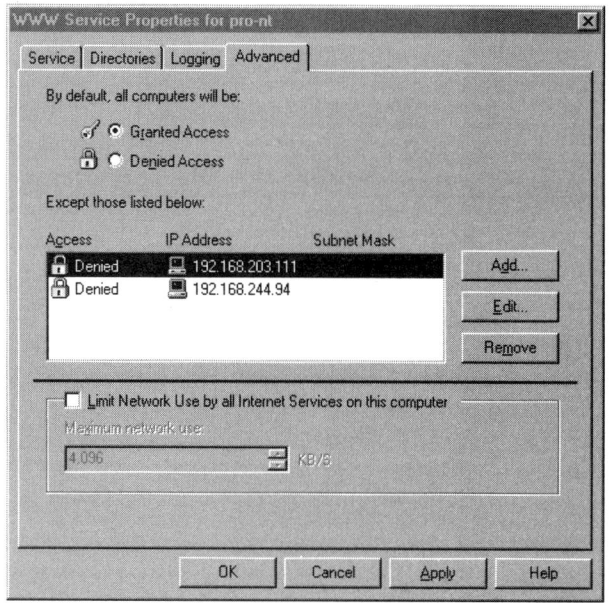

Encryption

The third type of security mechanism built into IIS is support for data encryption. IIS supports Secure Sockets Layer (SSL) version 3, a public key encryption protocol that provides for secure transmission of HTTP requests and responses. By implementing SSL on your Web sites, you can ensure that sensitive information such as credit card numbers, financial information, or private customer-related data will be kept private. How you configure IIS to use SSL will depend upon which version of IIS you plan to implement.

Configuring Encryption on IIS Versions 2 and 3 For IIS versions 2 and 3, you must generate a key pair and certificate request file using the Key Manager application that comes with IIS. When you generate a key and certificate, you will be prompted to input information about your organization, as well as the bit length of the key and a password. Figure 8.9 illustrates the form for creating a certificate request. If you plan to offer SSL-enabled pages to non-U.S. users, you should select a key length of 512 bits. For other applications, remember that the length of the key corresponds to the complexity of the encryption. The higher the key length, the more secure the transmission.

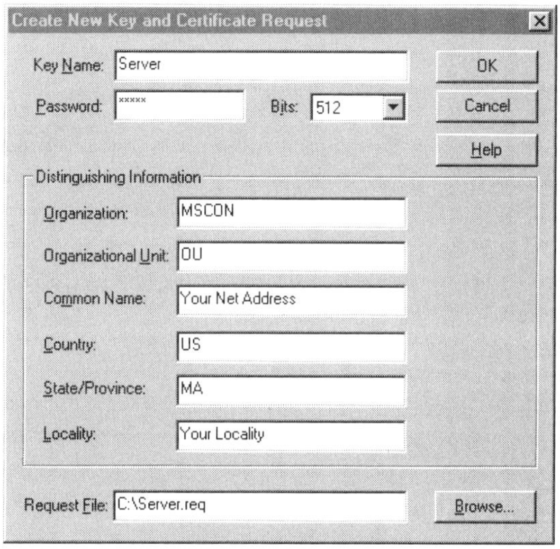

FIGURE 8.9

Requesting a certificate with Key Manager

Once you have generated the key pair and the request certificate, the next step is to submit the certificate request to a certification authority. A certification authority is a trusted third-party organization that will generate a valid certificate to be used on a public network such as the Internet. Certificate authorities operate on the concept of trust. If your organization trusts the certificate authority, and your customers trust the certificate authority, then your customers can trust that the encrypted information sent between you and them really comes from you. Typically, submitting a request for a certificate is as simple as sending an electronic mail message and submitting payment for the certificate. The certificate authority will generate the certificate and send it back to you. One such certificate authority is Verisign, Inc. (www.verisign.com).

The next step is to install the certificate and the key pair onto the IIS server using the Key Manager application. If you plan to implement virtual servers on your IIS server, you can use a single certificate for all of the virtual servers, or you can implement a separate certificate for each of the virtual servers. Installing the certificate is a relatively simple process. Once the installation is complete, both the key pair and the certificate will be stored in the registry.

The final step for implementing SSL is to configure IIS to require SSL transmissions. You can configure IIS to require SSL from the root directory or from individual directories, but keep in mind that any SSL-encrypted transmissions are more computation intensive than non-encrypted transmissions, so you should only configure documents and directories that require security for SSL transmissions. Longer key lengths translate to higher communications overhead.

Configuring Encryption on IIS Version 4   Configuring encryption on IIS Version 4 is a different process than in previous versions, because version 4 includes its own digital certificate server. With the Microsoft Certificate Server, organizations can become their own certificate authority of interorganizational certificate creation. However, if the organization plans to create an Internet-based IIS site, they should work in conjunction with a recognized certificate authority.

If you choose to install and configure the Certificate Server, you will have the option to take on the responsibility of managing all of the key requests from users throughout your network. Since each certificate from a commercial certificate authority may cost hundreds of dollars, the benefits of maintaining your own internal certificate authority can become obvious if you plan to manage a number of servers.

Generating key requests from IIS is similar to the way it was done in previous versions, with the exception that you'll be given the option to submit the request directly to your Certificate Server.

It's a good idea to implement SSL encryption if you plan to implement basic HTTP authentication so that the username and password information may be encrypted via SSL.

IIS and SNMP

Another aspect of server management that you should consider relates to the operational state of the IIS server itself. Microsoft has provided a number of SNMP Management Information Bases (MIBs) to utilize with IIS so that you can monitor critical IIS operational information.

Simple Network Management Protocol (SNMP) is a protocol that was developed to allow network administrators to remotely manage any type of network device, such as a server, router, printer, or hub. In a typical SNMP implementation, information about all of the managed network devices is collected by a single workstation, usually referred to as a *management console*. Each managed device loads a piece of SNMP software, called an *agent*. Information about the managed device can get to the console in one of two ways. Either the console can send a request, called a *GET*, to the device for the information, or the device can send an alert, called a *trap*, to notify the console that a predetermined threshold has been exceeded.

SNMP is an optional service that requires that TCP/IP be installed on the NT server you want to monitor. The basic NT agent can be "extended" by incorporating additional MIBs such as those provided for MS IIS, WINS, DHCP, etc. The agent will need to be configured to identify trap destinations (the management console or consoles) and the community name (used for security purposes).

The Windows NT Server 4.0 Resource Kit includes MIBs for the three primary IIS services: FTP, Gopher, and HTTP, as well as a general IIS MIB, called INETSRV. Once you have compiled these MIBs on your network management console, you'll be able to view a wide variety of performance values, such as the number of current connections, number of bytes transmitted, and number of files sent. Use the MIBCC.EXE utility that comes with the Resource Kit to compile the MIBs.

IIS SNMP functionality is limited to read-only, meaning you can view all related SNMP statistics and configuration information, but you cannot change IIS configuration parameters through the SNMP agent.

Reporting Utilities for IIS

SNMP information can be helpful to determine the operational state of your IIS server and basic server statistics, but it does not tell you very much about who is using your IIS site, where they came from, and how they use your site.

In IIS version 3.0, Microsoft bundled a special version of Seagate Crystal Reports, called Crystal Reports for Internet Information Server 4.5. Crystal Reports for IIS includes a number of predefined reports that have been specifically designed for IIS activity logs. Reports can be generated from standard IIS log files or from logs stored on a SQL Server or other ODBC database, and then published as HTML files that can be viewed by any Web browser.

One of the most useful features of Crystal Reports for IIS is its ability to dynamically generate Web reports through an Active Server Pages-based Web engine. Authorized users can specify the type of report to generate, the log to generate the report from, and the start and end dates for the report data. Figure 8.10 shows a graph that was dynamically generated as the result of the report request.

In IIS version 4, Microsoft bundled a subset of its Site Server product, called Site Server Express. Site Server Express includes two components: the Usage Analyst and the Site Analyst.

Usage Analyst is a reporting tool, similar to Crystal Reports for IIS. With Usage Analyst, administrators can import log files from IIS or from any other

FIGURE 8.10

A sample Crystal Reports for IIS graph

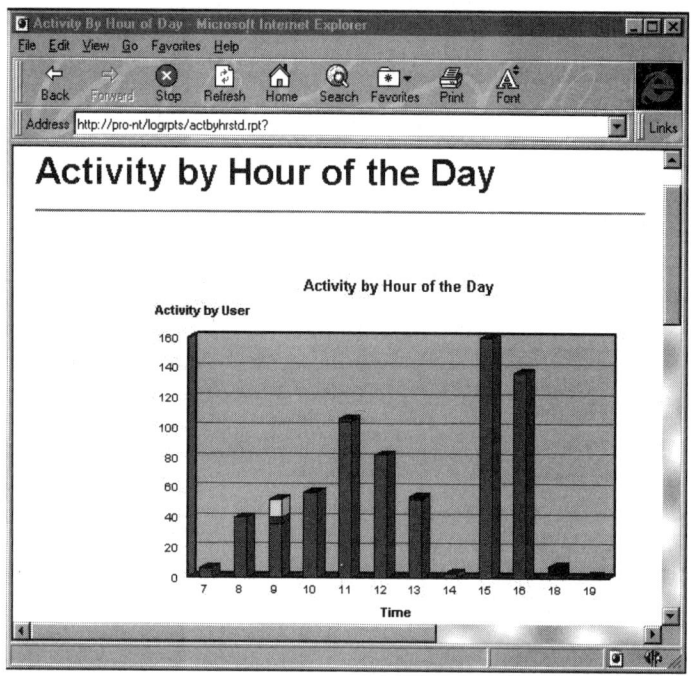

Web server that supports IIS or NCSA style logs. Once a log file has been imported, Usage Analyst can generate a number of predefined reports including the top 20 requested documents, daily visit trends, usage summaries, and bandwidth usage.

Site Analyst is a tool designed to provide comprehensive Web site structural analysis. Once configured, Site Analyst will explore through a Web site, checking for errors and invalid links, as well as missing objects (such as images) or links to other sites. After the exploration is complete, Site Analyst will create a visual map to the site, as shown in Figure 8.11. In addition, Site Analyst can generate site statistic reports in HTML format for viewing through a Web browser.

Another reporting tool for IIS is WebTrends, by e.g. Software, Inc. (www.webtrends.com). WebTrends is similar to Crystal Reports for IIS, in that it is designed to provide analysis of Web server log files. However, WebTrends includes a larger number of predefined reports than Crystal Reports for IIS and provides some additional reporting functions for intranet-related IIS sites.

WebTrends can analyze log files on the IIS server itself, or you can configure it to download log files from other IIS servers via HTTP or FTP. Unlike

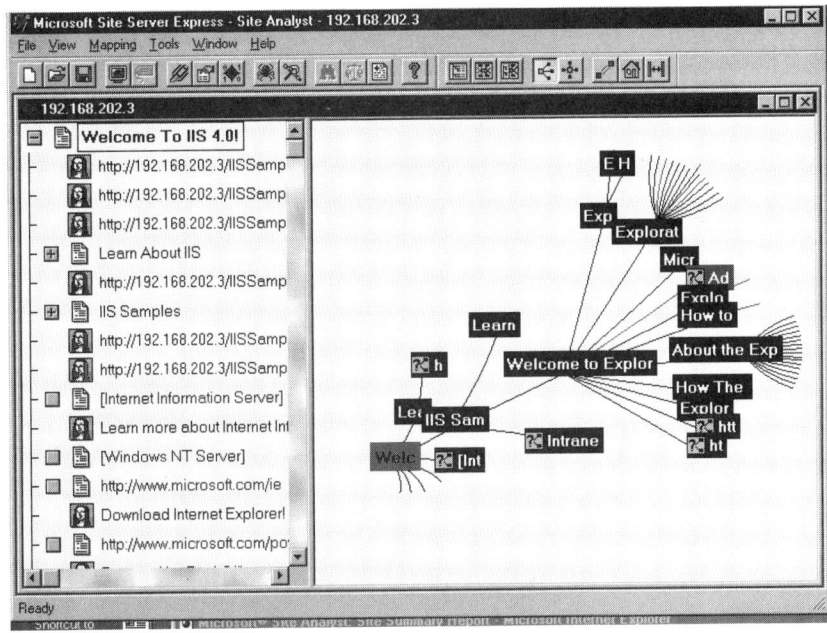

FIGURE 8.11

A Site Analyst Web site visual map

Crystal Reports for IIS, which utilizes Active Server Pages for dynamic report generation, WebTrends is able to run as a Windows NT service. You can schedule large reports to run automatically in the background so that they are available immediately upon request. Web administrators can view reports from the WebTrends program itself, or they can access the WebTrends engine through their Web browser. Figure 8.12 shows a sample WebTrends report.

IIS Design Considerations

Now that you understand some IIS fundamentals, let's discuss some issues and features you should consider before you begin to design an IIS implementation. IIS provides a number of unique features that you can leverage to extend the functionality provided by your design.

FIGURE 8.12
A sample WebTrends report

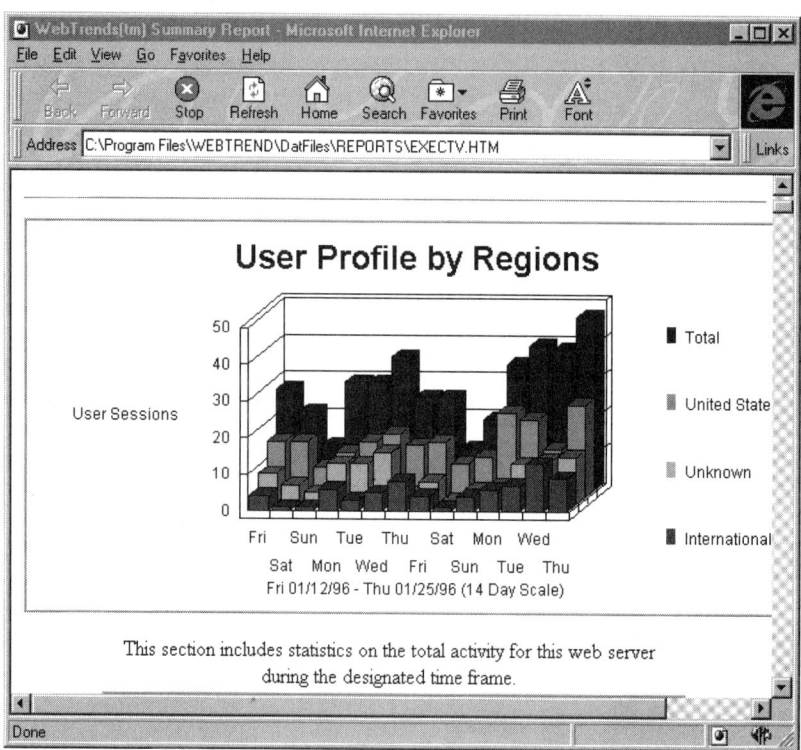

Utilizing Virtual Directories

As we discussed earlier in this chapter, IIS has the ability to serve documents not only from subdirectories of the Web server root directory, but also from virtual directories that have been logically mapped to actual subdirectories that do not exist off the document root. For example, if your server document root directory was called \WWWroot, IIS would interpret all HTTP requests relative to the \WWWroot directory. If a user submitted the URL http:\\www.server.com\docs\index.htm, IIS would look for the docs subdirectory of the WWWroot directory. The docs directory may be an actual, physical subdirectory of WWWroot, or it may exist only as a pointer to some other subdirectory on the IIS server itself, or on a totally different server.

The real advantages to utilizing virtual directories become apparent when you realize that a virtual directory can be created to point to any network file system that can be referenced by a UNC (Universal Naming Convention) name. For example, you can load the Gateway for NetWare services on your IIS server, mount a NetWare volume, and create a virtual directory that points to a subdirectory on the NetWare volume. Suddenly, users can access files on the IIS server or on your NetWare servers, all through their Web browser.

> ### A Virtual Directory: The Missing Link
>
> One client of ours had a large number of Microsoft Word files stored on their NetWare file server that they wanted to make available through their IIS server. However, they also wanted to allow users to search for documents using selected keywords. By creating a virtual directory to the NetWare file server and configuring the Microsoft Index Server to index the Word documents in the virtual directory, users could search for the documents they needed and download or view the files with a click on a hyperlink.

By designing an IIS implementation that utilizes virtual directories, you can significantly expand the scope of the content provided by the IIS server. You can create virtual directories that correspond to departmental shared file areas to enable each department to manage their own Web documents, or you can create virtual directories that map to existing legacy data. As you are creating your IIS design, keep in mind that it may be more efficient in the long run to point IIS to the data instead of moving the data to existing IIS subdirectories.

Creating Virtual Servers

Another extremely useful IIS feature is the ability to masquerade as multiple, unique Web servers, called *virtual servers*. Each virtual server looks like an entirely separate, independent Web server to users, and each server can have its own unique DNS name. For example, you can configure a single IIS server to masquerade as both the www.sales.company.com Web server and the www.marketing.company.com Web server.

To implement virtual servers, you must first configure your NT IIS server to have multiple unique IP addresses. You can add up to five unique addresses through the Network applet within the control panel, and you can configure additional addresses by modifying the registry.

Once you have configured the multiple IP addresses, you link a directory to the virtual server IP address within the Directory Properties dialog box of the WWW Service Properties section of the Internet Service Manager application. Input the name of the directory, then select the Virtual Server checkbox and input the IP address that will correspond to the directory itself.

When a user submits a request to the IP address of the virtual server, IIS will match the IP address to the directory of the virtual server, and it will respond with the file from the appropriate directory.

Virtual servers are extremely useful in situations where server hardware resources are limited and your customers need to support multiple, low-volume Web servers. For example, many Internet Service Providers offer virtual Web servers for their customers because they can support many users' virtual servers on a single, physical IIS server.

As you design virtual server implementations for IIS servers, consider the overall impact to the server hardware. If the servers will be extremely busy, or if they will use Active Server Pages, authentication, or encryption, keep the number of virtual servers to a minimum and keep an eye on performance statistics.

Load Balancing with DNS

As a Web site becomes more popular and network traffic to the server increases, eventually you will reach the point when no amount of performance optimization or hardware upgrades will suffice. One method you can utilize to address the need for additional IIS hardware resources is to create multiple mirror sites to your existing IIS site. By creating duplicate sites to your existing site, you can gain a higher level of performance as well as some additional fault tolerance. If your original server crashes or becomes otherwise unavailable, you will have additional, duplicate servers already online.

By balancing, or distributing, the Web traffic to multiple IIS servers, you can double, triple, or quadruple the number of hits your site can effectively accommodate. One of the technical hurdles you must overcome before you can mirror IIS servers is to provide a way to efficiently distribute the HTTP requests across all of the mirrored servers while providing a single, easy-to-remember host name to your users. One of the most frequently used techniques is called "round-robin" DNS. To implement round-robin DNS, you must create a CNAME resource record for each of the mirrored IIS servers. For example, you would normally give each IIS server a unique address (A) resource record, such as www1.company.com, www2.company.com, and www3.company.com. To implement round-robin, you would create three CNAME records, one for each of the IIS hosts, with the canonical name value of www.company.com. Once this is configured and a user submits a request for www.company.com, the DNS server will send a list of all hosts that have a CNAME of www.company.com. When the next user attempts to resolve www, the DNS server will send the list again, but this time it will change the order of the host names. (The name that was at the top of the list in the first request will be moved to the bottom of the list.) Since most client software will send the HTTP request to the first host name they receive, the requests will be balanced among all of the hosts.

In this chapter, we discussed the services available with the Microsoft Internet Information Server, such as FTP, HTTP, and Gopher. In the next chapter, we'll look at tools and products you can use to implement other Net services, such as DNS, Mail, and News.

CHAPTER 9

DNS, Mail, and News

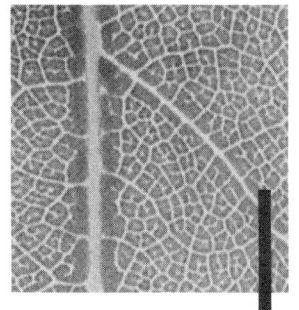

nternet Information Server is a powerful tool for publishing information to a large audience, but you'll need to plan to implement a number of other, auxiliary services that will augment your intranet, Internet, or extranet server.

First and most importantly, you'll need to implement a naming service so that your users can locate servers and services like your IIS server. In Chapter 5 we discussed one such naming service: the Windows Internet Naming Service (WINS). While WINS is a good choice on networks with Windows clients only, it is not an open standard in the spirit of the TCP/IP protocols, so it cannot be used by computers other than Windows-based systems. To open your resources to a broader, cross-platform audience, you'll need to implement a more open naming service protocol so that other users can locate your systems. The naming protocol used by hosts on the Internet and within intranets is the Domain Name Service (DNS), which we discussed in Chapter 7.

Once your naming service is in place, you'll likely want to provide your users with some other open-standards-based tools, such as electronic mail and news discussion groups. We'll briefly describe some of the tools and protocols you can use to implement and manage an e-mail system that will enable your users to communicate internally—and externally to the outside world.

In this chapter, we'll discuss:

- Microsoft's DNS Server implementation tips
- How to integrate DNS, WINS, and DHCP
- Third-party DNS tools
- Open-standards-based mail and news tools

Let's begin with Microsoft's implementation of the Domain Name Service (DNS).

The Microsoft DNS Server

The Microsoft DNS Server was initially released as part of Microsoft's embrace of the Internet in NT Server 4. Microsoft DNS server is a full-featured DNS implementation that allows administrators to provide primary and backup DNS services for Internet, intranet, and extranet applications. Because it was developed according to RFC-specified standards, the Microsoft DNS server can work in coordination with other servers that follow the DNS protocol standards.

Since we discussed DNS concepts in detail back in Chapter 7, let's reintroduce some key concepts in review.

The Domain Name Service is a hierarchical, distributed name database that provides a mapping of easy-to-remember host names to their corresponding IP addresses. DNS is comprised of three elements, the domain name space, name servers, and resolvers. The *domain name space* is the tree-like structure that organizes host names according to subdivisions, called domains. *Name servers* contain portions, called *zones,* of the entire domain name space. A zone may contain a single domain, or it may contain multiple domains and subdomains. *Resolvers* are the software components that submit name-to-address translation requests to name servers.

To provide fault tolerance, at least two DNS servers should be designated for each zone: a primary name server and a secondary name server. The primary name server will become the focus for all administrative tasks, and the secondary server will periodically replicate all DNS database changes through a process known as a *zone transfer*. While it is possible to maintain a single-server DNS implementation, it is not recommended. In fact, a two-server fault-tolerant DNS implementation is required if you plan to connect to the Internet. Considering that the server utilization overhead of running a secondary DNS server is minimal, you should be able to run secondary services on one of a number of servers on your network.

You can add the DNS server service through the Services tab page within the Network applet of the Control Panel. Once you add the service, the installation process will automatically add the DNS Manager application to the Start menu of your server. Like other NT adminstrative tools, you can use DNS Manager to manage DNS services on the local server or on a remote server.

Doing It Right

While configuring an NT server to become a DNS server is not a complicated process, the steps you'll need to follow for a successful implementation may not be immediately obvious when you first view the DNS Manager main window, as shown in Figure 9.1. To simplify your configuration, we'll outline the process of establishing a zone and domain.

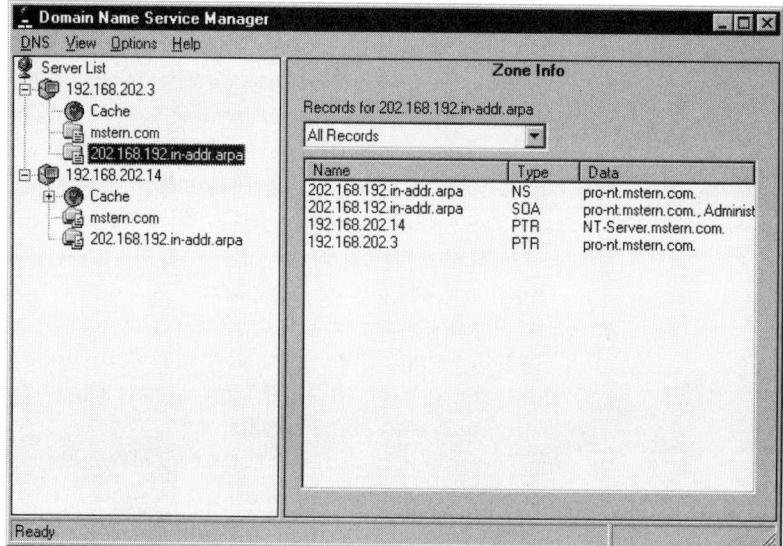

FIGURE 9.1

The DNS Manager application

At this point, if you have not already configured the DNS domain information for your server in the TCP/IP Protocol section of the Network Control Panel applet, you should do so. Select the DNS tab page within the Microsoft TCP/IP Properties dialog box, then input the domain name in which this server will exist. You'll need to reboot the server if you change this information.

Adding the DNS Server

Restart the DNS Manager from the Administrative Tools menu on the Start menu. DNS Manager is a Windows Explorer-like management tool: the left portion of DNS manager displays DNS objects such as servers, zones, and domains, and the right portion displays properties of the objects.

Highlight the Server List entry (identified by a globe on a globe stand) in the left-hand window. Then select the New Server option either by right-clicking the Server List object or through the DNS option on the menu bar. Input the IP address of the DNS server (the server on which you are working) in the Add DNS Server dialog box, and select OK.

Once the server object appears in the left window of DNS Manager to signify that the object has been created, double-click it to expand the view. You should see four objects: a Cache object (identified by a globe) and three folders (0.in-addr.arpa, 127.in-addr.arpa, and 255.in-addr.arpa). These three folders are the default reverse lookup zones. We'll discuss the function of the cache and the reverse lookup zones shortly.

You can view details for any of the objects by single-clicking that object. To view additional information for the object, right-click the object, and then select the Properties option.

Creating a Zone

Once you have created your DNS server, the next step is to create the zone that will contain your domain. Right-click the DNS server object, and select the New Zone option. Since this is the first DNS server, select Primary for the Zone Type, then select Next. In the Zone Info dialog box, input the name for your domain in the Zone Name field. The Zone File information will be filled in automatically, as shown in Figure 9.2. Click the Next button, and then select Finish to create the zone.

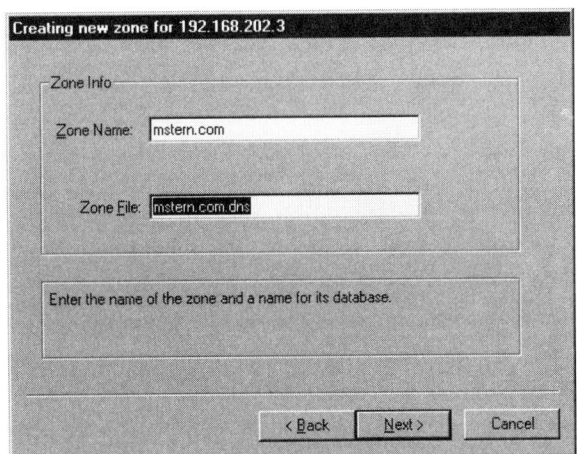

FIGURE 9.2

Inputting a new zone name

After the zone has been created, you'll notice that the DNS Manager now contains a folder for it. Highlight the zone with a single click, then view the zone information window on the right side of the DNS manager. You'll notice that at least three resource records have been created along with the zone: a nameserver (NS) record, a start of authority (SOA) record, and at least one address (A) record. If your server contains multiple IP addresses, an A record was created for each interface.

If you plan to use the virtual Web server feature of IIS, you'll want to make sure that the DNS names match up to the correct IP addresses. By default, when you create a new zone, DNS manager will automatically assign an A record with the host name of your NT server to all of the IP addresses on the server. For example, if you had three network interface cards, each with its own IP address, DNS Manager would create three A records with the same host name, one for each IP address. When a request from a Web browser was submitted to that host name, the DNS server could potentially return any one of those three addresses as a response. The end result would be that you could never predict exactly which IP address the browser would receive. While this functionality works great for "round-robin" purposes (see the last chapter), it will cause a problem in this type of scenario. Your best course of action is to leave only one of the newly created A records, and re-create the others so that they have unique names.

Each of these records fulfills a special role, and without them your DNS server will not operate properly. The nameserver (NS) record indicates the server which will provide DNS name services for the zone. If a zone has more than one name server (and all should have at least two), each name server will be indicated by an NS record. Only one server, however, will have primary responsibility for the zone, and that server will be identified by the start of authority (SOA) record. While the NS record merely identifies the host name for a name server, the SOA record contains additional information, such as the mail address for the DNS administrator and information that will be used by secondary DNS servers. For example, the SOA record contains the version number, or serial number, of the DNS database. Each time a record within the DNS database is modified, the serial number will be increased. When a secondary DNS server contacts the primary, it examines the serial number. If the current serial number is higher than the serial number of the secondary server's database, the secondary will request an update.

Other fields contained within the SOA record are the refresh interval (which identifies the frequency with which the secondaries will contact the primary), the retry interval (which informs secondaries how long to wait before attempting to recontact a failed server), the expire time (which defines the lifetime for DNS records on a secondary server), and the minimum time to live (TTL, the minimum amount of time that a host should cache information about a particular record).

Both the NS record and the SOA record utilize host names to identify servers, so your zone requires at least one address record to provide the name to address mapping to complete the zone. By default, DNS manager creates an address record for each IP address on your server.

Adding a Secondary Server

After you have created your primary DNS server, you'll need to create a secondary server for fault tolerance. Creating a secondary server is easier than creating a primary one. However, it will require that you have a second available DNS server. On the second server, follow the same procedure to install the DNS service. Once the service has been installed and the server rebooted, you can utilize the DNS Manager on your primary server to manage the secondary. Right-click the Server List object within DNS Manager, then select New Server. Input the IP address of the secondary server. Then right-click the new server object, and select New Zone. This time, instead of selecting Primary for the Zone Type, select Secondary. You will be prompted to input the zone name and IP address for the primary server. As a shortcut, you can drag the hand icon to point to an existing zone, and the fields will be filled in automatically. Complete the zone and file name information, then modify the list of IP masters (IP addresses for primary servers), as shown in Figure 9.3. The IP master is the host that the secondary server will contact to receive zone update information. Then select Finish to create the secondary server.

Don't Forget IN-ADDR.ARPA

Once you have created the primary zone and added a secondary server, you'll need to create another primary zone (the in-addr.arpa zone) to provide reverse lookup services for your domain. As we discussed in Chapter 7, the purpose of the in-addr.arpa zone is to enable processes to look up hostnames if they have an IP address of a host. For example, if you use logging on your IIS server, you can view the logs in one of two ways, either by the IP address of the browser or by the DNS hostname of the browsing machine. The way IIS generates the DNS hostname is by performing a reverse name lookup based on the in-addr.arpa zones.

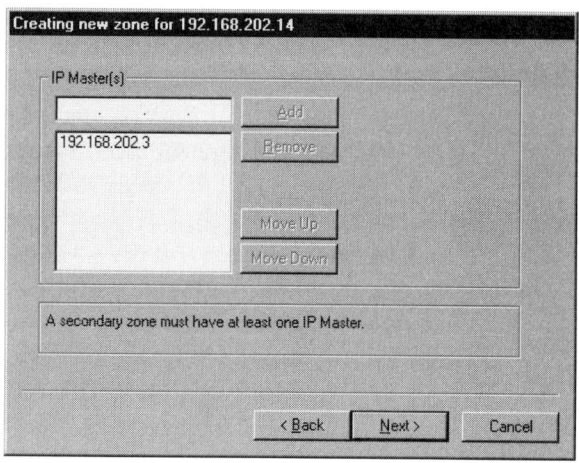

FIGURE 9.3

Input the address of the primary name server in the IP Master field.

Creating an in-add.arpa domain is similar to creating a regular DNS name. Follow all of the steps that you used to create your DNS domain, except this time, the name of the zone should be the IP address of your network, in reverse. For example, if your IP network address is 192.168.202.0, your in-addr.arpa zone name will be 202.168.192.in-addr.arpa.

Once you've finished creating the primary in-addr.arpa zone, you'll need to create a secondary server for the zone, using the same steps you followed to create your first secondary server. You can use the same NT server to provide secondary DNS services for your DNS zone as well as your in-addr.arpa zone.

Be sure to create a corresponding in-addr.arpa domain for your network *before* you create any additional address records, because once the reverse lookup domain exists, DNS Manager can automatically create records for it, called *pointer* or PTR records. Pointer records are the opposite of an A record; they list a IP address first, and then a DNS hostname. If you create the address records before you create the reverse lookup zone, you have to create the PTR records manually.

Adding Resource Records

Now that you've created your primary and secondary DNS servers, you can begin to populate the DNS database. To create DNS records, simply right-click the domain in which you would like the records to exist, then select New Host or New Record. The New Host option will allow you to create only an address (A) record. Use the A records any time you wish to create a simple IP address to hostname mapping. If you select New Record, you have an option to create any type of DNS resource record. The most common types of records (other than those we've already discussed) are CNAME records and MX records.

A canonical name (CNAME) record allows you to assign an alias name for a host that already has an address record. For example, you may have one NT server (called ptsnt01.company.com) that will provide FTP, DNS, and WWW services, so you can assign the names ftp.company.com, dns.company.com, and www.company.com as aliases to this server.

Alias records come in handy for these types of services, because they give you some flexibility if you need to switch a service to another system. Instead of having to delete and create a new address record, you can simply change the host DNS name in the CNAME record to point to the new server.

A Mail Exchange (MX) record is a special type of DNS resource record that identifies a default mail server for a domain. If a domain contains one or more MX records, any mail server that wanted to send mail to the domain would examine those MX records to determine which server provides mail services for the domain. An MX record contains three pieces of information: a domain name, a hostname, and a preference number. The domain name identifies the target domain, the hostname identifies the destination mail server for the domain, and the preference is a numeric value. Since multiple servers may provide MX services for a single domain, the preference value determines the order in which the servers will be contacted. Mail servers with lower preference numbers will be contacted first; if they are unavailable, the transmitting mail server will attempt to contact the server with the next highest preference value.

Remember that you do not need to create an address record for every host on your network, only those hosts that will provide services, such as FTP, WWW, or MAIL.

Working with the Cache File

As you explore the objects within DNS Manager, you may notice an object called CACHE. The CACHE object represents the cache file. The purpose of the cache file is to provide a listing of frequently accessed hosts, such as the root name servers. If your network is connected to the Internet, the Microsoft DNS service will use the cache file to determine the IP addresses for the Internet root name servers. Any time the Microsoft DNS server receives a

DNS request for a hostname that exists within another domain, it will forward the request to one of the root name servers.

The only time you may need to modify the cache file is if your network is not connected to the Internet, or if there is a firewall between your DNS server and the Internet. The reason you'll need to modify the file is that in either of these cases, the DNS server will not be able to contact the root name servers directly. To work around this problem, you'll need to replace the root name server NS records with NS records for the lowest level DNS servers on your network. Simply delete the existing root server NS records, and add new ones that instead point to your DNS servers. Once you have completed these changes, your servers will become the authoritative DNS servers for your network.

One additional step you can take is to configure your DNS server to forward all DNS requests for foreign domains to another DNS server. Right-click your DNS server object within DNS Manager, then select Properties, and then select the Forwarders tab page. Input the IP address of the DNS server to which you want the server to forward requests.

DNS/WINS/DHCP Integration

On the Internet, DNS has become the de facto naming service for locating computers across the network. However, there is one significant limitation that prevents many network administrators from taking full advantage of DNS as a naming service on their network: Most DNS servers will only provide name resolution for computers that have a permanent, static IP address. Since hosts that receive their IP address via DHCP do not permanently own their IP address, there is no mechanism in DNS to dynamically change the IP address for a host address (A) record. That means if you plan to assign addresses to workstations on your network via DHCP, your users will not have the ability to access other workstations using DNS hostname resolution. (That might not be a bad idea, as we'll discuss shortly). If your users plan to offer services such as the Microsoft Peer Web Services Web server on their workstations, users of non-Microsoft network clients may be unable to resolve the DNS name for the server.

Microsoft (and a number of other software providers) recognized this limitation of DNS and came up with a way to provide DNS services for DHCP-client workstations. Essentially, each of the products relies on some mechanism for the workstation to register its hostname when it receives its IP address upon boot-up. While each of the products performs this service in a slightly different way, each follows the same basic principles. For this discussion, we'll focus on Microsoft's implementation.

Microsoft provides DNS name services for DHCP-assigned workstations through an integration with the Windows Internet Naming Service (WINS), which we discussed in Chapter 5.

Essentially, here is the how the service works:

1. A workstation configured to be a DHCP client submits a DHCP address request upon boot-up.

2. The DHCP server responds with an IP address.

3. The workstation then registers itself with the WINS server, using its NetBIOS name as an identifier.

4. When a DNS request comes in to resolve the workstation's address, the DNS server will first search its database. If a resource record for the host is not found, the server (if configured to use WINS) will consult the WINS server for that DNS domain. When it contacts the WINS server, only the hostname information is transmitted, not the domain name. So if the DNS server wanted to resolve the hostname moby.company.com, it would send only the name "moby" to the WINS server.

5. The WINS server responds with the hostname and IP address, which the DNS server then formats as a DNS response to the request.

Configuring your NT DNS server to interact with WINS is a relatively simple process. First, you need to make sure that both the DNS and WINS services have been configured for your network and are working properly. Next, start the DNS Manager and right-click the zone on which you'd like to enable WINS/DNS integration. Select the WINS Lookup tab page, as shown in Figure 9.4. Then click the Use WINS Resolution checkbox, and input the IP address for the WINS server.

Once you've enabled WINS resolution for the zone, the DNS server will utilize WINS to resolve any hostname requests for hosts that are not contained within the DNS server's resource record database. Keep in mind that the WINS resolution will only work on the lowest-level domain in the zone, so if multiple subdomains exist within the zone, WINS lookups will not take place for those domains.

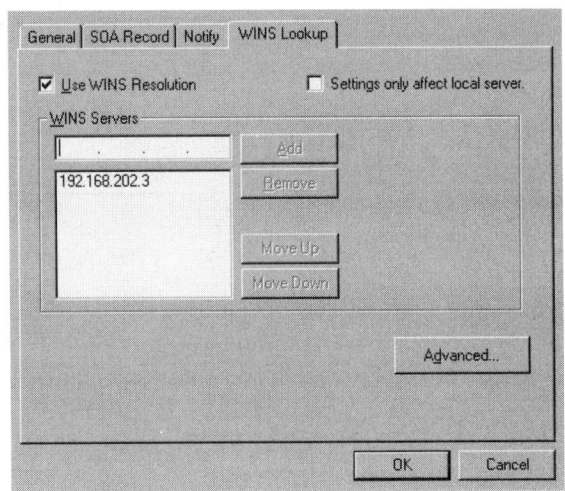

FIGURE 9.4

Enabling WINS/DNS Integration through the DNS Manager.

Dynamic DNS/DHCP Considerations

While the prospect of integrating DNS and DHCP to provide naming services for all of your workstations may sound intriguing, there are a number of issues you should consider before you attempt to implement this type of configuration.

First, reconsider whether or not every user on the network really needs a DNS name. Typically, network users require DNS to access other resources on the network. If your average network user will not provide any services, why do they need a DNS name? If no DNS name for their computer exists, it is less likely that the user would attempt to set up their own services, such as a Web or FTP server, on their workstation.

Some organizations limit the records in their DNS databases to an absolute minimum for security purposes. The primary reason for this is that system crackers may attempt to compromise a DNS server for the sole purpose of discovering more information about a given network. After all, what better tool could one use to obtain a directory of every computer on the network?

One compelling reason to employ DNS/DHCP integration is that it will allow network administrators to more easily track network and resource utilization by users with IP-addressed computers. For example, some firewalls provide logging features to track Internet usage by internal users. If each user's computer has a DNS name, the firewall can be configured to list the DNS name of the system instead of an IP address, which would make it easier for the administrator to identify exactly which user's workstation submitted the request.

Configuring Workstations for Dynamic DNS

The process for configuring client workstations for DNS/DHCP operation is also not complicated, but the exact procedures you'll need to follow may vary depending on whose DNS/DHCP product you plan to use. Virtually all of the products will use the computer's NetBIOS name to generate the DNS hostname. How you configure the NetBIOS name depends on the type of network client software being used on the workstation.

To configure the computer name on a Windows 95 or Windows NT workstation, select the Identification tab page within the Network applet of the Control Panel, as shown in Figure 9.5. Then complete the Computer Name field to identify the name of the computer.

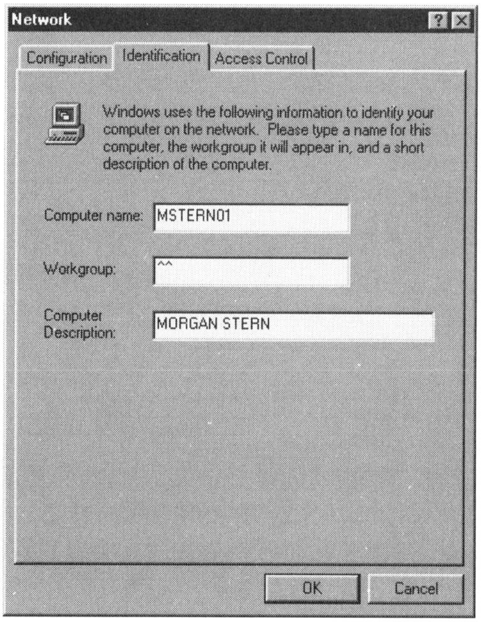

FIGURE 9.5

The Identification tab page of the Control Panel Network applet

Third-Party DNS Servers

While the Microsoft DNS server may be convenient to deploy because it comes free with NT Server 4, there are other factors that will influence your decision about which DNS service you deploy on your network.

One issue to consider is that your organization may have already deployed a DNS system that runs on another computing platform. For example, many organizations that maintain UNIX systems have already deployed DNS services based on the BIND or NAMED programs. If this is the case, you may not need to host DNS on your NT servers. However, you also may not have the flexibility you'd like because your administrators will not have access to the UNIX DNS servers. In such a situation, it might be helpful to implement a server on NT that would be more compatible with UNIX BIND.

Another factor that may influence your decision to avoid the Microsoft DNS server is the need for more flexibility in dynamic DNS/DHCP integration. Since the Microsoft DNS server only supports dynamic DNS through WINS, every workstation on your network would have to utilize Microsoft networking clients to take advantage of DNS/WINS integration.

There are other alternatives for providing DNS on your NT Servers, such as products available from third-party developers. In the next few pages, we'll examine two such products, although a number of other products exist on the market.

The first product, BIND for NT, is available as a free download from the Software.com Web site (http://www.software.com/prod/bindnt/bindnt.html). The second product, MetaIP from MetaInfo, Inc., combines DNS and DHCP management through a Java management program.

BIND for NT

BIND for NT is a free implementation of the Berkeley Internet Name Domain, the most widely used domain name server on the Internet. Originally, BIND was developed for the UNIX platform, so many organizations originally deployed DNS using BIND, and many administrators are familiar with BIND configuration and maintenance.

BIND relies upon a number of text configuration files for operation: a boot file, which contains instructions that the service will interpret when it initializes, and database (db) files, which contain information about the domains and resource records maintained by the server itself and pointers to other servers on the Internet.

Once you install BIND for NT, you can make configuration changes directly within the data files, and you can start, stop, and manage the service through a Control Panel applet, shown in Figure 9.6.

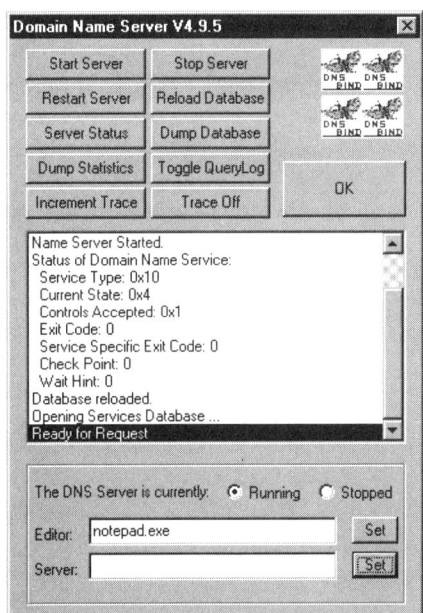

FIGURE 9.6

The BIND for NT Control Panel applet

The advantage of BIND for NT is that since it uses the same configuration files as its UNIX counterpart, your administrator can easily transfer configuration information between platforms. If an administrator is already comfortable working with BIND-style data files, they can enjoy the convenience of Windows NT server while still providing DNS services with BIND.

Note that although BIND is available from Software.com, it is non-commercial freeware. It is available on an as-is basis and is not supported by Software.com tech support. If you plan to implement BIND for NT, be sure to test it thoroughly before you deploy it on a production network.

MetaIP

Another commercial product is the MetaIP suite from Metainfo, Inc. MetaIP is a group of products developed to enable administrators of very large networks to gain control of the DNS and DHCP servers throughout their network. A Java-based management application, called the MetaIP/Manager (shown in Figure 9.7), provides network managers with a comprehensive graphical view of their entire DNS and DHCP environment. With this single utility, they can manage both DHCP and DNS.

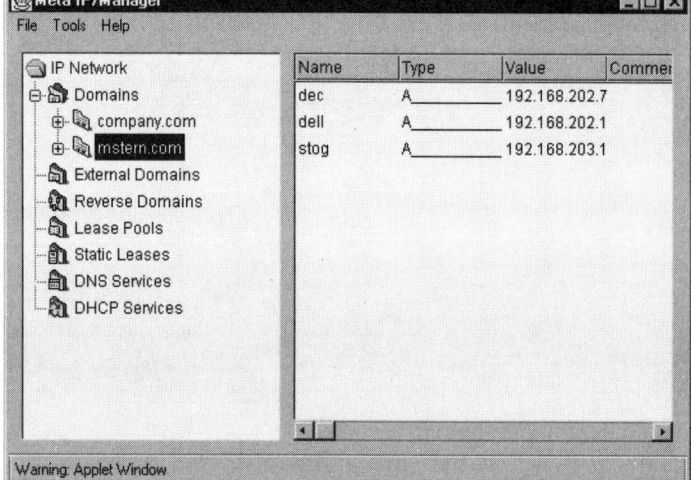

FIGURE 9.7

The MetaIP/Manager Java-based graphical user interface

One of the biggest advantages of MetaIP/Manager is that it has the ability to manage any BIND 8.1.*x*-compatible DNS server, so it can provide a single point of administration for an already existing DNS environment. This can be a significant benefit to DNS administrators because MetaIP/Manager gives them the ability to manage those DNS servers through a graphical utility instead of having to edit DNS text-based data files by hand. Because it is Java-based, IT managers can access it from any Java-capable computer on the network.

While it has the ability to interoperate with other vendor's servers, MetaIP also comes with its own DNS and DHCP server. The MetaIP/DNS server is a port of BIND 8.1.1, so it is fully compatible with other BIND 8.1.*x* name servers.

The MetaIP/DHCP Server includes a number of features not available in Microsoft DHCP. For example, MetaIP/DHCP has the ability to act as a primary or backup DHCP server, so that if one server fails, the other server will assume the role of assigning and managing DHCP addresses automatically. With other products, the only way to ensure fault tolerance is to install two DHCP servers and give them discrete, non-overlapping IP address pools. If one server fails, the other is still operational, but only half of the IP addresses are available to the user population. Both the primary and backup MetaIP/DHCP servers utilize the same database, so they are not prone to this problem.

Another interesting feature of MetaIP/DHCP Server is its support for dynamic DHCP/DNS updates. Essentially, this mirrors the functionality provided by DHCP/WINS integration, but since this feature can operate independent of WINS, the service does not have to rely on an existing WINS infrastructure. However, if your network already uses WINS, MetaIP will interoperate with it as well.

The MetaIP/Load Balancer is an add-on product to MetaIP that provides more sophisticated method than "round-robin" DNS for load balancing. As you remember from our discussion in Chapter 7, "round-robin" DNS works by assigning the same hostname to multiple physical systems, each with its own IP address. When a DNS name resolve request is received by the DNS server, it will pick one of the IP addresses from the group as the response. On the next request, the DNS server will respond with a different IP address. The downside to "round-robin" is that it's not a very sophisticated method of load balancing. Essentially, the task of rotating addresses is random and the DNS server does not attempt to determine if the server is available or to determine how much of a performance load the server is experiencing. The MetaIP/Load Balancer addresses both of these issues by periodically testing first to make sure that the server is operational, and then to determine the load level of the server. Once it determines the server under the least load, it will update the DNS record with the IP address of that server.

MetaIP incorporates a number of wizards to simplify installation, configuration, and population of the DNS and DHCP databases. It includes automatic support for reverse name mappings. For more information about purchasing the MetaIP products, visit MetaInfo's Web site (www.metainfo.com).

Design Considerations

Designing a successful DNS implementation will require you to consider a number of factors, such as the layout of your network, the flow of traffic through the network, and your organization's Internet strategy.

Looking at Your Topology

Determining the optimal placement for your primary and secondary DNS servers will, in large part, depend upon the topology of your local and wide area network. In this regard, planning your DNS server strategy is similar to planning the placement for other types of servers, such as your NT domain controllers and WINS servers. If your network contains a large number of remote sites connected to the corporate network with slow point-to-point links, you'll need to weigh the advantages and disadvantages of locating secondary servers at the remote sites.

The advantage of placing a secondary server at a remote site is that any of the DNS requests for an internal host can be served locally, on the secondary server, so no DNS request traffic has to travel over the wide area link. The only DNS-related traffic that will travel over the link would be requests for DNS hostnames that existed in domains other than what the secondary server maintained, as well as traffic associated with zone transfers between the primary and secondary DNS servers. The disadvantage of placing a secondary server at a remote site is that your staff will have to purchase and maintain a server that may exist in a site that lacks qualified personnel to manage the server. If the server is across town, this may not be a big deal. If the server is across the country, proper server management may become a problem.

Making the decision between deploying a remote DNS server or keeping DNS in a centralized location can be complicated. You'll need to consider the number of users at each remote site, but you'll also need to predict how (or if) these users will utilize the DNS server. Make a rough estimate of the number of total DNS requests per day for the site, and estimate how many of those requests will be for resources on your network and how many will be for resources on external networks such as the Internet. If the number of internal requests will comprise most of the DNS traffic and the number of requests is high, you should deploy the remote DNS server to reduce WAN utilization. If you are unsure, install a packet analyzer on your network for a few days and track DNS traffic.

Considering Your Internet Strategy

If your organization is already connected to the Internet, it's likely that you have some type of DNS service in place. Many organizations find it more convenient to have their Internet service provider maintain their primary and secondary DNS services off site. In fact, many ISPs will provide DNS services as part of their basic service offering.

One advantage of outsourcing your DNS services to a provider is that it will free up the technical staff from having to install, configure, and maintain primary and secondary DNS servers. In most small organizations, the IT staff is already working overtime, so outsourcing DNS will give them one less issue to worry about. The second advantage is that most service providers maintain multiple, redundant DNS servers, so that if one or two servers become unavailable, your corporate DNS service will remain up.

There are, however, some disadvantages to outsourcing DNS. First, your organization will lose some flexibility in its ability to make quick changes to the DNS database. Most Internet service providers will accept DNS record changes only through e-mail and will update their services once a day. If the number of DNS records you will maintain is relatively small, or if the DNS names will change infrequently, this is not such a big issue.

The second disadvantage to outsourcing DNS is that it will prevent your organization from using a DHCP/DNS integration product, because the software that most Internet service providers use for DNS will not support it.

One alternative that you might use, which will take advantage of some of the benefits of maintaining your own DNS and some of the benefits of outsourcing, is to maintain your own primary DNS server for your zone and have your service provider maintain secondary DNS services. This way, your staff will have the flexibility to make changes any time of day, and the changes will replicate to the secondary, service-provider-maintained server, which will provide a fault-tolerant backup for your server.

Some organizations maintain two sets of DNS services for their network; one for internal users and one for access by Internet users. In this type of configuration, the internal DNS system contains records for all of the systems that are private to the organization. The workstations within the organization are configured to point to this server as their primary DNS server, and the server is configured to forward requests that it cannot resolve to another DNS server, usually one on the Internet. A firewall or another mechanism is installed to block Internet users from accessing the internal DNS server, so confidential computer hostnames remain confidential. The second

DNS service contains a list of devices that are available to the Internet, such as the corporate external Web server, the mail server, and an FTP server. The server for the external service may be located within the corporate network or it may be maintained by the Internet service provider. To the Internet population, this DNS server is the primary DNS server for the domain, because they do not know about the internal, private DNS server.

If you plan to implement a dual-DNS strategy, be sure to configure all internal computers to look to the internal DNS server as the primary DNS server. Also, don't forget to install secondary DNS servers for both the internal and external DNS.

Mail and News Protocols: SMTP, POP3, IMAP, LDAP, and NNTP

While it would be difficult to do justice to all of the other open-standards-based products for electronic mail and discussion newsgroups in part of a chapter, we'd like to discuss some options to consider if you're faced with deploying an open electronic mail system.

In Chapter 7, we discussed some of the major mail protocols, such as the Simple Mail Transfer Protocol (SMTP), the Post Office Protocol version 3 (POP3), and the Internet Mail Access Protocol (IMAP). As you'll remember, SMTP is the protocol that defines communication between mail servers. It includes definitions for the format of e-mail messages, as well as the rules and commands for interaction between mail servers. The two other mail protocols, POP3 and IMAP, are client-server protocols: they define the interactions between mail users and their mail servers. When a user connects to an Internet mail server to download messages, their mail client is most likely using either POP3 or IMAP to contact the server, transmit authentication information, and retrieve mail messages.

If you've ever tried to send an e-mail message to someone on the Internet but you did not know their exact e-mail address, you'll appreciate the importance of the next protocol we'll discuss, the Lightweight Directory Access Protocol (LDAP). As its name implies, LDAP is a standard that defines client/server access to a directory service, such as an X.500 directory of users and resources. It is important to recognize that LDAP does not define the structure or contents of the directory, but instead it defines a standard for how a client can access that directory.

The reason it is important to mention LDAP in a section on electronic mail is that it is rapidly becoming the standard protocol to provide address-book-like functionality for open-standards-based electronic mail systems. One of the biggest limitations of deploying an open-standards-based mail system within an organization is that they lack a central, comprehensive directory of other users on the system—unlike most proprietary messaging systems that feature extensive, complete mail address databases for all users.

One approach that is gaining in popularity is to create a centralized, LDAP-ready database and to equip mail users with an LDAP mail client. When a user needs to send a mail message to someone, they can access their address book and perform a search for that user. The search request will be transmitted (using LDAP) to the directory, which will return the mail address for that person.

LDAP databases work well within organizations, but they can also be deployed for extranet or Internet applications as well. For example, many organizations that advertise themselves as Internet mail directories, such as 411 (www.411.com), have begun to offer LDAP access to their mail address databases so that Internet users can search for addresses directly through their mail client software.

Another messaging-related protocol that we covered in Chapter 7 is the Network News Transfer Protocol (NNTP). As we discussed, NNTP is the standard that defines both how News servers transmit messages to one another and how News clients can send and retrieve message headers and messages from a News server.

When most people think of the News service, they think of USENET, a loosely organized network of thousands of Internet-based discussion groups. USENET newsgroup topics span from the mundane to the useful to the bizarre. Because of the sometimes controversial subject matter contained within the groups, many organizations opted to offer a controlled subset of USENET newsgroups to their employees, while some have opted to block access to USENET altogether.

While the value of offering USENET to employees is debatable, the value of the functionality that News services can provide to an organization is clear. Internal, private corporate newsgroups can become valuable discussion groups for departments, individuals, and divisions. For example, an organization could create a News discussion group to help keep their national outside sales force in touch with one another. Because of their collaborative nature, discussion groups play a role that e-mail cannot. Electronic mail works well for one-to-one, or one-to-many correspondence, but it does not lend itself to ongoing, group-based collaborative conversations.

Choosing from Mail and News Server Options

If you've been involved in the network messaging arena for any length of time, you recognize that there is no shortage of messaging products to choose from. The problem isn't a lack of products, it's figuring out which one is the best for your organization.

The Big Debate: Proprietary vs. Open Messaging Systems

As recently as four years ago, organizations had only a few options for their electronic messaging systems. Back then, virtually all e-mail systems were closed, proprietary packages that worked well as a discrete, closed system. However, few of these systems had the ability to be seamlessly interconnected with mail systems from other vendors, and some couldn't connect to systems other than those from the same vendor.

If an organization wanted to connect their e-mail system to another organization's mail system, the project would have gone one of two ways. If both organizations used the same vendor's mail system, the connection process was relatively easy. If the organizations used different mail systems, the only way to establish a connection between the two was by using electronic mail gateways. While the gateways might provide basic mail transfer between the two systems, neither organization could take advantage of the full feature set of either mail platform. For example, users of one system were unable to view the address directory from the other system. To get a message to a user on the far end of a gateway, an employee might have to use a difficult-to-remember, cryptic e-mail address.

Later, as more vendors began to enter the messaging market, organizations had a new set of choices. Mail platforms came in one of two flavors. Either they were proprietary, closed systems that offered a rich, comprehensive feature set, or they were open-standards-based systems that lacked much of the sophistication of the proprietary platforms. An organization that selected a proprietary system could offer a full-featured product to their users, but the users might not be able to easily communicate with anyone outside the system. Employees that worked for organizations that selected open-standards-based systems could communicate with anyone else who used one of the other open-standards-based systems, but they didn't have access to many of the more useful features, such as folders or rules-based mailboxes.

Exchange 5: A Step in the Right Direction

In 1996, a new breed of electronic mail platforms reached the market. These platforms offered the rich feature set of the proprietary systems while incorporating support for many of the open standards, such as SMTP, POP3, IMAP, NNTP, HTTP, and LDAP into the core product. Now organizations could implement a system that would not only provide the latest features to their end users, but would also easily interoperate with systems from other vendors. Three such messaging systems were Lotus Domino, Novell Groupwise 5, and Microsoft Exchange 5. We'll discuss Exchange 5 as an example of one of the new hybrid mail systems—a system that uses a proprietary mail engine but effectively weaves support for open protocols into its core functionality.

Microsoft Exchange 5 was built upon many of the best features of its predecessor, Exchange version 4, but it also incorporated support for open protocols without the need for costly additional gateways or add-ons. Exchange 5 included support for HTTP, SMTP, POP3, NNTP, LDAP, and SSL. Exchange users were given the ability to access their mailbox in any number of ways: They could use the standard Exchange client; they could use any POP3-compliant mail client; or they could use their Web browser. They could participate in public folder discussions through the Exchange client, Outlook, or any NNTP-compliant news reader.

By providing a product that effectively incorporates open-protocol support, Microsoft, and other vendors, have given tremendous flexibility to organizations and to designers of messaging systems for those organizations. As a network designer, it's important for you to understand the capabilities of these products and to determine how to deploy them to best meet the needs of your organization.

Choosing a Third-Party Server

For some organizations, a hybrid mail system like Exchange may not be appropriate. A full Exchange deployment can be a significant undertaking, and some organizations may have requirements that are better met by a different vendor's mail system. There are a number of recent entrants to the open-standards-based NT mail systems market from vendors such as Netscape Communications (www.netscape.com), Software.Com (www.software.com), Qualcomm Inc.(www.qualcomm.com), and Ipswitch, Inc. (www.ipswitch.com). While the servers from these vendors all have been developed around open protocols, each offers a different combination of features, performance, and capabilities.

If you are considering a design that includes an open-protocol-based mail system implementation, here are some features to consider when evaluating servers.

Web-Based Client Access While nearly all mail servers offer POP3 client access, some of them also allow clients to access their mail messages through their Web browser via HTTP. Users typically access a Web page on the mail server, log in using their user name and password, and then are presented with a list of messages in their mailbox to read and respond to. Many of the early implementations of Web-based mail access suffered from limited functionality. For example, users could download attachments from incoming messages, but they couldn't create messages with attachments. Some of the newer versions support uploadable attachments.

Web-based client access provides a number of opportunities (and challenges) for messaging system designers. Many organizations want to give their employees the ability to access mail from the home or from the road. Web-based access minimizes the tools that an employee will need to get to their messages, because they only need Internet access and a Web browser. However, if it is easy for the employee to get to their mail, it's also easy for a non-authorized user to read that employee's mail. If you undertake a design that includes Web-based access (or any other type of access for that matter) to e-mail from the Internet, be sure to include the necessary security provisions, such as a firewall or virtual private network components, in the design.

IMAP4 Support IMAP4 offers a number of benefits over POP3-based client access, particularly for users who wish to access their mail over a low-bandwidth connection, such as a dial-up link. With an IMAP4 client, a user can download all of the subject lines for their messages, and then can select which messages to retrieve. In a POP3 scenario, all messages will be downloaded when a user connects to the mail server. If the number of messages is high, or if one of the messages contains a large attachment, the connection may have to remain active for a long time.

In order to take advantage of IMAP4, both the mail server, and the client software must support the protocol. As you evaluate vendor's products, be sure to match the client and server.

Mailing List Services Even with the advances in push technology, electronic mailing lists are still one of the most effective methods for distributing information to a group of individuals. In the past, maintaining a mailing list was a challenging undertaking because of the complicated software involved. Some of the newer crop of open protocol mail servers include a more sophisticated version of this mailing list software, so administering a list with one of these servers is a much less complicated process.

LDAP Support As we mentioned earlier in this chapter, LDAP provides users with the ability to search for electronic mail addresses quickly and easily. LDAP becomes extremely important if you plan to implement open-protocol mail servers throughout an enterprise network, because it provides the comprehensive enterprise-wide directory of users. Like IMAP4, both the client and the server must support LDAP in order for the service to work.

User-Configurable Some mail server products include features that can reduce the administrative overhead associated with day-to-day management by extending portions of the administrative functionality to the users. For example, some products allow users to set up vacation messages that will automatically be sent if someone sends them mail when they are out of the office, and some products will allow users to specify a second mail address to which all inbound mail should be forwarded.

Typically, these features are made available to end users through a Web interface or through a form they can transmit to the server through electronic mail. While the process of managing these features is relatively simple, this feature works well in environments where the average mail user has a medium to high level of computer experience.

Administrative Control of Mailbox Size One feature that is rare, but sorely needed, among open protocol mail servers is the ability for administrators to control the size of users' mailboxes.

Too often, a user or group of users will transmit and respond to messages that contain a large attached file without removing the file first. With each successive response, both the sender's and the receiver's mailbox grows. This can quickly get out of control, as these users consume all of the available storage space on the server. Once the server runs out of storage, it can no longer process other messages, effectively shutting down the service.

If administrators are given the ability to control the size of these user's mailboxes, they can set a threshold that will be adequate for normal daily usage but will prevent an individual user from shutting down the mail server.

Design Considerations

Designing an effective messaging system is a complex task that will require a significant amount of investigative work on your part. Before you begin to specify anything, be sure to clearly understand and document the organization's enterprise messaging needs. Be aware that electronic mail is a politically-charged issue. Many end users (particularly executives) are very sensitive about electronic mail, so be diligent about interviewing all of the appropriate parties to determine the real messaging needs.

Other areas you'll need to consider are things that will affect the volume of mail that the system will process. How many messages will be transmitted through the messaging system each hour, each day, each week? How many users will require their own mailboxes and electronic mail addresses? How much archive space does each user require to store old messages? Once you identify these types of requirements, you may find that the pool of potential products will become narrower. For example, if your users will require 25MB of archival storage space and you plan to house 500 mailboxes on a single server, you'll need to identify a mail server that can store 12.5GB of user mail messages. Some of the systems on the market may not meet that requirement.

In this chapter, we discussed how to implement the Domain Name Service within your network, as well as some alternatives for providing dynamic DNS for WINS and DHCP users. We also discussed many of the mail-related open protocols and some of the considerations for deploying systems based on these protocols. In the next chapter, we'll discuss measures you can take to protect the mail system (as well as the entire internal network), including firewalls and proxy servers.

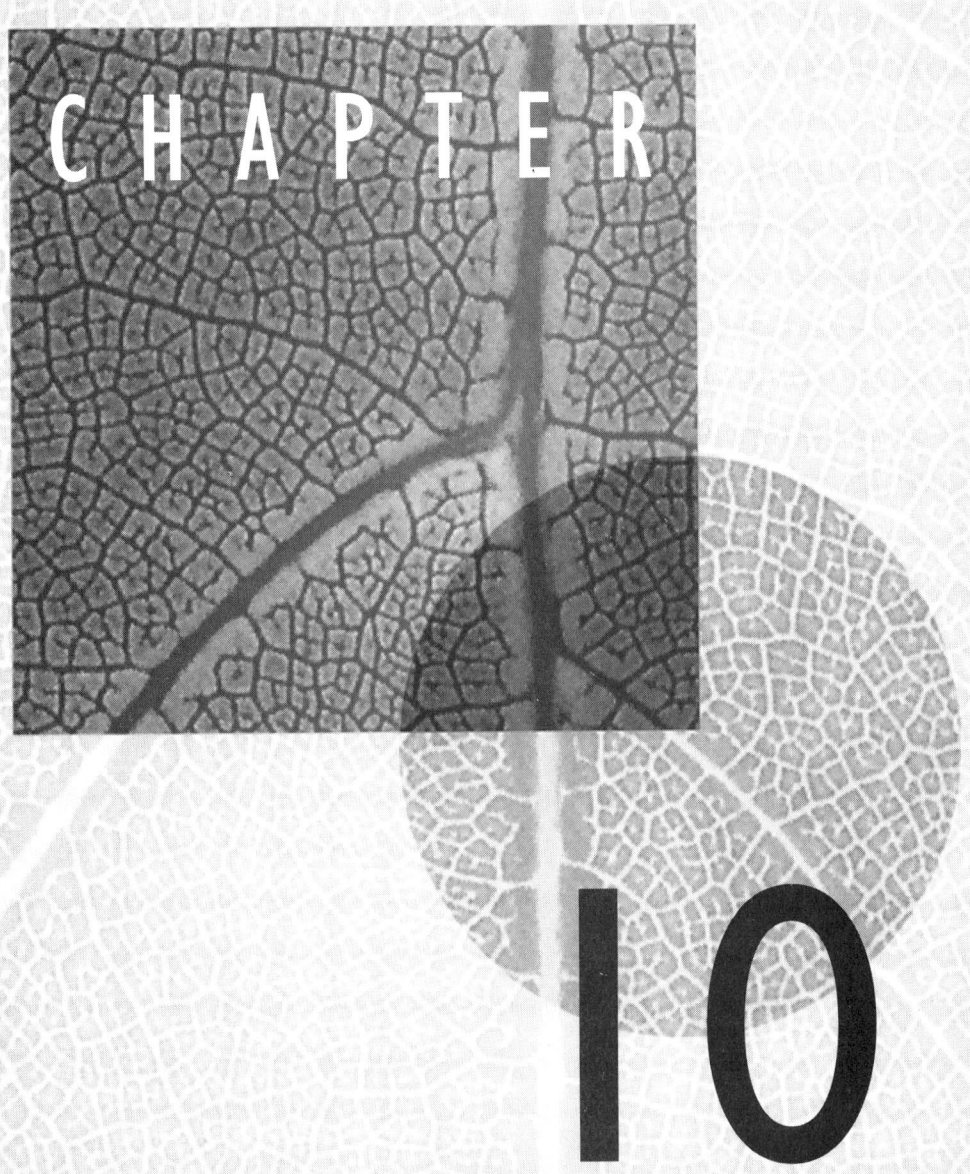

CHAPTER 10

Firewalls and Proxy Servers

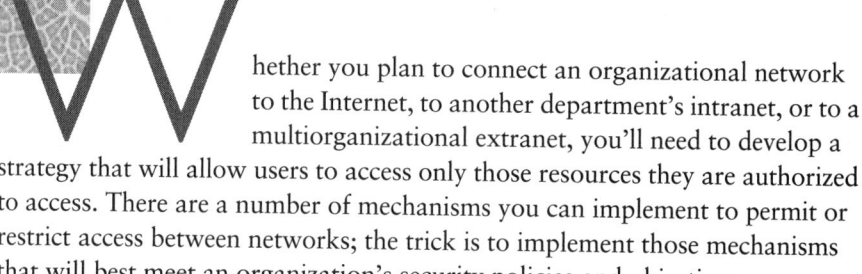

Whether you plan to connect an organizational network to the Internet, to another department's intranet, or to a multiorganizational extranet, you'll need to develop a strategy that will allow users to access only those resources they are authorized to access. There are a number of mechanisms you can implement to permit or restrict access between networks; the trick is to implement those mechanisms that will best meet an organization's security policies and objectives.

In this chapter we will discuss:

- The types of threats to protect against
- Steps to help an organization develop a security policy
- The difference between a firewall server and proxy server
- When to use a proxy server, firewall server, or both
- Firewall-1, an NT-based firewall server
- The Microsoft Proxy Server

While this chapter is not intended to be a comprehensive discussion of network security concepts and issues, our intention is to develop a conceptual framework that you can augment with network security information from other sources.

Most network security consultants agree that the most important element in your security implementation isn't which firewall server or proxy server you ultimately select, it is developing a proper corporate security policy and finding the devices which will enforce the policy. In this chapter, our goal is to describe how to develop the corporate policy, then give you pointers for ways you can enforce it.

Network Security Threats

There are two types of unauthorized access you will want to protect your network resources from. The first is that of external threats, or threats that come from users outside of your network such as users who may attempt to gain access to your systems through unsecured dial-up lines, or through your connection to the Internet (if you have one). The second type of unauthorized access (and the type that most organizations do not take as seriously, but should) comes from within your organization. These internal users may attempt to gain access to resources or servers to which they aren't allowed access. Let's examine each of these types of threats in more detail.

External Threats

When most people think about threats to their networks, they think about threats coming in from outside their networks—they probably picture lone, malicious system crackers intent on stealing their corporate secrets, or they might imagine a loosely organized group of young hackers looking to probe their networks for interesting information or credit card numbers.

While these images may sometimes be legitimate, there is another class of security threats that come from less malevolent origins. Improperly configured software may cause gateways to crash or may keep them so busy that they are unable to serve legitimate users. This type of threat is just as real as the one from system crackers, and it is often harder to prepare for.

These are the types of threats your network may be exposed to if it is connected to the Internet or if it contains dial-up access nodes:

- Curious people who want to see what resources and data they can access
- Malevolent people who want to destroy your resources or data
- Thieves who want to steal your resources or data
- Well-meaning people who unintentionally prohibit others' access to your resources through improper software configurations or improperly written software

Let's examine each of one of these types in more detail.

Curious People

The first type of external threat to your network comes from people driven by curiosity. They are mostly motivated by the challenge of breaking into your network. Once they have gained access, they may scan through the subdirectories of your computers looking for interesting files or information. They also may use your computers to access other systems on other networks in an effort to thwart those attempting to track them down.

These types of people may try to justify their actions by claiming that their intentions were only to gain more knowledge, not to cause destruction or steal information.

There are two types of problems these people can create. First, they may unintentionally cause damage to your computers by modifying critical system files in an attempt to cover their tracks. This can cause data loss, or in some cases, your system can crash.

The second threat is the loss of computing resources. While these people are poking around your network, they are using computing time which could otherwise have been used legitimately by applications or users on your network.

Once people like this have broken into your network, they are difficult to detect because they may log in using legitimate user IDs and may perform many of the same activities as your regular system users.

Malevolent People Out to Destroy Data

The second type of external threat comes from childish system crackers looking to amuse themselves, or from vengeful computer users with enough technical savvy to create havoc on your network.

System crackers frequently have the same motivation as writers of the computer viruses that spread like wildfire reformatting hard drives and deleting valuable data files. They consider it a challenge to break into someone's network, and once they are on the network they want to destroy and delete everything they see.

These people are usually easy to detect; unfortunately, by the time you detect them it is often too late to do anything about protecting your data. Your only recourse is to restore the lost data from tape. In some cases, certain files may be destroyed altogether while others have been modified to make it easier for the crackers to get back into your system at a later date.

Another group within this category are people who may hold a grudge against your organization for one reason or another, real or imagined. They may launch attacks aimed less at data destruction and more toward creating an annoyance for you and your users. One example of this type of attack is called *mail-bombing*. A mail-bomber will create an automated process that repeatedly transmits e-mail messages to your mail server from one or more locations. The incoming mail prevents your mail server from receiving any other legitimate mail, and the volume of the mail may fill up all of your storage space, causing the mail server to crash.

Thieves After Your Data

The third type of external threat comes from people who want to gain unauthorized access to your network in order to steal data from your organization. These people have very good system cracking skills and are hard to detect. They may be employed by a rival organization looking to steal corporate secrets, or they may be interested in stealing data, such as your customer information, in an attempt to get credit card numbers.

These people may access your corporate information either by breaking into a computer on your network or through the use of a *packet sniffer*. A packet sniffer, or protocol analyzer, can be placed anywhere on the Internet between your network and a computer system communicating with your network. Since most protocols, such as Telnet, do not encrypt the data they transmit across a network, the packet sniffer can capture any data sent via Telnet. A system cracker could intercept a legitimate user ID and password by capturing a Telnet session, and then use the ID and password to gain access to your network.

Well-Meaning People

The fourth type of external threat comes from people who have no intention of causing problems for you or your network. They may be running improperly configured applications or servers, or may have developed buggy programs.

For example, some older mail server implementations did not entirely conform to the SMTP protocol. When two of these types of mail servers attempted to communicate, mail message transmissions would fail and the server would attempt to retransmit the mail. Eventually it would give up and break the connection, only to reestablish the connection a few seconds later. This resulted in both mail servers being tied up trying to send one mail message. Mail from other sources never arrived, because the other mail servers could never get a connection.

Another example of this type of threat was the infamous *Internet Worm*. On November 2, 1988, a self-replicating program began to infect computers on the Internet by exploiting known loopholes in `sendmail` and `fingerd`, two Berkeley UNIX programs. Once the Worm infected a system, the system either crashed or froze up. The infection spread quickly, and the Internet was brought to its knees as administrators across the United States worked to isolate the program in an effort to stop its spread. After the smoke cleared, the Worm was discovered to be the work of Robert T. Morris, a Cornell University student. Morris' intention was to create a program that would quietly replicate itself throughout the Internet to demonstrate the inadequacy of computer security measures. What he didn't anticipate was that the Worm would replicate more quickly than he had planned, and that it would crash the computers it infected.

As you can see from these two examples, the threat from non-malicious, unintentional sources is just as real as the threat from curious hackers and system crackers. In fact, many times this type of threat is more difficult to prepare for because unintentional attacks cannot be anticipated. While it's relatively easy to implement measures like secure passwords, it's much more difficult to know if the mail software you have just purchased has an undiscovered bug.

Internal Threats

As you begin to develop your network security strategy, you must keep in mind that you not only need to protect your network from external threats, but from internal threats as well. Studies have shown that in most cases, the threats posed by internal users are much more dangerous to an organization than threats from the outside. Let's examine some of the types of internal threats.

Intentional Security Breaches

The first type of internal security threat is one of the most difficult to prepare for or to detect. This threat comes from members of your user community who wish to access network resources or data not intended for them. These users may try to access confidential or classified information, and then may save the information to a disk, transmit it over the Internet, or upload it to another computer over a modem.

To guard against this type of threat, you must first conduct an internal network security audit to make sure that users can access only the information that they require to do their jobs. If you create a system where they cannot access any other data, you'll limit the amount they can potentially steal.

The next step is to establish some means to control outbound network access (Internet or modem) and to log any transmissions or modem calls that occur. Some commercial firewall servers offer the ability to log outbound network access, and your telephone system may provide the ability to record basic telephone call information, such as the number that was dialed and the duration of the call.

Unintentional Security Breaches

Despite the devastating potential for intentional theft of data by your internal users, the more significant internal security threats comes from users who, unaware of your security policies, may transmit sensitive corporate information over insecure channels. The reason this threat is more significant is because of the frequency with which this type of security breach occurs.

For example, the widespread popularity of e-mail has made it easier than ever to transmit text and data files throughout the Internet. A user could send an Internet e-mail with an attached file that contained your customer list to a coworker at another site. If the file was not encrypted, it could potentially be intercepted and read by a third party. Incoming e-mail can pose a threat as well, especially when an attached program file might contain a virus.

Another threat can arise if network users are not properly educated on the configuration and operation of your Net servers. They may place sensitive corporate material on publicly accessible Web or FTP servers that your organization may not deem appropriate for the Internet community.

The third type of unintentional internal threat comes from naive or uninformed users who may give out passwords or other information that can be used by smooth-talking system crackers looking to break into your network. These hackers use a technique called *social engineering*. They may call one of your network users and impersonate another of your employees to gain login IDs or passwords in hopes of gaining unauthorized access to your systems. The only measure you can take to defeat social engineering is to educate your users never to give out their passwords or other login information over the phone or to anyone they do not recognize.

> ### It Never Hurts to Call Them Back
>
> A few years ago, I was a network administrator for a large corporate network. One of my responsibilities was to field help desk and support calls during the day. Frequently, I would receive calls from users asking to reset their passwords, add them to access groups, or disable accounts for employees who had left the company.
>
> One day, I received a call from a user at a remote office who said they had forgotten their password and wondered if I could tell it to them. I was initially suspicious because the call came from an outside phone line, so I told the user that I would have to call them back in five minutes. When I called the user, they claimed to have to never called me. In fact, their voice was different—it was definitely not the original caller. The caller ended up being a former employee who was trying to break in to the network through a dial-in connection; someone who thought they could use some social engineering to get enough information to gain access.
>
> I learned a valuable lesson that day. If you ever feel the least bit suspicious that someone is not who they say they are, don't tell them anything. And never, ever give out password information over the phone.

Developing Your Security Strategy

Now that you understand some of the threats your network will face, it's time to begin developing your network security strategy. We can break down the steps required to implement network security into the following tasks:

1. Determine your security objectives.

2. Develop a security policy.

3. Implement security measures in accordance with the security policy.

4. Conduct a security audit to test your implementation.

5. Continually monitor your security implementation.

Let's begin with the first step.

Determining Your Security Objectives

Before you can begin to establish network security, you need to determine not only what it is you want to protect, but why you want to protect it, how far you will go to protect it, and how much it would cost if security were compromised.

It might be helpful to write down your objectives on paper first. Begin with a few general statements describing how your organization will use your network resources. Try to be as complete as possible.

For example, if you plan to create a Web server that will provide general information to all of your employees, it's unlikely that you need to establish security for that Web server. However, if you plan to create a Web server for the human resources department that will contain employee information, you will want to be sure that the Web server will be accessed only by authorized personnel.

Once you have stated your plans for your network resources, develop a list that contains any concerns or potential concerns you might have. For example, if one of your intranet Web servers will contain sales information and your customer list, note your concerns about users from the Internet potentially gaining access to that server.

This is your chance to organize any issues you may have related to security and your network. You might find it helpful to speak with others in your organization as well. Speak with your manager or other managers to determine what types of concerns they have. By creating this list, you will able to inform your superiors about the possible risks as well as show them the steps you will take to minimize these risks. You will also be able to confirm that your plans are in line with the policies of upper management.

Assessing Your Risks

Once you have completed the list of your concerns, you should continue by developing an assessment of the elements of your network that will be at risk. The risk assessment list does not have to be a long, formal document; it should contain a description of the elements that might be at risk via your intranet, an extranet connection, or your Internet connection if you have one. Begin with a list of the devices that are configured with IP addresses, such as routers, servers, and workstations. Once you have gathered this information, create a second column that lists what each device does and the services available on each. For servers, indicate if the server is performing routing functions or running a service such as a Web server or FTP server. For workstations, list the type of TCP/IP stack software installed and whether the stack includes server applications. For example, Windows 95 and Windows NT Workstation users can implement Web and FTP servers on their workstations, so if any of your users plan to do so, you would want to make a note of it.

Also create a list of computers that have modems attached or access to a modem server.

This list will provide a starting point for you to develop your security implementation. It's a good idea to hold onto this list and modify it as you add or remove workstations or servers on your network so you can adjust your security strategy as needed.

What Needs to Be Protected?

The next step is to begin to evaluate the elements of your network that you want to protect. You should separate these elements into two categories: data and computing resources.

One way to do this is to use the list of network devices that you developed in the previous step and add a third column. In the column, describe the data that is either stored on the device or accessible through the device. For example, the hard drive on a workstation probably contains some applications and user data files. You should list that data, but you should also list the data on file servers to which the user has access.

By creating a list of network devices, you can see what the impact could be if a particular system were compromised, because once system crackers compromise a workstation, they can gain access to any resource to which that workstation has access.

This approach will help you to determine which systems require the most protection and to which users you should provide education on proper usage and security precautions.

How Far Will You Go to Protect It?

Once you have developed the list of network-accessible devices and the resources and data on those devices, you should begin to consider the techniques you will

> **And Don't Forget to Close the Window**
>
> Many times, organizations will spend thousands of dollars implementing an ultra-secure firewall while they forget about other network entry points, such as modem lines connected to users' workstations. This situation is reminiscent of a scene from a horror movie where a frightened teenager trying to escape from the ax murderer barricades himself in an old shack. He spends too much time trying to pile old furniture in front of the door and forgets about the open window that's right next to his head. When you decide to secure a network, think about every potential access point, not just the obvious ones like the Internet connection.

implement to protect your network. A number of factors will determine how far you should go to protect your data, but the most significant factor is the potential cost resulting from a security compromise.

At this point, it's important to have a clear idea of the scope of your security implementation, but you don't have to know the specifics of how you will implement it. Don't worry about the specific details such as what brand or type of firewall server you want to use. Focus on the business implications of a security compromise, not the network specifics.

How Much Would a Security Breach Cost Your Organization?

Finally, you should attempt to calculate the cost to your organization if your network were compromised. The total cost should include not only the value of the data, but also the cost associated with reinstallation and reconfiguration of the affected areas and the time involved in restoring the data. There are no hard-and-fast methods to determine this cost, but you should already have an idea of the value of your data and computing resources.

The value of your data should have a direct impact on the amount of money you spend on your security implementation. For example, if your network contains no valuable data, there is no point in spending tens of thousands of dollars to protect it. On the other hand, if your corporate network contains millions of dollars worth of data, you will want to make every effort to protect that data. You and your management should be willing to spend whatever is necessary to ensure the integrity of your network. In this type of situation, you may even want to consider taking steps to isolate your internal corporate data network completely from any externally accessible devices, such as modems or Internet routers.

Developing a Security Policy

Once you have determined what you want to protect on your network and avoid the cost of a security breach, you should begin to formalize your security objectives. Using the list of security objectives you created in the previous section, you should begin to develop an idea of the steps you will need to take to protect your network. Also consider your corporate culture: Do your users already maintain secure passwords and change them on a regular basis? Have you implemented adequate access rights on your network servers, or does everyone have the supervisor or administrator equivalent because you thought it would be too complicated to assign rights properly? Now is the time to address these issues, because from this point you will begin to develop your organization's security policy.

A good security policy will provide you and your users with a clear understanding of how your computers should be used, why they should be used a certain way, and who is responsible for doing what. It should be concise but complete enough to cover all the important issues.

A security policy will also protect you in case of a security incident. For example, if your policy states clearly that users must scan all of their own incoming e-mail attachments for viruses, then they will be the ones held responsible if their computers get infected. Without a formal policy, the fingers might be pointed at you instead.

Before you get uptight about creating a long, boring document full of legal terms, let's discuss exactly what a security policy is.

A Formal Statement of Your Objectives

As the heading says, a security policy is a formal statement of your organization's security objectives. *Formal* does not mean that it has to read like a contract or other legal document, just that you need to get your ideas down on paper in a format that can be read by management and your users. By creating a document that can be shared and read by everyone else in your organization, no one will be able to say "I didn't know" when a security issue arises.

Be realistic about the objectives you put into your security policy. Don't expect your users' behavior to change overnight just because a policy was put in place. No network is perfect—make sure your policy reflects a realistic attitude about your network, your users, and your job as an administrator.

No one should be expected to follow the guidelines of a security policy that is too idealistic. Fill your policy with "real-world" guidelines.

Your policy should begin with a paragraph that contains a general description of your organization. Discuss your organization's main business function, the general management structure, and any other relevant information. This will add background information so that reviewers and auditors outside of your organization can have a better idea of how your business operates.

Next, the policy should state the purpose of the network and the computing resources available on it. Describe why your organization has a network and the general uses for it. If your network has a connection to the Internet, include a section on your Internet connection and what your organization considers appropriate usage of the Internet. Be brief, because you will discuss specific details in a later section. The first few paragraphs should be included just as an introduction.

RFC 1244, the *Site Security Handbook*, describes seven issues that should also be addressed in your security policy:

1. Who is allowed to use the resources?

2. What is the proper use of the resources?

3. Who is authorized to grant access and approve usage?

4. Who can have system administration privileges?

5. What are the user's rights and responsibilities?

6. What are the rights and responsibilities of the system administrator versus those of the user?

7. What do you do with sensitive information?

As you address each of these issues in your security policy, avoid the temptation to create a laundry list of do's and don'ts. Try to create nontechnical descriptions for technical terms and concepts that you refer to, and give adequate explanations for the rules. Your users should understand not only what they can and cannot do, but also why they should or should not do it.

Who Is Allowed to Use the Resources? Your security policy should include a section that describes who is authorized to use the resources on your network. If different job functions are authorized to access different resources, be sure to state that here.

What Is the Proper Use of the Resources? Once you have established who is authorized to use the network resources, you must define the guidelines for how they are to use the resources. Use this section to describe authorized and unauthorized usage for both your internal network and your Internet connection, if you have one. For example, if your users are allowed to use corporate e-mail only for company business, state the appropriate uses of e-mail and the inappropriate uses.

You might want to include guidelines for account usage. For example, users should only log in to the system using the login name and password that is assigned to them. Sharing of accounts should not be tolerated, because you will lose the ability to track system usage by the login name. For example, if four people use the same login name and one person decides to delete everything on the system, you will have no way of determining which of those four people actually made the deletions.

Be clear that users are responsible for their own actions, regardless of the security measures implemented by the organization. For example, users need to choose secure passwords, even though you may not be able to force them to choose their passwords properly.

Be sure to describe how your rules will be enforced, who will enforce them, and the penalties for noncompliance in each of the sections of your security policy. Clearly define the course of action for enforcement for both accidental and intentional violations.

Who Can Grant Access and Approve Usage? Once you have determined who can use the resources and how they are to use them, you need to define who has authorization to give access to these users. A clear definition of who is authorized to give access and approve usage will clear up misunderstandings. For example, every organization usually has at least one technically adept user who steps outside of his or her job function to assist other users with computer-related problems. You want your policy to be clear that just because someone has the technical ability to give someone access to a resource doesn't mean that he or she has the *authority* to do so.

Who Can Have System Administration Privileges? The next section of your policy should state which users will have the ability to administer your entire system. They may be the same as those mentioned in the previous section, or it may be a different group of people. For example, in some organizations, a manager's approval is required before an individual can gain access to a particular resource or application. Once permission has been granted, a system administrator performs the actual changes to the system to allow that user to access the application.

What Are the User's Rights and Responsibilities? This next section will be important to your users because it will contain a detailed list of their individual rights and responsibilities. This section should include these kinds of topics:

- Password selection guidelines and restrictions
- Appropriate usage of computers during business hours
- Employee responsibilities not to disclose proprietary information
- Usage guidelines for network applications such as corporate e-mail
- A statement of the corporate policy regarding employee privacy for communications over company-owned equipment
- Usage guidelines for modems and dial-in access to the network
- User responsibility for backing up their own data (if applicable)

There may be other user-responsibility issues unique to your network that you will also want to include in this section.

System Administrator Rights vs. User Rights Once you have defined what the users' rights and responsibilities are, you will need to define the rights and responsibilities of the system administrator. This section should define what the system administrator can and cannot do. For example, an administrator needs access to network files in order to complete a tape backup, but does he or she have the right to view sensitive files such as payroll information or users' private files? Does an administrator have the right to monitor e-mail traffic between the Internet and the network?

Be sure to be as clear as possible in this section to protect your users, your administrators, and your organization.

What Do You Do with Sensitive Information? This section should describe the treatment of sensitive information stored on the network. You should include a definition of what information is to be considered sensitive, as well as where that information should be stored. Also include the procedures for backing up this data and for the handling and storage of the backups.

Keep in mind that your security policy should only describe the actual policies, not the technical implementations of security mechanisms. Your security policy is not the place to discuss the technical details of mechanisms such as your firewall server; it is a document that describes what your users should do and why they should do it. They don't need a lengthy discussion of *how* you plan to implement your network's security. For example, one well-meaning company almost when so far as to publish the supervisor password as part of their security policies.

The Importance of Corporate Review

Hopefully you have been working closely with management throughout the development of your security policy. If you have, the final policy should contain few (if any) surprises for management. However, if you have developed the policy on your own, you will want to be sure to present the completed version to all appropriate management members. A security policy must have the full support of corporate management to have a hope of being successful. Be sure to address any concerns or questions they might have. It's also a good idea to submit a copy of the security policy to your organization's lawyers for review *before* you implement it. They may have suggestions or concerns about some of the policies.

Once the security policy has been reviewed by management and your lawyers, you can begin the implementation. Make enough copies of the policy so that every employee can have his or her own copy. You may want to add a page at the end so that all employees can provide signatures to confirm that they have read and understand the policy. Work with your human resources department to see if they can provide the policy to new employees as well.

Once the policy has been completed, distributed, and returned with each employee's signature, you can begin the implementation of your official security policy. Some of the elements may already be in place, but now is the time to complete the job.

Be sure to review the security policy on a regular basis to determine whether you need to make changes or adjustments.

Implementing Security Strategies

Now that you have completed the security policy, let's examine some of the strategies, techniques, and technical elements you will use to implement it. We'll begin with a discussion of the four most common security strategies. A security strategy is an approach, or a *paradigm*, that shapes how network security is implemented. It is the set of assumptions that administrators use that will drive the mechanisms they put in place on their networks to prohibit unauthorized access.

These are the four most common security strategies:

- No security

- Security through obscurity

- Host security

- Gateway-based security

No Security

Most people wouldn't consider a no security strategy to be a strategy at all. Sadly, many networks are based on this strategy simply because their administrators take no precautions to secure their networks. These types of administrators assume that security is "somebody else's job" and may run their networks with the bare minimum of security. They may feel that passwords are a nuisance and that file access rights are too complicated to implement, so they allow most of their users to log in as GUEST or with accounts that have supervisor equivalence.

Networks based on the no security approach are accidents waiting to happen. For example, a misinformed user can accidentally delete entire subdirectories full of corporate data in an attempt to free up disk space.

As you can imagine, the no security approach makes it easier for users to access their applications, but it also makes it easy for system crackers and unauthorized users to gain access. If your network is based on the no security strategy, you'll need to change it before you implement your intranet.

Security through Obscurity

The security through obscurity approach is based upon the assumption that security can be achieved by hiding the details of an implementation from all users except those who must maintain it, similar to the "need to know" philosophy of most military intelligence agencies. The inner workings of the network are hidden from all except those who need to know them.

Security through obscurity falls apart quickly because these details don't remain obscure for very long, as the number of users who need access increases. Information spreads quickly by word of mouth, and soon the obscurity is gone. In addition, system crackers have learned to determine the types of applications and security precautions a network takes by examining the minute details they can gather from the behavior of publicly accessible services such as SMTP mail. Some of the more skilled system crackers can tell administrators more about their networks than the administrators are aware of.

Another element of security through obscurity is to attempt to keep quiet about known software bugs that may compromise a system's security. This approach seldom works, as evidenced by the Internet Worm attack described earlier. If you know about a software bug that poses a security threat, most system crackers will know about it also.

Fortunately, the security through obscurity approach has become less popular, as administrators and developers have embraced open systems and technology.

Host Security

The third security strategy, *host security*, still enjoys widespread use and may be a viable security strategy for some networks. Host security relies on the security that is provided by individual host systems, such as secure passwords, secure login ID combinations, and file access rights. Host security differs from gateway-based security in that it focuses on individual systems, not the entire network. An example of host security is when users authenticate to the local database of an NT server.

Host security provides a high level of security as long as your users choose passwords that are secure. The downside to host security is that it is cumbersome to maintain in larger network environments. If a user needs to have an account on 20 servers, that account has to be created 20 times. If all of the servers on a network run an application known to have a security bug, the software on each of the servers must be patched.

If your network is small, securing your hosts may be the only step you'll need to take to implement your security. Keep in mind that host security lacks the single point of control offered by a gateway-based security strategy implementation such as a firewall server.

Gateway-Based Security

The fourth security strategy is *gateway-based security*. The key element of a gateway-based security implementation is the focus on a gateway, or single point of entry, through which all incoming and outgoing traffic flows between two networks. The device or devices that control the traffic are usually referred to as a firewall because of their ability to act as a secure barrier between the networks.

Another example of gateway-based security is the user name/password authentication and dial-back functionality provided by some dial-up network devices. If your network contains any of these dial-up devices, you should use all of the security features they provide. If you are evaluating these types of products for your network, look for devices that provide features such as encryption, one-time password cards, and dial-back.

Gateway-based security provides a number of benefits over host security; the most significant of which is that it provides a single location for security fortification. While proper host security implementations require that all hosts on a network be secured and maintained, gateway-based security need only be implemented at one point—the firewall. Network traffic can be permitted or restricted by the firewall, and some implementations include the ability to log successful and unsuccessful access attempts.

Gateway-based security is more scaleable than host security for growing networks. As the number of servers and workstations increases, an administrator need only make modifications to the firewall, not to each of the systems within the network.

Some firewall implementations prohibit any traffic from traveling directly between the two networks. Internal network users must access specialized servers on the firewall called *proxy servers*. For example, users must configure their Web servers to submit all HTTP requests to the proxy server. The proxy server then interprets the request from the internal users and generates its own request to a target server. Once the proxy server receives a reply from the target server, it retransmits the information to the users. This type of implementation ensures that no unauthorized traffic can flow between the networks, because users never have direct access to the other network. All traffic must pass through the proxy.

Another type of firewall implementation, called *packet filtering*, allows only certain types of IP traffic to travel between the two networks. Packet filtering requires a high level of TCP/IP protocol knowledge because the access controls are based on IP addresses and port numbers unique to each of the individual TCP/IP protocols. For example, if administrators wished to provide NFS file system sharing to their network users, they would have to configure the firewall to deny inbound access to port 2049, the NFS port.

We'll discuss proxy servers and firewalls in much more detail later in this chapter. Just remember that if you choose to implement a firewall that allows any type of inbound traffic, you must also implement some level of host security within your network to protect the resources accessible to the outside world.

Balancing Ease of Use with Security

While you are considering which type of network security you should implement, try to strive for a solution that provides a sufficient level of security while remaining relatively easy to use. After all, your goal is to provide access to your users, not make them have to jump through hoops just to use their Web browsers.

Just remember that with any solution, there are going to be trade offs. An implementation that is extremely easy to use may not be as secure a solution, but your users will use it more often. An ideal solution balances ease of access with the need for security so that neither area is compromised too much.

Guidelines for a Secure Network

Regardless of whether you choose to implement host-only security on your network or a combination of host and gateway-based security, there are a few guidelines that you should follow to ensure that your network is secure:

- Establish a mandatory password policy.
- Educate your users.
- Maintain a regular tape-backup strategy.
- Continually test your network security.

Passwords Are a Must

Aside from implementing a firewall, ensuring that every account on your network contains a secure password is the most significant measure you can take to secure your network. Here are some password- and account-related suggestions:

- Conduct regular audits of your Windows NT domains, UNIX passwd files, NetWare binderies, or NDS trees to clean out any old or unused IDs.

- If you use special accounts for nonhuman network users such as tape backups or mail gateways, make every effort to give these accounts secure passwords or at least restrict to the absolute minimum the access rights these accounts have.

- When you create user accounts, make use of restrictions such as minimum password length, time and station restrictions, concurrent login restrictions, forced periodic password changes, etc.

- Enable intruder detection on your server so that invalid login attempts will lock out accounts.

- If you must maintain high-profile accounts such as GUEST, at least assign a password to the account and monitor account usage. Remove GUEST from every group possible, and assign access rights directly.

Educating Users

Another measure, and one that is frequently overlooked, is user education. Your security policy, if it is properly written, will go a long way toward educating your users on safe networking.

You may also want to distribute a memo or e-mail that describes the right way and the wrong way to select a password. Explain that good passwords are seven to eight characters long, contain numeric and mixed case alphabetical characters, and are easy to remember. They should not contain the user's name, date of birth, or telephone number (or those of any friends or relatives), company-related words, etc. They should be easy for the user to remember, but hard for someone else to guess. Passwords should never be written down.

Another way to educate users is to develop a quick training session to introduce them to your network. You can describe how the network applications work as well as their proper usage. Also include a nontechnical discussion of network security threats such as viruses and unauthorized network access. Throughout the session, be sure to explain not only the proper procedures, but also the reasons behind the procedures. Your users are more likely to use their computers responsibly if they understand why they should.

Regular Backups Are Mandatory

If you are not already certain that your network is being backed up on a regular basis and the data on the tapes is valid, you need to stop reading and get a reliable tape backup system in place now. Keep in mind that any backup system is worthless unless you are certain that the data can be restored once it's on tape. Try to implement a system that ensures that your tapes are clearly labeled and kept in a safe place. Create a disaster plan and schedule drills so you can determine how long a full restore will take should you have a complete server failure.

A tape backup is your last line of defense in case of catastrophic system failure, inadvertent file deletion, or a malicious system cracker attack, so make sure you back up frequently and regularly. Most organizations try to get full backups whenever possible in an effort to limit the number of tapes required for a full restore. If full backups are not practical for your network, consider upgrading to a faster backup technology such as a DLT tape drive. If an upgrade is not an option, avoid the temptation to do incremental backups. Do a full backup whenever possible, then do differential backups between full backups. Since a differential backup will catch all of the data changes since your last full backup, a complete restore will only require two tape sets. If you go with incremental backups, you will have to use every tape set since the last full backup for a full restore.

Be sure to test your backup system on a regular basis—it's better to learn about a problem with your tape backup system during a test, rather than after your file server's hard drive crashes. Any test of your tape backup system should include some file restores from tape. You want to be certain that you can not only back up your data but also restore it.

Test, Test, Test!

Finally, once your security implementation is in place, test it thoroughly and continue to test it on a regular basis. As your network grows, you may need to revisit some of your security mechanisms. Your reasons for choosing one implementation over another may have changed altogether depending how your network has grown or changed.

Enforcing Your Security Policy

Once you have worked with your organization to develop the corporate security policy, the next step is to design the mechanisms that will enforce the policy. For the remainder of this chapter, we'll discuss two of the most frequently implemented security mechanisms: firewall servers and proxy servers. We'll discuss the issues you'll need to consider before deploying a firewall server or proxy server, and we'll describe some of the products on the market that run on Windows NT.

It is important to recognize that effective network security does not begin and end with a firewall. A firewall is a tool, and like all tools it must be used properly. In this situation, the firewall is the tool that will enforce the policies that you and the management of your organization have developed. Firewalls that have been installed without regard for corporate policies are, in some respects, worse than no firewall at all because they lull network administrators into a false sense of security. If the firewall has not been configured to meet the corporation's communication requirements, it may contain unnecessary potential entry points for system crackers.

How Does a Firewall Work?

Contrary to what many firewall vendors might say, the term *firewall* does not strictly refer to a single device, it refers to an implementation (that may be comprised of one or more devices) that provides a single point of control to permit or deny the flow of traffic between networks. For example, some corporations use filtering rules configured on multiple routers for their firewalls. Technically, it is the configuration of the hardware, not the hardware itself, that is the firewall.

For a firewall to be effective, all traffic that flows between the two networks must pass through it. The firewall examines the traffic and compares it to the set of rules for which is has been configured. If the traffic matches the rules for traffic that can be transmitted between the networks, the firewall forwards the traffic. If the traffic matches the rules for traffic that should be blocked, the firewall blocks the traffic. While firewalls from different vendors may have a slightly different set of features such as access logging and network address translation, all of them perform this basic function.

For the purposes of this discussion, we'll use the term *firewall server* to refer to any one of the class of products being sold as firewalls on the commercial market, and the generic term *firewall* to describe the implementation of one or more of these and other related products.

Access Logging

Most commercial firewall server implementations provide access logging so you can monitor the traffic that passes between the networks, allowing you to make adjustments in the firewall server configuration as needed. The level of logging varies from firewall server to firewall server; some provide the ability to control which types of protocols will be logged and the amount of detail the logs provide, others only track the IP address and port number of the traffic.

Some firewall servers also offer the ability to monitor access to TCP and UDP port numbers on a given network interface. Once the number of attempted accesses to a particular port number exceeds the value you have preconfigured, it can notify you of a possible attempted break-in on your network. These attempts are based on a technique called *port scanning*.

System crackers utilize programs, called *port scanners,* that can quickly scan the entire range of TCP and UDP ports. The scanner logs any responses, which the system cracker can then use to attempt to compromise the network through one of the services. For example, SMTP mail servers operate on TCP port number 25. A system cracker could configure a scanner to check port number 25 on every host within a network address. If an SMTP server were configured and operational on any one of the hosts, it would respond to the port scanner. The cracker could then attempt to compromise each system that was running SMTP by utilizing a known security hole in older SMTP implementations.

Configuring Port Monitors

Configuring port monitors can be tricky because port access is a normal part of networking. The key to configuring a port monitor is to tune your configuration to avoid excessive false alarms.

If you have an Internet connection, your Internet service provider may offer firewall-based security included in your monthly fee, or they may offer it at extra cost. Unless you are willing to make an ongoing commitment to configuring and maintaining your firewall, you may want to consider using your service provider's security services. Even if you do choose to implement a firewall server yourself, you may want to use your service provider's security to provide an extra level of security. Be sure to find out exactly what kind of security services they are going to implement. Determine in advance who will be liable for security breaches and what your organization will be responsible for providing. Communicate your expectations clearly—explain exactly the purpose of your Internet connection, the types of services you want to provide to the Internet community, and what you don't want Internet users to access on your network.

Network Address Translation

Another feature found in many firewall servers is known as *Network Address Translation* (NAT). A firewall server configured to perform address translation will examine all of the network traffic that is bound for external destinations and will rewrite the source IP address of the IP packets. When it receives the return packets from the external destination, it will examine the destination IP address and rewrite the destination to match the original sending host. For example, if an internal host (address 192.168.202.75) wanted to access a Web server on the Internet, all of the traffic would first have to pass through the firewall server. As the firewall server receives the packets from the internal host, it rewrites the source address of each packet from 192.168.202.75 to 10.1.1.22 (the IP address of the firewall) and sends each to the destination Web server. When the Web server receives the packets, it thinks that they originated from 10.1.1.22, so it sends return packets to the firewall server's IP address. The firewall server, recognizing that these packets were sent in response to the Web request from 192.168.202.75, rewrites the packet with .75 as the destination address, and transmits the information back to the original host. This process is illustrated in Figure 10.1.

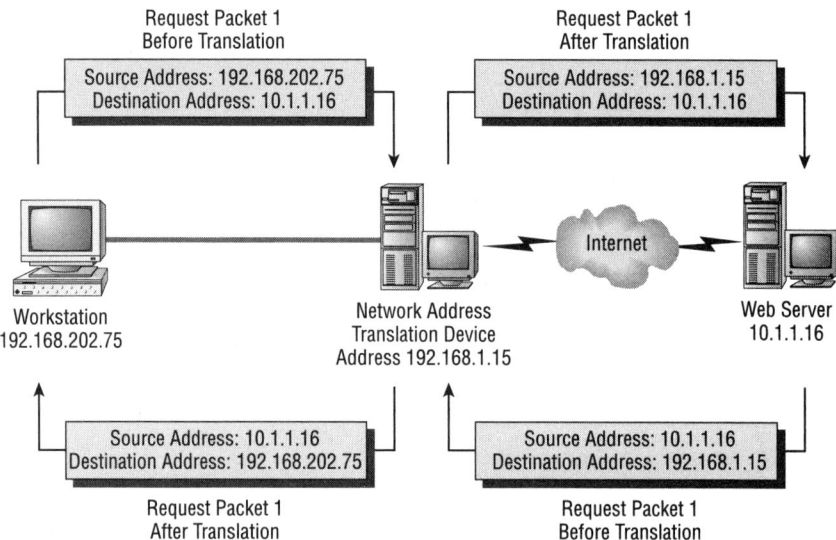

FIGURE 10.1

Network Address Translation in action

The concept of Network Address Translation may sound confusing, but it actually performs a very important function. To illustrate this function, imagine the following scenario.

The Capo di Monti Winery decides to connect their network to the Internet. For years, the Capo di Monti network has routed TCP/IP traffic to thousands of its users whose workstations have been configured with non-registered IP addresses. Once the Internet connection has been put in place, they'll have two choices: They can either spend hundreds of hours readdressing their entire network, or they can use network address translation on their firewall server to translate between the internal network and the Internet. Since the external interface on the firewall server will be configured with a registered IP address that Capo di Monti obtained from their Internet service provider, all traffic traveling between the Capo di Monti network and the Internet appears to be coming from a registered address.

One other benefit that Network Address Translation can provide is that it can hide information about hosts on the internal network since no addresses from the network will ever travel on the Internet, only traffic from the firewall's address. System crackers use information such as IP addresses of internal hosts in an effort to compromise a network's security, so in this situation, NAT prohibits anyone from knowing about the internal structure of the network.

Another advantage of some NAT implementations is their ability to translate many internal addresses into a single registered address. For example, the Capo di Monti Winery could have hundreds, even thousands, of users accommodated by only a few addresses from a registered Class C network address.

Network Address Translation should not be confused with a proxy service. In a NAT implementation, the contents of packets are transmitted "as is" to their destination, and only the source or destination address is modified. A proxy server, which we'll discuss shortly, actually transmits the request to the destination on behalf of the internal host.

Implementing a Firewall

The two most prevalent types of firewall implementations are firewall servers configured as *dual-homed hosts* and standard IP routers configured with packet filtering rules. A dual-homed host is a computer configured with firewall server software and two network interface cards, one connected to network A and one connected to network B. The firewall server software on the host may provide packet filtering, application proxies, or a combination of the two.

The default setting on a dual-homed host is to disallow all traffic to pass between the two networks. Therefore, a conscious effort must be made to allow traffic to pass. This is an affirmative process, which requires the association of a desired result with a specific action. The opposite approach, or the denial process, allows all traffic until denied and is much less secure.

The biggest limitation to installing a dual-homed host firewall server is the cost. Commercial firewall server software prices range from a few thousand dollars to tens of thousands of dollars, depending on the features they offer and, for some, the number of internal network users they will support.

The other type of firewall implementation is through the configuration of access lists and filtering rules on the preexisting routers. Packet filtering is a popular approach with administrators of smaller networks because it doesn't cost anything to implement other than the time required to configure the rules.

Packet Filtering Concepts

Packet filtering relies on a set of rules that a network administrator configures on his or her network router. The router may be a standalone unit, or it may be a Windows NT server configured to route TCP/IP traffic.

Some routers, such as those made by Cisco, provide filtering through the use of access lists. Access lists are programmed into the router's configuration and applied to the router's individual network interfaces. Below is an example of an access list that could be applied to an Internet-connected network interface.

```
access-list 101 permit tcp 0.0.0.0 255.255.255.255 0.0.0.0 255.255.255.255 established
access-list 101 permit tcp 0.0.0.0 255.255.255.255 0.0.0.0 255.255.255.255 eq 20
access-list 101 permit tcp 0.0.0.0 255.255.255.255 0.0.0.0 255.255.255.255 eq 21
access-list 101 permit tcp 0.0.0.0 255.255.255.255 0.0.0.0 255.255.255.255 eq 25
access-list 101 permit udp 0.0.0.0 255.255.255.255 0.0.0.0 255.255.255.255 eq 53
access-list 101 permit tcp 0.0.0.0 255.255.255.255 0.0.0.0 255.255.255.255 eq 53
access-list 101 permit tcp 0.0.0.0 255.255.255.255 0.0.0.0 255.255.255.255 eq 80
access-list 101 permit udp 0.0.0.0 255.255.255.255 0.0.0.0 255.255.255.255 eq 80
end
```

The following is the format for an access list of this type:

```
access-list #  permit/deny  protocol  source-address source-mask
destination-address  destination-mask  operator  port
```

The first line in the access list admits any traffic that is sent in return to connections initiated by the internal network. The remaining lines admit traffic from the Internet to services offered on the network, such as FTP, SMTP, DNS, and HTTP. Any other traffic that does not match one of the above criteria will automatically be denied.

The main advantage to using packet filtering is that it can be implemented using hardware that you already have; there is no need to purchase additional software or hardware. Packet filtering is transparent to your users, because they are able to use applications like Web browsers without having to change the configuration to accommodate a proxy server.

The main disadvantage to using packet filtering is that proper implementation is complicated and requires in-depth knowledge of the inner workings of the TCP/IP protocols. Improperly configured packet filtering rules can be dangerous because they may lull an administrator into a false sense of security.

In addition, packet filtering does not offer the same level of control as some firewall products. For example, if you configure packet filtering on your NT server, you will not have the ability to permit traffic to flow in one direction through the server. So if you want to block incoming Web traffic, it will be blocked outbound as well. Most firewall products, on the other hand, will let you specify different sets of rules for inbound and outbound traffic.

Exceptions often need to be made, and managing all these exceptions can create an "unmanageable" environment as the filtering rules become more and more complicated with each change

How Does a Proxy Server Work?

A proxy server is another type of security device used by many organizations who wish to connect their internal corporate network to an insecure network such as the Internet. There is a considerable amount of confusion in the market as to the difference between a firewall and a proxy server. We hope to clear up some of that confusion right now.

As we discussed earlier, the term *firewall* refers not only to a single physical device, it may refer to a group of devices that provide a single point of administration and traffic control between two networks. So far, most of the firewall server products we have discussed have been single devices, but that doesn't mean that they are the only devices you can use in a security implementation. You may find that in some situations, your corporate firewall will be comprised of both a firewall server and a proxy server, a firewall server only, or a proxy server only.

As its name implies, a proxy server is a server that acts on behalf of client workstations on a network. In a proxy server scenario, a user submits a request for a remote resource directly to the proxy server, which interprets the request and then generates its own request to the remote resource on behalf of the client. Unlike a firewall server, which may route the request to the remote resource, the proxy server never passes traffic between the internal network and the external network. When the proxy server receives a response from the remote resource, it relays the information sent in the response back to the originating host. Figure 10.2 illustrates how a proxy server works.

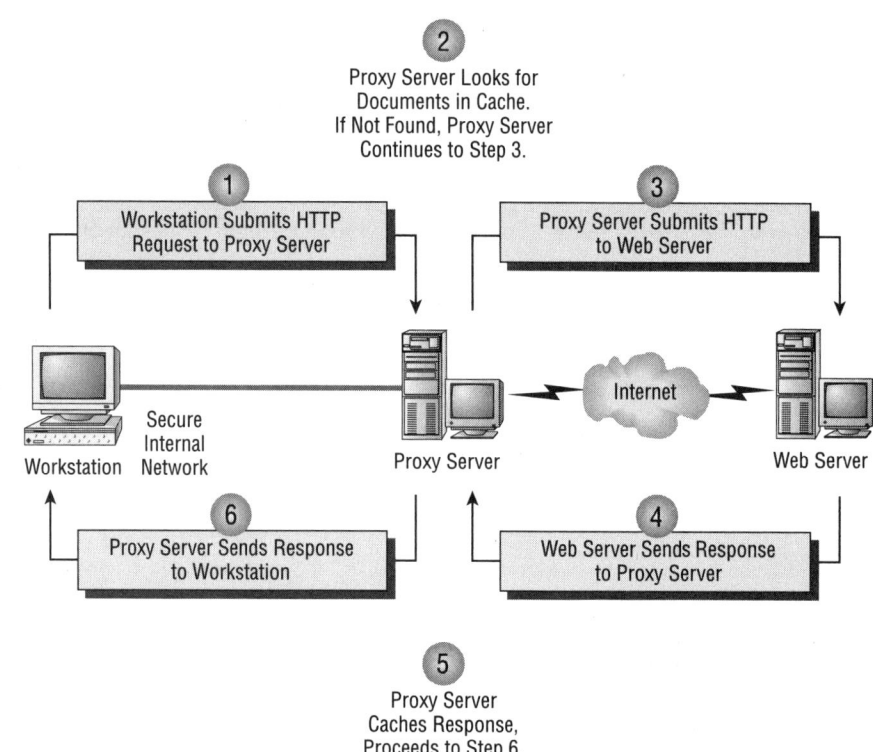

FIGURE 10.2

A proxy server acts on behalf of internal users.

A Proxy Can Control Traffic Based on User ID

The proxy server blocks all traffic between the internal and external networks, so it provides a control point for permitting or restricting outbound access to resources on the external network. For example, the Microsoft Proxy Server (which we'll discuss later in this chapter) has the ability to restrict Internet access by NT domain user or group accounts. If corporate policy dictates that only members of the executive committee can have unrestricted access to the Internet, an administrator can configure the proxy server to permit only those user accounts who are members of the executive committee group.

A Proxy Can Cache Frequently Accessed Content

Proxy server developers have extended the functionality of proxy servers by enabling them to cache large numbers of requested documents on the proxy server itself. For example, if a number of users on the corporate network access Microsoft's home page, the proxy server can cache the contents of the home page so that when the next user requests it, the proxy server can respond with the page immediately instead of having to go to Microsoft's Web site over a potentially slow WAN link.

The amount of pages that a proxy server can cache is configurable by the administrator and is limited only by the amount of physical storage on the proxy server itself. Utilizing a proxy server as a high-speed cache provides two benefits: it speeds up the Internet experience for end users, and it reduces the amount of traffic that has to flow over the WAN link, because the only requests that will be transmitted to the Internet will be for documents not contained in the proxy server cache.

A Proxy Can Provide Address Aggregation

Because the proxy server submits all of the client requests to servers on the Internet, all packets sent to the Internet contain the IP address of the proxy server, not the workstation that originated the request. In this respect, a proxy server is similar to the network address translation functionality provided by some firewalls, so an organization that currently uses non-registered IP addresses can implement a proxy server to avoid having to readdress their entire network.

Reverse Proxy Applications

Some proxy servers, such as version 2 of the Microsoft Proxy Server, include a feature known as a reverse proxy. A reverse proxy server performs the opposite function of a regular proxy server; it caches documents from a Web server on an internal network for access by users on the Internet. Figure 10.3 illustrates how a reverse proxy server works.

The advantage of a reverse proxy implementation is that it provides a shield between Internet users and the Web server. Users on the Internet access only the proxy server, not the Web server itself, so they never have an opportunity to compromise the Web server.

Proxy Server Limitations

One of the most significant limitations of most proxy servers is that their developers focused solely on developing proxies for outbound services (the notable exception being the reverse Web proxy). Therefore, proxy servers provide only half of the solution—an organization can control and protect its users as they access the Internet, but they have no flexibility for controlling inbound traffic from Internet users. The proxy server blocks everything.

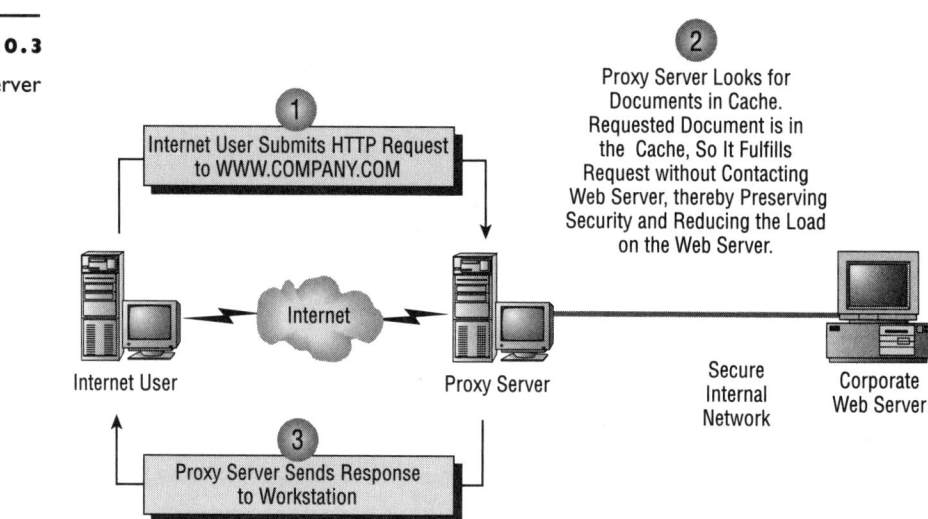

FIGURE 10.3

A reverse proxy server

Another limitation of proxy servers is that while all proxy servers work well for specific, core protocols such as HTTP and FTP, each application requires its own application on the proxy server itself. For example, some servers that have been configured to provide proxy services may run four or five servers: a Web server proxy, an FTP proxy, a SMTP hub, and a Telnet proxy. As the number of required services increases, so does the complexity of managing the proxy server.

A number of vendors, including Microsoft, have attempted to overcome this limitation by creating generic proxies that communicate directly with the Windows sockets interface (Winsock). The advantage of the Winsock proxy is that it can provide proxy services for virtually any Winsock-supported application.

A proxy server implementation will require some amount of configuration at every workstation that will use the proxy. Typically, this may involve some configuration within the user's applications, such as the Web browser or FTP client.

Proxy Servers vs. Firewall Servers

Now that you understand the basic differences between a firewall server and a proxy server, the question becomes: "Do I need a firewall server, a proxy server, or both?"

The answer to the question depends upon the requirements defined by your organization's security policy. By understanding how each device operates, you should be able to determine which one, or both, fits in with your organizational security objectives.

Here are some issues to keep in mind: Firewall servers work well in situations where network traffic requirements might be too complicated for a proxy server. For example, if an organization planned to offer a number of services to the Internet community such as an FTP server, Web server, and News server, as well as to establish a number of encrypted virtual private networks (we'll discuss VPNs in the next chapter) in addition to providing general Internet access to their users, the flexibility provided by a firewall server might be a requirement.

However, if a corporation only wants to establish an Internet connection so that their users can surf the Web and send e-mail, it may be more appropriate (and cost effective) to implement a proxy server.

Firewall servers are better at enabling organizations to implement somewhat complicated, custom security policies, while proxy servers are better for organizations that only want to provide outbound access.

NT-Based Firewalls

Now that you understand the processes and concepts you'll need to develop your organizational security policy, let's look at some examples of NT-based products that will enforce your policies. First, we'll discuss an NT firewall server, and later we'll discuss an NT proxy server.

Checkpoint Firewall-1: An NT Firewall

While early firewall servers were designed to run on UNIX systems, a new generation of servers has been developed that utilize NT as their platform. Many network administrators have implemented NT-based firewall serves because they find them easier to administer and maintain than their UNIX counterparts, particularly in organizations where NT is the dominant corporate OS.

Checkpoint Software Technologies was one of the first firewall vendors to release an NT-based firewall server. Offering virtually the same functionality as their market leading product, the Windows NT version of Firewall-1 combined powerful firewall features with the administrative simplicity of NT.

Firewall-1 Modular Components

Checkpoint built Firewall-1 as part of a modular security framework. It's available in a number of configurations, from a basic version that supports networks with up to 25 nodes to an enterprise version that includes support for router security management and virtual private network (VPN) encryption. Additional functionality is provided through the addition and combination of functional modules. The various component modules are described below.

Management Console Module   The Management Console Module is the central administration interface for all of the other modules. Through the management console, administrators can configure and monitor a single firewall or multiple components located on devices throughout the network.

Inspection Module   The Inspection Module is the component that provides the actual network security. It is responsible for examining all network traffic as it passes through a control device. It may also be responsible for maintaining and authenticating session information and auditing data.

Firewall Module   The Firewall Module combines the functionality provided by both the Management Console and Inspection Modules.

Encryption Module   The Encryption Module provides virtual private network-style encryption services for LAN-to-LAN and client-to-LAN encrypted sessions. Two types of encryption methods are supported: DES for domestic connections and a proprietary, non-restricted method called FWZ1. We'll discuss virtual private networks in much more detail in Chapter 11.

Connect Control Module   The Connect Control Module provides load balancing services for network servers such as Web or FTP servers. Administrators can increase effective throughput for a server by creating multiple, mirrored sites and defining them as a single, logical entity to the control connect module. When a request for the logical server is received by the Connect Control Module, it will relay the request to the most available physical server at that point in time. Other requests will be relayed to other servers, thereby distributing the request load across all servers in the logical group.

Router Security Management Module Administrators can take advantage of the Router Security Management Module to automatically generate packet filtering configuration scripts for Cisco, 3Com, and Bay Networks routers so that the routers can be used in conjunction with a firewall server to provide a higher level of security. Because the packet filtering scripts are generated from the same set of security rules that are used by the inspection module, network security can be enforced consistently throughout the network.

Stateful Inspection

The core architecture of Firewall-1 is based upon a technology called *stateful inspection*. Stateful inspection occurs at the network layer, when the Inspection Module examines each packet to determine whether to pass it through to its destination. The easiest way to describe how stateful inspection works is to compare it to standard packet filtering.

As we discussed earlier, a router that is configured for packet filtering examines every packet that passes through it to determine if that packet should be forwarded or discarded. The router compares information in the packet to information contained in the packet filtering rules. If the rules specify that the packet is permitted, the packet will be forwarded. If the rules specify that the packet is denied, the packet will be discarded. The primary elements of the packet that the router examines to make these determinations are the source address, destination address, and port number.

Stateful inspection takes packet filtering one step further. Instead of merely examining the source address, destination address, and port number, the Firewall-1 inspection module retains information about each communication session when it begins and compares information contained within each packet context within the entire session. If the packet is appropriate for the session and is permitted by the ruleset, the packet will be forwarded. If the packet is inappropriate, it will be denied. To use a real life example, if you were having a conversation with someone, you'd expect their answers to come after you asked the questions, not before (unless you were playing Jeopardy). If your friend started answering questions before you asked them, you'd most likely be somewhat confused or very surprised. Either way, it is not normal for someone to give you an answer before the question. The Firewall-1 Inspection Module uses stateful inspection to understand the rules of communication for TCP- and UDP-based protocols, so it can determine when a packet is appropriate or inappropriate.

The end result of stateful inspection technology is that it provides a more secure approach than standard packet filtering for both TCP and UDP communications.

Firewall-1 Rules Base

The Inspection Module uses stateful inspection to evaluate packets according to rules defined in the *rules base*. The rules base is a set of rules, defined by the firewall administrator through the administrative graphical interface, as shown in Figure 10.4.

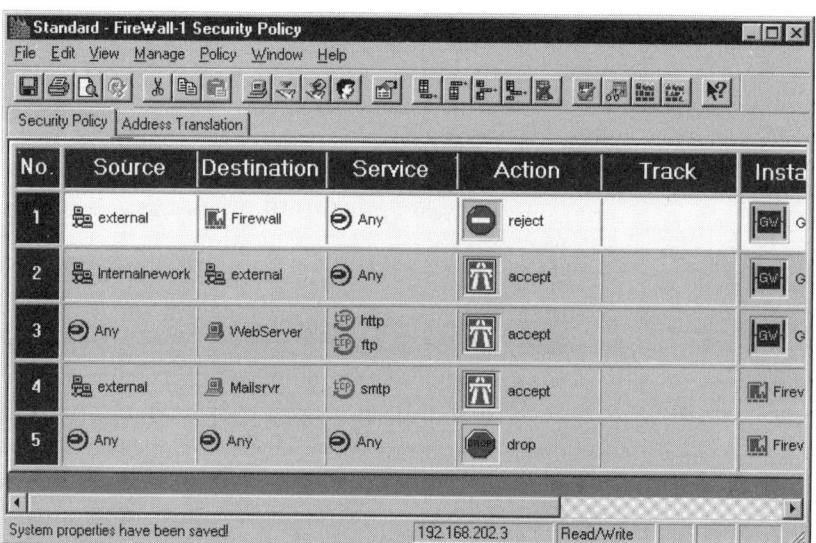

FIGURE 10.4

The Firewall-1 graphical administration interface

The rules base defines a set of actions and conditions. For example, one rule might specify that all inbound SMTP connections should be permitted only to the SMTP mail gateway, while another rule might specify that any inbound traffic on the FTP port will generate an alarm message to be sent through e-mail to the administrator. Any traffic that does not match one of the rules in the rules base is discarded.

A good rules base mirrors a corporation's security policy, because it is the primary mechanism for policy enforcement. It defines to the firewall how it should react to any type of network traffic.

Creating the Rules Base

The first step in creating the rules base is to define the objects which exist on the network, such as users, routers, hosts (workstations or servers), other firewall servers, and protocols. Once the network objects have been defined, they can be used within the rules in the rules base. After the user has finished adding rules, the management module evaluates the rules and determines which devices (firewall servers, routers) must be configured to enforce the rules properly.

Say, for example, that an organization's network had one Internet connection and two dedicated connections to business partners. For security purposes, the president of the company wants to place a separate firewall server on each of the three connections. An administrator would first define all of the connections, firewall servers, and external networks as objects through the management module. Then, they would define their rules, such as the connection to Company A will permit all traffic except FTP and Telnet, while the connection to Company C will only permit SMTP and Web traffic, and the Internet connection will allow unrestricted outbound traffic but only limited inbound traffic. Once all of the rules have been defined, the results can be distributed automatically to each of the three firewall servers. With this approach, the security policy is defined only once, and the management software takes care of implementing the rules on the firewall servers.

The Microsoft Proxy Server

In late 1996, Microsoft released version 1 of their Proxy Server. The Microsoft Proxy Server offered standard proxy services such as content caching and access restrictions based on NT domain user accounts and groups. It also provided two types of proxies, an application-level proxy (the Web proxy) and a circuit-level proxy (the Winsock proxy).

With the release of version 2 of the Proxy Server, Microsoft has taken a slightly different approach. Version 2 combines the features found in the original Microsoft Proxy Server along with some features found in most firewall servers, such as real-time alerting and logging along with dynamic packet filtering.

The new version also contained a number of other new features, including support for reverse proxies and support for the SOCKS protocol.

The Web Proxy

The Web proxy operates at the application layer and provides proxy services for HTTP, FTP, and Gopher. One advantage of using an application-layer proxy is that it is client independent. Any Web browser that supports a CERN-style application-level proxy will work with the Web proxy.

When a user attempts to access an Internet resource through the Web proxy, their Web browser submits a full HTTP request directly to the Web proxy. The proxy then creates an entirely new request to the destination Web server, which sends its response to the proxy server. The proxy server then retransmits the entire response back to the Web browser. All of this activity takes place at the application layer (in this case, all communication between the Web browser, proxy server, and Web server occur via the HTTP protocol).

While application-layer proxies provide a good level of client software independence, they can only support a limited number of protocols because a separate proxy must be created for each protocol.

The Winsock and SOCKS Proxies

The Winsock and SOCKS proxies belong to a different type of proxy called a *circuit-layer proxy*. Unlike application-layer proxies which must be application protocol specific, a circuit-layer proxy is designed to be flexible. While the Web proxy (an application-layer proxy) may only support HTTP, the Winsock proxy (a circuit-layer proxy) can support virtually any protocol.

When a user configures their workstation for the Winsock proxy, the installation program installs a special version of the Windows sockets dynamic link library (WINSOCK.DLL). Once installed, this DLL will communicate directly with the Winsock proxy any time a Winsock-compliant application is loaded on the user's workstation. For example, if the user loads a graphical Telnet application that utilizes Winsock, the DLL will establish a communications channel (referred to as a circuit) between Telnet and the Winsock proxy. The proxy then "stands in" for the client and establishes a connection to the destination Telnet server.

One of the advantages of a circuit-layer proxy is that it is extremely flexible. New protocols can be added to the proxy simply by defining the protocol and its port number and defining the list of users who can utilize that protocol.

Version 2.0 of the Microsoft Proxy Server added support for the SOCKS proxy service. SOCKS is an open protocol that defines standards for communication between client workstations and circuit-level proxies. The SOCKS protocol operates essentially the same way the Winsock proxy operates, except that it is not restricted to Windows client users. Any client application that supports SOCKS, on any platform, can work with the SOCKS proxy.

Reverse Proxy Support

As we discussed earlier in this chapter, a reverse proxy acts as an intermediary between external Internet users and servers located on a secured, internal network. For example, if a customer wanted to access the Capo di Monti Web site, they would enter a URL for the Web server (www.capodimonti.com). The DNS resource record would point to the proxy server, not the Web server itself, since the Web server was located on the secured network. The reverse proxy server would receive the document request, and then search for the requested document, first within its cache, and then on the Web server itself if the document didn't exist in the cache.

The reverse proxy serves two purposes; it isolates the Web server from external users, and it stores frequently accessed files within its cache, so that these documents can be served to the Web browsers more quickly.

Microsoft Proxy Server version 2.0 supports a number of reverse proxy features. Not only can it provide reverse proxy services for one Web server, but it can also provide services for multiple Web servers and for services other than HTTP.

The addition of reverse proxy support, along with the support for logging and alerting, extends the functionality of the Microsoft Proxy Server beyond traditional proxy servers. The combination of all of the features, along with functionality provided by products such as Routing and Remote Access Services (which we'll discuss in Appendix A), ends up creating a product that is somewhere between a proxy server and a firewall server.

In this chapter, we discussed how to develop a corporate security policy and some tips for securing your network. We also described some products that you can implement to enforce your newly created policy. In the next chapter, we'll describe another technology that you can use to secure network communications: virtual private networking.

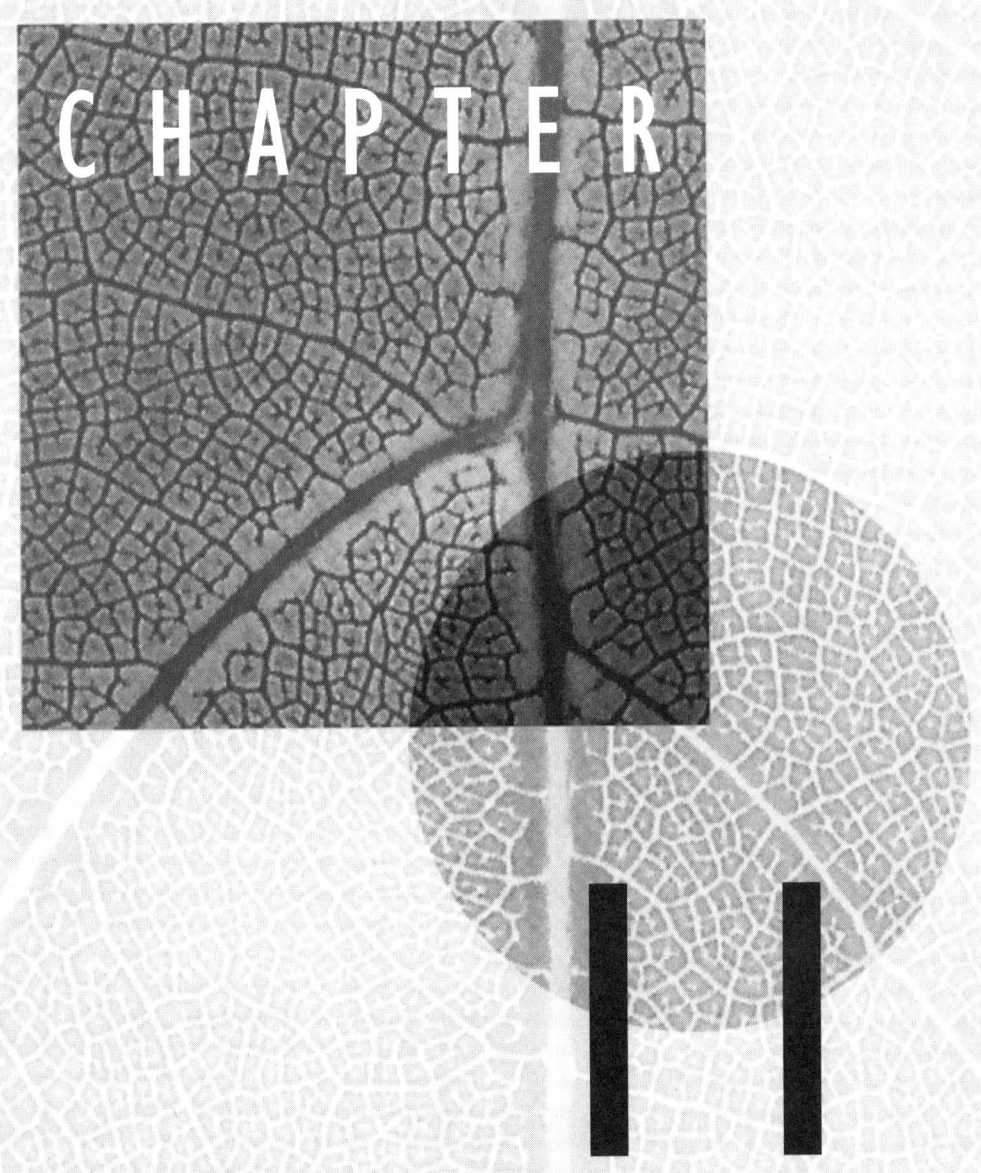

CHAPTER 11

Virtual Private Networking:
Private Conversations in a Public Network

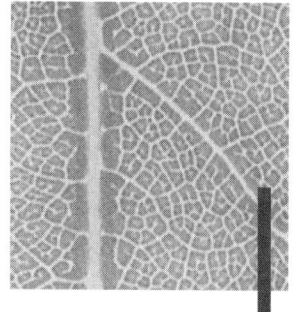

In the last chapter, we discussed how you can implement a firewall to protect your corporate network from unauthorized outside intruders. Firewalls are the best form of protection you can use to separate your network data and resources from unwelcome eyes. However, once the data leaves your network, it is essentially fair game. Anyone with a packet sniffer, or other network analysis device, can view the contents of the packets traveling to and from your network. For example, if you plan to implement a POP3 mail server so that your users can access their e-mail from within the corporate network or from the Internet, anyone can view the contents of the e-mail messages as they travel from the mail server to the user. Your user may be authorized to pass through the firewall to get to the mail server, and rightfully so, but if one of their e-mail messages contains sensitive information, someone could potentially intercept valuable corporate secrets.

Fortunately, you can protect information transmitted to authorized users who have connected to your network through a public network such as the Internet. By using encryption software from Microsoft or other third-party developers, you can create a *virtual private network* (VPN)—an encrypted communication channel that will effectively extend the security of your network over the Internet.

In this chapter, we'll discuss:

- The benefits of virtual private networks
- How VPNs work
- How to implement a VPN on NT Server
- Third-party VPN solutions
- Implementing a VPN with your firewall

Who Needs Encryption?

While the benefits of a firewall are usually immediately obvious to technology managers and network administrators, many times the benefits of encryption technology are not as obvious. This may be due to a lack of experience with encryption products, a lack of knowledge about encryption technology, or a lack of understanding about how to apply encryption technology when it fits. In this section, we'll discuss three scenarios in which the proper application of virtual private networks can increase data security while decreasing the cost of offering network access to remote users, to geographically dispersed offices, or to other organizations or corporations.

Leveraging the Internet as a Dial-Up Infrastructure

Home office and remote computing have created a number of challenges for the technology manager and the network administrator. The prospect of managing an extensive dial-up network infrastructure is not an attractive one. Even though products such as Remote Access Service (RAS) minimize the work associated with authenticating users and connecting them to the network, there is always the hassle associated with telecommunications carriers—and the costs associated with telephone lines, modem banks, and other equipment.

Many organizations have begun to outsource their dial-up infrastructure altogether by contracting with local and long-distance providers, who maintain their own networks of modems, phone lines, and authentication databases. In this type of scenario, remote users connect to a local point of presence (POP) maintained by the telecommunications company. Once connected, the user authenticates to the service and is then granted access to the corporate network, which is connected to the telecommunications provider through a high-speed WAN connection, usually a fractional or full T1 line.

Other organizations have looked to save more money by taking advantage of their existing Internet connection and the large number of Internet service providers (ISPs) who offer low-cost, flat-rate Internet access. In this scenario, users connect to the Internet through their ISP (to whom they pay a $19 per month flat rate) and then access resources on the corporate network through the company's Internet connection and firewall. Figure 11.1 illustrates a dial-up Internet connection to a corporate network.

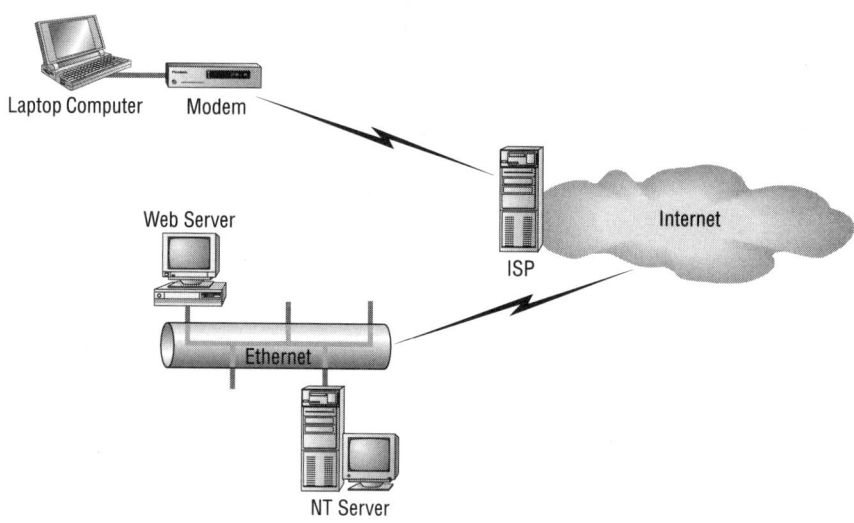

FIGURE 11.1

Accessing the corporate network through the Internet

The cost to the corporation of providing Internet-based remote access is minimal, since they already have a connection to the Internet, and most of their users already have an account with an Internet service provider. However, the security implications are not minimal.

First, remember that this type of connection entails some type of access from the Internet to the internal corporate network, so if any employee can access the corporate network from the Internet, that means that anyone on the Internet could potentially access the corporate network. It is always easier to deny all inbound traffic through a firewall; permitting selective access to internal resources creates a number of potential risks, so it should require an extremely high level of trust.

Every design should include a strong authentication mechanism to ensure that only authorized users have permission to pass through the firewall. Users should be equipped with one-time password mechanisms, such as SecurID card, to prohibit unauthorized users from stealing a user's login name and password.

Second, remember that any information that passes between a remote user and the corporate network can be intercepted at any point between the firewall and the remote user. If the user accesses any proprietary corporate information, such as a corporate database or electronic mail, that information could potentially be compromised. The only way to protect the information from unauthorized eyes is to keep it private by encrypting it while it travels between the user and the network, effectively creating a virtual private network.

 A SecurID card, or token, is part of a system developed by Security Dynamics and called Access Control Encryption (ACE). The token is a device, usually in the shape of a credit card or key fob, which has an LCD screen that displays a new, unpredictable access code number every 60 seconds. When a user authenticates to an ACE server, they are prompted to enter a personal identification number (PIN) as well as a password (the access number generated by the SecurID token). This combination of a number that only the user knows along with the number generated by the SecurID token is valid only for 60 seconds, so if the number were to be compromised, an unauthorized user could not use it later to access the system.

The Internet as WAN

Mergers, acquisitions, and plain-old corporate growth have all contributed to the change of the "typical" corporate network. Ten years ago, most corporate networks were single location LANs. Now, technical managers in many organizations must consider how to provide seamless network connectivity between multiple locations. The wide area network has become ubiquitous. For many corporations, as the number of wide-area links has increased, so has the telecommunications bill. Point-to-point links are extremely expensive, because each site must have a physical WAN connection to one or more sites.

Technologies such as frame relay help to reduce the overall cost of wide area networking, however, the cost for a frame-relay network increases in proportion to the number of Permanent Virtual Circuits (PVCs) required to connect each of the sites.

One alternative to point-to-point or frame relay connections is to use the Internet as the backbone connection between multiple corporate sites. In this scenario, each remote corporate site would maintain a full-time connection to the Internet. Network devices and resources would be configured to forward data to each of the other remote networks, using the Internet as the wide area link. By reducing to one the number of links that each site must maintain to access each other site, the overall cost to provide connectivity can be reduced significantly. Routers on the Internet will direct traffic between each of the sites, so multiple PVCs become irrelevant.

This alternative, however, is still subject to many of the same issues as Internet dial-up network access to an internal network. For example, in order to allow a remote site to gain access to the internal corporate network, some adjustments must be made to the firewall to selectively allow inbound traffic to the secured network.

The security risks of permitting inbound connections through a firewall are significant, so extreme measures should be taken to ensure that only authorized users can get in to access corporate resources.

Once you have resolved the issue of authenticating network connections from remote authorized networks, the issue of security as data travels between networks remains. If traffic travels unencrypted between the two networks, the potential that an unauthorized snooper could encounter valuable corporate information is increased, because the amount of traffic traveling between the two internal networks will be greater than in the Internet dial-up user scenario. Fortunately, many of the VPN encryption solutions work not only for dial-up connections, but also for network-to-network connections.

Before you begin to implement a network-to-network VPN over the Internet, you should consider some of the performance and bandwidth limitations associated with sending traffic over the Internet. Remember that the Internet is not owned or managed by any single organization; multiple organizations and ISPs provide Internet routing services, so no one can make guarantees about bandwidth. If your WAN will require consistent, dedicated bandwidth, you may want to avoid an Internet VPN. If, however, your network communication requirements are minimal and not time-sensitive, an Internet VPN may be a good solution. If your needs are somewhere in between, you may be able to negotiate a guaranteed bandwidth commitment if all of the sites are connected to the same Internet service provider. Providers can make this type of guarantee because the network-to-network traffic will never actually travel over the Internet; all communications will remain on the provider's network backbone.

Building Extranets

The explosion of corporate intranets has given the business community a sense of the vast information-sharing capabilities of Net-based applications. Using a simple Web browser, executives and employees can easily access a wide variety of applications and information resources. Many corporations, having moved many business functions to their intranet Web servers, have discovered that they can extend their business by offering this functionality to outside organizations and individuals. The extremely sensitive nature of the information that will be shared places a high requirement on security.

Typically, a corporation that wants to open portions of its network to other organizations will implement a dial-up infrastructure or will provision a series of point-to-point or frame relay links. The question of who ultimately pays for these connections is a matter of negotiation, but the costs can be significant.

As in the other examples, the alternative to dedicated dial-up or full-time connections is to use the Internet as the communications backbone. Remote users and corporations will first connect to the Internet and then will access the extranet resources. Each extranet participant pays for their piece of the connection, and the total overall cost remains low, particularly if each participant already has an Internet connection.

While the mechanics of providing outside access to internal Web servers are relatively straightforward, the security implications are not. Just as in the previous two examples, the issues of authentication and encryption are significant. However, the implications of connecting a totally separate organization or group of individuals to an internal corporate resource create a whole new set of security considerations. For example, who will become responsible for authorizing new extranet partners, maintaining the authorization accounts database, and monitoring extranet usage? A single person may become responsible, or a group of people may become responsible for these and other activities.

Establishing a virtual private network in an extranet environment may ultimately entail both of the types of connections we have already discussed. Connections to other corporate networks will be similar to the network-to-network VPN scenario, and connections to individuals will be similar to the dial-up Internet VPN scenario. Any data that will travel outside of the firewall must be encrypted to keep the secrets safe.

For more information on extranet design and implementation issues, see *Extranet Design and Implementation* by Pete Loshin (Sybex, 1997).

How It Works: Elements of a VPN

Now that you have an idea of some of the ways you can use VPNs to reduce costs, let's take a closer look at the elements that comprise a VPN. There are four primary elements to any VPN solution: a public network, a data source, a VPN server, and a VPN client. Figure 11.2 illustrates the elements of a VPN.

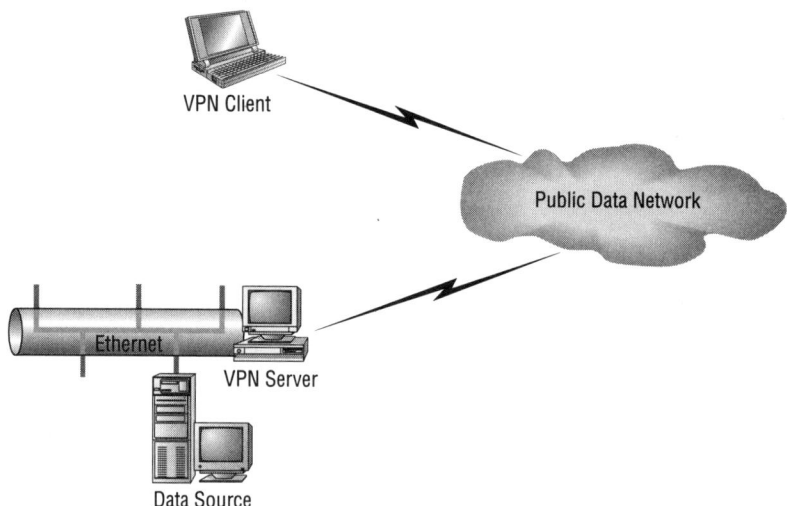

FIGURE 11.2

The elements of a virtual private network (VPN)

The Public Network

The first element, the public network, refers to any type of publicly available, packet-switched network. The most obvious example of a public network is the Internet. Public networks have a number of advantages over private networks based on point-to-point links. The two most significant advantages of public networks are their reliability and their relatively low cost to join.

Public networks like the Internet enjoy a high level of reliability, in large part due to redundancy. Between any two nodes on the Internet there are a number of potential routes, thanks to the large number of routers owned by the various Internet service providers. If any of those routers should fail, the other routers will automatically direct traffic around the failed link. The total time required for the packets to reach their destination may be longer, but the information will ultimately be delivered. Another contributor to the Internet's reliability is the TCP/IP protocols themselves. Protocols such as TCP have a number of provisions to guarantee delivery of information.

The second advantage of a public network is that it offers tremendous connectivity potential at a relatively low cost. In this regard, public data networks are similar to the public telephone network. The telephone network, by design, is a switched network. Once you connect your telephone at home to the public telephone network, you have the potential to call anyone else in the world who has a telephone on the network. If the public telephone network didn't exist, you would need to pay someone to run a separate telephone line between you and everyone you wanted to contact. As you can imagine, the cost for that many phone lines would be significant, to say the least.

Connecting to the Internet is like getting a network dial tone. Your single Internet connection gives users on your network the ability to communicate with anyone else on the Internet, and it gives anyone on the Internet the potential ability to communicate with users and resources on your network. With a single Internet connection you can avoid having to create a point-to-point link to each of your remote users and to all of your business partners.

Public data networks have their disadvantages as well, particularly in the area of security. Public networks, by nature, are accessible to anyone who can pay for the connection to their network. Once you have established a connection to the public network, anyone else will have the ability to reach your network. In addition, anyone who has access to the communications path between your network and a remote user can potentially intercept the transmission and view the contents of the communications.

While the benefits of a public data network like the Internet make it an attractive candidate for inter- and extra-corporate communications, the security risks tend to scare off many potential users. Two mechanisms are necessary to make the Internet a safe and suitable communication channel—a firewall (which we discussed in the last chapter) to protect against intrusions, and an encryption mechanism to provide secure transmissions of sensitive data.

The Data Source

The second element of a VPN is the data source. The data source may be a Web server, a client/server database, an e-mail server, or a file server. The data source is the resource that the VPN is designed to protect. Without a data source, setting up a virtual private network is pointless. Why go to the trouble and expense of protecting your network if there is no data to protect?

Many VPNs are designed to provide multiple data sources to users. For example, some corporations have deployed VPNs so their employees can access the corporate network from home. From home, these users can access any resource they might access from the office, including application servers, electronic mail, or groupware repositories.

Other VPNs are designed to provide a subset of the resources available on the network. For example, if an organization wanted to create an extranet Web server, they might develop a VPN that restricted remote extranet users to that Web server.

By using Windows NT domain accounts, access controls, and encrypted communications, you can adjust the levels and types of data sources available to VPN users. Through VPN software, such as Microsoft's PPTP (which we'll discuss shortly), users authenticate to your NT domain and become subject to any privileges or limitations associated with their domain account.

The VPN Server

The third element of a VPN is the VPN Server. A VPN Server is a software- or hardware-based device that manages all of the sessions between the internal network and the VPN users connecting through the public network.

A VPN connection may be between the VPN server and a VPN client workstation or another VPN server. These connections must first be defined within the VPN server configuration. Depending on the type of VPN software being configured, the definition process may include assigning network addresses and routing information for the connection, in addition to configuration of encryption keys or authentication information.

Most VPN server software includes a management application to view VPN connection status, to manipulate VPN activity log files, and to create new VPN connections or delete existing ones.

The process of encapsulating encrypted packets within IP packets to provide secure communications over an insecure network is called *tunneling*, and a VPN connection is frequently referred to as a *tunnel*. In a VPN environment, all communications between the client workstation and the data source are securely tunneled by the VPN server to travel over an IP network. When the client workstation sends a request or response, the VPN client software on the workstation encrypts the transmission, retunneling the communication. The tunneling process effectively creates a virtual point-to-point private link between the client and the server. Figure 11.3 illustrates a tunneling link.

Most VPN server software has the ability to tunnel multiple protocols within an IP packet. For example, users can communicate with devices using the IPX, IP, or NetBEUI protocols over a PPTP connection.

FIGURE 11.3
A VPN link is a virtual point-to-point connection on a public network.

The VPN Client

The fourth element of a VPN is the VPN client. The VPN client is usually a collection of drivers and software that must be installed onto any client workstation that requires a VPN connection. Configuration of the VPN client software varies from product to product, but it usually involves inputting the host name or IP address of the VPN server along with authentication information such as a login name or password.

After the client configuration has been completed, users can connect to the network via the VPN in a number of ways. In a dial-up scenario, a user would establish their Internet connection as usual, then activate the VPN client software to establish the tunneled connection to the VPN server. If the user wanted to establish the VPN connection from a LAN-connected workstation, they would simply activate the VPN client software.

In order for a VPN connection to work, both the server and the client must agree upon an encryption key. The method by which the key is determined varies according to the type of VPN software in use. For example, when a Microsoft PPTP client contacts a PPTP server, the client and server utilize the user's password as the encryption key. Other products may require some form of key sharing prior to the establishment of the VPN connection for the encryption process to work.

Once the connection has been established, the VPN client provides encryption and decryption services for the tunneled connection. Access to services at the far end of the tunnel is transparent to the end user—they can browse the network as if they were physically connected to the LAN. Within the internal network, devices will be able to access the VPN-connected device as if it were connected locally.

Putting It All Together

Now that you understand the elements of a virtual private network, let's review how they all fit together.

A virtual private network is a secure communications channel that is carried over a public data network. Data carried within a virtual private network is encrypted and encapsulated within the data portion of an IP packet. Virtual private networks are capable of delivering a variety of protocols, including IPX, IP, and NetBEUI, even though the primary protocol for communication between VPN devices is IP.

Four elements are required for a virtual private network: a public network, a data source, a VPN server, and a VPN client. In a typical VPN configuration, a VPN client will contact a VPN server over the public data network to establish an encrypted session. During this encrypted session, the user will access the data source as if their workstation were connected locally to the same network as the source.

For the remainder of this chapter, we'll examine two types of VPN software: Microsoft's Point-to-Point Tunneling Protocol (PPTP) and AltaVista's Tunnel.

Creating a VPN with PPTP

In June 1996, Microsoft, along with Ascend Communications, 3Com/Primary Access, ECI Telematics, and US Robotics—a group collectively known as the PPTP forum—submitted a draft of the Point-to-Point Tunneling Protocol (PPTP) to the Internet Engineering Task Force (IETF). PPTP was intended to become a standard for Internet software and hardware vendors who wished to provide secure, multiprotocol connections via the Internet.

PPTP, as its name implies, was developed to be an extension of the Point-to-Point Protocol (PPP). If you access the Internet through a dial-up connection, you may already be familiar with PPP. It is typically the protocol that provides connection services between your modem-equipped computer and an Internet access device. PPP is also one of the protocols that is frequently used between WAN-connected routers.

A PPTP client (or server) uses PPP to establish a connection to the PPTP server, to provide user authentication services, and to encapsulate data packets. Initially, PPTP was only supported on Windows NT Server 4 and NT Workstation, and only client-to-server connections were available. Today, PPTP is supported for NT Server and Workstation, as well as Windows 95, for client-to-server connections. Server-to-server connections are supported under the new Routing and Remote Access Service, formerly codenamed "Steelhead."

Since the PPP protocol provides initial authentication services, the PPTP service accepts the same authentication methods as does the NT Remote Access Service (RAS): the Challenge Handshake Authentication Protocol (CHAP), the Microsoft Challenge Handshake Authentication Protocol (MS-CHAP), and the Password Authentication Protocol (PAP) authentication scheme.

Normally, a PPTP user will authenticate to the PPTP server using the MS-CHAP authentication method. During the authentication process, the user's credentials are transmitted to the PPTP server to be validated against the information stored within the Windows NT domain. Once the user has been authenticated, the PPTP connection will be established, and all information transmitted through the connection will be encrypted by using the user's password as the encryption key. Since the client knows the user's password, and the server knows the user's password, the actual key need never be transmitted over the network, meaning its confidentiality is secured.

PPTP Server Configuration

To give you an idea of the process involved in setting up a VPN with PPTP, we're going to briefly walk through the steps for configuring both the PPTP server and the PPTP client.

PPTP is an extension of the Remote Access Service, so the majority of the server configuration steps must be completed through RAS management tools. If RAS is not already configured on your server, you should install it prior to the PPTP installation.

To enable PPTP on an NT 4 Server:

1. Go to the Protocols section of the Network applet within the Control Panel and click the Add button.

2. Select the Point-to-Point Tunneling Protocol, then select OK.

3. You'll be prompted to identify the number of virtual private networks that the server will process, as shown in Figure 11.4. Since each VPN connection will count as a separate virtual private network, you'll want to select a number that will be sufficient to serve your anticipated maximum number of concurrent connections. For example, if you anticipate a maximum of eight concurrent users, select 8 and click OK, then close the Network applet.

NT will review the bindings and save your changes. You may receive a prompt to insert your NT Server CD-ROM, so have it available just in case.

NT 4 Server can be configured to support a maximum of 256 simultaneous PPTP connections.

FIGURE 11.4

Configuring the number of virtual private networks

Once you have added the PPTP protocol and rebooted your server, your next step is to configure the VPN ports through the Remote Access Service:

1. Open the Network applet within the Control Panel and select the Services tab page.

2. Select Remote Access Service from the services list, then click the Properties button to view the Remote Access Setup Dialog box. This dialog box, as shown in Figure 11.5, displays a list of configured RAS ports.

3. Click on the Add button, then select one of the VPN devices from the list of RAS-capable devices, and click OK to add VPN to the list.

Repeat the process for each of the VPN devices that was created when you added the PPTP protocol.

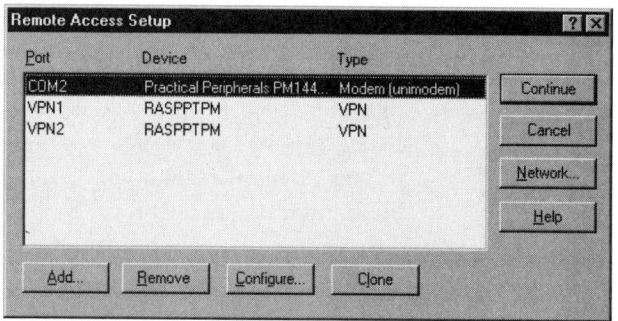

FIGURE 11.5

The Remote Access Setup dialog box

Next, you must configure the network properties of each of the ports:

1. Highlight one of the VPN devices in the device list, then click the Network button.

2. Within the Server settings section of the Network Configuration dialog box, select all of the protocols that the VPN device will permit.

3. Click OK to accept the changes, and repeat the process for each of the VPN devices.

4. When you are finished, select the Continue button from the Remote Access Setup dialog box, and close the Network Control Panel applet.

The NT server will review the bindings and prompt you to restart the server. Reboot your server to complete the PPTP server configuration process.

PPTP Client Configuration (Windows 95)

Configuring NT Workstation 4 for PPTP client operation is similar to configuring the NT Server, so we'll describe the configuration steps for a Windows 95 workstation to give you an idea of the process.

Before you can configure Windows 95, you must download a few files from the Microsoft Web site (www.microsoft.com/), because PPTP support was not included in the original Windows 95 package. Once these files have been installed, you can begin the configuration.

The file that you need to download is MSDUN12.exe (Microsoft Dial-Up Networking version 1.2). You may also need to upgrade your version of Winsock to a revised version of 1.1. The files are available from microsoft.com/Windows95/default.asp. Select the Windows 95 VPN Client link or go directly to microsoft.com/ntserver/info/pptp.htm.

To configure a Windows 95 workstation for PPTP client operation, go to the Dial-Up Networking folder, then select the Make New Connection wizard. You'll notice that in the first dialog box you'll have a new option in the Select a modem list, called Microsoft VPN Adapter, as shown in Figure 11.6. Give the connection a name, select the Microsoft VPN Adapter, and click the Next button.

Next, specify the VPN server that you wish to access. You can input either the IP address of the server, or its DNS name. Click the Next button, then click the Finish button to complete the configuration and to create the new connection.

FIGURE 11.6

Selecting the Microsoft VPN Adapter

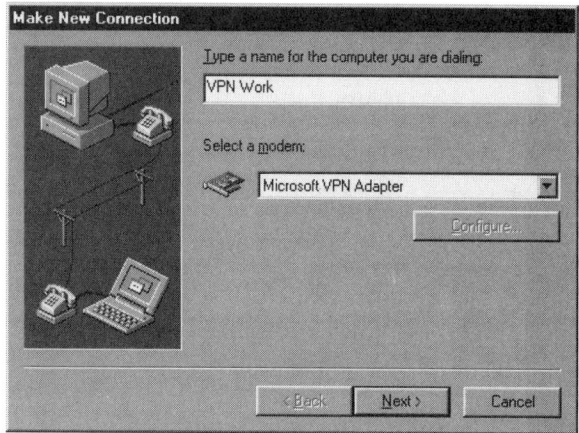

When you click the connection icon, you will receive a login prompt like the one shown in Figure 11.7. Enter a valid user name and password for the domain in which the VPN server exists, confirm the VPN server name, and click the Connect button. Once you have been authenticated, you can access any of the devices available through the VPN as if you were connected directly to the network.

FIGURE 11.7

Connecting to the VPN server

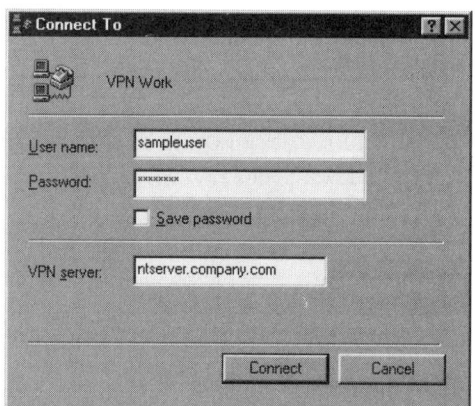

PPTP Design Considerations

If you plan to design PPTP implementations that provide connections over the Internet, you should specify that the Require Microsoft Encrypted Authentication and the Require Data Encryption options are selected to ensure that all authentication information will be sent in an encrypted format.

Another security precaution that you can implement is to set the Enable PPTP Filtering checkbox under the Advanced IP Addressing dialog box in the TCP/IP properties section of the Network applet in the Control Panel. Once you enable PPTP filtering, the network interface that is configured to filter will discard all non-PPTP packets that it encounters. This measure will ensure that only PPTP-authenticated traffic will pass through the PPTP server.

To implement PPTP along with a firewall, you will need to configure the firewall to forward all inbound TCP traffic with the destination port of 1723. The PPTP server itself should remain inside the firewall-protected network, not outside the firewall.

Third-Party Products

While PPTP services come free with NT Server 4, there are some issues that have prompted some organizations to consider other alternatives for their VPN. One of PPTP's strengths is that it is closely integrated with RAS, the NT domain structure, and the NT operating system itself. However, this close integration also forces implementers to rely solely on the domain accounts database for user validation. For some organizations, this requirement is not a big deal, because all of their users already have a domain account. Other organizations, however, may be forced to duplicate existing account information just for PPTP authentication.

The second concern expressed by some organizations is that the PPTP specification does not have a future, because of the announcement that Microsoft plans to merge the PPTP specification with Cisco's specification for Layer 2 Forwarding (L2F) to create a new protocol, L2TP. Early PPTP implementers are concerned that once L2TP becomes an official standard, PPTP will become obsolete and they will have to redesign their VPN implementation.

In this section, we'll take a look at one of the alternatives to Microsoft's PPTP: the AltaVista Tunnel.

AltaVista Tunnel

AltaVista Tunnel is similar to PPTP in that it is designed to provide a private, encrypted communication session between computers on a public network, but the implementation of the product has some noticeable differences from Microsoft's implementation. The AltaVista Tunnel software comes in two varieties: the Workgroup Edition, for providing encryption services for an entire network, and the Personal Edition, for providing encryption services for a single computer connecting to a workgroup server.

The Workgroup Edition can operate as a VPN server, a VPN client, or as both a server and a client. In a VPN server configuration, a Workgroup server supports connections from Personal Edition clients or from another Workgroup Edition configured as a client. A Personal Edition client can only communicate with a Workgroup Edition server.

Installation of the product is somewhat more complicated than configuring PPTP, and the software is not as tightly integrated with the NT operating system. For example, the AltaVista Tunnel does not rely on the NT Domain account database for authentication, as PPTP does. Instead, it uses a public key encryption scheme for all connection authentication. Additional software is included in both the Personal and Workgroup editions to simplify key management. Once a server key has been generated, the key file and a server configuration file can be distributed to the client user. The client user imports these files to establish the personal tunnel configuration. Next, the user initiates a connection to the tunnel server, and then inputs their password. Figure 11.8 shows the Personal Tunnel client dialog box during a connection to a Tunnel server.

Once the connection has been authenticated, the rest of the session is encrypted using secret key encryption to provide faster encryption and decryption. Every 30 minutes the client and the server negotiate a brand new session key.

In addition to encryption key generation functions, the Workgroup Edition management application provides options to define tunnels as inbound (to service connections from Personal Edition users), outbound (to provide one-way communication to a remote Workgroup server), or inbound/outbound (to provide two-way communications with a remote Workgroup server). One area in which the AltaVista Tunnel offers a much higher level of configuration control is tunnel definition. Each tunnel can be configured with a specific IP address; or addresses can be drawn from a range, and each tunnel can be configured with separate routing information and a unique port number.

FIGURE 11.8

The AltaVista Personal Tunnel client

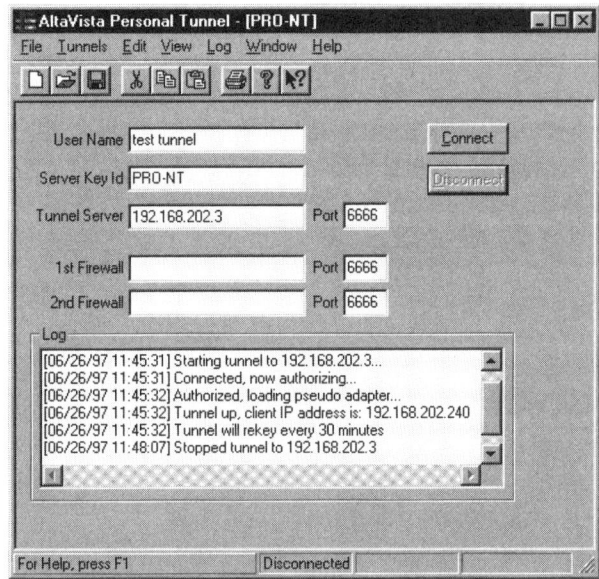

One of the more useful features of AltaVista Tunnel is its firewall support. During configuration, users can specify the DNS names (or IP addresses) and port numbers of firewalls that the packets must pass through to reach the tunnel server.

VPNs and Firewalls

The close relationship between the VPN server and the firewall has created a logical connection between these two devices. Many firewall vendors have begun to include VPN functionality within their standard product offering, and others have developed VPN add-ons for their firewalls.

Firewall vendors such as Checkpoint Software Technologies, Raptor Systems, Secure Computing, and Trusted Information Systems have included VPN technology within their firewalls. Features and capabilities vary from product to product, so review each vendor's documentation carefully. Some firewall/VPN solutions only provide network-to-network VPN capabilities when communicating with the same brand firewall. Others, like Checkpoint's Firewall-1, utilize encryption methods based on the open IPSec draft standards so they should, in theory, have the ability to communicate with VPN products from other vendors that support IPSec. As of this writing, the standards are still in the draft stage and are subject to change, so true interoperability between firewall vendors remains to be seen.

> IPSec is a group of security options for IP that are defined in RFCs 1825-29. These security options define open standards for encryption, authentication, and key management.

In this chapter, we've discussed the elements of Virtual Private Network technology, including two different VPN implementations from Microsoft and AltaVista. VPN technology is but one of the elements you'll need to consider as you begin to extend your network beyond its geographical boundaries. In the next part of this book, we'll discuss ways to extend your network through remote access.

PART IV

NT AS A REMOTE ACCESS PROGRAM

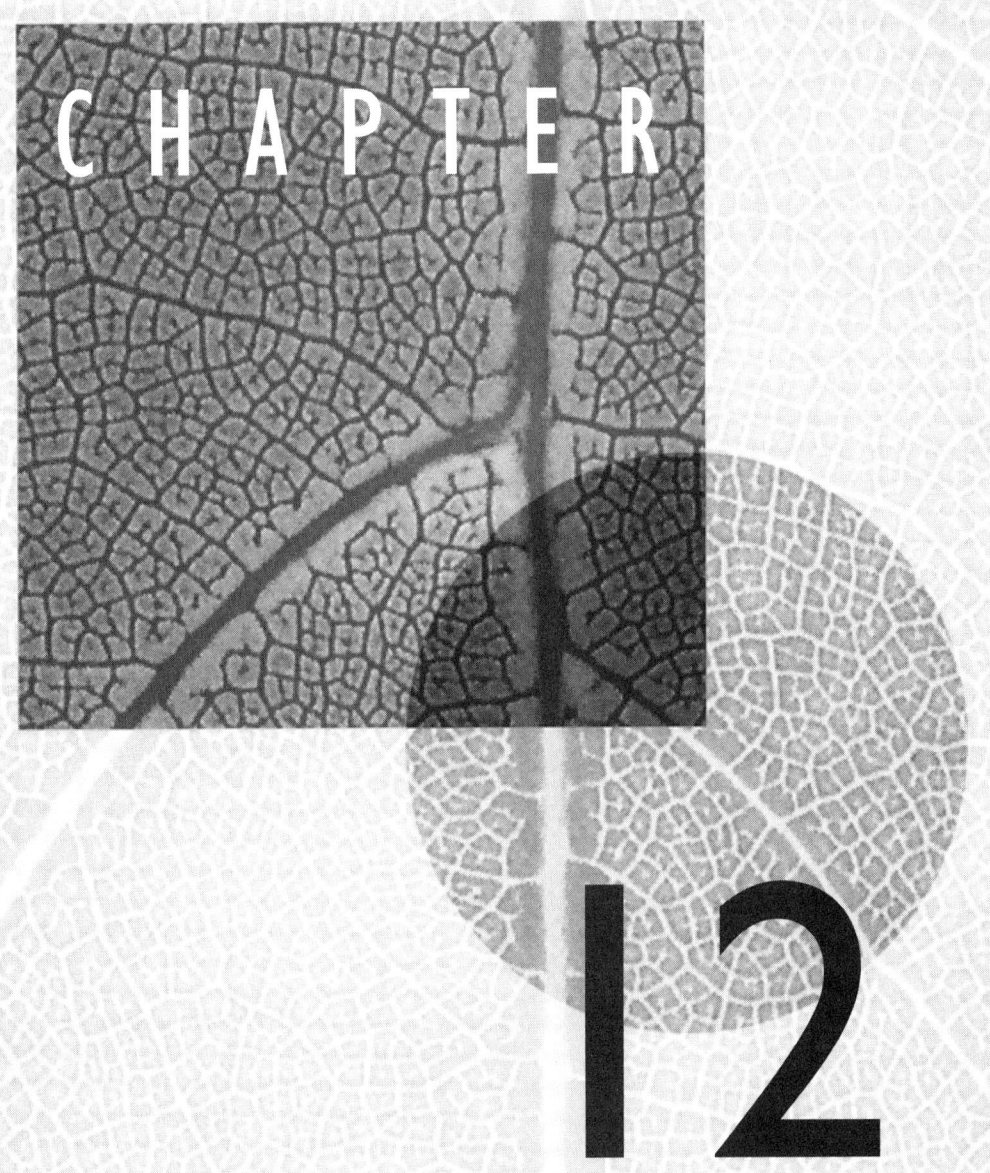

CHAPTER 12

Remote Access Concepts and LAN to WAN Design Issues

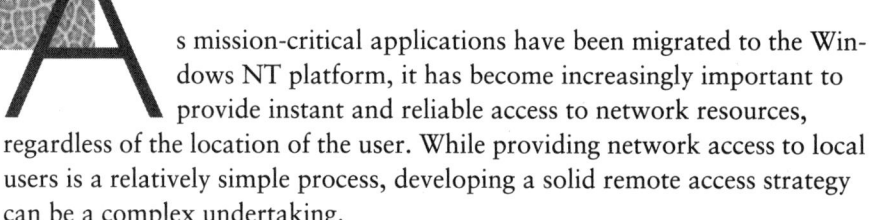

As mission-critical applications have been migrated to the Windows NT platform, it has become increasingly important to provide instant and reliable access to network resources, regardless of the location of the user. While providing network access to local users is a relatively simple process, developing a solid remote access strategy can be a complex undertaking.

A comprehensive remote access implementation can fulfill two roles: first, a remote access implementation can help to reduce the cost of providing network applications or resources to small, remote office sites; second, your remote access implementation will become the primary, centralized access method for mobile users or for clients of your organization.

In this and the next two chapters we will discuss remote access concepts, technologies, and implementations, including both remote node and remote control access methods. In this chapter we will cover the following:

- Remote access network technologies, such as Plain Old Telephone Service (POTS), ISDN, X.25, and the T-carrier system

- Remote access concepts

- Remote access network design principles

We'll begin with a detailed discussion of the various communication channels you'll have the opportunity to use as you design remote access systems. It is important to clearly understand the strengths and weaknesses of each of the technologies so that you'll be able to create the most effective and efficient designs.

Remote Access Network Technologies

Remote access connectivity can be provided via the Plain Old Telephone System (POTS), leased line system, T-carrier system, fractional T1 system, X.25 (PSDN system), ISDN, or frame relay system. Since the advent of laptops and their huge success, remote users have increasingly demanded better throughput and reliability in their connections to the "office." Many corporations that are forced to support a large pool of mobile users or remote locations have looked into access options that would reduce long distance costs, speed connections, and also provide ease of access and security benefits. Some of these new systems (from AT&T, Sprint, MCI, etc.) have provided some alternative options to the POTS method of direct dial-in. These systems vary from provider to provider but the fundamentals remain constant. They all provide local Point of Presence (POP) dial access numbers, which allow users to connect via a local number. They all provide security features (login ID, password, and filtering). The calls are routed through their private cloud (X.25 or frame relay), and terminated at the destination port (the user's corporate location), as shown in Figure 12.1.

However, the provider's connectivity cloud is just one piece of the total remote connectivity system. The chapters in this part of the book will discuss the other pieces to the puzzle and help you make the proper access method decisions—ones that would benefit your situation. The following sections will discuss each access method in detail.

Plain Old Telephone System (POTS)

The POTS network is the most familiar communication system in use today. There are millions of telephone lines in the United States, and the various switching systems that connect the voice and data calls have been designed to provide an extremely high level of reliability.

In technical terms, a POTS telephone channel is a specific frequency band (300 to 3,300 Hertz), called a *passband*, that has been optimized for voice communication. The bandwidth, which is measured in Hz, can be calculated by subtracting the upper and lower frequency limits (for example, 3,300 – 300 = 3,000Hz).

Any frequencies below 300Hz or above 3,300Hz would be attenuated and would not be transmitted with as great an amplitude as those frequencies within the passband.

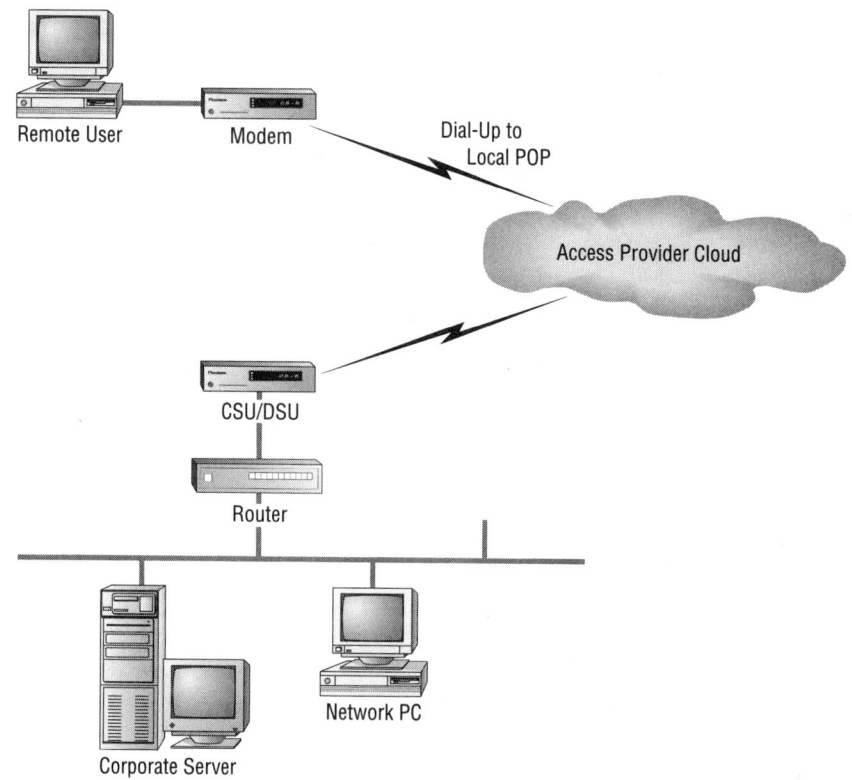

FIGURE 12.1 A typical provider-offered remote connectivity system

Data communication signals, however, are measured in terms of bits per second (bps), not Hertz, and therefore some kind of mechanism must be employed to associate the transmission channel characteristic (in Hz) to the data rate (in bps). This relationship is established using two theorems that were derived from early telegraph and telephone research.

The Nyquist Rate

Harry Nyquist, a researcher in telegraph transmission efficiency, published an equation called the Nyquist Rate that measured the transmission signaling rate in baud:

```
Nyquist Rate = 2B/s
```

where B is the bandwidth of the transmission channel.

Using this equation, you can see that a telephone channel bandwidth of 3,000Hz can support up to $2 \times 3,000$, or 6,000, baud.

Shannon's Capacity Theorem

Another scientist, by the name of Claude Shannon, continued Nyquist's research and created a study that showed how noise affects data transmission. Shannon took into account the signal-to-noise ratio of the transmission channel (measured in decibels, dB) and derived what is now known as Shannon's Capacity Theorem:

```
C = B log2 (1 + S/N) bps
```

A typical voice channel has a signal-to-noise ratio of 30dB (1000 : 1) and a bandwidth of 3,000Hz. If we substitute these values into Shannon's Theorem:

```
C = 3000 log2 (1 + 1000)
```

Since log2 (1,001) is approximately equal to 10, the theorem yields a maximum capacity of approximately 30,000bps.

Baud vs. Bits per Second

Let's take a step back from these equations to clarify a few points.

First the terms *baud* and *bits per second* are often confused. Modem designers, and others, will speak of those signals in terms of baud. When transferring data (such as a file), we refer to it as bits per second.

Second, upper limits of the data transmission characteristics of the telephone channel exist. These limits are 6,000 baud and 30,000bps. Thus, while it is possible to transmit data at rates greater than 30,000bps over twisted pair transmission media, it is not possible to do so using the PSTN. Modem technologies that provide up to 56,000bps do so because at least part of the connection between the two modems is over a digital telephone line, not a POTS line.

Third, it is correct to say, "I need a 9,600bps modem" instead of "I need a 9,600-baud modem." Because of the Nyquist Theorem, we know that a 9,600-baud modem could not transmit over the dial-up telephone network. What is really meant when someone says "9,600-baud modem" is a modem that transmits 2,400 signals per second (baud) and represents each signal with 4 bits, or

```
Modem speed = 2400signals/s × 4bits/signal = 9,600bps
```

There are current technologies, such as the V.34 standard, that push the upper limit of the Nyquist theorem. Any new technology will have to compensate for signal degradation with a process called *conditioning*. (Conditioning is a process that takes an incoming signal, removes the noise, and boosts the signal back to its original strength.) The other option is to use a digital medium instead of an analog one.

Leased Line Systems (Analog)

There are other options than the telephone dial-up method. One method would be to establish a permanent, constant transmission path, known as a leased line or private line. The end user has access to a telephone line (either 2-wire or 4-wire circuit) that is terminated at each end of the transmission path. The terminations can exist within the same city or across the country, connecting different Local Exchange Carriers (LECs) via one Inter-Exchange Carrier (IXC). When the transmission path is fixed, the user is guaranteed predictable transmission parameters. Conditioning, or correction for transmission problems, can be done on this fixed path.

The easiest way to describe the difference between a switched line and a leased line is to consider the way the telephone system operates when you make a telephone call. Each time you call your relatives on the other side of the country, you must first dial their telephone number. Once the number has been dialed, the telephone company will establish a connection between you and your relatives. This connection only exists for the duration of the call, and as soon as you hang up, the connection will be destroyed. In a leased line scenario, the connection will exist permanently, whether you are on a call or not. In some situations, leased lines have an economic advantage over dial-up lines. For example, let's assume that a leased line connection between two cities costs $500 per month. At a typical cost of $0.25 per minute, this would translate to 2,000 minutes or 33.3 hours of dial-up usage. So if a network requires use of the transmission facility more than 33.3 hours per month, a leased line would make more financial sense.

The T-Carrier System

The T-carrier system was developed by Bell Telephone Laboratories in the 1960s as a means of multiplexing voice signals onto a digital transmission line. The system was inspired by a telephone line capacity problem that developed in several cities. Signals were carried between switching offices on individual pairs of copper wire, one pair per conversation. These pairs were bundled into a large cable, with up to 3,000 pairs inside, and placed in a conduit under the city streets. As the city grew, so did the need for additional telephone circuits. Additional cables were placed, and the conduit runs eventually became completely full of cables. When all the conduit ductwork became congested, the telephone company was left with two choices: dig up the street and install additional conduits, or find a way to get additional capacity out of the existing copper pairs. Bell Systems opted for the second alternative and put their scientists to work to solve the problem. That was the birth of the T-carrier network.

The T1 circuit is a digital, full-duplex transmission system operating at 1.544Mbps. It can be used to transmit digital voice, data, or video signals. The complete circuit requires a 4-wire path (of copper) and is available only for point-to-point (not multipoint) connections. The T1 circuit, however, is not limited to copper-based, terrestrial communication channels. Many other transmission options are available, including 18 and 23 GigaHertz (GHz) microwave radio, fiber optic, infrared, and coaxial cables.

At either end of the T1 circuit is a customer-provided Channel Service Unit, or CSU, as shown in Figure 12.2. The CSU accepts the data from the Customer Premises Equipment (CPE) and encodes that data for transmission on the T1 circuit. Typical CPE would be a T1 multiplexer or a LAN bridge designed for T1-circuit-rate transmission.

Understanding Communications Terms

Multiplexing, in communications or signaling lingo, is a technique that allows multiple messages or signals to share a transmission channel. A device that performs multiplexing is called a multiplexer (or multiplexor). It selects a single output from several. The input channels are normally low-speed, while the output channel is high-speed, with enough bandwidth to accommodate the multiple slow channels. This device is often called a MUX. The multiplexer uses a predetermined strategy for combining multiple streams: Time Division Multiplexing (TDM) and Frequency Division Multiplexing (FDM).

TDM   In this technique, small slices from each input channel are sent in sequences, so that each input channel has some of the time on the output channel. If each *n* channel is given an equal time slice, then each channel gets only 1/*n* of the time on the output channel. There are variations of this technique:

- **ATDM:** Asynchronous time division multiplexing. Data is sent asynchronously.

- **STTM:** Statistical time division multiplexing. This technique polls ports and skips ports that have nothing to send.

- **STM:** Synchronous transfer mode. This technique is used in broadband ISDN and is also supported by the SONET architecture.

FIGURE 12.2

The T1-carrier network

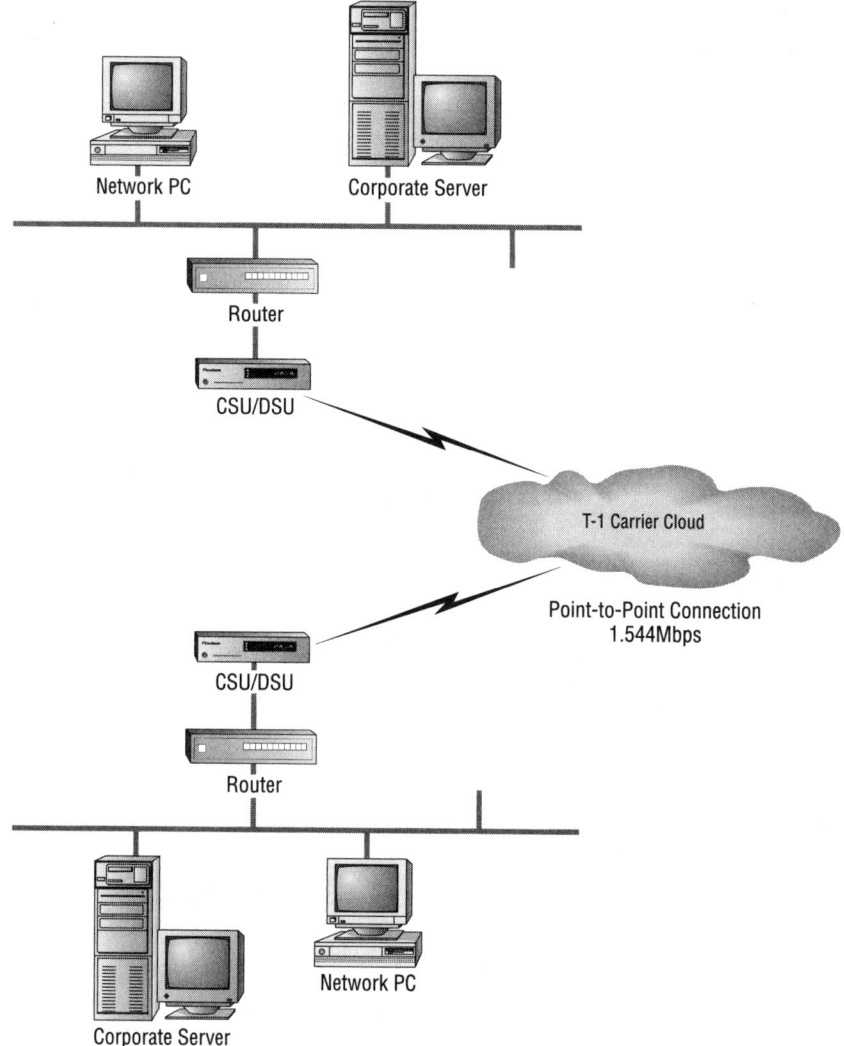

FDM In this technique, the output channel is divided into multiple smaller bandwidth channels. Each of these output channels is defined in a different frequency range, and each is allocated for transmitting one of the input channels. The output channels all have a capacity that is inversely proportional to the number of input channels.

CSU (Channel Service Unit) and DSU (Data Service Unit) are two components of a DCE (Data Communications Equipment) device. This device provides access to digital services or DDS, T1, and other types of lines.

The DSU performs the following tasks:

- Connects to the DTE (Data Terminal Equipment, usually a router or remote bridge) through a synchronous serial interface, which is a V.35 or an RS-422 connection. RS-232 connections are also possible for low speed services.

- Formats data for transmission over the digital line.

- Controls data flow between the network and CSU.

The CSU does the following:

- Terminates the long-distance connection at the user's end.

- Processes digital signals for the digital lines.

- Tests remote loopback on the lines.

- Serves as a buffer to keep faulty subscriber equipment from bringing down the digital service.

T1 circuits are found on more and more digital transmission facilities within North America. An existing hierarchy includes a number of different transmission rates. All of these facilities contain a specific digital signal level (DS) and all are based upon the DS0 channel, which operates at 64Kbps. This DS0 channel becomes the basic building block for ISDN (Integrated Services Digital Network) transmission, although the term used with ISDN for 64Kbps is a B (bearer) channel. Table 12.1 lists the various DS transmission rates.

The signal is referred to as DS1, while the transmission channel (over a copper-based facility) is called a T1 circuit.

TABLE 12.1 Digital Signal (DS) Transmission Rates	Signal	Carrier	Equivalent to Multiples of T1	Voice	Data Rate (Mbps)	Relationship between Data Rate and Signal (DS)
	DS0	N/A	N/A	1	0.064	N/A
	DS1	T1	1	24	1.544	24 DS0
	DS1C	T1C	2	48	3.152	2 DS1 multiplexed
	DS2	T2	4	96	6.312	2 DSC1
	DS3	T3	28	672	44.736	7 DS2
	DS4	T4	168	4032	274.760	6 DS3

The numerical differences in the values are due to framing information (we'll leave the explanation of that to another book).

Fractional T1 System

Fractional T1 (FT1) offers the network manager a range of digital bandwidth choices that are a fraction of a full T1 link. The service is designed for applications that have requirements greater than those provided by analog or DDS private lines, but may be less than a full T1 circuit. Fractional T1 circuits are configured in 64Kbps segments, up to the maximum of 1.544Mbps.

The financial benefits of FT1 service, plus the ease with which bandwidth may be added as business needs increase, provides an alternative to voice-grade, or digital, private lines. Customers can purchase a low-speed fractional T1, such as a 128 or 256Kbps connection, and increase bandwidth without having to replace the T1 line itself or any of the connecting equipment.

PSDNs: Packet-Switched Public Data Networks (X.25 Protocol)

Packet-Switched Public Data Networks (PSDNs), sometimes called Public Data Networks (PDNs) or Value-Added Networks (VANs), have been popular data transmission systems since their inception in the early 1970s. PSDNs are often referred to as X.25 networks. This use of the term is misleading. PSDNs are, in fact, packet-switched networks, and X.25 is the protocol of choice between most DTEs (Data Terminal Equipment) and the network.

The misconception lies in the fact that the X.25 protocols define an interface into the PSDN, not the internal protocols within the PSDN. The internal protocols and architecture of the PSDN may be considered proprietary to the network provider, as may the manner in which they route, switch, and store their customer's packets of information. PSDNs operate by accepting fixed-length packets of information (usually 128 octets in length) and routing these through the network to the desired location.

Network users can access the PSDN cloud (a public network provided by service providers, usually X.25 or frame relay, that provides permanent virtual circuit connections to subscribers to connect from one location to another), as shown in Figure 12.3, in several different ways. For high-speed applications, a synchronous leased line is provided between the customer's premises and the local PSDN node. Typical transmission rates are 9.6, 14.4, 19.2, and 56Kbps. Since most of North American PSDNs have access nodes in all major cities, the leased line becomes a local rather than a long-distance facility. Either the end user or the PSDN can contract with the LEC (Local Exchange Carrier) for the leased line. The terminal equipment (synchronous modems or CSUs) required by the type of facility (analog or digital) must also be obtained.

Dial-up access is also available and can be provided in two ways. The user can dial into the port with an asynchronous modem and then connect into another device, known as a PAD (Packet Assembler/Dissembler). The PAD functions similarly to a statistical multiplexer, taking the synchronous characters and placing them into packets of the appropriate length. At the receiving end, the PAD performs the opposite function, decomposing the packet and generating characters. Alternatively, the user can dial up using the X.32 protocol, which provides synchronous X.25 service over dial-up lines. This is often used when traffic volumes don't warrant a dedicated connection, but the error control capabilities of the X.25 protocol are still required or desired.

Integrated Services Digital Network (ISDN)

Integrated Services Digital Network (ISDN) is an all-digital transmission facility that is designed to gradually replace the analog PSTN on a worldwide basis. ISDN service to residences and small businesses is known as the basic rate, offering data throughput of 144Kbps. The transmission pipeline is

FIGURE 12.3

The PSDN network

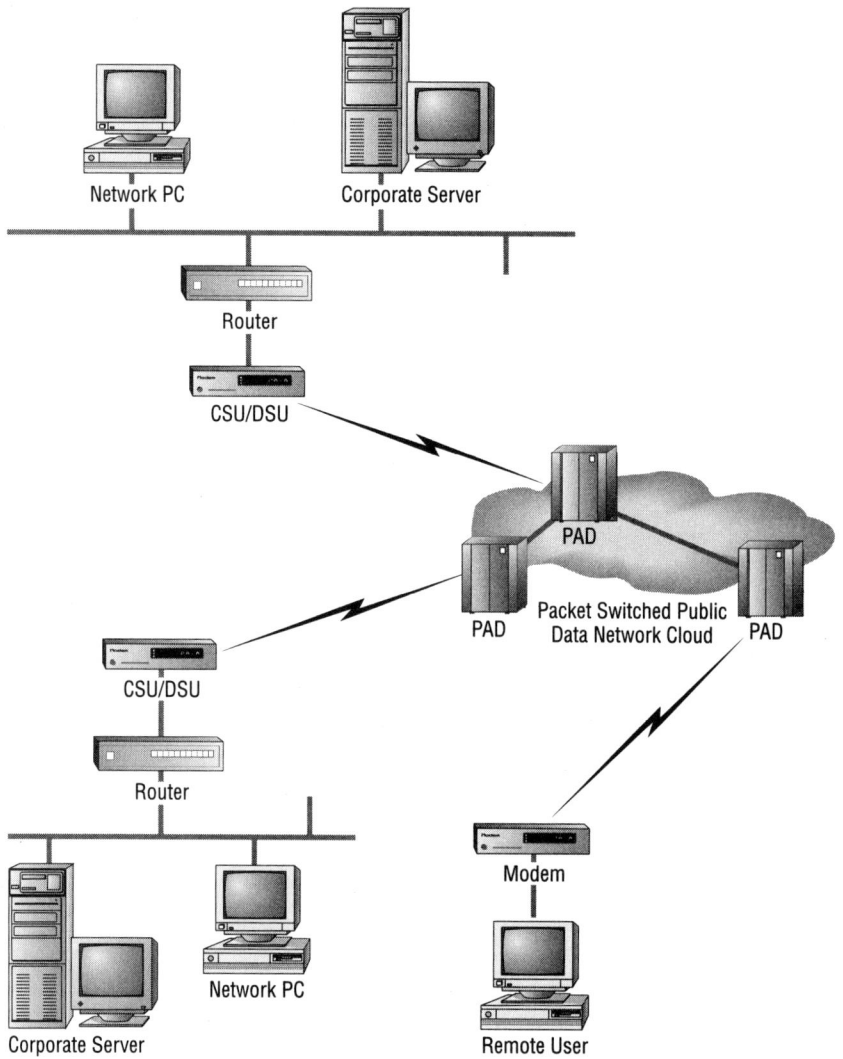

divided into two B (Bearer) channels offering 64Kbps throughput each, plus one D channel operating at 16Mbps. The B channels are for user information (carrying voice, data, or image communication). The D channel is used for signaling on behalf of the B channel, plus packet-switched data transmission. The primary rate has a data throughput of 1.536Mbps. It has the same structure as the DS1 frame, providing 24 of the 64Kbps channels. In most configurations, 23 of the channels are B channels, with the last channel designated a

D (signaling) channel. Primary rate interfaces are designed for businesses requiring higher bandwidth voice and data facilities. Figure 12.4 illustrates the ISDN network.

FIGURE 12.4 The ISDN network

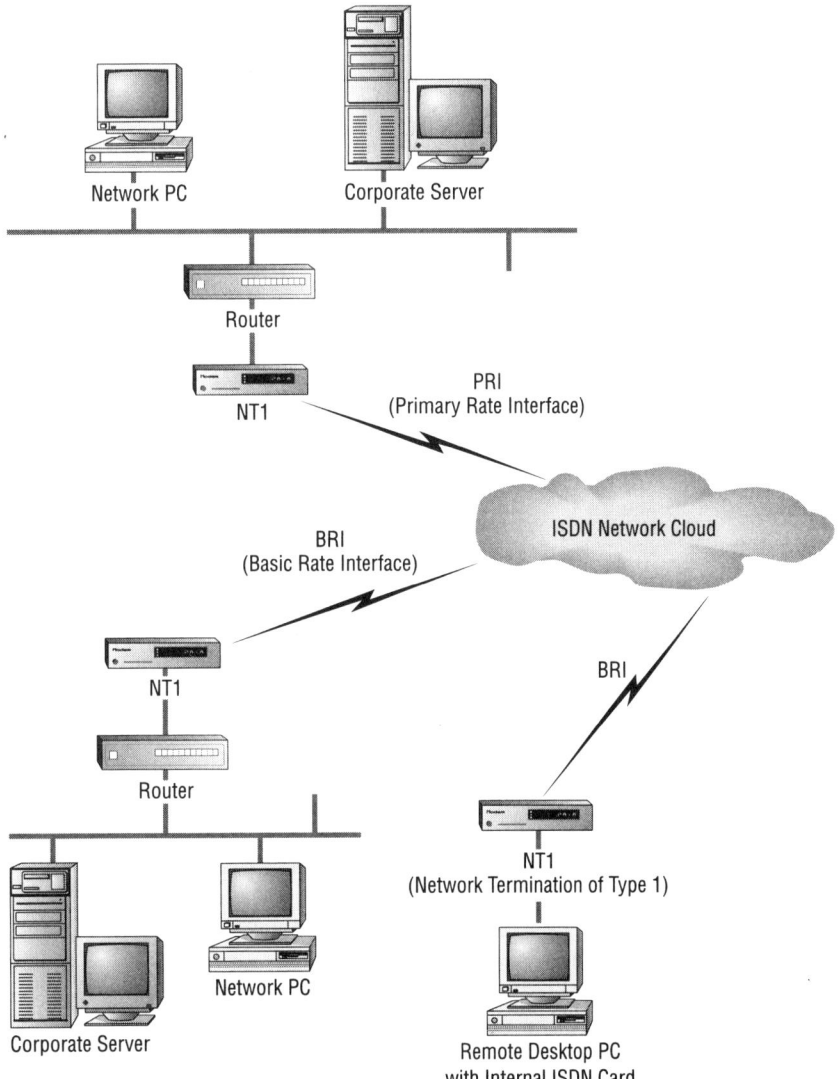

Frame Relay

Frame relay is a network interface standard derived from narrow-band ISDN technology and developed by the American National Standards Institute (ANSI) and the ITU-T (International Telecommunication Union-Telecommunication Standard Sector, formerly CCITT). Frame relay gets its name from its method of operation—the relaying of frames of information. Unlike X.25, which operates on both frames and packets of information, frame relay operates only on frames. The frame relay protocol operates at the Data Link Layer only, and does not include any network or higher layer protocol functions. As a result, the protocol overhead is much less, and with that, real-time processing time is reduced as well.

Frame relay is a connection-oriented service with standards that can implement both permanent virtual connections (PVCs) and switched virtual connections (SVCs). Access to frame relay service is available at rates up to DS1 (1.544Mbps), as shown in Figure 12.5. Frame relay service is available from most of the regional Bell operating companies, including Ameritech, Bell Atlantic (before and after the merger with NYNEX), BellSouth, and so on. Inter-exchange carriers providing frame relay include AT&T, CompuServe, MCI, Sprint, and WilTel.

A Frame Relay Access Device (FRAD), or Assembler/Disassembler, aggregates multiple data network access circuits (such as X.25, asynchronous, etc.) from terminals, hosts, and other network elements into a single frame relay access circuit, performing the frame packetizing function. It also has the capability to carry SNA and LAN traffic over a single interface or network access unit.

Remote Access Concepts

Traditionally, remote access was provided by software packages (such as ReachOut, pcAnyWhere), combinations of Network servers with specialized remote access modules imbedded in the NOS (such as NetWare Connect) and the traditional communications server (such as Citrix's WinFrame and WinView). But recently there has been an influx of new standalone products that more closely resemble routers. Some of these products have come from traditional router and bridge manufacturers, such as 3Com's Office Connect Remote (510, 520, 530); from traditional modem manufacturers, such as

FIGURE 12.5

The frame relay network

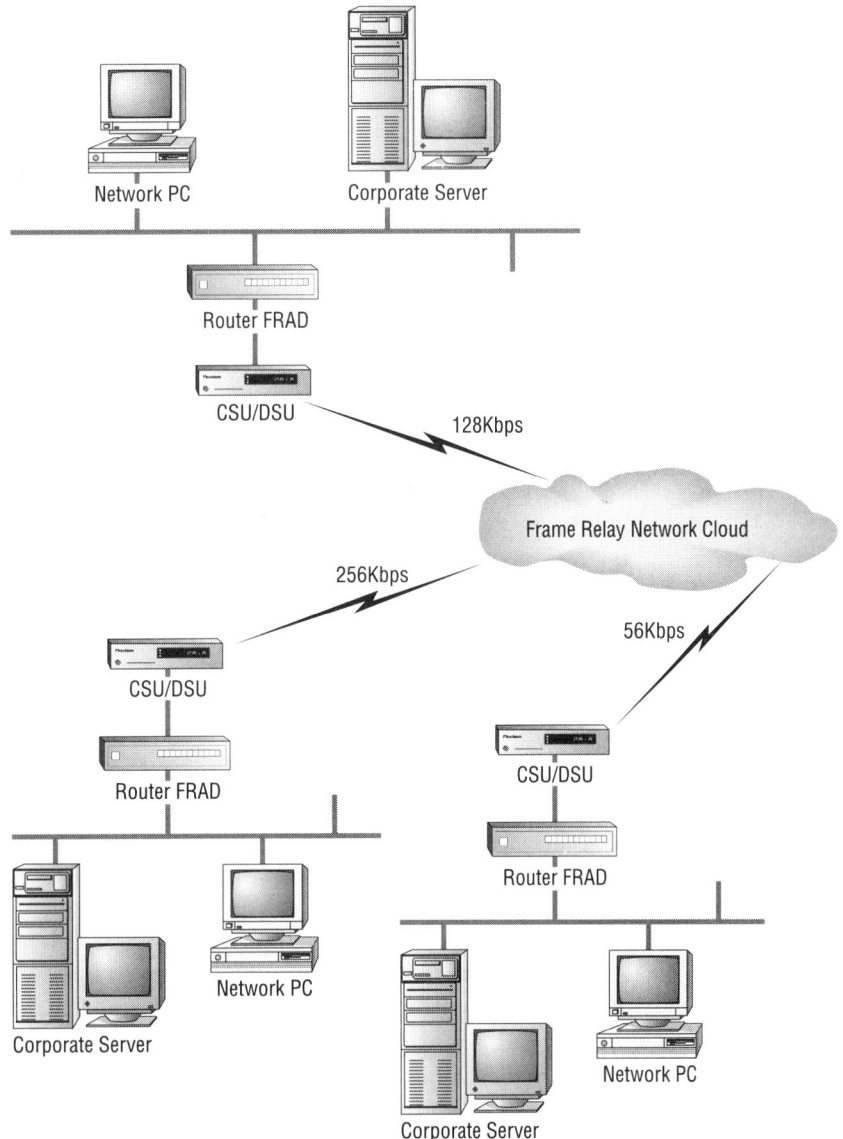

Multi-Tech System's MMLNOV2111; and from traditional communication hub manufacturers, such as Cubix Corporation's WorlDesk Commuter.

In order to understand a little of what is involved in the functions of a Communication Server (CS) or Asynchronous Communication Server (ACS), we'll briefly explain the concepts involved.

Communication Servers

The ACSs or CSs provide access to the LAN via the dial-up telephone network or allow users to share a modem on the LAN for outgoing data calls. An ACS can either be dedicated (with multiple ports) or non-dedicated (typically with one modem in a workstation). The practicality of the ACS lies in its ability to reduce the recurring monthly phone line charges.

The operation of an ACS is fairly straightforward. A serial port is driven by an LSI (Line Service Interface) device called UART (Universal Asynchronous Receiver/Transmitter). The PC controls this UART with ROM BIOS routines that are addressed through Interrupt 14 (INT 14H). However, to improve speed, some communication programs are written to address the UART directly, thus bypassing the INT 14H. With a networked communication requirement, the data that was intended to go to and from the serial port must be placed on the LAN instead. Several Application Program Interfaces (APIs) can be used for this purpose:

- **First API:** NCSI/NASI (Network Communications Services Interface/ Network Asynchronous Services Interface), developed by Network Products Corporation. Novell uses this interface in their NASC (NetWare Asynchronous Communication Server) product.

- **Second API:** Interfaces that send and receive their information via INT 14H calls that conform to IBM's standard INT 14H, as well as IBM's Extended 14H BIOS (EBIOS). These specifications are slow and do not allow the developer to control the line signals.

- **Third API:** The NetBIOS API (INT 5CH) used by IBM, as well as others.

- **Fourth API:** A hardware redirector card installed in each workstation needed to run non-network-modified software (the application reads and writes information directly to a COM hardware address). This card intercepts the write, sends the information down the network to the communication server, and then makes the received data available to the application to read as if it just came in from the local COM port.

The fourth API alternative is the most common and efficient method of communicating for communication servers. The servers that we will introduce in upcoming chapters will use this technology.

Next we will discuss the two primary remote access mechanisms: remote node and remote control access.

Remote Node

There is a great deal of confusion about how to best access a local area network (LAN) from a remote location. Of late, this confusion has boiled down to one simple question: whether the remote node or remote control technique is best. Both remote node and remote control utilize a WAN link that is typically a pair of high-speed modems connected via the Public Switched Telephone Network (PSTN). The basic difference between the remote node and remote control lies in where the actual processing takes place.

There are several ways to use remote connectivity technology. One method is to establish a remote node connection. Remote node is, as the name implies, a network node (workstation) placed at an extended distance from the local area network (LAN). In other words, it could be a user connecting his or her PC at home to the network at the office, as shown in Figure 12.6.

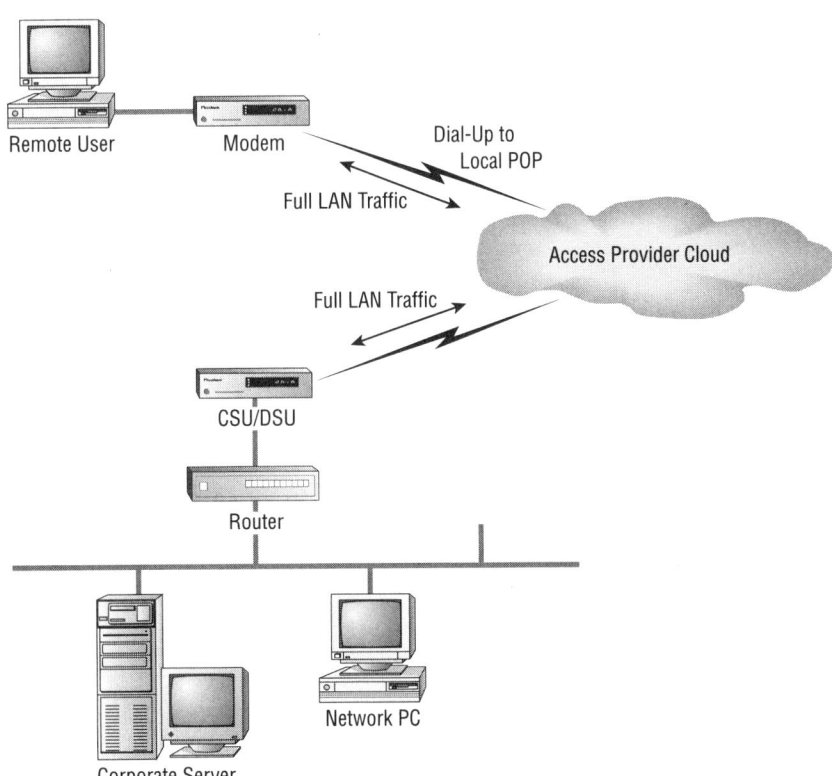

FIGURE 12.6
A remote node connection

A remote node implementation requires that protocol-dependent bridges and routers, or asynchronous multiprotocol bridges and routers, be installed. Protocol-dependent bridges only service a particular protocol. Multiprotocol bridges offer a wider range of connectivity. These connections support not only PC connectivity, but also peer-to-peer connectivity on the LAN, so a user has access to all services as if he or she were directly connected to the network.

This kind of connection allows the user to access their local devices (hard drive, printer, etc.) and local software (applications, protocol stacks, etc.). The local workstation is fully included in the link and acts as if it were directly connected to the network. This is ideal for situations where the user needs to run a front end on their local machine that communicates with the back end on a networked server. This is called a two-tier client/server system.

In a remote node session, all processing is performed at the remote site, so all the data must be transferred to the remote site and back. In this type of remote access, the speed of the WAN link is a very important factor. Typical examples of products that use remote node technology are Shiva's LANRover, Microsoft's Remote Access Services (RAS), and Novell's NetWareConnect.

Remote Control

Another method of performing a remote access is to use remote control connectivity. Remote control is, as the name implies, a method of taking control of an office workstation from a remote location. This software allows users to dial in and connect with a network, then take control of a computer on that network, and then perform their tasks as if they were physically sitting at that computer, as shown in Figure 12.7.

A remote node implementation requires that a host application be running on the host computer (the computer attached to the LAN), and that it be turned on and have access to a modem. In many cases, this will mean a modem directly attached to the COM port of the host computer; however, many of today's LANs have some sort of communications server that allows many users on a LAN to share a few modems. The communications server can be as simple as a software-only gateway that lets you share a modem on someone's LAN PC, or it can be as sophisticated as a dedicated server connecting many modems. The dial-up user (at the remote site) connects to the host computer by using client software. The actual network connections and applications reside on the host computer.

FIGURE 12.7

A remote control session

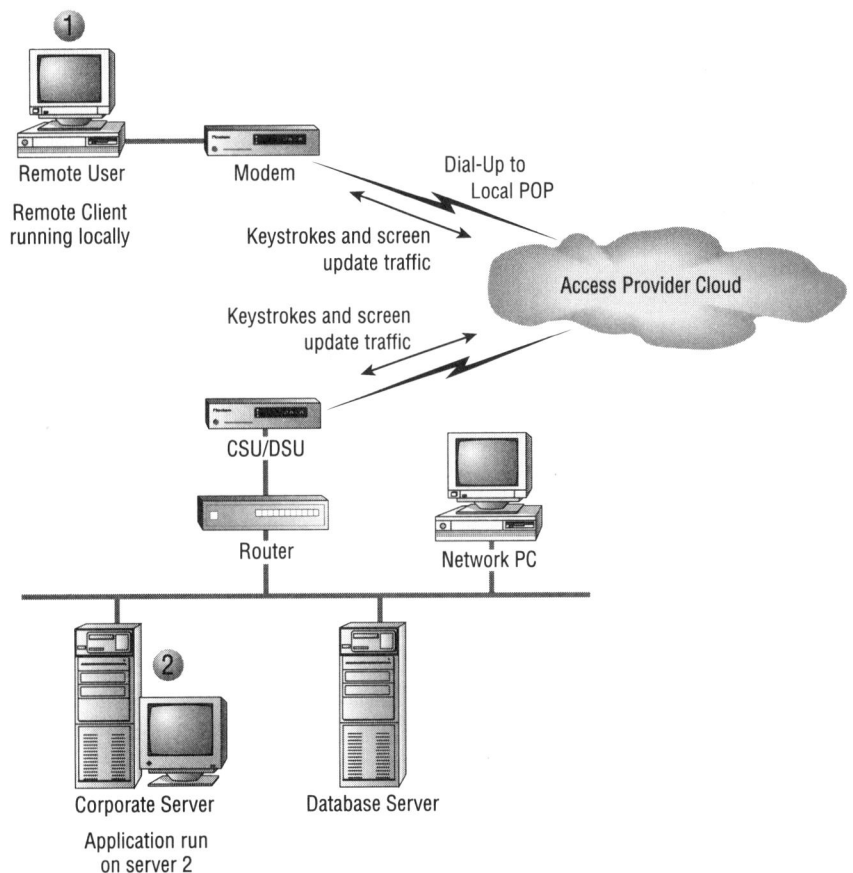

The host processor can be any LAN PC. For example, it could be the PC on your desk at work that you call up while at home or on the road, any other PC on the LAN that is available for a remote control session, or one of several PCs stacked in a wiring closet for that purpose (see Figure 12.8). It can also be a Single Board Computer (SBC) or MultiBoard Computer (MBC) mounted in a segmented backplane tower (Figure 12.9). You can also find products that provide multiple virtual DOS sessions in a single processor. They are adequate when only a small number of sessions are run simultaneously, or when the session does not involve any processor-intensive activities.

Typically, the remote control software has a host and a remote program. The host program is run on the application processor, and the remote program is used when the remote equipment is a PC. Normally, the remote equipment is a PC that requires the terminal emulation and special features

FIGURE 12.8

Accessing the network via a PC pool

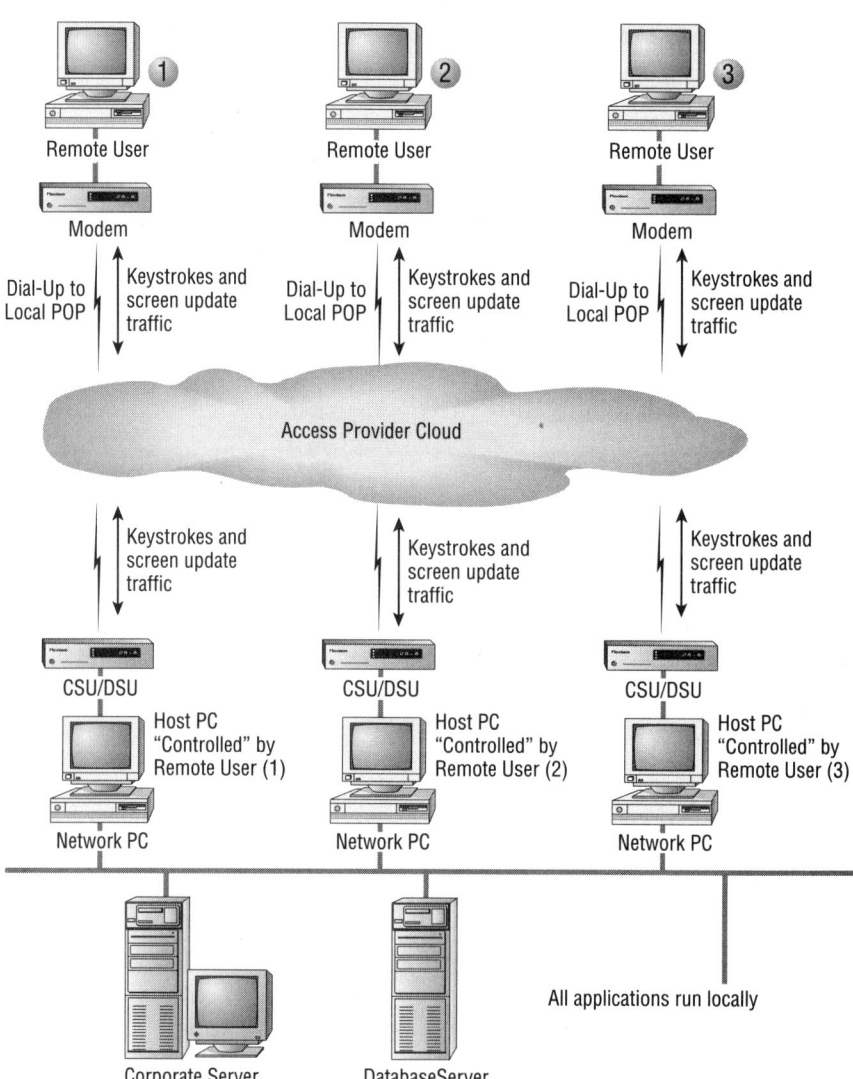

of the remote software, but the simple functions of passing keystrokes and viewing screen images make a dumb ASCII terminal appropriate for this situation, too.

Whether you are using a PC or a terminal as the remote equipment, a remote session works the same. When you type information, the keystrokes are sent to the host (the application processor), which processes these keystrokes as if they had been typed at the LAN PC's keyboard. The host software then

FIGURE 12.9

Accessing the network via an MBC

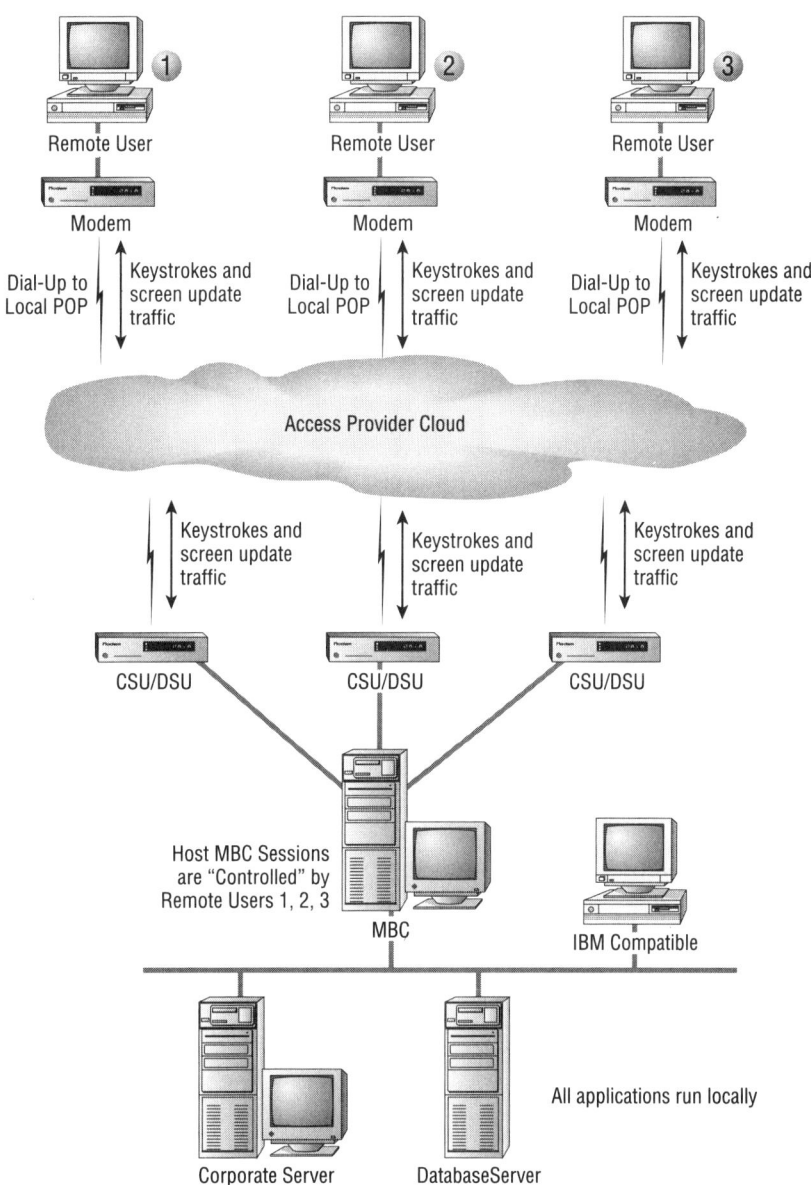

transmits any changes in its screen for the remote screen to display. The files and applications being used remain on the network, rather than being downloaded to the remote PC. Therefore, the only data that is actually transmitted between the remote site and its host are the keystrokes and the screen images. The remote and the host behave as if they were one machine, even though they may be separated by a great distance.

Typical examples of products that utilize remote control technology are Symantec's pcAnyWhere and Citrix's WinFrame and WinView.

Remote Node vs. Remote Control

We have discussed the different remote access methods and how they are used. However, how can you decide when to use a remote node versus a remote control access method? What are the inherent advantages and disadvantages of each technology?

As we have mentioned, there are fundamental differences in the two access methods. Because of the technology used in the remote node access method, more traffic is required to cross the remote access medium. All network traffic (not just the display and keyboard strokes) is transmitted over the communications line. Furthermore, to improve performance, it is necessary to install the applications on the client device and have only the shared data reside on the corporate LAN.

If the application is not resident on the client and it is run from a shared resource on the LAN, even more traffic must traverse the communications link. The client PC must download the entire application to the client before it can be executed. So, for example, if you used a networked program like Microsoft Word, Lotus 1-2-3, or Microsoft Access, you would need either to download the entire program to the remote PC or have the executable files (.EXE) installed locally on the remote node. Each remote user must purchase an individual copy to avoid violating the licensing agreement of the software package. If neither of the options mentioned above are followed (i.e., the *.EXE files are run from the server), the delay can become unacceptable.

Remote node can be slightly faster than remote control in opening Windows or a Windows application, as long as executable files are stored on the remote computer. However, when you try to open a file that is on the LAN, or you try to save a file to the host location once it has been modified, a remote control session is much more efficient. In a remote node session, the entire file must be transferred from the host to the remote PC when you open the file, and that same file has to be transferred back to the host PC (server) when you save it. If you intend to use any graphic-intensive application over a remote node session, you can load the application from the remote PC's hard drive (local) to speed up the application response time. However, you can still expect a long wait when you attempt to open a large file or place graphical images into a file from the network. Remote node works well for client/server database applications, when the response to a query is very small; but if the response is large, the data transfer to the remote location will take a long time. Generally, a remote node access method is best for LAN access of personal files that are not very large, or when the application has to reside on your local PC and the database it has to access is on the network.

Applications such as e-mail can be extended to non-networked PCs, since e-mail only requires transferring a few files. Both remote node and remote control perform well with normal-character e-mail. When you add Windows to the equation, remote node will service the Windows program faster, but if the mail includes large files and/or graphics, remote control will be faster. This is because the attached file is not transferred to the remote PC, but from the Post Office to the host PC on the network.

When you need to make the decision between a remote node or a remote control implementation, it is important to use the most efficient method of access for the applications at hand. Therefore, to sum up the guidelines for selecting the proper remote access method, you should follow these rules of thumb (outlined in Table 12.2).

TABLE 12.2 Access Method Selection Criteria

Task	Factor to Weigh	Solution
Access to office PC	Full use of office applications	Remote control method
Access to LAN data	Full LAN operations	Remote node method
File transfer	Light	Remote node method
E-mail	Light	Remote node method
Database lookup	Light	Remote node method
Database modifications	Heavy	Remote control method
Windows	Heavy	Remote control method
Spreadsheet	Heavy	Remote control method

In short, if you need to access an application on the network and you want to save your changes on your standard home directory on your network server, then use the remote control method. If you need to run an application that resides on your local PC but need to access data that is on the network, then you must use the remote node method. When you want to use your local applications and protocol stacks and access network applications simultaneously, you must use the remote node method. When remote users needed to access centrally administered applications that reside on a remote network, but wanted to save the data to their local hard drive, they traditionally had to resort to remote node connectivity. But some new developments in remote control technology have opened the door to more options.

New remote node and remote control technologies have increased the remote access efficiency. Also, with the advent of the new "remote access servers," or "communications servers," a new breed of hybrid access methods has emerged. Some of this hybrid technology is included in a new Microsoft NT-based remote access application package.

Remote Access: Emphasis on LAN to WAN Internetwork Design

Before we begin discussing and implementing a remote access system, it's important that we take a look at the overall impact of a remote access design on the efficiency of the accessed network, including both the wide area network (WAN) and the local area network (LAN). A system is only as good as its weakest link, and in most organizations the weakest link is the WAN. Typically, WANs are vulnerable to external sources (service providers, weather, and other accidents) and internal sources (routers). It is important, that all these issues are taken into account when designing a remote access system.

Enterprise-wide internetworks are rarely built from scratch. Instead, they evolve—perhaps from legacy systems—adding LAN, remote office, and remote access capabilities as required. Central to this remote access case, however, is the need to effectively use WAN transmission facilities. In this section we'll look at the requirements for implementing a sound LAN to WAN internetwork system.

Though we'll be mentioning remote access, we'll concentrate on defining the methodology in designing a basic LAN-WAN internetwork, since a remote access is an offshoot of this interconnectivity. A dial-in access is a scaled-down version of a dedicated WAN connection scenario (unless the user has money to spare). In other words, a single dial-in user will have a minimum impact on the accessed network. However, if we multiply the number of users connecting concurrently to the remote network, the impact will become noticeable. Furthermore, as the number of users connecting concurrently from a single site increases (to 100 or more), a dial-in solution is not cost effective.

To begin, let's assume that we have a system in which the network resources are located at different sites. New network requirements may have evolved since the initial installation. First, the network has invariably grown. A growth rate of 50 to 150 percent in the first year is not uncommon. Second, the network now needs to access other identified resources (a separate location). These other resources may be another LAN, a host computer, or a remote workstation, such as one belonging to a mobile user or a telecommuter. Third, the platforms requiring connectivity might not be the same; they may range from Macintosh to UNIX. All of these user requirements will invariably require the use of WAN facilities.

The topic of LAN/WAN and remote access interconnection is a broad one. There are many good products available. In order to put some structure into the study of this subject, this section will first investigate the design issues of LAN/WAN and remote access interconnectivity, addressing the question of how to determine the type of transmission facility required for a particular application. In our study of design issues, we'll look at analog and digital leased line issues only.

Designing the LAN/WAN Connection

Let's assume that the internetwork contains segments (or subnetworks) in dissimilar locations. The objective is to design the LAN/WAN transmission facilities required for this internetwork. Since this can be an involved process, we'll break it down into a number of smaller steps. You'll recall many of these steps from our discussion in Chapter 3:

1. Define the goals. Determine the functional goals for the internetwork, including costs, performance, maintenance and support, reliability, redundancy, and robustness. This last issue, robustness, is especially critical for LAN/WAN integration, as it addresses the ability of the internetwork to handle periods of heavy, or peak, usage.

2. Identify the components. Identify the hardware/software components at each location that must be incorporated into the internetwork. What LAN

hardware topologies (Ethernet, Token-Ring, etc.) must be connected? Are there any plans for converting one WAN architecture to another (such as replacing 10BASE-T with ATM)? What network operating system (such as Novell NetWare, Microsoft Windows NT, etc.) is implemented at each end node? Is TCP/IP enabled at any location?

3. Understand the applications. Consider the applications that are going to be internetworked (such as X.400, X.500, NFS, etc.). As with the hardware/software platforms, if there are common denominators at the application layer, the design job is much easier.

4. Project growth. Try to make an accurate projection of the growth that is expected to occur over the entire internetwork in the next few years (that is two to five years). Areas to consider are the number of local and remote locations, and the results due to mergers or acquisitions.

5. Analyze traffic. Determine the amount of internetwork traffic. Measure traffic on each segment and then calculate the amount of intersegment traffic. A flow chart often helps get the LAN/WAN design process off the ground. Figure 12.10 provides an adequate starting point.

6. Ask critical questions. How will this impact the business? What are the other options? What are the weak links and how do we minimize them? What platforms are involved? How many servers will be accessed? What software is accessed?

Leased Line Network Configurations

Designs for leased line networks in particular, and broadband networks in general, begin with an analysis of the LAN/WAN/LAN traffic patterns. Useful templates for this traffic analysis are shown in Tables 12.3–12.6. These templates were originally designed for Ethernet networks, but many of the principles can be applied to other network topologies and LAN/WAN interconnection designs. The analysis is broken down into four different worksheets.

Remote Host Server Resources

The worksheet shown in Table 12.3, Remote Host Server Resources, is designed to give a clear understanding of the host resources that are available to the remote user community. The parameters examined include:

- **Host Server Type:** The name (Citrix's WinFrame, etc.) of the host server.

FIGURE 12.10

The service selection decision flow chart

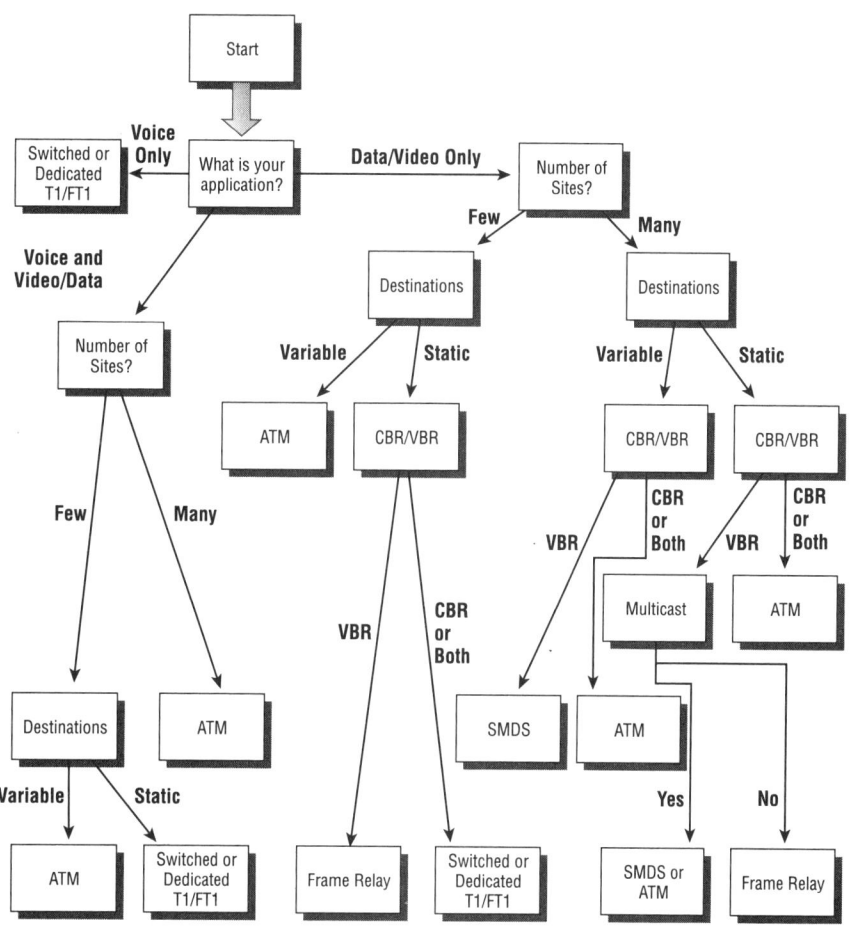

CSR(Constant Bit Rate): Video, Host-Remote, Real-Time Image
VBR (Variable Bit Rate): LAN-LAN, Non Real-Time Image

Courtesy of ADC Kentox

- **Protocols Used:** The protocols that the host server is supporting.

- **Applications:** The applications that can be accessed via the host server. It is important to designate the type of applications and whether they are pass-though (running on another server) or local to the host server.

- **Max Users:** What is the maximum number of concurrent users that the host server can support with its existing configuration? This means, "What is the limit before the throughput will drop to a crawl?"

- **Average Concurrent Users:** The average number of concurrent users that will attach to the host server.

- **Available Resources:** The difference between the maximum number of users and the average number of users. The amount of resources left for the remote user load.

TABLE 12.3 Remote Host Server Resources

Host Type	Protocols	Applications Running	Maximum Users	Concurrent Users	Resources Left

Ethernet Traffic Parameters

By completing the Remote Host Server Resources worksheet, you detail the remote host resources that are available for sharing by any remote devices and users of the wide area network. The second worksheet, Ethernet Traffic Parameters (Table 12.4), can be used either prior to a remote access integration or for troubleshooting the LAN/WAN internetwork. It details Ethernet traffic parameters. This information can be obtained using LAN protocol analyzers such as a Network General Sniffer.

Samples of traffic should be taken on the production network at a time of day that most accurately represents the typical amount of traffic on each segment. Multiple samples should be taken to establish trends in traffic flow, user activity, and traffic rates. When this has been accomplished, you should complete the Ethernet Traffic Parameters worksheet, using averages of these samples to derive numbers that are representative of the Ethernet environment. As mentioned before, these worksheets can be adapted and used for different networks (Token-Ring, etc.).

NOTE There are companies that provide remote monitoring and management of LAN/WAN traffic. They will also provide a history of trends of your LAN/WAN traffic flow.

TABLE 12.4 Ethernet Traffic Parameters

Site Name
Protocol
A : Number of Users
B : # of Packets per Sample
C : % of Total Ethernet Traffic
Multicast Traffic
D : # of Multicast Packets per Sample
C : % of Total Ethernet Traffic
F : % of Protocol Traffic
G : Average Packet Size
User Traffic
H : # of Data Packets per Sample
I : % of Total Ethernet Packet Size
J : Average Large Ethernet Packet Size
K : % of Large Packet Traffic
L : Average Medium Packet Size
M : % of Medium Packet Traffic
N : Average Small Packet Traffic
O : % of Small Packet Traffic
Average Traffic per User per Protocol
B/A = Total Number of Packets/Number of Protocol Users
G × F = Average Multicast Packet Size × % of Protocol Traffic
J × K = Average Large Data Packet Size × % of Large Packet Traffic
L × M = Average Medium Data Packet Size × % of Medium Packet Traffic
N × O = Average Small Data Packet Size × % of Small Packet Traffic
P = [(B/A)((G × F) + (J × K) + (L × M) + (N × O))] Average Number of Bytes per User for This Protocol

Remote Traffic Worksheet

The information from the Ethernet Traffic Parameters worksheet is then used in the Remote Traffic worksheet (see Table 12.5), which is a guide to estimating the bandwidth needed for effective throughput between two specific sites. By entering the information about each protocol operating at each site, and about the protocols that will traverse the link between the two sites, the required bandwidth can be adequately estimated. Parameters on the Ethernet Traffic Parameters and Remote Traffic worksheets may vary depending on the network topology and the LAN analysis tool used to gather the statistics. The following are some guidelines for completing the Remote Traffic worksheet:

- **Protocol:** The standard protocol that is being analyzed.

- **Number of users (1):** The number of users using the standard protocol when the analysis was taken.

- **% Total Standard Traffic (3):** The percentage of that protocol traffic.

- **# of Multicast Packets (4):** Number of multicast packets for this protocol.

- **% of Protocol Traffic (6):** The percentage of total protocol traffic for each type of packet.

- **# of Data Packets (8):** Number of packets containing user information.

- **Average Packet Size (10):** Mean packet size for this packet type. Suggested ranges:

    - **Large:** 1,000–1,518 bytes

    - **Medium:** 400–999 bytes

    - **Small:** 64–99 bytes

TABLE 12.5 The Remote Traffic Worksheet

Link Name					
Site Name			To Site		
Protocol	Traffic/ User	Traffic/User/ Sec	Bps/ User	Remote Users	Bandwidth Needed
		/x	*8		=
		/x	*8		=
		/x	*8		=
		/x	*8		=
		/x	*8		=
		/x	*8		=
		/x	*8		=
		/x	*8		=
		/x	*8		=
		/x	*8		=
		/x	*8		=
		/x	*8		=
		/x	*8		=
		/x	*8		=
		/x	*8		=
		/x	*8		=

Network Growth

The fourth worksheet in this group, Network Growth (see Table 12.6), takes information obtained from the preceding worksheets and allows you to project a design based on future requirements. The analysis is based upon the current peak bandwidth required per user, and the future need is projected with a standard calculation that yields the future bandwidth requirements. The designer can use this result to determine the transmission speed of the link between the two WAN locations. The growth calculation is important in order to avoid having the transmission facility hardware become obsolete.

TABLE 12.6 The Network Growth Worksheet

Link Name	
Site Name	
A = Peak Bandwidth Utilization of Link	
B = # of Current Users	
C = Peak Bandwidth per User	
C = A/B	
D = Additional Future Users	
E = Future Bandwidth Requirements	
E = C*(B+D)	
Future Bandwidth Requirements =	

The 80/20 rule estimates that in a typical network environment, 80 percent of a network's traffic remains local to that segment, while the other 20 percent of the traffic is directed to other segments. While this rule does not eliminate the need for an analysis of the traffic patterns, it may provide a starting point for a preliminary assessment of the transmission facility type and speed requirements. Also consider segments that will require redundant transmission paths for greater reliability.

The following are a couple of other steps that you may want to take:

- **Get Vendor Input:** Obtain input from both the WAN link providers (such as AT&T and CompuServe) and internetworking equipment vendors (such as Alpine CSI). These service providers may offer alternate solutions that you may not have considered.

- **Develop a Plan:** Develop an internetworking implementation plan. This would include establishing specific milestones for network design, equipment procurement, installation, cutover, and documentation elements.

Remember that the internetwork design will, by its nature, be a multi-vendor network. When something goes wrong there is always finger-pointing by the different vendors. The best defense against this situation is a strong offense: a thorough design, a well thought-out implementation plan, and the use of reputable vendors. With these goals in mind, let us take a closer look at an example of a remote node solution and an example of a remote control solution, and delve into detailed steps on how to use one of these new remote access servers as a solution in a remote access design.

CHAPTER 13

Designing a Remote Node Implementation

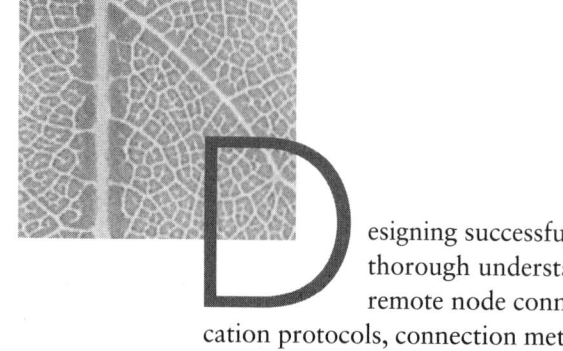

esigning successful remote node implementations depends on a thorough understanding of all the elements that comprise the remote node connection, including the access server, communication protocols, connection methods, and user requirements. Many organizations have chosen to use a free component of Windows NT for their remote node implementations: Microsoft's Remote Access Service.

In this chapter, we will:

- Introduce Microsoft's Remote Access Service (RAS)
- Focus on design and implementation considerations for RAS
- Describe the advantages and disadvantages of using a remote node service like RAS to provide dial-up access to your Windows NT network

Throughout the chapter, we'll use the term *remote link* to designate any link between a remote site and the corporate network. This includes WAN as well as dial-up links.

Windows NT Remote Access Service

Let's begin by taking a closer look at Microsoft's Remote Access Service, as well as the client components involved in establishing an RAS session.

What Is RAS?

Microsoft's RAS for Windows NT lets you connect to your office network from remote locations such as your home, a hotel, or any place with a telephone jack. (These days one can also make remote connections using wireless media). RAS is a dial-in/dial-out server software that enables users to dial in and log onto the NT server. NT clients can use RAS to dial out to outside services, such as their Internet provider or a bulletin board system (BBS). After a connection is established, the user can access all network resources as if the user were locally attached to the NT network or local database. For example, the user can:

- Access remote databases through the Windows NT Explorer
- Send and receive electronic mail
- Print files on the office printer

After the connection to the office network is made, the telephone link is transparent to the user. The user can access and view network resources in the same way as users in the office who are working on computers physically connected to the network.

Remote Node vs. Remote Control Revisited

In order to understand how NT RAS works, we are going to reiterate the distinguishable differences between the remote node and remote control access solutions.

Remote control solutions, such as ReachOut and pcAnywhere, connect using modems over standard telephone lines, but only screen updates and keystrokes are transmitted over the telephone line. All of the processing occurs at the host machine. Remote node uses the same access media but instead of transmitting screen updates and keystrokes over the line, the user is logged on to the network, and all network traffic is sent back and forth over the telephone line. While this allows the user to connect directly to the network and act as a full node on the LAN, the speed of the connection is but a fraction of the speed the user would experience were they connected at LAN speeds.

RAS takes full advantage of the processing power of the remote user's PC. In RAS (a remote node access solution), packets from the corporate LAN are sent across the asynchronous line to the remote PC, where the application executes locally. It's ideal for true client/server applications, such as e-mail, or groupware applications, such as Lotus Notes or Novell's GroupWise. It's also appropriate for quickly copying a file to the home office.

Even though the remote node approach is appealing to remote users and offers a great deal of flexibility, there are drawbacks. Performance depends on a variety of factors beyond simply the raw speed of the asynchronous link or the port speed of the server. In addition, security and accounting are issues that must be considered.

There are two distinct remote control technologies. However, they share a common root. The remote user dials in to an access server or a single PC on the network, and takes over that device (also called a *host*). The application processing then takes place on this host. The technologies differ in what they control on that host and how they run the application:

- In one technology, multiple users can dial into an application server and each user gets a "slice" of the server's CPU and RAM to run the application. These "slices" are called *sessions*. Processing takes place on the server, and only screen updates, keystrokes, and mouse movements are passed over the link to the remote user's PC. Citrix uses this technology.

- In the other technology, multiple users can dial into a communications server that houses multiple CPU boards, and each user controls one CPU board. Each board acts as a complete PC and processing takes place on that board. All traffic remains on the local network. CUBIX uses this technology.

Either of these remote control technologies is an ideal method for obtaining information from large databases keeping the processing local to the LAN, rather than attempting to send the entire database over the link. When the database search is completed, all that is sent to the remote user are the results.

Remote control also has additional benefits, specifically for the network manager. In remote control, if a user experiences problems while running a session on an application server, the help desk personnel can connect to the same application server and take over that user's session to perform diagnostics (called *shadowing*). In addition, security and management are easier because databases and systems being accessed still reside physically on the LAN.

However, remote control has its limitations. If the remote user is not using the same version of software as the gateway PC or host, problems may arise. If the remote user needs a specific application, it must be on the local PC in the appropriate version; otherwise, the remote user will be unable to perform the task.

RAS has a number of advantages and disadvantages. Because the remote user is logically attached to the network, the user can take advantage of true client/server computing. However, because data transfer rates are dependent on the limitations of the serial devices being used, large amounts of data may take a long time to move across the link.

Connecting through RAS

Remote Access Service can be as simple as using two modems and an analog connection or as complex as a pool of modems allowing up to 256 simultaneous connections to the RAS server. In general, establishing a RAS connection can be reduced to the following simple steps:

1. The user determines a need for some distant resource.
2. A connection, typically through a modem and telephone line, is established to a RAS server.
3. The user provides authentication (password) information to the server for verification.
4. Once the user is authenticated, the user has access to server facilities and can then attach file shares or use Internet applications (browsers), such as Microsoft's Internet Explorer or Netscape Navigator.

For dial-up connectivity the user needs at the minimum, the following:

- Two modems, one on the server side and one on the client side of the connection
- An analog telephone line

It is important to note that client systems always initiate RAS sessions. This means that the RAS software must always be running and waiting on the server system.

Compatibility between the server and client modems is essential for a trouble-free connection. Ideally, the same brand and version of modem should be used at either end of the connection link. When setting up the modems, select the same initial speed and enable the same features. If the same brand of modem is not available, choose a modem for the client with the same CCITT standard as the server's modem.

The RAS server can provide many services for a connected client, including the following:

- Routing of TCP/IP or IPX/SPX packets to non-RAS resources on the server LAN

- Routing the user's packets to the Internet for access to the WWW or other services
- Providing access to disk or printer resources local to the server
- Providing access to disk or printer services on other servers within the server's domain

Many applications can access the NT RAS. Network applications using the following protocols can access the NT RAS:

- NetBIOS
- IPC
- Named Pipes
- Mailslots
- LAN Manager APIs
- TCP/IP utilities
- RPC
- Sockets

RAS can use Point-to-Point Protocol (PPP) or the new extension to PPP, the Point-to-Point Tunneling Protocol (PPTP) that we discussed in Chapter 11, to frame and transport data over remote links.

Furthermore, RAS can support client services using NetBIOS, NetBEUI, TCP/IP, or IPX during an RAS session. Applications using Windows Sockets, NetWare APIs, and NetBIOS can run remotely using PPP as the framing mechanism. The use of PPP and SLIP provides interoperability with other PPP- and SLIP-enabled products.

RAS provides the functionality outlined in Table 13.1.

TABLE 13.1 RAS Functionality

Operating System	# of Ports	LAN Protocols	WAN Options
MS-DOS (RAS 1.1a)	1	NetBIOS/NetBEUI	Async, X.25
WFW 3.11	1	NetBIOS/NetBEUI	Async, X.25, ISDN

TABLE 13.1 (cont.) RAS Functionality	Operating System	# of Ports	LAN Protocols	WAN Options
	NT Workstation	1	NetBIOS/NetBEUI, IP, IPX	Async, X.25, ISDN, PPTP
	NT Server	256	NetBIOS/NetBEUI, IP, IPX	Async, X.25, ISDN, PPTP
	Windows 95	1	NetBIOS/NetBEUI, IP, IPX	Async, X.25, ISDN, PPTP

RAS-Supported Access Technologies

There are several technologies that are supported by RAS for accessing the server from remote locations. The access technology used is dictated by several factors:

- Cost
  - The corporation must justify the cost of utilizing one technology versus another.
- Bandwidth Requirements
  - High: ISDN (PRI), Frame Relay, ATM
  - Medium: X.25, ISDN (BRI)
- Low: Modems
  - Access Technology Available
  - Some service providers do not support all technologies, or do not support all of them at all geographic locations.

Some of the criteria used for selecting and justifying one technology versus another, will be discussed in the next chapter. The next section will revisit some of the familiar access technologies and visit some new ones.

ISDN Revisited

Integrated Services Digital Network (ISDN) carries voice and data by bearer channels (B channel) occupying a bandwidth of 64Kbps each. A delta channel (D channel) handles signaling at 16Kbps or 64Kbps. H channels are provided for user information at higher bit rates.

There are three types of ISDN service: Basic Rate ISDN (BRI), Primary Rate ISDN (PRI), and Broadband ISDN (B-ISDN).

BRI consists of two 64Kbps bearer channels (B channels) and one 16Kbps signaling channel (D channel) for a total of 144Kbps. This is sometimes referred to as 2B+D. The basic service is intended to meet the needs of most individual users.

PRI is intended for users with greater capacity requirements. Typically, the channel structure is 23 B channels (each one is 64Kbps) plus one 64Kbps D channel for a total of 1.544Mbps. This is sometimes referred to as 23B+D.

B-ISDN is still in development and is designed to support up to 150Mbps, but will be dependent on a complete optical fiber network. This could be the medium for High Definition TV (HDTV).

To use RAS with ISDN, you may need one or more of the following:

- **A network terminating device (NT1):** This serves as the network interface, providing line testing and diagnostic capability, as well as two-to-four wire conversion. Sometimes this is included in an ISDN modem.

- **A terminal adapter (TA):** This protocol converter adapts non-ISDN equipment, such as a computer, fax machine, or telephone, to the ISDN network. This can be an external box or a PC card.

- **Digital modems:** This is an ISDN TA that can emulate an analog fax/modem in order to interoperate with an analog modem or fax. When in emulation mode, the transfer rate is no longer at ISDN speeds, since the speed is controlled by the weakest link—the analog device at the other end of the connection.

- **An ISDN bridge:** Some TAs also function as Ethernet bridges to support connection to a LAN.

- **ISDN telephones:** ISDN phones have an internal TA, and most have an RS232 interface for a computer. So an ISDN telephone can be used to support simultaneous voice and data transmission over an ISDN link.

- **Inverse multiplexers:** For situations where more than 112Kbps of bandwidth is required, terminal adapters that perform inverse multiplexing are available. When quality video is required, an inverse multiplexer can combine multiple ISDN lines to provide the necessary bandwidth.

- **Wiring requirements:** ISDN was designed to work over standard copper twisted-pair wiring.

X.25 Revisited

X.25 is an international protocol used for wide area networks (WANs). Online services, such as America Online and CompuServe, may use an X.25 network to route subscriber connections to their services.

An X.25 network transmits data with a packet-switching protocol. This protocol relies on an elaborate worldwide network of packet-forwarding nodes that can participate in delivering an X.25 packet to its designated address.

To use RAS with X.25, you need the following:

- A modem for dial-up connections. You dial up to a point-of-presence port on the X.25 network, and your call is routed through the network to your destination, which is also attached to the X.25 network. Here the PAD (Packet Assembler/Disassembler) is located at the service provider's site.

- A smart X.25 direct interface card for direct connections. This card includes a PAD.

- A leased line for direct connections.

Point-to-Point Tunneling Protocol (PPTP)

As we discussed in Chapter 11, PPTP is an extension to the standard PPP that is used to create multiprotocol virtual private networks (VPNs) via the Internet. VPNs connect both branch offices and telecommuters into an enterprise-wide corporate network and can eliminate all long distance charges, along with the management and security responsibilities of maintaining private networks.

Other Connectivity Options

Many access providers, such as AT&T, MCI, and Sprint, are offering corporations access alternatives. In essence, the corporation is given a virtual private network within the provider's network. The corporation has a router installed at the corporate office which connects via X.25, frame relay, or ISDN to the provider "cloud." The corporation's remote clients are given local points-of-presence telephone numbers that will connect them to the provider "cloud." All traffic between these clients and the corporate network is managed by the provider. This solution may be advantageous in the following cases:

- The remote clients are located within long distance rate areas. If the clients are within the local calling area, the cost for X.25 connectivity is not justifiable. In other words, the cost of using standard dial-up rates must be greater than the cost for accessing an X.25 network.

- The corporation does not have the support personnel to manage the remote connectivity.

- The corporate network does not have a data security system installed.

The cost of subscribing to this system is inversely proportional to the telephone rates. For example, this solution would not be the best one for clients that are located within a metropolitan area. The cost of the subscription would be more than the costs incurred for local phone charges.

Designing a Remote Access Solution with RAS

Remote Access Service (RAS) can be used to allow remote users access to their network applications while still providing them with a high level of security. The RAS connection is transparent to Microsoft clients and the network applications. Figure 13.1 illustrates all RAS features and possible configurations. Actual implementations and configurations will vary and are discussed later in the chapter.

Server Preinstallation Considerations

If you plan to use Microsoft NT 4 Server for remote connectivity, you will need to consider the following issues:

1. How will the users access the RAS server?

   - LAN
   - WAN
   - Dial-up or Internet
   - Third-party service provider (such as AT&T's AWICS)

2. What type of client workstation will be used to access the RAS server?

   - Low-end PCs (Windows for Workgroups)
   - 32-bit workstations (Windows 95 or Windows NT workstation)

FIGURE 13.1

An overview of NT RAS

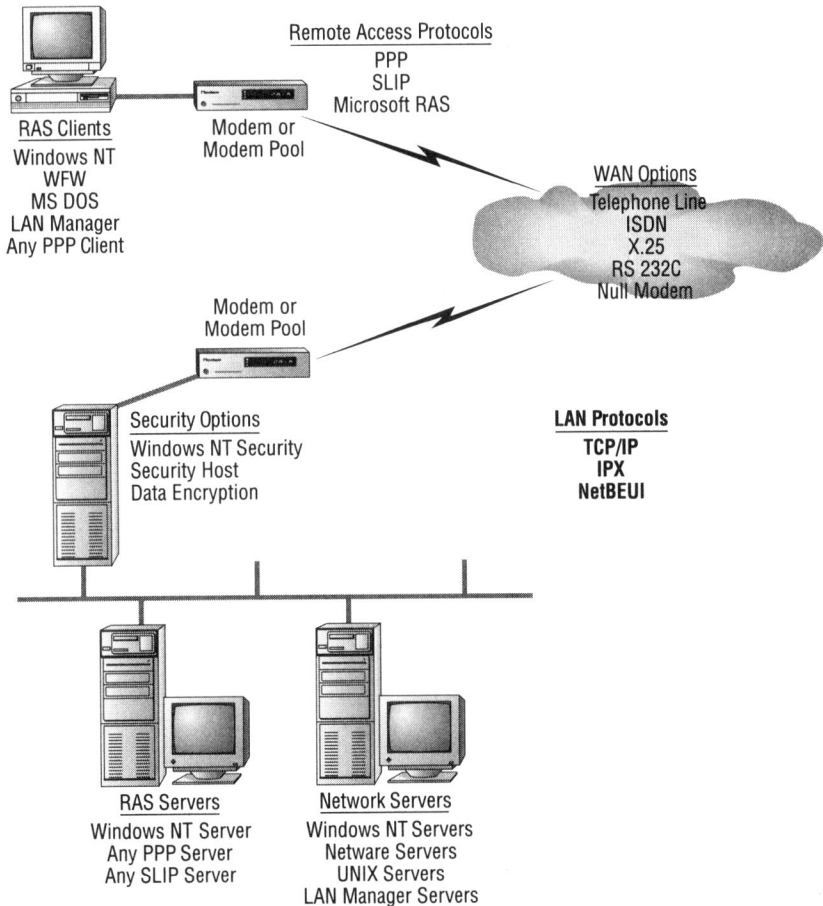

3. What standards are in place in the organization?

- Network operating system(s)
- Routed protocols and addressing
- Naming conventions
- Domain policies
- Application licensing
- Backup
- Security

4. How are users managed?

   - Where are shared Windows files kept?
   - Where are users' profiles loaded?
   - How are applications shared on the network?
   - How freely do users customize their own environment?

5. Do you want users to access only the machine they are dialing into, or do you want to give them access to the entire network?

6. Who will be allowed to dial into the network?

7. Will the RAS server be used as a gateway to the Internet?

Even though we will not delve into details on all of these questions (some of these questions have been covered in Chapter 3), getting clear answers to them up front can mean the difference between success and failure.

The following questions will be covered in detail and will focus on the RAS server preinstallation steps.

Predicted Number of Concurrent Users

Since the server will act as a file server, the same limitations that will present themselves in a file-server environment will manifest themselves in this environment. Each connection will take up approximately 2MB of RAM and approximately 1 percent of the CPU utilization (this is due to the fact that the CPU will be processing communication requests). Each user, when connected, is forwarded the specific executable requested and the client PC executes it. Since the RAS server's CPU will not be affected by the application processing, a bottleneck will arise from the network traffic coming across the link(s). These links incorporate the remote link as well as the LAN segments. The amount of processing required by each application resident on the RAS server will definitely need to be identified and extrapolated for the number of expected users. In order to make this decision, you may need to compare the impact on the network to the impact on the server to determine which will allow more concurrent users.

What Kind of Applications Will Be Accessed?

Each application contributes a specific load on the network. The network throughput is affected differently by each application, but one can roughly divide the application types into two categories: Some applications are truly client/server, and others are designed to be run on stand-alone PCs. The latter type of application does not lend itself well to a network environment. It expects that its I/O requests will be immediately answered and that there is a near infinite amount of network bandwidth available.

Some database applications are designed to reside on a single device. The front-end may be written in MS Visual Basic and the back-end database engine written in Paradox. Little if any consideration was given to optimizing the application for distributed processing. Only those designed to run in a two-tier environment operate well on multiple platforms. In two-tier applications, the front-end and back-end components have been specifically designed to minimize communication between them. It's therefore important to analyze the type of application that will be run on the RAS server or will be accessed via the RAS server (an application residing on another server on the LAN).

Applications Initiated on Another Server (Passthrough) or on the RAS Server

The location of the application affects the performance of the link as well. If all the pieces of the application are located on the RAS server, there is no network traffic generated on the local LAN. The traffic is restricted to the remote link between the RAS server and the remote PC. This reduces the number of potential bottlenecks, but the issues remain the same. However, if the application resides on another server on the LAN, the number of potential bottlenecks increases by N + 1. It is therefore desirable to install the applications on the RAS server whenever possible.

Connectivity Option Considerations

As we have seen, the potential bottlenecks are primarily the communication links between the remote user and the RAS server. It is after investigating and determining what type of application would be running on the RAS server, or accessed via the RAS server, that we can select the best type of remote link that would minimize the bottleneck(s) that the selected application would create. True client/server applications could potentially communicate efficiently over a 28.8Kbps dial-up line. However, applications that have been developed for standalone use would require at a minimum a switched 56Kbps or ISDN line. Applications that make numerous calls to a back-end would require a similar link.

Designing the Proper Hardware Configuration

Now that we have determined the type of applications that would be accessed, where they would be initialized, and the proper communication link required to provide an efficient link, the next piece of the puzzle would be the actual hardware devices that will have an impact on the overall efficiency of communication. Since the CPU of the server is primarily used by the communication requests, it would be more efficient if you could use bus-mastering multiport communication cards. Bus-mastering cards are cards that possess their own processors. This allows a greater number of communication requests to be processed directly on the card and lets the RAS server's CPU only process server service requests. NT supports multiple CPUs (up to four) on a RAS server. However, the effect on the efficiency of the CPU is as follows:

- For 1 CPU: A 30 percent reduction in efficiency
- For 2 CPUs: Provides a 95 percent increase in efficiency over one CPU
- For 3 CPUs: Provides a 15 percent increase in efficiency over two CPUs
- For 4 CPUs: Provides a 50 percent increase in efficiency over two CPUs

As we have learned, CPU utilization is at a minimum in a RAS (remote node) connection. On the other hand, RAM needs can be a factor. When applications make a call to the RAS's CPU, and another process is occupying the processor time, the requests have to be queued in RAM. If there is insufficient RAM the server will create a page file on the hard drive and perform a "page swap," which is essentially the server allocating a portion of the hard drive as RAM. This process of accessing the hard drive for needed RAM is considerably slower than real RAM. This would effect the overall performance of the RAS link. Therefore, answering all the previous questions would provide a good understanding of the minimum RAM requirements.

Pros and Cons of Protocols and Their Impact on Performance

The last piece of the puzzle is the network protocol that will be used to communicate. Some protocols contribute a larger portion of the traffic overhead on the remote link than do others. We will introduce each protocol and its impact on the RAS server.

- **NetBEUI:** RAS clients that run NetBIOS applications or need access to NetBIOS resources, such as file servers, on the remote network should always use NetBEUI. The NetBEUI protocol is the fastest and most efficient transport to access NetBIOS resources. With the RAS NetBIOS gateway enabled, clients have access to all remote NetBIOS resources even if they are not running NetBEUI. However, the NetBEUI protocol is not routable and corporations are reluctant to allow NetBEUI/NetBIOS traffic throughout their LAN.

- **IPX:** Clients that run Windows Sockets applications will need to use the IPX protocol if the applications run over the IPX protocol. An example of this would be the Client Service for NetWare that comes with Windows NT. However, Novell's IPX protocol in its native format produces a lot of traffic. It is considered a "chatty" protocol. Each request has to be acknowledged. IPX is best suited for LAN links. Novell has provided a method to reduce IPX traffic by creating the "packet burst" mode and the "large IPX packet" option.

- **TCP/IP:** RAS clients that run Windows Sockets applications need to use the TCP/IP protocol if the applications run over the TCP/IP protocol. It is possible for these clients to access a NetBIOS resource if the NetBIOS name can be resolved via the LMHOSTS file. However, it is much easier and more efficient to use the NetBEUI protocol to access NetBIOS resources. Furthermore, the IP protocol was designed for WAN links and does not require an acknowledgment for each request. This reduces overall network traffic. The IP (PPP) protocol is very well suited for WAN links.

Installing RAS on the Server

This section will describe how to install Microsoft's NT Remote Access Service on the computer. The default settings are usually adequate.

Installing Remote Access Service software is a relatively simple task. The installation is quite easy if you have followed the previous steps and prepared yourself first by following the steps mentioned in Chapter 12. RAS can be installed during a custom installation of Windows NT, or at any later time from the Network option applet in the Control Panel.

 If you are going to use the TCP/IP or IPX protocol with RAS, you should install the protocol before you install RAS, even though you have the choice to do so at the conclusion of the RAS setup. We recommend that you install TCP/IP first to make sure that it is set up and functioning properly—many problems with RAS and TCP/IP can be traced back to incorrect settings in the TCP/IP configuration.

Adding the RAS Software

The following is a list of steps to install the RAS software on an NT 4 server:

1. In Control Panel, select the Network option.

2. In the Network dialog box, click on the Services tab.

3. From the Network Services list, click the Add button. Select Remote Access Service from the Select Network Service dialog box. Then click OK.

   The installation program will prompt you for the path to the distribution files. It expects to use the same path from which you installed Windows NT. If the path of the installation media is different from the path presented, type the correct path and click the OK button. The RAS files will be copied to the computer.

4. In the Add Port dialog box, you will see a list of all ports available to the NT RAS (see Figure 13.2). If you have successfully installed a multiport adapter, ISDN card, frame relay card, X.25 card, or other device, these will be listed as well.

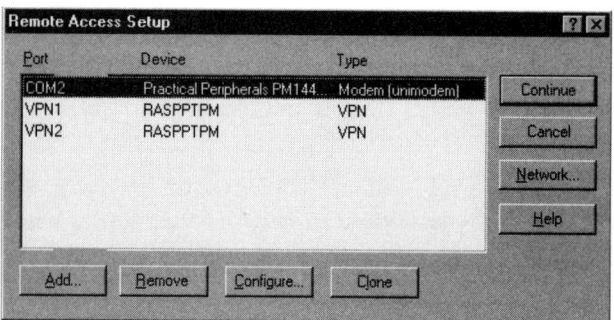

FIGURE 13.2

The Add Port dialog box

Designing a Remote Access Solution with RAS **429**

5. RAS Setup will offer to automatically detect the modem connected to the selected port. Click Cancel to manually select a modem or click the OK button to automatically select the modem. Sometimes, when attempting to detect a modem, RAS Setup may present a dialog box requiring you to select your modem from a short list of possible modems. This occurs only when RAS Setup cannot distinguish between two or more modems.

6. In the Configure Port dialog box, the modem detected will be highlighted.

Depending upon the type of modem you have, you might need manuals or other technical information about your modem to complete this step. Also, if the modem is external, make sure that it is turned on and hooked up to the system before using modem detection.

If RAS did not detect the modem or you have chosen to manually select the modem, select the device attached to the port from the list. Only modems that are supported are listed. If you are adding a port after initial RAS installation, you can use the Detect button to automatically detect the modem connected to the new port.

Configuring the Modem and Port

After you have selected the modem type, RAS requests information about how to configure the device's port. RAS needs to know whether the port should operate in a two-way mode, sending and receiving calls, or whether it should send only or receive only. You must also indicate whether you want to use modem features such as error control and modem compression. You configure the modem and port via the Configure Port dialog box (see Figure 13.3).

FIGURE 13.3

The Configure Port dialog box

The following list provides you with the steps needed to configure the modem and port:

1. In the Port Usage box, choose how the port is to be used.

   - Dial Out Only means the computer will be a RAS client only.

   - Receive Calls Only means the computer will be a RAS server only.

   - Dial Out and Receive Calls means the computer can be a client or server; however, the computer cannot do both at the same time.

2. To configure information specific to the type of device attached to the port, select the device from the list and choose the Settings button. The following options appear:

   - Enable Modem Speaker: Sets the modem speaker so that you can hear the modem during operation.

   - Enable Hardware Flow Control (RTS/CTS): Allows the modem to tell Remote Access software when the line is congested or clear so that the Remote Access software can temporarily stop transmitting data when necessary. *Handshaking* streamlines data transmission, prevents overrun errors, and improves overall data throughput.

   - Enable Modem Error Control: Detects errors on blocks of data through cyclic redundancy checks (CRCs). Modem error control causes the modem to retransmit garbled data, ensuring that only error-free data passes through the modem.

   - Enable Modem Compression: Compresses the modem-to-modem data stream, reducing the number of bytes transmitted and therefore reducing the transmission time. The reduction achieved depends on the amount of redundancy in the transmitted data.

You can use the default settings if you are unsure of the setting to choose.

Finishing the RAS Setup

When you have selected the kind of modem to use, how the port will be used, and which modem features to use, RAS setup displays the Remote Access Setup screen, so that you can tell the Remote Access software how to operate.

In the Remote Access Setup dialog box, configure RAS network-wide settings by choosing the Network button. You can also configure or reconfigure the ports, as desired, by highlighting the port you want to configure and using the buttons along the bottom of the port box.

Table 13.2 describes each button's use.

TABLE 13.2 Choices in the Remote Access Setup Dialog Box

Option	Use It To...
Add	Make a port available to RAS.
Remove	Make a port unavailable to RAS.
Configure	Change the remote access settings for the port, such as the attached device or the intended usage (dialing out only, receiving calls only, or both).
Clone	Copy the same modem setup from one port to another.
Continue	Proceed to the next step in Setup when you finish with this dialog box.
Cancel	Leave the Setup program.
Network	Configure RAS server-wide settings. Set network access to entire network or RAS computer only. Select and configure network protocols the RAS server will support. Select network protocols the computer will use for dial-out (client) and for dial-in (server) connections. Set authentication and data encryption options.
Enable Multilink	Enables Multilink functionality when you select the Enable Multilink check box. Applies to Windows NT Server computers only.

Dial-Up Networking Multilink combines multiple physical links into a logical bundle. This combined link increases your bandwidth. The most common use for it is to bundle ISDN channels, but you can also bundle two or more modems, or a modem and an ISDN line. To use Multilink both the clients and servers must have Multilink enabled.

Choosing Protocols for Dialing Out (Client)

If the computer that will act as the RAS server may also be used to connect to other servers, you'll need to choose which protocols to use for the dial-out sessions.

The Dial-out Protocols box sets the protocols used when this computer dials out as a RAS client to another computer. If you do not select a protocol in the Dial-out Protocols box, you will be unable to select that protocol later when you configure a phone book entry for dialing out.

Network LAN protocol settings apply to all RAS operations for all RAS-enabled ports. Also, RAS enables NetBEUI, TCP/IP, and IPX protocols on the RAS server by default, but you can adjust these bindings to allow RAS to use only certain protocols. Enabling all three protocols allows RAS clients to use any combination of protocols to access remote resources

In the Network Configuration dialog box, select the protocols for dialing out in the Dial-out Protocols box.

If no ports are configured for dial out, the Dial-out Protocols box will be dimmed.

Choosing Protocols for Receiving Calls (Server)

Choose the protocols for receiving calls in the Server Settings box. The Server Settings box sets the LAN protocols that the RAS computer can use for servicing remote clients. You must also configure parameters for each protocol that you want the RAS Server to support.

If no ports are configured to receive calls, the Server Settings box will not appear in the Network Configuration dialog box.

Choosing an Encryption Option

As part of RAS security, all authentication and logon information is encrypted before it is transmitted over the phone links. You can choose one of the following encryption options when setting up a RAS entry:

- Allow Any Authentication Including Clear Text: Permits connection using any authentication requested by the client (MS-CHAP, MD5-CHAP, SPAP, and PAP). This option is useful if you have different RAS Clients.

- Require Encrypted Authentication: Permits connection using any authentication requested by the client except PAP.

- Require Microsoft Encrypted Authentication: Permits connection using MS-CHAP authentication only.

- Require Data Encryption: Means that all data sent over the wire is encrypted.

Configuring the RAS Server to Use TCP/IP

Configuring the RAS Server for TCP/IP involves two configuration aspects:

- RAS requires its own basic configuration and IP address.

- RAS must be configured to supply IP addresses to RAS clients.

Before you begin be sure that TCP/IP is installed.

In the Network Configuration dialog box, enable the TCP/IP check box and click the Configure button to bring up the RAS Server TCP/IP Configuration dialog box as shown in Figure 13.4.

The RAS Server TCP/IP configuration options are as follows:

- **Allow Remote TCP/IP Clients to Access:** Select whether to allow TCP/IP clients to access the entire network or this RAS Server computer only.

- **Use DHCP to Assign Remote TCP/IP Client Addresses:** If your network uses Dynamic Host Configuration Protocol (DHCP) you should check this option to allow the DHCP Server to provide IP addresses to clients.

FIGURE 13.4

RAS Server TCP/IP Configuration dialog box

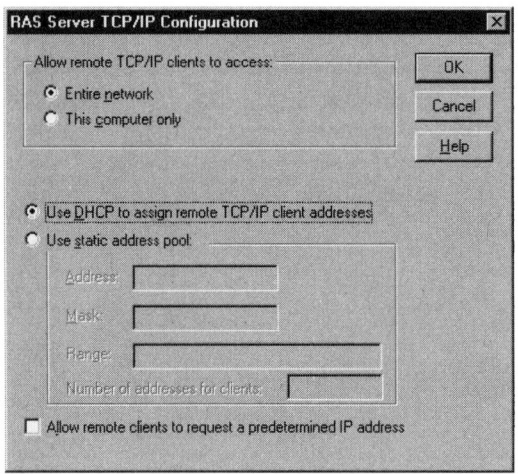

- **Use Static Address Pool:** Type the Begin and End IP addresses from the range allocated for RAS clients. These numbers should be assigned by the network administrator and should be entered in dotted decimal notation (such as 123.234.123.1)

- **Allow Remote Clients to Request a Predetermined IP Address:** RAS Servers can allow clients to request a specific address. Clients specify the address by entering it in Remote Access.

After selecting the appropriate options, choose the OK button to return to the Network Configuration dialog box. Now you can either click OK to end the protocol configuration process or select another protocol to configure.

Configuring the RAS Server to Use IPX

Make sure that the IPX protocol is installed before you configure the RAS Server to use IPX. If the IPX check box in the Network Configuration dialog box is selected, then the IPX protocol is installed.

You can follow these steps to configure the RAS server to use IPX:

1. Choose the IPX Configure button in the Network Configuration dialog box. The RAS Server IPX Configuration dialog box appears (see Figure 13.5).

FIGURE 13.5

The RAS Server IPX Configuration dialog box

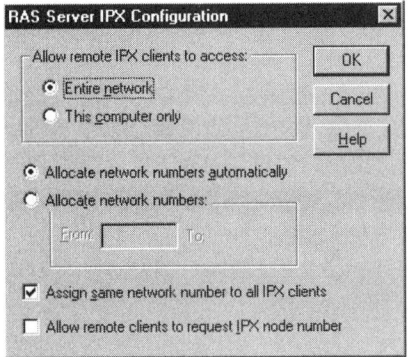

2. In the RAS Server IPX Configuration dialog box, select whether to allow IPX clients to access the entire network or the RAS Server only, and then select a method for allocating IPX network numbers:

- **Allocate Network Numbers Automatically:** The Windows NT RAS software uses the NetWare Router Information Protocol (RIP) to determine an IPX network number that is not being used on the IPX network. The RAS Server assigns that number to the remote client.

- **Allocate Network Numbers (Manual Override):** Manual assignments can be useful if you want more control of network number assignments for security or monitoring purposes. If you choose to allocate network numbers manually, type the first network number in the From box. RAS automatically determines the number of available ports and inserts the ending network number for you.

- **Assign Same Network Number to All IPX Clients:** Select this check box to assign the same network number to all IPX clients by using either the automatic or the standard allocation method.

- **Allow Remote Clients to Request an IPX Node Number:** Select this box to allow the remote client to request its own IPX node number rather than using the node number provided by the RAS Server.

Allowing a remote client to choose the node number is a potential security risk to your network. It allows a client to impersonate a previously connected client and access network resources accessed by the other client.

3. After selecting the appropriate options, choose the OK button to return to the Network Configuration dialog box.

Now you can either click OK to end the protocol configuration process or select another protocol to configure.

Configuring a RAS Server to Use NetBEUI

By default, Remote Access Setup enables NetBEUI and the NetBIOS gateway. The only configuration option you need to consider is whether NetBEUI clients can access the entire network or the RAS computer only. Choose one of these options in the RAS Server NetBEUI Configuration dialog box. Restart your computer after making any changes.

When to Use RAS

Increasingly, corporate networks are either integrating Microsoft's Windows NT into their existing Novell NetWare infrastructure, or they are migrating to Windows NT from Novell NetWare. In mixed environments, it is prudent to use the proper platform for the task. Using the most efficient platform to perform certain tasks will make the overall integration of the two NOSs more efficient. Novell NetWare has always been the leader in File and Print services, and its implementation of the X.500 directory structure has made NetWare Directory Services (NDS) an efficient and secure system. On the other hand, Microsoft's Windows NT is a NOS platform that has been specifically designed to function as an application server and does so efficiently.

When the remote access concept was introduced a few years ago, it was used sporadically by users in corporations, and it created few bottlenecks. So the systems were adequate for the job. But with mergers and acquisitions becoming so common, offices that were once considered local to a LAN have now become remote locations. This, in turn, creates a greater demand for remote access, and the users demand better performance. If we use the criteria enumerated and explained in the previous sections, we can see that RAS falls into the category of remote node service. Since RAS is incorporated into a NOS that has been specifically tweaked to function as an application server, RAS will provide greater efficiency in providing remote node services. Novell has its own version of remote node service, called NetWare Connect. However, this service is not integrated into the NOS and functions as an add-on feature or NetWare Loadable Module (NLM). When remote node is required or desired (and to follow the advice for minimizing bottlenecks), NT's RAS should be used whenever possible.

In this chapter, we discussed how to design a remote node implementation with the Microsoft Remote Access Service. While RAS is suitable for situations where the amount of data to be transmitted over the dial-up link is relatively low, there are situations where a RAS connection is not practical. In the next chapter, we'll discuss another approach to remote access: Citrix Winframe.

CHAPTER 14

Designing a Remote
Control Implementation

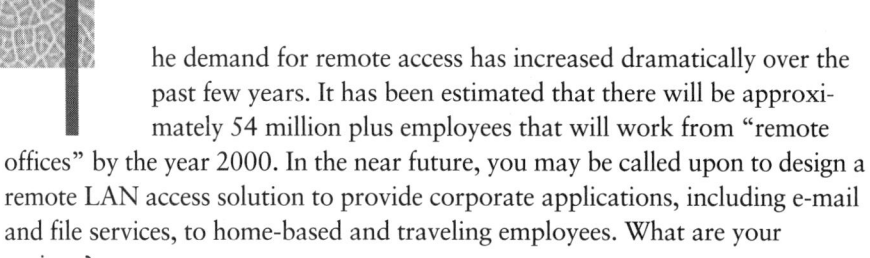

The demand for remote access has increased dramatically over the past few years. It has been estimated that there will be approximately 54 million plus employees that will work from "remote offices" by the year 2000. In the near future, you may be called upon to design a remote LAN access solution to provide corporate applications, including e-mail and file services, to home-based and traveling employees. What are your options?

In this chapter, we'll focus on planning a remote control implementation using an option that has gained immense popularity recently: Citrix's Enterprise Server, WinFrame.

We will discuss:

- WinFrame components such as the Intelligent Console Architecture (ICA)
- How to design a WinFrame remote access implementation
- Tips for troubleshooting your WinFrame installation
- What to expect in the next version of WinFrame

There are many remote LAN access solutions to choose from; however, only one will satisfy most of your requirements. The trick will be to select the best solution for your requirements, and minimize pitfalls when doing so.

As a start, you'll have to ask yourself the following questions:

- What type of remote access solution do I need? Remote node, remote control, or both? Which of the remote access solutions provide what I need?
- How much WAN bandwidth can I afford? What is the ease of implementation?
- How much administration is involved?
- What level of security is provided?

- How easy is the end-user operation (management, installation, etc.)?
- What is the speed of the network connection(s)?
- What level and extent of technical support is needed?
- What is the cost of ownership?

You should prioritize the questions in order of significance and rate the possible solutions by weight, based on their ability to satisfy your criteria.

Citrix WinFrame and Remote Access

Citrix WinFrame is a network operating system based on Microsoft Windows NT Server Version 3.51, with Citrix MultiWin multiuser extensions and remote control based on the Citrix ICA 3.0 protocol. WinFrame supports Windows applications remotely, regardless of a user's location or platform (286, 386, 486, or Pentium). However, WinFrame server is only supported on Intel-based platforms.

WinFrame has two basic components:

- The client software (WinClient) that resides on the user's PC, connects to the server, and initiates a Windows session.
- The server software that allows the WinFrame client to work in a private Windows NT session using a portion of the server's processor(s), RAM, and peripheral(s).

Throughout most of this chapter we've used Citrix WinFrame 1.6 for the examples. Any differences between version 1.6 and the newest version, 1.7, have been noted.

There are two ways to initiate a remote control session: The first by using a LAN connection, a WAN connection, or a RAS remote node connection. The second by using a dial-in connection directly to a WinFrame server via the Citrix ICA protocol.

 Microsoft has purchased parts of the WinFrame code, and will incorporate it in Windows NT 5. That release will retain the Windows, 95 GUI. Citrix will still provide support to their existing WinFrame server 1.6 and the new version 1.7. Furthermore, Citrix will continue to provide additional functionality to Microsoft's NT 5 application server. Some of that functionality includes dynamic load balancing, persistent caching, etc. These features are explained in detail in this chapter.

Because WinFrame uses a remote control system, it runs applications on the WinFrame server. Only the user's keystrokes, screen updates. and mouse movements—not the programs or data—are sent across the link. As we said in Chapter 12, remote control provides optimal performance for high-bandwidth legacy and database applications.

WinFrame can also provide remote node access in two ways: by remote node (based on Microsoft's RAS and WinFrame's Client Dial-In Manager, supplied with the WinFrame Client) or through third-party remote node software.

A remote node connection (versus a remote control connection) provides remote users with transparent access to all LAN and local resources as if they were directly connected to the LAN. Applications run on the remote PC, and use the workstation's available processor and RAM for fast user interface response.

Some applications, such as word processors, run best when used with remote node software because they are very efficient in utilizing network bandwidth and transfer only small amounts of data over the link. It is better to place those kinds of applications on remote PCs, providing the users with the flexibility to work off-line and copy files to and from the network when needed.

What Is ICA?

WinFrame provides enterprise remote computing to local and remote users through its advanced Intelligent Console Architecture (ICA) protocol. When you use the remote control feature of WinFrame, applications are loaded and executed on the WinFrame server (remote control). As the application runs, the WinFrame server intercepts the application's user interface (screen, keystrokes, and mouse) data, and transmits this data between the WinFrame server and the WinFrame client program running at the user's PC using the ICA protocol.

 More information can be found at Citrix's Web site at www.citrix.com/technology/icapos.htm and www.citrix.com/technology/icatech.htm.

Designing a Remote Access Solution with WinFrame

Because WinFrame is an application server integrated with Microsoft Windows NT 3.51 Server, it provides both remote control and remote node access for telecommuters and remote office workers. With this solution, users dial into the WinFrame server and access applications on the server or on another server, rather than on their local hard drives. Because of this server-based approach, WinFrame has often been called the first true network application server.

Most users experience a noticeable performance boost when first using WinFrame, because only screen refreshes, mouse positions, and key strokes are sent through the modem to the remote worker's location. This is in contrast to the remote node solutions, mentioned in Chapter 13, which send entire files over the phone line to remote users.

When to Use WinFrame

Citrix's WinFrame server is an authorized extension to Microsoft's NT 3.51 Server, so it not only has the same restrictions and requirements as Microsoft's NT 3.51 Server, but also has other restrictions. An application certified in Windows NT 3.51 does not necessarily guarantee successful implementation in WinFrame. Using the Microsoft hardware and software compatibility lists as a baseline is a good idea.

Since WinFrame is a complex but efficient application server, it is important to ask some specific questions before purchasing WinFrame as a remote access solution. However, when some of these questions cannot be answered and a definitive decision cannot be reached, a "proof of concept" project will have to be implemented.

How many remote users will need access to the corporate network?
The cost of ownership should offset the cost of a comparable solution using the traditional one-to-one remote control solution (such as ReachOut, PCAnyWhere, etc.). In other words, the cost of the hardware needed (such as one PC or CPU board for each remote user connection) and the cost of the software licensing (per user) must be greater than the cost of ownership of the WinFrame solution. Therefore, if the number of concurrent users is less than eight, it would be hard to justify purchasing a WinFrame solution. The approximate cost of the hardware and software for a Citrix WinFrame server solution for eight concurrent users is $14,000. This price is based on the following configuration: a Compaq Proliant 2500 6/200 with a Pentium Pro 200MHz CPU, 256KB cache, 128MB of RAM, 4.3GB hard drive, CTX 14-inch color monitor, mouse, keyboard, 10/100Base-T NIC, 8-port Comtrol RocketPort communications board and peripherals, US Robotics' Total Control MP/8 with 8 modems, APC SMART-UPS with Powerchute, and the WinFrame Enterprise server software (15-user base license).

How far away are my remote users? As we have proven in previous chapters, the fact that this is a remote control solution will provide significant throughput benefits when compared to remote node solutions, because of the inherent capabilities of a remote control connection. However, there is an immutable law of physics that cannot be overcome. Data cannot travel at faster than .85C, where C is the speed of light (299,792,458 miles/sec). Therefore, for large distances the latency due to the law of physics will become noticeable. For example, if we take a remote user in California connecting to a WinFrame server in New York, the latency due to distance will be approximately:

$L = D/V = 4000/158,340.03947 = .02526209$ seconds

Where:

D = Distance between LA and NY (4,000 miles)

$V = .85C = .85 * 186,282.39937841$ miles/sec $= 158,340.03947$ miles/sec

As you can see this is not significant, but as you increase the distance, the latency becomes noticeable in the form of the delay when pressing a key and seeing the result appear on the screen. It is important to consider the latency that remote users will tolerate. You must understand that the latency always factors into the throughput. However, at short distances that latency is minimal, and as distances increase, its effect on the total throughput increases.

What kind of WAN connectivity do I presently have? The type of WAN connectivity will affect the user's connectivity capabilities. For example, if the connectivity is via a traditional WAN connection (such as 56Kbps, frame relay, T1, etc.), the user can connect via the network connection option, using IPX, SPX, TCP/IP, or NetBIOS/NetBEUI. If, however, the connection is via asynchronous lines attached to the WinFrame server or to a modem pool server, the user, if using remote control, has only one choice of protocol connectivity: asynch. Furthermore, modem pools are notoriously unreliable because of the nature of modems and the multitude of standards.

It has been my experience that nine out of 10 asynchronous connection problems can be attributed to issues directly related to modems (such as modem strings, different modems on each end of the link, different modem handshaking configurations on each end of the link, etc.). If you anticipate a large number of users connecting to your site, and those users are connecting from a remote LAN, you should consider leasing or purchasing a traditional WAN connection.

What are my WAN connectivity options? If you've read the preceding comments, you will have seen that you should install a traditional WAN connection into your network if possible. However, if the users are not all colocated (centrally located) on a remote LAN, but are individual users at separate sites trying to connect to the corporate LAN, you have two choices: a normal telephone line or ISDN. ISDN would be cost effective and beneficial only if the user had an application that resided on the user's PC and had to access data on the corporate database. In that case, the user would only be capable of a remote node type of connection, and the increased throughput provided by an ISDN connection would offset its cost. However, most users can benefit from a remote control type of connection and don't require the bandwidth provided by an ISDN link. In that scenario it's advisable that you provide the following to minimize incompatibilities:

- A standard modem that will be at either end of the link (at the remote PC and at the server)
- A modem that is on the Windows NT 3.51 Server list of certified modems (Microsoft's NT 3.51 hardware compatibility list)
- A modem that is robust, reliable, and follows the international asynchronous communications standards
- A modem that has extensive management and diagnostic features
- The fastest modem that satisfies the four requirements we've listed

How easy is the WinFrame implementation? You have to weigh the cost of implementing a WinFrame solution, versus a traditional remote control solution. This advice has been given before, but since it is important, we'll reiterate it. The cost of ownership of a Citrix WinFrame server supporting 15 users (not concurrent) is approximately $24,000 over a 3-year period. Approximately half of this cost, $10,000, is due to the extensive installation and maintenance costs. The installation of the WinFrame NOS itself is relatively easy (comparable to the time it would take to install Windows NT 3.51), but the application setup can be complex, and the complexity increases as the application diverges from the standard off-the-shelf NT-ready application. Getting this solution up and running can be a time-consuming task. As you will see later in this chapter, there are many factors to consider when configuring a WinFrame server for maximum efficiency. However, when the installation is successful, you'll have the fastest and most sophisticated remote access system on the market.

How many administrative tools are included with the WinFrame server? Standard day-to-day administration of the WinFrame server is, for the most part, performed within NT 3.51. Adding and modifying remote users is performed in the standard NT 3.51 manner and without any interaction with WinFrame. However, WinFrame has additional administration features not found in Windows NT 3.51. They are composed of the WinStation Administration and the WinStation Configuration tools. The WinStation Administration tool provides the capability to view statistical data, such as incoming and outgoing traffic, in real time. It also offers the capability to view detailed client information, such as the build number of the Remote Application Manager for each user, the amount of client cache, and the client's network addresses. The WinStation Configuration tool provides capabilities, such as adding or editing WinStations (the virtual ports that the remote clients use to establish WinFrame sessions). This chapter covers those administrative tools and provides tips on configuration.

What level and extent of WinFrame technical support is needed? WinFrame technical support is provided through resellers that have been certified by Citrix. This means that the Citrix support engineers in the reseller's organization must have passed a certification class and test for Citrix WinFrame. This exam is similar to a Microsoft MSCE NT exam. The technical expertise to support the WinFrame solution is really only crucial during the actual installation and configuration of the system. The technical support will be crucial in providing end-user education on using the WinFrame interface (it may be different than the user's regular Windows interface, since WinFrame uses a Windows NT 3.51 or Program Manager interface), installing and configuring applications for each user, and stabilizing the WinFrame server (such as patches, service packs, etc.). Once the configuration and implementation has been accomplished, minimal maintenance is required. Unless new variables are introduced into the environment (such as new untested applications, a number of concurrent users beyond the configuration parameters, etc.), the system will remain stable.

What is the level of security provided by the WinFrame server? Essentially the security features of WinFrame are provided by Windows NT. Because WinFrame is so tightly integrated with NT 3.51, the security is more than sufficient in preventing access to those who don't belong on the network. Within NT, administrators can define certain hours of the day for remote users to access the network, and they can define what directories the user can see and whether a remote user can modify any of those directories. However, there is no way to password-protect the Remote Application Manager's configuration (the remote user's WinFrame Client piece), to prevent the user from modifying it. This means the user's rights and privileges must be carefully defined on the server to prevent any unauthorized activities.

How easy is the WinFrame client setup? The installation of the client piece, called the WinClient or Remote Application Manager, is quite straightforward. However, certain parameters must be provided to the user before installation, such as protocols to be used, name of the WinFrame server to attach to, etc. The Remote Application Manager requires extra user training to explain how to access files on the local drive, as well as those on the network, and to navigate through the application using command keys. As stated previously, since the Citrix solution runs on NT 3.51, if the remote PC is using an operating system that is using a GUI interface other than Program Manager, the users will have to learn how to use it. Unless the user has never seen the original Windows 3.*x* Program Manager, the transition should be a breeze.

Are my off-the-shelf applications Microsoft-NT-Server-3.51-certified? If they're not certified, have they been tested on an NT Server 3.51? As we said earlier, a good approximation of the compatibility of the applications with WinFrame is to first see if the applications are listed on the Microsoft NT 3.51 compatibility list. This will narrow down the number of variables when troubleshooting the application installation. In other words, you'll be able to eliminate the Windows NT 3.51 incompatibility issue and narrow it down to some tweaking and additional patching on the WinFrame side. Citrix technical support is reluctant to support any application installation that is not certified to run on Windows NT 3.51 Server or has not been successfully tested on a Windows 3.51 NT server. This being said, the application has to be installed in a particular manner, which is different than on a Windows NT 3.51 Server. If these steps are not completed, the application will not run properly. Missing these steps turns out to be the cause of 75 percent of installation problems.

Do I have many customized applications? Are any written exclusively for Windows 3.1? Nowadays, corporate applications that have to be accessed by remote users tend to be customized or specialized and are a crucial vehicle to performing the functions that are essential to the corporate business. Because of their nature, these applications are rarely NT 3.51 server certified, and therefore do not fall into the Citrix Supported installation category. More often than not, these application installations will have to be modified. This would include tweaking, modifying configuration files, etc. Most corporations do not have the skill level in house and will have to seek help from Citrix-certified technical support vendors.

For applications that have been written exclusively for Windows 3.1 (and have not been certified or tested on Windows NT 3.51), the installation will not always be successful. In other words, since the application has been written exclusively for Windows 3.1, its code may violate some of the Windows NT 3.51 Server restrictions and could therefore crash the server at any time. At other times, the code could be well-behaved (meaning it conforms to NT 3.51 server restrictions), but the overhead due to running in WoW (Windows on Windows) would cause the application to suffer a reduction in performance of approximately 25 percent. In order to minimize failure, the organization will need highly trained Citrix technical support (from a Citrix approved VAR), and the cooperation of programmers of the applications. Under this scenario, the Citrix technical support team would have the information needed to tweak and configure the server and application for the best performance on the WinFrame server. If any of those steps are missed, you run the chance of failure.

What will be the impact of WAN traffic on my WinFrame server?
The WinFrame server has been tweaked to provide processor priority to processing sessions. If the WAN link becomes bogged down because of traffic overload, the discarded packets (see the section on CIR) will increase and the server will have to process more retransmit requests. At some point, the server will disallow any new connections, even if the license limit has not been reached; or it will disconnect the last session connected, and the remaining sessions will respond sluggishly. Therefore, make sure that you have adequate WAN bandwidth for the amount of traffic you anticipate, and also plan for a realistic CIR.

What is the impact of WAN traffic on my LAN? Compared to the traffic that could be created between the WinFrame server and the file server or database server that the accessed applications have to communicate with, the traffic between the remote site and the server is minimal. Whether the application is placed on the server (local) or as a pass-through (on a separate file server), the application will be processed at the WinFrame server. The traffic will be generated by the data that has to travel between the executable and the data repository. If that data is local to the WinFrame server, there is no additional traffic on the LAN; however, if the data is found on another server, the traffic on the LAN can increase dramatically. In such a case, the traffic increase on the LAN is directly proportional to the amount of concurrent connections to that application on the WinFrame server.

What can I do to minimize LAN traffic bottlenecks on my WinFrame?
If the standard measures for LAN troubleshooting have been met (LAN analysis, resegmentation, etc.), there are additional measures that can be taken to alleviate the LAN bottleneck at the WinFrame server. As you know, every direct connection to the WinFrame server impacts its functionality. One method of relieving some of the traffic on the segment directly attached to the WinFrame server is to add an additional NIC. This will allow the server to load balance traffic between the two segments. However, you must make sure that each NIC does not have the same protocols bound to it. Each NIC must have a different protocol bound to it. If you have more than one WinFrame server on your LAN, you must allow the NetBIOS protocol to be bound to one of the NICs. The WinFrame servers identify their names using the NetBIOS/NetBEUI protocols.

 A proper WinFrame configuration is only valid for the environment it has been configured for. If the environment changes, no matter how slightly, the WinFrame configuration becomes obsolete and has to be reconfigured. It is important to keep the environment as clean and stable as possible, because all changes to the WinFrame's immediate environment impact the efficiency of the WinFrame server.

Now that you have read and understood all the issues we've covered, can you justify recommending a WinFrame server as a remote access solution? If the answer is "yes," then you have made a good choice. WinFrame is a highly sophisticated and efficient application server, and when installed and configured correctly it is the fastest remote access solution on the market. It will allow application management centralization (since the applications run on the server). If the applications are accessed from other servers, and the WinFrame server only acts as a pass-through vehicle (such as the application icons on the WinFrame server that point to applications residing on other servers), the application management will remain unchanged. Since WinFrame is based on Windows NT 3.51 Server, it essentially behaves as a standard Windows NT 3.51 Server and will conform to all NT domain guidelines.

Server Preinstallation Considerations

Let's assume that you have chosen the WinFrame server as the remote access solution for your corporation. What are your next steps?

In all successful system implementations, the success is due to careful planning. A WinFrame system is no exception. The importance of careful planning is even more crucial in a WinFrame deployment than in most.

Theoretical Minimum WinFrame Server Requirements

We'll guide you through the required planning steps to assure a successful WinFrame implementation, but first, you'll need to know the minimum standard system requirements for WinFrame 1.6 and 1.7:

- A personal computer using a 486, Pentium, or higher processor

- A minimum of 16MB of RAM (minimum operating system RAM requirement) plus 4 to 8MB per user

- A minimum of 90MB + Page File Size of free disk space

NOTE The Page File Size (PFS) is equal to 1.5 × installed RAM. For example, if we configure the server memory to support eight concurrent standard users (8MB of RAM per user), the PFS would be the following:
Installed RAM = 16MB + (8 × 8) = 80MB. PFS = 1.5 × 80MB = 120MB.

- A SCSI CD-ROM drive (for the WinFrame CD).

- A bootable 3.5-inch diskette drive (for the WinFrame boot diskettes).

- A minimum of one 32-bit network adapter (to allow WinFrame to be installed from the network, if the system does not contain a 3.5-inch diskette drive or a CD-ROM drive).

- A VGA or SVGA video adapter.

- An intelligent multiport adapter (for dial-in connections). This is optional, since you may only require LAN connections or have an existing dial-in remote node solution such as a Shiva.

- A mouse.

NOTE WinFrame supports computers with up to four *x86* processors. Any system with more than four *x86* processors requires a custom Hardware Abstraction Layer (HAL) from the equipment manufacturer.

A Sample WinFrame Project

To illustrate a WinFrame deployment project methodology, we will approach it as if Bachmann Consulting were implementing a WinFrame remote access solution for a corporation (Widget Corporation; a fictitious enterprise).

The Widget Corporation (Widget) has requested that Bachmann Consulting undertake a Citrix WinFrame pilot project, which is part of Widget's overall remote access project. The consultants will set up a lab environment and interview Widget WinFrame managers to gather configuration information.

This information will be used to formulate a standard template that will be distributed to all WinFrame locations at Widget.

During the pilot project a WinFrame server will be installed that will act as a test server. All application installations and configurations will be done on this server. Essentially, it will become the standard template server. This server will eventually be incorporated into the greater "remote access" scheme. Originally, the test server will have up to 16 33.6Kbps modems attached to it to provide dial-in capabilities via a hunt-group number (an 800 number). Other connectivity will be via IPX and/or IP, through Widget's WAN connection (frame relay).

Widget's WinFrame Capability Requirements

Widget users require access to specific application sets. The following is a list of the essential applications and their contacts (an administrator or user that has an in-depth knowledge of that application):

Application to Install	Contact
cc:Mail	John Doe
Notes	Jane Doe
MS Office 97	John Doe
Outlook	Jane Doe
Internet Explorer	John Doe
Netscape	Jane Doe
Adobe Acrobat	Jane Doe
Sybase (16-bit)	Jane Doe

Widget has requested that Bachmann Consulting recommend a location scheme for these applications that will allow remote users to access them efficiently. Furthermore, Widget is researching ways to outsource management of the WinFrame server(s) and provide local POPs to allow remote clients to connect to the WinFrame servers via a secured frame-relay cloud.

Planning Methodology (Discovery Phase)

Bachmann Consulting has decided to conduct a detailed discovery phase that will help in assessing the requirements of a successful WinFrame implementation.

Preliminary Tasks

The following tasks have been implemented and their results recorded.

Network Inventory Information on the present state of the network and its configuration will help in creating an efficient remote access design. The network diagram should provide the following information (where * indicates required information):

- *LAN Segments: *speeds, *IP Addresses, MAC addresses, *protocols, etc.
- *Servers: *location, number of cards, *NIC speed, CPU Speed, RAM, UPS, protocols, *OS versions
- *Applications: location

The network information was provided to Bachmann Consulting by Widget employees and the consultants reached the following conclusions:

- Network bandwidth between thin-clients and servers is adequate (switched 10Base-T and 100Base-T).
- No throughput overload is expected.
- Extensive use of Virtual LANs minimizes hops.

Application Inventory To assess the present state of applications and their locations, it is imperative that an application inventory be obtained. The information obtained from the software inventory will allow Bachmann Consulting to conduct an in-depth analysis of the interaction between the applications and the network. The consultants will then formulate a plan for integrating the applications into an efficient remote access system. The analysis will determine the following:

Nature of the Application

Is it a 16- or 32-bit application? Is the application IO or CPU intensive? Is it a 2- or 3-tier application?

Location of Applications

Are the applications pass-through or are they local to the WinFrame server?

Dependencies of the Applications

Does the application have any special requirements?

Application compatibility

Has the application been certified for WinFrame compatibility or Windows NT 3.51 Server compatibility?

Predicted Number of Concurrent Users

Because WinFrame is based on Microsoft's Windows NT 3.51 Server, it has the same restrictions, requirements, and limits. The number of total users supported by an NT server is restricted mainly by the disk space on the server. However, the number of concurrent accesses is restricted by the licensing and hardware setup.

WinFrame is efficient in handling multiple CPUs and performing load distribution. WinFrame load-balances evenly across the first three (3) CPUs (100 percent efficiency) and the efficiency degrades slightly on further CPUs (by 10 to 20 percent). Both WinFrame and Windows NT 3.51 Servers (straight out of the box) are limited to a maximum of 4 CPUs. However, when specialized, platform-specific custom HAL is used, they have both been shown to support up to 6 CPUs.

WinFrame acts as a workstation on the LAN for each remote WinFrame client, and all "workstation" processes are performed at the WinFrame server. These processes affect the server's CPU, RAM, I/O, and NIC I/O. This means that the server has to be configured correctly for the kind of "workstation" processes that are going to be initiated. Theoretically, the standard (efficient) limit for user connects per CPU is 45, but this number can fluctuate and is very dependent on the type of application that is run. In the past, database applications have been observed to run efficiently to a maximum of 8 to 14 concurrent users per CPU and per adequate RAM, depending on the database's algorithm. However, with the introduction of better drivers and better application codes (32-bit vs. 16-bit), those limits will increase. As in Windows NT, RAM seems to be a more important factor in determining application efficiency (speed) than CPU.

To optimize the server for a client/server-based application, the following changes would have to be made:

Real World Minimum Configuration

RAM: 55MB per CPU for the NT NOS, and 8 to 24MB per user.

(For a 45-user capacity, at 8MB per user, we would need a minimum of 470MB of RAM on a dual CPU system.)

CPU: Pentium 166MHz.

NIC: 10BASE-T (bus-mastering) or 16MB Token-Ring.

Typical Changes (to Improve Response Time)

CPU: Increase CPU speed and capacity (add more CPUs) and/or reduce the number of users connected per CPU.

RAM: Add more memory accordingly.

NIC: Change to 10/100 bus-mastering card.

Bus: Change to a higher bus speed motherboard.

Application: The changes needed would depend on the nature of the applications.

A WinFrame Configuration Example

The following numbers are theoretical and are *only for illustration*. The numbers are based on a proper LAN and WAN design and optimum throughput. The example also assumes that the database is located on a high-end, high-performance server.

Other assumptions include: A fast disk controller, a 32-bit bus-mastering NIC, Pentium Pro CPUs (166MHz or higher), a PCI bus, a fast BUS controller, fast disk drives, high network throughput (preferably switched 100Mbps), and the latest and greatest HAL and SMP drivers to support 4 CPUs. The users are limited to one session per connection. The application requires 16MB of RAM to function.

Table 14.1 illustrates the required RAM to support concurrent power users. In the real world, a power user (a developer, programmer, etc.) requires at least 16MB of RAM per session, and a standard user (a user running standard applications such as MS Word, Excel, PowerPoint, etc.) requires at least 8MB of RAM per session.

TABLE 14.1 RAM Required to Support Concurrent Power Users

# of CPUs	Required RAM	Number of concurrent Power Users (at 16MB/user)
1	0.811GB	46
2	1.404GB	69
3	2.290GB	101
4	3.360GB	135

Table 14.2 illustrates the number of concurrent power users supported with an installed amount of RAM and an increased number of CPUs.

TABLE 14.2 CPUs and Installed RAM for Concurrent Power Users

# of CPUs	Installed RAM	Supported Number of Concurrent Power Users (at 16MB/user)
1	512MB	29
2	512MB	29
3	512MB	28
4	512MB	28

As you can see, unless you add appropriate memory when adding CPUs, you will actually decrease the number of concurrent connections possible. The reason for this phenomenon, is that each additional CPU uses a percent of the available RAM. Therefore the applications have a smaller pool of memory to tap.

One must remember that the preceding examples are only to be used as approximate predictions. The results will vary slightly depending on several variables (application, network, etc.). However, the formulas used to obtain these figures have been used successfully in the past and the figures are a fair representation of the results obtained by most standard applications used in the industry.

Understanding the Applications

Bachmann Consulting has interviewed key application contacts and they have provided critical information about the users' and applications' requirements. The consultants developed the application requirements matrix shown in Table 14.3. We'll now review some of the questions the consultants asked.

How many concurrent users are anticipated?   The number of concurrent users directly affects the amount of RAM the server must, because the number of sessions directly affects the number of RAM slices utilized. In an application server, RAM is more significant than the number of CPUs. Therefore you must scale the amount of server RAM accordingly and correctly, in order to provide optimum session productivity. This piece is only the first variable in a five-variable factor that directly affects CPU and RAM configuration.

How many sessions per user?   If each user connects and only initiates one application, it is considered one session. In that instance, a session is equal to one connection. However, if a user connects to several applications at the same time, each initialization of an application is considered a session. In that instance, each session also occupies a slice of the server RAM and you must scale the server RAM accordingly. This is the second variable.

Approximate RAM per user?   Now the question is how much RAM the application or session itself needs to operate. This will determine the size of the server RAM slice that each session will occupy. This is the third variable.

16-bit or 32-bit code?   The final variable is the type of code that the particular session is written in. As you know, NT suffers a performance hit of 25 percent or more when running 16-bit code, compared to running 32-bit code. Therefore this factor has to be included when calculating the amount of RAM and CPUs required on the server. This is the fourth variable.

Pentium Pro or Pentium Processor?   Normally, a Pentium Pro CPU would be recommended. However, the type of application used on the WinFrame will affect the CPU's efficiency. An NT-coded 32-bit application will incorporate instruction code specifically written for the Pentium Pro processor, and will therefore run at 100 percent efficiency. A Windows 3.*x*-coded 16-bit application will not incorporate Pentium Pro instruction code, and will therefore run at 85 percent efficiency. A 16-bit application will run at 100 percent efficiency with a Pentium processor. NT-coded 32-bit applications do not run at 100 percent efficiency when running on a Pentium processor. You must

TABLE 4.3 The Application Requirements Matrix		cc: Mail	Notes	Office 97
	Concurrent Users	12	10	10
	RAM/User	8	8	8
	16-Bit or 32-Bit	16	16	32
	Operating System	Windows 3.1	Word for Windows	Windows 95
	Protocol	IPX	IP/IPX	IPX
	Local .ini File	Yes	Yes	Yes
	Local or Pass-through	Pass	Pass	Local
	NT 3.51- or WinFrame 1.6-compatible	Yes	Yes	Yes
	Database	No	Yes	Yes
	Code	?	?	?
	Remote Node	No	No	No
	On NetWare	Yes	Yes	Yes
	Other Applications	No	No	No
	Special Requirements	No	No	No
	Server Load	Minimal CPU	CPU	CPU, I/O
	2-Tier/3-Tier	2-tier	2-tier	2-tier

Outlook	IE	Netscape	Adobe Acrobat	Sybase Front-End
10	20	8	8	6
8	16	8	8	8
16	16	32	16	16
NT 4	Windows 95	Windows 95	NT 3.51+	NT 3.51+
IPX	IP	IP	IP/IPX	IP/IPX
Yes	No	Yes	Yes	Yes
Local	Local	Local	Local	Pass
?	Yes	Yes	?	Yes
No	No	No	No	Yes
?	?	?	?	PB
No	No	No	No	No
Yes	Yes	Yes	Yes	Yes
No	Yes	Yes	Yes	Yes
No	No	Yes	Yes	Yes
CPU	Minimal	Minimal	Minimal	CPU
2-tier	2-tier	2-tier	2-tier	2-tier

weigh the number of 16-bit versus 32-bit applications that will be running on your WinFrame server. If you anticipate using mostly 16-bit applications, you should configure a WinFrame server using a Pentium processor.

The next questions will affect the WAN remote access connectivity options and design.

What are the connectivity needs?   What kind of connection does the application being accessed require? Does the application require a virtual LAN connection, such as remote node? If it needs remote node, you will have to consider looking into other WAN links available for this kind of connection. The bandwidth requirements will be substantially higher than in a remote control link.

What kind of connectivity?   What kind of WAN links are in place at the present time? The available link capacity will determine the type and amount of connections your WAN network can support. Lately many service providers (AT&T, Sprint, MCI, etc.) are providing "public networks." These networks are essentially a frame-relay, X.25, or ISDN cloud. The service provider charges you access to their cloud. Here's the way it works.

The corporate network purchases or leases a router from the service provider. This router allows direct connectivity to the "public network." The remote users who want to access the corporate network have several options for connections.

- If colocated, they also acquire a router and connect into the same cloud.

- If not colocated, each user acquires a modem (analog or ISDN) and connects to the service provider's local point of presence (POP).

Once the remote user is connected to the cloud, the network routes the connection to the appropriate corporate destination. This kind of connectivity option can reduce costs, since your remote users only connect to a local POP and therefore do not incur long distance charges. However, this solution is more cost effective if your users are further away. In other words the long distance cost must be greater than your monthly "public network" charges. This sort of solution would not be cost effective within a metropolitan area.

Network card type?   If we want to minimize any bottlenecks, we also have to consider the capacity of the network card in processing packets to and from the network. If the network card does not contain its own processor, that duty will be delegated to the server's CPU, adding to its overhead. So it is advisable to install bus-mastering network cards. These cards have their own processor and therefore shield the server from having to process network I/O requests. In many instances, clients will be accessing applications which reside on application servers that are independent of the WinFrame server. In these scenarios, connect the application servers and the WinFrame server to a high-speed segment such as 100MB Ethernet or FDDI. This will minimize bottlenecks and latency.

Protocols?   The type of protocol used on a WAN link can sometimes affect the WAN throughput adversely. Netware's IPX/SPX protocols are excellent LAN protocols, but they are a handicap to WAN traffic. This is because IPX is a "chatty" protocol. In other words, for each data packet transmission it requires an acknowledgment packet. This creates overhead on the WAN link, and because the WAN link is already very sensitive to the amount of traffic, it is seriously affected by this "chatter." Novell has instituted two new features that minimize this "chatter," large packet protocol and packet burst. The first allows more data on a packet since a larger packet size is allowed, and the latter allows many packets to be sent before requiring an acknowledgment. This greatly reduces WAN traffic, but is still not the ideal WAN protocol to use. The best WAN protocol is the Internet Packet (IP) which does not require acknowledgments since the assurance of transmission is provided by TCP and other protocols. NetBIOS/NetBEUI are nonroutable protocols and are not usually allowed in corporate networks that have routing between their segments.

Internet access need?   If Internet access is needed, you must use TCP/IP as the common protocol and you must install it on the server. That is not a problem because, as we said before, the WinFrame server is similar to Windows NT 3.51 and has all the supported protocol stacks. However, the server has one network card and each user connection is viewed as a session, sharing a common IP number.

The remainder of the questions will affect the installation methodology and application performance.

Location of applications?   Applications can reside on the WinFrame server, or on another server. However, the location does affect the overall design of connectivity. The WinFrame server is designed to run applications locally, but applications that are I/O intensive will have a negative impact on the server's performance. The server is tweaked for applications that are RAM and CPU intensive. If an application is located on another file server, the application work flow is between the WinFrame server and the file server, therefore the link between the two servers could become a bottleneck and introduce delays.

Standard or custom applications? As was stated previously, a standard application may adhere to the NT OS requirements and run smoothly when run on NT. A custom application may not, and if it does run without a hitch, it may require manual changes to the installation.

Special needs for applications? Does the application need certain "hard-coded" parameters? For example, does the application specifically need the C: drive? Does it need to access the root of C:? Does it require each user to have their own installation of the application? Answering yes to any of these questions will affect the overall installation of WinFrame and its potential hard disk space. If the application has to be installed for each user that will access the WinFrame server, the hard disk space is dependent on the amount of space each such application installation needs per user. Also, WinFrame can have its hard drive designated as C: or any other drive. Once the drive letter has been decided upon during installation, the drive letter can be changed on the fly, but it will affect any application that has not been registered by WinFrame. That means that certain manually altered configuration files will have to be altered manually again to reflect the new drive letter.

There is another important aspect of the application requirement that has to be addressed before considering WinFrame as a vehicle for this application. Does the application run on IP only, and if so, does it require each connection to have an individual IP address? If the answer is yes, the application will not run correctly on the WinFrame server. That is because the WinFrame server, having only one card, will only provide one IP address. The first user connecting will acquire that IP address, but subsequent users will not have an address and the application will not function correctly.

Database applications/database code? Are any of the applications database applications? If so, where will they reside? Database applications can be very disk I/O intensive. In other words, they may make many requests to the drive. This is not the ideal type of application for an application server. There are other database applications that transmit a lot of information during information lookup requests. These databases would adversely affect LAN throughput if the application were to be accessed on another server via the WinFrame server. Applications that have both these characteristics would be better placed on a powerful UNIX server (such as a high-end SparcStation) with the link between the WinFrame server and database server being at least switched 10BASE-T.

Integrated NetWare security? Most corporations have an existing Novell NetWare network. It is sometimes desirable to keep all security management centralized, and if they already have a NetWare network then NetWare will probably fulfill their security needs. WinFrame can allow users to use the existing NetWare-based security as their network authentication. This provides centralized security management and adds another level of security, since the user has to log into the WinFrame server first. Users must essentially log in twice, first to the WinFrame server, then to the NetWare network or server. You can minimize this by having the users use their same NetWare authentication parameters (username and password) in WinFrame. That way, when the users log into the WinFrame server their authentication parameters are "passed through" to their preferred NetWare server, and they will not be prompted for a NetWare login and password.

Run login script? If you answered yes to the previous question, then you have the choice of having the user run their NetWare login scripts. This will provide the WinFrame users with their required drive mappings. It is important that a list of NetWare drive mappings be provided before the WinFrame server is installed, because of the issue of the drive letter that the WinFrame server will acquire as its own. Also, the WinFrame server will assign user drive letters first in descending order and then assign network drive letters in ascending order from the WinFrame drive letters. For example, if a user's C: drive is assigned the letter Z, then its D drive is Y, etc. If the server's C: drive is C: then the next server drive is D:, and after all the server drives have been assigned a letter, the network drives are then assigned their drive letters from the remaining unassigned letters in the alphabet. If the NetWare mapping requires a Z letter, you must manually reassign the user's PC drive to another drive letter, or you can go into the registry key and specify that the user's default drive letter is something other than Z:.

Individual preferred server? You can globally assign a preferred server by using the Set Preferred Server= command in the Command Prompt window, or by assigning the preferred server individually. In other words, each user can have their own NetWare preferred server (their authentication server, or home server).

Mandatory user profile? As in Windows NT 3.51, the administrator has the ability to assign profiles to users or groups of users. A profile sets the "look" of the individual's window. For example, if you want users from Department A to see an application icon and not allow any users outside of that department to see it, you create a profile and assign only users of the

Department A group to it. As the name implies, only the profile administrator can make changes to that profile, so when users are in that profile none of their settings will be saved when they exit the session. In other words, they cannot make any changes to the way the window looks.

Even though the administrator has rights to the mandatory profile, they must first rename the extension of the profile from *.man to *.usr before making any changes. Once the changes have been made they can save the file and then rename it with its original name.

Roaming profiles or local profiles in a domain environment? The advantages and disadvantages of each type of profile in a WinFrame Domain are the same as for the profiles in an NT 3.51 Domain. (See earlier chapters in the book for more information on these profiles.)

Group WinFrame servers in a domain? First, ask if the domain is an existing NT 4 domain? If so, see the tip in the troubleshooting section of this chapter. Second, if the domain is an NT 3.51 domain, then you have the following options:

- You can make the new WinFrame servers BDCs (Backup Domain Controller) of the NT PDC (Primary Domain Controller). This option would make a WinFrame server a PDC if the NT PDC went down. Depending on the number of users and servers in the domain, this would create a large amount of overhead on the WinFrame PDC and would render the WinFrame server inefficient for processing remote sessions.

- You can make the WinFrame server members of the domain, and you can administer the WinFrame users from the NT PDC. This minimizes administrative overhead.

A PDC is a server in an NT environment (domain) that acts as the central management server. This server controls all the security, resources, and user management throughout the domain (this includes other NT servers belonging to its domain). There can only be one PDC in a particular domain. A BDC of that domain is a "backup" to the PDC and "stands in" when the PDC is unavailable (down). There can be more than one BDC in a particular domain. (Please see earlier chapters for more information on these terms.)

If in a domain, should I create local or domain users? Creating domain users will facilitate user management, because you will be creating a single point of management (the PDC). However, there are certain instances when you want to confine the management to the WinFrame server. An example would be if you want to create user profiles exclusively for users that access the network via the WinFrame server. This WinFrame profile, or profiles, could be different than their profiles when the users are physically attached to the network.

Configuring the Hardware: RAM, Hard Drive, and the Rest

There are several factors that will affect the WinFrame server's efficiency: CPU utilization, I/O utilization, network bandwidth utilization, network throughput, application code, RAM availability, BUS throughput, and server hardware compatibility. Widget is presently utilizing a combination of switched fast and standard Ethernet topology. This kind of topology theoretically provides high bandwidth and minimizes bottlenecks. So the network configuration will not adversely affect the overall design of the WinFrame solution.

In this section, we'll focus on configuring the WinFrame server's hardware for efficiency. This will be achieved by using Bachmann's proprietary formulas for determining the number of CPUs and RAM, the server platform (such as Compaq 6000, etc.), the communication boards (such as DigiBoard, RocketPort, etc.), the drivers, and the latest service packs. The formulas will use the information obtained from the application matrix.

Updates

The first step is to download the latest Citrix service packs and the hot fixes (the appropriate ones). The service packs and hot fixes can be found at the Citrix Web site (www.citrix.com/support/ftpserve.htm) or at ftp.citrix.com. The following service packs for WinFrame 1.6 were available as of this writing:

- SP5_16S.EXE 15MB: To be loaded on any WinFrame server
- SP5_DOS.EXE 800KB: To be loaded on DOS clients
- SP5_W16.EXE 1MB: To be loaded on 16-bit Windows clients
- SP5_W32.EXE 1.3MB: To be loaded on 32-bit Windows clients

TIP There are also several hot fixes to download. The hot fixes are continuously being updated, so you have to check Citrix's Web site periodically. Service packs are not updated as often as hot fixes, since they contain all hot fixes from all previous service packs and any new hot fixes since the last service pack. These service packs are very large. When installing Service Pack 5 or any other service pack, first install the server pack, and then install the client pack. If that is not possible, you can upgrade the WinFrame client service pack prior to upgrading the server with the new service pack. The upgraded client can communicate with a server that has not had its service pack installed.

Hardware

The following parameters will affect the WinFrame server configuration (such as RAM/user, sessions/user, etc.). The other parameters, such as whether the application is a pass-through or if it requires local configuration files (.ini), will affect the installation procedure and its place in the network (where to locate the server in the infrastructure). We will look at each application's requirements and provide the minimum proper hardware requirements for the WinFrame server.

cc:Mail Requirements (RAM, CPU) Widget requires access for remote cc:Mail users (approximately 16 concurrent users). Using this requirement as a benchmark, Bachmann Consulting recommends the following minimum configuration:

Number of CPUs = 1
Sessions per user = 1
16-bit application
User RAM requirements = 8MB/user
Concurrent users = 16
The required minimum RAM for the WinFrame server will be:
RAM = 203MB

Notes Requirements (RAM, CPU) Widget requires access to Notes for remote users (approximately 24 users) in San Francisco and Fairbanks. Using this requirement as a benchmark, Bachmann Consulting recommends the following minimum configuration:

Number of CPUs = 1
Sessions per user = 1

16-bit application
User RAM requirements = 12MB/user
Concurrent users = 24
The required minimum RAM for the WinFrame server will be:
RAM = 363MB

MS Office 97 (Word, Excel, Access) Requirements (RAM, CPU)
Widget requires access for remote MS Office 97 users. Each application has different requirements. Using these requirements as a benchmark, Bachmann Consulting recommends the following minimum configurations.

Word 97
Number of CPUs = 1
Sessions per user = 1
32-bit application
User RAM requirements = 16MB/user
Concurrent users = 32
The required minimum RAM for the WinFrame server will be:
RAM = 582MB

Excel 97
Number of CPUs = 1
Sessions per user = 1
32-bit application
User RAM requirements = 16MB/user
Concurrent users = 24
The required minimum RAM for the WinFrame server will be:
RAM = 454MB

Access 97
Number of CPUs = 1
Sessions per user = 1
32-bit application
User RAM requirements = 16MB/user
Concurrent users = 8
The required minimum RAM for the WinFrame server will be:
RAM = 203MB

Outlook Requirements (RAM, CPU) Widget requires access for remote Outlook users (approximately 42 concurrent users). Using this requirement as a benchmark, Bachmann Consulting recommends the following minimum configuration:

    Number of CPUs = 1
    Sessions per user = 1
    16-bit application
    User RAM requirements = 8MB/user
    Concurrent users = 42
    The required minimum RAM for the WinFrame server will be:
    RAM = 411MB

Internet Explorer 3.02 Requirements (RAM, CPU) Widget requires immediate access for remote IE 3.02 users (approximately 10 concurrent users). Using this requirement as a benchmark, Bachmann Consulting recommends the following minimum configuration:

    Number of CPUs = 1
    Sessions per user = 1
    16-bit application
    User RAM requirements = 8MB/user
    Concurrent users = 10
    The required minimum RAM for the WinFrame server will be:
    RAM = 155MB

Netscape Requirements (RAM, CPU) Widget requires access for remote Netscape users (approximately 8 concurrent users). Using this requirement as a benchmark, Bachmann Consulting recommends the following minimum configuration:

    Number of CPUs = 1
    Sessions per user = 1
    32-bit application
    User RAM requirements = 8MB/user
    Concurrent users = 8
    The required minimum RAM for the WinFrame server will be:
    RAM = 134MB

Adobe Acrobat Requirements (RAM, CPU)   Widget requires immediate access for remote Adobe Acrobat users (approximately 14 concurrent users). Using this requirement as a benchmark, Bachmann Consulting recommends the following minimum configuration.

Number of CPUs = 1
Sessions per user = 1
32-bit application
User RAM requirements = 8MB/user
Concurrent users = 14
The required minimum RAM for the WinFrame server will be:
RAM = 187MB

SYBASE Requirements (RAM, CPU)   Widget requires access for remote SYBASE users (approximately 35 concurrent users). Using this requirement as a benchmark, Bachmann Consulting recommends the following minimum configuration:

Number of CPUs = 1
Sessions per user = 1
16-bit application
User RAM requirements = 8MB/user
Concurrent users = 35
The required minimum RAM for the WinFrame server will be:
RAM = 335MB

System Recommendations

Based on the numbers obtained above, the theoretical minimum amount of RAM required for the WinFrame server to accommodate all the concurrent connections would be 3.027GB.

However, unless you are using a high-end server such as a Compaq 6000, a single standard server (such as a Compaq 2500) cannot accommodate 3GB of RAM. Bachmann Consulting recommends that Widget acquire three WinFrame servers for the following reasons:

- Load balancing
- Flexibility
- Redundancy
- Fault tolerance

The servers should be configured in the following manner:

Server 1(PDC): 1GB RAM, 4CPUs, 100Base-T NIC
Server 2(BDC): 1GB RAM, 4CPUs, 100Base-T NIC
Server 3(BDC): 1GB RAM, 4CPUs, 100Base-T NIC

Additionally, the following network devices should be put in place:

Router 1 with two Frame Relay ports, 100BASE-T port
Router 2 with two Frame Relay ports, 100BASE-T port

What we have done is to prepare the server for the potential amount of load that it will receive and to provide a level of fault tolerance (two routers) to the system. This configuration will guarantee a minimum of n concurrent users, and enable the users to run their applications at optimum capacity. This does not take into account distance, which introduces latency, or other external problems such as modems and WAN speeds. You might wonder, "Is this overkill?" As we stated at the beginning of this chapter, there are criteria that the WinFrame solution must satisfy before you should consider using it. One of the most important questions is whether the cost of ownership, which includes all the hardware, software, and technical support costs, is justified. For example, you may only have 45 users that want to use a critical corporate application, but only 10 concurrent connections at any time. Does this justify incurring the cost of acquiring a WinFrame solution? Well it really depends on the cost to the corporation of not providing access to the critical applications.

You must weigh the benefits and drawbacks of a WinFrame solution. You might then say, "Well, what about having a traditional remote access solution, such as 3Com, PCAnyWhere, or something like that?" We'll repeat what was stated previously in the chapter. If the cost of installing a traditional remote access system is less than or equal to installing a WinFrame solution, and everything else is equal (such as same amount of productivity and features), then purchasing a WinFrame solution would not be justifiable. The advantages of WinFrame over other traditional remote access solutions becomes more obvious as the number of concurrent users increases and the amount of LAN or WAN bandwidth decreases. You also benefit by only having to spend money on centralized servers and not user hardware (except modems or other communication devices). An easy method to determine the cost of any solution is to add the number of users that are going to access your network from remote locations, and divide the cost of each solution (WinFrame or a traditional remote control solution) by that number. You can then compare the cost per user for your solutions.

Connectivity Options (ISDN, Frame Relay, Dial-In)

As we said before, WinFrame supports all the types of connections mentioned above. The question is what impact on performance each connectivity option has.

ISDN Integrated Services Digital Network is a service that provides WAN link bandwidth of either BRI (Basic Rate Interface), which is equivalent to 128Kbps, or PRI (Primary Rate Interface), which is equivalent to 1.536Mbps. This service is more expensive than regular Plain Old Telephone (POTs) lines so its use is only justified if it is required either to run the application(s) or for management and fault-tolerance purposes. If an application requires a remote node type of connectivity and the client is not colocated to others, it would be the only viable solution for that user. ISDN cards are very common, and service providers now have a better understanding of ISDN requirements than they did a few years ago and can install the client's ISDN line with a minimum of fuss.

Frame Relay Frame relay will provide WAN link speeds up to 1.544Mbps. Many service providers support them, and the lines are quite reliable. A frame relay solution is only cost effective if there are a number of users that are colocated (on a common LAN) that need to access a corporate LAN that does not exist on their LAN. Not only does frame relay provide seamless connectivity but it also eliminates some of the support problems that you would encounter with modem connectivity. It is important to plan carefully for frame relay service. The installation procedure can be trying at times. Once you have placed your order for frame relay service, it often takes at least two months to implement it. That is because a frame relay service commonly involves a service provider and a frame relay connection installer. Sometimes these two entities don't communicate effectively and you are caught in the middle when trying to troubleshoot a problem. There are several parameters that you must provide to the vendor, and these parameters must be well planned for or they will give you some headaches in the future. These parameters are:

- **PVC (Permanent Virtual Circuit):** This is a logical path (a virtual circuit) established between two locations. Since the path is fixed, a PVC is the equivalent of a dedicated line, but over a packet-switched network. This parameter directly affects the next one. So choose a PVC rate that is realistic for your WAN needs now and in the near future.

- **CIR (Committed Information Rate):** This is a bandwidth or information rate that represents the average level for your corporation. If your network activity exceeds this rate, the frame relay controller will mark your packets to indicate that they can be discarded if necessary. This means that if you do not select a high enough CIR, any packets above your CIR may be discarded, which could create potential problems in your remote access system (such as WinFrame server rebooting, slow response, users getting disconnected, etc.).

So what are your choices? Well, make sure that the PVC speed is realistic enough (high enough) and that you choose a realistic level of CIR. What you can do is select a perceived required CIR and have the service provider give you a detailed weekly report of your WAN traffic pattern. That way you can see whether you need to increase your CIR and/or PVC. It will also minimize your costs, since the price of your frame relay service increases as the PVC and CIR speeds increase.

Dial-In (Modem) This is the cheapest and most common method of connecting from remote sites. It is also the most unreliable. We're sure you've experienced disconnects and "modem unreachable" scenarios. That is because the modems have to translate from analog to digital and vice versa, on lines that are not always clean (noise-free), and between modems of different standards. The faster your connection the more unstable it becomes.

This solution is effective only in situations where you have users that are not colocated and do not need remote node connections. The amount of concurrent connections should not exceed 96 (the limit for modems supported by most common communication cards). Even if the card could support more connections, you are now creating a single point of failure (the server) and creating additional support headaches. Some corporations have installed a modem server (such as Ascend, Shiva LAN Rover, 3Com AccessBuilder, etc.) that manages the remote connections. This allows a greater measure of security and support management. These types of servers generally provide remote node connectivity. However, the users that connect via such a connection can still benefit from Citrix's WinFrame remote control speed by starting up their WinClient session after having connected via the remote node connection.

WinFrame Management Options

Now we're ready to delve into the management features of WinFrame. Instead of rehashing the product manuals, we'll provide some insight and tips so you can install the server correctly and with the fewest problems.

WinFrame Server Administration

We'll assume that you have already made the preliminary choices for server installation, such as the naming conventions, protocols, devices, file systems, and server type (PDC, standalone, or domain member).

As we said earlier, the WinFrame server (as seen in Figure 14.1) has the look and feel of a Windows NT 3.51 Server. When installing the server you have the choice of installing it as a server, a member of a domain, or a PDC of its own domain.

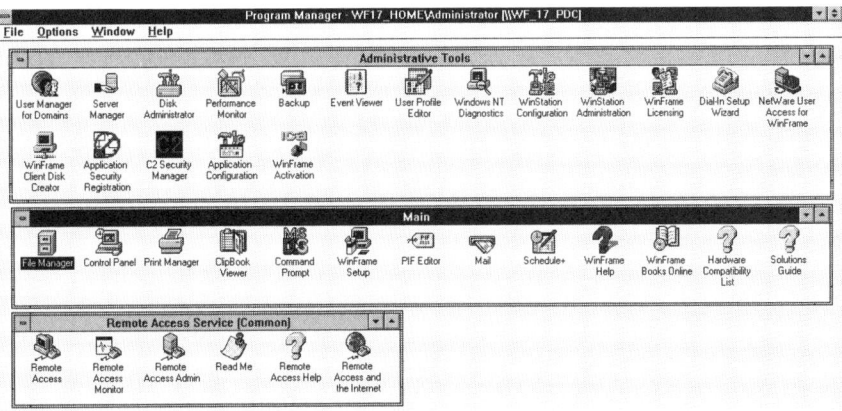

FIGURE 14.1

A WinFrame 1.6 Program Manager screen

In comparison to the Windows NT 3.51 Server Administrative Tools Group, there are a few additional items in WinFrame's Administrative Tools Group:

- **WinStation Administration icon:** This tool allows the WinFrame administrator to monitor, disconnect, and communicate with the WinFrame client connections.

- **WinStation Configuration icon:** This tool allows the WinFrame administrator to create and configure the WinFrame client connections.

> **Choosing a File System**
>
> You should think carefully about your choice of file system, since the two are not compatible. NTFS will allow a higher amount of security (user restrictions at directory and file levels) than FAT. When installing a WinFrame or Windows NT 3.51 Server, it is recommended that, in addition to the NTFS partition, a separate FAT partition be created where the boot files would be placed and provide a location for memory "core dumps." The information contained in the "core dump" is helpful to Citrix's technical support, when trying to troubleshoot server problems (screen freezes, crashes, etc.). Additionally, having a FAT partition allows the "core dump" to be retrieved even if the server cannot be rebooted. However, this feature can also be a detriment to the security of your server, because with FAT that partition is not protected from the network and is vulnerable to user manipulation.

- **NetWare User Access for WinFrame icon:** If you have a Novell NetWare 3.x file server on your network, you can migrate NetWare user IDs to your WinFrame server. There are two ways to migrate users:

  - The Migration Tool for NetWare (NWCONV.EXE). This utility moves all users and, optionally, moves files from a NetWare server to a WinFrame domain controller.

  - NetWare User Access for WinFrame (NW2NT.EXE). This utility presents you with lists of servers from which you can select users to be granted access to the WinFrame server. The user's password on the WinFrame server is automatically synchronized with the user's password on the NetWare server.

- **WinFrame Licensing icon:** This allows the WinFrame administrator to add licenses (allowed concurrent connections).

The following icons are found in the Main Group:

- **WinFrame Books On Line icon:** This provides access to WinFrame on-line books (from a CD-ROM).

- **WinFrame Setup icon:** This is (essentially) a renamed Windows NT Setup icon.

- **WinFrame Help icon:** This tool provides help information about WinFrame features. It is (essentially) a "how-to" help tool.

WinFrame User Setup

Some of the features and tasks required in setting up a user in WinFrame are similar to those found in Windows NT 3.51. However, there is an extra step in WinFrame that is not found in Windows NT 3.51: the NetWare setup task (see Figures 14.2 and 14.3).

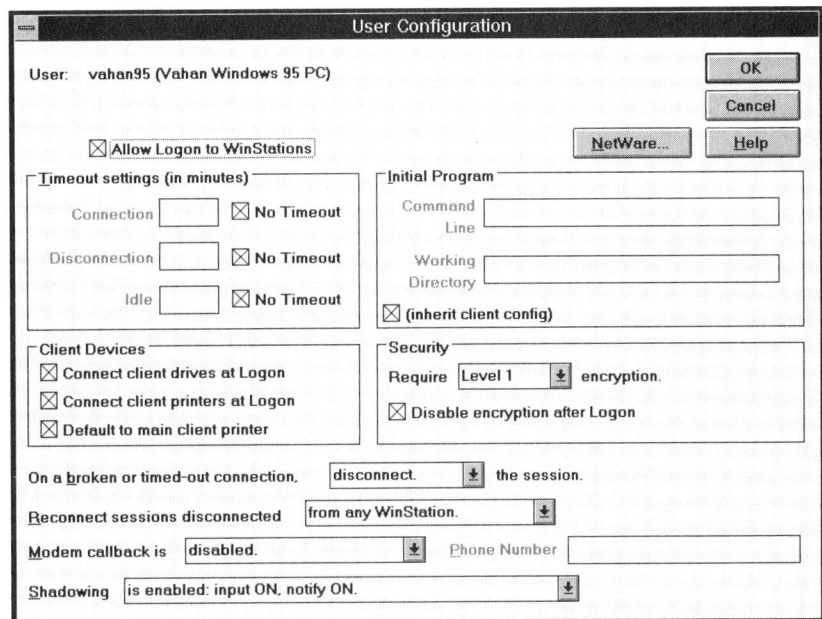

FIGURE 14.2

The User Configuration dialog box

WinFrame only allows bindery-emulation NetWare login. However, Novell's IntranetWare NT client supports Citrix WinFrame servers and allows users to attach to NetWare networks as NDS or bindery clients.

The NetWare Logon screen setup is directly related to the settings in the GateWay Service for NetWare toolbox (GSNW). This is also provided in Windows NT 3.51 Server.

FIGURE 14.3

The NetWare Logon Configuration dialog box

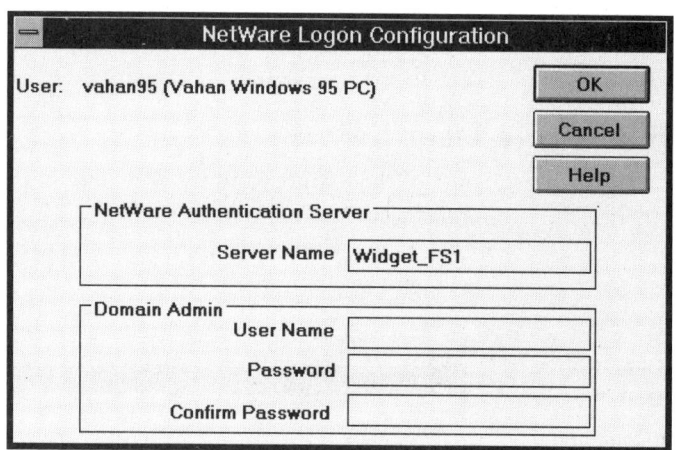

 The settings created in the GSNW box affect only the account under which you are logged on when you choose the settings. When other users log on, they are also prompted for a preferred server.

WinFrame Licensing

There are two licensing types. The first is WinFrame licensing which comes out of the box with a basic 15-user license. The license can be installed during the installation phase, or at a later date (this second option is available only in version 1.6), by opening the WinFrame Licensing tool (as seen in Figure 14.4). User upgrade licenses (to increase the number of concurrent connections) can always be purchased later. The upgrade licenses are additive. The second licensing type is Microsoft Client Access Licensing, which allows network and remote users to have access to the following Windows NT Server 3.51 Server features included in WinFrame:

- Remote Access Service (RAS). This feature allows you to combine remote node and remote control on the same WinFrame server, by working as a complement to the Remote Application Manager.

- File services for sharing and managing files and/or disk storage.

- Printing services for sharing and managing printers.

WinFrame Management Options **477**

Make sure you ask your Citrix reseller about your legal responsibilities for purchasing Windows NT licenses.

FIGURE 14.4

WinFrame 1.6 Licensing screen

WinStation Configuration

The WinStation configuration tool, as shown in Figures 14.5 and 14.6, allows the WinFrame administrator to create WinStations (connections) on the WinFrame server. The WinStation defines the attributes of a remote control session that will run on the WinFrame server. A WinStation is primarily associated with a network connection (IPX, SPX, TCP/IP, or NetBEUI).

If you are contemplating using RAS in conjunction with WinStation (remote node and remote control), you should first install RAS during the network setup portion of the WinFrame installation process, and select the asynchronous ports that you will dedicate to RAS. Ports cannot be shared between RAS and WinStation. You can then start WinStation configuration and select the remaining ports for WinStation.

When you are creating asynchronous WinStations, make sure you set the hardware flow control on the WinClient and the WinStation identically. This can be configured in the Advanced Async Configuration box.

If you have problems with modems synching up, try setting the Transmit Data parameter on both modems to When CTS Is On, and set the When Receive Buffer Is Full parameter to Turn off RTS.

FIGURE 14.5

WinStation Configuration dialog box

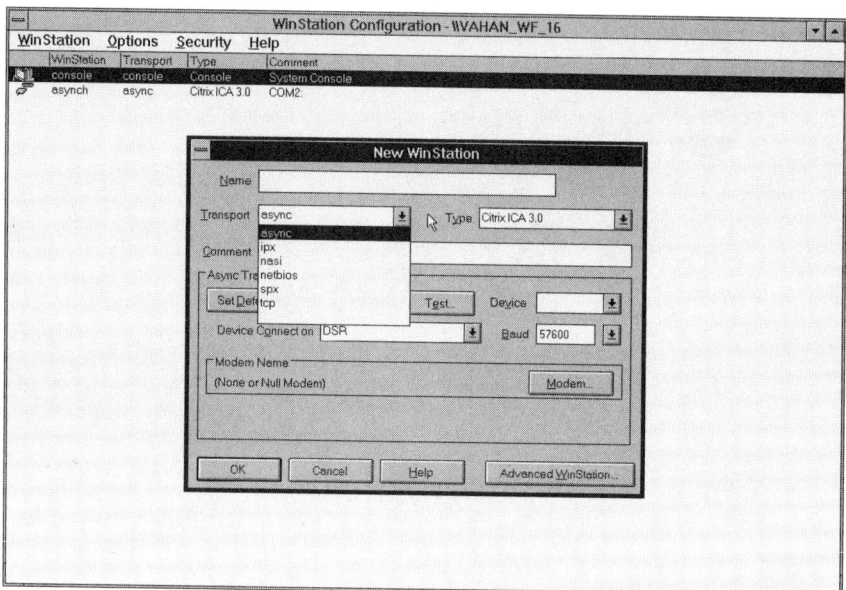

FIGURE 14.6

The Advanced Async Configuration dialog box

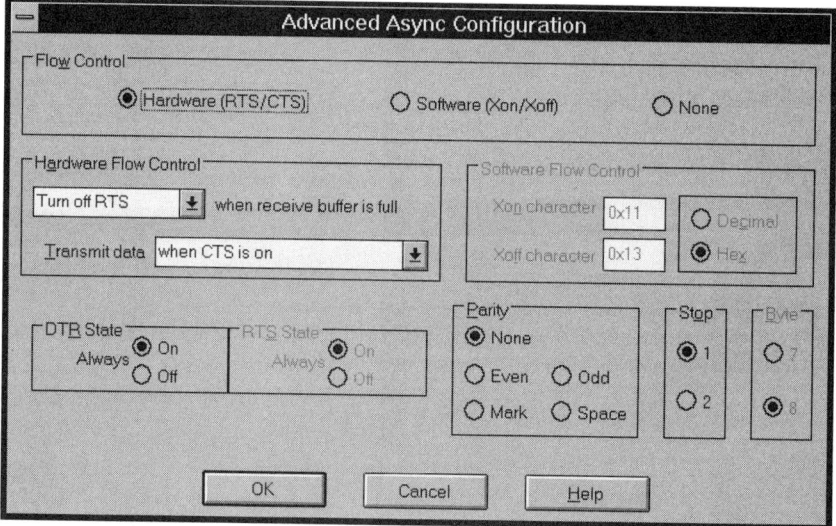

WinStation Administration

The WinStation Administration tool, as shown in Figure 14.7, allows the WinFrame administrator to monitor, send messages, disconnect, shadow, and troubleshoot WinStation connections. *Shadowing* allows an administrator, or any other authorized user, to take over a user's session, or in essence to "shadow" the session. This tool is used when the administrator is troubleshooting a user's connection.

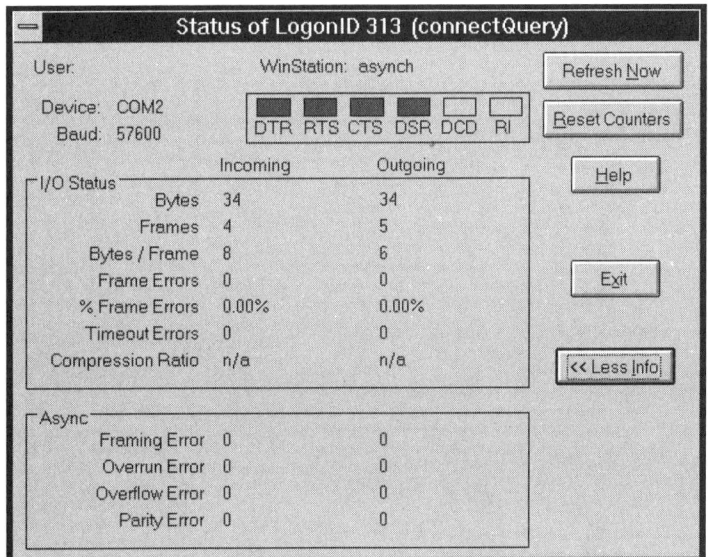

FIGURE 14.7

The WinStation Administration dialog box

Use the WinStation Administration tool when you want to disconnect users that have not logged off after their session. This will release licenses for others to use. You can also use it to reset the session when the connection has "hung."

WinFrame will not allow another connection if the number of WinStation licenses (connections) has been reached, that includes any type of WinStation configurations that you have created (IPX, TCP, Async, etc.)

The WinFrame Client Tool

There are three types of WinClients (Citrix's WinFrame client tool):

- **WinFrame DOS Client:** The WinFrame Client for DOS is used with DOS version 3.3 and above.

- **Win16 Client:** This is the WinFrame Client for Windows 3.1 and Windows for Workgroups 3.11.

- **Win32 Client:** This is the WinFrame Client for Windows 95 and Windows NT, as shown in Figure 14.8.

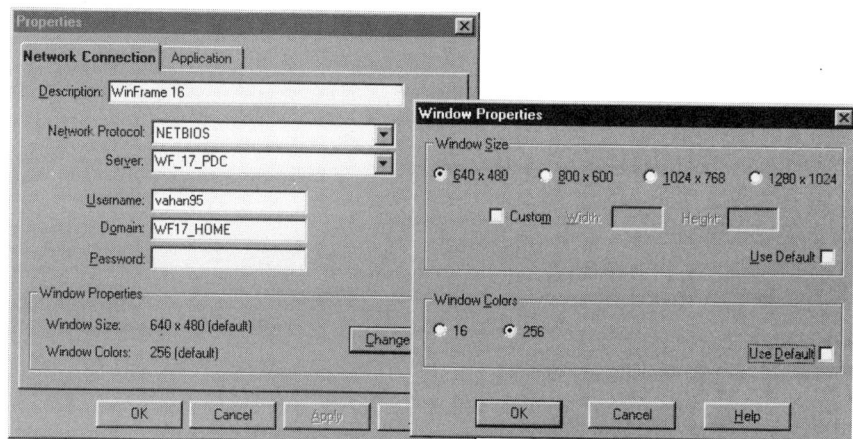

FIGURE 14.8
Client 32 Remote Application Manager screen

There are two components installed on the remote PC:

- **Dial Up Manager:** Provides remote node connectivity over a telephone line.

- **Remote Application Manager:** Provides remote control connectivity. This connection can be LAN (over a remote node or over a local network) or asynchronous (modem).

If you require IPX or TCP/IP remote connections, a "remote node plus remote control" session will be created with the WinFrame Win16 Client. The Dial-Up Manager will establish the remote node connection first and the Remote Application Manager will establish the remote control session on the WinFrame server.

NOTE The WinFrame Win32 Client includes only the Remote Application Manager.

The screen size and number of colors can be changed in the Remote Application Manager's Windows Properties box. The only restrictions are based on the video card of your remote PC.

TIP If you are going to have a remote node plus remote control session with WinFrame Win32 Client, install the remote node software first.

Other Client Support

WinFrame supports Macintosh and UNIX clients via third-party interfaces.

- **Insignia's NTRIGUE** (www.ntrigue.com): NTRIGUE delivers Windows 95-, Windows 3.x-, and Windows NT-based applications to PCs, X terminals, UNIX workstations, Macintosh computers, network computers, and Java desktops.
- **Wyse Technology's WinTerm** (www.wyse.com)
- **NCD** (www.NCD.com): NCD is porting Citrix's ICA thin-client software to its line of network computers.

WinFrame Questions and Troubleshooting Tips

Unfortunately, there will be times when you'll have to troubleshoot your server and server connections. The following is a list of questions with answers that may help you resolve some frustrating problems:

Q: I have a WinFrame server that has a lot of memory but my screen turns blue?

A: This is an NT 3.51 problem. The NT 3.51 kernel, straight out of the box, does not recognize more than 768MB of RAM. Therefore, even if you have installed more than 768MB of RAM, your application may "choke" when hitting the 768MB ceiling. This sometimes causes the server to "abend" which creates a blue screen. In order to rectify this problem, both Microsoft and WinFrame have produced their own patches. Citrix has a patch that you can download from their Web site. Install it, and follow the instructions.

Q: I have a Windows NT 4.0 Domain, can I have my WinFrame server join the domain?

A: Yes, since the WinFrame server acts as a Windows NT 3.51 Server. However, there are several issues you should consider: If you create users and profiles on the WinFrame server, they essentially have Windows NT 3.51 profiles. If the same users are also created on a Windows NT 4.0 PDC, their profiles will conflict when you make the WinFrame server part of the NT 4.0 domain. You can bypass that problem by making the WinFrame server a trustee of resource domain and have users log in twice, once on the WinFrame and once to the domain.

Q: I have users using Win 32 Client and IPX as their protocol, who are trying to connect through a WAN connection. They are unable to see their WinFrame server in their Win32 Network Connection Server box. How can I remedy this?

A: First, find out what kind of network card the WinFrame server is using. Find out by visiting the Citrix Web site and then see if there is a hot fix for this network card. If there is, install it on the server. Second, make sure your router has the proper IPX packet type filter enabled, since NetWare and NT have different versions of the IPX packet type.

Q: How can I audit users connecting to the WinFrame server?

A: By using the AUDITLOG.EXE command. Here are the steps required for auditing:

1. Log into the WinFrame server as an Administrator.

2. From the File pull-down menu in Program Manager, select Run. Click on Browse, and look for your WINFRAME directory. Double-click the auditlog.exe file, and click OK.

Make sure you have enabled the Logon\Logoff auditing features in the Audit Policy window. The Audit Policy window is found under Policies in the User Manager window.

3. The application will instantly minimize and create a log file in C:\WIN FRAME\LOGS called audit.txt.

4. Start Excel.

5. Choose File ➤ Open. Make sure the Type of File is set to *.txt.

6. The file is located in C:\WINFRAME\LOGS and is named AUDITLOG.TXT.

7. The text is comma delimited. Press the Next button.

8. Unselect the box next to Tab.

9. Check the box next to Comma.

10. Press the Next button two times.

11. Press the Finish button.

To clear the log, open a command prompt and type **auditlog /clear**.

The LOGS directory will be created in the directory where the WinFrame system files are installed (WINNT, WINFRAME, etc.)

Q: I have installed an application, but the application does not install correctly (for example, users do not get their configuration files)?

A: WinFrame is a complex operating system. Even though it has its roots in Windows NT 3.51, it is different enough to create problems if you install applications as if you would on an NT 3.51 server. There are two important commands needed when installing an application:

- CHANGE USER /INSTALL
- CHANGE USER /EXECUTE

To install a new application to the WinFrame server (for applications with an installation executable) follow these steps:

1. Log in as an Administrator or equivalent.
2. Start a Command Prompt session.
3. At the command prompt type **CHANGE USER /INSTALL**
4. Press the ↵ or Return key.
5. Exit the Command Prompt session by typing **EXIT**.
6. Follow the application's normal setup instructions.

Perform the previous steps once per each application to be installed, or you can cluster your application installations and perform the above steps once before installing all the applications.

Once the application has been installed, start a Command Prompt session again.

1. At the prompt type **CHANGE USER /EXECUTE** and press ↵.
2. Exit the Command Prompt.
3. Logout as Administrator.
4. Log in as each user who will use the application and execute the application.

For applications without an installation executable (without Install.exe or Setup.exe) follow these steps:

1. Log into the WinFrame server as Administrator.
2. Create an application directory in your global application directory (such as C:\APPS).
3. Copy all files for the application into the newly created directory (C:\APPS\WINWORD).
4. If there are *.ini files required for individual users, copy the *.ini files to each user's home directory on the WinFrame server.

5. Log off the WinFrame server.

6. Log in as a user who will access the application and test it.

This is the basic installation procedure and may not be the only procedure required for all application installations.

Q: My server was installed with a C: partition and a D: partition, and its performance is sluggish.

A: First find out how much space you have on your C: drive. Then look up your pagefile.sys file size and your virtual memory settings. The pagefile.sys file size should be 1.5 times your available RAM size. This is equivalent to the total RAM minus the RAM used by WinFrame (you can use the WinFrame Diagnostic tool and select memory).

If the required virtual memory size is too big for your primary drive do the following: Divide the total recommended virtual memory size (pagefile.sys) in half and place half on your primary drive and the rest on the secondary drive. If the primary drive still cannot accommodate the new virtual memory size, install the maximum size acceptable on the primary drive (C:) and install the remainder on the secondary drive (D:).

Q: My WinFrame server hangs when I attach to my Preferred NetWare Server and run through the NetWare login script.

A: Make sure that your NetWare login script does not refer to an application that scans a user's hard drive (such as virus scan). This will hang the server, since the user's C: drive has been assigned to the WinFrame server. However, there are several ways that you can avoid this pitfall:

Insert an exclusion statement in the NetWare login script, using a unique WinFrame identifier, such as the OS version label, MAC address, etc. The OS version label and MAC address can be obtained from the Windows NT Diagnostics Window by clicking on the Environment and Network boxes.

Q: What does the error *no more system ptes* mean?

A: It is an inherent problem with NT 3.51 where it is unable to deal with physical memory in excess of 768MB. There is a Citrix hot fix for this problem. This hot fix can be dowloaded from Citrix's FTP site (`citrix.ftp.com`).

Q: What is the procedure to upgrade my new HAL?

A: In order for the WinFrame server to function properly, it is important that the correct platform drivers (HAL) be installed. First find out the latest version that Citrix recommends of HAL for your server platform. Then proceed as follows:

1. Install the new HAL.
2. Reboot the server and reinstall Service Pack 5.
3. Reinstall the HAL before rebooting the server.
4. Reboot the server and install the hot fixes.
5. Reboot the server and reconfigure client printing settings.
6. Reset the WinStations.

Q: I have an application written for Windows 3.1 and its performance is very sluggish.

A: Make sure you have the latest hot fixes and service pack. You should install the service pack for the server first, and then install the hot fixes. Sometimes you have to reinstall third-party drivers (their latest version) after installing a service pack. Change the tasking parameter of the WinFrame server. Give equal priority to background and foreground applications. Last but not least, have the application programmer work with you so you understand the application requirements.

Q: How do I know which service pack I have installed?

A: Go to the top of the Program manager screen, click Help, and choose the About Program Manager line.

Q: Can I use the WinFrame Performance Monitor as a troubleshooting tool?

A: Yes, you can. This tool is the same as the tool found in Windows NT 3.51 Server. However, there are two monitoring objects that are provided with

WinFrame, that do not exist in Windows NT 3.51 Server's Performance Monitor. These objects are the following:

- **User:** This is used to monitor individual users. The information displayed is the sum of all processes and sessions for that user.

- **WinStation:** This is used to monitor individual WinStations. The information displayed is the sum of all processes for that WinStation.

Resources that can be monitored include the following:

- Microprocessor(s)
- Memory
- Hard disk(s)
- Networking hardware and software

You can then monitor how applications interact with each of the above resources, or monitor the overall load on each of these resources.

Q: What do I do when my WinFrame installation stops because it doesn't recognize the hard drive?

A: This problem is not specific to WinFrame, but applies to Windows NT 3.51 Server as well. To remedy this and continue with your installation, you must reboot the server, and as soon as the "blue screen" appears, press the F6 key. A new screen will appear and will state that it does not recognize the storage device. It will ask you to select a storage device from the list or one not listed. Highlight one that is listed or choose Other and press S. Follow the instructions.

Q: Can I access the WinFrame server through the Web with a browser?

A: Yes, you can, by taking advantage of the Web-based Application Launching and Embedding (ALE) feature found in WinFrame 1.6. There is a plug-in for Netscape Navigator and an ActiveX control plug-in for Microsoft Internet Explorer (3.02 and higher) that allows full-function Windows-based applications to be launched from or embedded in HTML Web pages. The application looks, feels, and performs as if it were running locally, but it is actually executing at the WinFrame server.

 The ActiveX plug-in for Microsoft's Internet Explorer can be downloaded from the Microsoft Web site (www.microsoft.com).

New Features in WinFrame 1.7

WinFrame 1.7 promises improved access, performance, and security for applications. Additionally, there will be two option packs to support load balancing and ICA encryption. These options will also be compatible with Microsoft's "Hydra/Hydrix."

As is the case with WinFrame 1.6, WinFrame 1.7 is based on Microsoft NT 3.51 Server, and contains all of the new features that were promised in WinFrame 2.0 (a version of WinFrame with a Windows 95 GUI that was supposed to be released in the summer of 1997, but whose release was affected by Microsoft's deal with Citrix).

The following are some of the features found in WinFrame 1.7:

- Persistent cache for clients
- New WinStation administration
- Installation changes including support for drive-letter remapping and upgrading from previous versions of WinFrame and NT
- New WinStation licensing scheme
- Cut and paste capability between WinFrame server and client workstation
- Client user interface changes
- New interface for load balancing applications, with the Application Configuration tool
- Improved client printing
- Automated client diskette creation tool
- Integrated security utilities
- WinFrame-specific additional performance monitor entries

 Citrix WinFrame 2.0 release has been canceled but at the time of this writing there is a new version of it, also with the Windows 95 GUI, but called WinFrame for Hydra/Hydrix (code-named "Picasso"). This was being codeveloped by Citrix and Microsoft. Hydra/Hydrix is Microsoft's version of the WinFrame component in Windows NT 5.

The following are some details on some of the features new to WinFrame 1.7:

- **System Security Enhancements:** This new feature provides more file, system, and application security. The WinFrame administrator can now secure specific files, directories, and system areas.

- **License Pooling:** The previous version of WinFrame was limited because when a server reached its license count, no other user could connect to that server. This creates a problem if that server is the only server with that particular application. This new feature allows servers in a cluster to share licenses. This simplifies administration and utilizes resources more efficiently.

- **Persistent Object Caching:** In WinFrame 1.6, when a user brings up an application, the application logo or other graphic-based startup image is downloaded via the network every time the user starts up that application. It is possible in the new release to choose to write to the hard drive any application's startup image, so that when you start that application again, the image will load locally.

- **Variable Protocol Compression Options:** The user now has the option of turning ICA protocol compression on or off based on the available bandwidth. Active ICA protocol compression is used for low-bandwidth dial-up and WAN links. It reduces bandwidth utilization. When using high-bandwidth LAN connections, compression is deactivated. This reduces server load and provides more efficient processor utilization on the server.

Two option packs are promised for WinFrame 1.7 thin-client/server system software and will be easy to migrate to the "Hydra Server" being codeveloped by Citrix and Microsoft:

- **Dynamic Load Balancing Option:** The load balancing GUI-based interface allows tweaking of the weighting factors for each server. This information is sent to the master browser and is then dynamically balanced. Information on the state of each server is sent to the master browser, which in turn knows where to send a client's request for connectivity. This feature is available as an add-on.

- **ICA Protocol Encryption Option:** This is an option that provides RSA encryption for the ICA protocol stream. Unlike current data scrambling techniques, this feature provides a higher level of security between the remote client and server.

In this section, our intention isn't to cover all the features in WinFrame 1.7 but instead to provide you with a peek at what improvements this advanced operating system will offer. As you have seen, these improvements are significant and will provide valuable managerial tools.

At the time of this writing, the new version of WinFrame was in the beta stage. By the time you read this book, WinFrame 1.7 will have been released and may include some features not present in the beta version.

In this chapter, we've discussed the concepts and techniques that you can use to design and maintain a successful WinFrame-based remote access implementation in your enterprise network, including performance considerations and integration with your existing infrastructure. In the next chapter, we'll discuss tools you can use to tune performance on any of the NT servers throughout your enterprise.

PART V

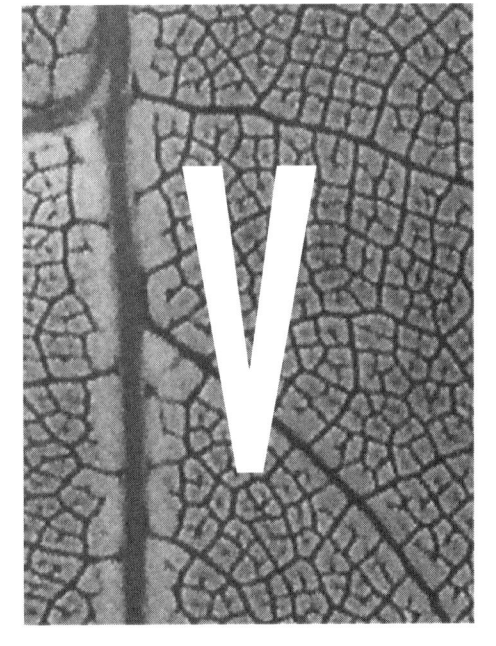

MANAGING THE NT ENTERPRISE NETWORK

CHAPTER 15

Performance Tuning and Optimization

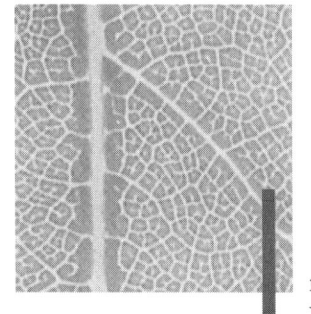
In Chapters 1 through 14 of this book, we have presented Microsoft Windows NT through the thoughts and words of design engineers. We'll continue in this spirit as we present our final chapter—on performance tuning and optimization. This chapter is designed to provide you with the necessary tools to evaluate areas of inefficiency and to remedy these situations through a logical process that conforms to all of the principles presented.

The principles and tools that produce high performance Windows NT enterprise networks include:

- A fundamental approach to performance tuning
- Performance tuning techniques
- Performance optimization techniques
- The task manager
- The performance monitor

This isn't so much of a "How to" guide, as it is a "What do" guide. In other words...

"The WAN engineers are screaming on the telephone that my Windows NT environment is clogging the network with MAILSLOT:BROWSE packets. *What do* I do to resolve this?"

If this sounds familiar, then we have no doubt this chapter will be of interest.

The Fundamentals of Performance Tuning

A solid plan for performance tuning and optimization begins with the basics. In the next two sections, we will explore the fundamental concepts by defining exactly what performance tuning is and, just as important, what it is not.

What Performance Tuning Is

We strongly believe that performance tuning begins in the earliest phases of network design. Truth be told, we have already covered the foundation of what constitutes a high-performance Windows NT network. When we discuss the principles of design—domain design, platform design, net design, and remote access—we do so in the spirit of performance and efficiency. The result is that our systems are built from the start to handle our business requirements. As such, when we tune for performance, we deal in small, incremental changes: the tweaking of a registry setting dealing with browsing or the adjustment of the size of the paging file. These tasks are examples of performance tuning, because they are operations that *maximize the performance of resources currently available.*

What Performance Tuning Is Not

Adding a second processor to a single processor system or adding one-half of a gig of memory does not constitute performance tuning. That is a *system upgrade* and, if conducted in the initial stages of implementation, is indicative of a misinterpretation of the demand for resources. We may need to go back to the business requirement phase of planning, discussed in Chapter 3, and the capacity planning phase, discussed in Chapter 5, to find out where we may have faltered.

If you find yourself in this situation, you would be best served by identifying the cause of this discrepancy so that you can adjust appropriately for *all* devices in the network. Finding that the cause of poor server performance is due to a business unit independently implementing a new imaging application is one thing. Discovering that this imaging application runs under the shared file model, is tied to the IPX/SPX protocol, must installed on a domain controller, and mandates that clients use Novell's IntranetWare Client for Windows NT, brings a different view to this issue. This example shows why it is important to wholly identify the cause of the discrepancy, so that you can subsequently identify all aspects of the network that may be affected.

The flow of commerce does not stop just because you are implementing a new enterprise network. Changes, such as the example of implementing a new imaging application just cited, can and will occur in the course of instituting a design. The only thing we can guarantee is that these changes will come at the worst possible time and be totally unexpected. Communication among members of the business community is going to be critical during the initial phases of deployment in order to reduce the impact that these impromptu changes have on your design.

In summary, major changes to a Windows NT server constitute a system upgrade, not a performance tuning measure. In the early stages of deployment, this is usually indicative of a change in the requirements of the business. This should be interpreted as a warning that the deployment process should halt long enough to identify the reason for the discrepancy between what was originally designed versus what is now required. This situation should not be handled as if it were a performance tuning event. The changes are neither small, nor incremental—characteristics which are normally associated with performance tuning.

In the sections that follow, we assume a basic understanding of the performance monitoring tools that accompany Windows NT: Task Manager and Performance Monitor. While we will discuss aspects of these tools, we won't cover their use and configuration in great depth. We recommend the *Microsoft Windows NT Resource Kit* (Microsoft Press) as a reference for those who would like additional information.

Where to Begin

When analyzing a system that is performing less than optimally, we need to first identify the bottleneck: that area of the system that is restricting the flow of bits with a negative impact on all other subsystems that follow. Those who have experienced the hunt for the elusive bottleneck soon discover that they never really locate it, as it always tends to be one step ahead of them. Our goal, then, is to move the bottleneck as close to the ends of our system as possible. In this location, it will be in contact with very few elements, so its impact will be lessened.

We invite you to examine with us those areas of a Windows NT system that are most often prone to bottlenecking. In the process, we'll examine the tools that will help you identify the cause of the bottleneck and the steps you'll need to follow to resolve it.

Inspecting Application Performance

One of the first things you'll need to inspect are the applications running on the Windows NT Server. In particular, you need to determine the characteristics

Zen and the Art of System Performance

When you get right down to the nitty-gritty details of system performance, you'll discover that it truly is a measure of perception. Our threshold for reasonable response time may be different than yours. If this is the case, then you may ask yourself, "If the system appears slow based on my perception, does that mean that the system really is slow?" The answer is yes—because perception is *truth*.

under which they are operating. A program that retains 40 percent of the total CPU time is going to have an impact on all others and therefore needs to be managed properly. The Windows NT Task Manager can assist you with your inspection.

Figure 15.1 provides a snapshot of the Windows NT Task Manager. We have selected the Processes tab and have enhanced the view to include most of the available counters. You can add or delete counters selecting View ≻ Select Columns from the menu.

FIGURE 15.1

The Windows NT Task Manager Processes tab

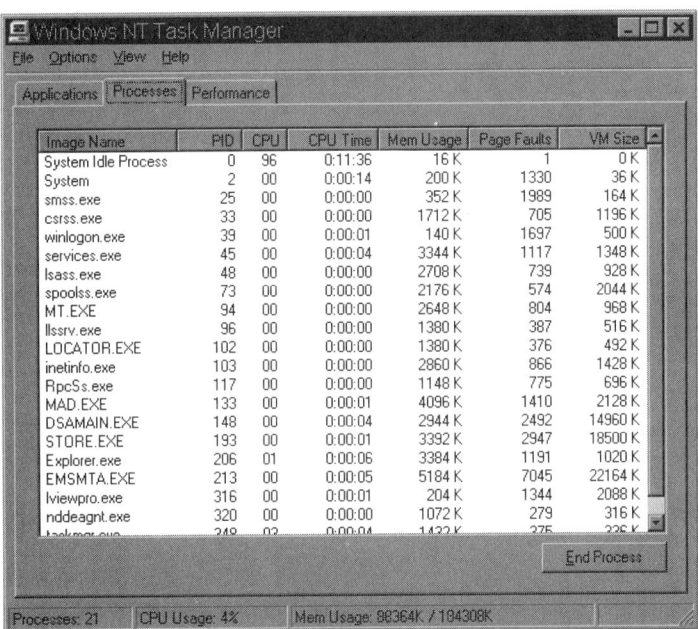

At the bottom of the Task Manager utility you'll notice a real-time view of total Processes, CPU Usage, and Memory Usage. The main window contains detailed information, including:

- **Image Name and PID:** The name of the image along with its process ID
- **CPU:** The percentage of CPU time that the process is utilizing
- **CPU Time:** The total time, since system initialization, that the process has been utilizing the CPU exclusively
- **Mem Usage:** The size of the working set for the process

Your objective in using this tool should be to identify those applications that heavily utilize system resources, especially memory and CPU time. Once identified, you'll need to determine whether they have a legitimate case for demanding those resources on the platform being inspected. If so, you'll need to upscale the platform as necessary to accommodate these applications.

If no legitimate reason can be given for the process's demand for system resources, then you'll need to determine an alternative course of action. This may include migrating the process to another platform or rescheduling the process to an off-peak time period.

Performance Tuning

At this point we are going to assume that you have an application with a legitimate reason for requesting the *lion's share* of resources from our system. This being the case, we'll explore a method for identifying, managing, and tuning this application to run efficiently on your system. We'll begin with nonpaged or physical *memory*, one of the areas most commonly addressed in performance tuning.

Memory

Windows NT has the ability to establish its nonpaged memory pool (physical memory, not including the virtual memory of the paging file) into one of four states. Each of these states uniquely characterizes the manner in which NT will allocate its nonpaged memory resources between network connections and applications. Identifying the state of the *server service* is one of the first items on your agenda when you suspect that the system may be lacking memory. Figure 15.2 shows the view of our system when we are examining the properties of the server service.

FIGURE 15.2

The server service properties

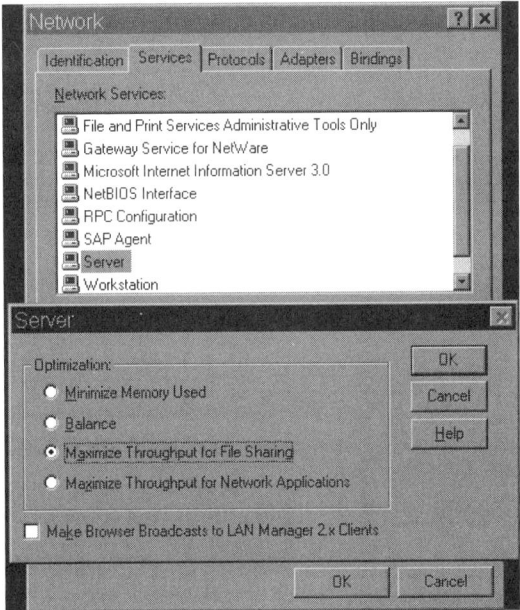

Let's examine each of the Server Service Properties in detail.

- **Minimize Memory Used:** Places the server service in a state where it will accommodate up to 10 simultaneous connections. While a *minimum* amount of memory is used for network connections, the majority is made available for applications.

- **Balance:** Supports up to 64 network connections.

- **Maximize Throughput for File Sharing (Default):** Supports over 64 network connections. Access to the file cache has a greater priority over user access to applications. This setting is best in instances where the server is primarily responsible for file sharing. It is counter-productive for servers running client/server applications, where the applications look to the server to manage their memory.

- **Maximize Throughput for Network Applications:** Supports over 64 network connections. Access to users' applications has priority over access to the file cache. Most effective in instances where the server is running a client/server application that passes responsibility for memory management onto the server platform where it resides.

To evaluate the state of memory further, turn to the Windows NT Performance Monitor. In particular you should focus on the objects and counters shown in Figure 15.3. Descriptions are included for each.

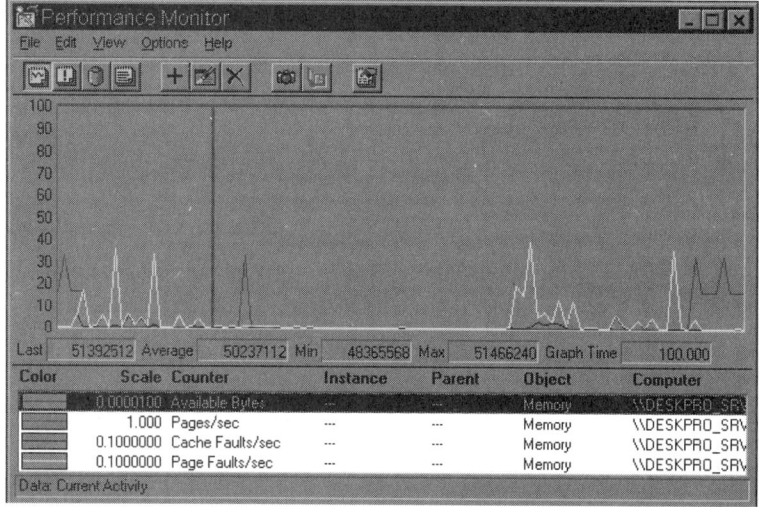

FIGURE 15.3

Evaluating nonpaged memory using Performance Monitor

Some of the pertinent objects and counters associated with memory tuning are as follows:

- **Memory: Available Bytes:** Displays the amount of free virtual memory, where the value should be greater than 1MB when the server service is set to Maximize Throughput for File Sharing or 4MB when the server service is configured to Maximize Throughput for Network Applications.

- **Memory: Pages/sec:** Number of pages read from or written to physical disk to resolve memory references that were not in nonpaged memory at the time of the reference. Look for instances where this value averages 10 or greater, while at the same time the Memory: Available Bytes counter continues to decrease. This is indicative of excessive paging due to insufficient memory. If both of these conditions are not met, meaning the Memory: Pages/sec averages 10 or greater, yet the Memory: Available Bytes counter is not decreasing, then you'll need to consider that the application is prone to excessive physical disk I/O. You may want to consider implementing a high performance RAID disk subsystem in order to meet the demands for information from the physical disk.

- **Memory: Cache Faults/sec** and **Memory: Page Faults/sec:** These counters are used for confirmation of whether your system needs additional memory. Look for instances where Memory: Page Faults/sec are greater than Memory: Cache Faults/sec. This, in conjunction with Memory: Pages/sec greater than 10, indicates that the system is paging excessively. The solution to this problem is to add additional memory.

Formulas abound detailing the ways and means of determining how much memory to add to a system that is undersized. We pondered whether to present a formula in this section and decided to forego it. Our decision is based on our experience that most clients determine how much memory they will add into a system based on the following criteria:

- The number of available free memory slots

- The current price per MB of RAM

- The next logical increment (usually in 128MB steps)

We also recommend that consideration be given to enhancing the size of the secondary cache (the L2 cache) at the same time as adding additional memory. This recommendation is based on the new demands being placed on the L2 cache, in particular its requirement of having to now map to a larger nonpaged memory area. This results in fewer instances where it will be able to immediately service the microprocessor out of its cache. This forces the microprocessor to wait while the L2 cache obtains the memory reference from nonpaged memory. It should come as no surprise that if the microprocessor is waiting, then everyone is waiting! L2 cache upgrades usually come in 256KB and 512KB increments.

Processor

Processor utilization is certainly a consideration for the engineer evaluating the performance of a system. We tend to favor the use of the Performance Monitor utility for this evaluation, focusing on the counters shown in Figure 15.4.

A description for our recommended counters follows:

- **Processor: %Processor Time [Instance]:** Monitor instances where the processor averages above 55 percent of its time servicing applications. This is usually indicative of a processor bottleneck. Schedule time to maintain this monitoring effort. Experience has shown that there tends to be an influx of applications that find their way onto Windows NT Servers over time.

FIGURE 15.4

Evaluating processor performance with the Performance Monitor

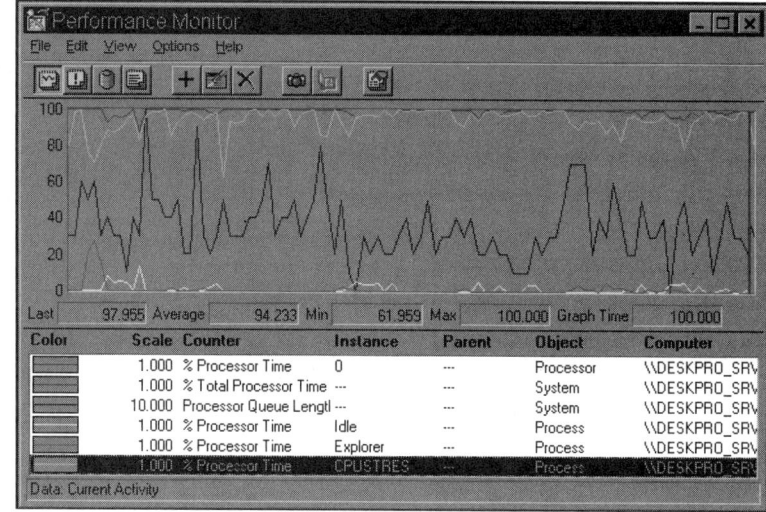

- **System: %Total Processor Time:** Useful for monitoring multiprocessor systems.

- **System: Processor Queue Length:** Instantaneous length of the processor queue, in units of threads. Threads that are currently executing are not counted. Only one queue is used, regardless of whether the system is single- or multiprocessor. A value greater than 2 is usually indicative of processor congestion.

- **Process: %Processor Time [Instance]:** Useful for monitoring individual processes in order to determine which is placing the greatest strain on the processor. In Figure 15.4, we are capturing *Idle* time, the Windows NT *Explorer,* and a utility designed to stress the CPU, called *CPUSTRES.* You'll notice that the utility CPUSTRES is grabbing an average of 94.2 percent of the processor's time.

When you have determined that a processor bottleneck is occurring, the question most often asked is, "Should I add an additional microprocessor or replace the existing CPU with one that is faster?"

In most instances, it is beneficial to add an additional microprocessor (scale horizontally) if the system is running a CPU-intensive, client/server database application. This strategy takes advantage of the SMP architecture that is an integral part of Windows NT.

In a case where the system is primarily responsible for file sharing, then the greatest benefit can be derived by replacing the existing microprocessor with a faster variant (scale vertically).

Physical Disk

We would be remiss if we did not include a section on disk performance. This area is slowly overtaking memory as the most common part of the system that becomes bottlenecked. We attribute this to the development of a richer set of database applications that are being asked to run on disk subsystem technology that has been around since God was a kid. (Well...we're sure you get the point.) Please refer to Figure 15.5 for a view of the counters pertinent to disk performance.

Windows NT requires that the counters for physical disk performance be initialized outside of the performance monitor utility. This is accomplished by issuing a **diskperf -y** at the Windows NT command prompt. The counters will be started the next time the system reboots. Once statistics are gathered, a **diskperf -n** should be issued. This will eliminate any overhead that may occur as a result of running these counters.

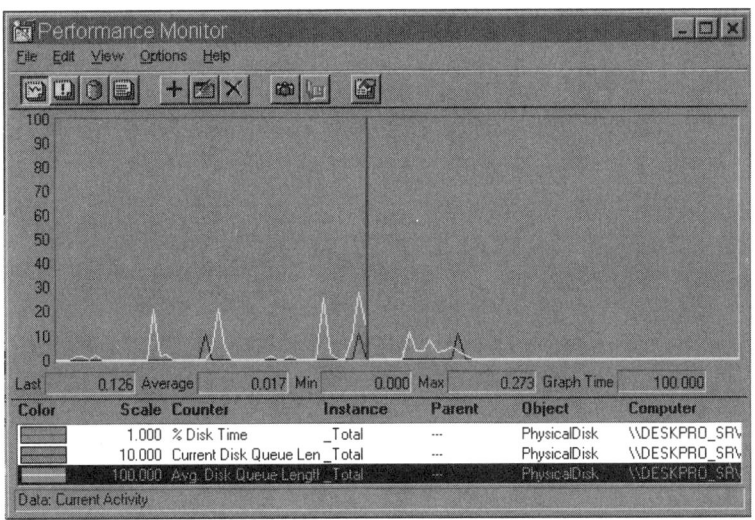

FIGURE 15.5

Evaluating disk performance

The physical disk objects and counters that we recommend monitoring are described below:

- **Physical Disk: %Disk Time [Instance]:** Measures the percentage of time that the physical disk is actively servicing read/write requests. The _Total instance provides information for all physical disks, otherwise each disk may be selected on an instance by instance basis. Any value above 65 percent should be cause for concern, indicating that the physical disk is a bottleneck in the system.

- **Physical Disk: Current Disk Queue Length [Instance]:** Measures the current number of read/write requests that are queued. The _Total instance provides information for all physical disks, otherwise each disk may be selected on an instance-by-instance basis. Observing this counter is useful if you suspect that access to your disk subsystem occurs in bursts. This value should not exceed 2 at any point in time.

- **Physical Disk: Avg. Disk Queue Length [Instance]:** Measures the average number of read/write requests that were queued during the sample period. The _Total instance provides information for all physical disks, otherwise each disk may be selected on an instance-by-instance basis. As is the case with the Current Disk Queue Length counter, this value should never be greater than 2.

The solution to resolving disk I/O bottlenecks can be found in comparing the technology that is currently within the system to what is emerging in the marketplace.

Evaluate your disks and controllers, IDE, EIDE, SCSI, SCSI-II, and Ultra-Wide-SCSI (in increasing order of performance). Controllers come in bus mastering (where the disk I/O operations are off-loaded from the microprocessor to the controller) and non-bus mastering variants. Most controllers also have an onboard cache that ranges from 4 to 32MB. The risk is low that data will be lost with caching controllers, as long as there is sufficient battery backup.

Consider the bus architecture that exists within the system. A PCI-based controller will provide better throughput than an ISA- or EISA-based controller.

Another option is to evaluate high performance disk subsystems from third-party providers. EMC, Storage Dimensions, and Stream Logic are vendors that span the cost/performance spectrum.

Optimization

When we use the term *optimization,* we are referring to the process of tuning our system proactively. Arguably, most of the default settings within Windows NT enable it to perform at an acceptable level in the majority of instances. Nevertheless there are a few areas that are worth a closer look. This portion of the chapter is devoted to those areas. We certainly don't recommend that any of these changes be made until ample time has passed to allow the network to settle down after implementation. Then after a reasonable period of monitoring, you may wish to experiment with some of these settings.

This is the place where we are supposed to insert the apocalyptic warning about making changes to the registry without first creating a backup. We're confident that you've been warned enough times about how it is harmful to your health, career, and social status, so we'll forego the extra verbiage.

Domain Controller Replication

The NetLogon service uses a 128KB buffer, by default, for replicating SAM database information between the PDC and BDC. In instances where the network is connected by low speed links (less than or equal to 64KB), it may be beneficial to reduce the size of this buffer.

Changes need to be made in the registry to the following keys, for instances where TCP/IP is the wide area networking protocol of choice:

- HKEY_LOCAL_MACHINE\SYSTEM\CurrentControlSet\Services\NetLogon\Parameters

- HKEY_LOCAL_MACHINE\SYSTEM\CurrentControlSet\Services\Tcpip\Parameters

You'll need to add the value shown in Table 15.1.

TABLE 15.1 Adjusting PDC/BDC Synchronization	Parameter	Type	Value
	ReplicationGovernor	REG_DWORD	0 to 100

This value holds a double meaning, indicating the percentage of the 128KB buffer that is used as well as the percentage of time that a replication request can be outstanding on the network. For example, a value of 50 refers to a 64KB buffer with an outstanding wait time of no more than 50 percent. A value of 25 refers to a 32KB buffer with an outstanding wait time of no more than 25 percent.

Browser Services

As mentioned in our introduction to this chapter, nothing eats up more wide-area bandwidth than the Windows NT browser service. As hungry as this service is, there are ways for us to control its appetite for our network resources.

Browser Synchronization Synchronization between the Domain Master Browsers and Master Browsers occurs every 12 minutes by default! It's difficult to justify this frequency on our Windows NT Servers, when chances are they aren't changing state or services all that often.

This default 12-minute update can be adjusted with the following key:

- HKEY_LOCAL_MACHINE\SYSTEM\CurrentControlSet\Services\Browser\Parameters

You will need to change the value shown in Table 15.2.

TABLE 15.2 Adjusting Browser Replication

Parameter	Type	Value (in seconds)
MasterPeriodicity	REG_DWORD	300 to 4,294,967

On average we set this value to two hours (7,200). This is set for every Windows NT Server within the enterprise network, as they all have the potential to become a master browser.

Browser Announcements Another area of consideration is the browser announcement cycle built into every Windows NT system. NT Workstations and Servers alike will announce themselves to a Browse Master on a 4-minute default cycle. This ensures that the most accurate depiction of devices and their shares are available. If bandwidth is more of a concern than accuracy (especially in installations where the nodes are not constantly changing states or services), you may wish to adjust the following parameter.

- HKEY_LOCAL_MACHINE\SYSTEM\CurrentControlSet\Services\LanmanServer\Parameters

You will need to change the value shown in Table 15.3.

TABLE 15.3 Adjusting Announcements

Parameter	Type	Value (in seconds)
Announce	REG_DWORD	1 to 65,535

You will need to determine the best value for these announcements within your own network, based on your perception of the frequency of change of the nodes and the shares that they advertise.

Please be aware of which protocols are being utilized within your network, and take care to include only those that are necessary. As you may recall from Chapter 4, a browser election occurs for every transport protocol that exists within the network. Announcements occur for each transport protocol within the network. By reducing the number of transport protocols, you reduce the number of announcements.

Print Services Windows NT nodes that share printers will continually announce their availability to other print servers on a 10-minute cycle. This occurs through the printer browse thread. In truth, these announcements aren't necessary once an ample period of time has been allowed for all devices to add the print share to their local printer list. Once this occurs, you can disable the printer browse thread on all those devices with printers to share. This will reduce the amount of browse traffic that the service generates:

- HKEY_LOCAL_MACHINE\SYSTEM\CurrentControlSet\Control\Print

You will need to add the value shown in Table 15.4.

TABLE 15.4 Disabling Print Services Announcements

Parameter	Type	Value
DisableServerThread	REG_DWORD	1

The change to disable the print browse thread will not occur until the next time the system is restarted. Please keep in mind that if an additional printer is added, or the existing one(s) changed, you will want to restart the service so that all nodes within the Windows NT network will have a chance to update their print list with these changes. After allowing a reasonable time period for this update to occur, you can go back and disable the print browse thread.

In summarizing this chapter, we would like to bring your attention to the manner in which we presented performance tuning and optimization. We chose to take a different tack than most, in that we did not immediately dive into the intricate details of establishing objects and counters within the Windows NT performance monitor. Nor did we choose to inundate the reader with secret views of the Windows NT registry, where the golden keys of performance tuning are kept. Instead, we chose to present a logical process for identifying and resolving performance issues.

We believe that most performance problems can be untangled using this approach. Digging too deeply, too quickly, into the bowels of Windows NT only tends to muddy the waters of our main objective—getting the server back to a *perceived* (perception is truth!) state of high performance. We encourage you to give this approach a try. We feel confident that you will be pleased with the results.

APPENDICES

APPENDIX A

The Future of NT

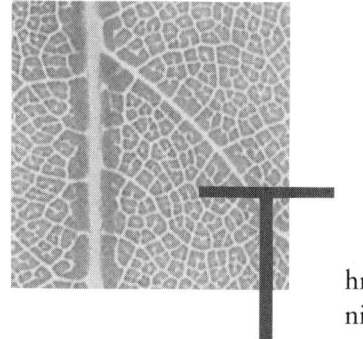

Throughout this book we've talked about the concepts, techniques, and tools that you'll use in all aspects of your enterprise network design. We've discussed how to design efficient domain structures, how to integrate NT into existing networks, how to use NT in an Internet, intranet, or extranet scenario, and how to design efficient remote access implementations.

By this point in, we've said all that we're going to say about NT's past and present. Now we're going to peer into the crystal ball to look at the future of NT. Fortunately for us, Microsoft has made no secret about where they plan to take NT, so you won't read any outrageous predictions.

Our intention is to provide you with some food for thought. By understanding the direction Microsoft has planned for Windows NT in the future, you can be a more effective network designer today.

In this appendix we will discuss:

- The future: NT 5
- Microsoft Active Directory
- Hydra
- The Zero Administration Initiative
- Routing and Remote Access Service
- Wolfpack Clustering Technology

The Future: NT 5

For the past several years, Microsoft has been promising the release of its super network operating system, code-named "Cairo." First spoken of with the release of NT 3.5, Cairo promised to provide better integration with Novell Netware than the NT 3.5 release. With NT 3.51 better NetWare integration was delivered, but 3.51 was not Cairo. Microsoft representatives promised that when the real Cairo was released we would know it. The real Cairo would deliver the Windows 95 user interface and would support storage restrictions on a per user basis. Then Microsoft released version 4.0 of Windows NT Server, which incidentally was not Cairo either. Oh, no, we were informed, although we now had the Windows 95 user interface, this version of NT was not Cairo. Cairo would provide a directory service, and Cairo would provide server mirroring.

When Microsoft announced server mirroring as a separate product codename "Wolfpack," most of us stood up and yelled, "What the heck is going on here? Is there really such a product as Cairo?"

In early 1997 Microsoft announced that they were dropping development of the Cairo network operating system. Instead, Cairo would be released as a series of technologies rather than a comprehensive network operating system. No kidding.

In light of this announcement, Microsoft proclaimed that their next generation network operating system would be known as Windows NT 5. Whether or not we view Windows NT 5 as the *real* Cairo there is no doubt that its release will be preceded by an entourage of leading edge technologies, like Wolfpack, Hydra, and Routing and Remote Access Service—to say nothing of a much-awaited enterprise directory service!

Active Directory

The Microsoft Active Directory is the most anticipated component of the NT 5 release. Through this service we can rid ourselves of domain modeling as we know it. Please notice we've purposely said *as we know it*, because the term domain still remains, although the meaning has changed. But wait, we're getting ahead of ourselves. Let's back up and introduce the characteristics of Active Directory.

The Microsoft Active Directory is composed of the following:

- DNS, X.500, and LDAP standards

- Hierarchical namespace

- Performance and scalability through partitioning
- Fault tolerance through multi-master replication
- Dynamically extensible schema
- Online backup and restore capabilities
- Open and extensible directory synchronization interfaces

The Active Directory can be viewed as having two components, one *physical* and the other *logical*. Both work cooperatively to provide a service that maps closely to the physical network infrastructure, while avoiding having that physical mapping determine the logical presentation of resources.

Site Structure

Sites are the physical organization of servers that provide performance and fault tolerance for the logical directory. It's important for us to recognize that the site is structured independently of the directory itself. Essentially, we are trying to group together server resources and the frequent users of those resources. In doing so we will need to keep aware of our network infrastructure, such that we do not separate users and resources by communications links that are incapable of supporting the requests for those resources. Figure A.1 illustrates a sample site configuration.

We have crafted sites around three locations, each interconnected to the other. Within the United States we have established sites in California and Rhode Island. Our third site is located in the European Community, in Italy. In Rhode Island we have Sales, Human Resources, Marketing, Engineering and Corporate Administration servers, with a similar configuration in Italy. In California we have servers established for Sales and Engineering only.

These sites are brought to life through the installation of a *Domain Controller Service* (yes, Service is correct), onto at least one of the servers within each site. These servers will then point to one another across sites, establishing a secure channel for replication of the directory. We'll have the opportunity to install the domain controller service onto additional servers in order to provide a measure of fault tolerance. All servers that are running the domain controller service will be interconnected into a spanning tree, providing integrity to the site configuration.

FIGURE A.1

A Windows NT 5 site configuration

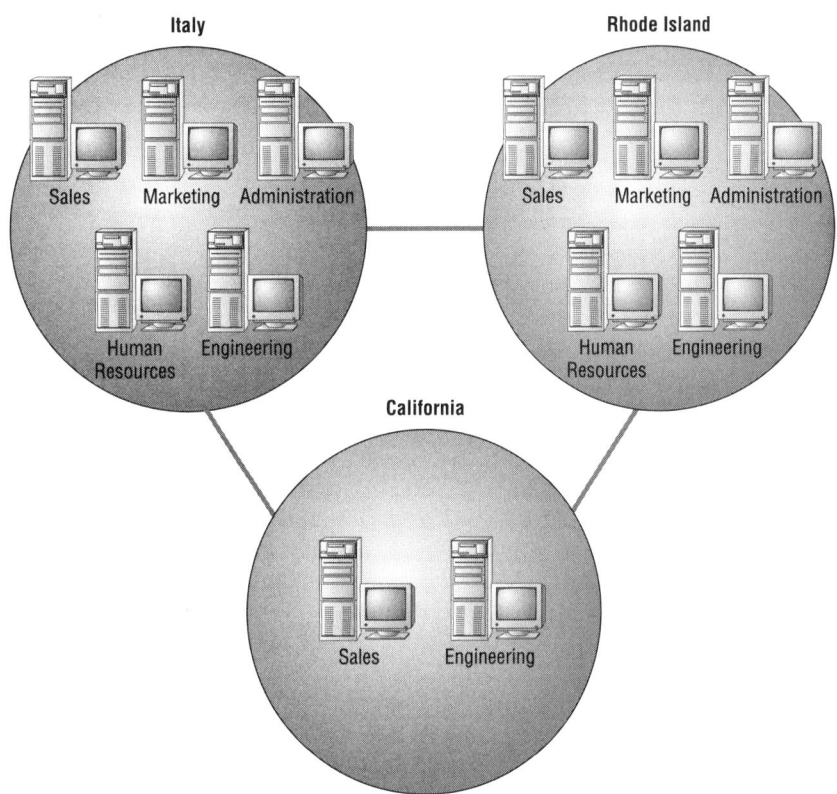

The replication services built into the Active Directory are much richer than what we've become used to in previous versions of NT. Active Directory supports multi-master replication, which allows us the opportunity to make changes to directory objects from any domain controller, not just the primary one. Changes will be propagated to all other domain controllers directly from the source where the modifications were made.

Directory Structure

With our site structure in place, we can begin to build our Active Directory. We will quickly recognize that this directory is constructed independent of the site configuration, and in most cases closely mirrors the organizational structure of the business. Figure A.2 provides a view of the Active Directory for the Capo di Monti winery. It's interesting to see how the directory structure is slightly different than our site configuration shown in Figure A.1.

FIGURE A.2

The Microsoft Active Directory configuration

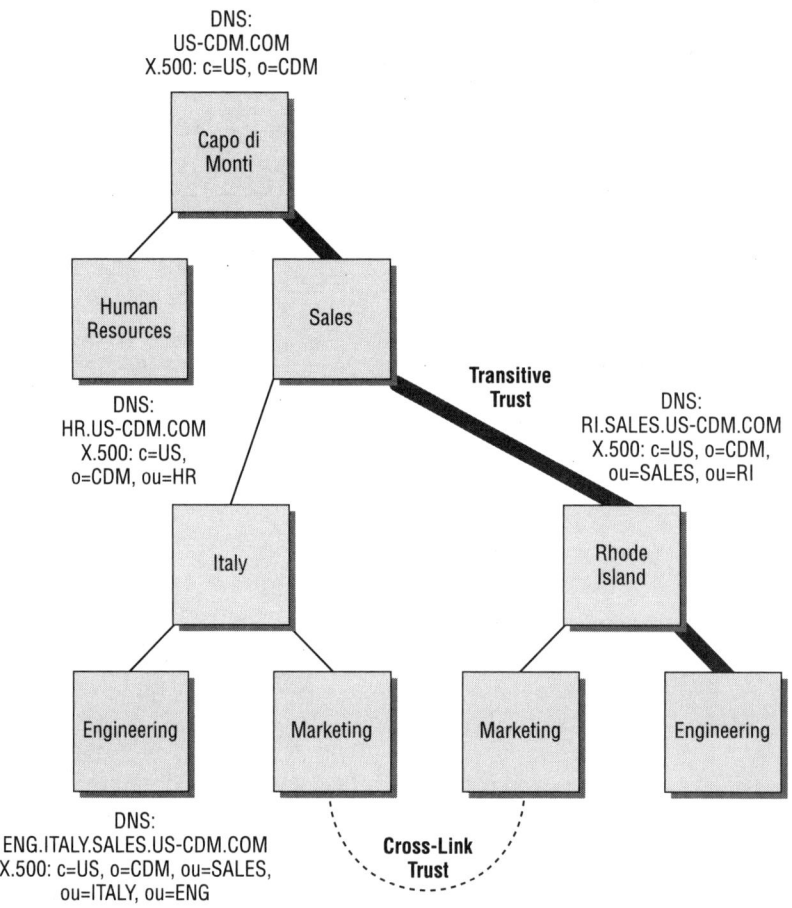

All sites in our example are brought together under nine *domains*. This decision was made based on assumptions regarding the nature of the business, as well as the desire for centralized administration. Within one of the domains—the Italy Engineering domain, for instance—we can establish an engineering *organization* along with several *organizational units*. These organizational units closely map to the departmental structure of our engineering business unit. Their role is to serve as containers for our user accounts and resource objects. Figure A.3 provides an expanded view of the engineering domain.

Like organizational units, domains are linked together through trusts. For the first time, Active Directory introduces the concept of *transitive trusts*. Transitive trusts will allow permissions to flow from one domain down through the

FIGURE A.3

The Microsoft Italy Engineering domain

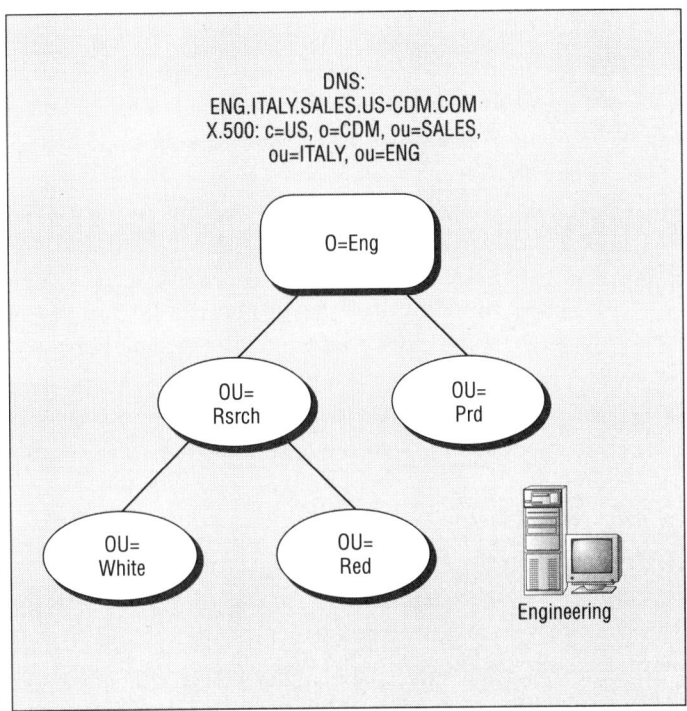

others, or from one organizational unit down through the others. In instances where the structure gets too deep, we can establish a cross-link trust between the low-lying components. The cross-link trust will enhance the performance of our directory by allowing requests to traverse this "shortcut," compared with the less direct route of having to walk up the tree and then down the alternate branch. Take another look at Figure A.2 for an illustration of transitive and cross-link trusts. You'll notice that a cross-link trust has been established between the marketing domains.

The Active Directory will adhere to DNS and X.500 conventions for name space. In our example, the top level domain name for DNS is US-CDM, while the top level name for X.500 is c=US, o=CDM. By referring back to Figure A.2, you'll be able to trace through the domain to view the remainder of the name space hierarchy.

NOTE We encourage you to compare the naming standards used in this example to those that were presented in Chapter 4. You may find it interesting that we were able to easily migrate our standards to the Active Directory name space.

Microsoft has a view of the future where we'll be able to pick up the entire domain we just presented and snap it into a standardized Global Active Directory. This Global Active Directory will be constructed entirely of domains—domains that may or may not be part of your company. All of the concepts we've presented will still be valid. Transitive trusts and cross-link trusts will still exist within the Global Active Directory. For instance, you may wish to establish a cross-link trust between your company's domain and a corporate domain that handles financing, or perhaps a domain belonging to the federal government. Then again, maybe not.

Administration

Administration of the Active Directory will occur through a new utility known as the Microsoft Management Console (described in detail later in this appendix). This utility will handle management of domains, users, groups, policies, servers, and workstations. The Active Directory is designed with an extensible schema, so in the future we'll be able to manage additional directory objects as well.

Renaming and moving of domains, domain controllers, and servers will be possible through the MMC. The promise is that all of this will occur without the need to reinstall the operating system. Finally!

The Microsoft Active Directory is promising to provide all that designers and administrators have been hoping for since first encountering the limitations of the domain architecture from which NT 4 takes its structure. By building on DNS and X.500, Microsoft hopes to establish the perception that they have designed a global directory structure built on open rather than proprietary, standards. Time will tell whether in this case perception really is truth.

Hydra

"Hydra" is the code name for the multi-user technology that Microsoft is developing (in conjunction with Citrix) to be released as an extension to Windows NT. As we discussed in Chapter 14, this technology will enable users of Windows-based terminals to use the Windows interface to access computing and data resources located on a NT-based server.

Hydra is but one of Microsoft's technologies for reducing the total cost of ownership for Windows-based systems. It is composed of three components: the Hydra server, the communications protocol, and the Hydra client. The Hydra server is, in most respects, similar to an NT server. It features the NT 4 interface (unlike Citrix Winframe which utilizes the NT 3.51 interface) as well as most of the NT 4 applications.

In a Hydra scenario, all applications and data are stored centrally on the Hydra server. Software and application upgrades occur directly on the server; no upgrades need to be performed on the users' workstations because users are accessing the server directly. When the user runs an application, the application runs on the server itself. By centralizing all processing and administration, many organizations can lower the cost to deploy new applications and to support existing ones.

Microsoft intends to use the T.120 remote protocol for all Hydra server-to-client communications. T.120 is a family of standards that define real-time, multipoint data communications that Microsoft has already utilized in their NetMeeting conferencing software. T.120 supports a wide variety of lower-layer network protocols and topologies and was designed to be platform independent.

The Hydra client will be what Microsoft calls a *super-thin client*. They have chosen to use the *super thin* terminology to differentiate the technology from typical *thin client* applications where an NC (network computer) runs an extremely small operating system capable of running network-downloaded applications written in Java. The super-thin client contains virtually no operating system; instead it contains only the code necessary to establish and maintain a communication session with the Hydra server. While a thin client may be subject to upgrade and maintenance requirements, the super-thin client never requires updates because it contains no operating system code.

 On a thin client, processing typically occurs on the client workstation; with Hydra technology, all processing occurs on the Hydra server itself. The super-thin client displays screen output and transmits keyboard input only.

Because of its heavy use of Citrix Winframe technology, Hydra is expected to contain many of the same features we discussed at length in Chapter 14. With Hydra, administrators will gain the ability to deploy NT-based applications throughout their network to users of NT, Windows 95, Windows 3.x, Macintosh, and UNIX.

The Zero Administration Initiative

Another technology that Microsoft has championed to reduce the total cost of ownership for Windows systems is the *Zero Administration Initiative*. The Zero Administration Initiative is an umbrella term for a number of features and products that Microsoft has already released, and plans to release, in upcoming revisions of Windows NT.

The goal of the Zero Administration Initiative is to extend the level of control for Windows network administrators so that they can more effectively manage their installed base of users and workstations. By equipping administrators with more efficient tools and methodologies for installing and maintaining their Windows workstations and applications, the amount of time required for managing end-user problems can be reduced, thereby reducing the cost of ownership for those systems. The tools that evolve out of the initiative may be in the areas of software distribution, configuration management, centralized administration, or update control.

The Zero Adminstration Kit

The Zero Administration Kit was the first of the Zero Administration Initiative technologies to be released. The kit is a collection of tools and methodologies that network administrators can utilize to simplify the end-user experience for users who don't have a lot of operating system and application experience.

By using existing Windows NT and Windows 95 components, such as user profiles and system policies, administrators can gain a very high level of control over the end user's Desktop. Elements such as the Run command, the Control Panel, and the Start menu can be eliminated or modified so that users cannot make configuration changes that could potentially cause their workstation to fail to operate properly.

Removing potentially dangerous elements from the end-user's Desktop allows users to focus more on using their business applications to be productive rather than fiddling with their Control Panel.

Microsoft has identified two primary operating modes for workstations managed by the Zero Administration Kit: the TaskStation mode and the AppStation mode.

Microsoft recommends the TaskStation mode for end users with relatively little computer experience who are responsible for working with a single business application. When a workstation that has been configured for TaskStation mode first boots up, the end user's application automatically starts up. Normal operating system environment elements, such as other icons or the start menu, are hidden from the user. When the user wishes to shut their machine down, they simply exit the application.

The AppStation mode is more appropriate for users with moderate computer experience who have a small set of defined applications that they work with. When a workstation that has been configured for AppStation mode boots up, the user can select only those applications that have been defined by the administrator from a reduced version of the Start menu. Users have the ability to start any of their approved business applications from the Program group on the start menu, and any changes to the menu must be initiated by the network administrator.

The kit comes with a number of script files, templates, and executables to allow administrators to customize either of the operating modes to suit their organization's requirements.

IntelliMirror Technology

Another component of the Zero Administration Initiative that has been announced by Microsoft is called *IntelliMirror*. IntelliMirror is a caching and synchronization technology that will automatically store user-specific information, such as data, applications, and desktop-specific configuration settings, on a centralized server. When a user authenticates to the network, they can access their own personal data and configuration from any workstation.

Another benefit of IntelliMirror technology is that it provides network administrators with a single location for archiving and managing all of their users' data and workstation settings. If a user's workstation has a massive hardware failure, the administrator can simply connect a new workstation to the network for the user to access. All of the data, applications, and configuration settings will be available immediately to the user on the new system.

IntelliMirror will work not only with workstations that are connected full-time to a network, but also with users who may connect to the network on a more periodic basis, such as laptop computer users. When a laptop user returns to the network, IntelliMirror will automatically synchronize the contents of their laptop to the image of the laptop on the server.

Microsoft Management Console

A third component of the Zero Administration Initiative is the *Microsoft Management Console* (MMC). The purpose of the MMC is to provide a single, centralized console for management of any of a number of network components. Microsoft developers envisioned the console as an environment—not as a single application—in which small customized management applets (called *snap-ins*) would run. These snap-ins would provide the different functional elements of the NT Server environment, such as the Internet Information Server.

With all of the server management elements centralized under a single graphical interface, server administration should become a much easier task for network managers.

The MMC console (shown in Figure A.4) looks similar to the Windows Explorer application. The frame on the left contains a list of folders, with each folder representing a discrete management element. When an administrator selects one of the folders, the frame on the left will display configuration options, performance statistics, or diagnostic information.

Microsoft has plans to make a version of the MMC that will work on both Windows NT and Windows 95.

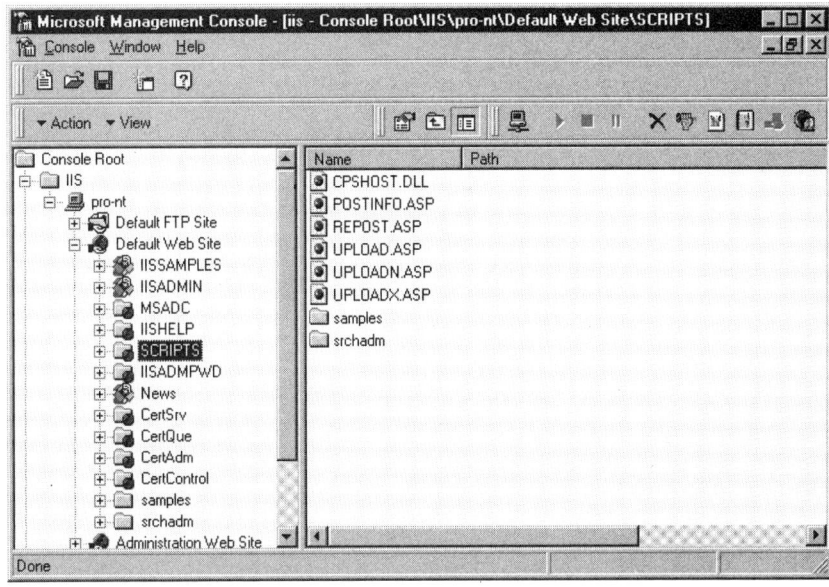

FIGURE A.4

The Microsoft Management Console graphical utility

Routing and Remote Access Service

The *Routing and Remote Access Service* (RRAS), formerly code-named "Steelhead," represents Microsoft's expansion into the enterprise, multiprotocol router market. Routing and Remote Access Service extends and unifies the functionality of two elements that were included with the NT Server 4 release—RAS, the remote access service, and the multiprotocol routing ability—both under a single administrative interface. In addition, RRAS includes a number of new features, such as support for demand-dial routing, RADIUS support, and enhanced PPTP. The Routing and RAS Admin graphical utility, shown in Figure A.5, provides a centralized point of administration for all of the features.

In addition to the Routing and RAS Admin utility, RRAS comes with a command-line configuration utility that can enable administrators to generate router configuration scripts which they can modify and transfer to other routers throughout their network.

FIGURE A.5

The Routing and RAS Admin utility

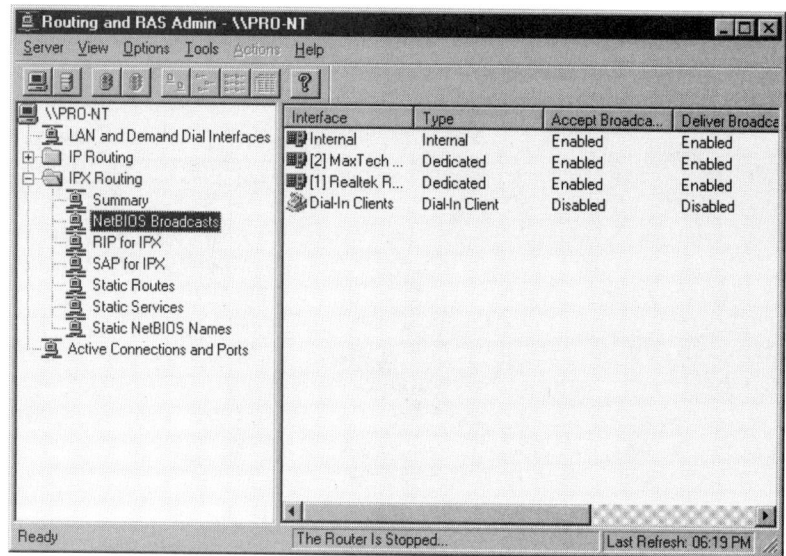

Microsoft has published a set of APIs in hopes that third-party developers will extend the functionality of RRAS to include support for additional protocols and additional management features.

Routing Protocol Support

While NT Server 4 included support for a few routing protocols, such as IPX Routing Information Protocol (RIP) and IP RIP version 1, RRAS includes support for two newer IP routing protocols—RIP version 2 and Open Shortest Path First (OSPF).

While the IPX and IP versions of the Routing Information Protocol (RIP) are different from one another, they are both based on a routing concept known as a *distance-vector algorithm*. Routers that use routing protocols based on a distance-vector algorithm make packet routing decisions based on updates received by their nearest neighbor routers. Periodically, these routers will broadcast information about the location of remote networks that they know about, including the distance to those networks. The distance between networks is normally measured in terms of *hops* (each router that a packet must pass through is considered a hop).

 Other protocols, such as the Open Shortest Path First Protocol, are called *link-state protocols,* because they maintain a table of the entire network, including the state of each router on the network. If a new router is added to the network, or if one fails, each router on the network transmits information to every other router on the network so that each one can calculate a new routing table. Link-state protocols are more network bandwidth efficient than distance-vector algorithms because they only transmit routing updates when a topology change occurs on the network instead of every 60 seconds or so.

Another supported routing feature is an enhanced relay agent for DHCP. As you remember, DHCP is a single-network broadcast protocol, and, as such, the requests by DHCP clients are not normally transmitted by routers to other segments. If both the DHCP client and server are connected to the same physical segment, this limitation is not a problem. However, if the client and the server are connected to different physical network segments, some mechanism (in this case the DHCP relay agent) is needed to propagate the DHCP requests to the remote DHCP server.

Demand-Dial Routing

One of the new features offered by RRAS is support for demand-dial routing. Demand-dial routing enables an administrator to define a dial-up routing interface that will only become active when the router receives packets that are addressed to the remote site defined within the interface. When RRAS detects these packets, it will initiate a dial-up connection to the remote site and transmit them. After a pre determined period of inactivity, the link will be terminated. Demand-dial routing can be a cost-effective alternative to leased-line or frame-relay connections between remote sites, particularly if the data transfer requirements between the sites are relatively small.

Microsoft has included a Demand-dial Interface Wizard to assist administrators in configuring new connections.

RAS Enhancements

Included with RRAS are a number of enhancements to Microsoft's already popular dial-up Remote Access Service (RAS).

As we discussed in Chapter 13, RAS is the NT service that handles remote-node dial-up access. The Routing and Remote Access Service manager utility replaces the previous RAS admin utility, so administrators can manage both their LAN-based routing functions and their dial-up remote access connections from a single point.

Routing and Remote Access Service (RRAS) also includes enhanced support for the Point-to-Point Tunneling Protocol (PPTP), which we discussed in Chapter 11. The version of RAS that shipped with NT Server 4 introduced support for PPTP over dial-up and LAN-based connections. This version allowed client workstations to connect to a RAS server and communicate securely through an encrypted session. However, PPTP support was limited only to client-to-server connections. In the Routing and Remote Access Service upgrade, Microsoft has included not only support for client-to-server connections, but also for server-to-server connections, so entire sites can connect to one another securely over a public network like the Internet.

Another new feature of the Remote Access Service is support for RADIUS authentication. With the version of RAS that shipped with NT Server 4, all users were forced to authenticate using account names and passwords from an NT domain accounts database. While this authentication method worked well for organizations that used NT as their only network operating system, it was less effective in organizations that used a variety of operating systems or organizations that had already developed a dial-in authentication infrastructure based on RADIUS.

The Remote Authentication Dial-In User Service (RADIUS) is a protocol that is designed to provide centralized authentication services for dial-in users. When users dial in to an organization's network, the remote access server will transmit the user's account name and password to a centralized RADIUS server, which will authenticate the user and will determine which services the user is authorized to access.

By combining the enhanced RAS functionality, along with support for multi-protocol routing and demand-dial connections, into a package that is available as a free download from their Web site (http://www.microsoft.com/ntserver), Microsoft has addressed the needs of small, mid-sized, and large organizations. While its routing abilities may not be on the scale of large, enterprise backbone routers, the Routing and Remote Access Service upgrade may become a popular alternative for dial-in and small-office routing applications.

Wolfpack Clustering Technology

Microsoft's Wolfpack makes its mark by offering the first clustering solution for Windows NT that is fully integrated into the operating system. Previous offerings for NT were often based upon proprietary hardware solutions (Marathon Technologies Endurance 4000) or third-party software add-ons (Vinca Standby Server and Octopus SASO).

The Wolfpack Concepts and Architecture

The first release of Wolfpack will adhere to the Phase 1 specification of Microsoft's phased approach to clustering for Windows NT Server:

- **Phase 1:** Automatic fail-over to the partner server. High availability is the major focus of this phase. A pair of servers will share a common disk subsystem. In the event of a server failure, the clustering software will reallocate the tasks (fail-over) to the active server. Whether or not the application and or client is aware of this fail-over is dependent upon the applications' support for the Microsoft clustering API's.

- **Phase 2:** High performance, load balancing, and availability through multinode clustering

Two NT servers will be interconnected in the interest of high performance and load balancing, as well as high availability. It is expected that over time this second phase will evolve to a third phase known as *massive parallelism*. In this third phase additional NT servers may be added to the cluster as the demands for processing power increase. Applications written to this distributed computing model will be able to take advantage of all NT servers within the cluster.

The current Wolfpack architecture (Beta 2), conforms to the phase 1 shared disk model. The cluster is built upon a pair of Windows NT Servers, version 4.0/SP3. These devices must share a SCSI bus that attaches to a common external disk subsystem. The server pair remains synchronized by monitoring each other using *heartbeat synchronization*. This communication can occur over the shared network or through a private Ethernet segment established between the server pair, known as the *server interconnect*. Figure A.6 illustrates the Wolfpack architecture.

FIGURE A.6

The Wolfpack architecture: Phase I

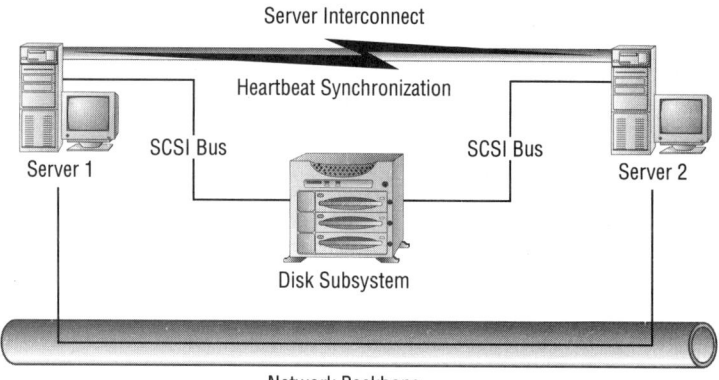

In the event of a resource or server failure, the *resource monitor* of the active server will determine through heartbeat synchronization that a resource on its partner server is no longer available, or, worse yet, that the entire server is no longer available. The *cluster service* will then take action based upon a pre-defined set of instructions. The action usually begins with a fail-over of NT resources and applications to the active server.

Which NT resources and applications fail-over is based upon the administrator predefining fail-over groups. The failure of a resource within the group will result in the entire group migrating to the active server. This ensures, for example, that if the License Logging service were to fail on one server, it would take all of the resources necessary to restart as it migrated over to the active server.

Whether or not this fail-over is transparent is dependent upon the application's ability to automatically restart. Microsoft's Internet Information Server meets the automatic restart criteria, while most current third-party products do not. This imbalance is bound to change as support for the clustering APIs is embraced by the development community.

Management of Wolfpack Clusters

The Cluster Administrator is the primary tool used to manage Wolfpack clusters for Microsoft Windows NT (see Figure A.7). We may run it from any NT server or workstation that is part of the cluster.

FIGURE A.7

The Wolfpack Cluster Administrator

The Cluster Administrator allows us to establish policies for failure detection and recovery. Additionally, we can manage NT services, file shares, and directory replication. Through this single utility, individual nodes can be brought into and out of the cluster for maintenance.

It's not unusual, during the monitoring of the NT cluster pair, to notice a disproportionate balance regarding the number of users connected to each server. Server 1, for example, may have 300 nodes attached to it, while Server 2 may only have 50. This discrepancy can be attributed to the lack of support for load balancing in phase 1 of the Wolfpack release. As a result, the clustered pair may perform less than optimally due to this imbalance.

Wolfpack takes us one step closer toward recognizing Windows NT Server as a platform capable of running mission-critical applications. Never the less, while high availability is a mandatory requirement, so is load balancing and high performance. If Wolfpack were to achieve the objectives of phase 2 prior to release, then we would certainly be a bit more excited over its arrival. Regardless of whether this occurs, we have confidence in the Wolfpack technology and look forward to the day when NT clustering will be commonplace within the enterprise.

APPENDIX B

The OSI Model

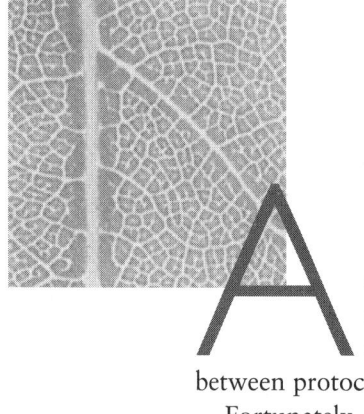As the number and types of networking protocols began to grow, it quickly became difficult for technologists to communicate with one another about the similarities and differences between protocols.

Fortunately, the *International Standards Organization* (ISO), an organization that determines international data communications standards, recognized the complexity of discussing network protocols and developed a tool called the *Open Systems Interconnection* (OSI) reference model. The OSI model is designed to assist the discussion of network protocols and technologies by providing a conceptual framework that can be applied to any type of data communication.

The Need for a Common Language

The goal of the ISO was to create a model that would enable users of different networks to discuss protocols using a common language. To create the model, the ISO distilled the elements common to all forms of network communication down to seven discrete functions. These functions became the seven layers of the OSI model. The ISO chose a layered approach that modeled the way data is manipulated during the communication process.

Within the OSI model, each layer describes a specific network activity (see Figure B.1). For example, the network layer is responsible for routing data between networks, while the physical layer describes the physical connections between nodes on a network.

It is important to remember that the OSI model is only a conceptual methodology used to describe the way computers communicate; it makes no attempt to dictate the rules for how communication is to be implemented (this is the job of protocols). By limiting itself to an abstract description of the functions, the

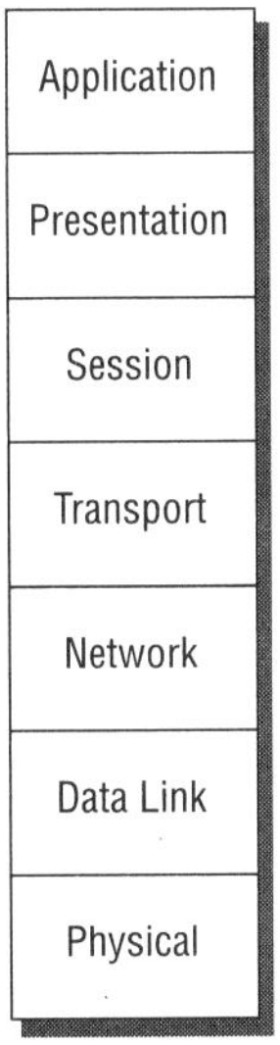

FIGURE B.1

The seven layers of the OSI model

| Application |
| Presentation |
| Session |
| Transport |
| Network |
| Data Link |
| Physical |

model creates a reference point that can be used to discuss particular implementations, each according to the functionality it provides.

The OSI layers are arranged hierarchically—each layer depends on the layers above and below it to provide data in a specific format, which it then processes and outputs to the next layer in the stack. The layer at the top of the hierarchy is the application layer; the lowest layer is the physical connections. As data is passed down through the layers, information is added to that data. Once the data is transmitted to another computer, it is then transferred back up through the layers.

The best way to illustrate this is to consider the processes that happen when an e-mail message is mailed to someone across the country. A user begins by typing a message into an e-mail application on his or her computer. The computer then translates the typed characters into a format it can understand. This data undergoes a series of translations that ultimately prepare it for transmission as a series of electrical impulses over a wire. Once those electrical impulses reach their destination, they are retranslated by the receiving computer into layers that can be read by a human. The e-mail message has traversed all the layers of the OSI model two times. It has gone down the layers at the sending end, and up the layers at the receiving end.

Encapsulation and Peer Communication

The two concepts critical to the OSI model are highlighted in Figure B.2. The first concept, *encapsulation*, describes the way data is modified as it travels from layer to layer. Each protocol within the layers adds information specific to its function to data it receives from previous layers. Some layers, like IP, may add a header to the data that contains IP-specific information, such as the destination or source address. In this way the data from the previous layer is encapsulated within the IP packet, which is then passed down to the next layer, until finally the data is encoded into a series of ones and zeros that are transmitted as electrical impulses across a network.

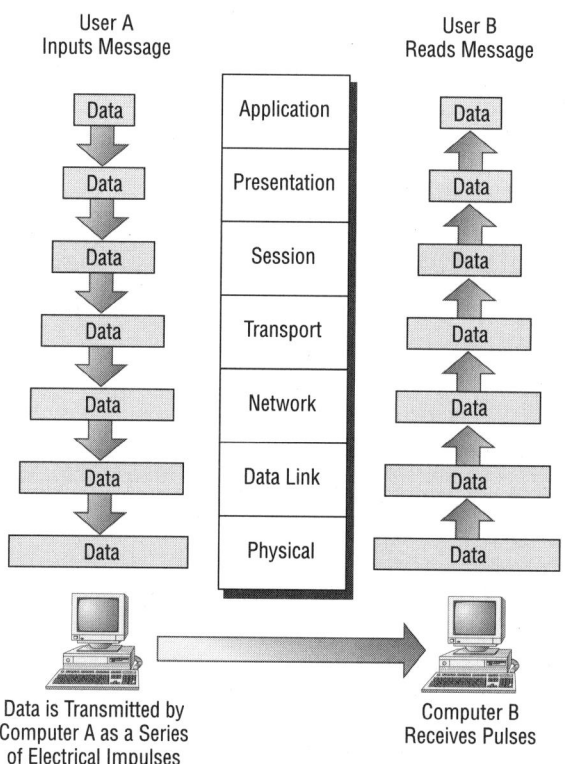

FIGURE B.2

Encapsulation is the process by which information to be transmitted over a network is converted into a data message.

Once a packet is received at the destination computer, the information goes up the layers. As it is passed up, each layer removes its portion of the data before it passes the information up to the next layer. The IP protocol on the receiving end removes the IP header and passes the packet to the higher-level protocols.

Encapsulation is a lot like the way an envelope is used to send a letter. The letter itself becomes encapsulated within the envelope. The outside of the envelope contains information such as the name and address of the recipient so the postal service can deliver the letter. When someone receives the letter, they decapsulate it by removing it from the envelope.

The second concept is *peer communication*. In any conversation between two computers, both computers need to use protocols that are compatible with one another. If you send a letter to someone in Microsoft Word format, that person needs to have a word processor that can read Word documents; otherwise the message will look like gibberish.

This concept also applies to lower-level protocols. If you are using a computer that utilizes the IP protocol as its network-layer protocol, you won't be able to communicate with people who are running IPX as their network-layer protocol, because the protocols are not compatible. For any successful network communication, the protocols in each of the layers must be compatible (see Figure B.3). Peer-layer protocols must be the same for any communication to work.

An OSI layer is similar to an organizational role within a corporation. Let's say Joe is the network administrator for Company, Inc. and he decides he doesn't like his job any more, so he quits. Company, Inc. then hires Rita to fill Joe's position—she becomes the new network administrator. Joe and Rita may not have anything in common other than their job; nevertheless they are both considered to be network administrators because during their time in the job they fulfill the same duties within the company. They both report to the vice president of operations, and they both manage the assistant network administrator.

If we compared Joe and Rita and their job to the OSI model, their position of network administrator would be considered a layer of the model and Joe and Rita themselves would be the protocols. The job description dictates the functions they need to fulfill, but each person may perform the job differently.

FIGURE B.3

The protocols that function at each layer on each computer (the peer layer) must be compatible for communication to be successful.

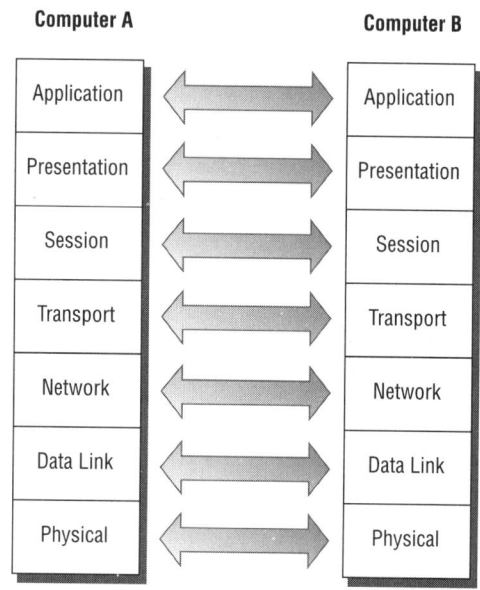

The Seven Layers of the OSI Model

Now that you have an idea of how the OSI reference model works, let's take a closer look at the individual layers of the model.

Starting from the bottom of the stack, the seven layers of the OSI model are the Physical layer, the Data Link layer, the Network layer, the Transport layer, the Session Layer, the Presentation layer, and the Application layer (see Figure B.4).

The Physical layer is the lowest layer of the model. It defines the physical characteristics of the hardware that carries the electrical transmissions of data. Specifications for voltage, electrical properties of the cable, and cable pinouts (the rules for which wire in a cable goes to which pin on a connector) are all included in the Physical layer. Some examples of Physical-layer standards are the IEEE 802 series and EIA-232D (an extension of RS-232, the standard that defines the electrical and mechanical specifications for connecting communication devices, such as modems, to computers).

FIGURE B.4

The OSI model and layer functionality

Layer	Function
Application	Provides Network Access to User and Applications
Presentation	Data Conversion
Session	Connection Establishment, Authentication
Transport	Data Integrity, Reliability
Network	Network Addressing, Routing
Data Link	Packet Creation, Transmission, and Reception
Physical	Defines Physical Characteristics of Communication Medium

The Institute of Electrical and Electronic Engineers (IEEE) is an organization that creates standards for telecommunications and networking. The 802 series of IEEE standards defines specifications for lower-layer network architectures such as Token Ring (802.5) and Ethernet (802.3).

The Data Link layer includes the processes for the creation, transmission, and reception of data packets. At this level, packets are considered *frames*. Frames are created according to the network architecture (such as Ethernet, ARCNET, and Token Ring) being used by the system. Each architecture requires its own unique frame type. Frames are addressed according to a hardware-defined address, called a MAC (*Media Access Control*) address. The MAC address is programmed into each network interface device by its manufacturer and generally cannot be changed by the end user. The value of the first portion of the MAC address is specific to each manufacturer; the value of the second portion of the MAC address is unique to each network interface card.

> **NOTE**
> A *frame* is an organized group of bits that act as the basic unit of communication for Data-Link-layer protocols. Frames contain information such as the source and destination addresses, frame type identifiers, and a data section that contains information passed down from higher-layer protocols. Network devices on a single segment must be configured to use identical frame types to communicate with one another.

Network architectures like Ethernet and Token Ring include both Physical-layer specifications and Data-Link-layer specifications. They do not include instructions for layers above the Data Link. Because the TCP/IP protocol suite is independent of the network architecture, we won't discuss these two layers in this book.

The Network layer specifies how addresses are determined on a network or internetwork. It also specifies how routes are discovered and how packets should travel to these routes. One additional function of the Network layer is the establishment and maintenance of logical connections between nodes. Two of the most widely used Network-layer protocols are IP and IPX (routing protocols). Network-layer addresses are defined in software by the individual protocols.

The Transport layer specifies how data integrity is maintained. It provides reliable communication in one of two forms—*connectionless* or *connection-oriented*. A connection-oriented communication session is one where a logical connection is established between the two end nodes. This connection may be a physical one, or it may only be a logical one. Data is then transferred in sequence until there is no more data to be sent, whereupon the Transport layer sends instructions to break the connection. In a connectionless communication, packets are sent independently of one another. Each packet contains a sequence number that the receiving end examines. Once the packets are received, they are reassembled according to this packet number.

Connectionless communications are seen in packet-switched environments. The TCP/IP protocol suite contains both connection-oriented and connectionless transport protocols—TCP and UDP, respectively. In NetWare, the SPX provides connection-oriented Transport-layer functionality.

Session-layer protocols are responsible for establishing connections, for authentication, and for maintaining the connection once it is established.

Presentation-layer protocols are responsible for converting data into appropriate forms for applications. There are few protocols that only provide

Presentation-layer functionality. Most of the functionality is handled by Session-layer or Application-layer protocols.

At the top of the OSI model is the Application layer. The Application layer is responsible for providing network access to the user and applications. Application-layer functionality is provided by both protocols and software. Some of these are FTP (file transfer protocol) and Telnet (a terminal emulation program).

Many of the higher-level protocols in the TCP/IP suite provide functionality from all three of the top layers.

APPENDIX C

Glossary

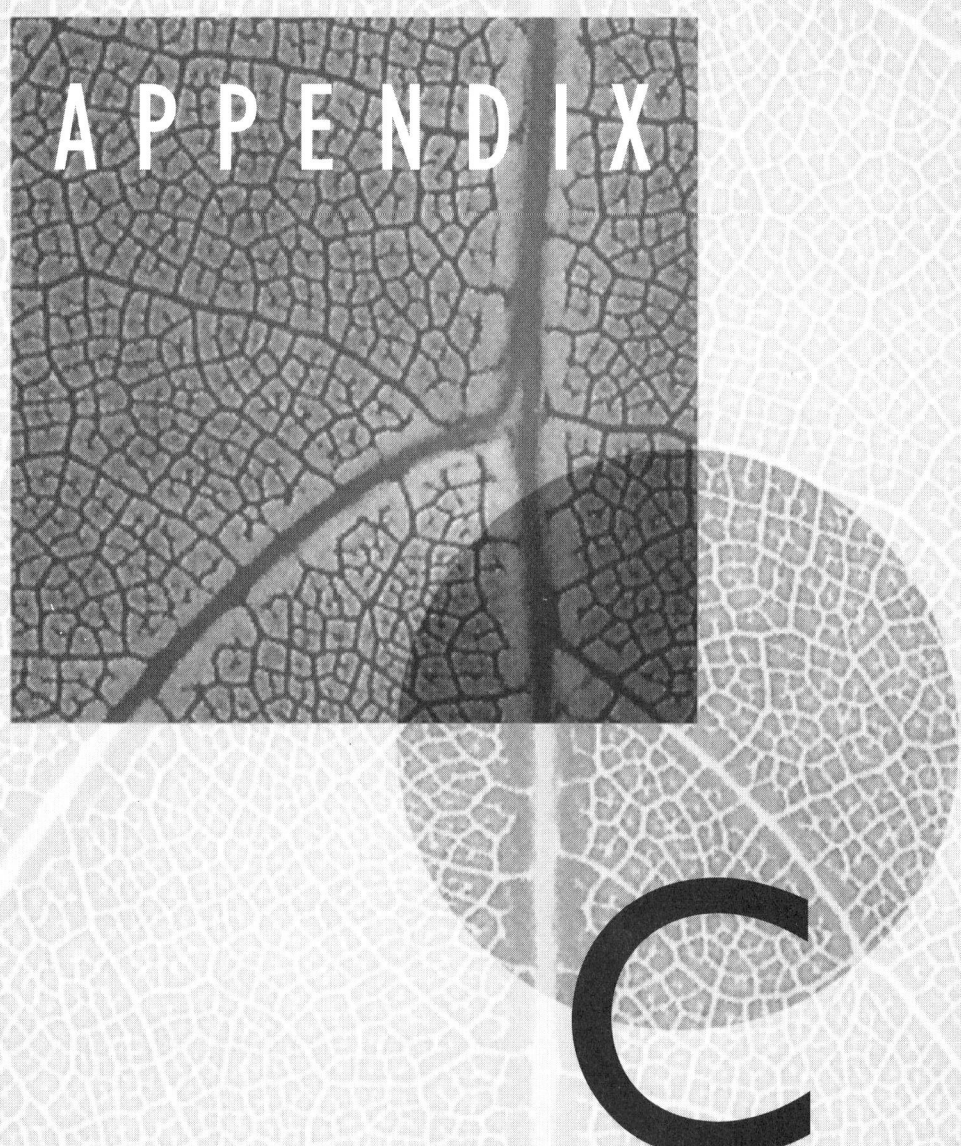

ActiveX A development framework, developed by Microsoft, that provides the equivalent of network Object Linking and Embedding (OLE) functionality.

API (Application Programmer Interface) An interface designed to allow programmers access to lower- or higher-level services by providing an intermediary layer that includes function calls to the services.

Application-level proxy A type of proxy in which security services are provided through the use of intermediate applications that have been specifically designed for a particular Internet service. For example, some firewall implementations provide an application-level proxy for HTTP traffic.

ARP (Address Resolution Protocol) The TCP/IP protocol that defines the mechanism for mapping a hardware MAC address to a software-defined IP address.

ARPAnet An experimental communications network created by the Department of Defense Advanced Research Projects Agency (DARPA), designed to improve communication between government agencies and to enable researchers to learn how to build networks that could withstand major disasters such as nuclear war or natural disasters. The ARPAnet would later become the Internet.

asymmetric multiprocessing A multiprocessing model in which a single processor is dedicated to supporting the operating system, while other processors may support peripheral systems, such as the disk or network subsystems. Some asymmetric multiprocessing systems support dedication of processors to individual subsystems, while others may distribute the processing load between them.

Backup Domain Controller (BDC) The Backup Domain Controller provides authentication services to a Windows NT network in the event of a failure of a Primary Domain Controller (PDC). In addition, Backup Domain Controllers can be deployed within a Windows NT network to assist in authentication services, thereby speeding up authentication response time.

bandwidth The term for the speed at which a network connection is capable of transmitting data, usually measured in bits per second (bps), kilobits per second (Kbps), or megabits per second (Mbps).

BIND (Berkeley Internet Name Domain) The most widely used Domain Name Service (DNS) server on the Internet.

bootp The Bootstrap protocol—a protocol developed to simplify IP address distribution to workstations. When a workstation that is configured to be a bootp client boots up, it broadcasts a request for its IP address to the network. The bootp server then examines the hardware address of the network interface and consults its database to determine if that system has already received an address. If so, the bootp server sends a response with the workstation's IP address. If the workstation has never received an address from the bootp server before, the server will select an address from a pool of available numbers.

certificate authority A trusted third-party organization that is used to verify the authenticity of a digital certificate. *See* digital certificate.

CGI (Common Gateway Interface) The standard that defines how a Web server may interact with other external applications and programs.

client The term used to describe a process or program that submits a request to a server in a client/server environment.

client/server The distribution of services and processing between a client and server element. Each is responsible for processing instructions based on its function, be it providing system services, as occurs at the Executive Services layer of Windows NT, or application services, as might occur when a Microsoft Exchange client communicates with an Exchange Server. The process usually begins when the client makes a Remote Procedure Call (RPC) to the server, instructing the server to begin its processing, and to only acknowledge the client once it has completed its task. Client/server is the antonym of *shared file*, whereby the majority of the processing occurs at the client, with the server constantly feeding the client information to sort through with the hope of finding the answer. The benefit of the client/server model is the reduction in the amount of communication traffic between the client and server elements. The detriment is the level of complexity that occurs in developing a model of this type.

compatibility The ability to operate on a variety of hardware platforms, communicate utilizing the most common transport protocols (TCP/IP and IPX/SPX), and interoperate with the leading network operating systems (Novell NetWare and UNIX). Consideration also needs to be given to the objective of being able to run both 32- and 16-bit applications designed for

DOS, Windows, OS/2, and POSIX. This characteristic of adaptability from the hardware to application layer is the definition of compatibility as applied to Windows NT.

connectionless   The term used to describe network protocols that begin communications without first establishing a logical, virtual connection between the two communicating nodes. Connectionless protocols do not provide guaranteed delivery. Normally, these guarantees are left up to higher-level protocols.

connection-oriented   The term used to describe network protocols that establish a logical connection between communicating nodes before the transmission of data begins.

context switching   The name for switching between the current task and dormant tasks in a multitasking environment.

cookie   A piece of information stored on a Web browser during a session with a Web server that may contain information such as the user's preferences, ordering information, or the number of times the user has visited that site.

current context   The name for the active task in a multitasking environment. Tasks other than the one currently running are considered to be *dormant*.

DARPA   (Department of Defense Advanced Research Projects Agency) The organization within the U.S. Department of Defense (DOD) that created the precursor to the Internet, the ARPAnet.

datagram   A basic unit of Internet Protocol (IP) activity. Datagrams contain a header, which includes a source and destination address as well as other IP control information, and a body, which contains data.

default gateway   The term for the router to which all traffic bound for other network segments will be forwarded unless another route is already known.

digital certificate   A digitally-signed electronic document that can be used to confirm the identity of the entity that possesses it. A digital certificate may contain information about a person or an organization, as well as a public encryption key.

distance vector algorithm   The algorithm used by RIP routers to develop routing tables. Based upon the notion of route costs and hop count, routers using a distance vector algorithm will always attempt to route traffic through the route with the lowest cost (usually the route that requires the data to pass through the least number of routers to reach its destination).

DNS (Domain Name Service) The TCP/IP standard developed to provide translation services for host names to IP addresses.

domain (NT) A logical, NetBIOS-named grouping of Windows NT clients and servers. The naming and establishment of a domain begins with the installation of a primary domain controller (PDC).

dual-homed host A host configured with two network interface cards, each connected to a different network. Dual-homed hosts are often used along with firewall software to provide network security.

Dynamic Host Configuration Protocol (DHCP) An IP address allocation protocol that enables hosts to obtain IP addressing information during network initialization. DHCP is similar to the bootstrap protocol (bootp) but it also includes the ability to reassign unused IP addresses after a predetermined time interval, as well as pass additional client configuration information beyond IP addressing. The DHCP standard includes backward compatibility for bootp clients.

encapsulation The term used to describe the process that data undergoes as it travels between functional layers of the OSI model. As data is passed from layer to layer, each software module adds information specific to its function to the data it received from the previous layer. Encapsulation is similar to the way a letter is placed in an envelope before it can be sent through the mail.

executive layer The executive layer is actually a set of objects working cooperatively as an interface between the system services and NT kernel. As requirements change, the object providing the service is the only one that needs to be updated. Objects requesting services can remain intact.

extensibility Flexibility in the Windows NT architecture such that it could adapt to the point where support for future microprocessor technology and hardware peripherals could be easily incorporated into the operating system.

extranet The term used to describe a meta-network that results from the linking of networks from multiple organizations.

firewall A mechanism or group of mechanisms designed to provide a single point of control to permit or deny the flow of traffic between networks.

flooding A process used by news servers to replicate news messages and groups to other servers.

FTP (File Transfer Protocol) A protocol within the TCP/IP family designed to provide file sharing and transfer services. FTP enables users of dissimilar platforms to transmit and retrieve files from one another using a common language.

gateway 1. Any device that operates at the Application layer of the OSI model to translate between data types. For example, a mail gateway might translate SMTP messages to be used with a proprietary mail system, such as cc:Mail. 2. Another term for a router on a TCP/IP network.

gateway-based security A security technique that places the security emphasis on a single gateway through which all inbound and outbound traffic between two networks must pass.

Gopher A distributed information service designed to hierarchically organize documents for later access by a menu-based Gopher client.

Hardware Abstraction Layer (HAL) A software layer that acts as an interface between the kernel and the computer hardware. The HAL provides NT with a level of hardware independence by establishing a set of virtual processors that communicate directly with the kernel.

host security A security technique that relies upon security provided by individual host systems, such as secure passwords and file access rights.

HTML (Hypertext Markup Language) The language that defines the markup elements of a Web document. HTML style elements are indicated by special markers, called *tags*.

HTTP (Hypertext Transfer Protocol) An Application-layer protocol designed to transmit documents between Web servers and Web browsers. It is considered to be a stateless protocol, which means that each transaction is considered to be a distinct and separate session.

hyperlink A pointer within an HTML document that, when selected, allows a user to jump to another point in that document or to another document altogether.

IETF (Internet Engineering Task Force) The organization within the Internet Society that handles issues relevant to the daily operation of the Internet. When an operational issue arises, the IETF creates a working group to address the issue.

Internet Protocol (IP) The Network-layer protocol that specifies the format for IP packets, called *datagrams*, as well as how datagrams should be addressed and transmitted throughout an IP network.

Internet worm A self-replicating program, launched on November 2, 1988, that disabled many computers on the Internet by exploiting known loopholes in two UNIX utilities.

intranet A corporate network that utilizes the open protocols and services associated with the Internet, such as WWW, FTP, and SMTP, to share corporate information and improve internal communications.

I/O manager The Executive-layer component that handles structured access to peripheral devices such as file systems, device drivers, and network drivers. The I/O manager is one of the only Executive-layer components that has the ability to communicate directly with the system hardware.

IPX/SPX (Internetwork Packet eXchange/Sequenced Packet eXchange) The Network- and Transport-layer protocols used by Novell NetWare servers for network communications.

kernel dispatcher Responsible for the prioritization and management of threads in a multitasking environment. The kernel dispatcher utilizes a 32-bit prioritization scheme for this purpose.

Kernel mode A mode of the NT operating system in which all instructions are allowed to run on the microprocessor. In Kernel mode, programs have full access to the processor, memory, and system hardware. Because they have complete access to the entire system, programs that run in kernel mode may jeopardize the integrity of the operating system if they are written incorrectly.

LDAP (Lightweight Directory Access Protocol) A standard that defines client/server access to a directory service, such as an X.500 directory of users and resources.

local procedure call facility The Executive layer component that manages client/server communication between objects within an NT system.

mail-bomb An automated process that repeatedly transmits e-mail messages to a mail sever, usually from one or more locations, and usually with the intent of overwhelming a mail server's ability to process mail.

MIB (Management Information Base) An organization of categories and a collection of status information maintained by an SNMP agent that can be queried by an SNMP management station.

monolithic A non-modular means of operating system development. Because it is comprised of a series of nested procedure calls, you can never tell where one process leaves off and the other begins.

multicast A special type of IP address that identifies a group of computers instead of a single computer. Multicasting is the technique of sending a single transmission to multiple computers.

multiprocessing The ability of a system to use more than one CPU for processing tasks. The two types of multiprocessing are asymmetric multiprocessing and symmetric multiprocessing.

multitasking The ability of a process to execute more than a task at a time.

name resolution The process of translating a host name into an IP address.

name server A server that contains IP address and host information about a given domain or group of domains. Name servers use this information to answer DNS queries from resolvers.

name space The term for the entire DNS hierarchy, including all of the host and domain names within it.

NetBEUI (NetBIOS Extended User Interface) It contains specifications for a transport protocol to support NetBIOS functions. Originally intended for small, workgroup networks, NetBEUI is non-routable and as such is not suitable for an enterprise network.

NetBIOS A software interface and naming standard originally developed by Sytek for IBM to support their PC Network LAN. NetBIOS acts as an API for processing network control directives. As a naming standard, NetBIOS specifies the rules for device and group naming on a network.

Network Address Translation (NAT) A service provided by a firewall or other network gateway device that rewrites source or destination addressing information on selected packets as they pass through it. Many organizations use Network Address Translation devices so that they can connect a network that contains non-registered IP addresses to a public IP network like the Internet.

News A discussion-oriented database service that allows users to communicate with one another within individual, topically-based discussion groups.

newsfeed The term for the process of transmitting articles/newsgroups between two news servers.

newsgroup A discussion database, usually focusing on a particular topic or subject, that is part of a news system.

newsreader A client application designed to access news databases and messages.

NFS A protocol developed by Sun Microsystems to allow access to file systems on remote hosts.

NNTP (Network News Transport Protocol) The TCP/IP protocol that defines the process for a newsreader client application to access news articles on an NNTP news server. The protocol also defines the interactions between news servers.

node 1. A computer or other connected device on a local or wide area network. 2. A branch point in the DNS name space.

non-pre-emptive A term that describes a type of multitasking environment where software services work in a cooperative fashion to request, share, and release resources. In a non-pre-emptive environment, an improperly written software module can overstep its limits and cause the entire system to crash. Novell NetWare 3.*x* is an example of a non-pre-emptive operating system.

Non-privileged Processor Mode *See* User mode.

Non-Protected mode Describes a state of the microprocessor where all instructions are allowed, if full access to memory is available, and if direct access to the hardware is permitted.

Object Manager The Object Manager is the component of the Executive layer that is responsible for the creation, securing, and auditing of objects. The Object Manager creates processes in which threads run.

Open Shortest Path First (OSPF) An interior link-state routing protocol designed for medium to large networks. OSPF routers gather routing information from all other OSPF routers on the network. Unlike with a RIP router, all information contained in an OSPF router's routing table is calculated from first-hand information since the OSPF router has communicated directly with each router on the network.

packet filter A device that screens all traffic flowing between two networks and permits or denies certain types of packets from passing depending on characteristics of those packets, such as the port address or IP address.

packet sniffer A device used to capture and decode network traffic as it travels through a network. Some system crackers use packet sniffers to capture unencrypted passwords sent across a network by legitimate users.

paradigm An approach, or stance, that determines how security is to be implemented within a network.

pass-through authentication Workstations with membership in a resource domain will contact the domain controller for the resource domain from which it will establish a secure connection. Through the trust relationship, the resource domain controller will pass the user authentication request to the most responsive master domain controller. This process is known as pass-through authentication.

performance The final design goal of Windows NT. Deals with optimizing various elements in the NT Kernel-mode layer, including the kernel itself, the executive services, and the networking components.

portability Windows NT was designed to be capable of operating upon a variety of hardware platforms with little modification to the operating system. Intel CISC and IBM RISC processors were equally supported during the initial release. This portable architecture proved valuable with the future release of the PowerPC microprocessor. In a very short period of time, Microsoft was able to *port* its operating system onto this new platform architecture.

ports   Numbers that Transport-layer protocols (TCP and UDP) use to deliver data to appropriate upper-layer protocols. For example, the TCP protocol will normally deliver any information addressed to port number 25 to SMTP.

PPTP   (Point-to-Point Tunneling Protocol) A protocol developed by Microsoft, Ascend Communications, 3Com/Primary Access, ECI Telematics, and US Robotics. PPTP was developed to become an extension to the Point-to-Point Protocol (PPP). With PPTP, devices can establish a virtual point-to-point connection over a network by encapsulating packets within regular IP packets. These encapsulated packets may be IP, IPX, or NetBEUI, and may be encrypted for security purposes.

pre-emptive   A term that describes a type of multitasking environment where the operating system is placed in control of system resources, such as memory and CPU cycles. In a pre-emptive environment, the operating system controls which software services can access these resources and for how long. Windows NT is an example of a pre-emptive multitasking operating system.

Primary Domain Controller (PDC)   A system that contains the master copy of the user accounts database for a Windows NT domain. The main function of the PDC is to provide access to the accounts database for user authentication.

primitives   The term for the lowest-level calls within an operating system.

Privileged Processor mode   *See* Kernel mode.

process   A virtual address space that connects to shared resources through handles. Threads execute within processes.

Process Manager   An Executive-layer service that is responsible for the creation and deletion of process objects.

Protected mode   Describes a state of the microprocessor where the instruction set is limited, access to memory is not allowed, and direct access to the hardware is not permitted.

proxy   A device or application that acts as an intermediary between two networks. For example, many firewalls include a proxy Telnet server to prevent any traffic from traveling directly between the Internet and an internal network. Users within the internal network establish a Telnet connection to the proxy server; they then create another session from the proxy server to a host on the Internet.

reliability   During the initial design, the internal architecture of Microsoft Windows NT was crafted such that it provided a solid foundation for handling exceptions in a predictable and structured manner. It was decided that at no time should an unexpected error condition result in the instability of another application program or, worse yet, the operating system itself.

remote control   The term for a remote access method in which a workstation establishes a dial-up or LAN connection to a workstation or server. The user assumes control of the network-connected workstation or establishes a session on the server. The only information that is transmitted over the dial-up link is keyboard input and screen output.

remote node   The term for a remote access method in which a workstation establishes a connection to the network through a dial-up link. When a workstation uses a remote node connection, it transmits and receives network packets as if it were connected directly to the local area network.

resource record   An entry within the files maintained on a DNS name server that identifies a particular network resource.

resource record type   An identification of the function of a particular DNS resource record. For example, the MX record type indicates that a particular resource record contains mail exchange information for a domain.

reverse proxy   A proxy server that has been configured to provide limited access for Internet users to a server that exists on an internal secured network. A reverse proxy may increase network performance because of its ability to cache frequently accessed files.

Routing Information Protocol (RIP)   An interior routing protocol based on a distance vector algorithm designed for moderate-sized networks. RIP routers gather routing information from neighbor RIP routers to develop their routing tables. Because of this, most of the information contained in a RIP routing table is calculated from second-hand information.

rules base A set of rules defined by a firewall administrator that the firewall uses to determine its enforcement policies.

scalability The ability of Windows NT Server to handle the future demands for processing power in support of mission-critical applications. Support for transaction-based processing as a foundation for commerce services is a current object that Windows NT hopes to scale toward.

schema A term used to define the objects that can be created, whose properties can be manipulated within Novell Directory Services.

security Windows NT is compliant with the C-2 security specification as defined by NCSC publication Department of Defense Trusted Computer System Evaluation Criteria, DoD 5200.28-STD, December, 1995. This book is commonly referred to as the *Orange Book*.

Security Reference Monitor (SRM) The component of the Executive layer that is responsible for setting and managing the security policy of the NT system. The SRM determines whether a request for accessing or creating an object is valid before authorizing the action.

segment (network) A logical, nonrouted network, such as a single ring in a Token Ring network.

segment (TCP) The basic unit of communication for the Transmission Control Protocol (TCP). Each segment is made up of a header, which contains information about the segment itself, and a body, which contains data.

server In a client/server environment, the server refers to the process or program that receives requests from clients, processes the requests, and returns the results to the client. In other instances the server can be any node that provides network services (i.e. resources for consumption by clients).

SMTP (Simple Mail Transfer Protocol) A TCP/IP protocol that provides for mail delivery and transfer. SMTP defines the rules for communication between SMTP mail transfer agents.

SNMP (Simple Network Management Protocol) A management protocol designed to allow TCP/IP network devices to exchange configuration and status information.

social engineering A technique used by some system crackers to gain passwords and account information from legitimate system users by impersonating another system user or administrator.

socket The term for the combination of an IP address and a port number. A socket uniquely identifies an application on a particular workstation.

SOCKS An open protocol that defines standards for communication between client workstations and circuit-level proxy servers.

SRI-NIC (Stanford Research Institute Network Information Center) The organization that maintained all hostname-to-IP address mappings in the early days of the Internet.

SSL (Secure Sockets Layer) A data encryption method developed by Netscape Communications, used for safe transmission of sensitive data between nodes on a TCP/IP network.

stateful inspection A process utilized by Checkpoint Technologies' Firewall-1 firewall inspection module. The inspection module examines each packet to evaluate whether the packet is appropriate given the context of the current network session, and permits or discards the packet based upon that evaluation.

stateless Used to describe any protocol in which each transaction is handled as an independent session. Stateless protocols, such as HTTP, do not track session information between transactions, so other methods are required to maintain a user's profile or activity within a particular visit to a Web site.

subnet mask The term for a grouping of bits that identify which portion of an IP address indicates the network address and which portion indicates the node address.

symmetric multiprocessing A multiprocessing model in which processing duties are spread evenly among all available processors. By distributing the duties to all available processors, the system cannot be bottlenecked by a single processor. A service, called a *dispatcher,* is responsible for scheduling threads to run on processors.

task A single objective to be accomplished by a microprocessor. The task may be to change the color of a pixel or open a file.

thread Threads run within a process. Their characteristics include: a processor state including the current instruction pointer, a stack for use when running in user mode, and a stack for use when running in kernel mode.

Time to Live (TTL) A mechanism that ensures that misdirected communications don't end up traveling endlessly through the Internet. For example, each IP datagram header contains a TTL value, measured as a unit of time. As the datagram passes through a router, this TTL value is decreased by a minimum of one second. Once the value reaches zero, the datagram is assumed to be undeliverable and is discarded. The Domain Name System (DNS) uses TTL values to indicate how long a DNS server should cache records obtained from other DNS servers.

Transmission Control Protocol (TCP) A connection-oriented Transport-layer protocol designed to provide guaranteed delivery of data on an IP network. The basic unit of information transmitted within a TCP packet is called a segment.

trap An error message generated by an SNMP agent and sent to an SNMP management device.

tunneling The process of encapsulating encrypted packets within IP packets to provide secure communications over an insecure network.

URL (Uniform Resource Locator) A standardized identifier of a resource or object on a network.

USENET A globally-distributed discussion database containing millions of messages within thousands of subject categories, called *newsgroups*.

User Datagram Protocol (UDP) A connectionless Transport-layer protocol designed to provide quick transmission of small pieces of information, called *datagrams*. Unlike TCP, UDP does not provide guaranteed delivery.

User mode A mode of the NT operating system in which direct access to memory, the microprocessor, and other system hardware is prohibited. Programs that are designed to run in User mode must work with other services (Kernel mode services) that are permitted to directly access the system hardware. Because they never have direct access to the hardware, an improperly written User mode application has no significant impact on operating system integrity.

Uuencode/Uudecode A group of applications designed to translate binary files into ASCII text files so they can be sent via SMTP e-mail.

virtual directory A feature of the Microsoft Internet Information Server that provides the ability to logically map a directory name to any other directory, whether located on the same server or on a different, network-connected server.

Virtual Memory Manager The Executive-layer component that enables the NT operating system to allocate memory beyond that which physically exists in the machine. The Virtual Memory Manager maps a virtual memory space to actual physical memory using pages that are 4KB. When the upper limit of available physical memory has been reached, the Virtual Memory Manager swaps the least used pages to hard disk.

virtual private network A term used to describe the use of encryption to provide secure communications between an internal corporate network and individual users or business partners over a public data network.

Windows Internet Naming Service (WINS) A naming service on an NT network that provides NetBIOS computer names to IP address mappings.

WINSOCK.DLL A dynamic link library that provides an API between TCP/IP protocol network software and TCP/IP applications.

XNS (Xerox Network Services) Developed by Xerox in their Palo Alto, California research center. XNS forms the foundation for many present-day networking technologies, such as the Ethernet protocol and the Banyan Vines network operating system.

zone A portion of the Domain Name Service (DNS) name space administered by a single individual or organization.

zone transfer The process by which secondary DNS name servers receive DNS information for a particular zone from the primary DNS server for that zone.

APPENDIX D

Acronyms

ACE:	Access Control Entry
ACE:	Access Control Encryption
ACL:	Access Control List
ACS:	Asynchronous Communication Server
AMP:	Asymmetric MultiProcessing
ANSI:	American National Standards Institute
ASF:	Active Streaming Format
ASP:	Active Server Pages
BBS:	Bulletin Board System
BDC:	Backup Domain Controller
BIND:	Berkeley Internet Name Domain
B-ISDN:	Broadband ISDN
bps:	bits per second
BRI:	Basic Rate Interface
BSD:	Berkeley Systems Development
CDFS:	Compact Disk File System
CERN:	Conseil European pour la Recherche Nucleaire
CHAP:	Challenge Handshake Authentication Protocol
CIO:	Chief Information Officer
CGI:	Common Gateway Interface
CPE:	Customer Premise Equipment
CRC:	Cyclic Redundancy Check
CS:	Communication Server

CSNW:	Client Services for NetWare
CSU:	Channel Service Unit
DAP:	Directory Access Protocol
DARPA:	Department of Defense Advanced Research Projects Agency
DC:	Domain Controller
DDE:	Dynamic Data Exchange
DHCP:	Dynamic Host Configuration Protocol
DIB:	Directory Information Database
DIT:	Directory Information Tree
DLC:	Data Link Control
DLL:	Dynamic Link Library
DLT:	Dynamic Linear Tracking
DN:	Distinguished Name
DNS:	Domain Name Services
DOD:	Department of Defense
DOS:	Disk Operating System
DS0:	Digital Signal level 0
DSA:	Directory System Agents
DSMN:	Directory Services Manager for NetWare
DSP:	Directory System Protocol
DSS:	Domain SAP/RIP Service
DTE:	Data Terminal Equipment
DUA:	Directory User Agents

EMWAC:	European Microsoft Windows NT Academic Consortium
FAT:	File Allocation Table
FPNW:	File and Print Services for NetWare
FT1:	Fractional T1
FTP:	File Transfer Protocol
GSNW:	Gateway Services for NetWare
HAL:	Hardware Abstraction Layer
HCL:	Hardware Compatibility List
HDTV:	High Definition Television
HPFS:	High Performance File System
HTML:	HyperText Markup Language
HTTP:	HyperText Transport Protocol
ICA:	Intelligent Console Agent
IDP:	Internetwork Datagram Protocol
IEEE:	Institute of Electrical and Electronic Engineers
IETF:	Internet Engineering Task Force
IIS:	Internet Information Server
IMAP:	Internet Mail Access Protocol
I/O:	Input/Output
IP:	Internet Protocol
IPX:	Internetwork Packet Exchange
ISAPI:	Internet Server Application Programmer Interface
ISDN:	Integrated Services Digital Network

ISO:	International Organization for Standardization
ISP:	Internet Service Provider
ITU:	International Telecommunications Union
L2F:	Layer 2 Forwarding
L2TP:	Layer 2 Tunneling Protocol
LAN:	Local Area Network
LDAP:	Lightweight Directory Access Protocol
LEC:	Local Exchange Carrier
LLC:	Logical Link Control
LPC:	Local Procedure Call
LSI:	Line Service Interface
MBC:	Multiboard Computer
MIB:	Management Information Base
MMC:	Microsoft Management Console
MS-CHAP:	Microsoft Challenge Handshake Authentication Protocol
MS/DOS:	Microsoft Disk Operating System
NADMINNT:	Novell Administrator for Windows NT
NAL:	Novell Application Launcher
NASC:	NetWare Asynchronous Communications Server
NAT:	Network Address Translation
NBF:	NetBEUI Frame
NBFP:	NetBIOS Frames Protocol
NCB:	Network Control Block

NCP:	NetWare Core Protocol
NCSA:	National Center for Supercomputing Applications
NCSI/NASI:	Network Communications Services Interface/Network Asynchronous Services Interface
NDIS:	Network Device Interface Specification
NDS:	Novell Directory Services
NETBEUI:	NetBIOS Extended User Interface
NETBIOS:	Network Basic Input Output System
NLM:	NetWare Loadable Module
NNTP:	Network News Transfer Protocol
NT:	New Technology
NTC:	NT Configuration Object
NTFS:	NT File System
NTLM:	Windows NT Challenge/Response
NWGINA:	Novell Workstation Graphical IdeNtification and Authentication
ODI:	Open Data-link Interface
OLE:	Object Linking and Embedding
OS/2:	Operating System/2
OSI:	Open Systems Interconnect
OSPF:	Open Shortest Path First
PAD:	Packet Assembler Disassembler
PAP:	Password Authentication Protocol
PDC:	Primary Domain Controller

PDN:	Public Data Network
PERL:	Practical Extraction Reporting Language
PID:	Process ID
POP:	Point of Presence
POP3:	Post Office Protocol version 3
POSIX:	Portable Operating System for Computing Environments
POTS:	Plain Old Telephone Service
PPTP:	Point-to-Point Tunneling Protocol
PRI:	Primary Rate Interface
PSDN:	Packet Switched Data Network
PVC:	Permanent Virtual Circuit
RAID:	Redundant Array of Inexpensive Disks
RAS:	Remote Access Service
RFC:	Request for Comment
RIP:	Routing Information Protocol
ROI:	Return on Investment
RPC:	Remote Procedure Call
SAM:	Security Accounts Management
SAP:	Service Advertisement Protocol
SBC:	Single Board Computer
SID:	Security ID
SLIP:	Serial Line Internet Protocol
SMB:	Server Message Block

SMP:	Symmetrical MultiProcessing
SMS:	Systems Management Server
SMTP:	Simple Mail Transfer Protocol
SNMP:	Simple Network Management Protocol
SOA:	Start of Authority
SPP:	Sequenced Packet Protocol
SPX:	Sequenced Packet Exchange
SQL:	Structured Query Language
SRI-NIC:	Stanford Research Institute Network Information Center
SSL:	Secure Sockets Layer
SVC:	Switched Virtual Circuit
TA:	Terminal Adapter
TCP:	Transmission Control Protocol
TCP/IP:	Transmission Control Protocol/Internet Protocol
TDI:	Transport Device Interface
UART:	Universal Asynchronous Receiver/Transmitter
UDP:	User Datagram Protocol
UNC:	Universal Naming Convention
URL:	Uniform Resource Locator
VAN:	Value Added Network
VDD:	Virtual Device Driver
VDM:	Virtual DOS Machine
VMM:	Virtual Memory Manager

WAN:	Wide Area Network
WCAT:	Web Capacity Analysis Tool
WINS:	Windows Internet Naming Service
WOW:	Windows on Win32
WWW:	World Wide Web
XNS:	Xerox Network Services

Index

NOTE: Page numbers in *italics* refer to figures or tables; page numbers in **bold** refer to significant discussions of the topic.

Numbers

12-minute heartbeat, 130
16-bit code, and WinFrame configuration, 457
32-bit code, and WinFrame configuration, 457

A

A (address) record, 296
abend, 482
access control, in Internet Information Server, **279**, *280*
Access Control Encryption (ACE), 361
Access Control List (ACL), 49
access lists, for packet filtering, 344
access logging, by firewalls, 253, **340–341**
access token, from Security Subsystem, 48, *50*
account objects, and database size, 97
accounts
    for nonhuman network users, 337
    security guidelines on, 330
acknowledgment packet, and WAN traffic overhead, 461
acronyms, **558–565**
Active Directory, 103, **513–518**
    administration of, 518
    directory structure, **515–518**, *516*
    site structure, **514–515**, *515*
Active Server pages, **268–269**
Active Streaming Format (ASF), 270
ActiveX, 542
    Active Server pages and components, 268
Add Port dialog box (Remote Access Service), 428, *428*
address (A) record, 296
address aggregation, by proxy, **347**
Address Allocation for Private Internets (RFC 1918), 161
Address Resolution Protocol (ARP), 542
administration
    control of end user Desktop, 521
    cost of, 64

Adobe Acrobat, hardware for WinFrame server, 468
Advanced Async Configuration dialog box, *478*
agents, 282
alias, 265
Allchin, Jim, 22
Alt. Profile script, 204
AltaVista Tunnel, **374–375**, *375*
Alt.Login script, 204
announcement cycle, for browsers, 506–507
anonymous FTP, 245
API (Application Programming Interface), 542
application groups, and naming standards, 112
Application layer in OSI model, 539
Application Programmer Interface, NetBIOS as, 174
application-level proxy, 542
applications
    compatibility with WinFrame, 447
    development vs. operating system development, 5
    hardware requirements for, 466–469
    improper configuration and mail server problems, 321–322
    inspecting performance, **496–498**
    installation on WinFrame server, **483–485**
    inventory in WinFrame planning, 453–454
    and RAS solutions, **425**
    server location and connectivity design, 461
    special needs and WinFrame implementation, 462
    understanding for WinFrame planning, **457–465**, *458–459*
    for Windows 3.1, performance in WinFrame, 486
AppStation mode, 521
architecting, 8
ARP (Address Resolution Protocol), 542
ARPAnet, 227, 542
assembler code, for Windows NT, 10
asymmetric multiprocessing, 542
asymmetrical operating system model, *33, 34*
asynchronous communication servers, 394
ATDM (Asynchronous time division multiplexing), 385
attachments to e-mail, 314
    sending binary files as, 277
    virus in, 323
AUDITLOG.EXE command, 482–483
authenticated process, *37*
authentication
    by IIS HTTP, 262–263, *263*, 277–278

by PPTP, 369
in Internet Information Server (IIS), 277–279
NDS, 196
pass-through, 146–147, *147*
authentication scheme, 93

B

BackOffice (Microsoft), 22
and domain design requirements, 94
backup browsers, **129–130**
browse list maintenance, 130
election process for, **131–132**
backup domain controllers (BDC), **142–148**, 464, 542
determining number by design, **144–148**
determining number mathematically, **143**
installation of File and Print Services for NetWare, 218
backups, scheduled, **338–339**
bandwidth, 542
as IIS bottleneck, **273**
and Internet as WAN, 362
for POTS, 381
Basic Rate ISDN (BRI), 420
baud, vs. bits per second, **383**
BDC. *See* backup domain controllers (BDC)

benchmark tools, Web sites for Web server tools, 276
Berkeley Internet Name Domain. *See* BIND (Berkeley Internet Name Domain)
bicycle racing, 191
binary-code, compatibility, **17**
binary file attachments, sending through electronic mail, 277
BIND (Berkeley Internet Name Domain), 543
DNS services based on, 304
for NT, 304–305, *305*
bits per second, vs. baud, **383**
blue screen, troubleshooting, 481, 487
Bootstrap (bootp) protocol, 165, 543
bottlenecks
identifying, 496
in IIS services, **272–273**
links between remote user and RAS server, 425
minimizing LAN traffic on WinFrame, 449
network card for WinFrame and, 460–461
from processor, 501
from RAID 5 stripes, 156
recognizing potential in network design, **66–67**
and secure connections, 147
brand-name components, vs. generic, **67–70**

Broadband ISDN (B-ISDN), 420
brother domains, 236
browsers
	election across wide area network, 128, *128*
	election packet, 132, *133*
	optimizing services, **506–508**
	sharing information among, 130–131, *131*
browsing, **125–135**
	backup browsers for, **129–130**
	domain master browsers and master browsers, **126–129**
budget, and network design, **63–65**
bugs, as security threat, 334
bus architecture, 504
bus-mastering multiport communication cards, 426
business requirements, and network design, **59–61**

C

C2 security, 15–16
C2CONFIG.EXE program, 15
C programming language, 10
cache, upgrading secondary, 501
cache file, DNS Manager and, **299–300**
Cache Manager, in I/O Manager, 44
caching
	to name servers, 240
	by proxy servers, 252, **346–347**
Cairo, 512–513
canonical name (CNAME) record, in DNS database, 299
cc:Mail, hardware for WinFrame server, 466
CCITT (now International Telecommunications Union), 115, 117
CD-ROM File System (CDFS), 18
certification authority, 264, 281, 543
CGI. *See* Common Gateway Interface (CGI)
Challenge/Response (NTLM) authentication, 263, 264, 278
Channel Service Unit (CSU), 385, 387
Checkpoint Firewall-1, **349–353**
	graphical administration interface, *352*
	modular components, **350–351**
	rules base, **352–353**
	stateful inspection, **351–352**
Checkpoint Software Technologies, 375
Chicago, 12, 19
child thread, 38
CIR (Committed Information Rate), 472
circuit-layer proxy, 354
Citrix. *See also* WinFrame (Citrix)
	and Microsoft, 32, 519
	WinView, 400
client, 543
	configuring in Windows 95, **371–372**

for e-mail, 242–243
Client Services for NetWare (CSNW), 191, 196
client workstation, for WCAT, 275
client/server database application, remote node for, 401
client/server model, **28–29**, *28*, 232–233, 543
Client/Server subsystem of Windows NT, 46, **50–51**
Cluster Administrator, **528–529**, *529*
CNAME (canonical name) record, in DNS database, 299
Committed Information Rate (CIR), 472
Common Gateway Interface (CGI), 543
    vs. Active Server code, 268
    and CPU load, 272
communication servers, **394**
compatibility, 543–544
    of file system, **17–18**
    of user interface, 18
    as Windows NT design goal, **14–18**
compression of modem-to-modem data stream, 430
Computer Browser services, 126
computing resources, decision to protect, **326**
concurrent users prediction, **424**
    and RAM requirements, 457
    for WinFrame, **454–456**
conditioning, 383

configuration, tuning in pilot project, 87
Configure Port dialog box (RAS), **429**, *429–430*
Connect Control Module (Checkpoint FireWall-1), 350
Connect To dialog box, for VPN server, 372
connection identifiers, 183
connection-oriented protocol, 160, 184, 538, 544
connectionless protocol, 160, 183, 184, 538, 544
console, 50
context switching, 36, 544
controller station, 275
cookies, 234
core dump, 153, 474
costs
    of dual-homed host firewall server, 343
    hidden, 64
    of security breach, **327–328**
    of WinFrame server solution for 8 concurrent users, 444
country, in domain name, 104
CPUs
    as IIS bottleneck, **272**
    Pentium Pro or Pentium, for WinFrame server, 457–460
    performance tuning, **501–503**
    on RAS server, 426

WinFrame handling of multiple, 454
criteria for success, 61
cross-link trust, 517
Crystal Reports for Internet Information Server, 283, *284*
CSU (Channel Service Unit), 385, 387
curiosity, as external threat to network, 320
current context, 36
Custer, Helen, 8
customer review, of pilot project, **89**
customers, and network design, 61
customized applications, WinFrame and, **448**
Cutler, Dave, 6, 22
Cyber Café, 108

D

DARPA (Department of Defense Advanced Research Projects Agency), 227, 544
data, decision to protect, **326**
Data Link Control (DLC) protocol, for NetBEUI, 177
Data Link layer in OSI model, 537–538
data source, in virtual private network, 365–366
database applications, 425
  and WinFrame implementation, 462
datagram, 544

DayStar Digital Genesis MP600, 33
default gateway, 544
Defense Advanced Research Projects Agency (DARPA), 227, 544
demand-dial routing, **525**
departmental groups, and naming standards, 112
design, definition, **59**
design goals, of Windows NT, **7–19**
Desktop, administrator control of end users', 521
device drivers, in I/O Manager, 44
DHCP (Dynamic Host Configuration Protocol), 160, **165–167**, 193, 545
  and DNS, 300
  enhanced relay agent for, 525
  for RAS, 433
dial-back functionality, 335
dial-up connection
  Internet as, **359–360**, *360*
  minimum connections for RAS, 417
  for WinFrame, 472
Dial-Up Networking Multilink, 431
digital certificate, 264, 544
digital modems, 420
Digital Signal (DS) transmission rates, 387, *388*
directory configuration, for IIS, 264–265
Directory Information Database (DIB), 115

Directory Information Tree (DIT), 104, 117
directory services, role of, **114–115**
Directory Services Manager for NetWare (DSNW), 192–193, **220–221**
  synchronization, *220*
Directory System Agents (DSA), 116–117
Directory System Protocol (DSP), 117
Directory User Agents (DUA), 117
disk configuration, for member server, *155–156*
disk controllers, and performance tuning, 504
diskperf command, 503
distance vector algorithm, 524, 544–545
Distinguished Name (DN), *118*, 118
distributed applications infrastructure, 22
distributed computing, 22
DN (Distinguished Name), *118*, 118
DNS database, adding resource records, **298–299**
DNS (Domain Name Service). *See* Domain Name Service (DNS)
DNS Manager, **294–295**, *294*
  and cache file, **299–300**
  WINS Lookup tab, 301, *302*
DNS name, user need for, 302
DNS Server (Microsoft), **293–300**
  creating zones in, **295–297**

DNS servers
  adding secondary, **297**
  configuring NT server as, **294–300**
  placement in network topology, 308
  third-party, **304–307**
DNS service, Internet strategy and, 309
documentation
  of maintenance procedures, 72
  for pilot process, **85**
Domain Contoller Service, 514
Domain Controllers (DC), 138
  consistency in file system access, 154
  disk partitions for, *151–152*
  hardware requirements, **150–154**
  installation of File and Print Services for NetWare, 218
  replication optimization, 505–506
domain design myths, **92–102**
domain master browser, **126–129**
  broadcast by, 130
  election process for, **131–132**
  synchronization with Master Browser, 506
domain models
  backup domain controllers in single, *144*, 144–145
  considerations in developing, 94
  multiple-masters, 101–102, *101*
  structure in Explorer, *140*
Domain Name Service (DNS), **235–242**, 293, 545
  design considerations, **241–242**

load balancing in IIS with, **288–289**
name servers, **237–239**, *548*
resolvers, **240–241**
vs. WINS, 168–169
domain name space, **236–237**, *237*, 293
domain (NT), 545
Domain SAP/RIP Service (DSS), 185, *186*
domains, 236. *See also* master domain model; multi-master domain model
in Active Directory, 516, *517*
backup browsers in, 129
grouping WinFrame servers in, 464
naming standards for, **104–105**
number of users for single, **96–99**
trusted and trusting, 119, *120*
Domino (Lotus), 313
DOS
vs. Windows (Microsoft), 9
WinFrame Client for, 480
Dr. Watson, exception handling by, 13
drive mappings in NetWare, and WinFrame server assignments, 463
DSA (Directory System Agents), 116–117
DSNW (Directory Services Manager for NetWare), 192–193, **220–221**
synchronization, *220*
DSP (Directory System Protocol), 117
DSU (Data Service Unit), 387
DUA (Directory User Agents), 117
dual-homed hosts, 253, 343, 545

dynamic DNS, configuring workstations for, 303
Dynamic Host Configuration Protocol (DHCP), 160, **165–167**, 193, 545
and DNS, 300
for RAS, 433
dynamic load balancing, in WinFrame 1.7, 489–490

E

election, for browsers, **131–132**
election packet, 132, *133*
electronic mail, **242–244**
design considerations, **316**
Exchange 5, **313**
LDAP (Lightweight Directory Access Protocol) for, 311
proprietary vs. open systems, **312–313**
remote node vs. remote control for, 401
third-party server, **314–316**
employees, USENET availability to, 311
encapsulation, **534–535**, *534*, 545
encryption
for ICA protocol stream, 490
in Internet Information Server, **280–282**
need for, **359–363**
in RAS, **433**

encryption key, for VPN connection, 367
Encryption Module (Checkpoint FireWall-1), 350
enterprise networks, xvii
    architecting, 8
enumeration, 125
environment subsystems, **48–53**, *49*
errors
    no more system ptes, 485–486
    Status_Nologon_Interdomain_Trust_Account, 121
Ethernet Traffic Parameters worksheet, **406**, *407*
European Microsoft Windows NT Academic Consortium (EMWAC), 260
exception handling process, in Windows NT, 13
Exchange 5, 313
Executive Layer, 30, **42–47**, 545
    access to, 32
Executive Services, 30
    optimizing, 18
    and reliability, 14
experimentation, and component selection, **69–70**
expire time, in SOA record, 297
Explorer, domain model structure in, *140*
extensibility, 545
    as Windows NT design goal, **9**
extranets, **229–230**, *231*, **362–363**, 545

F

failure, single point of, 79
FAT partition
    on NT server, 152–153
    for WinFrame, 474
fault tolerance
    backup browsers for, 129
    backup domain controllers for, 143
    for domain controller service, 514
    for name servers in zones, 238
    in network design, **77–79**
    for SAM database, 152
    secondary DNS server for, 309
    spare DHCP server for, 167
    and WINS servers, 168
fax boards, 62
File Allocation Table (FAT), support for, 17
File and Print Services for NetWare (FPNW), **216–218**, *217*
    to duplicate NetWare environment, **218–219**
    and shared apps & data for NetWare & NT clients, 219–220
file system
    compatibility, **17–18**
    in WinFrame, 474
File Systems component, of I/O Manager, 44

File Transfer Protocol (FTP), **244–246**, *246*, 546
  within IIS, 267
fingerd program, 322
Firewall Module (Checkpoint FireWall-1), 350
firewall servers, 340
  network address translation by, **341–343**, *342*
  vs. proxy servers, 348–349
firewalls, **252–254**, 335, 339, **340–345**, 546
  AltaVista Tunnel support, 375
  and cache file, 300
  Checkpoint Firewall-I, **349–353**
  effectiveness of, 340
  implementing, **343**
  implementing PPTP with, 373
  NT-based, **349–353**
  vs. proxy servers, 345
  software for, 75
  and virtual private networks (VPN), **375–376**
fixed costs, 64
flooding, 249
Fractional T1 system, **388**
frame relay, **392**, *393*
  for WinFrame, 471
frames, 537, 538
free virtual memory, displaying amount, 500

Frequency Division Multiplexing (FDM), 385, 386–387
FTP (File Transfer Protocol), **244–246**, *246*, 546
  MIB for, 283
functional groups, and naming standards, 112

G

Gates, Bill, 6, 8, 22
Gateway Services for NetWare (GSNW), 192, **214–216**, *215*
  for DSMN, 221
  for File and Print Services for NetWare, 217
gateway-based security, **335–336**, 546
gateways, 76, *77*, 546
generic components, vs. brand-name, **67–70**
geographical multi-master domain model, *100*, 101
GET (request), 282
GetBackupListRequest message, 131
Global Active Directory, 518
Gopher, **246–247**, 546
  MIB for, 283
  service in IIS, **267–268**
Graphics Device Drivers (GDD), in Win32K Manager, 47

Graphics Device Interface (GDI), in Win32K Manager, 47
Gray, Jim, 22
group accounts, naming standards for, **112–114**, *113*
Groupwise 5 (Novell), 313
Grove, Andy, 8
GSNW. *See* Gateway Services for NetWare (GSNW)
GUEST access rights, 337

H

handshaking, 430
hard drive
  performance tuning, **503–504**, *503*
  WinFrame install non-recognition of, 487
hardware
  generic components vs. brand-name, **67–70**
  operating system components with access to, 31
  platform and operating system portability, 10
  requirements for domain controllers, **150–154**
  specification sheets vs. reality, 74–75
Hardware Abstraction Layer (HAL), 11, *11*, 47, 48, 546
  upgrade for WinFrame server, 486

Hardware Compatibility List (HCL), from Microsoft, 149
heartbeat synchronization, 527
hidden costs, 64
hidden user account, for trusted domain, 120–121
High Performance File System (HPFS), 17
higher-layer protocols, 160
HKEY_LOCAL_MACHINE\SAM\SAM\Domains\Account\Users\Names, 122
HKEY_LOCAL_MACHINE\Security\Policy\Secrets, 122
HKEY_LOCAL_MACHINE\SYSTEM\CurrentControlSet\Control\Print, 507
HKEY_LOCAL_MACHINE\SYSTEM\CurrentControlSet\Services\Browser\Parameters, 134, 506
HKEY_LOCAL_MACHINE\SYSTEM\CurrentControlSet\Services\LanmanServer\Parameters, 505
HKEY_LOCAL_MACHINE\SYSTEM\CurrentControlSet\Services\NetLogon\Parameters, 505
HKEY_LOCAL_MACHINE\SYSTEM\CurrentControlSet\Services\Tcpip\Parameters, 505
hops, 524
host, 416
host-based applications, vs. client/server computer, 232

host security, **334–335**, 546
hot fixes, downloading for WinFrame, **465–466**
Hot Spare, 157
hours, estimating for installation, 71
HPFS (High Performance File System), 17
HTML (Hypertext Markup Language), 228, **235**, 546
HTTP (HyperText Transfer Protocol), 228, **233–234**, 546
    MIB for, 283
HTTP service, in Microsoft Internet Information Server (IIS), **262–267**
hybrid user account, 206
Hydra, **519–520**
hyperlinks, 233

I

I/O Manager, **44–45**, 547
ICA (Intelligent Console Architecture) protocol, **442**
ICA protocol compression, 489
IDP (Internetwork Datagram Protocol), 183
IEEE 1003.1 standards, POSIX subsystem for, 53
IETF (Internet Engineering Task Force), 368, 547

IMAP (Internet Mail Access Protocol), 242, **244**, 310
    support from third-party mail server, 314–315
in-addr.arpa domain, 239, **297–298**
Index Server, in IIS, **269–270**, *270*
INETSRV, 283
information sharing, among browsers, 130–131, *131*
infrastructure, leveraging existing, **65**
Insignia NTRIGUE, 481
Inspection Module (Checkpoint FireWall-1), 350
installation
    File and Print Services for NetWare, 218
    issues in network design, **70–74**
    Remote Access Service (RAS), **427–436**
    tuning in pilot project, 87
Institute of Electrical and Electronic Engineers (IEEE), 537
Integrated Services Digital Network. *See* ISDN (Integrated Services Digital Network)
integration
    Microsoft support for Novell NetWare, **190–193**
    Novell view on, **193–194**
Intel 80286 instruction set, OS/2 written to, 7

Intelligent Console Architecture (ICA) protocol, **442**
IntelliMirror technology, **521–522**
Inter-Exchange Carrier (IXC), 384
internal network, address translation between Internet and, 342
International Standards Organization (ISO), 117, 532
International Telecommunications Union (ITU), 115, 117
Internet, **227–228**, *231*
    address translation between internal network and, 342
    for remote user connection to corporate network, 359–360, *360*
    security policy on connection to, 329
    as WAN, **361–362**
    and Windows NT evaluation, 21
Internet Engineering Task Force (IETF), 368, 547
Internet Explorer, 21
    hardware for WinFrame server, 467
Internet Information Server, 21, 23. *See also* Microsoft Internet Information Server (IIS)
Internet Mail Access Protocol (IMAP), 242, **244**, 310
    support from third-party mail server, 314–315
Internet mail directories, 311
Internet Packet (IP) protocol, 461
Internet Protocol (IP), 158–159, 547

Internet Server Application Programmer Interface (ISAPI), 267
Internet Service Manager, *261*, 261
    Directories tab, *266*
Internet service providers
    DNS services from, 309
    firewall-based security from, 341
Internet strategy, and DNS service, **309**
Internet support by Microsoft, 226
Internet worm, 322, 547
Internetwork Datagram Protocol (IDP), 183
Interrupt 14 (INT 14H), 394
intranets, **228–229**, *231*, 547
IntranetWare (Novell), 172
IntranetWare Client for Windows NT, 193
inventories in WinFrame planning
    of applications, 453–454
    of network, 453
inverse multiplexers, 420
IP addresses, 159
    assigning to network nodes, 165
    listing in in-addr.arpa domain file, 239
    number of segments and, 161
IPSec, 375, 376
IPX Far Call Interface, 186
IPX node number request, by remote users, 435
IPX over TCP/IP, 187

IPX protocol, 482
   impact on RAS server, 427
   RAS server configuration for, **434–436**
IPX/SPX (Internetwork Packet eXchange/Sequenced Packet eXchange), **182–183**, 189, 547
   and interoperability, 189
   and WAN traffic, 461
ISAPI (Internet Server Application Programmer Interface), 267
ISDN bridge, 420
ISDN (Integrated Services Digital Network), **389–391**, *391*, **419–420**
   vs. telephone line, 445
   for WinFrame, 471
ISDN telephones, 420
IXC (Inter-Exchange Carrier), 384

J

JScript, 268

K

kernel
   maximum memory recognized, 481–482
   separation and division of, 30–31, *31*

kernel dispatcher, 547
   prioritization scheme for thread management, 39, *40*
kernel mode, 9, 29, 547
   Executive Layer in, 30, **42–47**
   optimizing, 18–19
   third-party developers' access to, 31
Key Manager, for IIS encryption, 280–281, *281*
keywords, 269

L

L2 cache, upgrading, 501
LAN (local area network), WinFrame and impact of WAN traffic on, 449
LAN Manager client, NetServerEnum API call from, 125
LAN-WAN internetwork
   connection design, **403–404**, *405*
   designing, **402–411**
   leased line configurations, **404–411**
LANRover (Shiva), 396
laptop user, and IntelliMirror, 522
latency, and remote control connection, 444
Launching and Embedding (ALE) feature, in WinFrame 1.6, 487
Layer 2 Forwarding (L2F) protocol, 373

LDAP (Lightweight Directory Access Protocol), 310–311, 548
　from third-party servers, 315
lease for IP address, 165
leased line systems, **384, 404–411**
　Ethernet Traffic Parameters worksheet, **406**, *407*
　Network Growth worksheet, **410–411**, *410*
　Remote Host Server Resources worksheet, **404–406**, *406*
　Remote Traffic worksheet, **408**, *409*
license pooling, 489
licensing, for WinFrame, **476**, *477*
link-state protocols, 525
listening state, 132
LMHOSTS file, 169
load balancing, in IIS with DNS, **288–289**
Local Exchange Carriers (LECs), 384
Local Procedure Call (LPC), 18, 46
Local Procedure Call Facility, **43**, 548
local profiles, in WinFrame domain, 464
Local Security Authority (LSA), 120, 121
Locality, as X.500 specification, 118
logical printer, vs. printing device, 108
login script
　for WinFrame, 463
　and WinFrame server hangs, 485
Login Script Variables, 205

logon screen, 48
Lotus Domino, 313
LSA secret object, maximum number, 122–123

M

MAC (Media Access Control) address, 537
Mach operating system, 9
Macintosh
　WinFrame support for, 481
　and WINS, 169
mail-bomb, 321, 548
Mail Exchange (MX) record, 299
mail servers, choosing, **312–316**
mailbox size, administrative control, 315–316
mailing lists
　vs. news systems, 248–249
　services from third-party servers, 315
maintenance, documentation of procedures, 72
maintenance plan, for net servers, **256–257**
management console, 282
Management Console Module (Checkpoint FireWall-1), 350
Management Information Base (MIB), 548

management needs, and network
   design, **72–73**
ManageWise (Novell), 194
massive parallelism, 527
master browser, **126–129**
   broadcast by, 130
   election process for, **131–132**
   preferred, **134–135**
   synchronization with Domain Master
      Browser, 506
master domain model, **96,** *139*
   backup domain controllers in,
      145–146, *146*
memory
   as IIS bottleneck, **272–273**
   nonpaged-pool, 123
   and number of anticipated WinFrame
      concurrent users, 457
   performance tuning, **498–501**
   for process, 37
MEMORY.DMP file, 153
messaging system, 23
MetaIP, **306–307,** *306*
MetaIP/Load Balancer, 307
MIB (Management Information Base),
   548
MIBCC.EXE utility, 283
microchips, exponential growth of transistor density, 7
microkernel, 30
Microsoft
   and Citrix, 32
   purchase of WinFrame code, 442
   support for NetWare, **190–193,**
      214–221
Microsoft Analysis tools, **273–275**
Microsoft BackOffice, 22
   and domain design requirements, 94
Microsoft Certificate Server, 282
Microsoft Client Access Licensing, 476
Microsoft Exchange server, 115
Microsoft Hardware Compatibility List
   (HCL), 149
Microsoft Internet Information Server
   (IIS), **260–289**
   Active Server pages, **268–269**
   core services, **261–268**
   design considerations, **285–289**
   directory configuration for, 264–265
   encryption configuration in version 4,
      282
   File Transfer Protocol (FTP) within,
      267
   Gopher in, **267–268**
   HTTP service, **262–267**
   Index Server, **269–270,** *270*
   management, **276–285**
   Microsoft Analysis tools, **273–275**
   NetShow, **270–271**
   optimizing, **271–276**
   reporting utilities for, **283–285,** *284*
   security, **276–282**
   and SNMP, **282–283**
   virtual directories in, 265, **286–287**

Microsoft Management Console (MMC), *262*, 518, **522**, *523*
   to configure directories, *266*
Microsoft NT 3.51 compatibility list of applications, 447–448
Microsoft Office 97, hardware for WinFrame server, 466
Microsoft Proxy Server, **353–355**
Microsoft Scalability Day, 22–23
Microsoft Script Debugger, 269
Microsoft Systems Management Server, 198
   design model for, 95
Microsoft Transaction Server, 269
Microsoft VPN Adapter, 371, *372*
MicroVAX workstation, 6
Migration Tool for NetWare, 474
minimum time to live, in SOA record, 297
mirrored server, fault tolerance in update process, 79
mission-critical applications, 529
modems
   for RAS, 417, **429–430**
   RAS Setup detection, 429
   for WAN connection, 445
monolithic, 548
monolithic operating system model, 27, *27*
MS-DOS
   and printer names, 108
   subsystem in Windows NT, **51**

MSDUN12.exe file, 371
multi-master domain model, *100*
   geographical, *100*, 101
   reasons for, **99–102**
MultiBoard Computer (MBC), 397
   to access network, *399*
multicasting, 271, 548
multiple CPUs, WinFrame handling of, 454
multiple-masters domain model, *101*, 101–102
multiplexing, 385
multiprocessing, 548
   monitoring systems, 502
   multiple processors for, *36*, 36
   symmetric, 32–41
multiprotocol bridges, 396
multitasking, 34–41, 548
multithreaded process, *38*
MUX, 385

N

NAdminNT. *See* Novell Administrator for Windows NT
NAL (Novell Application Launcher), 194, 198
name resolution, 240, *241*, 548
name servers, **237–239**, 293, 548
   cached information by, 240
name space, 548

NAMED program, DNS services based
    on, 304
nameserver (NS) record, 296
naming standards, **102–119**
    for domains, **104–105**
    for group accounts, **112–114**, *113*
    importance of, 103, 140
    maximum length, *101–102*
    NetBIOS as, **175–177**, *176*
    for printers, **108–110**, *109*
    for servers, **105–107**, *106*
    for user accounts, **110–112**, *111–112*
    for workstations, **107–108**
native transport protocols, **173–189**
    closing comments, **194–195**
    IPX/SPX, **182–183**
    NetBEUI, **174–177**
    NetBIOS over TCP/IP, **178–182**
    TCP/IP in NetWare environment,
        183–188
NBFP (NetBIOS Frames Protocol), 174
NCBs (Network Control Blocks), 181
NCD, 481
NCSC publication, Department of
    Defense Trusted Computer System
    Evaluation Criteria, 14
NCSI/NASI (Network Communica-
    tions Services Interface/Network
    Asynchronous Services
    Interface), 394
NDS. *See* Novell Directory Services
    (NDS)

NDS authentication, 196
NDS Event Monitor, 208
NDS Object Replication Service,
    208–209, *209*
NDS user accounts, synchronization
    with NT, 213, *213*
net servers, maintenance plan for,
    256–257
Net services
    design issues, **255–257**
    DNS (Domain Name Service),
        235–242
    electronic mail, **242–244**
    FTP (File Transfer Protocol),
        244–246, *246*
    Gopher, **246–247**
    NNTP (News protocol), **247–250**,
        311, 549
    security for, **250–254**
    Web protocols, **233–235**
NetBEUI (NetBIOS Extended User
    Interface), **174–177**, 548
    impact on RAS server, 427
    and interoperability, 189
    limitations, 157
    RAS server configuration for, **436**
NetBIOS, 549
    as interface, 174–175, *175*
    as naming standard, **175–177**, *176*
NetBIOS Frames Protocol (NBFP), 174
NetBIOS over TCP/IP, **178–182**
    browser broadcasts as frames, 129

NetBT. *See* NetBIOS over TCP/IP
Nets. *See also* extranets; Internet; intranets
  definitions, **227–230**
Netscape, hardware for WinFrame server, 467
NetServerEnum API call, from LAN Manager client, 125
NetShow, **270–271**
NetWare. *See also* IntranetWare (Novell)
  interoperability with Windows NT, **188–189**
  Microsoft support for, **190–193**, **214–221**
  TCP/IP in, **183–188**
NetWare Connect, 437
NetWare Logon Configuration dialog box, *476*
NetWare servers, Windows NT client access to, 214
NetWare User Access for WinFrame, 474
NetWare/IP, **185–188**
  client software (NWIP.EXE), 187, *188*
  server architecture, *187*
NetWare/IP domain of services, 185
NetWareConnect (Novell), 396
network, existing issues and design, 65
network address, in IP address, 162

Network Address Translation (NAT), 162, 549
  by firewall servers, **341–343**, *342*
Network applet (Control Panel), 165
  Identification tab, *303*
  TCP/IP Properties dialog box, 166
Network Basic Input/Output System (NetBIOS). *See* NetBIOS
network broadcasts, DHCP client requests as, 166
network components, side effects of adjusting, 66
Network Control Blocks (NCBs), 181
network design, **58–89**
  alternatives in, **80–81**
  assumptions in, 75
  bottleneck recognition, **66–67**
  budget and, **63–65**
  business requirements and, **59–61**
  fault tolerance and redundancy, **77–79**
  installation implementation issues, **70–74**
  leveraging existing infrastructure, 65
  and management needs, **72–73**
  organizational objectives in, **63**
  providing support, **73–74**
  scope, avoiding expansion, **65–66**
  simplicity in, **76**
  technology for its own sake, **61–62**
  upgrade requirements, 67
network drivers, in I/O Manager, 44

Network Growth worksheet, **410–411**, *410*
network infrastructure, and design options, **255–256**
network interface cards (NICs)
 for IIS server, 273
 for WinFrame server, 449, 460–461
network inventory, in WinFrame planning, 453
Network layer in OSI model, 538
Network News Transport Protocol (NNTP), **247–250**, 311, 549
network objects, in rules base, 353
network operating systems. *See also* WinFrame (Citrix)
 integration and interoperability, **190–195**
 matching client software, 198
network terminating device (NT1), 420
network topology, and DNS server placement, 308
networking components, optimizing, 19
New Technology File System (NTFS), 18
News, 549
news servers, choosing, **312–316**
newsfeed, 549
newsgroup, 549
newsreader, 248, 549
NFS protocol, 549
NNTP (Network News Transport Protocol), **247–250**, 311, 549

no more system ptes error, 485–486
node, 549
 in domain name space, 236
node address, in IP address, 162
non-aged memory pool, 498
non-PPTP packets, setting interface to discard, 373
non-preemptive, 549
non-preemptive multitasking environment, 13
non-privileged processor mode (user mode), 9, 29, 549, 555
non-protected mode, 29, 550
nonhuman network users, accounts for, 337
nonpaged-pool memory, 123
 calculations, *124*
 Performance Monitor to evaluate, *500*, 500–501
nonvolatile account, 203
Notes, hardware for WinFrame server, 466
Novell Administrator for Windows NT (NAdminNT), 194, **206–214**
 Integration Utility, **209–214**, *210*, *211*
 modules in, **207–209**, *208*
Novell Application Launcher (NAL), 194, 198
Novell Directory Services (NDS), 115
 managing NT objects within, 212–214

NT workgroup-user accounts replication to, 209
Novell Dynamic Host Configuration Protocol (DHCP), 193
Novell Groupwise 5, 313
Novell IntranetWare, 172
Novell IntranetWare Client for Windows NT, **196–199**
  integrated NDS and NT authentication, 197, *197*
Novell NetWare Client for Windows NT, release, 195
Novell NetWareConnect, 396
Novell Workstation Graphical Identification and Authentication (NWGINA) module, 200–201
  customizing, 204
  upgrade mode, 206
Novell Workstation Manager, 193, **199–206**
NT 4 Server
  enabling PPTP on, 369
  remote connectivity issues, **422–426**, *423*
NT Advanced Server 4.0,
  open-standards-based services in, 231
NT Bootloader files, FAT file system for, 153
NT Configuration (NTC) objects, 200, **201–206**
  Associations tab, 201, *202*

Client Upgrade tab, 205–206, *205*
Dynamic Local User tab, 201, *202*, 203
Identification tab, 201
Login Scripts tab, 204–205
Login Tabs tab, 204
Profile/Policy tab, 203–204, *203*
Welcome Screen tab, 205
NT File System (NTFS), 14
NT infrastructure, **138–169**
  capacity planning, **138–148**
  network protocol support, **157–169**
  platform design, **149–157**
NT server
  as browsers, 126
  FAT partition on, 152–153
NT user accounts, integrating to NDS, 211, *212*
NT workgroup-user accounts, replication to Novell Directory Services, 209
NTDOS.SYS, 51
NTIO.SYS, 51
NTLM (Challenge/Response) authentication, 263, 264, 278
NTRIGUE (Insignia), 481
NW2NT.EXE, 474
NWCONV.EXE, 474
NWGINA. *See* Novell Workstation Graphical Identification and Authentication (NWGINA) module

NWIP.EXE (NetWare/IP client software), 187, *188*
NWLink protocol, 190, 216, 221
    for File and Print Services for NetWare, 217
Nyquist rate, **382**

O

Object Manager, **43**, *550*
objectives, of pilot project, **84–85**
objects, implementing shared resources as, 30
obsolescence, planning, 8
open electronic messaging systems, vs. proprietary, **312–313**
Open Shortest Path First (OSPF), 524, 525, *550*
open standards, 227
Open Systems Interconnection (OSI) reference model, **532–539**, *533*
    encapsulation, **534–535**, *534*
    layers, **536–539**, *537*
    peer communication in, 535, *536*
operating system
    development, **6–7**
    development vs. application development, 5
    objectives for Microsoft, 6
operating system models, **26–41**
    asymmetrical, **33**, *34*
    client/server, *28*, **28–29**
    monolithic, 27, *27*
    symmetrical, **34–41**, *35*
optimization, **505–508**
    of browser services, **506–508**
    of Internet Information Server (IIS), **271–276**
    of print services, 507–508
organization, in Active Directory, 516, *517*
organizational objectives, in network design, **63**
organizational structure, and multi-master domain, 99
organizational units, in Active Directory, 516, *517*
organizationally autonomous multi-master model, *100*
OS/2
    development of, 7
    lack of portability, 10
OS/2 subsystem in Windows NT, **52**
OSI model. *See* Open Systems Interconnection (OSI) reference model
OSPF (Open Shortest Path First), 524, 525, *550*
Outlook, hardware for WinFrame server, 467
outsourcing DNS, 309

P

packet filtering, 336, **344–345**, 550
   by routers, 343
   vs. stateful inspection, 351
packet sniffer, 321, 550
Page File Size, 451
page swap, by RAS server, 426
paging, check for excessive, 500
paradigm, 550
parent thread, 38
partitions, **116**
   for domain controller, *151–152*
   FAT, 152–153, 474
   maximum NT objects in, 210
   for WinFrame server and performance, 485
pass-through authentication, 146–147, *147*, 550
passband, **381**
passwords, **337**
   and encryption, 264
   security for, 323, 324
   of trusted domain PDC, 121, 122
   user education about, 338
PC pool, to access network, *398*
pcAnyWhere (Symantec), 400, 415
PDC. *See* Primary Domain Controllers (PDC)
peer communication, in OSI model, 535, *536*

peer-to-peer networking, and workstation naming, 107
perception, and system performance, 497
performance, 550
   clone vs. brand-name components, 68
   inspecting for applications, **496–498**
   optimization in pilot project, 88
   as Windows NT design goal, **18–19**
   on WoW (Windows on Windows), 448
Performance Monitor
   to evaluate nonpaged memory, *500*, 500–501
   IIS objects added to, 274
performance tuning
   fundamentals, **494–496**
   hard disk, **503–504**, *503*
   memory, **498–501**
   optimization and, 505–508
   processor, **501–503**
peripheral devices, access handled by I/O Manager, 44
permanent virtual connection (PVC), 392
persistent object caching, 489
physical disk. *See* hard drive
Physical layer in OSI model, 536
pilot project, **82–89**
   customer review and sign-off, **89**
   determining impact, 88

documentation of process, 85
incorporating new product in, 75–76
learning from, 83
objectives of, 84–85
performance optimization in, 88
phases, **86–89**
planning, **84–86**
production network protection by, 83–84
purpose of, **82–84**
success defined for, **85–86**
plain old telephone system (POTS), **381–383**
Point of Presence (POP) dial access numbers, 381
point-to-point links, vs. public networks, 364
Point-to-Point Protocol (PPP), for RAS, 418
Point-to-Point Tunneling Protocol (PPTP), **368–373**, **421**, **526**
   client configuration in Windows 95, **371–372**
   design considerations, **373**
   for RAS, 418
   server configuration, **369–371**
pointer records, 298
policy groups, and naming standards, 112
port monitors, configuring, **341**
port scanning, 253, **340–341**
portability, 7–8, **550–551**
   as Windows NT design goal, **10–11**
Portable Operating System for Computing Environments (POSIX) subsystem, **53**
ports, 160, 551
   configuring for RAS, **429–430**, *431*
   for HTTP, 233
POSIX (Portable Operating System for Computing Environments) subsystem, **53**
Post Office Protocol version (POP3), 242, **244**, 310
Power Mac 9500/180MP, 33
power users, RAM to support, 455–456
PowerPC platform, 7–8
PPTP. *See* Point-to-Point Tunneling Protocol (PPTP)
pre-emptive, 551
preemptive multitasking environment, Windows NT as, 13
preemptive operating system, 39
preferred master browser, **134–135**
preferred server, assigning in WinFrame, 463
Presentation layer in OSI model, 538
Primary Domain Controllers (PDC), 138–139, 464, 551
   as domain master browser, 127
   installation of File and Print Services for NetWare, 218
   limitations of, **140–141**
   platform recommendations, *141*

Primary Rate ISDN (PRI), 420
primitives, 9, 551
print services, optimizing, 507–508
printers, naming standards for, 108–110, *109*
printing device, vs. logical printer, 108
priority boosting, 41
private networks, IP addresses for, 161
privileged processor mode, 29. *See also* kernel mode
Process Manager, 36, 43, 551
Process Monitor, 274
Process Viewer, 274, *275*
processes, 551
    prioritizing, 39–41
    and threads, 37–39
processor queue, instantaneous length of, 502
processors. *See* CPUs
production network, protection with pilot project, 83–84
programs. *See* applications
proprietary e-mail systems, 242
    vs. open, 312–313
Protected mode, 551
protected subsystem, 29
protocol-dependent bridges, 396
protocols
    for dial-out by RAS server, 432
    for Remote Access Service (RAS), 426–427, 432
proxy, 551–552

proxy servers, **251–252**, *251*, 336, 345–349, *346*
    address aggregation by, 347
    vs. firewall servers, 348–349
    limitations, 347
    from Microsoft, 353–355
    vs. Network Address Translation, 343
    user ID and traffic control by, 346
PSDNs (packet-switched public data networks), **388–389**, *390*
PTR records, 298
Public Data Networks. *See also* PSDNs (packet-switched public data networks)
public domain, 227
public network, in virtual private network, **364–365**
PVC (Permanent Virtual Circuit), 471

R

RADIUS authentication, 526
RAID 5 stripes, bottleneck from, 156
RAID controller, 152
    on member server, 156
RAM. *See* memory
Raptor Systems, 375
RAS. *See* Remote Access Service (RAS)
RAS Server IPX Configuration dialog box, *435*, 435

Rashid, Richard, 9
ReachOut, 415
read/write requests, measuring number queued, 504
ready state, 39
redundancy
   for name servers in zones, 238
   in network design, **77–79**
refresh interval, in SOA record, 297
registration, of client with WINS server, 167–168
registry, backup of, 505
Relative Distinguished Name (RDN), *118*, 118
reliability, 552
   clone vs. brand-name components, 68
   of Internet, 364
   of tape backup system, 338
   as Windows NT design goal, **12–14**
remote access connectivity, 381, *382*
   Citrix WinFrame and, **441–442**
   decision process, **440–441**
   Fractional T1 system, 388
   frame relay, **392**, *393*
   Integrated Services Digital Network (ISDN), **389–391**, *391*
   leased line systems (analog), **384**
   packet-switched public data networks, **388–389**, *390*
   plain old telephone system (POTS), **381–383**
   T-carrier system, **384–388**, *386*
   vs. WinFrame, 470
Remote Access Service (RAS), 359, 396, **414–422**
   access technologies supported, **419–422**
   advantages and disadvantages, 416
   connecting through, **417–418**
   enhancements to, **525–526**
   finishing setup, **430–431**, *431*
   functionality, *418–419*
   hardware configuration, **426**
   installing, **427–436**
   PPTP as extension, 369
   protocols and performance impact, **426–427**
   solution design with, **422–436**, *423*
   when to use, **436–437**
   and WinStation, 477
Remote Access Service (RAS) install, **427–436**
   adding software, **428–429**
   encryption option, **433**
   modem and port configuration, **429–430**
   protocols for dialing out, **432**
   protocols for receiving calls, **432**
   server configuration for IPX, **434–436**
   server configuration for NetBEUI, **436**

server configuration for TCP/IP, **433–434**
Remote Access Setup dialog box, *370,* 370
Remote Application Manager (WinFrame), 447
Remote Authentication Dial-In User Service (RADIUS), 526
remote control, **396–400,** *397, 398, 399,* 552
  vs. remote node, **400–402, 415–416**
Remote Host Server Resources worksheet, **404–406,** *406*
remote link, 414
remote node, **395–396,** *395,* 552
  connection with WinFrame, 442
  vs. remote control, **400–402, 415–416**
remote users
  bottlenecks between RAS server and, 425
  Internet connection to corporate network, 359–360, *360*
  IPX node number request, 435
  and WinFrame implementation, **444**
replication, **116**
  database size before corruption, 97
  NT workgroup-user accounts to Novell Directory Services, 209
  services in Active Directory, 515
Requests for Comments (RFCs), 228. *See also RFCs*

resolvers, **240–241**
resource domain
  backup domain controllers for, 146–148
  database size calculation, *151*
resource domain controller
  hardware, *153–154*
  sizing, 141–142
resource monitor, in Wolfpack, 428
resource record type, 552
resource records, 239, 552
  adding to DNS database, **298–299**
  creating for zone, 296
retry interval, in SOA record, 297
return on investment, **59–60**
reverse proxy, 251, **347,** *348,* 552
  support in Microsoft Proxy Server, 355
RFC 821, SMTP specifications, 243
RFC 822, for electronic mail message format, 243
RFC 1244 (Site Security Handbook), 329
RFC 1918 (Address Allocation for Private Internets), 161
risk assessment, and security objectives, **325–326**
Ritchie, Dennis, 10
roaming profiles, in WinFrame domain, 464
root directories, for IIS services, 265
root domain, 236

root name servers, 238
"round-robin" DNS, 288, 307
Router Information Protocol (RIP), 435
　　version 2, 524
Router Security Management Module
　　(Checkpoint FireWall-1), 351
routers, 159
　　for DHCP, 166
　　packet filtering by, 343
routing, demand-dial, **525**
Routing Information Protocol (RIP),
　　183, 185, 552
routing protocol
　　selecting, **164–165**
　　support in future Windows NT, **524**
Routing and Remote Access Service
　　(RRAS), 368, **523–526**, *524*
rules base, 553
running election state, 132, 134
running state, 39

S

SAP (Service Advertising Protocol), 185,
　　217
scalability, 553
scheduled backups, **338–339**
schema, 553
Schema Extension, in NAdminNT, 207,
　　208

scope of network design, avoiding
　　expansion, **65–66**
Seagate Crystal Reports, 283, *284*
search sites, 125–126
searches, of World Wide Web, 269
secondary cache, upgrading, 501
secondary DNS server
　　adding, **297**
　　at remote site, 308
　　service provider maintenance of, 309
secure communications, on insecure
　　network, 366
Secure Computing, 375
secure connections, and bottlenecks,
　　147
secure network, guidelines for, **337–339**
Secure Sockets Layer (SSL), 254, 554
　　authentication, 264, **278–279**
　　Client Authentication, 263, **278–279**
SecurID card, 360, 361
security, 13, 553. *See also* firewalls;
　　passwords; proxy servers
　　absence of, **333–334**
　　vs. ease of use, **336**
　　for extranets, 230
　　firewalls for, **252–254**
　　gateway-based, **335–336**, 546
　　host, **334–335**, 546
　　for Internet Information Server (IIS),
　　　276–282
　　for Internet as WAN, 362

Internet-based remote access and, 360
for Net services, **250–254**
proxy servers, **251–252**, *251*
subsystem, **48–50**
testing, 339
through obscurity, **334**
virtual private networks, 230, 254, *255*, 556
in WinFrame 1.7, 489
WinFrame and, 463
from WinFrame server, **447**
Security Accounts Management Database (SAM), 48
security breach, cost of, **327–328**
Security Dynamics, 361
security policy
corporate review of, **332–333**
development, **328–333**
enforcing, **339–349**
objectives statement in, **328–332**
and rules base, 352
user education about, **338**
Security Reference Monitor (SRM), **43**, 49, 553
security strategy
development, **324–336**
implementing, **333–336**
objectives in, **325–328**
security threats
external, **319–322**
internal, **322–323**

segment (TCP), 553
segments (network), 159–160, 553
assigning network numbers to, *164*, 164
identifying number in network, **161–162**
sendmail program, 322
sensitive information, security policy on, 332
server-based applications, vs. client/server computer, 232
server interconnect, 527
server service, identifying state of, **498–501**, *499*
server-side processing, 267
servers, 553. *See also* client/server model
designing for fault tolerance, 77
disk configuration for, *155–156*
hardware for, **154–157**
multiple services on, 256
naming standards for, **105–107**
virtual, **287–288**
for WCAT, 275
Service Advertising Protocol (SAP), 185, 217
service packs
determining installed version, 486
downloading for WinFrame, **465–466**
Service Properties dialog box, Advanced tab, 279, *280*

Session layer in OSI model, 538
sessions, 416
sessions per user, for WinFrame server, 457
SGML (Standard Generalized Markup Language), 235
shadowing, 416, 479
Shannon's capacity theorem, **383**
shared data, supporting for NetWare and NT clients, **219–220**
shared groups, and naming standards, 112
Shiva, LANRover, 396
sign-off of pilot project, **89**
signal-to-noise ratio, 383
Silicon Graphics, WebStone, 276
Simple Mail Transfer Protocol (SMTP), 242, 244, 310, 553
Simple Network Management Protocol (SNMP), 553
  and IIS, 282
simplicity in network design, **76**
  and redundancy, **78**
Single Board Computer (SBC), 397
single domain model
  backup domain controllers in, *144*, 144–145
  database size calculation, *151*
single point of failure, 79
Site Analyst, 284
Site Server Express, 283

skill levels, implementation requirements, 73
SMTP. *See* Simple Mail Transfer Protocol (SMTP)
snap-ins, 522
snAppShot tool, 194
SNMP (Simple Network Management Protocol), 553
social engineering, 323, 324, 554
sockets, 160, 554
SOCKS, 554
SOCKS proxy (Microsoft), **354**
software. *See* applications
source code
  compatibility, **17**
  viewing HTML, 235
speaker on modem, 430
Sphinx SQL server, 22
SQL server, 22
SRI-NIC (Stanford Research Institute Network Information Center), 235–236, 554
SRM (Security Reference Monitor), **43**, 49, 553
SSL (Secure Sockets Layer), 254, 554
  authentication, 264, 278–279
  Client Authentication, 263, 278–279
Standard Generalized Markup Language (SGML), 235
standard users, RAM to support, 455–456
standby state, 39

start of authority (SOA) record, 296
stateful inspection, 554
    in Checkpoint Firewall-1, **351–352**
stateless protocol, 554
    HTTP as, 234
static routing, 164–165
statistical time division multiplexing (STTM), 385
Status_Nologon_Interdomain_Trust_Account error, 121
Steelhead. *See* Routing and Remote Access Service
STM (synchronous transfer mode), 385
streaming multimedia, NetShow for, **270–271**
streamlining IIS services, **271–272**
STTM (statistical time division multiplexing), 385
subnet masks, **162–163**, 554
success, defining for pilot project, **85–86**
super-thin client, 519
switched virtual connections (SVCs), 392
SYBASE, hardware for WinFrame server, 468
Symantec, pcAnyWhere, 400, 415
symmetric multiprocessing, 32–41, 554
symmetrical operating system model, **34–41**, *35*
synchronous transfer mode (STM), 385

system administrator
    rights vs. user rights, 331–332
    security policy on privileges, 331
system crackers, **320–321**, 334
system resources, applications use of, 498
system upgrade, 495

T

T.120 remote protocol, 519
T-carrier system, **384–388**, *386*
tags in HTML, 235
tape backup system, reliability of, 338
task, 554
TaskStation mode, 541
TCP (Transmission Control Protocol), 159–160, 555
    firewalls to monitor access to port, 253, 340
TCP/IP applications, WinSock-compatible in Windows NT, 182
TCP/IP network, planning, **161–165**
TCP/IP Properties dialog box (Network applet), 166
TCP/IP protocol suite, **158–160**
    development, 228
    impact on RAS server, 427
    and Internet reliability, 364
    and interoperability, 189

in NetWare environment, **183–188**
NetWare Server support, **184–185**
and RAS install, 428, **433–434**
for WAN communication, 188
Windows NT implementation of, *180*, 180–181
TDI (Transport Device Interface), 181
TDM (Time Division Multiplexing), 385
technology
 best of breed, **79–80**
 and network design, **61–62**
telephone line
 vs. Integrated Services Digital Network (ISDN), 445
 plain old telephone system (POTS), **381–383**
telephone network, 365
terminal adapter (TA), 420
terminated thread, 40
text files, Gopher service to access existing, 268
theft, as external threat to network, **320**
third-party developers, access to NT kernel mode, 31
thread in news system, 249
threads (process), 555
 base priority of, **40–41**
 life of, 39
 prioritizing, 39–41
 and processes, **37–39**
thunking, 51

Time Division Multiplexing (TDM), 385
Time to Live (TTL), 240–241, 555
 in SOA record, 297
topology of network, and DNS server placement, 308
total cost of ownership, 64
transitive trusts, in Active Directory, 516
Transmission Control Protocol (TCP), 159–160, 555
 firewalls to monitor access to port, 253, 340
Transport Device Interface (TDI), 181
Transport layer in OSI model, 538
transport protocols, 173. *See also* native transport protocols
trap, 282, 555
Tri-Flex architecture (Compaq), 153
trust relationships, 93, **119–124**
trusted domain, 119, *120*
 response from, 123
Trusted Information Systems, 375
trusting domain, 119, *120*
trusts, limit to number, **122–124**
TTL (Time to Live), 240–241, 555
 in SOA record, 297
tunneling, 366, 555
two-tier client/server system, 396

U

UART (Universal Asynchronous Receiver/Transmitter), 394
UDP. *See* User Datagram Protocol (UDP)
Universal Naming Convention (UNC), 108
UNIX
  extensibility of, 9
  WinFrame support for, 481
  and WINS, 169
UNIX to UNIX Copy Protocol (UUCP), 249
URL (Uniform Resource Locator), 555
U.S. Department of Defense, 227
U.S. Federal Information Processing standard 1521, 53
Usage Analyst, 283–284
USENET, 247, 311, 555
user accounts
  integrating NT and NDS, 211, *212*
  naming standards for, **110–112**, *111–112*
  Novell Workstation Manager to manage information, 199
  recommended number of BDCs based on number of, *143*
  synchronization between NDS and NT, 213, *213*
User Accounts Database, 140

user-configurable mail server, from third-party servers, 315
User Configuration dialog box, for WinFrame, *475*
User Datagram Protocol (UDP), 159–160, 555
  firewalls to monitor access to port, 253, 340
user ID, and traffic control by proxy, **346**
user interface, compatibility, 18
User Manager for Domains utility, 120
  to add trusted domain, 121
user mode, 9, 29, 555
user-mode layer, compatibility in, 17
User Mode subsystem, *33*
user profiles, 196
  mandatory option in WinFrame, 463–464
user rights, vs. system administrator rights, 331–332
user upgrade license, for WinFrame, 476
users. *See also* authentication
  association with NT Configuration object, 201
  auditing connections to WinFrame server, 482
  education on security policy, **338**
  individual rights and responsibilities in security policy, 331

maximum number for single
    domain, **96–99**
need for DNS name, 302
personalized profile of, 204
power vs. standard, RAM to support,
    455–456
predicting number of concurrent, **424**
security policy on authorized,
    330–331
setup in WinFrame, **475–476**, *475*
transmission of sensitive data, 323
UUCP (UNIX to UNIX Copy Protocol),
    249
UUencode/Uudecode, 277, 556

V

V.34 standard, 383
Value-Added Networks. *See also*
    PSDNs (packet-switched public data
    networks)
Vaskevitch, David, 22
VBScript, 268
vendors
    reliable, **67**
    support from, 74
Verisign, Inc., 281
virtual directories, 556
    in IIS, 265, **286–287**
Virtual DOS Machine (VDM), 51

Virtual Memory Manager (VMM), 14,
    43, 556
virtual private networks (VPN), 230,
    254, *255*, **358–376**, 556
    configuring number of, 369, *370*
    elements of, **363–368**, *364*
    and firewalls, **375–376**
    Point-to-Point Tunneling Protocol
        (PPTP) for, **368–373**
    third-party products, **373–376**
virtual processors, 47
virtual servers, **287–288**
virus, in attachments, 323
Volatile User account, 203
VPN Client, **367**
VPN connection, 366, *367*
VPN Server, **366**

W

warranties, 68–69
Web Capacity Analysis Tool (WCAT),
    274–275
Web pages, dynamic generation, 229
Web protocols, **233–235**
Web Proxy (Microsoft), **354**
Web reports, dynamically generated by
    Crystal Reports, 283
Web servers
    communication with, 234

implementation for Windows NT, 260
Secure Sockets Layer (SSL) for, 254, 278–279
Web sites for benchmark tools, 276
Web sites
   for BIND for NT, 304
   for Citrix, 443
   for mail servers, 314
   for MetaInfo, 307
   Microsoft, 488
   for third-party WinFrame interfaces, 481
   Verisign, 281
   for Web server benchmark tools, 276
   WebTrends, 284
WebBench (Ziff Davis), 276
WebStone (Silicon Graphics), 276
WebTrends, 284–285, *286*
wide area network (WAN), 402
   browser elections across, *128*, 128
   Internet as, **361–362**
   and WinFrame decision process, 445
   and WINS server, 168
Win16 subsystem, in Windows NT, **51–52**
Win32 subsystem, pre-Windows NT 4, 45
Win32K Manager, **45–47**, *46*
WinClient (WinFrame), 441, 447
Window Manager, in Win32K Manager, 47

Window NT Challenge/Response (NTLM) authentication, 263, 264, 278
Windows 3.1, WinFrame Client for, 480
Windows 95
   16-bit applications on, 19
   PPTP client configuration in, **371–372**
   and printer names, 108
   WinFrame Client for, 480
   workstations and NAdminNT, 209
Windows (Microsoft), vs. DOS, 9
Windows Internet Naming Service (WINS), 556. *See also* WINS (Windows Internet Naming Service)
Windows NT
   172, *172*
   16-bit application support, 19
   design goals, **7–19**
      compatibility, **14–18**
      extensibility, **9**
      performance, **18–19**
      portability, **10–11**
      reliability, **12–14**
   evolution, **20–21**
   exception handling process, 13
   FPNW to duplicate NetWare environment, **218-219**, –219
   future direction, **21–23**

implementation of TCP/IP, **180–181**, *180*
internal architecture, *42*
interoperability with NetWare, 188–189
lack of peripheral support in first release, 12
modular approach with, **29–32**
network protocol display, *179*
network services display, *179*
Novell support for, **195–214**
synchronization with NDS user accounts, 213, *213*
Web server implementations for, 260
Windows NT 3.1, support for NetWare, 190
Windows NT 3.5, support for NetWare, 191–192
Windows NT 3.51, and NetWare, **192–193**
Windows NT 4, and NetWare, **193**
Windows NT Advanced Server 3.1, **20**
Windows NT - Enterprise Edition, 23
Windows NT future
    Active Directory, **513–518**
    Hydra, **519–520**
    Routing and Remote Access Service, **523–526**, *524*
    Wolfpack clustering technology, **527–529**, *528*
    Zero Administrative Initiative, **520–522**

Windows NT Server Directory Services, 93
Windows NT Services for NetWare, 193
Windows NT Task Manager, *497*, 497–498
Windows Sockets (WinSock), 181–182, 354, 556
Windows on Win32 (WOW), 51
WinFrame 1.6 Program Manager, *473*
WinFrame 1.7 new features, **488–490**
WinFrame (Citrix), 400, **441–442**
    administrative tools with server, 446
    client setup, **447**
    configuration validity, 450
    downloading service packs and hot fixes, **465–466**
    file system for, 474
    handling of multiple CPUs, 454
    and impact of WAN traffic on LAN, 449
    initiating remote control session, 441
    installation non-recognition of hard drive, 487
    Intelligent Console Architecture (ICA) protocol, **442**
    licensing, **476**, 477
    management options, **473–481**
    Microsoft purchase of code, 442
    question and troubleshooting, **481–487**
    technical support levels, **446–447**

user setup, **475–476**, *475*
when to use, **443–450**
WinFrame Client tool, **480–481**
WinFrame for Hydra/Hydrix, **489**
WinFrame Performance Monitor, **486–487**
WinFrame sample project, **451–472**
   capability requirements, **452–454**
   connectivity options, **471–472**
   hardware configuration, **465–470**
   predicted number of concurrent users, **454–456**
   system recommendations, **469–470**
   understanding applications, **457–465**, *458–459*
WinFrame server
   administration, **473–475**
   application installation on, **483–485**
   auditing user connections to, **482**
   connection by Win32 Client, **482**
   drive assignments, NetWare drive mappings and, **463**
   impact of WAN traffic on, **449**
   partitions and performance, **485**
   processor for, **457–460**
   security provided by, **447**
   sessions per user, **457**
   theoretical minimum requirements, **450–451**
   troubleshooting blue screen, **481**
   WAN remote access connectivity options, **460**
   in Windows NT 4.0 Domain, **482**

WINS (Windows Internet Naming Service), **556**
   and DNS name services for DHCP-assigned workstations, **301**
   vs. Domain Name Service (DNS), **168–169**
   to find servers, **167–169**
Winsock proxy (Microsoft), 348, **354**
WINSOCK.DLL, 181–182, 354, **556**
WinStation Administration tools, 446, **479**, *479*
WinStation configuration, **477**, *478*
WinStation Configuration tools, **446**
WinTerm (Wyse Technology), **481**
WinView (Citrix), **400**
Wolfpack clustering technology, 513, **527–529**, *528*
workgroups, backup browsers for, **130**
workstations
   configuring for dynamic DNS, **303**
   naming standards for, **107–108**, *107*
World Wide Web
   accessing WinFrame server through, **487**
   for client access to mail messages, **314**
   searches, **269**
WoW (Windows on Windows), application performance on, **448**
WWW Service Properties dialog box, Advanced tab, **273**
Wyse Technology, WinTerm, **481**

X

X.25 protocol, 389, **421**
X.500 Directory Service, **114–119**
    communication among fundamental components, 117, *117*
X.500 naming standards, 102
Xerox Network Services (XNS), 182–183, *556*

Z

Zero Administrative Initiative, **520–522**
Ziff Davis, WebBench, 276
zone transfers, 238, 293, 556
zones, 556
    creating in DNS server, **295–297**
    for domain database, 237
    for name servers, 293

SYBEX BOOKS ON THE WEB!

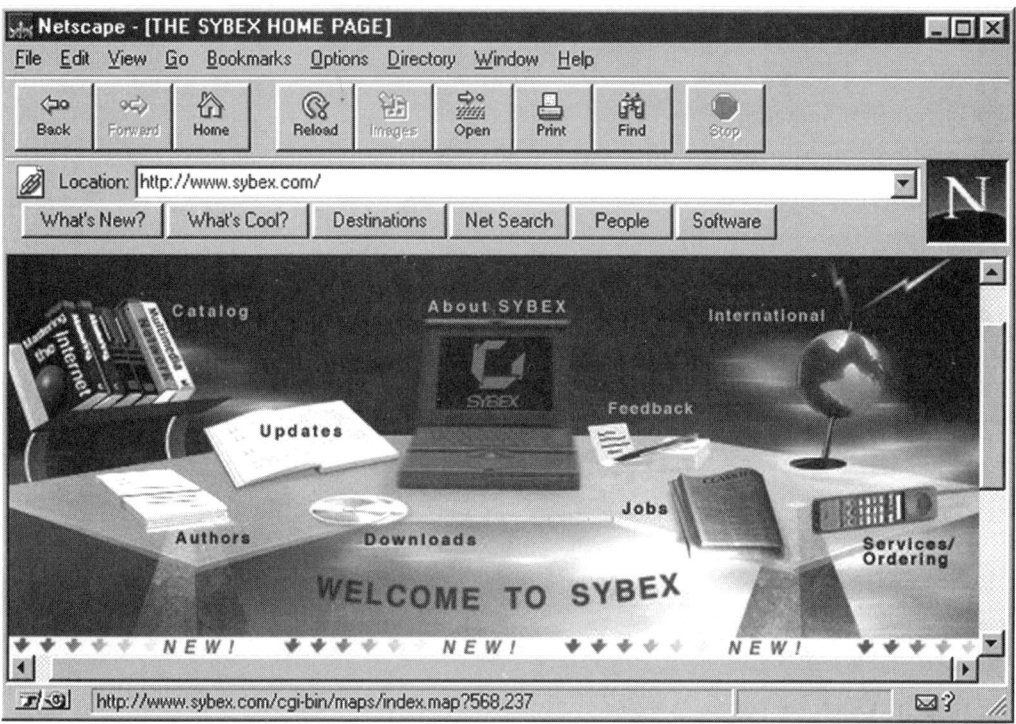

Presenting a truly dynamic environment that is both fun and informative.

- download useful code
- e-mail your favorite Sybex author
- preview a book you might want to own
- find out about job opportunities at Sybex
- order books
- learn about Sybex
- discover what's new in the computer industry

http://www.sybex.com

SYBEX Inc. • 1151 Marina Village Parkway • Alameda, CA 94501 • 510-523-8233